MW01273006

THE GLOBALIZED RULE OF LAW

THE GLOBALIZED RULE OF LAW
Relationships between International and Domestic Law

CHIEF EDITOR:
Oonagh E. Fitzgerald

The Globalized Rule of Law: Relationships between International and Domestic Law
© Irwin Law Inc., 2006

Published in 2006 by

Irwin Law
14 Duncan Street
Suite 206
Toronto, Ontario
M5H 3G8

www.irwinlaw.com

Design: Heather Raven

ISBN-10: 1-55221-122-3   ISBN-13: 978-155221-122-9

Library and Archives Canada Cataloguing in Publication

Fitzgerald, Oonagh E., 1955–
      The globalized rule of law : relationships between international and domestic law / chief editor, Oonagh E. Fitzgerald ; editorial board, Elisabeth Eid ... [et al.].

Includes bibliographical references.
ISBN 1-55221-122-3

1. Law—Canada. 2. International law—Canada. 3. International law. 4. Law—International unification. I. Eid, Elisabeth II. Title.

KE448.G56 2006   349.71   C2006-902883-4
KF385.ZA2G56 2006

The publisher acknowledges the financial support of the Government of Canada through the Book Publishing Industry Development Program (BPIDP) for its publishing activities.

We acknowledge the assistance of the OMDC Book Fund, an initiative of Ontario Media Development Corporation.

Printed and bound in Canada.

1 2 3 4 5   10 09 08 07 06

Table of Contents

Introduction and Acknowledgments

OONAGH E. FITZGERALD

The purpose of the book is to engage the reader, whether student, teacher, government policy-maker, parliamentarian, lawyer, judge, diplomat, or citizen to think deeply about how law is evolving in our globalizing world and to consider how each one of us might influence this evolution in positive ways.

Domestic, international, and transnational laws are competing, conflicting, harmonizing, blending, and merging. This creates difficulties in the courtroom while judges and lawyers try to make sense of the confusing array of domestic laws and international and bilateral agreements, resolutions, and declarations. It causes problems for policy-makers and diplomats trying to respond to domestic and international policy pressures and to project Canadian values onto the world stage. It raises concerns for citizens and parliamentarians seeking to ensure democratic representation in important decision-making processes that may take place within or beyond our borders. It presents challenges for students and teachers because, although there is much in domestic law and international law that is clear and well documented, the intersection and interplay between these bodies of law are still evolving and remain areas of doubt and confusion.

The papers in this collection examine the relationships between international and domestic law from different angles and through a variety of lenses. Not all contributors agree with each other about the appropriate treatment of international law by governments, parliamentarians, or the courts—the views expressed are those of the individual authors and not of the various institutions with which they may be affiliated. We did all agree, however, that there needed to be a clearer and broader understanding of the impact of international law on domestic law and policy, in order to be able to use law more effectively in international and domestic litigation and dispute settlement, policy development, and decision-making.

For the authors gathered in this collection, this project has had a rather lengthy gestation. It originated in the first roundtable between international law academics and Justice officials in October 2003, where participants discussed the key issues they were struggling with in the practice and teaching of international law. The topic of the relationship between international and domestic law quickly surfaced as one that was generating interesting new legal analysis and causing the most difficulty in government legal practice.

A one-day brainstorming session in June 2004 produced a long list of ideas for papers to elucidate this issue. In October of that year participants gathered to discuss outlines of their papers, and we could see that providing a wide range of perspectives on the relationship between international and domestic law would help to increase understanding and awareness of this issue. Authors proceeded to research and write their papers and gathered again in June 2005 for a two-day symposium at McGill University, where the draft papers were presented and discussed. In the ensuing months the papers were finalized and reviewed by an editorial board, last revisions were made, and here we are.

Along the way there have been many sources of inspiration and guiding hands. Some years back, Morris Rosenberg, then deputy minister, commissioned Stephen Toope to study and make recommendations as to how the Department of Justice might better organize and position itself to provide high-quality, strategic, and coordinated international law advice to the government of Canada. Stephen Toope wrote a seminal report recommending a stronger leadership role for the department, centred on a core group of international law experts who could give guidance and, where necessary, coordinate the work of Justice lawyers practising international law in the federal government.

The project really became a possibility when Morris encouraged me, as Special Advisor for International Law appointed to implement Stephen's report, to reach out to the academic community and make connections between its work in international law and what the Department of Justice was doing in this field. The roster of participants at the roundtables and symposium is a veritable who's who of international law in Canada, and even those who have not contributed a paper to this collection, contributed much by way of probing questions, brilliant insights, and challenging discussion. While the book is a culmination of our collective efforts, the process of getting here was at least as important as the result. The worlds of academe and of government law practice are no longer distant and isolated but have become richly interconnected and collaborative. Therefore, we all owe a special debt of gratitude to both Morris and Stephen for having had the strategic vision that made this kind of inspiring partnership conceivable and possible.

This project is the product of collaboration and partnership by many academics and government officials and they all deserve to be congratulated for their valuable and varied contributions to the collective product. Let me begin by expressing my sincere appreciation to the other members of the project's editorial board composed of Elisabeth Eid, director of the Human Rights Law Section of Justice, Don Fleming, currently dean of the Law Faculty at the University of New Brunswick and president of the Canadian Council for International Law, Anne Warner La Forest, past dean of the Law Faculty at the University of New Brunswick and scholar-in-residence at the Department of Justice in 2004–5, Armand de Mestral of the Law Faculty of the University of McGill, and Lorraine Pelot, senior research officer at the Law Commission of Canada. Their expert advice was crucial in developing the overall framework for the book project and in reviewing and commenting on all draft papers.

Next, I sincerely appreciate the conscientious and able assistance of three counsel within the Public Law Sector of the Department of Justice, Anik Beaudoin, Mimi Lepage, and Angela Arnet-Connidis, who, along with Anne Warner La Forest, contributed their expertise, inspiration, energy, and enthusiasm to this project on a continuous basis. I would like especially to acknowledge the substantial contribution made by Tania Nesrallah, who was my administrative assistant on this project. Without her organizational skills and *savoir faire* the roundtables and symposium likely would not have been nearly so successful in generating excitement and momentum. Without her attention to detail, personal charm and humour, and good-natured cajoling, I know there would have been fewer contented contributors and fewer final papers. I am also very grateful to Vanessa Van Rooijen, Helena Moore, Marie Lemieux, and Lucille Rochon for their able assistance at various points in completing the project.

I gratefully acknowledge the ongoing support of my deputy minister, John Sims, and the members of the deputy minister's team, who welcomed and encouraged visiting academics and participants over the life of the project and humoured me in my desire to see this project to completion. Similarly, I thank Carolyn Kobernick, chief counsel, Public Law, for supporting the project as it came to fruition.

Let me express my appreciation for the support this project received from some important Canadian institutions. I wish to thank the Law Commission of Canada, its past and current presidents, first, Nathalie Des Rosiers and more recently, Yves leBouthillier, as well as Bernard Colas and Lorraine Pelot, for their interest in globalization's impact on law and for their encouragement. I am especially indebted to Lorraine for her untiring collaboration and practical advice throughout. Thanks are due to the Executive Committee of the Canadian Council of International Law for ongoing interest, guidance, and moral support for the project. I would like to thank all Canada's law schools and the law deans who generously offered up their international law experts to participate in this government–academic partnership. Much appreciation is due to Dean Nicholas Kasirer and the University of McGill Faculty of Law for generously providing us with the venue for our memorable symposium of June 2005, and I am grateful to Nathalie Des Rosiers and the Law Faculty of the University of Ottawa for their encouragement and interest in co-hosting a conference based on the project.

I sincerely thank the individual authors, both academic and government, for their steadfast commitment to this project and for their patience and persistence with me when I was occupied with other work responsibilities. It has been an honour and great privilege to work with such excellent and inspiring teachers and colleagues. This project gave me a front-row seat to hear the debates of some of Canada's best international lawyers and a glimpse at the enormous potential of government–academic collaboration.

I also acknowledge and thank the many other academics and government officials who participated at various stages in the development of this project, contributing their energy and excitement, and thereby helping to create the momentum we needed to complete the work. I hesitate to mention all the names for fear of being called a shameless name-dropper, or of missing any one of the early contributors, or of unfairly associating their names with the later product. I only wish to say they all made unforgettable and uniquely insightful contributions to the exploration and shaping of this project, and without their participation in the early brainstorming sessions the end product would not be nearly as good as in fact it is.

Thanks are also due to Jeff Miller and Alisa Posesorski and their colleagues Heather Raven and Aimee Coueslan at Irwin Law for their enthusiasm for this project and their skillful and meticulous attention to the many aspects of ensuring a high-quality publication. Finally, on behalf of all the authors, let me express the deep gratitude and appreciation due to our families and friends who support, inspire, and encourage us in all our endeavours.

Our discussions throughout the life of this project revealed that there are still more angles on the relationships between international and domestic law than those examined in this book, such that there may be future opportunities to mine further our sources of inspiration, and even expand our partnership both nationally and internationally, in order to write a sequel. For example, time and circumstance did not permit a full examination of the issues of federalism and regional governance, or a comprehensive comparative analysis of the domestic implementation of international law in other legal systems, and there may be more issues to explore regarding new actors in international law, such as corporations' emerging roles and responsibilities under the UN Global Compact initiative. Through continued connection and collaboration among those who share an interest in what becomes of the rule of law in a globalizing world, we are surely more able to exert a positive influence on the law's coherent and principled development at home and abroad.

Oonagh Elizabeth Fitzgerald
April 2006, Ottawa

Part One:

WHAT IS INTERNATIONAL LAW AND HOW DO WE FIND IT IN CANADA?

Section A:
INTRODUCTION TO THE ISSUES SURROUNDING THE RELATIONSHIP BETWEEN INTERNATIONAL AND DOMESTIC LAW

The Use and Abuse of International Legal Sources by Canadian Courts: Searching for a Principled Approach

HUGH M. KINDRED

A. INTRODUCTION

That international law is a source of law in Canada is undeniable, but as soon as one asks *how*, disputes begin. The source of uncertainty is, unfortunately, the absence of almost any reference to international law and relations in the Canadian Constitution, compounded by inadequate guidance by the courts. As a result, Canadian legal practice has drifted from case to case in an eclectic application of legal perspectives that, at one extreme, have denied the relevance of international law, to the other extreme of indiscriminate reference to all manner of international legal sources. Into such a fluid context this chapter will try to clear a way through distracting precedents to the underlying legal principles and to clarify the implications of their operation in Canadian courts.

The problems of internalizing international law in Canadian law are not new, but they are persistent. Indeed, if anything, Canadian courts have put new twists on the old problems, but without resolving them. Since the problems have not been solved, perhaps the basic principles said to underlie judicial practice in this area are inadequate. In that light, this paper will re-examine the principles involved around four recurrent questions, as follows:

1. Is international law binding within Canada?
2. Why treat customary and conventional international law differently?
3. Is legislative transformation of conventional international law really necessary?
4. How should different international legal sources be employed?

Familiar as the first three questions may be, they need to be rehearsed again in order to reach the focus of the paper in Question 4 about the employment of the wide range of binding and non-binding international legal sources. They are not limited to customary laws and conventions but also include a great variety of other material sources, such as preparatory histories, United Nations' documents and subsequent state practice. Through the exploration of Questions 1 to 3, the paper will establish a perspective on the domestic internalization of international law. This perspective will then be used to provide a principled basis for practical conclusions to Question 4, on the appropriate use of international legal sources.

B. QUESTION 1—IS INTERNATIONAL LAW BINDING WITHIN CANADA?

The purpose in raising this question in this paper is to recall some constitutional underpinnings to the way Canadian courts are organized.[1] These, it will be asserted, fundamentally affect attitudes and approaches to determining the sources of Canadian law.

There is no doubt that international law is binding *on* Canada; the query is how it impacts *in* Canada. International law itself decrees that both customary and conventional international rules must be obeyed, yet it leaves each state to determine for itself how the obligations will be fulfilled.[2] This power is but an aspect of state sovereignty, that is, the right of every state to establish its own internal social, political, and constitutional organization, subject to the restraints of international legal standards such as the protections for human rights.

In Canada, the exercise of sovereignty is dispersed. It is exercised by various bodies with differing powers under the *Constitution Acts, 1867–1982.*[3] There is a so-called separation of powers between legislative, executive, and judicial organs, as well as a division of jurisdiction between federal

---

1 Both Karen Knop and Stephane Beaulac have written eloquently in disagreement over this question; see Karen Knop, "Here and There: International Law in Domestic Courts" (2000) 32 N.Y.U.J. Int'l L. & Pol. 501; see Stephane Beaulac, "National Application of International Law: The Statutory Interpretation perspective" (2003) 51 Can. Y.B. Int'l L. 225.

2 "*Pacta sunt servanda*": Vienna Convention on the Law of Treaties, 1155 U.N.T.S. 331 (1969) art. 26.

3 *Constitution Act 1867,* (U.K.), 30 & 31 Vict., c. 3 and *Constitution Act, 1982,* being Sch. B to the *Canada Act 1982* (U.K.), 1982, c. 11. These and all the other Canadian constitutional documents are reproduced in R.S.C. 1985, App. 3.

and provincial authorities. The courts, as a body, are part of this structure: they are creatures of the Canadian Constitution, either by federal or by provincial powers of creation.[4] The appointed judges are domestic law officers of the Crown who are constitutionally bound to apply the law of the land, that is, the various federal and provincial laws of Canada.

This particular sovereign choice of constitutional arrangements in Canada points directly to the process for applying international law binding on Canada. If any particular rule of international law has become the law of Canada, Canadian courts are duty-bound to apply and enforce it. Such an analysis leads to the key question about *how* to determine the impact of international law within Canadian law. On this crucial issue, the Constitution is next to silent: it contains only one explicit and now irrelevant provision in section 132 on Empire treaties.[5] Thus the task has fallen to the courts to determine what impacts international law has within Canada. As keepers of the constitutional process, it is they who control the solutions to the next three questions.

C. QUESTION 2—WHY TREAT CUSTOMARY AND CONVENTIONAL INTERNATIONAL LAW DIFFERENTLY?

If international law has any impact domestically—which without doubt it has, though *what*, as well as *how*, have still to be answered—why should separate sources of that law be treated differently? It is well known that two principal sources of international law, as declared in Article 38(1)(c) of the *Statute of the International Court of Justice*, are treaties and custom and that both are equally obligatory according to their terms.[6] Yet it is said, both by courts[7] and

---

4 *Constitution Act 1867, ibid.,* ss. 92(14) and 101. See Peter W. Hogg, *Constitutional Law of Canada,* 4th ed., looseleaf (Scarborough, ON: Thomson, 2004) at 7-1 to 7-4 and 1-15 to 7-22.

5 Plus an admonishment in the Preamble to operate "a constitution similar in principle to that of the United Kingdom": *Constitution Act 1867, ibid.*

6 *Military Activities In and Against Nicaragua (Nicaragua v. United States),* [1986] I.C.J. Rep. 14.

7 For example, *Ref. Re Foreign Legations, (sub nom. Reference Re: Powers of Ottawa (City) and Rockcliffe Park)* [1943] S.C.R. 208; *Saint John v. Fraser-Brace Overseas Corp.,* [1958] S.C.R. 263; *Re Newfoundland Continental Shelf, (sub nom. Reference re: Seabed and subsoil of the continental shelf offshore Newfoundland)* [1984] 1 S.C.R. 86; *Bouzari v. Iran (Islamic Republic)* (2004), 243 D.L.R. (4th) 406 (Ont. C.A.).

commentators,[8] that customary international law may be adopted by Canadian courts as directly applicable rules of Canadian law, but that treaty
provisions must be transformed, generally, by some legislative act, in order
to become part of Canadian law and so enforceable by Canadian courts.

If this is the practice, it is reasonable to ask, what is the principle of it?
Why should customary international law be adopted as part of the law of
Canada upon its discovery (subject only to clearly conflicting legislation)[9]
while treaties require an intervening act of transformation? Law is law:
in the international realm both sources of obligation are equally binding,
so where is the logic or wisdom in differentiating between them in the
domestic legal order?

The reasons commonly given to justify the differing regard for international obligations are two fundamental features of the Constitution: the
supremacy of Parliament[10] and the federal/provincial division of powers.[11]
Indeed, the courts have the responsibility and authority to filter all Canadian laws through the net of these constitutional principles, striking down
any that are judged to be *ultra vires*. And this is true of internationally
sourced laws as well, seeing that, as argued under Question 1, international obligations on Canada are applicable by the courts only to the extent
that they are laws of Canada.

Considering the supremacy of Parliament principle first, it does not
demand that all Canadian laws be legislated. Neither domestic common
law nor international customary law is sourced in legislation, yet both are
operable as soon as they are ascertained. Surely the fundamental point
about the supremacy of parliament is that no Canadian law, whether statutory, code, common law, or international in origin, may stand in force if
the appropriate legislature, federal or provincial, passes legislation that
contradicts it. For sound democratic reasons,[12] the ultimate power of the

---

8   For example, Ronald St. J. Macdonald, "The Relationship between International Law
    and Domestic Law in Canada" in Ronald St. J. Macdonald, Gerald L. Morris, & Douglas
    M. Johnston, eds., *Canadian Perspectives on International Law and Organization*, (To-
    ronto: University of Toronto Press, 1974) at 88; Gibran van Ert, *Using International Law
    in Canadian Courts* (The Hague; New York: Kluwer Law International, 2002) at 137–70,
    who, of all commentators, have written most thoroughly on this particular issue.

9   On which, see more below at note 12.

10 See Hogg, above note 4 at 12-1 to 12-4.

11 See Hogg, *ibid.* at 5-3 to 5-22.

12 Joanna Harrington, "Redressing the Democratic Deficit in Treaty Law Making: (Re)
    Establishing a Role for Parliament" (2005) 50 McGill L.J. 465.

legislature is to control the body of Canadian law by reform and repeal, both adding to it and subtracting from it. In this way the supremacy of Parliament is fully acknowledged and respected even as international law—or customary international law at least—seeps into Canadian law without the intervention of legislation.

The second principle, the federal/provincial division of powers presents a different order of concern. Obviously, treaties may, and increasingly do,[13] involve provincial areas of authority, so the federal government, in exercising its treaty-making power,[14] may readily be seen to step into provincial jurisdiction and onto political toes. But equally customary international law may interfere with provincial authority. Obviously, customary international law is not of the Canadian government's making alone, but still provincial authority is impacted without the provincial legislatures or executives having control, or even say, in the matter. Recall the *Ref. Re Foreign Legations,*[15] in which the Ontario *Assessment Act* for the taxing "of all real property in Ontario" was read down by the Supreme Court of Canada to exclude foreign states' diplomatic premises because customary international law granted them immunity from the local jurisdiction.

So, if customary international law can be adopted without any transformative action, why should treaties not be also? After all, the provincial legislatures or federal Parliament, depending on the subject matter, can always legislate to overrule or vary the operation of applicable international law, whether customary or conventional. Their supremacy of control over the laws of Canada within their individual jurisdictions is not challenged or diminished, and the provinces will not lose any of their constitutional shares of plenary powers. This is not a new idea,[16] but it is a principled and a practical one. The principles have just been outlined. The practicability lies in the courts' control of the constitutional process and their readiness to develop it.

In the absence of explicit provisions in the *Constitution Acts,* already noted, Canada's participation in international law and relations progressively developed during the birth and slow separation of the new country

13 See Hugh M. Kindred, "Making International Agreements and Making Them Work within a Multicultural Federal State: The Experience of Canada" in Stephen Tierney, ed., *The Long Road: Constitutionalism and Cultural Pluralism in Canada,* not yet published.
14 Both to conclude and to ratify treaties, by reason of Crown prerogative: on which see Hogg, above note 4 at 1-14 to 1-16 and 11-1 to 11-4.
15 Above note 7.
16 See Macdonald, above note 8.

from British imperial authority. As a result, Canada adopted, *mutatis mutandis*, the constitutional conventions of the United Kingdom, all of which have received the imprimatur of the Supreme Court.[17] But Canadian practice does not have to stay the same, and certainly it need no longer follow the British model. In exercise of Canada's sovereignty, the courts could nudge the continuing development of the foreign relations law of Canada along a more productive path. Indeed, there is some evidence that they are inclining this way in their recent decisions, as will be discussed under Question 4. But before that question can be addressed, it is necessary to review the changing regard of the courts for treaty implementation.

D. QUESTION 3—IS LEGISLATIVE TRANSFORMATION OF CONVENTIONAL INTERNATIONAL LAW REALLY NECESSARY?

The repetitious recitation by the courts that Canadian law cannot be altered by binding treaty provisions without domestic implementation cannot be denied,[18] but the incantation begs the questions: What constitutes this transformation? How deliberate and explicit must implementation be? What form must or may it take?

To clarify the core issue, let it be recognized, first, that not all conventional international laws need to be implemented. If they do not affect the rights and duties of persons within the reach of Canadian laws, then there is no need for their incorporation into Canadian law. The provisions of peace treaties, defence pacts, and other agreements that deal exclusively with Canada's foreign relations are typically given as examples.

Second, sometimes governments may implement treaty provisions by executive action. Orders-in-Council and other regulatory directives may

---

17   See, for example, Duff C.J.C.'s judgment in the *Labour Conventions Case*, *(sub nom. Reference Re: Weekly Rest in Industrial Undertakings Act (Canada))*, [1936] S.C.R. 461.

18   For example, *Attorney General for Canada v. Attorney General for Ontario (Labour Conventions Case)*, [1937] A.C. 326 (J.C.P.C.); *Baker v. Canada (Minister of Citizenship and Immigration)*, [1999] 2 S.C.R. 817; *Suresh v. Canada (Minister of Citizenship and Immigration)*, [2002] 1 S.C.R. 3 at para. 60. On the whole topic, see the finely nuanced discussions of Jutta Brunnée & Stephen Toope, "A Hesitant Embrace: The Application of International Law by Canadian Courts" (2003) 51 Can. Y.B. Int'l L. 225; Louis LeBel & Gloria Chao, "The Rise of International Law in Canadian Constitutional Litigation: Fugue or Fusion? Recent Developments and Challenges in Internalizing International Law" (2002) 16 Sup. Ct. L. Rev. (2d) 23; and René Prevost, "Le juge mondialisé: légitimité judiciaire et le droit international au Canada" in Marie-Claire Belleau & François Lacasse, eds., *Claire L'Heureux-Dubé à la Cour suprême du Canada 1987–2002* (Montreal: Wilson & Lafleur, 2004) at 569.

be enough to give domestic effect to a treaty's provisions,[19] but no government official, from the prime minister down, can make regulations without statutory authority. There has to be enabling legislation that grants appropriate regulatory power to the minister, board or tribunal else their attempts to make regulations or to impose rulings may be declared *ultra vires* upon judicial review. Implementation of treaty obligations by the exercise of government regulatory power is, therefore, an indirect or subsidiary act of delegated legislation.

Thus, the business of implementing treaties comes back to legislative action and, in particular, two questions about what form it may take and how explicit it should be. The responses of the courts have been much influenced since 1977 by the views of then Chief Justice Laskin when, in *Vapor Canada*,[20] he expressed the opinion that "the exercise of [the treaty implementing] power must be manifest in the implementing legislation and not be left to inference. The court should be able to say, on the basis of the expression of the legislation, that it is implementing legislation."[21] If taken at face value, Laskin C.J.C.'s approach would severely limit the occasions when treaty provisions could be said to have been implemented into Canadian law. His standard is not far short of requiring an explicit statement of the legislature's intent in the statute in question "that it is implementing legislation." That standard is readily satisfied when, following common law practices of drafting, the statute states that so many articles of the treaty annexed in a schedule to the Act "shall have the force of law."[22]

The legislature's intent is less obvious but potentially still "manifest" when, following the civil law's prevalent drafting tradition, the treaty's provisions are incorporated into the text of the legislation but without reference to their international source. In cases of doubt, however, may the Court compare the statute with the treaty? Laskin C.J.C.'s answer, on the continued assumption of the literal interpretation of his stated opinion, would surely have been no. However, Armand de Mestral has suggested

---

19 For example, see *Rousseau Metal Inc. v. Canada* (1988), 80 N.R. 74 (F.C.A.), which dealt with government procurement standards under GATT.

20 *MacDonald and Railquip Enterprises Ltd. v. Vapor Canada Ltd.*, [1977] 2 S.C.R. 134. See also *Capital Cities Communications Inc. v. Canadian Radio-Television Commission*, [1978] 2 S.C.R. 141.

21 *MacDonald and Railquip Enterprises Ltd. v. Vapor Canada Ltd.*, *ibid.* at 171.

22 For example, *Marine Liability Act*, S.C. 2001, c. 6, s. 41 and Sch. 3, implementing the Hague-Visby Rules on the Carriage of Goods by Sea.

a different and more contextual interpretation of Chief Justice Laskin's views. He has pointed out:

> What most judges and commentators have failed to notice is that Chief Justice Laskin adopted this position in *Vapor Canada* essentially for constitutional reasons relating to the peace, order and good government power and not for reasons of treaty law. Chief Justice Laskin was of the view, contrary to the *Labour Conventions Case*, that Parliament possessed the jurisdiction to legislate to implement any treaty, by virtue of the general power in the *Constitution Act 1867* section 91, but that this power could only be triggered by an explicit statement of Parliament's intention to implement a treaty. His concern was with the exercise of the general power, not with treaty law as such, but this has led many to believe that implementation can only be effected by an explicit statement of the intention to do so.[23]

This is a possible and reasonable reading of Laskin C.J.C.'s expressed opinions in light of his further remarks in the *Vapor Canada* case.[24]

Be that as it may, the Supreme Court of Canada has moved on in later cases to a much more flexible approach, which has not been widely noticed. In *National Corn Growers Association v. Canada (Import Tribunal)*[25] the courts were engaged in the judicial review of the interpretation by the Canadian Import Tribunal of the *Special Import Measures Act (SIMA)*[26] in light of the GATT Code on Subsidies and Countervailing Duties.[27] This led the various justices to opine whether *SIMA* implemented the GATT Code. Their opinions differed. Iacobucci, then Chief Justice of the Federal Court of Canada, said "it is the wording of the implementing legislation which is of paramount importance."[28] He compared *SIMA* and the GATT Code to show that when Parliament wished to incorporate the treaty provisions, it had done so deliberately and precisely, but that it had not done so in the section under review. MacGuigan J., on the other hand, considered "the Act is so enmeshed with the Code that it must be taken to be an implementation

---

23 Commentary by Armand de Mestral in Hugh Kindred & Phillip Saunders, eds., *International Law Chiefly as Interpreted and Applied in Canada*, 7th ed. (Toronto: Emond Montgomery Publications, 2006) at 235.

24 Above note 20 at 171–72.

25 (1988), 58 D.L.R. (4th) 642 (F.C.A.), aff'd [1990] 2 S.C.R. 1324.

26 R.S.C. 1985 (1st Supp.), c. 23.

27 GATT B.I.S.D. (26th Supp.) 56 (1980).

28 Above note 25 at 650 (F.C.A.). He accepted that *SIMA* was passed with the general intent of implementing Canada's obligations under the GATT Code: *ibid.* at 649 (F.C.A.).

... of it."[29] Though these justices differed in the outcome of the case, what is significant for present purposes is that both of them compared the treaty with the act in order to determine whether the one incorporated the other. In other words, they both breached the barrier against looking beyond the statute. Such a step might be thought obvious but was, in fact, a significant change of practice.

Compare the view of Wilson J. when the case reached the Supreme Court. She did not think it appropriate to look beyond the statute.[30] However, Gonthier J., writing for the majority, accepted that *SIMA* implemented the GATT Code. He observed that "it was not disputed in either of the courts below that the Canadian legislation was designed to implement Canada's *GATT* obligations."[31] He went on to interpret the implementing legislation by reference to the treaty provisions. His comments about the lower courts were much more generous and general than Iacobucci C.J.'s remarks in the Federal Court of Appeal had been. Perhaps Gonthier J. wanted to move quickly past the implementation issue to get to the interpretation question at the heart of the case, on which he had significant views to express. The upshot, it seems, is that implementation remained some sort of requirement but its determination had become much less certain. It could be said from the case that, far from requiring manifest intent of treaty incorporation, the Supreme Court would assume a statute is implementing legislation if its language is redolent of the treaty's provisions.

Yet the uncertainty surrounding treaty implementation persists in the Supreme Court. *Gosselin v. Quebec (Attorney General)*[32] is a recent example. In a class action, Ms. Gosselin argued that a regulation under the Quebec *Social Aid Act* of 1984 violated her rights under the *Canadian Charter* sections 7 and 15(1) and under the *Quebec Charter of Human Rights and Freedoms* section 45. The Supreme Court affirmed the views of the courts below that the regulation was constitutional. In measuring the regulation in question against the standard of the *Quebec Charter* three of the judgments interpreted the scope and intent of the rights expressed in section 45 by reference to international human rights laws. They used the *International Covenant of Economic, Social and Cultural Rights* (ICESCR), to which Canada is a party. Chief Justice McLachlin, writing for the majority of five,

---

29   *Ibid.* at 671 (F.C.A.).
30   *Ibid.* at 1349 (S.C.C.).
31   *Ibid.* at 1371 (S.C.C.).
32   [2002] 4 S.C.R. 429.

took the view that, despite the similarity of the rights expressed in the *Quebec Charter* and the ICESCR, their differences in particulars indicated that the *Quebec Charter* did not afford the same rights found in the ICESCR.[33] LeBel J., in dissent, agreed on this point, saying "[t]he apparent similarity between s.45 and art. 11(1) of the Covenant does not necessarily mean that the Quebec legislature intended to entrench the right to an acceptable standard of living in the *Quebec Charter*."[34] To the contrary, L'Heureux-Dubé J., also in dissent, stated she was fully in agreement with the dissenting judgment of Robert J.A. in the Quebec Court of Appeal that the *Quebec Charter* "was intended to establish a domestic law regime that reflects Canada's international commitments."[35]

Once again, the Supreme Court showed itself divided over the issue of whether a certain statute was intended to be implementing legislation. Noticeably, yet again, all the justices, who addressed the point, explored the international treaty in order to determine the scope and purpose of the legislation, and were not content with reviewing the language of the act alone. In addition, two refinements of the implementation issue may be teased out of this case. First, these judgments confirm the suggestion, made in light of the *National Corn Growers* case, that courts will assume a statute is implementing legislation if its language reflects an international obligation. L'Heureux-Dubé J. thought it did and both McLachlin C.J.C. and LeBel J., who ultimately thought it did not, only reached that decision by a close comparative examination of the differences in detail between the domestic and the international texts. In other words, all three justices subscribed to the idea that the apparent similarity between statute and treaty provisions is sufficient to imply legislative implementation until it is dispelled. Nowadays therefore, the starting presumption is that similarity between domestic and international provisions signals implementation, and that affirmative proof is not necessary; rather proof to the contrary is required.

The second refinement takes note of the fact that McLachlin C.J.C. and LeBel J. did not speak in terms of implementation at all. They simply applied the international covenant, the ICESCR, accepting it without question as the relevant standard by which to judge the scope of the *Quebec Charter* right, which they both found wanting. This approach implies that for some

---

33   *Ibid.* at 495–96.
34   *Ibid.* at 655.
35   *Ibid.* at 517, quoting Robert J.A. in [1999] R.J.Q. 1033 at 1099 (Que. C.A.).

purposes, such as statutory interpretation, implementation of international treaty obligations is irrelevant. This proposition is relevant to Question 4 on the issue of international legal sources, but it also addresses the core of Question 3 on whether legislative transformation of conventional international law is really necessary. One more example of a common situation may not resolve the question decisively but will add to the growing evidence towards a negative answer. The contemporary approach of the Supreme Court of Canada comports with Canadian administrative practice towards treaty provisions that are already reflected in existing Canadian law.

Often no express legislative action on a treaty is taken because the law officers of the Crown determine that existing Canadian laws are fully consistent with its provisions.[36] In light of the *Canadian Charter* and its provincial counterparts, this situation is particularly representative of the status of international human rights covenants and treaties to which Canada is a party. Few, if any, have received deliberate implementation by specific legislation. Yet in delivering periodic reports, as required by some of these treaties, to international human rights supervisory bodies, like the UN Human Rights Committee, the federal government regularly represents that Canadian law fulfils Canada's international obligations.[37] Assuming such representations are accurate, they add another and different strand of uncertainty to the question about the need for implementation. If implementation is taken to mean, as it has been assumed to mean in the discussion of Question 3 so far, specific legislative transformation, then in these situations it obviously cannot be said to have occurred. But if implementation simply means incorporation in Canadian law by interpretation—or perhaps re-interpretation—of relevant and existing legislation, then these situations must be said to have passed the test of domestic acceptance.

Surely, the Crown officer's position is sound in both principle and practice. Why waste the effort and scarce time of Parliament and the legislatures to enact anew what already exists as law? Regrettably, the practice

---

36 Armand de Mestral, a former law officer, has commented: "Frequently, Law Officers of the Crown will deem it unnecessary to initiate new legislation because the substance of the treaty can be found in pre-existing common or statute law, or in statutory authority that can be used to make the necessary regulations in order to ensure implementation." See Kindred & Saunders, above note 23 at 207. See also Irit Weiser, "Effect in Domestic Law of International Human Rights Treaties Ratified Without Implementing Legislation" [1998] 27 C.C.I.L. Procs. 132.

37 See, for example, Anne F. Bayefsky, *International Human Rights Law: Use in Canadian Charter of Rights and Freedoms Litigation* (Toronto: Butterworths, 1992) at 53–56.

16 HUGH M. KINDRED

of not doing so has yet to be squarely faced and determined by the courts. Reflecting Chief Justice Laskin's views, courts have been apt to ignore treaty obligations in the absence of specific legislation. Advocates for the domestic protection of international rights have had to resort to legislative history and other extrinsic evidence to try to demonstrate that particular legislation was intended, at least in part, to take account of international treaty provisions even though they are not mentioned. The *Canadian Charter* is a good example. Strong arguments have been made that in its making Canadians' international human rights were intended to be respected.[38] But there are judicial indications that arguments about intentions of the legislatures may no longer be necessary. As Dickson C.J.C. said in 1989 of the *Canadian Charter*, it "should generally be presumed to provide protection at least as great as that afforded by similar provisions in international human rights documents which Canada has ratified."[39] In the past fifteen years, the courts have accepted this proposition and moved beyond its confines of the *Canadian Charter*, as will be discussed under Question 4. Meanwhile, note how well Chief Justice Dickson's presumption aligns with the suggestion above that similarity of statute and treaty raises an assumption of implementation.

To summarize the discussion of Question 3, one may safely say that the principle of implementation of treaty obligations has progressively shifted in meaning and function. Moving from the requirement of manifest legislative intent on the face of a specific statute, implementation may now be a passive act.[40] That is, implementation may be presumed whenever the provisions of a treaty in force against Canada are similar to the provisions of a statute on the same subject matter, whether that statute was pre-existing or subsequently enacted. This understanding of treaty implementation does not deny the need for transformation of conventional international law, but it does very greatly diminish the previous requirements. Plainly, this position is not the courts' firm and final proposition on treaty implementation. The change in judicial attitudes displays a trend that is not yet fully worked out, and that is consistent with the opportunity open to the courts, as discussed in answer to Question 2, to develop the constitutional prin-

---

38 See generally Bayefsky, *ibid.*; William A. Schabas, *International Human Rights and the Canadian Charter*, 2d ed. (Scarborough, ON: Carswell, 1996).

39 *Slaight Communications Inc. v. Davidson*, [1989] 1 S.C.R. 1038 at 1056.

40 It has also been described as "implicit implementation": see Elisabeth Eid & Hoori Hamboyan, "Implementation by Canada of its International Human Rights Treaty Obligations: Making Sense Out of the Nonsensical" in this text, Chapter 13.

ciples controlling the internalization of international law. In essence, what the courts have done towards resolving the treaty implementation question is to turn it, very largely, into a matter of interpretation of domestic and international legal sources, which is the subject of Question 4.

E. QUESTION 4—HOW SHOULD DIFFERENT INTERNATIONAL LEGAL SOURCES BE EMPLOYED?

Judicial recourse to international legal sources has been incredibly varied from court to court and case to case. Nevertheless, two propositions will be ventured about the general character of this judicial practice. For most of the twentieth century Canadian courts shied away from international law. Perhaps ignorant of its relevance or unsure of how to handle it, they tended to disregard it and even to treat it with the contempt of exclusionary nationalism. During the last decade, in which the case of *Baker v. Canada*[41] may conveniently be treated as a turning point, judicial attitudes changed and the pendulum of opinion swung to the other extreme. Nowadays courts are likely to refer to every available international legal source indiscriminately in pursuit of inclusive globalism. Detailing the basis for these propositions would be long and tedious and, indeed, the evidence would be conflicted. This paper will simply illustrate them in order to demonstrate the enormity of the change in curial practice, as a stepping stone to the important question: How *should* the courts employ international legal sources in the twenty first century?

In the bad old days, making reference to international law could be anathema to judicial ears. Take *Gordon v. R. in Right of Canada*[42] decided in 1980 as an example. Gordon was charged with unlawfully fishing within Canada's declared 200-nautical-mile fishing zone but outside its territorial sea. Gordon argued in his defence that he was fishing in the high seas, beyond Canadian jurisdiction, with freedom of navigation and fishing obtained under international law. In fact, at the time, though the UN Law of the Sea Convention had not been concluded, evidence was amassing that the exclusive regulation of 200-nautical-mile fishing zones by coastal states, like Canada, was acceptable practice in customary international law. But the court was not interested in international law. It held:

---

41 *Baker v. Canada (Minister of Citizenship and Immigration)*, above note 18.

42 [1980] 5 W.W.R. 668 (B.C.S.C.) aff'd [1980] 6 W.W.R. 519 (B.C.C.A.).

[W]here Canada asserts jurisdiction over an area of the sea and purports to limit access thereto, from the standpoint of domestic law the access is in fact limited for a special purpose, and even if the law of Canada contravenes "customary international law," if Parliament, as here, has acted unambiguously, the courts of this country are bound to apply the domestic law.[43]

This kind of exclusionary parochialism has not been eradicated from Canadian courts even after the asserted change in judicial attitudes. Another example, this time involving treaties rather than customary law, is *Pfizer Canada Inc. v. Canada (Attorney General)*[44] in 2003. Pfizer sought judicial review of the refusal of the Minister of Health to list certain Canadian patents under the Patented Medicines regulations. The case turned on the meaning of "a filing date" in the regulations. The Federal Court of Appeal declared itself satisfied that the meaning was amply clear in the regulations and so it refused to resort to three relevant treaties, basing its opinion "on the long-established jurisprudence that while Parliament is presumed not to intend to legislate contrary to international treaties or general principles of international law, this is only a presumption: where the legislation is clear one need not and should not look to international law."[45]

Turning from exclusion of international legal sources to universal inclusion, a particularly exorbitant example was the trial court judgment in *Re Alberta Union of Provincial Employees and the Crown in Right of Alberta.*[46] The case concerned the right to strike within the public service. In the report of the case, extensive reference was made to a wide variety of international legal sources. They included:

- *Treaty of Versailles*;
- ILO Convention 87, ratified by Canada;
- *International Covenant on Economic, Social and Cultural Rights*;
- *Universal Declaration of Human Rights* (a UN General Assembly resolution);
- ILO case no. 893;

43   *Ibid.* at 670–71 (B.C.S.C.).
44   (2003), 224 D.L.R. (4th) 178 (F.C.A.).
45   *Ibid.* at paras. 13 and 20. See also *Schavernoch v. Foreign Claims Commission*, [1982] 1 S.C.R. 1092 at 1098.
46   (1980), 120 D.L.R. (3d) 590. (Alta. Q.B.).

- ILO Reports of the International Labour Conferences in 1977 and 1978.

No one need doubt the relevance of the contents of these materials to the issue before the court, but how were they applied? After thirty pages spent rehearsing the contending parties' arguments around these materials, the court delivered a one-and-a-half-page judgment that failed to explain what distinctions had been drawn between the different types of international sources, if any, or what use had been made of them.[47]

These examples of parochial exclusion and global inclusion of international legal sources are not models of judicial practice because they are unprincipled. A successful search for a principled approach to the use of international legal sources in the welter of diverse cases needs to pay attention to two sustaining canons of statutory interpretation. The older of the two is the presumption of legislative conformity with international law. The more recent and more expansive of them is the contextual approach to interpretation.

1) The Presumption of Legislative Conformity with International Law

The presumption of legislative conformity demands that judges seek an interpretation of a statute that is consistent with all relevant international laws, whether customary or conventional, that are binding on Canada.[48] The presumption has a substantial history, though it is chequered by those occasions, previously illustrated, when the courts refused to consider relevant international law. But in recent years it has been acknowledged openly and frequently at the highest judicial level.

An early Canadian example of the application of the presumption is *Re Arrow River* in 1932.[49] Though they did not name the presumption, the Supreme Court justices each strove to find an interpretation of the *Lakes and Rivers Improvements Act* of Ontario that was congruent with the Webster-Ashburton Treaty. The case is a very instructive example of the scope of intertextual reading. One of the first clear statements of the presumption

---

47 And see *Dunmore v. Ontario (Attorney General)*, [2001] 3 S.C.R. 1016 at 1050 for a more recent example of recourse to ratified treaties without explaining the basis on which they were invoked.

48 See the excellent discussion of the presumption by van Ert, above note 8 at 99–136.

49 *Re Arrow River and Tributaries Slide and Boom Co. Ltd.*, [1932] 2 D.L.R. 250 (S.C.C.).

was made in 1968 by Pigeon J. in *Daniels v. White and the Queen*[50] when he declared "the rule of construction that Parliament is not presumed to legislate in breach of a treaty or in any manner inconsistent with the comity of nations and the established rules of international law. It is a rule that is not often applied because if a statute is unambiguous, its provisions must be followed even if they are contrary to international law."

The presumption was expressed very strongly in the Supreme Court in *R. v. Zingre*[51] in 1981 by Dickson J., as he then was, when he stated: "It is the duty of the Court, in interpreting the ... Treaty and ... Act to give them a fair and liberal interpretation with a view to fulfilling Canada's international obligations." This is a powerful affirmation of the presumption on three counts. First, it designates the application of the presumption as a "duty" of the courts: no stronger statement of its legal force could be made. Secondly, it is not content with a passive approach by which courts check that their interpretation of a statute is not inconsistent with international law: it demands that they endeavour actively to "fulfil" the international law along with the legislation. Thirdly, Dickson J.'s statement refers to "Canada's international obligations" thus including all sources of international law, not just treaties.

Recently the presumption of conformity with international law has been reiterated frequently by the Supreme Court in, for example, *National Corn Growers Association v. Canada (Import Tribunal)*,[52] *Ordon Estate v. Grail*,[53] *R. v. Sharpe*,[54] *Spraytech*[55] and *Canadian Foundation for Children, Youth and the Law v. Canada (Attorney General)*.[56] In the last case in 2004 the presumption was again presented as an affirmative responsibility of the courts with respect to all sources of international law. Chief Justice McLachlin wrote: "Statutes should be construed to comply with Canada's international obligations."[57]

---

50 [1968] S.C.R. 517 at 541. See also *C.A.P.A.C. v. CTV Television Network*, [1968] S.C.R. 676.
51 [1981] 2 S.C.R. 392 at 409–10.
52 Above note 25 at 1371 (S.C.C.).
53 [1998] 3 S.C.R. 437 at 526.
54 [2001] 1 S.C.R. 45 at 75.
55 *114957 Canada Ltée (Spraytech, Société d'arrosage) v. Hudson (Town)*, [2001] 2 S.C.R. 241 at 266.
56 [2004] 1 S.C.R. 76.
57 *Ibid.* at 100.

The presumption of conformity is not an absolute rule for the simple reason that, as discussed above in Question 2, the constitutional doctrine of the supremacy of Parliament demands that a court give effect to a statute that cannot be reconciled with international law binding on Canada but, rather, contravenes it. This canon of construction is presumptive, not absolute, because it is rebuttable. It is one of several aids to the courts, yet it is a particularly significant one as it supports the contextual approach to statutory interpretation, discussed below. Further, as Dickson J. and McLachlin C.J.C. declared, it places a serious duty on courts to take affirmative action. The earlier views of Pigeon J. when he qualified "the rule of construction" by saying it is "not often applied because if a statute is unambiguous, its provisions must be followed even if they are contrary to international law,"[58] are now outdated. In the last three and a half decades since Pigeon J. gave his opinion, there has been an upsurge in treaty making which has affected matters of daily life rather than diplomatic relations much more than in the past.[59] As a result, there are many more occasions when domestic and international laws address the same subject. Whenever they do, it is no longer enough, if it ever was, to stop from considering international legal sources because a statute appears on its face to be clear, plain, and unambiguous. That is a passive response that permits the kind of exclusion of international law that occurred in *Gordon's* case. It was expressly rejected by Gonthier J. in *National Corn Growers*[60] and contravenes the affirmative duty explained by Dickson J. in *R. v. Zingre* and reiterated by McLachlin C.J.C. in *Canadian Foundation for Children*. It also runs counter to the practice of contextual interpretation, the second sustaining canon of construction for consideration.

2) The Contextual Approach to Statutory Interpretation

Judicial interpretation of statutes in context is a relatively recent practice. Previously, the literal approach to statutory interpretation, alias the plain meaning rule, along with its variants in the event of ambiguity or other lack of clarity in the legislative phraseology, was the extant method of the courts for a very long time. It required them to seek the intention of the

---

58 See *Daniels*, above note 50.

59 See Kindred, above note 13.

60 Above note 25 at 1371 (S.C.C.): "The ... suggestion that recourse to an international treaty is only available where the provision of the domestic legislation is ambiguous on its face is to be rejected."

legislature primarily, if not exclusively, in the words of the statute alone. It excluded a rich source of material evidence extrinsic to the statutory text, such as its legislative history, scholarly commentary, and all international legal sources. Now the literal approach, together with its clutter of exceptions and addenda, has given way to the contextual approach to statutory interpretation.

The acknowledged authority on statutory interpretation in Canada in the English language, *Driedger on the Construction of Statutes*, has declared there is but one "modern" principle:

> There is only one rule in modern interpretation, namely, courts are obliged to determine the meaning of legislation in its total context, having regard to the purpose of the legislation, the consequences of proposed interpretations, the presumptions and special rules of interpretation, as well as admissible external aids.[61]

In a symbiotic relationship, the courts have quoted Driedger's text while successive editions of Driedger have reformulated the governing principle in light of the courts' pronouncements.[62] Certainly, a series of Supreme Court judgments has consistently voiced and supported the "modern" method of interpreting statutes from *Hills v. Canada (Attorney General)*[63] in 1988 forward.[64]

The significance of the guiding force of the contextual approach to statutory interpretation is the inclusiveness of the methodology. Reference to the total or entire context of the statute in question demands the courts have recourse to any and all relevant international legal sources. Combined with the presumption of statutory conformity with international law, a powerful new engine of what might be called internationalized justice[65] is at work in Canadian courts.

---

61 Ruth Sullivan, *Driedger on the Construction of Statutes*, 3d ed. (Markham, ON: Butterworths, 1994) at 330.

62 Compare 3d ed., *ibid.*, and 2d ed. (Toronto: Butterworths, 1983) at 87.

63 [1988] 1 S.C.R. 513.

64 See also *2747-3174 Quebec Inc. v. Quebec (Régie des permis d'alcool)*, [1996] 3 S.C.R. 919, *Verdun v. Toronto-Dominion Bank*, [1996] 3 S.C.R. 550, *Royal Bank of Canada v. Sparrow Electric Corp.*, [1997] 1 S.C.R. 411, *R. v. Hydro-Québec*, [1997] 1 S.C.R. 213, *Re Rizzo & Rizzo Shoes Ltd.*, [1998] 1 S.C.R. 27, *R. v. Gladue*, [1999] 1 S.C.R. 688, *R. v. Sharpe*, [2001] 1 S.C.R. 45, *Chieu v. Canada (Minister of Citizenship and Immigration)*, [2002] 1 S.C.R. 84.

65 Or globalized justice: see, for example, Anne-Marie Slaughter, "Judicial Globalization" (2000) 40 Va. J. Int'l L. 1103. See also Gérard V. La Forest, "The Expanding Role of the

3) Nourishing the Interpretation of Statutes with Ratified Treaties

Yet the "modern" methodology of statutory interpretation also begets a modern problem - the indiscriminate application of international legal sources. When should a court invoke a particular document or source of international law? How should it be deployed? The courts have barely addressed these questions and are in need of guiding principles. The resort to contextual interpretation, after all, involves reference to extrinsic evidence, which, like all evidence, bears different degrees of credibility, weight, and relevance.

Fortunately, there is guidance to be found in international law itself. A primary source is the *Vienna Convention on the Law of Treaties*,[66] particularly articles 31 and 32 on the interpretation of treaties. Overlooked for many years, the courts have now adopted these articles as the appropriate principles for interpreting treaty obligations that have been incorporated into Canadian law.[67] But their Canadian application has not been extended to treaty obligations on Canada that have not been legislatively implemented. For their use, initial and limited guidance was provided by the renowned *Baker* case.[68] In it, Justice L'Heureux-Dubé, writing for the majority of 5-2, expressly undertook a contextual approach to statutory interpretation and implicitly applied the presumption of statutory conformity with international law. After reciting that international conventions are not part of Canadian law unless they have been implemented by statute, Justice L'Heureux-Dubé went on to declare that the values reflected in them may be used to inform the contextual interpretation of a statute. Her judgment

---

Supreme Court of Canada in International Law Issues" (1996) 34 Can. Y.B. Int'l L. 89; William A. Schabas, "Twenty-Five Years of Public International Law at the Supreme Court of Canada" (2000) 79 Can. Bar Rev. 174; Knop, above note 1; Stephen Toope, "The Use of Metaphor: International Law and the Supreme Court" (2001) 80 Can. Bar Rev. 534; David Dyzenhaus, Murray Hunt & Michael Taggart, "The Principle of Legality in Administrative Law: Internationalisation as Constitutionalisation" (2001) 1 O.U.C.L.J. 5; Irit Weiser, "Undressing the Window: Treating International Human Rights Law Meaningfully in the Canadian Commonwealth System" (2004) 37 U.B.C. L. Rev. 113 at 116–20.

66 Above note 2.

67 See *Re Regina and Palacios* (1984), 45 O.R. (2d) 269 (C.A.); *Thomson v. Thomson*, [1994] 3 S.C.R. 551; *Pushpanathan v. Canada (Minister of Citizenship and Immigration)*, [1998] 1 S.C.R. 982.

68 *Baker v. Canada (Minister of Citizenship and Immigration)*, above note 18.

contains a fine demonstration of this new technique in relating the *UN Convention on the Rights of the Child* to the *Immigration Act*.[69]

The significance of the new interpretive technique lies in the narrowness of the distinction between implemented and unimplemented treaty obligations. The letter of the law of the *UN Convention on the Rights of the Child* could not be applied directly alongside the *Immigration Act* for lack of statutory incorporation, but the spirit of the principles of the Convention were employed to influence the interpretation of the Act. The technique exhibits strong features of adoption of the treaty even though it has not been formally and explicitly transformed.[70]

Subsequently the Supreme Court demonstrated the power of this technique in *Suresh's* case.[71] Suresh, who was a member of the Tamil Tigers, which the Canadian government considered a terrorist group, appealed a deportation order on the grounds that he risked torture if returned to Sri Lanka. The order was made pursuant to the *Immigration Act*, which incorporates article 33 of the *Convention on the Status of Refugees* by which a state shall not return or *refouler* a refugee except where there are reasonable grounds for regarding him or her as a danger to the security of the host country. The Supreme Court deployed two ratified but unimplemented treaties, the *International Covenant on Civil and Political Rights* and the *Convention Against Torture*, to read down the scope of the section of the *Immigration Act* that implemented the exception to *non refoulement* in the *Convention on the Status of Refugees*. Though the article of the Refugee Convention had the force of a statute in Canada, the subsequently ratified treaties, even though they had not been actively transformed into Canadian law, occasioned a new interpretation of the existing statutory provision.[72] The remarkable development of this technique confirms the concluding

---

69 For fuller comments on the interpretive technique employed in *Baker*, see Hugh Kindred, "The Use of Unimplemented Treaties in Canada: Practice and Prospects in the Supreme Court" in Chi Carmody, Yuji Iwasawa & Sylvia Rhodes, eds., *Trilateral Perspectives on International Legal Issues: Conflict and Coherence* (Baltimore, MD: American Society of International Law, 2003) 3 at 22–26.

70 The case provides no evidence whether the Convention might have been passively incorporated, as discussed above at note 40.

71 *Suresh v. Canada (Minister of Citizenship and Immigration)*, above note 18. See also *Ahani v. Canada (Minister of Citizenship and Immigration)*, [2002] 1 S.C.R. 72. And see Stephane Beaulac, "The *Suresh* Case and Unimplemented Treaty Norms" (2002) 15 R.Q.D.I. 221.

72 More precisely, the two ratified treaties impacted the act through the medium of the *Canadian Charter*. The ICCPR and the CAT substantiated a norm of international law

observation to Question 3 that the issue of legislative implementation has largely, but not completely, been transformed into a matter of statutory interpretation.[73]

4) Using Soft Law Sources in the Courts

It is noticeable that *Baker* and *Suresh* both involved treaties to which Canada is a party. One might expect ratified treaties to carry considerable weight of influence even if not directly applicable. By comparison, how should the courts treat other international legal sources that do not contain binding obligations for Canada? They might be, for example:

- multilateral treaties in force, but not ratified by Canada;
- *travaux préparatoires* of treaties that may or may not be in force for Canada;
- UN resolutions of various kinds and effects;
- guidelines, general comments, and interpretive handbooks issued by executive bodies within the UN, other universal and regional IGOs and treaty compliance bodies, of which Canada may or may not be a state party;
- foreign state practice around a multilateral treaty;
- foreign and international judicial decisions on a multilateral treaty;
- foreign and international arbitral awards on a multilateral treaty;
- scholarly commentaries on international law.

Treaty obligations are the hard edge of this large collection of international legal sources that quickly shades off to soft law. International lawyers understand the elusive yet significant category of "soft law," but the term does not seem to be familiar to domestic counsel and courts, who have yet to develop the analytic tools to handle it.[74]

---

that informed the contents of the Canadian principles of fundamental justice in the *Canadian Charter* s. 7, which in turn circumscribed the scope of the *Immigration Act*.

73 An alternative interpretation of *Suresh's* case also buttresses this conclusion. Although the ratified treaties in question had not been explicitly transformed into Canadian law, they might be considered to have been passively implemented by existing legislation and the *Canadian Charter*, and so the legal issue was simply a matter of statutory interpretation informed by the relevant international law.

74 Justice LeBel of the Supreme Court admitted as much: see LeBel & Chao, above note 18 at 62–64. See also the observations of Weiser, above note 65 at 141; and Eid & Hamboyan, above note 40.

At this point, notice must be taken of the way these soft law sources operate. They do not create binding obligations for Canada and, apart from multilateral treaties to which Canada is not a party, they are not law for any other state. Most often, they are the experience and (state) practice around a treaty, and, as such, they are an intrinsic yet subsidiary part of it. Consequently the use of such international sources is a further step removed from the interpretation of the statutory provisions in question. They function as interpretive aids for the treaty which, in turn, is the interpretive standard or aid[75] for the legislation before the court. This distinction in the status and function of soft law is most important, yet it is hardly ever expressly noted and honoured by the courts.

A rare example was *Quebec (Minister of Justice) v. Canada (Minister of Justice)*.[76] In this reference case, Quebec challenged the validity of a number of sections of the federal *Youth Criminal Justice Act* (*YCJA*). One of the four questions presented to the court asked: "Are the legislative provisions proposed in the *YCJA* compatible with full compliance with international treaties ratified by Canada?" The treaties placed before the Quebec Court of Appeal were the *Convention on the Rights of the Child* and the *International Covenant on Civil and Political Rights*. In addition the Court was referred to three international instruments that were drawn up prior to the two conventions and adopted by the UN General Assembly. They were the UN Standard Minimum Rules for the Administration of Juvenile Justice (known as the Beijing Rules), the UN Guidelines for the Prevention of Juvenile Delinquency (known as the Riyadh Guidelines), and the UN Rules for the Protection of Juveniles Deprived of Their Liberty. Developed by deliberation multilaterally and then adopted by UN resolution, these instruments are classic examples of non-binding international directives, or soft laws.

What was the court to do with these international legal sources? Both attorneys-general proposed, and the court accepted, that the two ratified treaties had to be interpreted in light of these instruments, which, in turn, had to be considered in light of the observations and recommendations of the Convention implementation committees.[77] This is an appropriate, double-sided proposition about the interpretation of treaties. The prior instruments provided contextual references for the interpretation of the

---

75 This depends on whether the treaty has been formally incorporated into Canadian law.
76 (2003), 228 D.L.R. (4th) 228 (Que. C.A.).
77 *Ibid.* at para. 119.

provisions of the conventions, yet their assistance was moderated by any observations made about their provisions by the bodies set up to oversee the performance of the conventions. This double aspect or feedback loop is true of all interrelated international legal materials, but an important distinction must be observed accordingly as the legal sources are mandatory or only hortatory in nature. Soft laws may influence the interpretation of hard laws, like ratified conventions, but they cannot modify, amend or overreach their provisions. The Quebec Court of Appeal made careful note of the impact of this distinction when it said:

> [I]t is worthwhile reiterating that the only coercive provisions in international law for the signatory States are those in the Convention and Covenant. The others are merely instruments for interpreting the philosophy and wording where necessary. The distinction is important in this case, since, to the extent that the wording and interpretation of a provision of the Convention do not reflect the philosophy or the wording of the instruments that preceded or followed the Convention's ratification, those instruments are irrelevant to the question we have been asked. It must immediately be pointed out that, for example, article 3 of the Convention ... does not necessarily reflect all the rules adopted prior to it.[78]

The contribution of *Quebec (Attorney General) v. Canada (Attorney General)* to the issue of using international legal sources is an important first step. In particular, the distinction between hard law and soft law sources needs to be imbibed by Canadian courts generally. But further guidance on the interrelationship of hard and soft legal sources is also necessary. The principled use of international soft law sources in domestic courts has yet to be addressed by them. In this, international law itself can offer help.

Just as the Canadian courts have consciously adopted the provisions of articles 31 and 32 of the *Vienna Convention on the Law of Treaties* as the appropriate principles for the interpretation of ratified treaties brought before them, so they might usefully be employed to determine the contextual significance of related soft law sources. After initially exhorting faithfulness to the text of the treaty, the articles provide an organized structure for prioritizing access to related but subsidiary sources as means to achieve a contextualized interpretation. Article 31 specifies the kinds of subsidiary instruments that constitute the immediate context of the treaty and they relate to that any subsequent agreements or practice of the parties to the

---

78   *Ibid.* at para. 127.

treaty. Article 32 describes further supplementary aids to interpretation, which include the treaty's *travaux préparatoires,* along with the circumstances in which they may be used.

It is not appropriate in the context of this paper to explore the details of the rules to be found in Articles 31 and 32, but it is important to point out that these articles of the Vienna Convention address the use of all the commonly available soft law sources surrounding a treaty that might come before Canadian courts. The contents and mode of application of the articles are well known to international lawyers but need to be brought to the attention of domestic counsel and courts. A resolution of the question about how to employ international legal sources in Canadian courts may be found in international law itself if one is prepared to look there.[79]

F. CONCLUSION

The diagnosis in this paper reveals a remarkable change in the attitude of the Supreme Court of Canada towards the use of international legal sources. The inclusivity of its modern approach is a welcome development that is fully in tune with, and perhaps leading, the global trend towards more internationalized justice. Yet by no means have all the problems surrounding the use of international legal sources been resolved, and the implications of the developments so far for the Canadian legal system have yet to be widely understood and absorbed.

In the absence of constitutional clarity over the impact of international law domestically, the courts have rendered contradictory precedents containing confusing ideas about the role of international law as a source of law in Canada. More recently the Supreme Court of Canada has shown concerted leadership and given explicit directions, at least on how to handle conventional international law that is binding on Canada. The Court continues to maintain a clear line of distinction between those ratified treaties that have been implemented in Canadian law and those that have not, thus protecting the fundamental Canadian constitutional values of representative democracy as divided between federal and provincial spheres of operation. Yet it has sharply narrowed the margin of difference on both sides of

---

79   Compare the illuminating analytical framework proposed by Irit Weiser, above note 65 at 143–55. See also the thoughtful analysis of similar issues about the role of international law in *Canadian Charter* cases in Anne Warner La Forest, "Domestic Application of International Law in *Charter* Cases: Are We There Yet?" (2004) 37 U.B.C. L. Rev. 157.

that clear line by reducing the significance of the act of legislative transformation of treaty provisions into Canadian law.

The actions of the Supreme Court show that implementation of a treaty no longer needs to be an affirmative transformation made manifest in explicit legislation. Rather, they demonstrate the practice of a passive approach that accepts the implicit implementation of ratified treaty provisions in the presence of legislation that applies the same rights and fulfils the same obligations. Backed by the presumption that the legislature does not intend to legislate contrary to international law, members of the Supreme Court have declared it a duty of the courts to seek an interpretation of a statute that comports with Canada's obligations under ratified treaties whenever possible, unless the contrary intent of the legislature is demonstrated. But this description of what the Supreme Court has been doing in a collection of recent cases has not yet been explicitly recognized and propounded in any judgment.

While the Supreme Court has been reducing the burden of demonstrable implementation of treaties binding on Canada, it has also been enhancing the impact of ratified but unimplemented treaties. Rather than ignore them, as courts have often done in the past, the Supreme Court now expects courts to employ the spirit and values underlying a relevant ratified treaty as aids in the interpretation of related statutes and delegated administrative powers, in addition to rights under the *Canadian Charter*. This new practice has received explicit judicial formulation as well as demonstration in practice. As a result, Canadian courts are bound to take much more attentive account of ratified treaties, whether implemented or not.

Curial reference and use of the wide range of international legal sources other than ratified treaties has not yet received the same degree of judicial care and scrutiny. The inclusion of non-binding international instruments and precedents as extrinsic yet material aids in the interpretation of Canada's laws is, indeed, a welcome consequence of the Supreme Court's modern contextual approach to statutory construction. But crucial distinctions between different types of sources recognized internationally have yet to be acknowledged domestically. Hardly has the non-binding character of soft law been recognized, let alone the variance in evidential weight and effect of the different sources, or the differing ways they may legitimately be asserted as interpretive aids. These refinements to the inclusive use of international legal sources in Canadian courts have yet to be propounded, but, as with the domestic adoption of international practices in the interpretation of treaties, so, in due course, the courts could usefully take guidance from international experience in handling the great wealth of soft law sources. While the courts are profitably set upon a course of contextual interpretation, they have yet to clarify all its implications for the use of international legal sources, as they might, by adapting fully to the techniques afforded by the international legal process.

Implementation and Reception: The Congeniality of Canada's Legal Order to International Law*

ARMAND DE MESTRAL AND EVAN FOX-DECENT

A. INTRODUCTION: *PACTA SUNT SERVANDA*—PACTS MUST BE RESPECTED

The degree to which international law is integrated and respected within a particular state's domestic legal order depends importantly on the nature of the relationship between the state's domestic law and international law. In this paper we reconsider the relationship between Canada's domestic law and the international treaties that Canada has ratified but that Parliament is alleged to have failed to implement. Two central doctrines animate the judiciary's present approach to such treaties. The first doctrine is that these instruments are not binding as a matter of domestic law because Parliament alone has domestic law-making authority, and this authority would be usurped if the executive could unilaterally make law by ratifying treaties.[1] The second doctrine is that ratified but unimplemented conventions inform the legal context within which Parliament's laws are presumed to

---

* We are indebted to T. Tankut Soykan for invaluable research assistance, to Gibran van Ert for fruitful comments and suggestions, and to the Social Science and Humanities Research Council for the financial assistance that made this paper possible.

1 *Capital Cities Communications Inc. v. Canadian Radio-Television Commission*, [1978] 2 S.C.R. 141 [*Capital Cities*]; Iacobucci and Cory JJ.'s partial dissent in *Baker v. Canada (Minister of Citizenship and Immigration)*, [1999] 2 S.C.R. 817 at 821 [*Baker*]; *Suresh v. Canada (Minister of Citizenship and Immigration*, [2002] 1 S.C.R. 3, 208 D.L.R. (4th) 1 at para. 60 [*Suresh*]: "International treaty norms are not, strictly speaking, binding in Canada unless they have been incorporated into Canadian law by enactment."

operate, and thus interpretations of domestic legislation that are consistent with international law are to be preferred.[2]

The principal rationale underlying the first doctrine is based on a separation of powers argument that concerns democratic accountability. Parliament provides an institutional forum in which proposed domestic legislation is debated, and Members of Parliament are accountable to their constituents for the laws they vote for and against. Notwithstanding these elemental truths, we argue that the demands of democratic accountability can, and should, be met by an understanding of international law that is less dismissive of its domestic effect than the approach suggested by the first doctrine, even when this doctrine is tempered by the second. We argue that, in a multitude of cases, treaties can be understood to have been implemented and otherwise received into Canada's common law independently of whether Parliament has passed an Act for the express purpose of implementation. As a consequence, ratified treaties ought to be understood to be binding on the executive (ministers, frontline decision-makers, boards, tribunals, commissions, agencies, and so on) unless Parliament explicitly signals through legislation that some or all of a treaty's provisions are of no or limited effect.[3] More specifically, our claim is that the obligations found in ratified treaties ought to enjoy the same legal status as common law obligations found in other areas of public law, such as the duty of procedural fairness.

In short, our argument is that although Parliament can and should play a much more active role in defining the contours of the ongoing rela-

---

2   *Baker, ibid.* at 860–61. For a thorough discussion of the tension and interplay between these two ideas, see Gibran van Ert, *Using International Law in Canadian Courts* (The Hague: Kluwer Law International, 2002). For the argument that domestic law *must* be interpreted in a manner that conforms with Canada's international legal obligations (as opposed to the idea that courts *may* interpret domestic legislation in a manner consistent with such obligations, so long as there is no direct conflict, to resolve ambiguities and to "inform" the way in which statutory discretion must be exercised), see Stephen J. Toope & Jutta Brunnée, "A Hesitant Embrace: The Application of International Law by Canadian Courts" (2002) 50 Can. Y.B. Int'l L 3 [Toope & Brunnée]. In a sense, and with a few modifications, we think that our argument is the logical endpoint of Toope and Brunnée's view that ratified treaties ought to be viewed as binding upon courts and public bodies seized with interpreting domestic law and determining the proper exercise of discretionary powers.

3   There may be constitutional constraints as well, either as a result of Canada's federalism or by virtue of the *Canadian Charter of Rights and Freedoms,* Part I of the *Constitution Act, 1982,* being Sch. B to the *Canada Act 1982* (U.K.), 1982, c. 11 [*Charter*]. For the sake of economy, we do not discuss such constraints, and note simply that the provisions of treaties would have to conform to Canada's Constitution to have legal effect.

tionship between international and domestic law (we make some concrete recommendations on how this might transpire in the final section below), it is time to reverse the presumption that Parliament must do something explicit following ratification of a treaty in order for a treaty to serve as the basis for legal duties that constrain the administration's exercises of public powers. Parliament always retains authority to strike down particular provisions of ratified treaties, but requiring Parliament to express its will in such a way strengthens rather than weakens Canada's democratic legitimacy.

B. HARMONIZING THE INTERNATIONAL AND DOMESTIC EFFECT OF INTERNATIONAL LAW

The constitutions of some countries subordinate domestic law to international law;[4] others give all treaties a status equal to statutory enactments provided they are approved by the legislature;[5] still others establish a special

---

4   For instance, according to art. 94 of the Netherlands' constitution, "Within the Kingdom, legal regulations in force shall not be applicable if such application is incompatible with provisions of treaties that are binding on all persons or of resolutions by international organizations." Nonetheless, it must be noted that art. 91(3) of the Dutch constitution states that if there is a conflict between a certain provision of an international agreement and the constitution, such an international agreement must be approved by the legislature with the same qualified majority necessary for changing the constitution. *Constitution of the Kingdom of the Netherlands*, 1983 (as amended to 2002). The status of international agreements is even higher in the Turkish constitution. Article 90 (5) explicitly states that compatibility of an international agreement with the Constitution cannot be challenged before the Constitutional Court. Moreover, ratification of such agreements is not subject to the approval of any qualified majority in the legislature. Article 90(5) also stipulates: "In case of contradiction between international agreements regarding basic rights and freedoms approved through proper procedure and domestic laws, due to different provisions on the same issue, the provisions of international agreements shall be considered." *Constitution of the Republic of Turkey*, 1982 (as amended to 2001).

5   Article 133 of the Constitution of Mexico states: "[the] Constitution, the laws of the Congress of the Union that emanate therefrom, and *all the treaties that have been concluded and shall be concluded in accordance therewith by the President of the Republic, with the approval of the Senate*, shall be the Supreme Law of the whole Union" [emphasis added]. The Political Constitution of the United Mexican States, 1917 (as amended to 2003). Moreover, pursuant to Article 53 of the French constitution, "Peace treaties, commercial treaties, treaties or agreements relating to international organization, those that commit the finances of the State, those that modify provisions which are matters for statute, those relating to the status of persons, and those that involve the cession, exchange or addition of territory, can be ratified or approved only by virtue of an Act of Parliament." *The Constitution of France*, 1958 (as amended to 2003).

procedure for the approval of a limited category of treaties by the legislature.[6] The Constitution of Canada is silent on everything relating to international law, except for the implementation of the largely spent category of
"Empire Treaties"[7] and the recently adopted provision in the *Charter* ensuring that Canadian courts may exercise jurisdiction over war crimes committed abroad.[8] This is an unfortunate omission, all the more so with the
ever increasing globalization of the work of government, human rights,
business, and the lives of ordinary Canadians. It is unfortunate that at a
time when some 40 percent of the Statutes of Canada are adopted to implement international commitments in whole or in part,[9] the very *concept*
of implementation is shrouded in confusion, and the courts have only recently begun to come to grips with an issue long resolved in many other
comparable jurisdictions.

If there is any clear logic underlying the approach of the courts it is
founded upon a dualist approach that, implicitly or explicitly, sees domestic and international law as constituting two different legal systems. According to this approach, international law, at least in the form of a treaty,
can have effect in the Canadian legal system only if it is accompanied by
an explicit act of transposition or transformation through which the international rule is made part of the Canadian legal system, that is, "implemented." Implementation occurs through a deliberate act of the legislature
that subjects the treaty to the will of Parliament. According to this assumption, without appropriate implementation, the international treaty rule is
at best a rule binding the executive in some other sphere unrelated to Canadian domestic law. The unity of law itself, particularly the unity of the
rule of law, is thereby neglected in favour of an approach which denies
international law—especially treaty law—from having the force of law, despite it being one of the primary sources and inspirations of contemporary
law-making in a host of different fields.[10]

---

6 Section 2(2) of the United States of America's Constitution stipulates: "[the President]
   shall have Power, by and with the Advice and Consent of the Senate, to make Treaties,
   provided two thirds of the Senators present concur ..." U.S. Const. art. II, s. 2.
7 *Constitution Act, 1867* (U.K.), 30 & 31 Vict., c. 3, s. 132, reprinted in R.S.C. 1985, App.
   II, No. 5. Now *Constitution Act, 1982*, Sch. B of the *Canada Act, 1982* (U.K.), 1982, c. 11
   [*Constitution Act, 1982*].
8 *Charter*, above note 3, art. 9.
9 Authors' estimate is based on review of revised federal legislation.
10 These fields include, for example, transportation by air, sea, rail, and road, communications and telecommunications, international trade, environment, food safety, health,
   education, human rights, the conduct of armed conflict, and movement of people.

Customary law is an interesting exception to the dualist approach in the Anglo-Canadian-American legal tradition, an exception that finds its origins in cases dating back to the eighteenth century,[11] when Lord Mansfield and other leading common law judges affirmed that "the Law of Nations will be affirmed as much in England as in any country."[12] This is an affirmation that sits well with the common law, based as it is on custom. International custom is seen as being "adopted" by the common law as a rule of English law without the need for any act of transformation. Canadian courts appear to have accepted this position on customary international law;[13] certainly it is the position of the Ontario Court of Appeal.[14] But some authors have noted disturbing *dicta* in certain recent cases that suggest a judicial approach that confuses customary international law with treaty law, *dicta* that might thereby impose a duty of explicit transformation on customary rules as well as on treaties.[15]

Here we consider several issues related to the implementation of international treaties in Canadian law where the relationship between the two appears to be particularly dysfunctional, despite efforts of many courts in recent years to respond to ever increasing pleas based on international law.[16] One of the principal areas of judicial activity and concern has been that of human rights as reflected in the *Charter;* the search for the meaning of different provisions of the *Charter* has been intense and has inevitably led Canadian advocates to examine the many international human rights treaties to which Canada is a party. As a result, some commentators suggest that there is a particularly close relationship between these treaties

11   *Heathfield v. Chilton* (1767), 4 Burr. 2015; *Schooner Exchange v. McFaddon* (1812), 7 Cranch 116 at 146 (U.S.S.C.).

12   *Heathfield v. Chilton, ibid.* at 2016.

13   *Ref. Re Foreign Legations, (sub nom. Reference Re: Powers of Ottawa (City) and Rockcliffe Park)* [1943] S.C.R. 208; *Saint John (City) v. Fraser-Brace Corp.,* [1958] S.C.R. 263.

14   *Re Regina and Palacios,* (1984), 45 O.R. (2d) 269 (C.A.) *[Re Regina and Palacios]; Bouzari v. Islamic Republic of Iran,* [2004] O.J. No. 2800 (C.A.) *[Bouzari].*

15   Toope & Brunnée, above note 2 at 26.

16   See *Re Regina and Palacios,* above note 14; *Bouzari,* above note 14; *National Corn Growers Assn. v. Canada (Import Tribunal),* [1990] 2 S.C.R. 1324 *[National Corn Growers]; Baker,* above note 1; *Ordon Estate v. Grail,* [1998] 3 S.C.R. 437; *United States of America v. Public Service Alliance of Canada et al.* (1992), 91 D.L.R. (4th) 449 (S.C.C.) *[Public Service Alliance]; Suresh,* above note 1; *114957 Canada Ltée (Spraytech, Société d'arrosage) v. Hudson (Town),* [2001] 2 S.C.R. 241, 2001 SCC 40; *Ahani v. Canada (Minister of Citizenship and Immigration),* [2002] 1 S.C.R. 72, 2002 SCC 2; *Schreiber v. Canada (Attorney General),* [2002] 3 S.C.R. 269, 2002 SCC 62.

and the *Charter* that should be reflected in a higher degree of receptivity to these treaties than might be the case for other categories.[17] Whatever the case to be made for special sensitivity to the commands of international human rights treaties,[18] we suggest that the difference is one of degree but not of kind, and that the general issue of the relationship of treaty law to Canadian law needs to be faced and resolved.

As noted already, the central assumption of Canadian judges has been that for treaties to have legal effect in Canada they must be legislatively implemented. This has been and remains the central paradigm. But, as we argue later, implementation is a profoundly ambiguous concept, at least as it is currently applied by the courts in Canada today. In this respect, one point needs to be made at the outset of this article relating to the Canadian approach to implementation: there has been a hardening of the criteria for judging implementation. There has been little explicit discussion but the *dicta* concerning the necessity of explicit implementing legislation appear to have hardened in the last twenty years. At first blush this is curious, given the ever increasing number of treaties that Canada has ratified and given the fact that in the United Kingdom the courts appear to be relaxing the requirement of implementation.[19] There seem to be two reasons for the trend in Canada. The first is legislative; the second is judicial.

During the Trudeau years, the Government of Canada virtually ceased to submit multilateral conventions and bilateral treaties to the scrutiny of Parliament. Previously it had been the custom to table most treaties and to seek parliamentary support before ratification of most important multi-lateral instruments. During the Trudeau years a decision appears to have been made to go back on this practice and to assert that treaty-making was a purely executive function in which Parliament played no role at all until it came time to implement the treaty. It is perhaps not entirely coincidental that at that time the Government of Canada was locked in a debate with the Government of Quebec over provincial participation in international rela-

---

17   See John H. Currie, *Public International Law* (Toronto: Irwin Law, 2001) at 223–25.

18   David Dyzenhaus, "The Politics of Deference: Judicial Review and Democracy" in Michael Taggart, ed., *The Province of Administrative Law*, (Oxford: Hart Publishing, 1997) at 279.

19   *Trendtex Trading Corp. Ltd. v. Central Bank of Nigeria*, [1977] Q.B. 529 at 553–54 (C.A.); *R. v. Bow Street Metropolitan Stipendiary Magistrate, Ex parte Pinochet Ugarte (No. 3)*, [1999] 2 W.L.R. 827 (H.L.).

tions.[20] Be this as it may, from that time forward the federal position has been to assert that Parliament and the provincial legislatures have no place in the decision to negotiate or ratify a treaty. Arguably, Trudeau's vision of the exclusively executive nature of treaty-making has influenced judicial thinking on the matter.

The second factor shaping judicial attitudes has come from the top of the judiciary in the form of *dicta* by Chief Justice Bora Laskin relating to treaty implementation. In several cases[21] Laskin C.J.C. asserted that specific and explicit language should be used by Parliament to indicate its intention to implement a treaty. This idea was picked up by his successor as Chief Justice of Canada, Brian Dickson.[22] The net result was that Canadian judges, taking their cue from the Chief Justices, have looked carefully for Parliament's explicit intention to implement a treaty and, if they find none, have often concluded—sometimes with extraordinary consequences[23]— that the treaty in question is an "unimplemented treaty." What has been missed is that Laskin C.J.C., in making his statement about implementation, was not concerned so much with the process of ensuring congruence between Canadian and international law as he was to create an opening to apply the Peace Order and Good Government (POGG) power of section 91 of the *Constitution Act, 1867* to treaty implementation. By extending the POGG power in this manner, Laskin C.J.C. sought to give Parliament the authority to implement any treaty, regardless of subject matter, in ef-

20 See Hon. P. Martin, Secretary of State for External Affairs, *Federalism and International Relations* (Ottawa: Queen's Printer, 1968) at 11–33; Hon. Mitchell Sharp, Secretary of State for External Affairs, *Federalism and International conferences on Education: A Supplement to Federalism and International Relations* (Ottawa: Queen's Printer, 1968).

21 Particularly *MacDonald v. Vapor Canada Ltd.*, [1977] 2 S.C.R. 134; *Capital Cities*, above note 1.

22 See *Schneider v. British Columbia*, [1982] 2 S.C.R. 112, 139 D.L.R. (3d) 417.

23 See *Ahani v. Canada (Attorney General)*, [2002] 156 O.A.C. 37 at paras. 18–20, 58 O.R. (3d) 107, 208 D.L.R. (4th) 66 (C.A.) [*Ahani*], where Laskin, J.A. expresses the view that the *International Covenant on Civil and Political Rights* is an unimplemented treaty, despite the fact that federal and provincial governments spent ten years negotiating the legislative changes required to ensure full Canadian implementation before ratification, despite the source of inspiration this treaty provided for the *Charter*, and despite the fact that decisions of the UN Human Rights Committee acting under the *Covenant* have led to important legislative changes, as in *Auclair c. Labelle Mini-Excavation Inc.*, 2003 QCCRT 163 [*Auclair*]. See also *International Covenant on Civil and Political Rights*, G.A. res. 2200A (XXI), 21 U.N. GAOR Supp. (No. 16) at 52, U.N. Doc. A/6316 (1966), 999 U.N.T.S. 171 (entered into force 23 March 1976) [ICCPR].

fect rewriting the *Labour Conventions Reference*.²⁴ Laskin C.J.C., like many jurists of his generation,²⁵ considered this decision to have hampered the emergence of a strong central government, and it is likely that he wished to overrule it indirectly through this means. Unfortunately, Canadian judges have applied Laskin C.J.C.'s *dicta* to another aspect of treaty implementation—the idea that implementation is necessary for treaties to have domestic effect—and have used implementation to set a threshold that unduly restricts the role that treaties might otherwise play in Canadian law.

The result of this ever stricter insistence that treaties require explicit legislative implementation to have domestic effect has been to expand the category of "unimplemented" treaties in Canada. Thus, despite the fact that the ratification of the *Convention on the Rights of the Child*²⁶ (CRC) was the object of considerable negotiation between the federal and provincial governments in order to ensure that Canada would be in a position to fulfil its obligations under the CRC (negotiation that resulted in the conclusion that Canadian law was fully compatible with the CRC), in the absence of specific implementing legislation, the Supreme Court of Canada and lower courts assumed in *Baker*, without discussion, that the CRC was an "unimplemented treaty."²⁷

A further result of this trend is to place Canada in potential violation of its international obligations. Rather than developing principles of interpretation designed to ensure congruence between the Canadian and international legal orders, Canadian courts have, perhaps unwittingly, widened the gap that separates them. The *Vienna Convention on the Law of Treaties*²⁸ and customary international law require that states fulfil their treaty commitments in good faith and prohibit states from pleading constitutional impediments in mitigation of their international obligations. Furthermore, the *Vienna Convention on the Law of Treaties*, to which Canada is bound and which is widely understood to reflect customary international law in this respect, states in its Article 24: "Every treaty in force is binding upon the parties to it and must be performed in good faith." By the act of ratifica-

---

24 *Labour Conventions Case (sub nom. Attorney General for Canada v. Attorney General for Ontario)*, [1937] A.C. 326, [1937] 1 D.L.R. 673 (J.C.P.C.).

25 See F.R. Scott, "The Consequences of the Privy Council Decisions" (1937) 15 Can. Bar Rev. 485; "Labour Conventions Case" (1956) 34 Can. Bar Rev. 114.

26 *Convention on the Rights of the Child*, 20 November 1989, 1577 U.N.T.S. 3 (entered into force 2 September 1990) [CRC].

27 *Baker*, above note 1 at 860–61. See also *Ahani*, above note 23 at paras. 18–20.

28 (1969) 1155 U.N.T.S. 331 (entered into force 1980).

tion the Government of Canada commits the state to abide by the treaty. Ratification is both the individual act of one state and also the principal constitutive act of participation that brings into existence the edifice of the international law-making community. To fail to respect the obligations of a ratified treaty is to weaken the whole structure of public international law. Good-faith performance suggests that all the law-making organs of a state should participate in ensuring respect for a ratified treaty.[29] Contemporary Canadian practice is fraught with the danger that different organs of the state will not always work together and that Canada, a country that has always prided itself in supporting the rule of law at the international level, will find itself in violation of its treaty obligations.

In Canada, the current understanding of unimplemented treaties places the burden of ensuring and proving implementation on the executive (or worse, on the executive's adversaries in the context of litigation), and in the face of cases of deemed inadequate implementation the courts tend to hold that the separation of powers precludes them from giving effect to a treaty's terms. The result is a sense that the courts view legislative implementation as the primary or even sole means of reception, as a problem of other orders of government, and one about which they take themselves to have surprisingly little say, given that they are at least partially responsible in that they have raised the bar so high with respect to what counts as implementation.

The most serious result of all is the pervading sense that legality is divisible into watertight compartments and that Canadian courts have scant duty to ensure respect for legality within the international legal order. Canadian courts appear to assume that their duty is only to the Canadian legal order. This is surely wrong. Canada is part of the international legal order. It is entirely bound by customary international law. It is a member of the United Nations. As a sovereign state, Canada, like all other United Nations members, bears primary responsibility for enforcing international law and will continue to do so for the foreseeable future. It participates in virtually every international law-making conference, most of which produce treaties that both codify and develop public international law. To assert that these treaties, when ratified by Canada, are incapable of producing effects in the Canadian legal order unless they have been the object of a specific

---

29 See generally Ian Brownlie, *Principles of Public International Law*, 6th ed. (Oxford: Oxford University Press, 2003) at 582; Currie, *Public International Law*, above note 17 at 120.

legislative enactment that gives explicit effect to every word in the treaty is to gravely oversimplify a complex legal process, and ultimately to do a disservice to both the Canadian and the international legal orders. Respect for the rule of law, we argue below, requires judges to consider themselves responsible to both legal orders.

Canada has a proud record of commitment to the rule of law at the domestic and international levels and yet our courts continue to act as though the two legal orders were completely separate. What is required is a greater sensitivity to both international customary and treaty law to ensure as high a degree of congruence as possible between international and domestic law. The interpretive presumption takes its bearings from exactly this imperative. The Parliament of Canada can still decide to implement a treaty in a particular way or restrict particular rules, but the onus should be reversed so that it is assumed that Canada intends to comply with its international obligations, rather than positing a rule that appears to hold a large variety of treaties to be unimplemented and hence incapable of producing legal effects in Canada. In other words, in the absence of express legislative indications to the contrary, public officials and administrative tribunals must respect the requirements of the treaties that the Government of Canada has ratified.

Much has been written on the doctrine of legitimate expectations and the idea that such expectations are created by the ratification of a treaty.[30] The High Court of Australia in 1995 made reference to legitimate expectations in *Minister of State for Immigration and Ethnic Affairs v. Teoh*,[31] but restricted its application of the doctrine to the legitimate expectation of children to the continued presence of their father, an expectation that was said to arise from Australia's ratification of the CRC. The *Teoh* decision met with a barrage of criticism in the Commonwealth Parliament, where it was alleged that the High Court's use of legitimate expectations involved illegitimate executive law-making. Successive Australian governments have attempted to introduce legislation to condemn and restrict the courts' ability to use legitimate expectations to give effect to international conven-

---

30   See Mark Jennings, "The Relationship between Treaties and Domestic Law," online: www.dfat.gov.au/treaties/workshops/treaties_global/jennings.html; see also Charlsworth, Chaim, Hovell, & Williams, "Deep Anxieties: Australia and the International legal Order" (2003) 25 Sydney L. Rev. 423 at 431–38.

31   (1995) 128 A.L.R. 353 [*Teoh*].

tions.[32] In England, where the doctrine of legitimate expectations has long been accepted in administrative law,[33] the courts have begun to build on the theory in relation to international treaties in a more positive fashion than elsewhere.[34]

It is plausible to suggest that ratification signals the intention of the government to be bound by the treaties it ratifies, and that this public display of the government's intention is sufficient to give rise to a legitimate expectation and (therefore) to a presumption that the state intends to respect the obligations of the treaty in its domestic as well as in its international dealings. Sadly, this argument remains underdeveloped in Canadian jurisprudence. The Supreme Court in *Baker* made no mention of *Teoh*, and held that Canada's ratification of the CRC:

> did not give rise to a legitimate expectation on the part of Ms. Baker that when the decision on her H & C application was made, specific procedural rights above what would normally be required under the duty of fairness would be accorded, a positive finding would be made, or particular criteria would be applied.[35]

The Court nonetheless left dangling the possibility that legitimate expectations might do some work in a different context involving a ratified treaty, concluding that "[i]t is unnecessary to decide whether an international instrument ratified by Canada could, in other circumstances, give rise to a legitimate expectation." In Part VI we suggest that the Court in *Suresh* adopts implicitly the view of legitimate expectations we urge here.

---

32 See Australian Lawyers for Human Rights, online: www.alhr.asn.au/html/documents/teoh_opinion.html; Teoh and Human Rights in Australia, online: www.dcian org/html/teoh.html; see also Heerey, "Storytelling, Postmodernism and the Law" (2000) 74 Australian L.J. 681.

33 See David Wright, "Rethinking the Doctrine of Legitimate Expectations in Canadian Administrative Law," (1997) 35 Osgoode Hall L.J. 139.

34 *R. v. North and East Devon Health Authority; Ex Parte Coughlan*, [2001] Q.B. 213. The English Court of Appeal upheld the right of a disabled woman to remain in a purpose-built care facility on the grounds that the health authority had promised her that she could remain there as long as she wished. This promise was held to give rise to a substantive legitimate expectation that could not be frustrated unless the overriding public interest required it. The court also found that by reneging on its promise the health authority had breached Ms. Coughlan's right to respect for her home, a right based on Article 8 of the European Convention on Human Rights and Fundamental Freedoms.

35 *Baker*, above note 1 at para. 29. We discuss *Baker* in greater detail later in Part V.

C. THE MANY MEANS OF IMPLEMENTATION

Implementation is a complex concept. It is accomplished by different means in different countries according to differing constitutional requirements and differing legal traditions. It is thus important that domestic courts accept that they have a duty to promote respect for Canada's international legal obligations: to do this they need to develop techniques of interpretation and enforcement that are sensitive to the demands of the international system as well as the domestic legal order.

From the perspective of international law, there are degrees of implementation that may be required by a treaty. The experience of the European Union (EU) is instructive in this regard. The highest degree of implementation reflected in state practice is probably that required in EU law by the concept of "direct *application*"[36] with respect to regulations, the highest form of legislative enactment in this legal system. A regulation must be given direct application; it must be treated exactly like the highest form of legislative enactment in every member state. Not only does it bind the government and all public officials, it is also enforceable before the domestic courts at the behest of public and private persons and it produces full legal effect between citizens *inter se*. The next highest and related degree of implementation in EU law is reflected in the concept of "direct *effect*,"[37] a jurisprudential creation of the European Court of Justice (ECJ). Not all rules of the European Community (EC) Treaty[38] have direct effect and few of the rules of the Treaty on EU[39] have this status. Only those treaty rules that are sufficiently explicit and precise have direct effect, and they are often posed as negative commands and subject to explicit time limits for entry into force, to be applied by the domestic courts against governments at the be-

---

36   Article 249 (2) of the European Community Treaty [ECT] states: "[A regulation] shall be binding in its entirety and directly applicable in all Member States." EC, *Consolidated Version of the Treaty Establishing the European Community* O.J. C. 325, (24 December 2002).

37   See Case 26/62, *NV Algemene Transporten Expeditie Onderneming van Gend en Loos v. Nederlandse Administratie der Belastingen*, [1963] E.C.R. 1 [*van Gend en Loos* case].

38   See, for example, ECT art. 10 (ex art. 5), arts. 87 to 89 (ex arts. 92 to 94), art. 96 (ex art. 101), art. 97 (ex art. 102), art. 101 *et seq.* (ex art. 104 *et seq.*) and art. 108 (ex art. 107).

39   It can be argued that the provisions of arts. 6(1) & (2) have direct effect, although this has not been tested by the ECJ because art. 46 of EU Treaty excludes its competence to deal with second and third pillar acts of the Union.

hest of citizens.[40] In certain circumstances treaty rules may have direct effect between citizens, but the rules of directives[41] only have "vertical" direct effect between citizens and governments or citizens and the Union itself.[42] "Horizontal" direct effect between persons has always been denied to directives, although the ECJ has gradually relaxed this rule and has found different reasons for accepting various forms of limited "horizontal" or "indirect" direct effect.[43] Decisions[44] have direct effect and direct application but exclusively upon those persons to whom they are addressed.

Subsequent to developing these rules with respect to EU treaties and EU legislative instruments, the ECJ has also dealt with many requests to give direct effect to other treaties to which the EC has become a party. The ECJ has accepted that some sufficiently explicit commands of treaties binding upon the EU can have direct effect,[45] particularly treaties providing for accession of new members, but it has steadfastly refused to grant direct effect to any provisions of the GATT and subsequently the WTO "covered agreements."[46] In the view of the ECJ, the contingent nature of the GATT/WTO agreements and the fact that they are subject to future negotiation and adjustment suggest that the duty of implementation assumed by the EU does not require the granting of direct effect.

The experience of the EU over the past forty years is therefore instructive as what may be required by the duty to implement a treaty, and examination of other international treaties reveals an immense range of expectations as to what is required for implementation of a treaty. An armistice or a peace treaty may require some legislation, but above all they

---

40   *Van Gend en Loos* case, above note 37 at 12–13, Case 6/64, *Costa v. ENEL*, [1964] ECR 585 at 593–94.

41   Art. 249(3) of the ECT, above note 36.

42   Case 152/84, *Marshall v. Southampton and South-West Hampshire Area Health Authority (Teaching)*, [1986] E.C.R. 723, [1986] 1 C.M.L.R. 688.

43   Case 14/83, *Von Colson and Kamann v. Land Nordrhein-Westfalen*, [1984] E.C.R. 1891, [1986] 2 C.M.L.R 430; Case C-91/92, *Faccini Dori v. Recreb*, [1994] E.C.R. I-3325, [1995] 1 C.M.L.R. 665; Case C-188/89, *Foster v. British Gas plc*, [1990] 2 C.M.L.R. 833.

44   Art. 249(4) of the ECT, above note 36.

45   EU Accession Treaty with Spain and Portugal (1985).

46   Cases 21-24/72, *International Fruit Company v. Produktschap voor Groenten en Fruit*, [1972] E.C.R. 1219; Case C-149/96, *Portugal v. Council*, [1999] E.C.R. I-8395; Case C-307/99, *OGT Fruchthandelsgesellschaft*, [2001] E.C.R. I-3159; Cases C-300 and 392/98, *Dior v. Tuk Consultancy*, [2000] E.C.R. I-11307, Cases T-18/99, *Cordis Obst und Gemüse Großhandel v. Commission*, [2001] E.C.R. II-913; *Bocchi Food Trade International v. Commission*, [2001] E.C.R. II-943; *T. Port GmbH v. Commission*, [2001] E.C.R. II-981.

require an end to hostilities between armies. At the other end of the scale, a treaty such as the Danzig Agreement[47] requires the creation of legal effects directly in the domestic legal system, as do the EU treaties discussed above. Between these two extremes are a host of treaties requiring that governments put appropriate measures into place to ensure that the treaties are respected. Traditionally, double taxation treaties are implemented verbatim by domestic legislatures.[48] Many treaties relate to actions that can only be taken by governments between themselves, but more and more treaties envisage the establishment of domestic regulatory systems to ensure respect for their obligations. Treaties in the field of transportation, communications, energy sharing and conservation, and environmental protection[49] are particularly relevant in this regard. Treaties dealing with the definition and the protection of human rights may involve interstate reporting or dispute-settlement obligations. However, they can also require the establishment of domestic regulatory commissions, and changes to domestic private and public law that are enforceable by public officials and by the domestic courts. In all these cases, while something like direct effect may not be required, arguably, all those charged with treaty enforcement must be sensitive to the global standards that are set by these treaties.

It is the practice of the Department of Foreign Affairs and International Trade and other concerned departments to ensure that the obligations of a treaty can be fulfilled by the federal or provincial governments before depositing the instrument of ratification.[50] Legal officers attempt to take stock of a treaty's obligations and the correlative capacity of the appropriate governments to fulfil these obligations. Normally, the federal Department of Justice will be called on to prepare an opinion as to the potential constitutional issues that may arise, and as to the existence of sufficient legal authority, whether constitutional, statutory, or common law, to ensure full

---

47 *Danzig Railway Officials Case: Jurisdiction of the Courts of Danzig, (Adv.Op.)* (1928), P.C.I.J. Ser. B, No. 15.

48 See *Taxation Act,* L.R.Q., c. I-3 and *Income Tax Conventions Implementation Act,* S.C. 1997, c. 38; *Income Tax Conventions Implementation Act,* S.C. 1998, c. 33; *Income Tax Conventions Implementation Act,* S.C. 1999, c. 11

49 *British Commonwealth Merchant Shipping Agreement,* 10 December 1931, Can. T. S. 1931/7; *Agreement on an International Energy Program,* 18 November 1974, T.I.A.S. 8278; *Cartagena Protocol on Biosafety to the Convention on Biological Diversity,* 29 January 2000 (entered into force 11 October 2003).

50 "Some Aspects of Canadian Treaty Law and Practice," 19 External Affairs, No. 9 (September 1967) 369 at 375.

implementation. If federal or provincial legislation is required, this will entail obtaining a Cabinet decision to prepare such legislation or to seek the assistance of the provinces and territorial governments to prepare the requisite legislation. This is a lengthy process, entailing policy analysis as to the desirability of ratification and, subsequently, extensive legal analysis of the treaty, constitutional law analysis, legal analysis of common law and existing statutory and regulatory provisions, organization of the legislative and regulatory agenda, and, finally, preparation of the appropriate administrative arrangements. Different treaties may have special requirements as to their implementation and these will have to be followed. In the relatively common case that Canadian law (Constitution, statutes, regulations, and common law) contains sufficient authority to permit the fulfilment of treaty obligations, it is normally not the practice of the Government of Canada to seek the adoption of new legislation.[51]

Canadian administrative and legislative practices reveal at least thirteen methods of implementing treaty obligations. The list that follows is by no means exhaustive, but simply illustrates some of the more common means of treaty implementation.

1. Incorporation textually of the whole or part of a treaty, giving the text of the treaty the force of law;
2. Scheduling the text and referring to all or part;
3. Specific implementation by reference or incorporation of particular treaty provisions;
4. Translating the treaty into Canadian statutory language;
5. Adding a statement in text of intention to implement;
6. Adding a statement in text of intention to approve a treaty;
7. Adding instructions for interpretation giving priority to a treaty;
8. Adopting provisions which provide for the adoption of implementing regulations or decisions by the Governor-in-Council, a minister, or an independent tribunal;
9. Adopting regulations with the purpose of implementing;
10. Reliance upon a rule or provision of the Constitution;
11. Reliance upon pre-existing federal and provincial legislation;
12. Reliance on the common law, including the Royal Prerogative; and,

---

51 Maurice Copithorne, "Canada" in Monroe Leigh *et al.*, ed., *National Treaty Law and Practice*, vol. 3, (Washington, DC: American Society of International Law, 2003) at 5.

13. Reliance on the intention of the treaty—self-executing or specifically non–self-executing to determine the effect of the treaty in the legal system.

1. Incorporation textually

Some treaties are incorporated into Canadian law by making the whole treaty text part of the law. A good example is provided by the *Tax Conventions Implementation Act, 2004 (Tax Conventions Act)*,[52] which gives force of law to five recently concluded double taxation agreements with foreign countries. The *Tax Conventions Act* states: "The Convention is approved and has the force of law in Canada during the period that the Convention, by its terms, is in force."[53] It further states that, subject only to the *Income Tax Act*, this Act and the Convention have priority over any other inconsistent Act of Parliament.[54]

Another means of using treaty language is found in many definitions of terms derived from treaties. There are instances in Canadian laws where the exact words of the international definition have been used to give effect to the treaty in various statutes, such as definitions of waters subject to national jurisdiction pursuant to the *United Nations Convention on the Law of the Sea*.[55]

In these cases, implementation implies that the terms and provisions of the relevant treaties have the status and effect of domestic legislation. As we will see later, there is tension between this kind of rights-determining authority and the idea that, pursuant to the constitutional separation of powers, only the legislature has law-making authority to make and repeal domestic law.

---

52 S.C. 2005, c. 8.
53 *Ibid.*, s. 3.
54 *Ibid.*, s. 4(1).
55 *Oceans Act*, S.C. 1996, c. 31, s. 14(a) defining the rights to be exercised in the Exclusive Economic Zone of Canada states: "[S]overeign rights in the exclusive economic zone of Canada for the purpose of exploring and exploiting, conserving and managing the natural resources, whether living or non-living, of the waters superjacent to the seabed and of the seabed and its subsoil, and with regard to other activities for the economic exploitation and exploration of the exclusive economic zone of Canada, such as the production of energy from the water, currents and winds ...."

2. Scheduling the text and referring to all or part

A further approach consists of scheduling the whole treaty, but the legislation gives effect only to certain articles listed in the legislation. One notable example is the *Foreign Missions and International Organizations Act*[56] that states:

> 3. (1) Articles 1, 22 to 24 and 27 to 40 of the Vienna Convention on Diplomatic Relations, and Articles 1, 5, 15, 17, 31 to 33, 35, 39 and 40, paragraphs 1 and 2 of Article 41, Articles 43 to 45 and 48 to 54, paragraphs 2 and 3 of Article 55, paragraph 2 of Article 57, paragraphs 1 to 3 of Article 58, Articles 59 to 62, 64, 66 and 67, paragraphs 1, 2 and 4 of Article 70 and Article 71 of the Vienna Convention on Consular Relations, have the force of law in Canada in respect of all foreign states, regardless of whether those states are parties to those Conventions.

Perhaps the best example of incorporation of part of a treaty by reference is found in the *Immigration and Refugee Protection* Act (*Immigration Act*),[57] which explicitly incorporates Article 1Fc of the *Refugee Convention*.[58] With respect to the prior version of this Act, Bastarache J. stated: "Since the purpose of the Act incorporating Article 1Fc is to implement the underlying Convention, the Court must adopt an interpretation consistent with Canada's obligations under the Convention."[59]

3. Specific implementation by reference or incorporation of particular treaty provisions

One example of this technique is the *Act to amend the Patent Act and the Food and Drugs Act (The Jean Chrétien Pledge to Africa)*,[60] which states in a definition that "General Council Decision" means the decision of the General Council (of the WTO) of 30 August 2003 respecting Article 31 of the TRIPS Agreement, including the interpretation of that decision in the General Council Chairperson's statement of that date.

Another example is found in the *Act to implement the North American Free Trade Agreement Act (NAFTA Act)*,[61] which states in section 21:

---

56 S.C. 1991, c. 41, s. 3.
57 S.C. 2001, c. 27.
58 *Convention relating to the Status of Refugees*, 14 December 1950, 189 U.N.T.S.150, (entered into force 22 April 1954) [*Refugee Convention*].
59 *Pushpanathan v. Canada (Minister of Citizenship and Immigration)* (1998), 160 D.L.R. (4th) 193 at para. 51 [*Pushpanathan*].
60 S.C. 2004, c. 23, s. 21.02.
61 S.C. 1993, c. 44.

21. (1) The Governor in Council may, for the purpose of suspending in accordance with the Agreement the application to a NAFTA country of benefits of equivalent effect pursuant to Article 2019 of the Agreement, by order, do any one or more of the following:

> (a) suspend rights or privileges granted by Canada to that country or to goods, service providers, suppliers, investors or investments of that country under the Agreement or any federal law, except under Chapter Nineteen of the Agreement or under any provision of the Special Import Measures Act enacted by Part II;
>
> ...

A further example of specific implementation by reference or incorporation of treaty provisions that become directly operative is found in statutory references to the procedure of international trade tribunals, before which individuals or companies are allowed to appear. Among the best examples are Article 1904[62] or Chapter 11 Part B of the *North American Free Trade Agreement Between the Government of Canada, the Government of Mexico and the Government of the United States*,[63] which for all intents and purposes are directly effective as a result of the *NAFTA Act*.

4. Translating the treaty into Canadian statutory language

One of the most common forms of implementation is to transpose the language of the treaty into a new form, more closely approximating Canadian statutory language. Several reasons explain the relative popularity of this approach. Perhaps the most important is the need to have the language of the enactment approximate the language used in related statutes. In the case of legislation dealing with trade remedies, this may also be explained by the desire to have the law on all fours with Canadian administrative law, which forms the basic regulatory matrix and deep structure of the law. Another reason may well be the distrust of those responsible for legislative drafting in Ottawa or provincial capitals of treaty language that is unfamiliar or which, as is often the case, appears to lack a sufficient degree of clarity and precision. A particularly significant example is the *Special Import*

---

62   This article sets the right to appeal to a bi-national panel in respect of AD/CV duty decisions of domestic tribunals. *Ibid.*

63   17 December 1992, Can. T.S. 1994 No. 2, 32 I.L.M. (entered into force 1 January 1994) [NAFTA]. This Part creates a right to call for the creation of an arbitral tribunal to determine private rights under Chapter 11 Part A on the protection of investors and investments. *Ibid.*

Measures Act.[64] This Act was first adopted to implement the results of the 1979 Tokyo Round of Multilateral Trade Agreements to regulate dumping and the imposition of countervailing duties. It was the object of a leading decision on the implementation of treaties, *National Corn Growers,*[65] in which Justice Gonthier stated that treaties behind legislation may be consulted in the case of ambiguity or to reveal underlying ambiguities that might be latent, but not patent. However, he prefaced his opinion by stating that in the face of a clear difference the statute must prevail. The Act has subsequently been amended to reflect the results of the 1994 Uruguay Round of Multilateral Trade Negotiations, the 1988 Canada–United States Free Trade Agreement, and the 1993 NAFTA.

5. Adding a statement in the text of intention to implement

A number of Acts contain language stating that the intention of the Act is to implement a treaty. One might assume that this would be interpreted as a clear direction to the courts to give effect to the treaty. However, it appears that Canadian courts simply treat such declarations as merely statements of fact and evidence that Parliament is doing its duty to implement the treaty. Thus, despite including the express statement in the *NAFTA Act* that "[t]he purpose of this Act is to implement the Agreement," NAFTA has never been given direct effect by Canadian courts despite several efforts to argue the case.[66]

It appears that a clear statement of intention to implement a treaty is deemed to be essentially declaratory in nature and is not sufficient to ensure that the treaty in question will have any significant dispositive effect. In the face of a clear difference between the language of the statute and the treaty, according to many decisions,[67] the statute must prevail, even if no clear intention is stated to depart from the treaty. It seems that Canadian courts would feel much more comfortable basing themselves strictly upon a statute rather than upon the treaty behind the statute. Arguably, the

---

64 R.S.C. 1985 (1st Supp.), c. 23.

65 See above note 16.

66 *Industries Hillenbrand Canada Ltée v. Québec (Bureau de normalisation),* [2002] J.Q. no 3811 at para. 191 (C.S.); see also *Pfizer Inc. v. Canada,* [1999] 4 F.C. 441 at para. 45 (T.D.), aff'd [1999] F.C.J. No. 1598 (C.A.); see also *UL Canada inc. v. Québec (Procureur géneral),* [1999] R.J.Q. 1720 (C.S.); *Les Entreprises de rebuts Sanipan v. Québec (Procureur général),* [1995] R.J.Q. 821 (C.S.).

67 *National Corn Growers,* above note 16; *Capital Cities,* above note 1; *Pushpanathan,* above note 61; *Baker,* above note 1.

courts are more comfortable with the statement quoted above in the *Tax Conventions Act* section 4(1) giving force of law to a treaty.[68]

6. Adding a statement in text of intention to approve a treaty

It is not the usual practice in Canada to submit treaties to Parliament or the provincial legislatures, with the exception of Quebec,[69] for the purposes of ratification. At best they are tabled and very occasionally (as with such politically sensitive treaties such as NAFTA or the Kyoto Protocol)[70] they may be debated and approved on motion by the appropriate minister. Very exceptionally a provision is added in the legislation itself "approving" the treaty. Thus the *NAFTA Act*[71] states that "[t]he Agreement (NAFTA) is hereby approved." This did not constitute Canadian ratification and a separate instrument was deposited according to the requirements of the treaty process. It seems that this provision has been considered to be strictly declaratory and political in nature and it does not appear to have been given weight by any court.

7. Adding instructions for interpretation giving priority to a treaty

A number of statutes instruct the courts to give force of law to the treaty and to give priority to the treaty over conflicting legislation or require that other federal law be interpreted in a manner consistent with the treaty. One example is the *NAFTA Act*. Section 3 of this Act states:

> For greater certainty, this Act, any provision of an Act of Parliament enacted by Part II and any other federal law that implements a provision of the Agreement or fulfils an obligation of the Government of Canada under the Agreement shall be interpreted in a manner consistent with the Agreement.[72]

Another example of the same manner of implementation is found in the *Tax Conventions Act*,[73] section 4(1) which states:

> Subject to subsection (2), in the event of any inconsistency between the provisions of this Part or the Convention and the provisions of any other

---

68   Above note 54.
69   *Loi sur le ministère des relations internationales*, R.S.Q., c. M-25.1.1.
70   *Kyoto Protocol to the UN Framework Convention on Climate Change*, 11 December 1997, 37 Int. Leg. Mat. 32 (entered into force 16 February 2005) [Kyoto Protocol].
71   See above note 61, s. 10.
72   *Ibid.*
73   Above note 52.

law, the provisions of this Part and the Convention prevail to the extent of the inconsistency.

8. *Adopting provisions which provide for the adoption of implementing regulations or decisions by the Governor-in-Council, a minister, or an independent tribunal*

Many Acts of Parliament contain express authority for the Executive to adopt regulations for the purpose of implementing both a treaty and the decisions of major intergovernmental organizations. Perhaps the best known is the provision of the *United Nations Act* (*UN Act*),[74] which empowers the executive to adopt regulations for the purpose of implementing mandatory sanctions adopted by the Security Council under article 41 of the Charter of the UN. Similarly, the *NAFTA Act* empowers the executive to make regulations implementing the Act. The same Act contains language empowering regulatory boards to issue general orders or to take decisions pursuant to NAFTA.[75] Another example of a grant of broad authority to adopt implementing regulations is found in the *Canada Shipping Act 2001*,[76] which states:

> 35. (1) The Governor in Council may, on the recommendation of the Minister of Transport, make regulations
>
> (d) implementing, in whole or in part, an international convention, protocol or resolution that is listed in Schedule 1, as amended from time to time, including regulations
>
> > (i) implementing it in respect of persons, vessels or oil handling facilities to which it does not apply:
> >
> > (ii) establishing stricter standards than it sets out, or
> >
> > (iii) establishing additional or complementary standards to those it sets out if the Governor in Council is satisfied that the additional or complementary standards meet the objectives of the convention, protocol or resolution;

In the same vein, the *Tax Conventions Act*,[77] states: "[t]he Minister of National Revenue may make any regulations necessary for carrying out the

---

74 R.S.C. 1985, c. U-2, s. 2.
75 Above note 61, ss. 120–120.5 concerning the National Energy Board; ss. 201–218 respecting the Canadian International Trade Tribunal.
76 S.C. 2001, c. 26.
77 Above note 52, s. 5.

Convention or for giving effect to any of its provisions." As a result of this authorization the Consolidated Regulations of Canada are filled with statutory instruments whose purpose is to ensure the implementation of various treaties.[78] But it is by no means clear that the failure to respect the terms of the treaty has ever been successfully invoked to declare a domestic regulation to be *ultra vires* the treaty. By the same token, it is far from clear that Canadian courts would regard the adoption of a regulation as a case of implementation or that the rules of interpretation set out in *National Corn Growers* could be invoked to refer to the treaty underlying the regulation. And, at least until *Baker,* discussed later in this chapter, it was unclear whether an independent administrative body was under any obligation to be guided by the language of a treaty that either underlies or relates to the regulations it administers.

9. *Adopting regulations with the purpose of implementing*

Nothing compels the executive to make use of a regulatory power that is specially delegated within a statutory scheme to authorize the promulgation of treaty-implementing regulations. But, so long as the regulatory authority derived from the statute is sufficiently broad, it may provide a basis for the adoption of regulations whose purpose will be to give effect to the treaty.[79]

---

78 The number must run to several hundreds, including: *Anti-Personnel Mines Convention Implementation Act,* S.C. 1997, c. 33; *Chemical Weapons Convention Implementation Act,* S.C. 1995, c. 25; *World Trade Organization Agreement Implementation Act,* S.C. 1994, c. 47; *Civil International Space Station Agreement Implementation Act,* S.C. 1999, c. 35; *Comprehensive Nuclear Test-Ban Treaty Implementation Act (not in force),* S.C. 1998, c. 32; *Biological and Toxin Weapons Convention Implementation Act (not in force),* S.C. 2004, c. 15; *United Nations Act,* R.S.C. 1985, c. U-2; *Income Tax Conventions Implementation Act,* S.C. 2001, c. 30; *Canada-Chile Free Trade Agreement Implementation Act,* S.C. 1997, c. 38; *Canada-Costa Rica Free Trade Agreement Implementation Act,* S.C. 2001, c. 28; *Canada-Israel Free Trade Agreement Implementation Act,* S.C. 1996, c. 33; *Canada-United States Free Trade Agreement Implementation Act,* S.C. 1998, c. 65; *Income Tax Conventions Implementation Act,* S.C. 1999, c. 11; *Income Tax Conventions Implementation Act,* S.C. 1998, c. 33; *Income Tax Conventions Implementation Act,* S.C. 1997, c. 38; *Income Tax Conventions Implementation Act,* S.C. 1996, c. 27; *Income Tax Conventions Implementation Act,* S.C. 1995, c. 37.

79 A sample of some of the more important of these regulations includes: *Procurement Review Board Regulations,* S.O.R./89-41; *Schedule 1 Chemicals Regulations,* S.O.R./2004-155; *Administrative and Technical Staff of the Embassy of the United States and Families Duty and Tax Relief Privileges Order,* S.O.R./93-391; *Administrative and Technical Staff of the Embassy of the United States and Families Privileges and Immunities Order,* S.O.R./93-384; *African Development Bank Privileges and Immunities Order,* S.O.R./84-360; *Agence de la Francophonie and the Institut de l'énergie et de*

Such regulations, we claim, ought to be interpreted as implementing a treaty's provisions such that those provisions place the executive under a statutory obligation to comply with them, since there is, in this case, direct statutory authorization of the implementing regulations.

10. *Reliance upon a rule or provision of the Constitution*
The *Charter* contains extensive protections of fundamental civil and political rights. It was drafted bearing in mind the *Universal Declaration on Human Rights* (UDHR), the *European Convention on the Protection of Fundamental Freedoms*, and the two United Nations Covenants on civil and political and economic and social rights. It is in part for this reason that it was not judged necessary to adopt a special act to implement the obligations of the ICCPR when Canada decided to ratify this treaty after some ten years of federal–provincial negotiations to ensure that Canada could fulfil its obligations under the ICCPR. Canada is surely able to assure the international community that, on the basis of the constitutional right to life entrenched in section 7 of the *Charter* and provisions in its *Criminal Code*, genocide will be severely punished if it were ever practised in Canada. The constitutional guarantee of freedom of association has been invoked in support of labour rights before the Supreme Court of Canada.[80] Torture is banned by the *Charter*, and so the absence of a special law implementing the *Convention against Torture and Other Cruel, Inhuman or Degrading Treatment or Punishment*[81] is not a failure to implement or an indication that Canada acquiesces in torture.[82]

---

l'environnement de la Francophonie Privileges and Immunities Order, S.O.R./88-574; *Asian Development Bank Privileges and Immunities Order*, C.R.C., c. 1305; *Caribbean Development Bank Privileges and Immunities Order*, C.R.C., c. 1306; *European Communities Privileges and Immunities Order*, C.R.C., c. 1308; *Regulations Clarifying the Application of Provisions of the Convention on the Privileges and Immunities of the United Nations*, S.O.R./2002-195; *Order Designating the Minister for International Trade as Minister for Purposes of Sections 1 to 9 and Parts I and III of NAFTA Implementation Act*, SI/94-8; *United Nations Afghanistan Regulations*, S.O.R./99-444; *United Nations Iraq Regulations*, S.O.R./90-531; *United Nations Liberia Regulations*, S.O.R./2001-261; *United Nations Rwanda Regulations*, S.O.R./94-582; *United Nations Sierra Leone Regulations*, S.O.R./98-400; *United Nations Suppression of Terrorism Regulations*, S.O.R./2001-360.

80 See *Public Service Alliance*, above note 16 at 476.
81 *Convention against Torture and Other Cruel, Inhuman or Degrading Treatment or Punishment*, adopted 10 December 1984, entered into force 26 June 1987, Can. T.S. 1987 No. 93 [*Convention against Torture*].
82 One reading of the *Suresh* case might suggest that there is doubt as to whether Canada has fully implemented the *Convention against Torture*, since the Supreme Court of

11. Reliance upon pre-existing federal and provincial legislation

We recognize that, in light of the courts' frequent designation of certain treaties as "unimplemented," it is problematic to claim that a treaty can be deemed implemented on the basis of pre-existing legislation. Yet this issue requires far more serious examination than it has received. It is certainly the practice of the federal Department of Justice to presume that legislation on the books can be read to satisfy Canada's international treaty obligations. As indicated already, Judges of the Ontario Court of Appeal have described the ICCPR as being an unimplemented treaty despite the fact that its ratification was preceded by some ten years of federal provincial negotiations, whose purpose was to ensure that Canadian law at the federal and provincial levels guaranteed respect for the obligations of the treaty.[83] The characterization by the Supreme Court of Canada in *Baker* of the CRC as being unimplemented is equally problematic. Unless one is to assume that Canada ratified the CRC in a frivolous manner, and without contemplating the need to respect its

---

Canada's judgment permits *refoulement* under some conditions to a place where there is a serious risk of torture, whereas the ban on such *refoulement* under the Convention is absolute. However, this assessment may not be correct, for it glosses over a distinction that can be drawn between Canada's positive law (including the *Charter*) and the judiciary's interpretation of it. Perhaps the Supreme Court simply misinterpreted the *Charter* in *Suresh*. If so, then the *Charter*—properly interpreted—is capable of providing a domestic legal basis for full implementation of the *Convention against Torture*, and thus Canadian positive law (though not its jurisprudence) is in full compliance with the Convention. We prefer this understanding of the relationship between *Suresh* and the Convention because it permits judges at a later date to bring Canada's jurisprudence in line with its international commitments, and to do so without the prompt of a constitutional amendment or some other change to Canada's positive law.

83 See, for federal statutes, *Canadian Human Rights Act*, R.S.C. 1985, c. H-6; *International Centre for Human Rights and Democratic Development Act*, R.S.C. 1985, c. 54 (4th Supp.); *Canadian Multiculturalism Act*, R.S.C. 1985, c. 24 (4th Supp.); *Canadian Race Relations Foundation Act*, S.C. 1991, c. 8. See, for provincial statutes, *Human Rights Code*, R.S.O. 1990, c. H.19; *Religious Freedom Act*, R.S.O. 1990, c. R.22; *Charter of human rights and freedoms*, R.S.Q., c. C-12; *Human Rights Code*, R.S.B.C. 1996, c. 210; *Civil Rights Protection Act*, R.S.B.C. 1996, c. 49; *Multiculturalism Act*, R.S.B.C. 1996, c. 321; *Human Rights, Citizenship and Multiculturalism Act*, R.S.A. 2000, c. H-14; *Saskatchewan Human Rights Code*, S.S. 1979, c. S-24.1; *Human Rights Code*, C.C.S.M., c. H175; *Manitoba Multiculturalism Act*, C.C.S.M., c. M223; *Human Rights Act*, R.S.N.B. 1973, c. H-11; *Defamation Act*, R.S.N.B. 1973, c. D-5; *Human Rights Act*, R.S.N.S. 1989, c. 214; *Multiculturalism Act*, R.S.N.S. 1989, c. 294; *Defamation Act*, R.S.N.S. 1989, c. 122; *Human Rights Act*, R.S.P.E.I. 1988, c. H-12; *Defamation Act*, R.S.P.E.I. 1988, c. D-5; *Human Rights Code*, R.S.N.L. 1990, c. H-14; *Human Rights Act*, R.S.Y. 2002, c. 116; *Human Rights Act*, S.N.W.T. 2002, c. 18.

terms, one must assume that the issue of the compatibility of Canadian law with the Convention was considered seriously by law officers of the Crown at the federal and provincial levels. Why does specific new legislation have to be adopted in order to win the accolade of "implemented treaty," when existing legislation provides all the authority required to implement?

The reason, we think, is that some judges have accepted the argument that just because the executive has ratified a treaty and has sufficient delegated authority to comply with its terms, this is not reason enough to think that the executive and its various agencies in fact have a legal obligation to do so. Much of the remainder of our paper is dedicated to arguing that the executive does have such an obligation, and that the presence of pre-existing legislative authority to comply with treaty obligations denotes the presence of discretionary public authority that (in the absence of clear legislation to the contrary) must be exercised in accordance with the provisions of international law.

12. Reliance on the common law including the Royal Prerogative
The same question as the one asked above can be posed when the rules of the common law provide a sufficient basis for performance of Canada's obligations under a treaty. As was argued in the case of *Operation Dismantle Inc. v. Canada*,[84] if the Royal Prerogative in foreign affairs can give rise to a potentially unconstitutional infringement of the *Charter,* why can it not be used to protect human rights or other obligations assumed under human rights treaties? Yet it is by no means clear that Canadian courts would accept that a treaty becomes implemented if the Crown intends to implement by using the Royal Prerogative or some other rule of the common law.

13. Reliance on the intention of the treaty—self-executing or specifically non–self-executing to determine the effect of the treaty in the legal system.
Another important consideration concerning implementation is sensitivity to the purpose and terms of the treaty itself. Some treaties on their face appear to require that their very words be given direct effect. [85] Others do not.[86] Many require only administrative action by one or more govern-

---

84 [1985] 1 S.C.R. 441.
85 NAFTA, above note 63, art. 1904, c. 11, s. B.
86 ICCPR, above note 23.

ments.[87] Some clearly require major legislative changes.[88] Others require that discretionary decisions of ministers or administrative tribunals reflect the policy of the treaty.[89] All this suggests that the treaty itself cannot be ignored and frequently must be dispositive when courts are asked to determine whether there has been adequate implementation for the treaty to give rise to legal obligations. The more Canadian courts sense that the rule of law requires respect for the rule of law at the international as well as the domestic level, the more they will look to the treaty itself.

D. THE SEPARATION OF POWERS AND THE SPECTRE OF EXECUTIVE LAW-MAKING

In the Westminster tradition, ministers and their delegates typically exercise legal authority on the basis of statutory grants that empower them to implement public law regimes. The treaty-making power is distinct, however, as there is no requirement in Canadian law that the executive (usually the federal executive) consult with its legislative counterpart prior to entering into a treaty. A democratic deficit appears to afflict the Canadian treaty-ratification process because the process does not require prior or subsequent parliamentary review and approval. As noted above, Parliament currently plays virtually no role in defining the executive's mandate to negotiate entry into a treaty. It would seem that giving ratified but unimplemented treaties direct domestic effect would only make matters worse by letting the executive unilaterally "enact" law without Parliament's assent.

Now, clearly there is merit to the idea that Parliament and its relevant committees should play a greater role in treaty ratification, and we make some specific recommendations about how this might take place in the final section. In addition to contributing to the transparency and openness of a relatively opaque process, a requirement that Parliament, and where appropriate the provincial legislatures, should play a role in defining the executive's mandate to negotiate entry into a treaty, or assent in some way prior to its ratification, would add to the treaty's democratic credentials. In the tradition of a sober second thought, involving Parliament would give

---

87 *Canada-US Treaty on Extradition* (signed 3 December 1971, Amended by Exchange of Notes 28 June and 9 July 1974; in force 22 March 1976). CTS 1976/3.

88 *Cape Town Convention (International Interests in Mobile Equipment)*, (16 November 2001) (entered into force 1 April 2004); *International Interests in Mobile Equipment Act (Aircraft Equipment)*, 2002, S.O. 2002, c. 18, Sch. B.

89 *Refugee Convention*, above note 58.

our elected representatives an opportunity to reflect on particular treaties and to consider reservations and other nuances that may not occur to the executive acting alone. And, of course, if Parliament developed a practice of unabashedly implementing treaties (before or after formal ratification) using the first technique described above—textual incorporation of a treaty's terms—then the controversy over whether such treaties had domestic effect would all but vanish. For the sake of argument, however, let us assume that reform in this area is likely to be slow, and that for some time to come we will be living with, at least, the possibility that the executive may ratify treaties that Parliament has not implemented with sufficiently explicit legislation for judges to be left with no doubt that, in fact, the treaty has become a full-fledged part of our domestic law.

The substantive question underlying the rationale of the separation of powers, then, is whether democratic accountability is undermined if ratified treaties are given domestic effect without Parliament having enacted legislation that explicitly implements them. The more formal and constitutional question is whether courts and public actors are barred, as a matter of law, from being bound by the terms of treaties that do not enjoy explicit implementation in the wake of ratification, notwithstanding that there may be sufficient legislation in place prior to ratification to enable compliance with, and therefore implementation of, a treaty's terms. In this section we suggest that neither the formal nor the substantive arguments against giving ratified treaties domestic effect are as compelling as they may first appear.

With respect to the formal separation of powers itself, the main constitutional worry that preoccupies courts is that neither they nor the executive has authority to impose legal obligations independently of the legislature. However, common law courts have a long history of enforcing public law obligations against the executive in the absence of express statutory language. The duty of procedural fairness is one such obligation.[90] This duty requires administrative agencies to use fair procedures to permit individuals to know and reply to the case against them, and it applies independently of whether the legislature has provided for such procedures in the agency's enabling statute. Below we will compare this common law duty of public law with the obligations arising from ratified treaties. At this junc-

---

90 See, for example, *Nicholson v. Haldimand-Norfolk Regional Board of Commissioners of Police*, [1979] 1 S.C.R. 311; *Board of Education of the Indian Head School Division No. 19 of Saskatchewan v. Knight*, [1990] 1 S.C.R. 653 [*Knight*]; *Baker*, above note 1.

ture we wish simply to point out that the separation of powers does not entail that *all* legal obligations to which the executive is subject must have some basis in legislation. The administration is subject to some legal duties that have no explicit basis in statute.

The substantive concern over democratic accountability also overshoots the mark. Given the particularities of Canada's first-past-the-post electoral system and a Parliamentary tradition of voting along party lines, the Government of Canada tends to rule as a majority in the House of Commons for a four- to five-year term. The same is true at the provincial level. Minority governments are relatively rare, and they tend to be short-lived because their budget legislation can be voted down by a unified opposition, the effect of which is to bring about a general election. In the normal course of law-making, ministers draft and table legislation that almost invariably passes in the House as a matter of course, due once again to the majority the government usually enjoys in the House and the tradition of voting along party lines. Ministers are not required to submit proposed legislation to public scrutiny and debate before tabling it in the House, although an opportunity to review proposed statutes does arise once they are tabled.[91] But the upshot is that in Canada's present legal and political system, the executive through its ministers has a virtually free hand, within constitutional limits, to determine the content of its citizens' legal rights and obligations.

The characteristics and practices of Canada's parliamentary tradition may well disclose a lamentable disregard for public input and consultation in the law-making process. However, these deficiencies do not impugn the legality of legislation that is enacted by Parliament at the behest of the executive. Furthermore, once proposed legislation is enacted into law, members of the opposition (members of the formal Opposition as well as members of other parties that do not comprise the government) remain free to monitor and comment on the ongoing effect of legislation.

Similarly, when the executive ratifies a treaty (and sometimes prior to ratification), members of the opposition have the opportunity to scrutinize its measures and criticize the obligations that the government has

---

91 The First Nations case is a notable exception, but one grounded in the entrenchment of treaty and Aboriginal rights in s. 35 of the *Constitution Act, 1982*, above note 7. Recent jurisprudence suggests that the Crown does have a constitutional duty to consult with First Nations if "the Crown has knowledge, real or constructive, of the potential existence of the Aboriginal right or title and contemplates conduct that might adversely affect it." *Haida Nation v. British Columbia (Minister of Forests)*, 2004 SCC 73 at para. 35 [*Haida*].

assumed through ratification. If the government's ratification proves un-popular, it could withdraw from the treaty. Further, if the government falls in an election, a subsequent government can withdraw from the treaty or enact legislation that limits the treaty's domestic effect. All of these pos-sibilities remain available, and together they ensure that, substantively, the democratic deficit alleged to attend recognition of the binding nature of ratified treaties, when compared with law-making through legislation in the normal course of events, is not as significant as it may first appear.

Still, some may worry that giving ratified treaties domestic effect is dangerous from a democratic point of view because ratification does not require formal debate on the House floor, whereas the legislative process does. We have four replies. First, much can be done through reforms to parliamentary procedures to remedy this concern, and we offer some sug-gestions in this regard towards the end of this chapter. In Australia, for example, a dedicated parliamentary committee reviews all proposed treat-ies pre-ratification. South Africa's constitution requires Parliament's prior approval for most treaties, and in the UK the convention known as the "Ponsonby Rule" requires that treaties be tabled in both Houses of Parlia-ment at least twenty-one sitting days prior to ratification.[92]

Second, our claim is not that the terms of implemented treaties should have the same legal status as legislation. Rather, their status should be equivalent to common law obligations that explicit legislation (but only explicit legislation) can supersede and restrict. There is no doubt, for in-stance, that Parliament can pass legislation that has the effect of expropria-tion, but the common law requires compensation for expropriation unless the statute explicitly bars such claims.[93] Roughly speaking, we suggest that treaty provisions operate in much the same way as the common law doc-trine that controls expropriation.[94]

---

92 For fruitful discussion of the Australian and U.K. cases, see Joanna Harrington, "Redressing the Democratic Deficit in Treaty Law Making: (Re-)Establishing a Role for Parliament" (2005) 50 McGill L.J. 465.

93 See, for example, *Authorson v. Canada (Attorney General)* (2002), 58 O.R. (3d) 417 (Ont. C.A.), rev'd 2003 SCC 39.

94 Our proposal may appear to be a radical departure from current doctrine. However, it is interesting to note that a similar suggestion was made more than thirty years ago by Canada's eminent international jurist R. St. J. MacDonald: "As to the separation of powers between the crown [the executive] and parliament, it is submitted that this could be preserved while still enabling (and forcing) Canada to fulfill her international obligations by according ratified but unimplemented treaties a status superior to com-mon law but inferior to statute." Ronald St. J. MacDonald, "The Relationship between

Third, our argument is limited to asserting the domestic effect of a treaty's terms as against solely the executive, its tribunals, agencies, and frontline decision-makers. We do not think that, without more, an unimplemented treaty ought to have legal effects as against private parties or in disputes between them. However, private parties who confront administrative agencies may rely on the terms of such treaties, much as Mavis Baker, who attempted to rely on the terms of the CRC that require the state to regard children's best interests as a "primary consideration" in administrative proceedings that affect them.[95]

Fourth, the substantive concern over a democratic deficit proceeds from the assumption that democratic legitimacy rests almost entirely on respect for legislative procedures that enable the will of the majority to operate. We have already suggested that our electoral system combined with Parliament's ability to monitor ratification and its consequences provide significant procedural and political safeguards against an executive that ratifies a treaty without Parliament's prior assent. The will of the majority is not left to the caprice of a politically unaccountable executive: ministers need to get re-elected too. But there is a deeper issue in play.

The deeper issue has to do with the assumption that democratic legitimacy is reducible to giving effect to the will of the majority. As many others have argued, majoritarianism alone supplies an impoverished conception of democratic legitimacy.[96] Majorities as well as dictators can engage in ruthless domination—the so-called tyranny of the majority. It is this latent

---

International Law and Domestic Law in Canada" in Ronald St. J. MacDonald *et al.*, eds., *Canadian Perspectives on International Law and Organization* (Toronto: University of Toronto Press, 1974) at 127. For clarity, we do not think that it is helpful to suggest to judges that they need to invent a space between the common law and statute law within which international law is supposed to operate domestically. It is enough that international law be received into the common law for it to bind the executive while still being subordinate to clear and express legislation that seeks to limit its scope. Furthermore, MacDonald thought that his proposal "would require or, at least, would be best accomplished by a constitutional amendment." (*Ibid.*) An implicit aim of our paper is to show that no such constitutional amendment is necessary, though of course one would certainly be welcome, and indeed we make such a recommendation below in Section H.

95 *Baker*, above note 1 at 841.

96 See, for example, David Dyzenhaus, "Constituting the Rule of Law: Fundamental Values in Administrative Law" (2002) 27 Queen's L.J. 445 at 501–2; H. Richardson, *Democratic Autonomy: Public Reasoning about the Ends of Policy* (New York: Oxford University Press, 2002).

feature of unrestrained populism to which the liberal, republican, and rationalist strands of contemporary democratic theory respond.[97] The liberal strand speaks to the protection of fundamental rights and interests, such as those protected in the *Charter*. Republicanism concerns the separation of powers, but from the standpoint of ensuring checks and balances so that no particular branch of the state—not the legislature, the executive, or the judiciary—accumulates unconstrained power that lends itself to abuse. From the republican perspective, judicial review is less about protecting cherished liberal rights than it is about limiting the threat of domination posed by concentrations of power. The rationalist aspect of democracy relates to the idea that democratic rule is accomplished through a process of people reasoning together with one another about the proper ends of policy, and not through resorts to force or naked assertions of individual self-interest. We do not elaborate further on these components of democratic theory; we note them simply to illustrate the poverty of a conception of democracy that relies exclusively (or almost exclusively) on majoritarianism.

To sum up, giving domestic effect to a ratified treaty is consistent with populism so long as Parliament retains authority to restrict the scope of the treaty's terms once it is ratified. Further, if the treaty touches on human rights, then giving it domestic effect contributes to the liberal ideal of protecting such rights, and to that extent contributes to Canada's democratic legitimacy. Similarly, the republican strand of democracy is strengthened by requiring the executive to respect domestically the obligations it assumes on the world stage. Republicanism is strengthened in the first instance because these treaty obligations place constraints on executive power and therefore make its abuse more difficult, and secondly, because deviation from international norms requires Parliament to justify such deviations publicly through the legislative process. Thus, consistent with the ethos that motivates republicanism, Parliament's power is constrained in the sense that its statutes are expected to operate in conformity with the provisions of international law, unless Parliament explicitly declares otherwise. This public justification requirement dovetails with, and contributes to, the final aspect of democratic governance canvassed above; collective reasoning about public goals. By requiring Parliament to be explicit about

---

97 We adopt these categories from Richardson's "republican-liberal-populist-rationalist" conception of democracy, or "democracy as democratic autonomy" for short, the point of which he summarizes as "collectively reasoned self-rule...collective reasoning about public ends, the ends of policy." *Ibid.* at 17–19.

its intent to contravene international law, the government must expose its intent to the public scrutiny that attends the legislative process.

It may seem that reliance here on the public scrutiny supplied by the legislative process is at odds with our view that such a process is not necessary for ratified treaties to have domestic effect. However, as we will now attempt to show, there is good reason to think that ratified treaties ought to have domestic effect, regardless of whether Parliament takes explicit steps to implement after ratification occurs (steps that may well be redundant, if enabling legislation already exists), and that any curtailment of such effect must be premised on clear legislative words rather than the executive's discretion.

E. MAKING SENSE OF THE PRESUMPTION OF LEGALITY

There is considerable tension between the idea that ratified treaties cannot give rise to legal obligations without explicit implementation, on the one hand, and the presumption of legality that instructs judges and officials to interpret domestic law in conformity with international law, on the other. The tension can be put thus: If Parliament is the sole legitimate source of law, then what is the reason for interpreting domestic legislation so that it is consistent with the dictates of ratified treaties? International comity cannot be the reason, because the issue is the domestic rather than international effect of treaty obligations, and in many cases the relevant domestic effect engages matters in which other nations and their citizens have no material interest (for example, the calculation of property taxes).

The presumption of legality that inheres in international law suggests that this body of law has some authority independently of any Act of Parliament. If this were not the case, there would be no reason to use international law as an interpretive lens. While we do not have space to defend a comprehensive account of the basis of the authority of international law, presumably part of such an account would include the fact that such law reflects the international community's consensus on the constitutive and substantive contents of the rule or law, which is to say, a consensus on the best legal principles and institutional modes through which public authority may legitimately interact with the people subject to it. As we discuss later, this consensus suggests that obligations arising from ratified treaties ought to enjoy common law status within Canada. For now, however, we limit our discussion to merely the implications that flow from the presumption of legality as a vehicle for statutory interpretation.

To say that international law can inform the proper interpretation of domestic legislation is to say that, in some cases, it is capable of giving rise to legal obligations where such obligations might not otherwise have been found to exist. In *Baker*, for example, L'Heureux-Dubé J. looked to the international law to support her view that immigration officers determining an application for relief from a deportation order on humanitarian and compassionate grounds must pay close attention to children's best interests.[98] While she referred to the objectives of the *Immigration Act* and to ministerial guidelines, neither of those sources made specific reference to children nor to a requirement to "consider children's best interests as an important factor, give them substantial weight, and be alert, alive and sensitive to them."[99]

Article 3 of the CRC, on the other hand, stipulates that in "all actions concerning children ... the best interests of the child shall be a primary consideration."[100] While L'Heureux-Dubé J. was cautious not to adopt the exact language of "primary consideration" found in the CRC, she found that the "values and principles of the Convention recognize the importance of being attentive to the rights and best interests of children when decisions are made that relate to and affect their futures."[101] She also noted that the preamble from the Convention recalls language from the UDHR, and cited it for the proposition that "childhood is entitled to special care and assistance."[102] Finally, she observed that the preamble from the United Nations *Declaration of the Rights of the Child* (1959) affirms that the child "needs special safeguards and care."[103]

L'Heureux-Dubé J. framed this analysis within the four corners of the two controlling doctrines mentioned in our Introduction. She cited *Francis v. The Queen*[104] and *Capital Cities* for the doctrine that ratified, but unimplemented treaties "are not part of Canadian law."[105] But she also cited

---

98 Subsection 14(2) of the *Immigration Act*, R.S.C. 1985, c. I-2 (repealed, now s. 25(1) of the *Immigration and Refugee Protection Act*, S.C. 2001, c. 27) gives the minister authority to exempt an individual from the usual requirements and regulations concerning immigration if the minister is satisfied "that the person's admission should be facilitated owing to the existence of compassionate or humanitarian considerations."

99 *Baker*, above note 1 at 831.

100 See above note 26.

101 *Baker*, above note 1 at 821.

102 *Ibid.* at 861.

103 *Ibid.* at 862.

104 [1956] S.C.R. 618.

105 *Baker*, above note 1 at 861.

the following passage from the leading text on statutory interpretation in support of the idea that international law "may help inform the contextual approach to statutory interpretation and judicial review":[106]

> [T]he legislature is presumed to respect the values and principles enshrined in international law, both customary and conventional. These constitute a part of the legal context in which legislation is enacted and read. *In so far as possible, therefore, interpretations that reflect and respect these values are preferred* (emphasis by L'Heureux-Dubé J.).

Our argument, then, is that taking the contextual approach seriously places intolerable strain on the idea that ratified treaties "are not part of Canadian law."

It is interesting to note that the subject of Iacobucci and Cory JJ.'s partial dissent was the majority's use of international law to support its finding that the immigration officer had exercised discretion unreasonably and, therefore, illegally. The dissenters worried that reference to the underlying values of the CRC would permit Baker:[107]

> to achieve indirectly what cannot be achieved directly, namely, to give force and effect within the domestic legal system to international obligations undertaken by the executive alone that have yet to be subject to the democratic will of Parliament.

Now, on the facts in *Baker*, the immigration officer who reviewed Baker's application at first instance, wrote notes that were so riddled with prejudice and stereotype that they gave rise to a reasonable apprehension of bias, and so the court could have confined its review to this ground alone. However, the court clearly wished to convey more than a message that immigration officials should not be so foolish as to write case notes that disclose bias and other irrelevant considerations.[108] For the first time,

---

106 *Ibid.*, citing Ruth Sullivan, *Driedger on the Construction of Statutes*, 3d ed. (Markham, ON: Butterworths, 1994) at 330. As an aside, Toope and Brunnée suggest, see above note 2 at 45, that the *Baker* Court could have found that "the best interests of the child" test has evolved into a norm of customary international law, and as such is directly binding within Canada's domestic law without the need for transformation. Arguably, the same may be said of many if not most human rights norms.

107 *Baker*, above note 1 at 866.

108 For argument that the Court wished to ensure that people in Baker's position were not subject to the arbitrary good fortune of gaining access to notes such as the ones that surfaced in *Baker*, nor to the caprice of an administration sufficiently wise to couch

the court held that a common law duty to give reasons applied generally if an administrative decision implicates important interests, and that such reasons may be subject to review on a standard of reasonableness (the more deferential standard of patent unreasonableness had been the norm for review of discretion). But the most important aspect of the decision for present purposes, as indicated earlier, is that L'Heureux-Dubé J. needed to turn to international law to explain just what a reasonable exercise of discretion would entail in the given circumstances because neither the object of the *Immigration Act* nor the minister's guidelines spoke directly to the idea that children's best interests must be given special regard.

Indeed, the prevailing jurisprudence developed by the Federal Court of Appeal in *Langner v. Canada (Minister of Employment and Immigration)*,[109] a case relied on by that same court in the decision that *Baker* overturned, took the following view of children's interests in deportation proceedings:[110]

> [T]he appellants are essentially asking this court to do nothing less than to declare that the mere fact that these people, who otherwise have no right to remain in Canada, have had a child in Canada prevents the Canadian Government from executing a deportation order that has been validly made against them. In short, one would need only have a child on Canadian soil and argue that child's Canadian citizenship rights in order to avoid the effect of Canadian immigration laws and obtain indirectly what it was impossible to obtain directly by complying with those laws....
>
> The appellant parents' decision to take their children to Poland with them or to leave them with family members living in Canada is a decision which is their own to make and which, to all appearances, they will make in the best interests of the children. The Canadian Government has nothing to do with this decision, which is of strictly private interest....
>
> Counsel for the appellants also contended that removal of the parents would be contrary to the international obligations contracted by Canada when it ratified the Convention on the Rights of the Child. Even if these international obligations had been incorporated into Canada's domestic law by legislation, which is not the case, we need only look to articles 9 and

---

its motives in language that lacks the stench of prejudice, see David Dyzenhaus, "The Deep Structure of *Roncarelli v. Duplessis*" (2004) 53 U.N.B.L.J. 111.
109 [1995] F.C.J. No. 469 (C.A.).
110 *Ibid.* at paras. 4, 6, and 11.

10 of that Convention to find that, here again, Mr. Grey's arguments are entirely devoid of merit.

Notice the similarity in apprehension and even language between this *dictum* and the partial dissent in *Baker*: both express concern about litigants obtaining indirectly, through reliance on children's best interests, what they could not obtain directly. One of us has argued that this concern is ultimately a concern about the non-statutory source of the obligation to have due regard for children's best interests.[111] The worry over sources, however, ought to have led the partial dissenters in *Baker* to dissent to the common law duty to give reasons, as well as to the equally common law requirement that those reasons be capable of standing up to a somewhat probing examination. These common law duties, whether informed or not by international law, have no explicit basis in statute, and thus they ought to be suspect to judges preoccupied with anchoring public law duties in statute law. In other words, the partial dissenters in *Baker*, to be true to the rationale underlying their dissent, should have affirmed *Langner* and the Federal Court decisions that subsequently relied on it.

Given this jurisprudential backdrop and the role that the CRC played in the majority's reasons in *Baker*, it is fair to say that the Convention did *part* of what the dissenters in *Baker* feared: it gave rise to a new obligation (or at least to an obligation that had been denied rather than affirmed by the courts) to exercise discretion in a manner that is "alert, alive, and sensitive" to children's best interests.

We say that the CRC did only *part* of what the dissenters feared because, with respect to the views of a very compassionate and innovative judge, we deny that the Convention was unimplemented in the sense that there was insufficient legislative authority on the books for the decision-maker to comply with the Convention (the *Immigration Act* itself provided ample discretion). Further, we deny that the Convention's ratification was not subject to the will of Parliament. Before and after the Convention was ratified, Parliament could have signalled its disapproval or could have restricted the application of some or all of its terms. Parliament's failure to take any such measure should be interpreted as a willingness to permit the terms of the Convention to operate with the force of the common law, just as legislative

---

111 David Dyzenhaus & Evan Fox-Decent, "Rethinking the Process/Substance Distinction: *Baker v. Canada*" (2001) 51 U.T.L.J. 193 at 232–36.

silence is presumed to be filled with common law duties, such as the duty to give reasons and the other dictates of procedural fairness.

Returning to the immediate argument, our claim is that *Baker* presents a case in which a court is willing to use international law for the purposes of controlling discretion in a way that gives rise to a legal obligation that had no explicit basis in the relevant statute. *Baker* is not a case in which resort is made to international law for the purposes of deciding between competing, but reasonable interpretations of an ambiguous statutory term. Rather, it is a case about the exercise of a broad discretion in which the only concrete statutory indications are that a favourable discretion may be exercised on the basis of nebulous and undefined humanitarian and compassionate considerations. At the very least, *Baker* stands for the proposition that where a broad statutory grant of discretionary power is at issue, legal obligations that condition the exercise of the power may be inferred from international law, and that these obligations apply as a matter of common law independently of Parliament explicitly implementing them in the controlling statute. So in this sense, ratified treaties *are* a part of Canadian law insofar as they are capable of giving rise to legal obligations that public officials and judges alike are bound to respect and enforce. In short, taking seriously the contextual approach urged in *Baker* implies giving domestic (and sometimes dramatic) effect to ratified treaties.

The significance of *Baker* lies not in the result that the complainant was granted relief from a deportation order, for the court did not find that Baker had a substantive right to remain in Canada just because she had Canadian-born children. Rather, the court held that Baker had a right to have the decision-maker exercise his discretion in a manner that was "alert, alive, and sensitive" to her children's best interests. In the circumstances, this right entailed that if the officer wished to make an adverse determination, then he must have and provide weighty reasons capable of justifying the inevitable impairment of the children's best interests. Thus, the CRC played a vital role in establishing the justificatory burden the decision-maker must satisfy in order to exercise discretion in a manner that is both reasonable and lawful.

The real issue that *Baker* leaves unanswered is not the threshold question of whether ratified treaties can have domestic effect (they can and do), but rather the extent to which such treaties can establish a justificatory threshold that the executive and its agencies must meet in order to exercise discretion lawfully. Now, *Baker* could be interpreted as simply an extension of the interpretive presumption to discretionary grants of power that are already circumscribed by express statutory language, because the Convention was used in *Baker* to inform the proper use of a discretionary power that was to be exercised on the basis of humanitarian and compassionate considerations found in the discretion-conferring text of the *Immigration Act*.[112] The question we will now explore is whether ratified treaties can impose autonomous legal obligations on the executive and its decision-making bodies, obligations that arise independently of the express words found in the relevant domestic statute that authorizes administrative action. We believe that they can, and turn to an argument in support of this view.

F. TREATIES WITH FIRST NATIONS AND THE HONOUR OF THE CROWN

The honour of the Crown may seem an odd place to look to affirm the domestic effect of treaties because historically the courts referred to the Crown's honour in ambivalent ways that reflect the two doctrines that underpin today's dualism. The ambivalence has oscillated between, on the one hand, the interpretative presumption concerning international law, and on the other, the idea that ratified but unimplemented treaties have no domestic effect. Consider the *dicta* of Lamont J. (for himself and Cannon J.) in *Arrow River & Tributaries Slide & Boom Co. v. Pigeon Timber Co.*[113] The case dealt with whether the Ashburton-Webster Treaty between Great Britain and the United States of America[114] could restrict an Ontario company from charging tolls authorized by Ontario law. Lamont J. cited the Second Divisional Court below for the proposition that:[115]

> because a former Sovereign had been party to the treaty and His Majesty was in honour bound to uphold it, and, as the Act in question was passed in His Majesty's name, it should not be given a construction inconsistent with the terms of the treaty if it could fairly be otherwise interpreted.

However, Lamont J. quickly went on to affirm the dualist thesis:[116]

---

112 Note that this is no small extension of the presumption, since it extends the presumption into a realm of judicial review (review of discretionary decision-making) that had previously been subject to only limited curial scrutiny. For discussion of the significance of this extension, see Dyzenhaus, Hunt, & Taggart, "The Principle of Legality in Administrative Law: Internationalisation as Constitutionalisation" (2001) 1 O.U.C.L.J. 5.

113 [1932] S.C.R. 495 [*Arrow River*].

114 Signed at Washington, D.C., on 9 August 1842.

115 *Arrow River,* above note 113 at 509.

116 *Ibid.* at 510.

The treaty in itself is not equivalent to an Imperial Act and, without the sanction of Parliament, the Crown cannot alter the existing law by entering into a contract with a foreign power. For a breach of a treaty a nation is responsible only to the other contracting nation and its own sense of right and justice.

Notice that even within the affirmation of dualism the judge refers to a nation's "own sense of right and justice." One place where the Canadian sense of right and justice expresses itself is in the principle of the honour of the Crown that informs First Nation treaty interpretation. We suggest that it is time for this principle to water the roots of the international-domestic law nexus from which it originated.

In the nineteenth and much of the twentieth century, the courts held that First Nations could make only limited claims on the basis of treaty either because the treaty obligations amounted to nothing more than a "personal obligation" undertaken by the Crown's representative rather than the Crown itself,[117] or because First Nations were not deemed to have the requisite status to enter into treaties.[118] It was not until *R. v. White and Bob*[119] that Canadian courts affirmed that First Nation treaties gave rise to obligations enforceable against the Crown, and that such obligations could only be extinguished through federal legislation.

Many years later, in the pre-*Charter* case of *R. v. Taylor and Williams*,[120] the honour of the Crown first took hold as the underlying justification to the contemporary "liberal and generous" approach to interpreting First Nation treaties.[121] The Ontario Court of Appeal found that "[i]n approaching the terms of a treaty ... the honour of the Crown is always involved and no

---

117 *Attorney-General for Ontario v. Attorney-General for Canada: Re Indian Claims*, [1897] A.C. 199 at 213 (J.C.P.C.).

118 *R. v. Syliboy*, [1929] 1 D.L.R. 307 at 313 (N.S. Co. Ct.), where the court held that "[t]he savages' rights of sovereignty even of ownership were never recognized." Interestingly, even the *Syliboy* court conceded that "[h]aving called the agreement a treaty, and having perhaps lulled the Indians into believing it to be a treaty with all the sacredness of a treaty attached to it, it may be the Crown should not now be heard to say it is not a treaty." *Ibid.* at 314.

119 (1964), 50 D.L.R. (2d) 613, 52 W.W.R. 193 (B.C.C.A), aff'd (1965), 52 D.L.R. (2d) 481n (S.C.C.) [*White and Bob*].

120 (1981), 62 C.C.C. (2d) 227, leave to appeal to S.C.C. refused, [1981] 2 S.C.R. xi [*Taylor and Williams*].

121 See, for example, *Simon v. The Queen*, [1985] 2 S.C.R. 387 [*Simon*]; *R. v. Sioui*, [1990] 1 S.C.R. 1025 [*Sioui*]; *R. v. Badger*, [1996] 1 S.C.R. 771; *R. v. Marshall*, [1999] 3 S.C.R. 456 [*Marshall*].

appearance of 'sharp dealing' should be sanctioned."[122] Thus, literal interpretations are to be avoided, ambiguities are to be resolved in favour of the Aboriginal party, First Nations' understandings of the treaties are to be taken into consideration, and extrinsic evidence may be relied upon as part of the interpretive exercise.[123]

The liberal and generous approach to First Nation treaty interpretation proceeds from the assumption that Crown agents (often local military commanders[124] or governors[125]) were capable of binding the Crown, and that the obligations that arose were and are enforceable against the Crown, notwithstanding a wholesale lack of statutory implementation. Indeed, as indicated earlier, the presumption concerning the legal effect of First Nation treaties runs in the opposite direction: First Nation treaty rights remain in force unless such rights were abrogated by clear and express federal legislation prior to their entrenchment in section 35 of the *Constitution Act, 1982*. Prior to the constitutionalization of Aboriginal treaty rights in 1982, they imposed (or are now deemed to have imposed) common law duties on the Crown, and as such they could be extinguished or restricted by nothing less than an explicit Act of Parliament. There is no reason to think that ratified international treaties should not enjoy exactly this status. What the First Nations case shows is that the honour of the Crown can, and should, have domestic as well as international application.

The Supreme Court has recently used language in a non-First Nations context that echoes the idea that the executive's assumption of treaty obligations cannot be rendered a nullity by the inconvenience such obligations may later pose to the executive. In *Suresh*, the Court considered the effect of Canada's ratification of the *Convention against Torture* on deportation

---

122 *Taylor and Williams*, above note 120. In recent years the honour of the Crown has come to be associated with the Crown-First Nation fiduciary relationship, and more specifically with the idea that the Crown owes Aboriginal peoples a duty to consult if Aboriginal rights may be infringed by Crown legislative or administrative action, a duty that is owed even prior to a judicial determination that an Aboriginal right is in fact at stake. See *Haida*, above note 93; *Taku River Tlingit First Nation v. British Columbia (Project Assessment Director)*, [2004] 3 S.C.R. 550.

123 See cases cited above at note 121, and also Leonard Rotman, "Taking Aim at the Canons of Treaty Interpretation in Canadian Aboriginal Rights Jurisprudence" (1997) 46 U.N.B.L.J. 1.

124 See, for example, *Sioui*, above note 121.

125 See, for example, *White and Bob*, above note 119; *Simon*, above note 121; *Marshall*, above note 121.

proceedings that threatened to *"refoule"* an individual to a state where he faced a serious risk of torture. The Court held:[126]

> It is only reasonable that the same executive that bound itself to the CAT intends to act in accordance with the CAT's plain meaning. Given Canada's commitment to the CAT, we find that the appellant had the right to procedural safeguards ...

Following *Baker*, the Court looked to five contextual factors to determine the content of the Crown's duty of procedural fairness:[127]

> (1) the nature of the decision made and the procedures followed in making it, that is, "the closeness of the administrative process to the judicial process"; (2) the role of the particular decision within the statutory scheme; (3) the importance of the decision to the individual affected; (4) the legitimate expectations of the person challenging the decision where undertakings were made concerning the procedure to be followed; and (5) the choice of procedure made by the agency itself.

The significance of the *dictum* that "[g]iven Canada's commitment to the CAT ... the appellant had the right to procedural safeguards" is underscored by its exact location in the court's judgment, for the *dictum* occurs precisely at stage four of the *Baker* analysis, where the court inquires into whether Suresh had a legitimate expectation that certain procedures would be followed on the basis of Canada's ratification of the *Convention Against Torture.* Although the Court does not explicitly use the words "legitimate expectation," this is the first time in Canadian jurisprudence that judges have cited the rationale underlying legitimate expectations in support of procedural safeguards. This rationale, we contend, is part and parcel of the idea that ratification triggers the honour of the Crown, and that in this context the honour of the Crown has direct legal implications.

Of course, there are significant differences between the positions of First Nations and non-Aboriginal Canadians vis-à-vis the executive and its exercise of the treaty-making power. Aboriginals are parties to the relevant treaties; non-Aboriginals are not. First Nations alone entered into treaties in a manner that facilitated European colonization of Canada, and Native peoples relied on treaties in consideration for the land and rights they surrendered (or were taken to have surrendered). Further, First Nation treaty

---

126 *Suresh*, above note 1 at para. 119.
127 *Ibid.* at para. 115.

rights enjoy constitutional protection under section 35(1) of *The Constitution Act, 1982*. In these and other respects, the relationship between the Crown and First Nations is commonly referred to as *sui generis*. The question, then, is whether differences such as these should matter from the perspective of the honour of the Crown and its capacity to place itself under obligation on the basis of the commitments it makes through ratification.

Our view is that the differences are properly reflected in the distinct content of the relevant treaties and the rights contained therein, but that the honour of the Crown can give rise to claims against the executive in both cases. In each case the honour of the Crown is engaged because in each case the Crown is presumed to enter into treaties for the benefit of the people subject to its authority, Aboriginal and non-Aboriginal alike. It is for this reason that in the Aboriginal context 'no sharp dealing' is to be countenanced or otherwise assumed in the process of treaty interpretation, despite the fact that the Crown treated with First Nations for the purposes of extending and entrenching its very own sovereignty. The honour of the Crown, properly understood, is just a metaphor for the idea that the legitimacy of the Crown depends upon the Crown keeping the commitments it makes for and on behalf of the people it represents.

If the courts are willing to play a role in upholding the honour of the Crown in the First Nations case, as we believe they should, there is no reason for them to shirk this responsibility when the Crown, through the executive, enters into international treaties on behalf of all Canadians, including Canada's Aboriginal peoples. Viewing the honour of the Crown in this manner lends coherence to the principle's application, for it is a principle found explicitly in international law, as *Arrow River* attests, and one that has since been used to inform the proper attitude of the Crown and the courts to the treaty claims of First Nations. The principle affirms the Crown's legitimacy by subjecting the Crown to the obligations it assumes, and as a consequence the honour of the Crown can subject the executive to domestically enforceable legal obligations whenever the executive ratifies treaties of any sort. The status of these obligations, we argue now, is the same common law status that Aboriginal treaty rights had prior to their constitutionalization in 1982, and which public law duties, such as the duty or procedural fairness, have today.

G. THE STATUS AND EFFECT OF TREATY OBLIGATIONS

As indicated already, in many cases there is law in place that grants the executive authority to conduct administration in a manner consistent with Canada's treaty obligations. In yet other cases, it is arguable that Canadian law already requires the executive to act in conformity with international law, and thus the quest for further and more explicit implementation in these circumstances is misguided from the start. However, in some cases treaties will contain terms and provisions that attribute obligations to the executive and its agencies that have no apparent or explicit basis in existing statutes, notwithstanding statutory powers delegated to the administration that make compliance with treaty obligations possible. In this section we suggest that such obligations ought to be understood to impose common law duties on the executive and its subordinate decision-makers (including the full range of boards, tribunals, commissions, and agencies that operate in the public sector), and that the content of such obligations is informed in part by the degree to which they have been implemented or otherwise received into Canada's domestic legal order. In other words, ratification and the commitments implicit in the interpretive presumption dispose of the threshold issue of whether or not international law imposes legal duties on the executive, whereas implementation and reception, properly understood, suggest not only an affirmative answer to the threshold question, but important things about the content and effect of such obligations in practice.

The division of labour we are proposing, between issues of threshold and content, is a division familiar to Canadian administrative lawyers versed in the duty of procedural fairness. Before determining *which* procedural safeguards are due in a given administrative decision-making context (the content of procedural fairness), courts first determine whether *any* such protections are due at all (that is, whether the threshold has been met).[128] If the threshold conditions are satisfied, inquiry turns to the content of the duty, an inquiry that takes its bearings from the five *Baker* factors cited previously.[129]

It bears emphasizing that while a statutory scheme and a delegation of authority must be present for the duty of fairness to apply, courts address

---

128 *Knight*, above note 90 at 669–77. A duty of procedural fairness may apply independently of statutory indications, but for the duty to apply the decision must be "administrative" rather than "legislative" in nature, an important interest must be at stake (such as an immigration or employment interest), and the decision must be "final" in the sense that no further appeal within the statutory scheme is possible.

129 Above note 127.

both the threshold and content issues even if there is no support for procedural safeguards to be found in the relevant legislation. The reason they do so is that they take fairness to be an integral part of the common law, and thus capable of giving rise to public legal obligations without the prompt of positive law.[130] But there is a deeper or at least more explicit reason, we contend, to suppose that both public law duties such as fairness as well as treaty obligations ought to apply presumptively against the executive.

The reason flows from a substantive conception of the rule of law[131] that requires public authority to have an alert and attentive regard for the human dignity of the people subject to it. Thus, procedural fairness is due because letting people know and respond to the case against them treats them as participants in (rather than objects of) decision-making processes, and as a corollary reduces the likelihood of arbitrariness. Similarly, a concern for human dignity is exactly the premise that underwrites human rights conventions, and so respect for the principles contained in such conventions follows from the idea that the administration ought to have due regard for the dignity of the people subject to its jurisdiction. Respect for human rights principles flows from the Kantian idea that the concept of law implies treating people as worthy of respect in their own right, as well as from Kant's related view that governing through law entails enshrining rights in a regime of equal freedom.[132] Respect for human rights follows from these ideas because such respect is both a precondition and an aspiration of a substantive conception of the rule of law that seeks to guarantee the equal freedom of everyone subject to the law.

---

130 As L'Heureux-Dubé put it in *Knight*, above note 90 at 683: "Like the principles of fundamental justice in s. 7 of the *Canadian Charter of Rights and Freedoms*, the concept of fairness is entrenched in the principles governing our legal system."

131 For discussion of the difference between substantive and formal conceptions of the rule of law, see Paul Craig, "Formal and Substantive Conceptions of the Rule or Law" [1997] P.L. 467. Roughly, a formal conception holds that the rule of law goes to the manner in which laws are formulated and enforced rather than to the substantive content of particular laws. On the formal understanding, a baldly discriminatory statute would not violate the rule of law on account of its discriminatory substance, whereas any statute may infringe the rule of law if it authorizes retroactive sanctions, or if its provisions are not made public, or if it is excessively vague. A substantive conception of the rule of law, on the other hand, is sensitive to content, and may hold (for example) that flagrant violations of human rights are also violations of the rule of law.

132 For a much more elaborate articulation of the Kantian view of law in exactly this context, see Alan Brudner, "The Domestic Enforcement of International Covenants on Human Rights: A Theoretical Framework" (1985) 35 U.T.L.J. 219.

The Supreme Court of Canada's approach to international law in the context of interpreting the *Charter* fits comfortably with this conception of human rights and the rule of law. In *Slaight Communications Inc. v. Davidson*[133] the majority held that:

> Canada's international human rights obligations should inform not only the interpretation of the content of the rights guaranteed by the Charter but also the interpretation of what can constitute pressing and substantial s. 1 objectives which may justify restrictions upon those rights.[134]

Moreover, Dickson C.J., writing for the majority, reaffirmed his *dictum* from *Reference Re Public Service Employee Relations Act (Alberta)*[135] that "the Charter should generally be presumed to provide protection at least as great as that afforded by similar provisions in international human rights documents which Canada has ratified."[136] Thus, issues of implementation pose no obstacle to courts that use international law to inquire into, for example, the content of open-textured principles of fundamental justice found in section 7.[137]

Recognition of "unimplemented" international law as a guide to *Charter* interpretation, however, is recognition that such law, via the *Charter*, may play a significant role in restricting the operation of ordinary legislation. If international law did not have the capacity to play this role, then using it as an interpretative guide in this context would be meaningless. But if treaties the judiciary considers to be unimplemented really can play a role in limiting the operation of statutes, then this is a further reason to believe that they have the normative capacity to give rise to default legal obligations that the executive is bound to respect, and which courts are therefore bound to enforce. If a lack of explicit implementation cannot block international law from playing a constructive role in determining the constitutional limits of domestic legislative authority, and if (as we contend) Canadian judges have adopted far too restrictive a view of implementation, then there is no reason to think that an alleged failure to implement (or worse, an alleged failure to implement in a certain way) ought to preclude international law from placing analogous constraints on domestic executive authority. The most

---

133 [1989] 1 S.C.R. 1038 [*Slaight Communications*].
134 *Ibid.* at 1056.
135 [1987] 1 S.C.R. 313.
136 *Slaight Communications*, above note 133 at 1056.
137 See, for example, *Suresh*, above note 1 at 5–6.

appropriate status for those constraints to assume is the status enjoyed by common law obligations, for recognising that international law has such authority is to recognise the very substantial role it does and should play in setting constitutional limits on both legislative and executive authority.

Now, admittedly, even in the *Charter* context, where the presumptive authority of international law has been explicit since at least *Slaight Communications*, it is an authority relative to the interpretation of exiting and domestic positive law, that is, the *Charter*. Moreover, the kinds of international instruments called upon to guide interpretation relate to human rights and the specification of human rights principles. We need to say more to support the further propositions that 1) the terms of allegedly unimplemented treaties give rise to autonomous common law duties, duties that apply independently of the explicit provisions in a given statute; and that 2) such duties apply even if the treaties concern matters unrelated to human rights. We defend these propositions in turn.

1) The Autonomous Domestic Operation of International Law

Conventional wisdom holds that for the executive and its subordinate agencies to exercise legal powers at all, they must do so *intra vires* a particular grant of statutory authority or, somewhat exceptionally, on the basis of the prerogative. We wish to situate our argument within the bounds of this conventional understanding of delegated power, and so we do not argue that the executive has authority on the basis of international law to undertake substantive policy initiatives, which themselves have no basis in domestic legislation. Whether such an argument can be made and sustained (perhaps on the basis of doctrine concerning the pre-constitutionalized common law status of First Nation treaties) is largely beside the point because in virtually every important area of human endeavour there is a public law regime that controls its development. When we speak of the autonomous domestic operation of international law, then, we do not refer to rules and principles that stand free of all domestic law, but rather to rules and principles that can influence both the interpretation of domestic law as well as the exercise of broad discretionary powers, much as the duty of procedural fairness attaches autonomously to the operation of statutes, which themselves may contain no explicit provision of procedural safeguards.

Consider, for example, a case such as *Baker*, but assume for the moment that the relevant provision of the *Immigration Act* stipulates simply that the minister has discretionary authority to exempt an individual from the usual requirements and regulations concerning immigration. That is, suppose that the minister can exempt an individual on the basis of a discretion that the statute does not condition by reference to the existence of humanitarian and compassionate (or any other) considerations. In our view, the CRC would still be relevant to the proper exercise of this discretion, with the result being that children's best interests would have to be treated as a "primary consideration," or, to use L'Heureux-Dubé J.'s proxy, as special interests toward which the decision-maker must be "alert, alive, and sensitive." The Minister can still adduce reasons to show that, in a given set of circumstances, other considerations outweigh the children's best interests (perhaps the applicant is a dangerous criminal and his children are near majority). However, we contend that a number of factors overdetermine that the common law duty to give reasons (a duty that applies independently of international law, as a matter of procedural fairness) includes a substantive duty to take account of the significance that international law gives to children's best interests. These factors are: the normative authority of international law that underlies the interpretive presumption in human rights cases, confirmation by the executive prior to ratification that Canada's legal framework is consistent with the CRC, the act of ratification itself that binds Canada internationally, and Parliament's implicit assent to ratification. The lack of a specific domestic statutory anchor in terms of humanitarian and compassionate considerations is of no consequence.

One of the advantages to conceiving of public law as intrinsically concerned with the justification of exercises of public power is that this conception permits us to see the manner in which the terms of international conventions can function as legal principles, whether or not they are expressed as principles or as rules. Some scholars sympathetic to the domestic enforcement of human rights treaties have argued that human rights principles require no implementation because they inhere in the universal reason of the common law, and therefore do not require a legislative act in order to have legal authority.[138] Human rights rules, on the other hand, consist in a mix of reason and contingency, and therefore it appears that they cannot be brought into domestic law without being subject to the will of the legislature. For example, the principle against cruel and inhuman punishment can be assumed as an *a priori* principle of reason applicable to all human societies, whereas a rule derivable from this principle such as "one person per cell" does not seem to have this universal flavour, since we

---

138 Brudner, above note 134 at 235–7.

can readily imagine situations where more than one person per cell is the more humane option.

Once we see that the imperatives of international treaties, generally speaking, express limited rather than absolute rights from which some derogation is possible, we see that the focus of our inquiry shifts fruitfully from the overdetermined threshold question of whether a particular provision applies to a relevant set of circumstances to the more interesting content question of what reasons must be offered to justify an infringement of the right. In the case above, pointing out that prisoners generally prefer to share cells than be kept separate would be one such justifiable infringement of the rule "one person per cell," and of course the reason we think the infringement may be justifiable is that the reason given for infringing the rule appeals implicitly to the underlying principle that proscribes cruel and inhuman punishment.

We say that the threshold question, here as in *Baker*, is overdetermined just because human rights are at stake and human rights instruments are evoked. Arguably, the authority implicit in these instruments, in virtue of their subject matter and its connection to human dignity, is sufficient to render their terms mandatory and primary considerations[139] in decision-making contexts in which human rights are at stake. But many treaties concern matters that do not bear directly on human rights, and so an appeal to human rights cannot be relied on to support the idea that their terms, too, deserve to be treated as capable of placing the executive and its officials under legal obligation.

2) Non-Human Rights Treaties

The argument in favour of giving domestic effect to non-human rights treaties flows from the multitude of considerations canvassed above, all of which apply equally to the domestic enforcement of human rights conventions. In summary:

First, a failure to give effect to ratified treaties would make a mockery of Canada's assumed international obligations as well as the practice of federal and provincial administrations that labour to ensure that Canada's laws comply with such treaties prior to their ratification.

---

139 Administrative lawyers distinguish mandatory relevant from mandatory primary considerations in that the former is indifferent to the weight that must be accorded the consideration, whereas the latter implies that significant (but not insurmountable) weight is due.

Second, and related, Parliament may enact laws that do not specifically implement the exact terms of a treaty by incorporating it into an existing statute, but there are many means of implementation, and evidence of any of these in a particular case adds to the argument that the relevant treaty's terms ought to be given domestic effect. Courts can and should take account of existing law such that the presence of discretionary grants of authority that enable compliance with a treaty's terms count for, rather than against, using international law to contribute to the justificatory burden the administration must discharge to exercise its discretion in a manner injurious to protected interests.

Third, the honour of the Crown is engaged whenever the Crown enters into treaties for and on behalf of the people subject to its authority, and this holds true independently of the subject matter of a particular treaty. The honour of the Crown implies that the executive must be held accountable domestically for the obligations it assumes internationally.

Fourth, the interpretative presumption is already being used by judges to impose obligations on the executive that have only a tenuous basis in statute, and which lend substance to the common law duty to give reasons which itself may have no support in the relevant legislation (for example, *Baker*). Looking beyond the four corners of a statute to impose obligations grounded in international law is no more threatening to the separation of powers than holding administrative bodies to an autonomous duty of procedural fairness.

Each of these considerations speaks to the growing integration of international and domestic law, and each speaks to the need to embrace international law as a vital component of the rule of law.

H. REFORMS THROUGH THE LEGISLATURE AND THE EXECUTIVE

In the authors' view, while much has been done by creative judicial reasoning in recent years and while much more will certainly be done in the future, there is a case to be made for more guidance from the legislative branch at the federal and provincial levels. Subject only to the restrictions of the Constitution, parliamentary supremacy allows considerable scope for a broad incorporation by reference of international law or for otherwise directing the courts and the executive branch to give greater weight to international treaty law in defined contexts. Perhaps the ultimate example of the exercise of parliamentary supremacy is found in the *European Com-*

munities Act [140] of the UK Parliament, by which the EC treaties (existing and future) and all other EC law (existing and future) would have the force of law in the United Kingdom. The only limit to this delegation is set by the implicit capacity of Parliament to alter the *European Communities Act* at some future time. Many other less drastic approaches can be envisaged in Canada in order to promote the more harmonious coexistence of the Canadian legal order and public international law. Some of these approaches are set out in the following paragraphs.

1. The first and most far-reaching possibility would be a constitutional amendment that would state the place of customary and conventional international law in Canada as well as determine the authority to implement treaties. From the perspective of this article, the central question would be the weight to be given to a duly ratified treaty in the face of competing legislation and regulations and the deference to be paid to a ratified treaty by an official or administrative tribunal.

2. Related to the first approach would be consideration of a constitutional amendment that would provide for ratification of treaties by a reformed Senate in which the provincial governments as well as the federal government would be represented. This is the system in the federal government of Germany, but other federations such as Mexico and also unitary states such as France provide for approval of treaties by their respective parliaments, thus ensuring that the elected representatives of the people have an explicit opportunity to accept or reject the treaty.

3. A non-constitutional approach using existing institutions and procedures would be to rethink the role of Parliament in the process of treaty

---

140 *European Communities Act 1972* (U.K.), 1972, c. 68):

    Sec. 2. General implementation of Treaties.

    (1) All such rights, powers, liabilities, obligations and restrictions from time to time created or arising by or under the treaties, and all such remedies and procedures from time to time provided for by or under the treaties, as in accordance with the treaties are without further enactment to be given legal effect or used in the United Kingdom and shall be recognized and available in law, and be enforced, allowed and followed accordingly; and the expression "enforceable Community right" and similar expressions shall be read as referring to one to which this subsection applies.

    ...

    (4) ... any enactment passed or to be passed, other than one contained in this Part of this Act, shall be construed and have effect subject to the foregoing provisions of this section.

approval and also in the process of determining the general negotiating mandate of the executive in particular treaty negotiations. It is still the practice to seek approval of Parliament for treaties of peace. Happily, Canada has not been in a declared war since the end of hostilities against Germany and Japan, so this is not a major source of precedent. As mentioned above, until the Trudeau years it was the practice to submit major treaties to the scrutiny of Parliament before their ratification and most treaties were at least tabled in Parliament. Simply to return to parliamentary scrutiny in a more consistent fashion with respect to all important treaties and tabling every treaty would help to show parliamentarians, the courts, and the public that treaties are an important source of law. Setting aside specific blocks of parliamentary time to debate international agreements would also satisfy the same purpose. The more Parliament is seen to approve the ratification of a treaty, the harder it will be for courts to suggest that treaties are reserved to the executive and that they do not have the assent of the legislative branch as well.

4. A further step in the direction of parliamentary scrutiny would be to involve Parliament not only in the treaty approval process but also in the decision to open negotiations. Parliament cannot conduct negotiations but it can certainly authorise them, approve the broad negotiating mandate and even be informed of progress in a timely fashion. This can be done by amending the Rules of Procedure or by including the grant in categories of statutes. It is common for the United States Congress to pass international trade legislation that envisages the executive returning for a specific negotiating mandate and, when the negotiation is complete, returning to Congress for an affirmative vote in both Houses on the treaty and any implementing legislation that may be needed.[141] One could envisage a similar procedure for trade treaties and the adoption of comparable procedures in other contexts.

5. A very few Canadian laws listed above[142] do contain a general statement of approval or of the intention to approve a treaty. In some cases it would be helpful to include in statutes more specific and directed language which would both affirm the intention to implement and require that courts and administrators give primacy to the treaty in the case of

---

141 Known as the "fast track" procedure as the vote in Congress involves a simple yes or no and any amendments are precluded thus facilitating a rapid and clear decision.
142 Above note 61.

a conflict between the treaty and the relevant legislation. This practice should not be occasional but should be carefully followed with every law devoted to the implementation of a treaty. Clear and specific indications from Parliament or a provincial legislature concerning the status of a treaty can only be of assistance to judges and all others responsible for public decision-making.

6. A rather specific policy but, nonetheless, one which can be of considerable importance, would be the adoption of a more consistent litigation strategy by governments respecting the status of treaties. It may have been a convenient defence at the time to assert in the *Baker* and *Ahani* cases that the treaties were unimplemented and thus could not produce legal effects, but in the broader context the argument presented by the Crown, which internationally had pledged to respect these major treaties, must surely be seen as ill advised and contrary to the honour with which it is presumed to act. The consistent adoption of positions designed to assert a closer relationship between domestic and international treaty law would do much to promote respect for the rule of international as well as domestic law.

7. Beyond specific rules as to the place of a particular treaty in domestic law, it would seem advisable to adopt a more general and coherent set of rules by amending the *Interpretation Act* at the federal and provincial level, as well as the legislation governing foreign relations, to state clearly what is meant by implementation, for instance, to state that a treaty should be considered to be susceptible of implementation by either specific or pre-existing general legislation. Such legislation could also state that Canadian laws should be interpreted in the light of the treaties that they implement unless there is specific language in the law requiring an interpretation that does not square with the treaty. The legislation should also state that there is a general presumption of compatibility of Canadian law with international treaty law to which Canada is a party.

8. Finally, specific legislation requiring administrators and administrative agencies to make their decisions in a manner compatible with Canada's treaty obligations would greatly encourage courts exercising the power of judicial review to ensure greater respect for Canada's international treaty obligations.

I. CONCLUSION

Pacta sunt servanda is not only a central principle of public international law, it is a universal principle of law to be found in all major legal systems. It is a principle of Canadian civil and common law. It is to be found in a host of federal and provincial statutes. For this and for the other reasons given, it is incumbent on the Canadian judiciary to adopt an approach to public international law that promotes respect for *pacta sunt servanda* by recognizing that Canada's treaty obligations regulate the exercise of executive power in the domestic as well as the international sphere.

What Is Reception Law?

GIB VAN ERT*

The purpose of this short essay is to suggest the existence of a new body of law. Were the law statutory in origin, this would be fairly easy. One would simply refer to the new Act and structure discussion of it around the terms it defines, the classifications it establishes, the powers it creates, and so on. One could even express ideas numerically, for example, "section 39 is subject to section 116." But the new body of law I propose to introduce derives mainly from the common law, and speaking about the common law is hard to do. How does one describe tort, for instance? Is it a "branch" of the common law? A "body" of common law? Is it even a coherent category, given the extraordinary variety of law we file under its name—from trespass to negligence to defamation to *Rylands v. Fletcher*?[1] What is it that connects these various causes of action enough to bring them under one name and distinguish them from other bodies or branches of the common law? These are questions we can usually ignore. But when one proposes, as I do, to suggest the existence of a new body of common law, they leap to the fore. Indeed, they are positively discouraging. The intertwining threads of history, procedure, legal reasoning, and legal practice, which found the distinctions we draw between branches of common law learning, appear so knotted that they cannot be loosened enough to add a new strand. The

---

*   I am grateful to Anthony Aust and the participants in the Department of Justice conference on international and domestic law (16–17 June 2005, Montreal) for their insights and suggestions.
1   (1866), L.R. 1 Ex. 265; (1868), L.R. 3 H.L. 330.

result leads to conservatism in the common law. Without the words to describe innovations when they appear, they become difficult to see at all.

A second difficulty in putting forward a new branch of the common law lies in the word *new*. The common law develops by accretion. To call something that grows over time "new" invites criticism. One can try to identify a turning point or a coming-of-age, but this may prove arbitrary or subjective. The most one may be able to say is that something is "emerging."

Yet another difficulty in heralding the arrival of a new body of common law derives from the presence of civil law systems within leading Commonwealth jurisdictions. To describe a body of law as "common" may suggest to some, quite understandably, that it has no application, or at least an attenuated application, in such jurisdictions as Quebec and Scotland. Yet, as we will see, the body of law I will explore in this essay is public in nature, and common law doctrines are current in these jurisdictions despite their civil law character.

I begin this way to make clear that I am well aware of the difficulties I face in suggesting the existence of a new branch of the common law. I nevertheless think it worthwhile to try to depict the jumble of evidentiary, interpretive, and constitutional rules that govern the interaction of domestic law and public international law in the Commonwealth tradition as a branch or body of law. And since it is largely judge-made law, and could seemingly be swept away entirely by codifying legislation,[2] the qualifier *common* seems generally appropriate. Naming this branch of law is perhaps not that important, but the label *reception* has been used and is as good as any.[3]

The advantage of identifying reception as a body of law can (and should) be questioned. Indeed, I am of the view that, more than any other factor, what will determine whether reception does indeed establish itself as a recognized branch or body of law will be the usefulness of thinking of it in this way. If the label I am proposing here proves to be only a label for labelling's sake, it will not stick. But I think there are practical advantages in describing reception as a body of common law. To do so may provoke debate about the legitimacy of the alleged category and the true content (if

---

2   Whether in Canada such legislation would fall within federal or provincial jurisdiction is a question I am happy to duck.

3   Stephen Toope has suggested that *reception* misleadingly implies a purely passive scheme, whereby the state only receives international norms and does not participate in their development. I agree that reception may have that misleading connotation, but I cannot think of a more appropriate term.

any) of reception law. Identifying reception may encourage us to view it in its totality, rather than fixating on particular rules within it, and to think systematically about what its rules are and should be. And we may simply understand the interaction of domestic and international law in Canada, the UK, and similarly constituted legal systems better when we think of it as a body of law, rather than merely a collection of distinct, if occasionally overlapping, rules. In his preface to *English Private Law*, the late Peter Birks observed: "there is no body of knowledgeable data which can subsist as a jumble of mismatched categories. The search for order is indistinguishable from the search for knowledge."[4]

I have mentioned the difficulty in describing reception as new. The leading features of reception law (assuming for the moment that such a thing exists) are in fact centuries old. The rule that customary international law is incorporated by the common law dates back to 1737.[5] The interpretive presumption that statutes conform with international law was first enunciated, as best I can determine, in 1817.[6] The rule that Parliament is sovereign to violate international law was acknowledged, at least in *obiter dicta*, as early as 1861.[7] The rule that common law courts take judicial notice of international law is hard to date with precision but was declared and applied by the US Supreme Court in 1871.[8] The requirement that treaties be implemented by legislation before taking domestic effect was established by the late-nineteenth century, if not earlier.[9] In short, for some time now English and English-derived law has managed just fine without recognizing reception as a distinct body of law. Why then should reception be recognized now?

The answer, I suggest, lies in the nature of modern treaty-making. It is commonplace that international law-making accelerated a great deal in the twentieth century because of increased reliance on treaties, particularly multilateral treaties and treaties of a law-making character.[10] Furthermore,

---

4 Peter Birks, ed., *English Private Law* (Oxford: Oxford University Press, 2000) at xxxi–ii.
5 *Buvot v. Barbuit* (1737), Cas. t. Talb. 281, 25 E.R. 777.
6 *Le Louis* (1817), 2 Dods. 210 at 239, 165 E.R. 1465 at 1473–74.
7 *The Annapolis—The Johanna Stoll* (1861), Lush. 295 at 306, 167 E.R. 128 at 134; see also *Colquhoun v Brooks* (1888), 21 Q.B.D. 52 at 57–58 (also *obiter*).
8 *The Scotia* (1871), 14 Wall. 170. On the difficulty in finding express judicial pronouncements on the rule, see H. Lauterpacht, "Is International Law Part of the Law of England?" (1939) *Transactions of the Grotius Society* 51.
9 For example, *The Parlement Belge*, [1878–89] 4 P.D. 129.
10 Brownlie succinctly defines law-making treaties as those that "create legal obligations the observance of which does not dissolve the treaty obligation": Ian Brownlie, *Principles of Public International Law*, 5th ed. (Oxford: Oxford University Press, 1998) at 12.

treaty parties increasingly committed themselves to ensuring the conformity of their domestic laws with international norms established in the treaties they concluded. This process continues, of course, today. The areas of heretofore domestic law into which such treaties have ventured are many. Human rights, trade, environmental protection, labour standards, crime, migration, taxation—these are only the most obvious examples. Such inward-looking treaties have inevitably influenced domestic legal developments, whether by prompting the adoption of new legislation or by other, more subtle means.

In states operating within the Commonwealth tradition, the rise of inward-looking treaties has raised questions that are not new, but are more numerous and more pressing than they have ever been. Questions include: Can this court properly have regard to this treaty? Can this administrative tribunal properly have regard to this treaty? Is this treaty implemented in domestic law? Can I use this treaty to challenge an administrative decision? Must this statute be interpreted in conformity with this treaty? Must the common law be interpreted in conformity with this treaty? Can the legislature violate this treaty? Can the executive violate this treaty? These questions (and others) are the stuff of reception law. The more frequently the questions arise, the more useful it will be to have thought through the answers in a systematic way, viewing both question and answer in context—including the state's obligations at international law; the constitutional imperatives of Westminster-model parliamentary democracy; the respective roles of the legislative, executive, and judicial branches in the performance of the state's international obligations; and the proper forum and procedure for the resolution of these questions.

Assuming, then, that there is reason to think about reception issues in a more systematic way, what might this system look like? What are the doctrines and principles that constitute reception law? I have referred to them already. There are, in my view, four founding doctrines upon which the structure of reception law rests.

The first doctrine is essentially a rule of evidence, though one of peculiar importance: common law courts take judicial notice of the rules and requirements of public international law. Indeed, for evidentiary purposes, common law courts generally treat international law the same as they treat legislative enactments, common law decisions, and other sources of domestic law. The courts may have regard to applicable international laws of their own motion and will not hesitate, in proper cases, to construe a treaty (according to international treaty interpretation rules) just as they would take notice of and interpret a statute, regulation or common law rule. By contrast, common law courts generally require foreign law to be pleaded and proved in evidence. In short, common law courts treat foreign law as a question of fact but international law as a question of law.[11] I do not say that the doctrine of judicial notice of international law is uncontroversial or universally observed.[12] But the rule exists. Indeed, it is the necessary foundation of all other reception rules.

The second basic doctrine of reception law is the presumption of conformity. This is a rule of statutory interpretation whereby courts presume that legislatures do not intend their enactments to place the state in default of its international legal obligations. Where two interpretations of a law are possible, courts operating in the Commonwealth tradition will prefer the internationally lawful interpretation unless the language of the enactment clearly admits of no other interpretation. While the rule is often described as a presumption of legislative intent, in its application it tends more to resemble a rule of judicial policy to the effect that the court will not, by its decisions, bring the state into violation of international law unless given no other option. The chief difficulty with the rule lies in knowing how far to apply it; at what point must a court conclude that the presumption is rebutted and the law in question is contrary to international law?[13]

The third underlying doctrine of reception law is difficult to characterize, but might perhaps be described as constitutional in the unwritten, English sense. It is the rule or judicial practice of incorporating norms of customary international law into the common law. The incorporation doctrine provides that customary international laws are directly enforceable in common law courts as rules of the common law. The doctrine essentially equates customary international law with the common law such that by establishing the existence of a custom one establishes a parallel, common

---

11   The position is slightly different in Quebec. Article 2807 of the *Civil Code of Quebec* provides that "international treaties and agreements applicable to Québec but not contained in a text of law, and customary international law, shall be pleaded". Yet Quebec courts nevertheless take judicial notice of all law in force in Quebec, including custom and treaties: Claude Emanuelli, *Droit international public: contribution à l'étude de droit international selon une perspective canadienne* (Montreal: Wilson & Lafleur, 1998) at 61 and 95.

12   See, for example, Gibran van Ert, "The Admissibility of International Legal Evidence" (2005) 84 Can. Bar Rev. 31.

13   On the presumption generally, see Gibran van Ert, *Using International Law in Canadian Courts* (The Hague: Kluwer Law International, 2002) at 99–136.

law rule. Having been incorporated as a common law rule, the custom is seemingly subject to encroachment or repeal by statute. Like the presumption of conformity, incorporation is a judge-made doctrine that serves to promote the harmonization of domestic and international law. Incorporation is not uncontroversial. The rule itself is increasingly accepted in Canada[14] and indisputably established in the UK,[15] but there remain questions about its ambit. For instance, does the common law incorporate rules of *jus cogens*—which are, after all, only an entrenched form of custom—in the same way as ordinary customs, or does it accord them some pride of place analogous to their special status in international law?[16]

The fourth founding doctrine of reception law, I suggest, is the requirement that treaties be implemented by legislation before (or perhaps instead of) taking direct effect in domestic law. This again is a constitutional rule in the unwritten sense of the word. The rationale for this rule—which is so different in tenor from the other three doctrines—stems from the source of treaty obligations in Westminster-model constitutions like those of Canada and the UK. Treaties derive not from Parliament but from the Crown. They are made by the executive in exercise of the Royal Prerogative over foreign affairs. At common law, the legislative branch has no necessary part in their negotiation, consideration or adoption. As a result, the common law accords them no direct legal consequence. To gain such effect, they must be implemented by the legislature. Of the four doctrines I have outlined, this may be the most uncertain. While the principle is clear and largely uncontroversial, its application frequently proves difficult. What does implementation consist in? What sort of legislative language is required? How can one tell whether a treaty has been implemented or not? How far may the presumption of conformity be applied before conflicting with the implementation requirement? In the case of federal constitutions like Canada, which jurisdiction has authority to implement the treaty?

---

14   For example, *Bouzari v. Islamic Republic of Iran* (2004), 71 O.R. (3d) 675 at para. 65 (C.A.).

15   An *obiter dictum* illustrates the point. In *Campaign for Nuclear Disarmament v. Prime Minister and others*, [2002] EWHC 2759 at para. 23 (Q.B.), Simon Brown L.J. observed that the first of the applicant's difficulties was in its "invocation of the principle that the common law encompasses also customary international law." "Correct although this undoubtedly is," said his lordship, "I have difficulty in understanding how it avails the applicant here."

16   This question has been raised, but not answered, in some recent Canadian cases. See the discussion in Mark Freeman and Gibran van Ert, *International Human Rights Law* (Toronto: Irwin Law, 2004) at 162–64.

These are some of the questions to which the implementation requirement gives rise.[17]

I have identified these four rules as foundational because they appear to me to be the primary means by which public international law is received into domestic law in Canada, the UK, and similarly constituted common law jurisdictions. But they are not the only rules of reception law. One significant rule that I have not depicted as a founding doctrine is that the legislature may enact laws violating the state's international obligations. Legislatures are said to be "sovereign" to violate international law, meaning that a court may not invalidate primary legislation on the basis of its lack of conformity with the state's international obligations. To describe this rule as a founding or basic doctrine of reception law would be an overstatement, for the power of Parliament to violate international law is rarely ever used. Other reception rules may be developing. There is, for instance, a body of law suggesting that the executive's entry into treaty obligations may engender legitimate expectations of procedural rights.[18] Specific reception rules may develop in respect of certain laws. For instance, the Supreme Court of Canada's jurisprudence on the interaction of international human rights law and the *Charter* has so far failed to apply the presumption of conformity in a consistent fashion, but has elaborated specific roles for human rights treaties under sections 7 (protection of life, liberty, and security of the person) and 1 (justification of *Charter* violations).[19]

This, in broad outline, is the system according to which public international law is received by domestic law in Canada, the UK, and various

17 This is not to suggest that a so-called monist approach to treaties, whereby they take direct effect in domestic law without implementation, would be any less confusing; see Anthony Aust, *Modern Treaty Law and Practice* (Cambridge: Cambridge University Press, 2000) at 151 and 156–57.

18 See, for example, *Minister of Immigration and Ethnic Affairs v. Teoh* (1995), 183 C.L.R. 273 (H.C.A.); *Thomas v. Baptiste*, [1999] 3 W.L.R. 249 (P.C.); *R. v. Secretary of State for the Home Department ex p Ahmed and Patel*, [1998] I.N.L.R. 570 (Eng. C.A.); *R. v. Secretary of State for the Home Department ex p Gashi and Djoka*, unreported, 15 June 2000 (Eng. Q.B.D., Collins J.); *R. (Lika) v. Secretary of State for the Home Department*, [2002] EWCA Civ 1855 (Eng. C.A.); *Ibrahim v. Secretary of State for the Home Department*, 2002 SLT 1150 (Scot. Ct. Sess. O.H.), *Khairandish v. Secretary of State for the Home Department*, 2003 SLT 1358 (Scot. Ct. Sess. O.H.) and *In re McKerr*, [2004] 1 W.L.R. 807 at paras. 50–52 (H.L.), Lord Steyn. In Canada, a different but arguably similar effect was given to a treaty in *Baker v. Canada (Minister of Citizenship and Immigration)*, [1999] 2 S.C.R. 817. I am grateful to Roger O'Keefe for many of these references.

19 See Freeman and van Ert, *International Human Rights Law*, above note 15 at 196–202.

other Commonwealth jurisdictions. The reader will note that I have given this short account of reception without once mentioning the two words that have so often dominated previous discussions of the question, namely, *monism* and *dualism*. It is frequently said, largely on the basis of the implementation requirement, that Commonwealth legal systems are dualist. But one might just as well cite the judicial notice, presumption of conformity, and incorporation of custom rules in support of the conclusion that such systems are monist. I doubt any of this advances our understanding of reception very much. I also suspect that to use these terms in this way oversimplifies the theoretical debate between monists and dualists. To my mind, monism and dualism are more of a hindrance than a help when trying to understand the Commonwealth (or at least the Anglo-Canadian) position. My short account of reception law, given above, suggests that these terms have no necessary role in the discussion of these questions.

It is, however, remarkable that of the four doctrines I have identified, three tend strongly towards the harmonization of domestic and international law. What is more, these three doctrines all concern matters generally within the judiciary's sphere of activity: the proof of facts and law, legal interpretation, and the content of common law rules. The judiciary, by means of judicial notice, admits public international law into domestic legal controversies. The judiciary, by means of the presumption of conformity, ensures internationally compliant interpretations of laws and requires the legislature to make itself irresistibly clear before attributing internationally unlawful intentions to it. The judiciary, by means of the incorporation doctrine, brings the common law into conformity with customary international law, thus avoiding the hypocrisy of holding Parliament up to international standards it does not meet itself. The depiction of reception as a systematic body of law bears its first fruit: viewing matters in this light, we discover that the predominant role of the judges in the reception system is (or at least has so far been) to work towards the harmonization of domestic and international law. This may come as news to the judges themselves!

In the light of the rest of the reception system, the implementation requirement may seem like something of an aberration. All the more so the rule that Parliament is sovereign to violate international law. Both these seeming aberrations derive from the same principle, namely that laws (or at least positive laws; the common law is something of an exception) are properly made by citizens in Parliament assembled and not by the Crown nor even by that committee of Parliament, the Cabinet, that exercises the

Crown's powers. This principle has gone unquestioned for some time. But one could question it. In the twenty-first century, is any useful purpose still served by permitting the legislature the power to violate the state's binding treaties, or for that matter its obligations under customary international law? For the courts to deny Parliament this sovereignty would be revolutionary in theory but would probably not have much practical effect, given how rarely legislatures actually exercise their power to enact internationally unlawful laws. Likewise, in an era of democratically elected legislatures and democratically responsible Cabinets, is there still any point in denying direct legal effect, or at least some indirect legal effect, to the treaties Cabinet concludes? This line of thinking may inform some of the legitimate expectations jurisprudence mentioned above.

I do not intend to answer these questions, or even to imply any personal dissatisfaction with the status quo. I wish only to suggest that like other branches of the common law, reception is not without its controversies and inconsistencies. It has developed over time and will continue to do so. But is there such a thing as reception at all? And is it, as I have suggested, a body or branch of the common law? The answer to these questions will depend in part on our academics. Textbook writers in particular have had a central role in shaping our understanding of the common law. If academics see merit in regarding reception as a body of law, and a body of common law at that, its more general recognition may follow. But what is most likely to be determinative is whether reception, as I have introduced it, proves useful. I am inclined to think it will.

Section B:
CANADA'S INTEREST IN INTERNATIONAL LAW
AND WHY IT IS RELEVANT TO CANADIANS

Canada's External Constitution and Its Democratic Deficit

4

STEPHEN CLARKSON AND STEPAN WOOD[*]

One of the international system's most striking developments during the last half-century is the vast proliferation of international organizations (IOs). These IOs are generally presented *individually* as addressing almost every imaginable policy issue concerning the global public domain, such as managing international air traffic, dividing up the universal radio wave spectrum, establishing a law of the sea, or lending to developing countries.

By their very nature, all international phenomena have a domestic incidence. At the same time as they create a transnational sphere of governance, multilateral institutions created by governments necessarily affect the internal affairs of the signatories, whether this is the pricing of drugs for their HIV/AIDS victims, the treatment of their Aboriginals, or the size of their foreign debt and the interest payments they have to make on it.

This chapter argues that the best framework within which to understand Canada's relationship with these evolving instances of global governance is to reframe these IOs in terms of two constitutional expressions of their *collective* significance.

First, the steady accumulation of intergovernmental agreements and organizations has constituted a complex but substantial world order, which we can best conceptualize as comprising an emerging global constitution.

---

[*] Much of this analysis evolved through our collaboration as virtual professors at the Law Commission of Canada on the paper "Governing Beyond Borders: Law for Canadians in an Era of Globalization."

Second, and simultaneously, the global constitution restructures the legal order of every participating state by adding an external constitution to its domestic constitution, albeit in varying ways and to different degrees.

These two propositions need both to be amplified by defining *constitution* and by elaborating the complexities raised by this expanding dialectic reality in which the international has domestic roots and the local has global effects.

A. DEFINING A CONSTITUTION

A constitution is the set of fundamental rules and institutional practices according to which any organization—whether a small club or a large state—governs itself. Reduced to its essential features, a constitution demonstrates four main components. It typically sets out: the guiding *principles* that guide the community's collective life; the main *rules* that govern members' behaviour; the *rights* of community members vis-à-vis governing authorities; and the functions, scope, and limitations of the collectivity's executive, legislative, and judicial *institutions*.[1] In the realm of politics and public law, constitutions are associated almost exclusively with the nation-state[2]—an inward-looking understanding that needs to be supplemented by appreciating how international commitments also affect the domestic constitutional order. At the same time, as international governance arrangements have become more powerful and pervasive, it has become plausible to talk about them collectively as giving a constitutional character to the global community.

B. THE GLOBAL CONSTITUTION

Any consideration of the emerging global constitutional order must preemptively recognize its fragmentary, disconnected, imbalanced, heterogeneous, and multifarious nature. International organizations range in their territorial scope from bilateral to regional to global, and in their size from tiny to huge. Some are relatively autonomous, while others are little more than agents for their member states. Some may be quite insignificant, while others exercise substantial influence over world developments,

---

1   For example, Joel Bakan *et al.*, eds., *Canadian Constitutional Law*, 3d ed. (Toronto: Emond Montgomery, 2003) at 3–4; *Black's Law Dictionary*, 5th ed. (St. Paul, MN: West, 1979).

2   Peter W. Hogg, *Constitutional Law of Canada*, student ed. (Scarborough, ON: Carswell, 2004) at 1; Patrick Monahan, *Constitutional Law*, 2d ed. (Toronto: Irwin Law, 2002) at 3.

as well as over national governments. They vary from relatively informal secretariats to bricks-and-mortar organizations with their own buildings, permanent civil service, insignia, and flags (for example, the UN Development Program). They include ad hoc arrangements for cooperation in a specific functional area (for example, international fisheries management regimes) and general-purpose political structures complete with the organs of a would-be world government (the United Nations itself).

The general trend shows that many international institutions enjoy expanding competences in sectors that once were the exclusive domain of states. Beyond enlarging its range, thanks to the formal decisions of their member states, the global order has acquired some autonomous capacity to evolve. Although typically established by some kind of intergovernmental agreement, an international organization may take on a life of its own with implications for its founders. For instance, new rules that bind member states may be introduced in the course of an international body such as the World Health Organization (WHO) carrying out its responsibilities. When international tribunals make judgments to resolve a dispute between two governments, they often establish new norms that can impact all other countries, however far away. International commissions reach decisions about new problems with significant consequences in member states. For instance, food safety issues have become burning questions for the once obscure Codex Alimentarius Commission in Rome. Although highly technical, the questions surrounding the approval or labelling of genetically modified (GM) foods produced for human consumption involve the fate of many countries' agricultural economies as well as the profitability of some of the world's largest corporations, which have invested billions to develop seeds impervious to certain insects or plant diseases. Because of public concerns about the health implications of hormone-treated livestock and GM fruits and vegetables, agribusiness and governments are defending their positions at the Codex in the face of non-government organizations and experts who represent the often opposing interests of consumer and producer groups.

In sum, the hugely complex, multi-institutional international order can be analyzed in terms of the four basic components of a constitutional order.

1. **Norms or principles** range from the vague (the aspiration for peace) to the specific (responsibility to protect). This chapter will restrict itself to such norms governing the economic behaviour of governments as national treatment and most favoured nation.

2. **The rules** emitted by IOs are multitudinous but more specific and forbidding, for example, preventing states from exploiting children. Since

these rules are negotiated in a power-based process, they naturally reflect the interests of the dominant powers.

In the economic sphere, a great many of the rules reflect American norms. When the members of the World Trade Organization (WTO) reached an agreement in 1997 on the liberalization of their telecommunications sectors, the US trade representative Marlene Barshefsky exulted that the United States had just universalized its *Telecommunications Act of 1994* (*New York Times*, 7 February 1997). The WTO's Trade-Related Aspects of Intellectual Property Rights (TRIPs) Agreement supported the interests of American, European, and Japanese big pharma, entertainment, and information-technology industries, but threatened those of the emerging economies.

3. **Rights** in the global constitution are generally expressed in very general terms, such as the right to justice or education or shelter.

In the economic side of the global constitution, rights become much more specific. Many bilateral investment treaties establish the right of foreign investors not to have their property expropriated by the host government.

4. **Institutions** can be found that are powerful, well financed, and sophisticated as in the partly supranational, partly intergovernmental, structure created by the various treaties that built the European Union into its own constitutional order. Other international institutions are quite flimsy. Whether strong or weak, international institutions can be analyzed as a global collectivity or as individual institutions in terms of their five principal functions.

a) Legislature. Taken as a totality, world institutions have a spotty and uneven legislative capacity, because their rule-making record is weak. The General Assembly of the United Nations is a major global debating forum, but its capacity to legislate has been contained by the UN's executive, the Security Council. The European Parliament's mandate has grown but remains inferior to the European Commission's substantial legislative capacity, which manifests itself in the form of hundreds of directives that its member states are bound to implement.

The WTO was born in 1995 with a vast number of rules already decided as a result of eight years' worth of intergovernmental negotiations. Its institutional ability to delete, amend, or add new rules takes the form of the biennial meeting of its members' trade ministers. However, the requirement that WTO decisions be made by consensus makes it extremely difficult to reach any decision acceptable to all—currently 148—member states. As a result, new rules for the WTO are made following years-long negotiating "rounds" between the member-governments, as in the current Doha Round, named for the site of the ministerial meeting that launched it in 2001. The North American Free Trade Agreement (NAFTA)'s trade commission has virtually no rule-making authority: any rule changes must be negotiated by the continent's three states.

b) Executive. Most institutions have an executive group charged with managing day-to-day operations as well as making critical decisions such as whether the United Nations should endorse a pre-emptive war against Iraq. Putting all international organizations together, one of their second constitutional functions is the executive—largely because nation-states have been reluctant to allow devolve much decision-making authority beyond their control.

The WTO has no executive to speak of, while NAFTA's merely consists of periodic meetings of the three countries' trade ministers.

c) Administration. If it is to operate, an organization needs a staff to implement decisions and deliver the action for which it is mandated. The Organization for Economic Cooperation and Development (OECD), UNESCO, and, of course, the United Nations have personnel totalling in the thousands. Aggregating them all would show a considerable—but heterogeneous and disconnected—international civil service, many elements of which are supranational in the sense that their civil servants' careers are independent of their member governments' control.

The WTO has an extremely lean administration: a mere five hundred people operate this globally crucial institution. NAFTA has no central administration at all. Each of the three signatory states maintains a small office to keep track of NAFTA-related paperwork and each federal government assigns civil servants to staff a few working groups that deal with some of NAFTA's minor, outstanding business.

d) Judiciary. Norms and rules are subject to diverse interpretations. Administrative actions cause compliance complaints. As a result, no organization can operate for long without having to resolve conflicts generated by its own mandate, measures, and mechanisms. Dispute settlement varies from the highly structured European Court of Justice, whose rulings have direct effect in each member state of the EU, to the largely ineffectual arbitration processes established in the International Labour Organization (ILO).

As we will shortly see when looking at the domestic impact of global economic norms and rules, the WTO's and NAFTA's judicial capacities can have decisive effects.

e) Enforcement. The European Commission's directives can be enforced through the rulings of the European Court of Justice, which have direct effect in the domestic legal system of the EU's member states. By contrast, the conventions of the ILO are unenforceable except by moral suasion.

Compliance with the WTO's dispute settlement rulings tends to be high, in large part because its rules permit economic retaliation against states that do not comply with its judgments. WTO rulings are also effective in part because a member considers it in its interests to comply with an adverse judgment, on the expectation that its counterparts will comply when it wins a ruling against their trade protectionism.

This is not the place to develop a more extended analysis of the global constitution in all its kaleidoscopic components and uneven functioning. The point of this section is to emphasize that, taken as a whole, existing international organizations create a global governance system which Canada has to take seriously, and for two reasons.

- First, as an agent in—or subject of—globalization, Ottawa participates in efforts to reform existing elements of the world order and develop new components as needs arise. Canada may have lost relative position in the global hierarchy of states over the last few decades, declining from being the seventh largest economy to battling with Brazil for ninth place, but it remains a player in the upper-middle range of semiperipheral states that can make a difference in the shadow of the more powerful states that bestride the centre of the world's power system. During the Uruguay Round of negotiations to reform the GATT, for instance, Ottawa made the original proposal that led to the new WTO receiving a powerful judicial capacity.
- The second reason why Canadians should take the global constitution seriously is that, as objects of globalization, their own political system is significantly affected by having imposed on it what this chapter calls a supraconstitution—to the explication of which we will now turn.

C. CANADA'S SUPRACONSTITUTION[3]

Because of the many IOs' cumulative domestic impact, the global constitution necessarily impinges on the constitutional order of every member

---

3   Much of this analysis is adapted from Stephen Clarkson, "Canada's External Constitution under Global Trade Governance," in Ysolde Gendreau, réd., *Dessiner la société par le droit/Mapping Society Through Law* (Montreal: Les Éditions Thémis, 2004) at 1.

state but to a degree that depends on its inherent power. In this section, we will focus on the extent to which two international economic institutions—the global WTO and the continental NAFTA—have contributed to creating an external constitution for Canada.

The main thrust of economically focused regimes established in the past half-century is the liberation of international trade and investment from member governments' control. Through global, regional, or bilateral agreements, states commit themselves to dismantling barriers to the movement of goods, services, and capital (but generally not labour) across borders; to revoking policies that favour domestic over foreign producers, goods, or services; and to eliminating all forms of government intervention that distort market competition. All this is implemented in the hope of reaping the benefits of comparative advantage, more efficient production, lower prices, and greater consumer choice of goods and services.

Although presented at the time as a commercial agreement, the Canada-United States Free Trade Agreement (CUFTA)[4] was historically significant as a step towards a new global investment regime, with fundamental implications for the structure of corporate-state relations, and the effective constitutionalization of an international corporate "personhood" complete with powerful individual rights.

CUFTA also became a polarizing moment in Canadian politics. On one side, was the business community, which saw the agreement as necessary to its survival in a world characterized by declining tariff protection and increasing challenges from competitors exploiting economies of scale in global markets and minimal labour costs in Third World countries to achieve lower production costs. On the other side, was a broad coalition of civil-society organizations led by the labour unions and the women's movement, which saw CUFTA as a death warrant to the activist state on whose public services and programs they believed their collective well-being depended.

NAFTA, which was signed in 1993 and came into force in 1994, in effect continentalized CUFTA's bilateral regime by incorporating Mexico into its then toughened set of rules. Driven by Washington's demands that its two neighbours open up their economies by cutting back their governments' controls, NAFTA strengthened CUFTA's investment provisions, extended its rules on services, and added powerful intellectual property rights that were of particular importance to American brand-name phar-

---

4   CUFTA came into force in 1989.

maceutical transnational corporations (TNCs). NAFTA partially institutionalized the two peripheral economies' hitherto informal integration as territorial extensions of the American marketplace. It is worth noting that NAFTA became almost as divisive in American politics as CUFTA had been in Canada. Fearing the loss of jobs to Mexico because of that country's low wages and weak enforcement of environmental and labour standards, American environmental organizations and trade unions followed their Canadian comrades by launching a similarly futile campaign against the business-led agenda for continental economic integration.

A year after NAFTA had established a continental economic régime, the long Uruguay Round of the GATT negotiations came to a successful end with the establishment of a new global economic order in the form of the WTO, which transformed global governance by projecting to the global level the trade and investment rules wanted for their TNCs by the core capitalist countries. Taken together, the WTO and NAFTA superimposed on Canada's already existing internal legal order an external constitution which can in turn be analyzed in terms of its norms, rules, rights, and institutions.

1) Norms

The WTO and NAFTA establish general principles that are to guide state behaviour. National Treatment (NT) is a supraconstitutional norm in the sense that it controls government actions because it has been incorporated as a superior legal principle in general terms, but not as legislation applying to specific public policies. For instance, there is no Canadian law saying that the federal government must treat foreign-owned furniture companies at least as well as it treats Canadian-owned furniture firms. But now that these trade agreements have extended the national-treatment principle from goods to investments and then to services, if any federal or provincial or municipal government discriminates in favour of a nationally or provincially owned firm—whether one that manufactures goods or one that offers services, the government of Canada is liable to legal attack by another government belonging to NAFTA or the WTO that deems one of its companies in Canada to have suffered from unequal or discriminatory treatment. In other words, although not implemented in specific statutory texts, NT is a supraconstitutional principle on the basis of which NAFTA partners may litigate.

Along with National Treatment, the Most Favoured Nation (MFN) norm in GATT's Article I rules out discriminating among trading partners, even for reasons of social or environmental policy. NT and MFN have become supraconstitutional along with countless other international commitments that Canada has made by signing, for instance, the many conventions on labour rights sponsored by the ILO. What makes NT and MFN more important than other norms in the global constitution is the fact that they can be enforced, as we will shortly see.

The domestic impact of these supraconstitutional norms is also growing because the judicial interpretation of the WTO's principles has proven far more expansive and intrusive than that of identical norms had been under the GATT. Even when government measures are formally neutral vis-à-vis nationality, for instance, the WTO may strike them down if, in practice, they are deemed to bias competitive conditions in favour of domestic service providers (national treatment) or of particular foreign providers (most favoured nation).[5]

When trying to assess the democratic implications of a country's supra-constitution, it helps to distinguish *process* legitimacy from *outcome* legitimacy. The insertion of authoritative new norms into the Canadian political order raises legitimacy issues, both in terms of process and outcome. The imposition of major constraints on the capacity not just of the federal, but also of provincial and municipal governments as a result of a negotiating process characterized by secrecy and non-transparency took place with a minimum of informed public debate. This absence of a democratic deliberation concerning a major shift in the parameters of the political order contrasts with the extensive engagement not just of the political parties, the media, and interest groups—the normal actors in a political process—but also of the highest court of the land from 1980 to 1982 when Prime Minister Pierre Trudeau led a campaign to patriate the domestic Canadian constitution into which he intended to introduce a *Charter of Rights and Freedoms*.

Normative additions to the Canadian legal order from NAFTA and the WTO had direct consequences in terms of their outcome legitimacy. National treatment for investment spelled the end to a whole generation of industrial development policies centred on the targeting of subsidies to domestic corporations or sectors to improve their competitive performance in order to boost their exports. It also called into question the capacity of the Canadian state to impose environmental regulations and bolster its

---

5   Scott Sinclair, *GATS: How the WTO's Expanded General Agreement on Trade in Services Will Erode Democracy* (Ottawa: Canadian Centre for Policy Alternatives, 2000) at 44.

cultural industries through favouring domestic entities in the private sector. In this way, supraconstitutional norms have had direct, delegitimizing impacts on the domestic legislative and administrative order without most of the public—and even much of the government apparatus—understanding this had happened.

2) Rules

When we speak of Canada's external constitution, we also refer to those rules at the international level that can be said to form part of the ensemble of fundamental practices by which Canadian society is governed, and from which domestic Canadian laws and policies may not derogate. Identifying all such rules is bound to be a monumental task, given the hundreds of international commitments Ottawa has signed. To illustrate the substance of Canada's supraconstitutional rules, we focus on those contained in CUFTA, NAFTA, and the WTO.

Continental economic integration was paid for by North America's two weaker partners with diminished political autonomy. While CUFTA and NAFTA did achieve somewhat reduced American tariffs for Canadian exporters, the price Ottawa had to pay for a partial opening of the US market was to accept constraints on the Canadian state's regulatory capacity. The federal government was no longer allowed to manage a two-price system that supplied petroleum products for domestic industry and consumers at lower prices than the export price charged to American importers. No new cultural policies could negatively affect the commercial interests in Canada of American entertainment corporations.

CUFTA introduced rules reducing Canadian governments' capacity to regulate investments, whether foreign or domestically owned. Another innovation incorporated in CUFTA was to have trade rules extend far beyond the rules for buying and selling physical goods by including services, which cover an enormous range of activities, from those traditionally in the private sector (for example, banking, advertising, engineering, and tourism) to those normally provided by governments as public goods (for example, education, health care, and public utilities). Even if they were not provided directly by the public sector, many of these services are closely regulated by governments (including environmental, labour, health and safety, and consumer protection regulation) and may fall under international rules for services if they have any commercial characteristics that make them competitive with potential foreign providers of the same service.

By the very act of signing CUFTA, NAFTA, and the WTO, Canada also undertook to make immediate changes in a wide range of legislation and regulations. CUFTA's investment chapter raised the exemption for a review of a foreign takeover from $5 to $150 million (CUFTA 1988). This required Canadian implementation legislation to make the appropriate amendment to the *Investment Canada Act.*

The WTO's and NAFTA's trade principles can also be understood as supraconstitutional because they extend legal protection to foreign corporations—which, for instance, might consider demands on investors in the Arctic to be too onerous or the subsidization of only Canadian firms discriminatory. If they do feel aggrieved, they can press their home government to launch a suit against Canada through NAFTA's dispute settlement panels or the WTO's dispute settlement board. When Canada persisted in showering public largesse on its champion aircraft builder, Bombardier, to boost its exports, and Brazil lodged a complaint at the WTO on behalf of its own regional airplane builder, Embraer, the dispute panel in Geneva found Canada to have acted illegally. Ottawa was obliged to mend its ways.

While free trade was extremely controversial in the late 1980s, CUFTA's process legitimacy was actually quite considerable. Although secret, the negotiation process was the subject of intense media and public interest. Once the agreement was published, fierce debate over its various provisions continued for months, reaching their climax in the 1988 federal election campaign whose results—a majority of seats (if only a minority of votes) for Prime Minister Brian Mulroney's Progressive Conservative government—gave the accord an ultimate parliamentary legitimacy. Nevertheless, CUFTA's practical outcome—the loss of hundreds of thousands of industrial jobs in the Canadian economy's manufacturing centres—left it highly unpopular among the labour unions and a number of popular grassroots movements, which continue to deem "free trade" an illegitimate expression of globalization.

The WTO's and NAFTA's rules are so comprehensive that, in their implementation legislation, their members had to change hundreds of existing laws. In the WTO's agreement on agriculture, member states committed themselves to transform such quantitative restrictions as import quotas into tariffs, which were then to be reduced. Canada duly proceeded to "tariffy" its protective regulations for farmers in central Canada.

Benefiting from much less public debate and information, the process legitimacy of the WTO's and NAFTA's rules remains dubious. Their outcome legitimacy is difficult to assess in any comprehensive way, since the effects of these rules may take years to become evident.

Previously, changes in laws and regulations were made by governments within the institutional and legal framework established by their internal constitutions and in response to demands by the electorate or by specific functional constituencies. NAFTA rules are also supraconstitutional in the sense that the signatory governments have to change their laws and regulations in a context that makes them irreversible. Unlike normal amendments to statutes made by sovereign legislatures, which can further amend or revoke their acts in response to changing domestic considerations, statutory amendments incorporating international trade norms can be validly changed only if the external regime changes its rules by international agreement. What would otherwise be democratically legitimate measures could subject that government to sanctions or penalties if they are deemed by the appropriate arbitration procedures to violate the international agreement in question.

In this respect, not only has the *political* order been changed by the amendments, but the *legal* order has been altered by introducing legislative and regulatory changes over which Parliament no longer exercises sovereignty. This is what free trade's proponents meant when they described NAFTA as "locking in" neoconservative rules—despite the fact that the neoconservative model is no closer to being accepted as a sustainable societal contract in Canada than it is elsewhere.[6] Even if more activist political parties were to win power, they would find their hands tied by these internationally negotiated and domestically implemented political limits to which their predecessors had committed them.

Another type of rule whose enforcement is contingent on foreign complaints is the prohibition of governments from imposing conditions on foreign investors, requiring them to make export commitments, to find local sources for their manufacturing needs, to transfer technology to domestic partners, or to guarantee set levels of employment.[7] To be precise, these standards do not actually *prevent* governments from imposing performance requirements on foreign investors or subsidizing domestic

---

6   Tony Clark, *Silent Coup: Confronting the Big Business Takeover of Canada* (Toronto: J. Lorimer, 1997).

7   Ha-Joon Chang, "Transnational Corporations and Strategic Industrial Policy" in Richard Kozul-Wright & Robert Rowthorn, ed., *Transnational Corporations and the Global Economy* (Tokyo: The United Nations University, 1998).

firms—just as traffic laws do not prevent a motorist from speeding. But any federal or provincial government that violates these NAFTA or WTO norms is vulnerable to a partner state initiating a legal action that could result in economic sanctions to compensate for the damage from which its corporations claim they have suffered.

The global constitution's rule book is never finalized. A chronic state of flux results from the intergovernmental processes of continually nego-tiating new global rules. At the WTO's Doha Round, for instance, Canada was pressed by countries trying to obtain better access to the Canadian market for their agricultural products. As a result, Ottawa's negotiators agreed ultimately to abandon both the marketing boards (which guarantee protection from foreign competitors for chicken, dairy, and egg farmers in central Canada) and the Canadian Wheat Board (which gets Western grain farmers the best price on the world market by marketing their wheat collec-tively). Canada is also under severe pressure from the United States to al-low, through raising its commitments to the General Agreement on Trade in Services, the entry of transnational enterprise into its public health and education systems. This international context of constant pressure to make further concessions creates an instability that necessarily puts the external constitution's legitimacy in continuing jeopardy. If central Canadian farm-ers realize that their government cannot protect the marketing boards on which their entrepreneurial calculations depend, their cultural security vanishes.

3) Rights

The corollary of a limit on government may be a right for the citizen. In contrast with the EU, which does create direct rights for citizens in mem-ber states—for instance to sue their own governments before the Euro-pean Court of Justice, the only "citizens" whose rights in Canada were expanded under NAFTA were corporations based in the United States or Mexico. Under the WTO's Trade Related Investment Measures agreement, rights were also created for all corporations based in states belonging to the WTO, not to their citizens. The national treatment principle and the right of establishment made it easier for firms owned in one country to do busi-ness throughout the continent. What makes NAFTA supraconstitutional in this regard is its creation of a right in Chapter 11 that gives non-Cana-dian NAFTA corporations the power to overturn such regulations as those designed to secure the health and safety of the citizenry by taking member governments to international commercial arbitration in alleged cases of expropriation.[8]

CUFTA's Article 1605 provided that no government may "directly or indirectly expropriate or nationalize," or take "a measure tantamount to expropriation or nationalization" except for a "public purpose," on a "non-discriminatory basis," in accordance with "due process of law and minimum standards of treatment," and on "payment of compensation."[9] NAFTA's Chapter 11 contained an identical provision. In the face of Canada's *Charter of Rights and Freedoms* that deliberately excluded property rights (on the grounds that they would excessively enhance corporate power which was already adequately protected by the common law), this provision created a property right for foreign corporations that was understood neither (apparently) by the government nor (certainly) by the public.

Unlike rights in their internal constitution, this right was not available for Canadian corporations in Canada, where it can only be enjoyed by American and Mexican companies. The more citizens' groups understood that foreign corporations had been given invasive rights to nullify domestic legislation that were unavailable to Canadian enterprise, the more NAFTA's Chapter 11 became delegitimized, both in terms of its process and its outcomes. Also contrasting with a national constitution, the new justiciable empowerment accorded to transnational corporations subjects them to no balancing obligations. For instance, there are no continental-level institutions with the clout to regulate, tax, or monitor the newly created continental market that has proceeded to emerge.[10] NAFTA's Chapter 11 expanded the scope of investment rights without requiring TNCs to promote the public interest by protecting the environment or public health.[11]

---

8   Richard C. Levin & Susan Erickson Marin, "NAFTA Chapter 11: Investment and Investment Disputes" (Summer 1996) 83 NAFTA: Law and Business Review of the Americas 82 at 90.

9   CUFTA 1988, Canada–U.S. Free Trade Agreement, Article 1605.

10 Stephen Blank & Stephen Krajewski, "U.S. Firms in North America: Redefining Structure and Strategy" (February 1995) 5(2) North American Outlook 9.

11 Steven Shrybman notes that the powerful private enforcement machinery of international investment treaties has now been invoked by several transnational corporations to assail water protection laws, water export controls, and decisions to re-establish public-sector water services when privatization deals have gone sour. See Steven Shrybman, "The Impact of International Services and Investment Agreements on Public Policy and Law Concerning Water" (Paper presented at From Doha to Kananaskis: The Future of the World Trading System and the Crisis of Governance, conference at Ro-

One minor exception to NAFTA's non-provision of rights to citizens is the process established under the North American Agreement on Environmental Cooperation for citizens to submit complaints challenging any member government's "persistent failure" to enforce its environmental laws. However, the mechanism established to investigate these complaints and the possibilities of enforcing any finding on a delinquent government are so weak as to be almost meaningless beyond the value of the publicity and the potential shaming effect that the citizen submission process and ultimate factual findings might have on a delinquent government. Similarly, the North American Agreement on Labour Cooperation established elaborate mechanisms formally dedicated to facilitating citizens' challenging a member government for failing to apply its labour laws. In practice, trade unions in the three countries have concluded that the scant results achieved by pursuing the complicated process have not been worth the expensive efforts needed to pursue a complaint.

Other WTO agreements also contained rights for international corporations but none for citizens, other than investors. Its agreement on Trade Related Aspects of Intellectual Property Rights (TRIPs) required that all member states amend their intellectual property legislation and change their judicial procedures in conformity with TRIPs' stipulated norms.[12]. The external and constitutional quality of these rights can be seen in their giving transatlantic pharmaceutical firms the legal justification to have the EU successfully take a case to the WTO against Ottawa because its drug legislation did not give European big pharma the full patent benefits that they claimed were now their due.[13]

4) Institutions

With the major exception of the European Union, whose various institutions' decisions can directly affect the behaviour of its member states' individuals and corporations, global governance acts indirectly through influencing the behaviour of the nation states that have constructed its vari-

---

barts Centre for Canadian Studies, York University and Munk Centre for International Studies, University of Toronto, 1-3, 7 March 2002) [unpublished].

12 Christopher Kent, "The Uruguay Round GATT, TRIPS Agreement and Chapter 17 of the NAFTA: A New Era in International Patent Protection" (1994) 10 Canadian Intellectual Property Review at 711–33.

13 World Trade Organization, *Canada—Term of Patent Protection: Report of the Panel* (Geneva: World Trade Organization, 2000).

ous organizations. It would be surprising if, in Canada's case, the WTO and NAFTA would not have some indirect effects on its political institutions as well as their relationship with civil society.

Beyond inhibiting federal and provincial governments' previous capacity for policy action, provincial government powers are deeply affected by NAFTA and the WTO. For instance, only the federal government may launch a trade dispute and appear in its hearings, even when a provincial grievance or measure is the issue. NAFTA and the WTO may also have altered Canadian federalism's relative powers by realigning them between the two levels of government. By making Ottawa responsible for ensuring the provinces' conformity to its provisions, NAFTA arguably restored to the Canadian constitution a federal power of disallowance that had fallen into disuse. In this way it may possibly alter—to a potentially dramatic degree—the country's delicate constitutional balance.[14] NAFTA norms also create constitutional abnormalities at the level of interprovincial relations. The application of national treatment and investor-state conflict resolution to subcentral governments creates the anomaly that provinces, territories, and municipalities have to give NAFTA investors non-discriminatory treatment, whereas the Canada *Constitution Act, 1982* does not prevent them from discriminating against Canadian investors from other provinces.

Global and continental rules have differing impacts on different parts of Canadian society. Take the country's two geographically determined types of agriculture. To the extent that the Prairie Provinces are exporters of grains and livestock, their farmers can expect to benefit from the WTO's agreement on Sanitary and Phyto-Sanitary (SPS) standards whose supraconstitutional norms limit *other* states' capacity to use health regulations to impede imports. As illustrated by the North American dispute with the European Union over its refusal to allow the import of beef raised with a growth hormone, the SPS norms, if successfully applied, should make it easier for Canadian cattle ranchers to expand their export markets. In contrast, farmers in central Canada—who supply a protected market of national consumers thanks to the quotas established by government-enforced marketing boards for eggs, milk, and poultry—can be expected to suffer under the WTO rules as their quantitative barriers are turned into

---

14   Andrew Petter, "Free Trade and the Provinces" in Marc Gold & David Leyton-Brown, eds., *Trade-Offs on Free Trade: The Canada–U.S. Free Trade Agreement* (Toronto: Carswell, 1988) at 141–47.

tariffs, which are subsequently cut to allow more foreign competition in the Canadian market.

An efficient public health system has become a defining characteristic of Canadians' sense of national identity. If the privatization of publicly provided services is the product of the services provisions in NAFTA and the WTO's GATS (the General Agreement on Trade in Services), Canadian society may risk losing a prime social institution that has played a major role in defining its identity and so threatening its cultural security.[15] Should the impact of continental and global free trade norms cause the accelerated commercialization of health care with consequently increased inequality in the treatment of rich and poor, a central element of Canadian political culture will have been jeopardized. In this scenario, the external constitution's democratically inaccessible rule-making institutions would not just be of dubious process legitimacy in themselves but would help delegitimize the country's domestic political outputs.

Instead of developing its social and community cohesion, Canada appears to be polarizing into a society of those who can succeed in the globalized system and a society of those left behind. If this perception is linked to the norms and practices of global and continental governance regimes, serious repercussions may be felt in the legitimacy of the country's own representative system.[16] If the external constitution has "hollowed out" the institutions of the Canadian state to the point that it risks being seen as incapable of defending its citizens' interests,[17] the Canadian political system will lose credibility at the same time as neoconservative globalization loses legitimacy. Much hangs on the capacity and effects of judicial rulings concerning the conformity of domestic regulations with the supraconstitution.

5) Adjudication

For a foreign government to litigate a case against Ottawa presumes that global governance boasts adequate judicial capacity. This ability on the

---

15 Arup writes that "the main thrust of the GATS is deregulatory: it attacks non-conforming national government measures." See Christopher Arup, *The New World Trade Organization Agreements: Globalizing Law Through Services and Intellectual Property* (Cambridge: Cambridge University Press, 2000) at 96.

16 Stephen McBride & John Shields, *Dismantling a Nation: The Transition to Corporate Rule in Canada*, 2d ed. (Halifax: Fernwood, 1997).

17 Harry Arthurs, "The Hollowing Out of Corporate Canada?" in Jane Jenson & Boaventura de Sousa Santos, *Globalizing Institutions: Case Studies in Social Regulation and Innovation* (London: Ashgate, 2000).

part of one state to pursue another for violating some supraconstitutional norm varies widely depending on the IO's own constitution. Global *environmental, human-rights,* and *labour* governance is notably bereft of adjudicatory sinew. The strength of global *economic* norms, rules, and rights is due to the muscularity of the WTO's dispute-settlement mechanisms. Whereas the WTO was endowed with an impressive apparatus for adjudicating intergovernmental disputes, NAFTA was created without a supranational judiciary. Instead, North American governance is distinguished by some precarious dispute-settlement processes whose supraconstitutional impacts vary from minor (for general disputes between member states) to negligible (for trade disputes between exporting and importing states) to substantial (for disputes between transnational corporations and host states).

a) NAFTA

i) Chapter 20: General Disputes

Continental dispute settlement was meant to depoliticize conflicts between the three governments through having their differences resolved by neutral arbitrators applying common rules. In this spirit, NAFTA's Chapter 20 provides for bi-national panels to be struck when the member states have been unable to resolve their differences related to issues generated by the agreement. Although Chapter 20 dispute settlement was considered expeditious at first,[18] later decisions have proven unable to settle conflicts without resort to power politics.[19] For example, when it lost a panel decision to Canada in a wheat case,[20] Washington responded by threatening to launch an investigation into Canadian wheat exports. Closure was only achieved when US pressure caused the Canadian government to give way by agreeing to limit wheat exports during 1994–95 to 1.5 million tons.[21] If such Chapter 20 rulings are unable to constrain the continental hegemon, it becomes futile for its neighbours to submit general issues to NAFTA

---

18 William J. Davey, *Pine and Swine* (Ottawa: Centre for Trade Policy and Law, 1996) at 65.

19 Vilaysoun Loungnarath & Céline Stehly, "The General Dispute Settlement Mechanism in the North American Free Trade Agreement and the World Trade Organization System: Is North American Regionalism Really Preferable to Multilateralism?" (2000) 34 J. World T. 43.

20 *Interpretation of Canada's Compliance with Article 701.3 with respect to Durum wheat sales,* (1993), CDA-92-1807-01 (Ch. 18 Panel).

21 Davey, *Pine and Swine,* above note 18 at 65.

arbitration. Continental governance then gets delegitimized, being unable to deliver for its weaker members the rights for which they "paid" when negotiating the original compact. In this respect, the judicial function of NAFTA is faulty as an aspect of North American governance because it fails to have supraconstitutional effect in the US legal order.

ii) Chapter 19: Trade disputes

Had NAFTA created a true free trade area, its members would have abandoned their right to impose anti-dumping (AD) or countervailing duties (CVD) on imports coming from their partners' economies. In their place, problems of predatory corporate behaviour would have been dealt with by establishing continentwide antitrust and competition policies. The United States refused such a real levelling of national trade barriers that would have created a single continental market. It simply agreed to cede appeals of its trade-protectionist rulings to bi-national panels that were restricted to investigating whether the administration's AD or CVD determinations properly applied *domestic* trade law.[22]

Written into NAFTA's Chapter 19, this putatively binding judicial expedient turned out to be almost as disappointing as its critics had predicted. When the United States' CVD action against Canadian softwood lumber exports was remanded for incorrectly applying the notion of subsidy as defined in US law, Congress simply changed its definition of subsidy to suit the Canadian situation. Beyond softwood lumber's long-lasting evidence,[23] Canada has not had a satisfactory experience in using Chapter 19 to appeal other American trade determinations. In 1993, for instance, there were multiple remands in five cases, which led the panels to surpass their deadlines significantly. Furthermore, problems have arisen over the lack of consistency in Chapter 19 panel decisions, which have shown differing degrees of deference to agency decisions.[24] Although AD and CVD jurisprudence may have been ineffective in helping the peripheral states constrain their hegemon, the opposite is not necessarily true. Canadian trade agencies have had to become more attentive to American interpretations of the standards they apply in AD or CVD determinations out of a

---

22 Leon Trakman, *Dispute Settlement under the NAFTA* (New York: Transnational, 1997) at 277.

23 Robert Howse, "Settling Trade Remedy Disputes: When the WTO Forum Is Better Than the NAFTA" (June 1998) C.D. Howe Institute Commentary 111 at 15.

24 Michael Trebilcock & Robert Howse, *The Regulation of International Trade*, 2d ed. (New York: Routledge, 1999) at 83.

concern for what the bi-national panels, which necessarily include American jurists, may later decide on appeal.

Thus Chapter 19 confirms the experience of Chapter 20, that NAFTA's judicial function is asymmetrical in its impact. On the one hand, it does not have supraconstitutional clout over the hegemon's behaviour. On the other, it is used to enforce NAFTA rules in the periphery where it has some effect on Canadian administrative justice. However, when these processes don't satisfy Washington, it can still exercise its raw power to achieve its objectives.

iii) Chapter 11: Investor-State Disputes
With NAFTA's Chapter 11, Canada constricted the authority of its national courts by accepting the jurisdiction of private international arbitration when American (or Mexican) corporations claim that action (or inaction) by a federal, provincial, or municipal government has an effect "tantamount to expropriation" of their property. (By the same token, of course, Chapter 11 also gives Canadian companies the right to sue US or Mexican governments.) Although barely noticed when NAFTA was debated in the public domain before its ratification, a then obscure dispute mechanism has established a powerful new zone of adjudication to enforce Article 1110's corporate rights. Under these investor-state tribunals, American (or Mexican) corporations with interests in Canada can initiate arbitration proceedings on the grounds of expropriation against a municipal, provincial, or federal policy that harms their interests. These "investor-state" disputes are taken for arbitration before an international panel operating by rules established under the aegis of the World Bank's International Convention on the Settlement of Investment Disputes between States and Nationals of other States, or the United Nations Commission on International Trade Law for settling international disputes between corporations.[25] Since these forums operate according to the rules and procedures of international commercial law, Chapter 11 disputes actually transfer the adjudication of disputes over government policies from the realm of public law to commercial law.[26]

---

25 Gary Horlick & F. Amanda DeBusk, "Dispute Resolution Under NAFTA: Building on the U.S.–Canada FTA, GATT and ICSID" (1993) 27 J. World T. 21 at 52.

26 For example, in the *Metalclad* case, the tribunal ruled that the local municipality had exceeded its constitutional authority—a judgment that hitherto only the judges of the Supreme Court of Mexico had the power to make. Patrick Dunberry, "The NAFTA Investment Dispute Settlement Mechanism: A Review of the Latest Case Law" (March 2001) 2 Journal of World Investment 151.

Written by trade law specialists in closed hearings with virtually no opportunity for public input, Chapter 11 panel decisions have taken a fairly broad view of what is "tantamount to expropriation" and what counts as "property," going well beyond what is considered an impermissible taking in Canadian law and effectively restricting governments' ability to regulate transnational capital in what they see as the public interest. Since Chapter 11 allows American TNCs to take legal action directly without having to wait for their government to initiate arbitration proceedings, these firms gain the ability to short-circuit what may be lengthy diplomatic negotiations when they consider themselves to have been subject to abuse in the neighbouring jurisdiction as well as to avoid having to make their case in domestic tribunals where the pleadings would be more transparent and the rulings subject to appeal before superior courts. The threat of an adverse Chapter 11 ruling is sometimes enough to prompt Canadian governments to repeal offending laws without waiting for a decision (as was the case when the Canadian government rescinded its ban on the suspected neurotoxin, the gasoline additive MMT). The result of the various Chapter 11 cases that have been decided is the public awareness that TNCs from the US or Mexico have greater rights vis-à-vis the Canadian government than do domestic Canadian corporations or citizens.

Chapter 11 arbitrations both shrink the scope of the Canadian judicial system and overlay it with supraconstitutional processes that conflict with many of its historic values.

- *Transparency* is the first victim in this secret world of commercial arbitration: even the existence of a case may be kept secret, and the public may never learn what has happened or why.
- *Neutrality* is the second legal value that falls by the wayside. Since the plaintiff investor has the right to appoint one of the three arbitrators, the defending government already faces a bench that is substantially weighted in favour of corporate rather than public values.
- *Judicial sovereignty* is a third victim of this extraordinary addition to the Canadian legal order. As the corporate plaintiff and the defendant state choose the panel's chair by consensus, it is likely that there will be just one Canadian in tribunals adjudicating suits launched against federal, provincial, or municipal governments' policies.

With its intrusive judicial institutions, this dynamic continental economic regime creates new levels of uncertainty for domestic governments whose elected officials cannot be sure how measures they propose to implement might be judged in some future trade tribunal. Many critics of the new external constitution have talked about a "regulatory chill," particularly in light of NAFTA Chapter 11 rulings on environmental matters that have given complaining businesses the benefit of the doubt and shown little deference to democratically-sanctioned government regulations. This suggests that, when a norm of international corporate law comes into conflict with a Canadian legal standard, the latter is likely to be overridden by the former to the profit of transnational corporate autonomy and with the decline in legitimacy of global economic governance in the public's eyes.

b) The WTO

In contrast with NAFTA's judicial processes, which are weak at the governmental level and strong at the corporate level, the WTO's dispute settlement body excludes corporations from directly using its services and gives governments a powerful tool with which to enforce the global regime's economic rules even against the most powerful non-compliant state. Indeed, the key to the WTO's singular importance lies in the power and neutrality of its dispute-settlement mechanisms. Unlike NAFTA's Chapter 19 and 20 panels, WTO panelists are chosen from countries other than those involved in a particular dispute. Their rulings are not based on the contenders' own laws, as they are in NAFTA's AD and CVD cases but on the WTO's international rules. They make their judgements quickly on the basis of the WTO's norms that they interpret in the light of the international public law developed by prior GATT jurisprudence.

The composition of its panels enhances the WTO's legalistic rigidity.[27] Panelists adjudicating WTO disputes are either trade lawyers and professors of international law who tend to stick very close to the black letter of the WTO's texts they are interpreting, or they are middle-level diplomats who take their cues from the Secretariat's legal staff. In either case, they know full well that their judgment will be appealed by the losing side and that the judges on the Appellate Body will be responding to highly refined legal reasoning.[28]

---

27 J.H.H. Weiler, "The Rule of Lawyers and the Ethos of Diplomats' Reflections on the Internal and External Legitimacy of WTO Dispute Settlement" (2001) 35 J. World T. 191 at 194.

28 Raj Bhala, "The Myth About *Stare Decisis* and International Trade Law" (1999) 14 Am. U. Int'l L. Rev 845 at 847; David Palmeter & Petros C. Mavroidis, "The WTO Legal System: Sources of Law" (1998) 92 Am. J. Int'l L. 398 at 405.

While WTO Appellate Body rulings are not formally precedent-setting, it is generally recognized that the logic of one panel's decision can be carried over from case to case as the situation dictates. Palmeter and Mavroidis also note that the Appellate Body "operates on a 'collegial' basis. While only three of the seven members sit on any one 'division' to hear a particular appeal, and the division retains full authority to decide the case, views on the issues are shared with the other Appellate Body members before a decision is reached. Consequently, members of the Appellate Body, in confronting prior decisions, are far more likely to be confronting their own legal logic, or that of their close colleagues, than are WTO panellists. This relationship seems likely to lead to a stronger attachment to the reasoning and results of those decisions."[29] Under these conditions, "soft" arguments defending cultural autonomy or environmental sustainability hold little weight against the "hard" logic of the WTO's rules.

While the WTO's rules create new supraconstitutional norms for member states to accept, their meaning cannot be anticipated with any certainty. In referring to one contentious concept in trade law, the WTO's Appellate Body memorably compared the notion of "likeness" to "an accordion, which may be stretched wide or squeezed tight as the case requires." This judicial flexibility did not guarantee cultural sensitivity, as Canadians discovered when the WTO ruled that *Sports Illustrated Canada* (though filled with American content) was "like" *Maclean's* magazine (which was written by Canadian journalists for a Canadian readership).[30] This judgment meant that several key policy instruments, which had successfully promoted a Canadian magazine industry for several decades, were declared invalid.[31] The permanent threat of a WTO court challenge of their regulations means that national policy-makers can only be sure that they will never know what this supreme court of commercial law will decide until a trade dispute concerning this policy is heard.[32]

As any student of federalism knows, a system containing more than one order of jurisdiction creates conflicts between the cohabiting authori-

---

29 Palmeter & Mavroidis, *ibid.*
30 World Trade Organization, *Canada—Certain Measures Concerning Periodicals: Ruling by the Appellate Body* (Geneva: World Trade Organization, 1997).
31 Daniel Schwanen, "The Summer of Our (Canadian) Content: Thinking About Canada's Response to the WTO Magazine Decision" (29 June 1998) C.D. Howe Institute Backgrounder at 29.
32 Robert Howse & Donald Regan, "The Product/Process Distinction—An Illusory Basis for Disciplining Unilateralism in Trade Policy" (2000) 11 Eur. J. Int'l Law 249 at 268.

ties. Whether the WTO rulings' supraconstitutional superiority over their own constitutional norms will be accepted by Canadian courts remains to be seen. No case has yet been brought to Canada's Supreme Court to test whether a ruling by a global or continental dispute panel takes precedence over a Canadian norm.[33] The introduction of a supraconstitution with judicial muscle suggests that continuing clashes between the external and internal constitutional orders must be expected. If, as further global limits on government are negotiated in the Doha Round, the federal government agrees to let education and health care be brought under the aegis of the GATS, it would affect the provincial constitutional order more than the federal. This action might also be of dubious constitutional validity since it would lead to a change in the norms governing the provinces without the appropriate amendment having been made in Canada's internal constitution.

Conflict can also be anticipated between the global and continental orders. The United States, for instance, challenged Canada's tariffication of its agricultural quotas as a violation of its NAFTA obligations.[34] The NAFTA panel ruled that the WTO's tariffication imperative prevailed.[35] Other conflicts between the two regimes' norms are bound to occur, complicating their constitutionalizing impact on their members.

The WTO's dispute-settlement system may be superior to NAFTA's in many respects, but multilateralism does not necessarily present Canada with a real escape from US pressure. Indeed, much of the constraint that the WTO imposed on the Canadian state in the first few years of its existence was an application of US-driven demands that Canada comply with US-inspired WTO rules on behalf of US-based pharmaceutical and entertainment oligopolies.

The judicialization of trade rules has affected international cooperation on regulation in other areas, such as the environment. Before 1990, many governments, including Canada's, considered trade sanctions a legitimate tool for enforcing multilateral environmental agreements and pushed for their inclusion in such agreements. These governments (and many supportive NGOs and business groups) wished to apply the "teeth" of the trade

33 A constitutional challenge launched by the Canadian Union of Postal Workers and the Council of Canadians to NAFTA's Chapter 11 investor-state arbitration process is working its way through the Ontario court system and may ultimately land in the Supreme Court of Canada for resolution.
34 Trebilcock & Howse, *Regulation of International Trade*, above note 24 at 267.
35 *In the Matter of Tariffs Applied by Canada to Certain US-Origin Agricultural Products* (1996), CDA-95-2008-01 (Arbitral Panel).

regime to the enforcement of environmental treaties. They achieved a breakthrough in 1987 with the Montreal Protocol on ozone-depleting substances, which allowed member states to impose general trade sanctions against other member states that violate their obligations under the Protocol. Ten years later, when states were negotiating the Kyoto Protocol on climate change, the Canadian and many other governments had reversed their position and actively opposed the inclusion of trade sanctions as an enforcement tool in the agreement. Few governments will now openly support the use of trade sanctions in multilateral environmental agreements. The conclusion of the WTO agreements in 1994 led many governments, which were unwilling to take the risk of adverse trade rulings, to fear that the use of trade sanctions to enforce multilateral environmental agreements may violate their trade-law commitments. In this way international trade rules have taken primacy over, and inhibit more robust action to enforce, international rules in other areas, such as environmental protection. These other areas are thus denied the legal and political "teeth" reserved for the rules of economic globalization.

6) Enforcement

As with other trade treaties, NAFTA has no enforcement capacity other than the parties' sense of their long-term self-interest. If one member state does not comply with the judgments that it loses, it cannot expect its partners to do the same. Under the extreme asymmetry prevailing in North America, the hegemon is largely unconstrained by such prudential considerations. The United States remains able to flout the trade agreements' rules as interpreted by its judicial processes, something that Washington has repeatedly done with both Canada and Mexico.

Like NAFTA, the WTO has no police service capable of implementing its judicial decisions. But unlike NAFTA, the enforcement provisions supporting its dispute settlement rulings are significantly stronger.[36] Once the final decision on a trade dispute has been handed down in which a signatory state's laws or regulations have been judged in violation of a WTO norm, the offending provisions are supposed to be changed by the defendant or compensation paid to the plaintiff state. A non-compliant state is

---

36 Ostry called the DSU "the strongest dispute settlement mechanism in the history of international law." See Sylvia Ostry, "The Future of the World Trading System: Beyond Doha" in John J. Kirton and Michael J. Trebilcock, eds., *Hard Choices, Soft Law: Voluntary Standards in Global Trade, Environment and Social Governance* (Aldershot and Burlington, VT: Ashgate, 2004).

much more likely to be brought to "justice" by a litigant state because failure to abide by a WTO dispute ruling gives the winning plaintiff the right to impose retaliatory trade sanctions against the disobedient defendant. This retaliation can block any exports of the guilty state. The amount of the damage inflicted by the retaliation can equal the harm caused to the complainant by the violation. This self-enforcement system works better in the WTO where there is greater symmetry among the major powers, confirming that the global economic regime has a far more substantial supraconstitutionality for its members in its judicial dimension than does the regional NAFTA.[37]

The global constitution has an uneven incidence, depending on the size of the state. The weaker it is, the more difficult it is to resist. For smaller countries on the periphery of the world power system, financial organizations—notably the International Monetary Fund (IMF) and the World Bank—have unapologetically and even dictatorially impinged directly on the internal policies of their weaker members, insisting that they radically restructure their governments. Having well-governed financial institutions—and long experience in floating its currency—Canada has not been subject to the humiliation of these enforced disciplines.

It has, however, been the object of a process of external oversight that keeps the Canadian state's behaviour under transnational scrutiny. The United States Trade Representative's Office keeps federal and provincial policies under regular review, reporting annually to Congress about Canadian compliance with the obligations it assumed in NAFTA and the WTO. The WTO's Trade Policy Review Mechanism reviews Canada's policies every two years. This surveillance mechanism presses Ottawa to ever greater transparency before the epistemic community of trade liberalizers in conformity to their neoconservative ideology. At these encounters, Canada's trading partners cannot force it to make changes, but they ask about governmental measures that interfere with their investments or trade and so put Canada's governing elite on the defensive if it is caught practising discrimination.

---

37 Robert Howse, "The Canadian Generic Medicines Panel-A Dangerous Precedent in Dangerous Times" (July 2000) 3 Journal of World Intellectual Property at 493–508.

F. WHAT TO DO?

That the multilateral institutions of global governance are currently facing a significant set of challenges, or even a crisis, has by now become a relatively uncontroversial point of departure. In many accounts, this crisis of legitimacy centres on the processes of decision making in multilateral institutions, which remain largely state-driven and shielded from direct input from or accountability to citizens and non-governmental organizations. The crisis label also refers to widespread concern about the lack of substantive fairness of the policies adopted by these multilateral institutions, which are seen as contributing to the exacerbation of inequalities in the world economy between the richer countries of the North and the poorer countries of the South. While most agree that a crisis is being faced and even that it involves questions of the multilateral economic institutions' perceived legitimacy and accountability, there is no consensus on how to respond.[38]

As with domestic constitutional borders, the supraconstitution is not a fixed entity but one that is constantly evolving as new rules are negotiated and judicial decisions are made by international trade and investment dispute settlement. The malleability of the country's external constitution raises a question about whether Canada should attempt to change it as a result of deliberate, proactive intervention. In other words, to the extent that Canada is an agent of globalization, what should be its program of action? The answer to this question depends both on assessing the global constitution's strengths and weaknesses and on defining Canada's national interest. In the view of many, the global order's excessively powerful economic norms and institutions serve the interests of the major powers and their transnational corporations. They may even perpetuate the vicious circles that keep the poor in poverty by denying them the very policy tools, such as the tariffs and industrial subsidies, that big powers used in the nineteenth and twentieth centuries to industrialize their own economies. The corollary weakness of transnational governance is to be found in the other institutions of the global constitution, principally the IOs defending human, labour, and ecological rights.

---

38 Ruth Buchanan & Andrea Long, "Contested Global Governance: States, the World Trade Organization, and Global Civil Society" (Report prepared for the Law Commission of Canada "Governance Relationships in Transition" Program, December 2002) 1.

Recommendation: Twenty years ago, a similar study to this one could well have recommended that the government of Canada establish a full inventory of the country's international obligations to be used as an essential tool by its own policy-makers, by judges working in the judicial system, and for the general public's enlightenment. Now that NAFTA and the WTO have given international economic agreements supraconstitutional weight, what is even more urgently needed is a constantly updated document that details exactly what comprises Canada's external constitution.

While the implications of many of its norms, rights, rules, and institutions remain unclear, public officials as well as the general public, business people as well as civil society organizations need to have just as authoritative information about their external legal order as they do about the Canada *Constitution Act, 1982*. While most citizens will not know or care about most of their domestic constitution, accurate information becomes critical to them when an issue becomes significant—rights for same-sex couples, for instance. Similarly, vast areas of the country's external obligations are of little interest either to officials or citizens, who need nevertheless to have access to authoritative information when the need arises.

Recommendation: Following this analysis, Canada should strive to re-balance the global constitution in order to bolster weak environmental, labour, and human rights by giving them equivalent weight to its already robust economic rights.

If Canada's external constitution is not to become a source of political illegitimacy in its domestic politics, Ottawa must move both to bring transparency to this largely hidden reality and to join with other like-minded countries in rebalancing the evolving norms and institutions of global governance. While the Departments of Foreign Affairs and International Trade must play the lead role in the latter endeavour, the Department of Justice has the responsibility to deal with the former.

Understanding the Question of Legitimacy in the Interplay between Domestic and International Law

5

OONAGH FITZGERALD[*]

A. INTRODUCTION

This chapter examines the question of legitimacy that arises in the relationship between international and domestic law and considers why domestic lawyers, judges, lawmakers, politicians, and government policy-makers at times are reluctant to accept international law completely into domestic law and policy.[1] Written from the perspective of a government lawyer advising a government client about how to mediate among international law obligations, domestic constitutional constraints, and international and domestic policy priorities, the paper explains why legitimacy questions are indeed relevant (and legitimate), but offers some practical answers to assuage uncertainties and allow us to function reasonably well within the evolving matrix of international and domestic law.

---

* The author acknowledges the generous assistance in preparation of this paper of Anik Beaudoin, Counsel, Public International Law Section, Department of Justice Canada, who reviewed an early draft and greatly assisted in developing conference speaking notes from that draft. The assistance of Tania Nesrallah, Administrative Assistant to the Special Advisor International Law, is also gratefully acknowledged. The views expressed are those of the author alone, and do not represent the position of the Department of Justice.

1 Jutta Brunnée & Stephen Toope, "A Hesitant Embrace: The Application of International Law by Canadian Courts" (2002) Can. Y.B. Int'l L. 3. These authors have made concerted efforts to familiarize the judiciary with international law to reduce their level of discomfort using international law in deciding cases.

The chapter begins by considering how questions about the legitimacy of international law arise in practice. Second, the chapter examines legitimacy questions relating to evolving notions of sovereignty, representation, and enforcement of international law. Third, the chapter identifies and analyzes potential ingredients of legitimacy, core concepts that provide a workable foundation for international law's legitimacy.

Because international law is still in development and somewhat imperfect as a legal order, legitimacy questions are raised quite fairly. With increasing interconnection between international and domestic law, a national government needs to understand international law to position itself to influence outcomes, both domestically and internationally, and to effectively reconcile international and domestic priorities. For this it may need a working appreciation of how the legitimacy of international law can be founded in collective security, state consent, and evolving notions of sovereignty.

B. HOW LEGITIMACY QUESTIONS ARISE IN PRACTICE

The question of legitimacy arises in the creation, interpretation, application, and enforcement of international law, and wherever particular international law principles encounter other systems of law, such as domestic constitutional law, federal and provincial statutes and regulations, bilateral and regional treaty law, customary international law, and international treaties on overlapping issues. The question is relevant to a national government because it deals with international and domestic law obligations and policy priorities on a daily basis. The government legal advisor observes that clients absorb and react to legal advice through a process of assessing the legitimacy of the legal rules under consideration. Some questions relevant to a client's assessment of legitimacy on receiving advice about a matter of international law are: Is the rule expressed clearly in an international treaty that Canada has ratified and expressly implemented into domestic statute law? Is the rule still current and readily applicable and responsive to present circumstances? Are there competing or inconsistent international rules? Is the rule honoured by Canada's treaty partners? Is compliance with the rule reasonably enforceable? Is the rule expressed in a Resolution of the UN Security Council? Is the rule well known to be part of customary international law? Is the rule expressed clearly in an international treaty that many other states have ratified, but which Canada has not? Has the rule developed over time through resolutions, declarations, advisory opinions of international bodies, and writings of international jurists? Is there consistency between Canada's international obligations and any domestic laws on the same subject?[2]

There can be uncertainty about the relationship between aspects of international and domestic law relevant to a particular fact situation. As an example, a lawyer advising on the applicability of the *UN Convention on the Law of the Sea*[3] would focus on the specific relevant articles of the Convention and the fact that it is binding on Canada since we have recently ratified it and, anyway, many of its provisions are considered customary international law. The lawyer would also consider any international enforcement mechanisms that may be relevant and explain how these would operate in the circumstances. The lawyer would ascertain whether domestic law is consistent with the provisions of the Convention, and consider how domestic courts might deal with any ambiguities or divergence between the international and domestic rules. This would involve explaining that a court likely would apply a presumption that domestic law conforms to international law where possible, but would give effect to a clearly expressed legislative intent to diverge from the international rule, if applicable. This kind of analysis may reveal that there is scope for debating the correct interpretation of the domestic and international legal rules. Assuming the government is committed to acting in conformity with both the applicable international and domestic rules, it may nonetheless have certain interpretative preferences.

---

2   Clients may also have legitimacy concerns about aspects of domestic law: Do they have confidence that the lawyer articulating the rule speaks authoritatively for the Department of Justice? Does the rule apply clearly to the situation, does it make obvious good sense, and does it accord with what the client wants to do? Is the rule found in a well-known, well-respected, familiar source of authority? For example, is the rule clearly expressed in one of the Statutes of Canada, officially published in the Canada Gazette? Is the rule clearly expressed in a definitive majority decision of the Supreme Court of Canada, clarifying points of ambiguity? Is the rule gleaned from interpreting the majority and minority reasoning in a series of judicial decisions? Is the rule supported by foreign sources? For example, is there a similar or identical rule expressed clearly in the statute law of the United States, the United Kingdom, Australia, France? Is there a similar or identical rule expressed clearly in definitive majority decisions of the highest courts of the United States, the United Kingdom, Australia, France? Is there some support for the rule to be gleaned from interpreting the majority and minority reasoning in judicial decisions of the United States, the United Kingdom, Australia, France?

3   10 December 1982, ratified by Canada on 6 November 2003.

It also appears possible to have a domestic law that conflicts with inter-national law upheld as constitutionally valid by our courts. In the *Suresh* case, the Supreme Court of Canada recognized that the international law rule prohibiting return to torture was absolute, but noted that the right in section 7 of the *Canadian Charter of Rights and Freedoms* was not absolute.[4] Rather, section 7 was subject to balancing, such that there was a possibil-ity "in exceptional circumstances" for return to torture to be justifiable under the *Charter*, even if it could never be justifiable under the *Convention against Torture*. When Canada was invited to report on its compliance with the Convention, the UN Committee against Torture was unimpressed by Canada's legal conundrum and emphasized that domestic law could not excuse failure to comply with international law obligations.

The possibility of contradictions between domestic law and interna-tional legal obligations raises additional legitimacy questions, in giving advice to a government client, but in some contexts may be viewed as a nec-essary safety valve to protect national interests even at the expense of inter-national relations.[5] For example, with the global terrorism threat post-911 policy-makers in some Western democracies have raised questions about the continued relevance or applicability of longstanding international law rules and sought to reshape domestic law according to new paradigms.[6]

4   *Suresh v. Canada (Minister of Citizenship and Immigration)*, [2002] 1 S.C.R. 3 (S.C.C.).
5   Paul B. Stephan, "The New International Law—Legitimacy, Accountability, Author-ity, and Freedom in the New Global Order" (1999) 70 U. Colo. L. Rev. 1555 at 1583–84. Stephan suggests two complementary approaches that:

a state might take to enhance its power to hold international lawmakers account-able for their actions while not inflicting too great an injury on the international legal system as a whole. First, a state might structure its internal lawmaking pro-cesses so as to make it difficult to enter into binding international commitments [having strict rules of legislative endorsement]. Second a state might resist inter-national customs that it has not unambiguously embraced as binding in cases where it seeks to develop new international norms [restraining courts from impos-ing international rules in the absence of clear support from the other branches of government]. In other words, states should seek to contribute to a dynamic pro-cess that in some instances will repudiate old customs in favour of new, presum-ably more desirable practices.

See also UN Human Rights Committee views on Quebec signage laws (*Communica-tion No. 455/1991: Canada. 15/08/94. CCPR/C/51/D/455/1991(Singer v. Canada)*) and Ontario's separate (Catholic) school system (*Communication No. 694/1996: Canada. 05/11/99. CCPR/C/67/D/694/1966 (Waldman v. Canada)*).
6   Anne Orford, "The Destiny of International Law" (2004) 17 L.J.I.L. 441 at 453 quotes Anne-Marie Slaughter, then president of the American Society for International Law,

C. LEGITIMACY CHALLENGES

> Only universal organizations like the United Nations have the scope and legitimacy to generate principles, norms and rules that are essential if globalization is to benefit everyone.[7]

It is only fitting that the Secretary-General of the United Nations would expound the legitimacy of the United Nations system, but we need to dig further to deconstruct the notion of legitimacy. It is helpful to begin with J. Habermas' definition:

> Legitimacy means that there are good arguments for a political order's claim to be recognized as right and just; a legitimate order deserves recognition. *Legitimacy means a political order's worthiness to be recognized.* This definition highlights the fact that legitimacy is a contestable validity claim; the stability of the order of domination (also) depends on its (at least) de facto recognition. Thus, historically as well as analytically, the concept is used above all in situations in which the legitimacy of an order is disputed, in which, as we say, legitimation problems arise. One side denies, the other asserts legitimacy. This is a *process.*[8]

There are sovereignty, representational, and enforcement dimensions to the question of the legitimacy of international law, all of which may contribute to ambivalence about accepting international law completely into domestic law and policy.

---

when she wrote in defence of the US government's abandonment of the UN Security Counsel process, with regard to getting support for the invasion of Iraq:

> By giving up on the Security Council, the Bush administration has started on a course that could be called "illegal but legitimate" ... even for international lawyers, insisting on formal legality in this case may be counterproductive.... The United Nations imposes constraints on both the global decision-making process and the outcomes of that process, constraints that all countries recognize to be in their long-term interest and the interest of the world. But it cannot be a straitjacket, preventing nations from pursuing what they perceive to be their vital national security interests.

A.-M. Slaughter, "Good Reasons for Going around the UN" *New York Times* (18 March 2003) 453.

7   Secretary-General Kofi A. Annan, *Partnerships for Global Community: Annual Report on the Work of the Organization* (New York: United Nations, 1998) at 81.

8   J. Habermas, "Communication and the Evolution of Society" quoted in Thomas M. Franck, "Legitimacy in the International System" (1988) 82 Am. J. Int'l Law 705.

1)   Evolving Sovereignty Dimensions of Legitimacy

Paul Stephan contrasts what he calls traditional international law governing relations among sovereigns with new international law that subordinates the role of the sovereign state, supplanting national law with international rules and standards.[9] This legal transformation is more complex than simply replacement of domestic law by a new international legal order, as Boaventura de Sousa Santos explains:

> We live in a time of porous legality or of legal porosity, multiple networks of legal orders forcing us to constant transitions and trespassings. Our legal life is constituted by the intersection of different legal orders, that is, by interlegality. Interlegality is the phenomenological counterpart of legal pluralism, and a key concept in the postmodern conception of law.[10]

---

9   Stephan, "The New International Law," above note 5 at 1556–57:

Traditionally conceived, international law governed the relations among sovereigns. A treaty or custom would create some right or obligation owed by one sovereign to another. Even in those cases where the subject of one sovereign might invoke one of these rights against the other sovereign, the individual or group seeking the protection of international law derived its claim from its sovereign's rights. As a general matter, and with important exceptions, it did not provide a body of substantive rules that people, rather than states, could invoke when conducting their affairs.

...

[I]n the years since World War II, we have seen the emergence of a different sort of international law, one that subordinates the role of the sovereign state. The end of the Cold War has brought about a quickening of this process. International organizations increasingly promulgate substantive rules to govern private transactions.... [I]n important if sometimes subtle ways, international bodies have supplanted national law with international rules and standards.

10   Boaventura de Sousa Santos, "Toward a New Common Sense: Law, Science and Politics in Paradigmatic Transition" (1995) quoted and discussed in William Twining, *Globalisation and Legal Theory* (London: Butterworths, 2000) at 194. Twining (at 239–40) refers to Santos' seven types of legal transnationalization that warrant attention: 1) The transnationalization of nation-state law, for example, movements to harmonize or unify branches of municipal law and programs of structural adjustment; 2) The development of legal regimes of regional integration; 3) Transnational commercial regulation, much of it involving non-state law, which Santos calls "global capital's own law"; 4) The Law of People on the Move, that is, the regulation and rights of migrants, refugees, and displaced persons; 5) The Law of Indigenous Peoples; 6) Cosmopolitanism and human rights; 7) Genuinely global law—the common heritage of mankind (*ius humanitatis*).

William Twining points out that globalization requires us to look at law in the modern world from multiple perspectives "to include not only municipal legal systems and traditional public international law, but also global, regional, transnational, and local orderings that deserve to be treated as 'legal' for given purposes and the relations between them."[11] There are no longer "black box" self-contained spheres of law, but rather, growing interdependence in which even the most local of issues can best be viewed "in ever-widening contexts, up to and including the world and humankind in general."[12] Twining argues: "Globalisation does not imply homogenisation," but rather it generates multiple interpretations and requires acute sensitivity to the implications of ethical, legal, and cultural pluralism.[13]

This intertwining and intersecting of international law means that it is relevant to Canadians on a daily basis. It is no longer just a distant phenomenon, but rather it shapes local experience even as local events try to reshape and redraw international law in more favourable ways. Law's globalization, begun in earnest over a century ago, has generated a vast infrastructure of international, regional, and bilateral treaties and institutions, as well as domestic-implementing legislation and regulation that underlie many of our daily personal and business transactions.[14] It includes: safety standards for international travel and transportation by sea and air; copyright, trademark, and patent protections; economic statistics and accounting standards; pharmaceutical identity, standards for food and drug safety, and public health protection measures; labour standards; core intellectual property rules and trade liberalization rules; and rules on sales and carriage of goods; mail and telecommunications across national borders; meteorological forecasting; environmental protection, pollution and damage control—to name a few. Beyond the commercial domain we find an extensive infrastructure of UN Conventions and international institutions (some dating back to fifty or one hundred years ago), regional and bilateral treaties, and domestic-implementing legislation establishing fundamental and universal prohibitions and protections relating to human security, humanitarian law, and human rights. These examples provide but a brief

---

11   Twining, *ibid.* at 87–88.

12   *Ibid.*

13   *Ibid.*

14   Mark W. Zacher, *The United Nations and Global Commerce* (New York: United Nations, 1999).

glimpse of the all-pervasive ways in which international law shapes and influences our lives and the policy choices of government decision-makers.

International law provides enhanced predictability in international relations, focusing on how the international community views a set of circumstances as consistent with or contrary to the established norm or within a grey zone of interpretative uncertainty; it also channels disputes into prescribed procedural and remedial avenues. Law at the international level, therefore, is potentially useful to all nations—they will try to shape it to be most helpful to their own national interests and perspectives. International trade law provides an example of an ever increasing body of law where states' common interest in securing access to markets and facilitating investment has led to the development of international, regional, and bilateral agreements, with similar terms and conditions aimed at removing protectionist measures that impede the free flow of capital, goods, and services, and providing a focused channel for resolution of trade disputes.[15] Nations all seek to secure for themselves an international legal environment that suits their national interests, although those with greater power tend to be more successful at shaping international law to suit their objectives. Groups of less powerful nations with a common goal may also develop agreements that meet their own domestic needs and preferred vision of international law.[16] Canadian negotiators seek to exert influence by leveraging Canada's geopolitical alliances, its two official languages, and its two legal systems to bridge differences and suggest compromise approaches for international treaties and model laws.[17]

2) Representational Dimensions of Legitimacy

The international legal system may be subject to legitimacy questions because of perceived inadequacies in how states are represented internation-

---

15   The General Agreement on Tariffs and Trade, the World Trade Organization, the North American Free Trade Agreement, and Mercosur are examples of international and regional trade liberalization instruments.

16   The Convention on the Prohibition of the Use, Stockpiling, Production and Transfer of Anti-Personnel Mines and on their Destruction, 18 September 1997 (the Ottawa Protocol) is an example of international law being developed by lesser powers, at the initiative of committed NGOs, and without the support or leadership of the major powers.

17   This is especially useful in relation to negotiations at the Hague Conference on Private International Law where Canadian delegates have been able to leverage our bijuralism and bilingualism.

ally and how international law speaks for and represents the interests of all nations and all people.

The text of a new treaty is generally articulated by government officials who may be highly expert in the particular subject matter of the treaty under negotiation, but may not be well positioned to perceive the broader and longer-term implications of the new agreement for the whole developing system of international law and governance. As well, the finalized treaty is likely the product of compromise between competing policy objectives and perspectives and may be intentionally unclear in order to paper over these differences and encourage states to sign and ratify. An international instrument may have unforeseen implications that only come to light after several years of jurisprudential development and that may not be compatible with individual state parties' current domestic priorities. Decades ago, when the executive decision was taken to ratify an international treaty, it may have seemed consistent with the state of Canadian law; but over the ensuing years the legal landscape shifts, as the international obligation is interpreted and applied around the world, and the scope for government policy and programs becomes ever more constrained. For a domestic policy-maker unfamiliar with this history, the evolution of international law may sometimes feel like an external constitutional straitjacket.

Parliamentarians may or may not have been engaged in a meaningful way in the development of a new treaty obligation. There has been substantial political and democratic accountability with respect to trade agreements: a federal election was fought over the decision to enter the *Canada–US Free Trade Agreement*, and the federal government has been meticulous in passing implementation legislation for trade agreements, thereby providing a clear legislative role for parliamentarians in respect to such treaties. However, the federal government has tended to take a less transparent and accessible approach to the implementation of international human rights conventions, relying on the existence of federal, provincial, and territorial human rights codes, quasi-constitutional and constitutional provisions, and the current state of human rights protection in the country. This approach may have been reasonable in the 1970s, when Canadian understanding and expectation of such international instruments was that they would help raise world standards of human rights protection, but it likely added little for Canadians who, it was understood, already enjoyed such protections. Today, however, uncertainty about implementation has led to confusion and contradiction within government and before the courts. The fact that the interpretation of these standards has also evolved and, in a few instances, advanced beyond the current state of human rights protection in Canada (notwithstanding the rights revolution brought about by the *Canadian Charter of Rights and Freedoms*)[18] may have exacerbated bewilderment about the power and legitimacy of international law.

Parliamentarians may have views about international law and try to become engaged on the questions of negotiation, ratification, accession, and implementation of international treaties, but unless the government of the day chooses to involve them, either through debates or the introduction of a bill to implement a treaty, their role is limited to parliamentary committee study, question period debate, Opposition day motions, private members' bills, etc. In other words, there is not an established parliamentary role in the absence of a need for implementing legislation. Thus, although the federal and provincial legislatures were at the core of Canada's decision to include the *Charter* in the newly repatriated Constitution, they have been left somewhat on the periphery of debate about international human rights instruments.[19]

As citizens, each of us may view our relationship to our nation differently, through the lens of our multiple identities. We may each see ourselves best represented by specific, diverse, and often overlapping collectivities, which are identified by party, province, region, culture, ethnicity, tribe, family, faith, language, gender, colour, disability, profession, etc.[20] Nego-

---

18   Address by Irwin Cotler, then Minister of Justice and Attorney General of Canada, 17 November 2004, Main Estimates for the Department of Justice Canada.

19   Hon. Raynell Andreychuk, Chair C (Saskatchewan), and Hon. Landon Pearson, Deputy-Chair Lib. (Ontario), of the Senate Standing Committee on Human Rights have made considerable efforts to enhance parliamentary engagement on international human rights issues, most recently in relation to children's rights.

20   James Tully, *Strange Multiplicity: Constitutionalism in an Age of Diversity* (New York: Cambridge University Press, 1995). Tully's focus is on the complexity within a state, but his writing has interesting implications for the international context. He describes how modern constitutionalism supplanted ancient recognition of custom, tradition and culture by applying the conceit that the new constitution is created by equal individuals in a state of nature desiring to form one uniform political association, and accepting "as authoritative a set of threshold, European institutions, manners, and traditions of interpretation within which they deliberate and reach agreement on a [progressive, politically and legally uniform] constitution" (at 63; discussed from 62–69).Tully writes (at 190–91):

> If a liberal constitution is to provide the basis for its most important values of freedom and autonomy, it thus must protect the cultures of its members and engender the public attitude of mutual respect for cultural diversity that individual self respect requires. To put this differently, the primary good of self respect requires

tiation of legal instruments at the international level is not well suited to capture and reflect the complex tapestry that is Canadian identity.

Joanna Harrington's chapter in this text argues that there are representational deficiencies in how international law is made because Parliament's role has not been sufficiently developed and recognized.[21] Josee Boudreau, Stefan Matiation, and Gib van Ert explore the potential involvement of First Nations in shaping Canada's international law obligations in their chapters.[22] Recently parliamentarians have advocated for a stronger provincial role and a stronger parliamentary role in treaty-making.[23] For several years the federal public service has studied ways to enhance and manage effectively parliamentary and provincial involvement in the treaty-making or treaty-approval process. During the last federal election there was discussion and debate about providing for greater provincial involvement in the representation of Canada on the international stage.

The difficulty in finding solutions to the representation challenge indicates the complexity of managing the development of international and domestic law in the postmodern world. It is neither practical nor strategic for a nation such as Canada to go to international meetings with a hundred disparate voices representing its many selves: the nation's position would be too incoherent to have any influence. On the other hand, people's identities often cross international boundaries so it is possible that diverse Canadian voices might help to represent people around the world who are not well represented by their own state.

As a multicultural nation, Canada should model these broad representational values on the international stage. When Canadian delegations reflect our multicultural, multi-faith, officially bilingual, naturally mul-

---

that popular sovereignty is conceived as an intercultural dialogue. The various cultures of the society need to be recognised in public institutions, histories and symbols in order to nourish mutual cultural awareness and respect. Far from being a threat to liberal values, the recognition and protection of cultural diversity is a necessary condition of the primary good of self respect, and so of the individual freedom and autonomy that it underpins, in a manner appropriate to a post-imperial age.

21 See Chapter 6.

22 See Chapters 7 and 12.

23 For example, Daniel Turp, former MPP for Beauharnois–Salaberry, now a Parti Québécois MNA, presented Private Members' Bill C-214 in 1999; Francine Lalonde, the MPP for La Pointe-de-l'Île, introduced Private Members' Bill C-313 in 2001; Jean-Yves Roy, MPP for Haute-Gaspésie–La Mitis–Matane–Matapédia, introduced Private Members' Bill C-260 in 2004.

tilingual, federated, bi-jural and gendered selves, they help all to see that there may be better ways of representing the peoples of the world.[24] Just as domestic notions of constitutionalism and democracy evolve to meet the changing values of a nation, so too the institutions and instruments of international governance may need to evolve to address changing global values.[25] Through the process of debating and discussing international law's legitimacy, weaknesses may be identified and legitimacy-enhancing solutions found.

3) Enforceability Dimensions of Legitimacy

It might be suggested that international law lacks legitimacy in that it is more like a simple form of social structure than a developed legal system because it lacks: clear rule hierarchy—a legislature, courts with compulsory jurisdiction, and centrally organized sanctions; secondary rules permitting a rule to change and adapt through legislation and court decision;

---

24 Tully, *Strange Multiplicity*, above note 20 at 109–10, refers to Wittgenstein's "philosophical investigations" in which he illuminates the multifaceted perspectives on rules by analogy to tennis games and entering a city from an unfamiliar gateway, to demonstrate how understanding requires dialogue between various perspectives:

> The final aspect of Wittgenstein's two arguments I wish to draw to your attention is that his examples of understanding a general term by assembling examples always take place in dialogue with others who see things differently. The dialogical character of understanding is one of the many things he wishes to convey by calling the activity of understanding a "language game," for, like playing tennis, we grasp a concept by serving, returning and rallying it back and forth with other players in conversations. Indeed, it is precisely the analogy between the use of words in dialogue and games like tennis that Wittgenstein thought of emphasising by selecting as a motto for the Philosophical investigations, the line 'I'll teach you differences' uttered by Kent to Oswald in King Lear, for the dialogue between them, in which the differences are taught and learned, is based on the analogy between word play and tennis play.
>
> ...
>
> To understand a general term, and so know your way around its maze of uses, it is always necessary to enter into a dialogue with interlocutors from other regions of the city, to listen to their 'further descriptions' and come to recognise the aspects of the phenomenon in question that they bring to light, aspects which go unnoticed from one's own familiar set of examples.... Understanding, like the Philosophical investigations itself, is dialogical.

25 See, for example, UN reform and the *Report of the Secretary General's High Level Panel on Threats, Challenges and Change,* and the earlier initiative on *The Responsibility to Protect.*

and "a unifying rule of recognition specifying 'sources' of law and providing general criteria for the identification of its rules."[26] Despite such formal weaknesses, states generally act as if they are bound by their treaties, thereby providing circumstantial evidence of a rule of recognition.[27]

The UN Security Council has substantial law-making and enforcement powers, but it is unable to act if it cannot achieve agreement among its five permanent members, each of whom has a veto power. When it can achieve unanimity, its resolutions have immediate and extensive reach. For example, Resolution 1373, passed days after the terrorist attacks of September 11th, 2001, called on all states to take immediate and concerted action to stop terrorism. By means of Canada's *United Nations Act*[28] and *Regulations* that implement UN resolutions, aspects of this and related antiterrorism resolutions dealing with terrorist financing have had virtually immediate effect in Canada. Additional specific federal legislation was also required to address the details of prohibitions against terrorism in a manner consistent with Canadian criminal, human rights, and constitutional law principles.[29]

The UN General Assembly does not have direct law-making power but can shape how international law develops and is interpreted through the passing of declarations,[30] or it may pass a resolution condemning a particular course of action.[31] The UN General Assembly may also help to shape

---

26 H.L.A. Hart, *The Concept of Law* (Oxford: Clarendon Press, 1961) at 209, cited in Thomas M. Franck, "Legitimacy in the International System," above note 8 at 751. Alvarez argued that Franck had misinterpreted Hart and that Hart viewed international law as obligatory regardless of whether there were organized sanctions and a system of threats to discourage non-compliance: Jose E. Alvarez, "The Quest for Legitimacy: An Examination of *The Power of Legitimacy Among Nations* by Thomas M. Franck" (1991–92) 24 N.Y.U.J. Int'l L. & Pol. 199 at 250.

27 Franck, "Legitimacy in the International System," *ibid.* at 756. He cited the advisory opinion of the International Court of Justice [ICJ] on 26 April 1988 to the effect that it was "the fundamental principle of international law that it prevails over domestic law" (rendered at the request of the United Nations General Assembly with respect to a conflict between US law requiring the closure of the PLO Observer Mission, and the terms of the UN Headquarters Agreement: [1988] I.C.J. Rep. 12 at para. 57.)

28 R.S.C. 1985, c. U-2.

29 See the *Antiterrorism Act*, S.C. 2001, c. 41 (formerly Bill C-36).

30 For example, see the UN General Assembly Resolution 217A (III) of 10 December 1948, adopting and proclaiming the *Universal Declaration of Human Rights.*

31 At the 60th General Assembly (42d meeting) by GA 10413, the GA decided that the United Nations would:

    designate 27 January—the anniversary of the liberation of the Auschwitz death camp—as an annual International Day of Commemoration to honour the victims

international law by seeking an advisory opinion from the International Court of Justice about the legality of a particular course of action.[32]

If a state fails to meet its obligations under a particular treaty that includes an individual complaints mechanism, an individual may be able to bring a complaint before the treaty body, which body may issue an advisory opinion. It is generally recognized that such opinions are not binding on the state party, although they may be highly persuasive and, indeed, definitive in the interpretation of the provisions of the particular Convention. The state thus retains the option of not following the advisory opinion but risks being censured when presenting periodic reports under that Convention. As well, domestic courts may opine on the matter, adding pressure to comply with the international law standard.

Professor Thomas Franck argued that coherence in the application of a rule was a key indicator of legitimacy and a key factor in explaining why rules compel obedience, demonstrating this by contrasting the development at international law of the right to self-determination, the notion of state equality, and the most-favoured-nation, free, and non-discriminatory system of trade.[33] International trade law seems to be an area where states share a sufficiently strong common interest in securing access to markets, facilitating investment, and ensuring reasonable international economic stability and predictability that they were able to develop a substantial body of international, regional, and bilateral agreements with very similar terms

---

> of the Holocaust, and urged Member States to develop educational programmes to instil the memory of the tragedy in future generations to prevent genocide from occurring again.
>
> Rejecting any denial of the Holocaust as a historical event, either in full or in part, the 191-member Assembly adopted by consensus a resolution condemning "without reserve" all manifestations of religious intolerance, incitement, harassment or violence against persons or communities based on ethnic origin or religious belief, whenever they occur.

32   On 8 December 2003, the United Nations General Assembly adopted Resolution ES-10/14 referring to the International Court of Justice questions pertaining to the *Legal Consequences of the Construction of a Wall in the Occupied Palestinian Territory* (ICJ Advisory Opinion issued on 9 July 2004).

33   Franck, "Legitimacy in the International System," above note 8 at 741, referring to R. Dworkin, "Law's Empire" (Cambridge, MA: Belknap Press, 1986) at 176–224:

> The costs to its legitimacy of applying a rule incoherently arise in three related, but different, senses. First, incoherence nullifies the flawed act of validating or withholding validation. Second, it undermines the standards, rules and processes for bestowing status or validity. Third, it derogates from the legitimacy of the institution that is charged with validating.

and conditions, and relatively effective dispute-settlement mechanisms.[34] Beyond the realm of trade law there are international dispute-resolution mechanisms of a binding nature, such as the contentious issues jurisdiction of the International Court of Justice (ICJ),[35] as well as specialized treaty bodies with jurisdiction to issue advisory opinions.[36]

If a state's treaty partner does not comply with a treaty obligation, and if the treaty lacks a mandatory, independent, and effective dispute-resolution mechanism, the offended state party may find itself with few real avenues of recourse. Often treaties provide recourse mechanisms but require the consent of both parties to use them. Even if the treaty provides a unilateral avenue of recourse, it may be illusory in that invoking it would only exacerbate what presumably is already a delicate diplomatic situation, without offering any prospect of enforcement.[37] This can lead domestic policy-makers and lawmakers to question the value of the treaty as a binding legal instrument and, more generally, can undermine the sense that international law is real law. It starts to be viewed as merely hortatory, a guide to action, not law.

A government lawyer is in an awkward position trying to explain to the client that a treaty is binding even though the state has no effective enforcement mechanism to ensure its treaty partner complies. Canada is a principled and pragmatic advocate of a rules-based international system, habitually abiding by its international law obligations and supporting rule of law at both the international and domestic level, but one can see how such a position is tested when other states take a more flexible approach (ranging from creative

---

34 While normative debates continue about the impacts and consequences of free trade and about the accessibility and fairness of trade dispute settlement procedures, Chapter 11 of the *North American Free Trade Agreement* provides an example of how international panel decisions can be enforced by national courts, thereby integrating international and domestic law.

35 By virtue of Article 93 of the *UN Charter*, all 191 UN member states are automatically parties to the *Statute of the International Court of Justice*. While the court only has jurisdiction by consent of the state (Article 36 of the *Statute*), many have agreed to its jurisdiction for contentious issues.

36 An example would be the jurisdiction of the UN Human Rights Committee to hear complaints under the *International Covenant on Civil and Political Rights* [ICCPR], by virtue of the *First Optional Protocol* to the ICCPR.

37 For an example of this, see the Canada–US *Boundary Waters Treaty* (1909), art. IX, which permits unilateral reference of a question to the International Joint Commission, for examination but not for decision, and art. X, which permits joint reference of a disagreement to the ICJ for decision.

interpretation to outright non-compliance) vis-à-vis their treaty obligations.[38] Thus, while Canadians and Canadian policy-makers are becoming progressively more accustomed to the all-pervasive nature of bi-national, regional, and international law, feelings of ambivalence remain.

There are informal sanctions that may carry even more weight than the available legal remedies: pressure of conformity with like-minded states, criticism from recognized interest groups, domestic public pressure, etc.[39] The combined legal and non-legal consequences may take years to manifest and reach a level of sufficient pressure to induce greater conformity between international and domestic law. The ongoing debate about the legality of various aspects of the US Guantanamo Bay detention facility illustrates how this multi-faceted dialogue about international law and domestic law obligations can unfold. The intensity and uniqueness of this example also illustrates a key dynamic: such instances are rare and are likely to be confined to matters of singular importance to a state's sovereign interests.[40] It is in such cases that proponents might be tempted to argue that the state's position is, above all, "legitimate," regardless of the strength or weakness of its "legal" foundation.[41]

38 Canada's longstanding efforts to develop an effective fisheries management regime for the waters off the coast of eastern Canada, through the North Atlantic Fisheries Organization, the *United Nations Convention on the Law of the Sea*, 10 December 1982, and the *United Nations Fisheries Agreement* (Agreement for the Implementation of the Provisions of the United Nations Convention on the Law of the Sea of 10 December 1982, Relating to the Conservation and Management of Straddling Fish Stocks and Highly Migratory Fish Stocks, September 1995), illustrate the challenges in achieving effective agreements.

39 Alvarez, "The Quest for Legitimacy," above note 26 at 229, 233.

40 The only Canadian example in recent history was the "turbot war" and the ongoing pressure to enforce a system of custodial management in the Grand Banks that would push the limits of existing international rules.

41 Dencho Georgiev, "Politics or Rule of Law: Deconstruction and Legitimacy in International Law" (1993) 4 Eur. J. Int'l L. 2, contrasts these two concepts (at 11–12):

    A concept which seems capable of taking account of the existence of contradiction and indeterminacy within law is the concept of legitimacy. Legitimacy in its simple original meaning implies conformity with law. Unlike legality however, it denotes accordance with basic principles of law, and not with all specific rules of law. Legitimacy has also the connotation of contestability: of a "contestable validity claim," of a "claim to be recognizes as right and just," of "worthiness" to be recognized.

    …

    Legitimacy, unlike legality refers to the "ought" and not just to the "is" of law. Moreover, one could say that it incorporates the "ought" into the "is" of law.

Although we can identify the sources of normative obligation and the relative weight to be given to different sources of international law, it is also worth considering why sovereign states generally feel obliged to obey international law.[42] Franck observed, "[T]he perception of a rule as legitimate contributes to the chances of compliance."[43] The source of law or its pedigree is, after all, only one indicator of whether it will be obeyed.[44] Franck argued that some evidence of the hierarchy of rules to support the legitimacy of the international legal system could be found in the rule of *pacta sunt servanda*, the duty to perform international treaty obligations in good faith, articulated in Article 26 of the *Vienna Convention on the Law of Treaties*, and the universally recognized equality of nations.[45] He concludes that even without a coercive world government, the rules of international law have developed sufficient coherence, hierarchy, and rules of recognition to "exhibit a powerful pull to compliance and a self-enforcing degree of legitimacy."[46]

Alvarez argues that there may be more practical explanations for why states comply with their international legal obligations other than the perceived legitimacy of the international legal order. He suggests that states may be motivated to comply by "perceptions of fairness or justice, social necessity, fear of sanctions by one state, groups of states or even a non-governmental organization or domestic coalition, self interest (either long-term or short-term), or merely habit or tradition."[47] He considered Franck's

---

42 Stephan, "The New International Law," above note 5 at 1555. Stephan notes that international law academics tend not to be very critical of international law, and tend to favour its expansion without much reflection on its impacts on other fundamental legal and political principles. He urges academics to subject international law to a more critical analysis.

43 Franck, "Legitimacy in the International System," above note 8 at 706.

44 *Ibid.* at 705. Franck asks the fundamental question why "states obey laws in the absence of coercion," as distinct from other studies that investigate the sources of normative obligation, examining "the origins of rules—in treaties, custom, decisions of tribunals, *opinio juris*, state conduct, resolutions of international organizations, and so forth— to determine which sources, qua sources, are to be taken seriously, and how seriously to take them."

45 UNTS Regis. No. 18,232 UN Doc.A/CONF.39/27 (23 May 1969); UN Charter Article 2(1); *The Antelope* (1825), 23 U.S. (10 Wheat.) 66 (Marshall J., explaining why the court would not impose recent abolitionist laws on owners of a foreign slave-trade ship captured on the high seas).

46 Franck, "Legitimacy in the International System," above note 8 at 759.

47 Alvarez, "The Quest for Legitimacy," above note 26 at 229, 233. He cites Inis Claude, Jr., who contended it was a mistake to equate legitimacy with legality ("Collective

quest to establish the legitimacy of international law to be like chasing a will-o'-the-wisp.[48]

A related legitimacy issue is that the method of international legal argumentation is rendered doubtful by its incessant struggle between legal supremacy and state will. For government lawyers this is a challenging point to explain to a client who may be attracted to the notion that international law is only the will of the state that agrees to be bound by it, and yet repelled by the difficulty of dealing with other states that adopt this attitude. Koskenniemi, an international lawyer from the Finnish public service, contends that international legal argumentation is like a game of "snakes and ladders," comprised of mutually contradictory ascending and descending lines of argument, and that neither kind of argument satisfies its counterpart, so that legal reasoning is nothing but political positioning dressed up as law.[49] In effect, he concludes that legitimacy questions about

Legitimization as a Political Function of the United Nations" (1966), 20 Int'l Org. 367 at 369). Rather, "the process of legitimization is ultimately a political phenomenon, a crystallization of judgment that may be influenced but is unlikely to be wholly determined by legal norms and moral principles."

48 Alvarez, "The Quest for Legitimacy," *ibid.* at 255: "Franckian legitimacy is probably fated to join that melange of 'positivist and naturalistic, consensualistic and non-consensualistic, teleological, practical, political, logical and factual arguments' which make up the 'happy confusion' of modern international legal arguments," quoting from Martti Koskenniemi, *From Apology to Utopia: The Structure of International Legal Argument* (Helskinki: Finnish Lawyers' Publishing Company, 1989) at 47.

49 Koskenniemi, *From Apology to Utopia, ibid.* at 41–42:

The two patterns—or sets of arguments—are both exhaustive and mutually exclusive. A point about world order or obligation can either be "descending" or "ascending" and is unable to be both at the same time. The former is premised on the assumption that a normative code overrides individual State behaviour, will or interest. As a legal method, it works so as to produce conclusions about State obligations from this code. The latter is premised on the assumption that State behaviour, will and interest are determining of the law. If State practice, will and interest point in some direction, the law must point in that direction, too. This view starts from the given existence of State behaviour, will and interest and attempts to produce a normative code from them. Either the normative code is superior to the State or the State is superior to the code. A middle position seems excluded.

From the ascending perspective, the descending model falls into subjectivism as it cannot demonstrate the content of its aprioristic norms in a reliable manner (i.e., it is vulnerable to the objection of utopianism). From the descending perspective, the ascending model seems subjective as it privileges State will or interest over objectively binding norms (i.e., it is vulnerable to the charge of apologism).

Consequently, international legal discourse cannot fully accept either of the justificatory patterns. It works so as to make them seem compatible. The result,

international law are well founded and insurmountable.[50] He is critical of the notion that international law is founded on the consent of states ("voluntarism" or "consensualism").[51] He points out inconsistencies and incoherence in trying to build international legal argument about *jus cogens*, customary international law, or any other source of law on notions of express or implied consent, unilateral declaration, acquiescence, or estoppel.[52] From this, Koskenniemi concludes that international lawyers cannot offer their clients a coherent theory of international law but should rely on their core (domestic) lawyering skills to provide the best analytical advice possible in the particular, difficult, and uncertain circumstances of an international dispute.[53]

---

however, is an incoherent argument which constantly shifts between the opposing positions while remaining open to challenge from the opposite argument. This provides the dynamics for international legal argument.

50   *Ibid.* at 48:

In other words, my argument is that international law is singularly useless as a means for justifying or criticising international behaviour. Because it is based on contradictory premises it remains both over- and underlegitimizing: it is over-legitimizing as it can be ultimately invoked to justify any behaviour (apologism), it is underlegitimizing because incapable of providing a convincing argument on the legitimacy of any practices (utopianism).

51   *Ibid.* at 200, 270 *et seq.*

52   *Ibid.* at 459:

The contradiction between the demands for concreteness and normativity accounted ... for the way in which legal argument arranged itself in crucial doctrinal areas. There was always a "descending" argument which attempted to ensure the law's normativity and this was always countered by an "ascending" one which provided for the law's concreteness. The former led beyond State will in a manner which seemed vulnerable because non-concrete (utopian); the latter led into particular State will and seemed unacceptable because non-normative (apologist). To seem acceptable, doctrines tended constantly towards a reconciliation. They looked at normativity from the perspective of concreteness and concreteness from the point of view of normativity. To make an ascending point you had to give a descending justification; and to verify or justify your descending argument, you had to produce an ascending point.

53   *Ibid.* at 496–97:

The international lawyer should take seriously the partial character of his experience. He possesses no more objective information about what solutions to offer than the parties in the conflict he deals with. There is no one, coherent explanation of international society, no indivisible legal system which he could rely upon. Uncertainty and choice are an uneradicable part of his practice. Denying this, he will retreat into assimilation or phantasy. Accepting it, he can re-establish an iden-

As Koskenniemi seems to imply, legality and legitimacy can both be double-edged swords when dealing with international law; not only do states like to maintain some latitude in interpreting their own international law obligations, but they also like to be able to rely on other states acting as though bound by their respective international law obligations.[54] In giving advice to a client the lawyer will likely focus on legality points and only address legitimacy concerns if the legal advice is questioned.

Consideration of the consequences of non-conformity can raise many questions about the legitimacy of international law simply because they are often more political than legal. Thomas Franck questioned whether the legitimacy of international law can be sustained on similar grounds as the legitimacy of domestic law: "Why should rules, unsupported by an effective structure of coercion comparable to a national police force, nevertheless elicit so much compliance, even against perceived self-interest, on the part of sovereign states?"[55]

There may be some differences, but arguably there are also some fundamental elements of the legitimacy conundrum that are applicable at both the domestic and international level. For example, when Alexander Hamilton described the US judiciary as the least dangerous branch of

---

tity for himself as a social actor. This involves a refusal to engage in discussions about general principles or lawlike explanations of international conduct. Rather than be normative in the whole (and be vulnerable to the objections of apologism-utopiansim) he should be normative in the small. He can attempt, to the best of his capability, to isolate the issues which are significant in conflict, assess them with an impartial mind and offer a solution which seems best to fulfil the demands of the critical programme... In this way, he can fulfil his authentic commitment, his integrity as a lawyer.

54 Dencho Georgiev, "Politics or Rule of Law," above note 41 at 12:

The concept of legality refers to a static, one-dimensional vision of law in which the distinction legal-illegal is expected to give a definite, determinate answer about whether a given behaviour corresponds to it or not. This distinction cannot tolerate indeterminacy and contradiction, and has to assume that they do not exist, approaching them technically by applying certain rules and procedures in order to be able to present a non-conflictual picture of law.

"Legitimacy," on the other hand, having the connotation of the "contestable validity claim," is capable of referring to something which has the potential of being "legal" and yet is not, not yet, or not fully recognized as being "legal." It has the potential of being "legal" because it corresponds to certain rules or principles which are perceived as basic but yet the claim, because of various circumstances, is not being recognized, so it does not have "real" legality.

55 Franck, "Legitimacy in the International System," above note 8 at 707 (his emphasis).

government, he raised the question of how it is that courts are able to secure compliance with their rulings.[56] It is not the presence or absence of a
strong enforcement mechanism, such as a domestic or international police
force, that determines legitimacy. It is whether the rules are accepted and
believed in, and this depends on both good process in making the rule and
good substantive content of the rule.[57]

States normally respect both binding rulings and advisory opinions,
but if they do not, they expose themselves to criticism by the relevant treaty
body, the broader international community, and domestic constituents.
The mere fact that international law's enforcement is imperfect or incomplete does not necessarily impair its legitimacy. As Louis Henkin put it,
"[A]lmost all nations observe almost all principles of international law and
almost all of their obligations almost all of the time."[58] As D'Amato argues,
law—whether domestic or international—is not at its essence simply "a
rationale for the application of force," and the fact that some states periodically disobey rules of international law "does not itself mean that those
rules are not rules of 'law,' because even in domestic society some people
(for example, criminals) break the law from time to time."[59]

D. POTENTIAL INGREDIENTS OF LEGITIMACY

With such polarized views in academia about the state of international law
it is no wonder that clients occasionally raise questions about its legitimacy.

---

56   Alexander Hamilton,The Federalist Papers No. 78. It is ironical that Hamilton was to
     die at the hand of the US Vice-President Aaron Burr in a duel apparently fuelled by
     intense political rivalries, suggesting constitutional theory was not then the bloodless
     pursuit of academe it has since become. *Marbury v. Madison* (1803), 5 U.S. (1 Cranch)
     137 (U.S.S.C).

57   See also Hans Kelsen, *Principles of International Law*, 2d ed., rev. and ed. R.W. Tucker
     (New York: Holt, Rinehart and Winston, 1966) at 13–14, who describes how inter-
     national law, like domestic law, creates "collective security" and that self-interest in
     collective protection engenders adherence to the law.

58   L. Henkin, *How Nations Behave*, 2d ed. (New York: Columbia University Press, 1979)
     at 47, cited in Anthony D'Amato, "Is International Law Really 'Law'?" (1985) 79 Nw.
     U.L. Rev. 1293 at 2.

59   D'Amato, *ibid.*, at 2 and 5. D'Amato argues that enforcement is not really the hallmark
     of law, citing examples of domestic litigation in which enforceability of a judgment
     that goes contrary to the government interest, really depends on the government ac-
     cepting to follow the court ruling—judgments are not and do not need to be backed up
     by force, except in a very narrow band of cases in criminal matters. Just as govern-
     ments comply with the rulings against them made by their domestic courts, so too do
     they generally comply with international law.

The lawyer will focus on legality as it is understood under both international and domestic law, but may still need to assuage the client's doubts about the legitimacy of this law. Notwithstanding these doubts, there are a few related core ideas—collective security, state consent, and evolving notions of sovereignty or statehood—that are capable of providing a framework for understanding the legitimacy of international law.

1)   Legitimacy Founded in Collective Security

Hans Kelsen suggests that international law, like other legal systems, is at core a coercive order founded on the need for collective security.[60] He describes how establishing collective security creates a social order of the community, with binding mutual obligations even where there are no formal governing institutions to police compliance. This is because the international community puts social pressure on individual states to comply, notwithstanding weak or incomplete enforceability.[61] Anthony D'Amato focuses less on international law as coercion than as a system of reasonable assumptions that states can rely on in the conduct of their affairs.[62] He suggests that international law polices itself by the meta-rule: "That it is legal to deter the violation of an entitlement by threatening a counter-violation of the same or a different entitlement. This latter enforcement action

---

60   Kelsen, *Principles of International Law*, above note 57 at 4: "Thus the antagonism of freedom and coercion—fundamental to social life—supplies the decisive criterion. It is the criterion of law, for law is a coercive order."

61   Kelsen, *ibid.* at 13–14:

> In a strict sense, collective security is a characteristic of every legal order, however decentralized. In establishing a force monopoly of the community, it is the purpose of every legal order to protect certain interests of the individuals subjected to it by providing for coercive acts (sanctions) to be applied as reactions against violations (delicts) of these interests. The security thus afforded its subjects by a legal order is collective security because it is a security established by a social order. By regulating the mutual relations of individuals, every social order creates certain social relations among these individuals and in this manner brings about a certain collectivization constituting a community as a collective body. The collective character of the security established manifests itself, first, in that the use of force is forbidden by the legal order which is equally valid for all members of the community constituted by the order, and, second, in that the reaction against an illegal use of force is a collective action. It is a collective action because it is an action performed by organs of the community and is therefore imputable to the community, even if the individuals concerned are not special organs.

62   D'Amato, above note 58 at 13.

is the 'physical sanction' provided by the international legal system, just as the rule regulating police, prison officials, sheriffs, etc., are its domestic legal equivalents."[63]

2) Legitimacy Founded in State Consent

State consent to be bound by a rule of international law is one of the cornerstones of legitimacy.[64] Bodansky describes "legal legitimacy" as that which "connects an institution's continuing authority to its original basis in state consent."[65] Such consent carries with it the fundamental principle *pacta sunt servanda*.[66] First, a state will only be bound by treaties it chooses to ratify, although also, it must not act inconsistently with any treaty it has signed but not yet ratified. Second, generally a customary international law rule may bind the state without any explicit demonstration of consent, but not if the state expressly and consistently has refused to be so bound.[67]

---

63 *Ibid.*

64 Brunnée & Toope, "A Hesitant Embrace," above note 1 at 13:

> In the practice of international law, and in much of the literature, the role of state consent in the creation of international law remains predominant. Within this framework, the ultimate question is whether or not states have agreed to a binding treaty rule or have demonstrated the practice and *opinio juris* necessary to show the existence of a rule of customary law.

65 D. Bodansky, "The Legitimacy of International Governance: A Coming Challenge for International Environmental Law?" (1999) 93 Am. J. Int. Law 596 at 605. Bodansky notes three basic theories of legitimacy (at 612): 1) source-based (for example, from God, from custom, from consent etc.); 2) procedural (for example, fair and open procedures, qualified adjudicators, etc.); and 3) substantive (for example, success in achieving intended results).

66 Brunnée & Toope, "A Hesitant Embrace," above note 1 at 14. They note the starting point for a definition of international law is art. 38 of the *Statute of the International Court of Justice*, which states that there are three main sources of international law: treaty, custom, and general principles, with decisions of domestic courts and doctrine written by qualified publicists being subsidiary sources of law. By virtue of art. 26 of the *Vienna Convention on the Law of Treaties*, treaty obligations must be performed in good faith: "By becoming a party to a treaty, a state pledges that it will uphold and implement all the provision of the treaty."

67 This is a simplification of a complex field, and it should be noted that there is debate about how customary international law operates in various circumstances, such as when faced with a persistent objector, or a new state actor. See, for example, D'Amato, above note 58 at 11. D'Amato contends that consent is not a complete explanation of how international law binds states because otherwise we would see states withdrawing consent every time any international law rule was inconvenient for them and we would see new states picking and choosing their obligations whereas we see them seeking

Third, a state will be bound by Resolutions of the UN Security Council even if it does not participate directly in its decisions because by joining the United Nations the state has already agreed to the supreme law-making role played by the Council.[68] Fourth, a state will be bound by the rulings of any international organization of which it is a member, if that was a term of membership.[69]

The consensual process by which a state becomes bound by international law is deliberative and intentional. In Canada the authority to negotiate and commit Canada to international treaties rests with the federal government and derives from the Royal Prerogative. A negotiating mandate is usually sought from the federal Cabinet for Canadian participation in an international negotiation. Where the substance of the treaty involves matters of both federal and provincial jurisdiction, consultations are held to obtain the views of the provinces, and provincial representatives sometimes join the Canadian delegation to the international negotiation. Once the text of a treaty is

---

acceptance by the other states according to the existing terms of international law and its system of entitlements.

68   Article 2(4) of the UN Charter provides: "All members shall refrain in their international relations from the threat or use of force against the territorial integrity or political independence of any state, or in any other manner inconsistent with the purposes of the United Nations." In the face of an armed attack, art. 51 makes clear that: "Nothing in the present Charter shall impair the inherent right of individual or collective self-defense if an armed attack occurs against a member of the United Nations, until the Security Council has taken measures necessary to maintain international peace and security." With respect to Security Council actions under Chapter VII, art. 39 stipulates: "The Security Council shall determine the existence of any threat to the peace, breach of the peace, or act of aggression and shall make recommendations, or decide what measures shall be taken in accordance with Article 41 and 42 to maintain or restore international peace and security." Article 42 provides for the use of armed force, the exercise of which is binding on all member states: "Should the Security Council consider that measures provided for in article 41 would be inadequate or have proved to be inadequate, it may take such action by air, sea, or land forces as may be necessary to maintain and restore international peace and security." See also Jason Reiskind, "International Law through the Prism of Justice," paper presented to the Department of Justice Public International Law Conference (September 2005).

69   Bodansky, note 65 at 604:

In considering the legitimating role of state consent, two types of consent should be distinguished: (1) specific consent to particular obligations or decisions—for example, by ratifying a treaty, joining consensus on a UN resolution, or accepting a court's jurisdiction in a particular case; and (2) general consent to an ongoing system of governance—for example, by ratifying a treaty such as the UN Charter, which creates institutions with quasi-legislative and adjudicatory authority.

finalized, Canada will not ratify it until it has ascertained that there is support for ratification among federal departments responsible for the subject matter of the treaty and provinces and territories (if it also involves matters of provincial and territorial jurisdiction); relevant federal, territorial, and provincial laws must also be in compliance or have been amended to be in compliance with the new treaty obligations. If the treaty includes a "federal state clause," it will be possible to ratify with only some provinces ready to accept the new treaty obligations, because the others can join at a later date if they so desire. Ratification of the treaty is done by the federal executive, by Order-in-Council. Occasionally, very important treaties are the subject of parliamentary debate, but Parliament's constitutional role (and that of the provincial legislatures) in the treaty ratification process is to pass any legislation needed to implement the new treaty obligations.

3) Legitimacy and Evolving State Sovereignty

The third concept that helps to frame our understanding of the legitimacy of international law is the evolving concept of state sovereignty or statehood. The sovereignty and intrinsic equality of states underpin both the idea of an international community of states founded on common concern for collective security and the idea that states become bound by international law through their own consent. However, conceptions of sovereignty have evolved considerably over the past one hundred years, along with the development of a new kind of international law that qualifies state sovereignty and starts to recognize the individual.

Paul Stephan points out that the building of imperial empires "blurred the line between subjects of a sovereign and foreigners entitled to the protection of international law."[70] Development of notions of universal human dignity and human equality in the late-nineteenth century would throw into doubt the claim that slavery could be tolerated by civilized imperial nations and eventually destroy the underpinnings of colonialism. The *Treaty of Versailles* that ended the First World War recognized nationality as distinct from citizenship, thus implying there may be some people who, based on nationality, have a right to remove themselves from a state's sovereignty.[71] With the development of global economic relations in the nine-

---

70 Stephan, "The New International Law," above note 5 at 1568.
71 *Ibid.* at 1569: "Once international law embraced a principle of national self-determination, it necessarily and significantly intruded into the relationship between a state and those persons over whom the state exercised sovereignty."

teenth and early-twentieth centuries, foreign investors wanted their home sovereigns to intercede, as agents of the foreign investors, in order to prevent host states from nationalizing foreign investments.[72] Concurrently, the international war crimes tribunals established after the Second World War "articulated new standards governing the minimum obligations of a sovereign to its subjects."[73] After the horrific abuses of total war and genocide, the international community finally took seriously the human side of international law, and produced fundamental human rights instruments to set clear limits on states and establish stewardship responsibilities on the international community through the UN Security Council, General Assembly, and specific treaty bodies.

Stephan considered the ending of the Cold War to be the most important event in quickening the development of a new kind of international law that subordinates the role of the sovereign state: "International organizations increasingly promulgate substantive rules to govern private transactions.... [I]n important if sometimes subtle ways, international bodies have supplanted national law with international rules and standards."[74]

Neil MacCormick explores the implications of this trend in the context of the European Community, finding that traditional aspects of sovereignty have been subordinated to the supreme European community law, creating a new kind of "constitutional pluralism":

---

72   *Ibid.* at 1570:

> Once international law was seen as encompassing appeals made by sovereigns as agents for private persons, it became easier to ask whether the discipline might recognize substantively identical claims where the sovereign dropped out of the controversy. A path opened for treating the regulation of the relationship between host states and foreign investors as part of international law without regard to the investor's home state.

73   *Ibid.* at 1571.

74   *Ibid.* at 1574, and at 1556–57. Both East and West blocs had formed multilateral blocks of cooperation, whereby there was some subordination of sovereign integrity to create "intracamp homogeneity" for collective strength. Stephan suggests that each side in the Cold War "invoked the aspirational instruments that had accompanied the postwar settlements as a basis for assigning legal content to its ideological critique of its opponent." Polarized perceptions of international law tended to encourage a strict separation of domestic and international law (dualism) both in the east and west. With the end of the Cold War, writes Stephan (at 1576): "the apprehension that full incorporation of universal international rules into domestic law would leave a nation exposed to its adversaries has dissipated with the disappearance of general adversarial conditions."

Classically, state-law was home-made. Even when norms had an extraneous history through a reception or an inheritance from colonial rule, the mark of sovereign independent statehood was that the power to change received or inherited law was fully autochthonous, exercisable within state territory by organs established for that very state by its own constitution. The development of European Community law has wrought a profound change in this for the Member States. The Treaties, and norms validly made under the Treaties, and interpretative principles acknowledged by the ECJ, are all now recognized as part of the law of each of the member-states. Each state has amended its criteria of recognition to include validity-in-EC-law as a criterion of validity domestically. Moreover, the concept of the 'supremacy' of EC law has entailed its being a high-ranking criterion, ranking above legislation and all subordinate forms of law locally.[75]

MacCormick suggests that legal unification could equally have been achieved without resorting to the idea that European law constituted a new *sui generis* legal order, by relying on general principles of international law. The obligations of European states under this body of regional international law would have been to ensure their domestic laws met their international obligations. Individuals' rights deriving from this regional international law "would have been mediated through national law."[76] He cites the UK *Human Rights Act, 1998*[77]—cautiously implementing the *Eu-*

---

75 Neil MacCormick, *Questioning Sovereignty: Law, State, and Nation in the European Commonwealth* (Oxford: Oxford University Press, 1999) at 115. He explains this evolution (at 106–7):

> Critical decisions in the formative period of the Community held that the Community constituted a new legal order. First, this was characterized as a new legal order of international law. But later the concept of "international law" was dropped, and there was said to be simply a new legal order, or an order *sui generis*.
>
> The norms of this order include express treaty norms, norms made under powers conferred by the Treaties, and norms explicated as tools to assist interpretation of the Treaties, under the guise of fundamental legal principles applicable in EC law.... All such norms have been held directly applicable and directly effective (in appropriate cases) so as to confer rights and obligations on citizens of the member states now also "citizens of the Union"). The law of the Community has been held to enjoy "supremacy" over domestic law. Correlative with this assertion of supremacy has been the doctrine that the member states in acceding to the Community necessarily transferred to it a part of their "sovereign rights."

76 MacCormick, *ibid.* at 107.

77 UK Statutes, 1998, Chapter 42.

ropean Convention on Human Rights[78]—as an example of how to domes-
ticate obligations undertaken through an international convention, while
leaving unimpaired the ultimate constitutional authority of the state's own
legislative and judicial organs.

The extent of legal integration being experienced in Europe goes beyond the Canadian experience to date, and we have a tendency to deal with
the relationship between international and domestic law in a dualist fashion, more like the approach embodied in this UK *Human Rights Act*. The
vast growth of Canada's international law obligations has substantially affected both the content of our domestic laws, and the policy choices open to
government decision-makers. However, the way international law becomes
part of domestic law in Canada is still determined by Canadian constitutional, statutory, and common law rules. It does not just flood into domestic
law, swamping governments and citizens alike with new and unexpected
rules. Rather, it flows in only as permitted, through designated executive,
judicial, and legislative channels.

MacCormick asks whether in losing sovereignty through ever extending international commitments, a democratic state abandons popular self-
government and creates a democratic deficit, as Euro-skeptics have argued.
He responds by questioning whether the state is always the best representative of the people when segments of a population may have affinities that
extend beyond national borders and national interests. MacCormick views
the loss of state sovereignty in the development of European Community
law and the notion of subsidiarity, as opening opportunities to strengthen
democracy and interconnection in Europe.[79] This notion of larger communities connecting and gathering strength through international law should
resonate with Canadians, given our multicultural and varied identities. It
suggests that what international law may require to be given up by a state
in terms of sovereignty or local democracy may be compensated for by a
greater common purpose and richer representation. In this sense, state

---

78 Rome 1950.
79 MacCormick, above note 75 at 125, 134. He writes (at 135):

> The doctrine of subsidiarity requires decision-making to be distributed to the
> most appropriate level. In that context, the best democracy—and the best interpre-
> tation of popular sovereignty is one that insists on levels of democracy appropriate
> to levels of decision-making.... The demise of sovereignty in its classical sense
> truly opens opportunities for subsidiarity and democracy as essential mutual
> complements. It suggests a radical hostility to any merely monolithic democracy.

sovereignty is not so much subordinated to international law as it is *sublimated* willingly to the collective purpose.

E. CONCLUSION

Thus, the government lawyer can reassure her client: collective purpose, subordinated sovereignty, and state consent are the three pillars to the temple of international law. Having attempted to reassure the government client that there is at least a legitimate foundation for the international law that binds Canada, she can proceed to advise in the particular case.

This brief consideration of questions of legitimacy indicates that international law is still in development, imperfect and incomplete, and its relation to domestic law uncertain. As such the legitimacy questions are raised quite fairly; trying to find answers to them helps in navigating the complex interplay and interconnection of domestic and international law and politics. Government lawyers and government decision-makers need to understand both international law's weaknesses and its legitimacy founded in collective purpose, state consent, and evolving sovereignty, in order to influence outcomes both domestically and internationally, and effectively manage international and domestic priorities.

Part Two:
PROCEDURAL AND INSTITUTIONAL ROLES

Section A:

STATE ACTORS AND THE DEMOCRATIC DEFICIT

6

The Role for Parliament in Treaty-Making

JOANNA HARRINGTON

A. INTRODUCTION

The judgment in *Baker v. Canada*[1] has become a "cause célèbre" for both administrative and international lawyers in Canada, with many of the latter embracing (if only hesitantly)[2] the majority's approach concerning the interpretive use of the underlying values of an unimplemented treaty. Far less attention is paid to the dissent of Iacobucci J. who viewed the new approach as inconsistent with past jurisprudence on the status of international law within the domestic legal system[3] and feared its impact on "the balance maintained by our parliamentary tradition."[4] He further opined that the new approach would enable a litigant "to achieve indirectly what cannot be achieved directly, namely, to give force and effect within the domestic legal system to international obligations undertaken by the executive alone that have yet to be subject to the democratic will of Parliament."[5]

Such concerns about the democratic credentials of executive law-making by treaty are nothing new, as evidenced by the intent in the US Consti-

---

1   [1999] 2 S.C.R. 817 [*Baker*].
2   See further, Jutta Brunnée & Stephen J. Toope, "A Hesitant Embrace: The Application of International Law by Canadian Courts" [2002] Can. Y.B. Int'l Law at 3, later published as "A Hesitant Embrace: *Baker* and the Application of International Law by Canadian Courts" in David Dyzenhaus, ed., *The Unity of Public Law* (Oxford: Hart, 2004) at 357.
3   *Baker*, above note 1 at para. 79.
4   *Ibid.* at para. 80.
5   *Ibid.*

tution to subject the president's treaty-making power to Senate approval.[6] However, as the volume of treaty-making has grown,[7] so has its scope, with treaties now covering an endless range of subjects as diverse as trade, climate change, and crime—all with clear implications for domestic law and policy. This in turn has prompted greater interest in the executive's prerogative to make treaties in a Westminster-model democracy, with the writings of David Marquand in 1979 contributing the term *democratic deficit*[8] as the catch-phrase for critiquing the absence of parliamentary oversight, albeit that Marquand was referring at the time to the functioning of the European Community.[9]

Yet, despite the impact of treaty-making, including the occasional controversy, law-making by treaty remains an executive act in countries that follow the British constitutional tradition. The common law imposes no obligation to inform or involve Parliament, albeit that Parliament is the ultimate law-making authority in a Westminster-model democracy. Of course, optics or politics may compel an executive to seek parliamentary approval for a treaty prior to its ratification or accession, but the lack of a legal requirement for such involvement grounds complaints that a democratic deficit exists, whatever may be the correct definition of democracy (a subject beyond the scope of this chapter). Moreover, in federal Commonwealth states, such as Australia and Canada, and even quasi-federal states such as the UK, an additional deficit exists because there is no requirement for the central executive to involve the legislative or executive branches of the subnational units in the treaty-making process.[10] This is so even when part

6 Article II(2) of the U.S. Constitution provides that the President "shall have the Power, by and with the Advice and Consent of the Senate, to make Treaties, provided two thirds of the Senators present concur."

7 The UN's treaty collection contains over 50,000 treaties, many of which remain in force. See the website of the UN Treaty Database, online: untreaty.un.org/English/overview.asp. Canada's treaty collection consists of 3,873 treaties as of 1 October 2005: Canada, Foreign Affairs Canada and International Trade Canada, *Examples of Current Issues of International Law of Particular Importance to Canada* (October 2005) at 46.

8 David Marquand, *Parliament for Europe* (London: Jonathan Cape, 1979) at 64–66.

9 The term *democratic deficit* is used more broadly today, without attribution to Marquand, to refer to various aspects of the lack of executive accountability to either Parliament or citizens in both the domestic and international arena. See, for example, Canada, Privy Council Office, *Ethics, Responsibility, Accountability: An Action Plan for Democratic Reform* (Ottawa: Government of Canada, 2004).

10 On the "federal democratic deficit", see Joanna Harrington, "Redressing the Democratic Deficit in Treaty Law Making: (Re-)Establishing a Role for Parliament" (2005) 50 McGill L.J. 465 at 497–507 and Joanna Harrington, "Scrutiny and Approval: The Role

of the subject matter of the treaty falls within the legislative competence of the subnational body—a position not without controversy as evidenced by the provincial opposition to Canada's ratification of the *Kyoto Protocol to the United Nations Framework Convention on Climate Change*.[11]

There are, of course, two ready responses to proposals to grant Parliament a role in treaty-making. The practical response is that in a Westminster democracy, the executive comes from the party with the most seats in Parliament, absent a minority situation, and thus the executive reflects (or controls) what would be the wishes of Parliament. The legal response is that a treaty does not have domestic legal effect until Parliament so chooses through the enactment of implementation legislation, and thus Parliament retains its primary responsibility for law-making. But law-making by treaty does not always require the enactment of legislation, with implementation by regulation and implementation through reliance on pre-existing law being two means that avoid additional parliamentary involvement. Moreover, once ratified, treaties are clearly binding under international law, and their legal character, along with the reciprocal nature of the international legal system, puts pressure on a state's domestic institutions to ensure compliance. It may also lead to judicial circumvention of the traditional rule on domestic effect, as illustrated by the judicial modification of the doctrine of legitimate expectation in Australia,[12] new rules on statutory interpretation

---

for Westminster-Style Parliaments in Treaty Making" (2006) 55 Int'l & Comp. L.Q. 121 at 148–57.

11 11 December 1997, UN Doc. FCCC/CP/1997/L.7/Add.1, (1998) 37 I.L.M. 22 (entered into force 16 February 2005) [Kyoto Protocol]. Canada ratified the Kyoto Protocol on 17 December 2002, after a motion calling on the government to ratify the treaty was passed by a vote of 196 to 77: *House of Commons Debates* (10 December 2002) at 2524–25. Parliament did not, however, examine the text of the Kyoto Protocol prior to adopting the call to ratify. Some have argued that a constitutional convention was breached in ratifying the Kyoto Protocol without provincial support: Allan Gotlieb & Eli Lederman, "Ignoring the Provinces Is Not Canada's Way" *National Post* (3 January 2003) A14.

12 See *Minister of State for Immigration and Ethnic Affairs v. Teoh* (1995), 183 C.L.R. 273 (H.C.A.) [*Teoh*]. But see Wendy Lacey, "Prelude to the Demise of *Teoh*: The High Court Decision in *Re Minister for Immigration and Multicultural Affairs; Ex parte Lam*" (2004) 26 Sydney L. Rev. 131. The British Court of Appeal has rejected the *Teoh* route, with Laws L.J. opining that it would "amount, pragmatically, to a means of incorporating the substance of obligations undertaken on the international plane into our domestic law without the authority of Parliament": *European Roma Rights Centre v. Immigration Officer at Prague Airport*, [2003] E.W.C.A. Civ. 666, [2004] 2 W.L.R. 147 at para. 101.

in New Zealand,[13] and new uses for the underlying values of an unimplemented treaty in Canada.[14]

Treaty law would thus become the purview of the executive branch and the courts, but not Parliament, were it not for certain reforms. These reforms include the adoption in Australia of a dedicated parliamentary treaty committee to ensure the pre-ratification scrutiny of all treaty actions and the enactment in South Africa of a constitutional rule requiring Parliament's prior approval for treaties of significance. They also include the much earlier development in the UK of a treaty tabling procedure, modified in the 1990s to enhance Parliament's scrutiny opportunity, and the development of mechanisms to involve the representatives of subnational units in treaty-making. But not all Commonwealth states are so-minded to embrace reform, with Canada serving as an example of a state with virtually no required or institutionalized parliamentary involvement, whether federal or provincial, in the treaty-making process.

And yet, if one looks back at the Westminster model for treaty-making as it developed in its home country, it is evident that the desire to provide for some parliamentary role is longstanding. A review of the historical record shows that this desire originated with the efforts of British antiwar MPs in the late 1910s, who sought to secure greater parliamentary control over treaty-making in reaction to the impact of treaties of alliance on World War I. The purpose of this chapter is to acknowledge this history, as well the more recent reforms, through an examination of the current pre-ratification roles for Parliaments in treaty-making in Westminster-model democracies, with the UK, Australia, Canada and South Africa being chosen as comparable countries of focus given their shared legal heritage and similar parliamentary systems.[15]

---

13 See *Tavita v. Minister of Immigration*, [1994] 2 N.Z.L.R. 257 (C.A.) suggesting that ratified but unincorporated treaty obligations are mandatory relevant considerations. Subsequent cases, however, suggest a less enthusiastic approach: see *Puli'uvea v. Removal Review Authority* (1996), 2 H.R.N.Z. 510 (C.A.). See further, Claudia Geiringer, "*Tavita* and All That: Confronting the Confusion Surrounding Unincorporated Treaties and Administrative Law" (2004) 21(1) N.Z.U.L. Rev. 66.

14 *Baker v. Canada*, above note 1 at paras. 69–71.

15 For the practice in other states, including civil law states, see Stefan A. Riesenfeld & Frederick M. Abbott, eds., *Parliamentary Participation in the Making and Operation of Treaties: A Comparative Study* (Dordrecht: Martinus Nijhoff, 1994) and the proceedings of a symposium on the subject in vol. 67:2 of the Chi.-Kent L. Rev. See also the series on *National Treaty Law and Practice* published by the American Society of International Law.

B. TREATY-MAKING IN COMMONWEALTH STATES

Treaties take various forms, go by various names, and can concern an un-limited range of subject matters, but as express agreements between states that create legally binding rights and obligations, treaties are also "a form of substitute legislation"[16] in the international legal system. As expressed by the Latin maxim *pacta sunt servanda*, now codified in article 26 of the *Vienna Convention on the Law of Treaties*,[17] every treaty in force is binding upon its parties and must be performed by them in good faith. By bind-ing states to each other, treaties constitute a significant component of the international legal order and their faithful observance is "perhaps the most important principle of international law."[18]

Given the binding quality of treaty law, the most important stage in the treaty-making process is when the state parties express their consent to be bound. This can be done by a variety of means so long as the method cho-sen clearly signifies a state's intention to assume the legal obligations in the treaty. With bilateral treaties, the expression of consent often coincides with the adoption of the final treaty text, but with multilateral treaties, a state usually expresses its consent through a formal process of ratifica-tion,[19] or accession,[20] typically accomplished by the deposit of a declaration of consent some time after the treaty's adoption. This pause in the process, between the treaty's initial adoption and later ratification, enables a state to take whatever steps are necessary, if any, to secure domestic approval for the treaty and to enact any legislative changes needed to ensure compli-ance.[21] It also gives a state time if it so desires to gauge public opinion about

---

16 Malcolm N. Shaw, *International Law*, 5th ed. (Cambridge: Cambridge University Press, 2003) at 89.

17 23 May 1969, 1155 U.N.T.S. 331, (1969), 8 I.L.M. 679 (entered into force 27 January 1980) [*Treaties Convention*].

18 *Restatement (Third) of the Foreign Relations Law*, §321 (1986) [*Third Restatement*].

19 *Treaties Convention*, above note 17, arts. 2(1)(b), 14, and 16. I refer here to "ratification" in the international law sense and not in the sense of a domestic procedure required in some states.

20 Accession has the same legal effect as ratification, but is the term used when a state becomes bound to a treaty already negotiated and signed by other states: Anthony Aust, *Modern Treaty Law and Practice* (Cambridge: Cambridge University Press, 2000) at 81 and 88; *Treaties Convention, ibid.*, arts. 2(1)(b) and 15.

21 Since a state cannot invoke the provisions of its domestic law as justification for its failure to perform a treaty obligation (*Treaties Convention, ibid.*, art. 27), it is common practice for states to insist that any necessary legislative changes be in place before a treaty is ratified. See, for example, the guidance on this point in *Treaties and MOUs:*

the new treaty commitments, with the possibility existing that a strong negative reaction might persuade a state to withhold ratification.

As for where the power to make treaties resides within a state, this is determined by the constitutional law of the particular state, and varies from state to state. For states that follow the British constitutional tradition, the power to conduct foreign relations, including the power to make treaties, is one of the Royal Prerogatives retained by the Crown and carried out by the executive branch, usually through the minister responsible for foreign affairs. Since prerogative powers, by definition, provide the executive with the power to act without Parliament's consent,[22] treaty-making, including treaty ratification, is, at common law, a wholly executive act. Of course, statute law can change this, as will be discussed in relation to South Africa.

As for a treaty's domestic implementation, the dualist view of treaties as co-existing but functioning separately from domestic law[23] means that a treaty that purports to change existing domestic law has no domestic legal effect unless and until the treaty obligations are "incorporated"[24] or "transformed"[25] by the enactment of domestic legislation.[26] For some, this distinction is lost in practice given the degree of executive control over Parliament, but the distinction in law between treaty-making and treaty implementation and the corresponding distinction between the roles of the executive and Parliament remains part of the British, and Commonwealth, constitutional tradition.[27]

Australia and Canada, however, are federal states, and their federal character adds a further dimension to the debate about the democratic creden-

Guidance on Practice and Procedure, 2d ed. (London: Foreign & Commonwealth Office, 2000) (Revised May 2004) at 7, online: www.fco.gov.uk/Files/KFile/Treatiesand-MOUsFinal,0.pdf [*Treaties and MOUs*].

22 A.V. Dicey, *Introduction to the Study of the Law of the Constitution*, 10th ed. (London: Macmillan, 1959) at 425; Anthony W. Bradley & Keith D. Ewing, *Constitutional and Administrative Law*, 13th ed. (London: Longman, 2003) at 246–50, 309.

23 Bradley & Ewing, *Constitutional and Administrative Law, ibid.* at 310. See further, Sir Robert Jennings & Sir Arthur Watts, eds., *Oppenheim's International Law*, 9th ed. (London: Longman, 1992) at 53.

24 This is the term used in the UK: Aust, *Modern Treaty Law*, above note 20 at 150–51.

25 This is the term used in Canada, with incorporation being one of the means of transformation: John H. Currie, *Public International Law* (Toronto: Irwin Law, 2001) at 205. For the somewhat interchangeable use of both terms, see Ian Brownlie, *Principles of Public International Law*, 6th ed. (Oxford: Oxford University Press, 2003) at 41–45.

26 *Canada (A-G) v. Ontario (A-G)*, [1937] A.C. 326 at 347 (J.C.P.C.) [*Labour Conventions*].

27 See generally J.E.S. Fawcett, *The British Commonwealth in International Law* (London: Stevens & Sons, 1963) at 16–32.

tials of treaty-making. With respect to Canada, the responsibility for treaty implementation is divided according to the country's constitutional division of powers. Treaties must therefore be implemented by the level of government that has constitutional responsibility for the particular subject matter of the treaty,[28] notwithstanding the lack of accountability between the federal treaty-maker and the provincial legislatures and the potential problems this poses for treaty compliance, absent federal state clauses, and reservations alleviating federal responsibility for provincial non-performance. This rule is either criticized for holding the federal government hostage to provincial demands, or praised for protecting provincial autonomy and encouraging federal-provincial collaboration in the treaty-making process, but it is probably here to stay. As a result, if a role were to be accorded to the Canadian Parliament in the making of treaties, it would be logical to accord a similar role to the provincial legislatures where the subject matter of the treaty falls within that body's area of legislative competence.

By contrast, in Australia, the Commonwealth Parliament has the ability, authorized by an express "external affairs" power in the Australian Constitution,[29] to enact any legislation necessary to bring into effect Australia's treaty obligations, even when the subject matter of the legislation falls within the constitutional competence of the six state Parliaments.[30] The Constitution further provides that the Commonwealth law prevails to the extent of any inconsistency with any state law.[31] Thus, Australia takes the opposite position to that taken in Canada, with the Australian approach ostensibly placing the value of treaty compliance above any possible encroachment on areas of state responsibility.

C. THE BRITISH MODEL FOR PARLIAMENTARY INVOLVEMENT IN TREATY-MAKING

Ironically, the adherence to a strict separation of powers between the executive and Parliament in treaty-making and implementation does not in fact match the actual practice of the UK, where provision has long been made for some parliamentary involvement in the making of treaties by the ex-

---

28 *Labour Conventions*, above note 26.
29 *Commonwealth of Australia Constitution Act, 1900* (U.K.), 63 & 64 Vict., c. 12, s. 51(xxix) [Australian Constitution].
30 See generally Tony Blackshield & George Williams, *Australian Constitutional Law and Theory*, 3d ed. (Sydney: Federation Press, 2002) at 774–801.
31 Australian Constitution, above note 29, s. 109.

ecutive. Under a conventional practice, known as the "Ponsonby Rule," all treaties requiring ratification[32] must be presented before both Houses of Parliament for at least twenty-one sitting days (rather than calendar days)[33] before the actual ratification takes place, thereby enabling any member of either House to call attention to the proposed treaty action and stimulate public debate. This laying before Parliament is effected by the deposit of a Command Paper,[34] published in one of three series by the Foreign and Commonwealth Office (FCO): the Country Series (for bilateral treaties), the European Communities Series (for treaties between member states of the European Union), and the Miscellaneous Series (for multilateral treaties). A fourth series, known as the Treaties Series, contains the texts of all treaties that have come into force for the UK.[35]

The rule does, however, have some exceptions. Treaties that explicitly call for parliamentary approval in order to come into force are handled outside of the Ponsonby process,[36] as are treaties that are not subject to ratification in the international sense, although these treaties are later laid before Parliament upon their entry into force via publication in the Trea-

---

32 This term has been interpreted broadly to include treaty accessions, approvals and acceptances: House of Commons Information Office, *Treaties* (House of Commons Factsheet No. 14, Procedure Series, Revised June 2003) at 3, online: www.parliament. uk/documents/upload/p14.pdf [H.C. Factsheet No. 14]. The rule also applies to treaties amending treaties and, since January 1998, treaties coming into force by the mutual notification of the completion of constitutional and other procedures by each party: "The Ponsonby Rule" (London: Foreign & Commonwealth Office, 2001), online: www. fco.gov.uk/Files/kfile/ponsonbyrule,0.pdf.

33 Twenty-one *sitting* days can be considerably longer than twenty-one *calendar* days since sitting days need not be continuous.

34 Command Papers are presented to Parliament as "by command of the Queen". They serve as a vehicle through which the government can bring forward matters deemed to be of interest to Parliament, the presentation of which is not required by statute. See further, Sir William McKay, ed., *Erskine May's Treatise on the Law, Privileges, Proceedings and Usage of Parliament*, 23d ed. (London: LexisNexis U.K., 2004) at 261–62.

35 Since January 2002, recent treaty texts are also available online: www.fco.gov.uk/treaty.

36 Section 12 of the *European Parliamentary Elections Act 2002* (U.K.), c. 24, for example, requires any treaty increasing the powers of the European Parliament to be approved by a specific Act of Parliament for ratification to take place. The UK Parliament has established extensive, sophisticated and systematic methods for the scrutiny of European Union developments. See further Priscilla Baines, "Parliamentary Scrutiny of Policy and Legislation: The Procedures of the Lords and Commons" in Philip Giddings & Gavin Drewry, eds., *Britain in the European Union: Law, Policy and Parliament* (New York: Palgrave Macmillan, 2004) at 60–96 and Adam J. Cygan, *The United Kingdom Parliament and European Union Legislation* (The Hague: Kluwer Law International, 1998).

ties Series.[37] Bilateral double taxation agreements are also exempt from the Ponsonby process, since there is a statutory requirement to expose such treaties to parliamentary scrutiny when the draft Order-in-Council providing for the taxation relief is laid before the House of Commons for approval.[38] These too are later published in the Treaties Series. Lastly, the Ponsonby Rule allows for exceptions when other means of consulting or informing Parliament can be used instead, although this is rare.[39]

As for the origins of the rule, it has existed since 1924, when it began life as an undertaking given on behalf of the first government of Ramsay MacDonald by Arthur Ponsonby, then Under-Secretary of State for Foreign Affairs,[40] during the Second Reading of the *Treaty of Peace (Turkey) Bill* in the House of Commons.[41] Ponsonby was familiar with international affairs, having worked in the diplomatic service prior to his first election as an MP in 1908,[42] and he had long campaigned for greater parliamentary control over treaty-making as an author[43] and as a leading member of the Union of Democratic Control (UDC), a prominent antiwar organization,[44] whose 1914 manifesto expressly stipulated "No Treaty, Arrangement, or Undertaking shall be entered upon in the name of Great Britain without the sanction of Parliament."[45] As a minister in 1924, Ponsonby gave an undertaking to inform the House of all other "agreements, commitments and

---

37 Above note 35.

38 U.K., H.C., *Parliamentary Debates*, 6th ser., vol. 4, col. WA 82 (6 May 1981).

39 "The Ponsonby Rule," above note 32.

40 Knowing that Labour was unlikely to stay in office for longer than a few months, Ponsonby had successfully urged MacDonald to serve as his own foreign secretary, noting that the "extraordinary combination of circumstances" would allow them "to have control of the F.O. [Foreign Office] and to begin to carry out some of the things we have been urging and preaching for years". Letter from Ponsonby to MacDonald cited in David Marquand, *Ramsay MacDonald* (London: Jonathan Cape, 1977) at 300.

41 U.K., H.C., *Parliamentary Debates*, 5th ser., vol. 171, cols. 2001–2006 (1 April 1924).

42 He had also been long exposed to the workings of government, being the son of the Sir Henry Ponsonby, the Private Secretary to Queen Victoria, and the great grandson of Lord Grey, Prime Minister from 1830 to 1834. See further, Raymond A. Jones, *Arthur Ponsonby: The Politics of Life* (London: Christopher Helm, 1989).

43 Arthur Ponsonby, *Democracy and Diplomacy: A Plea for Popular Control of Foreign Policy* (London: Methuen and Co., 1915).

44 See further, Marvin Swartz, *The Union of Democratic Control in British Politics During the First World War* (Oxford: Clarendon Press, 1971) and Sally Harris, *Out of Control: British Foreign Policy and the Union of Democratic Control, 1914-1918* (Hull: University of Hull Press, 1996).

45 Reprinted in Swartz, *The Union of Democratic Control, ibid.* at 42.

understandings which may in any way bind the nation to specific action in certain circumstances."[46] The undertaking was later withdrawn during the Baldwin Government of 1924–29, but reinstated when MacDonald was re-elected prime minister in 1929, and has been observed ever since, apart from rare cases of emergency.[47] While failure to follow the practice carries no legal sanction, it would subject the government to criticism, given the longstanding nature of the convention.

Some have taken the view that the Ponsonby Rule is of "limited value"[48] since the government is not legally bound to find valuable parliamentary time to debate a motion deploring its intention to ratify a treaty, and if it did find time, it is unlikely that the government would be defeated. This, of course, assumes the government holds a majority. Moreover, although there is no rule flowing from the Ponsonby procedure that requires Parliament to debate the proposed treaty action, and parliamentary time is limited, it may still be difficult for the Leader of the House to resist a debate on an important or controversial treaty that has been laid before Parliament. Ponsonby himself admitted as much in his original announcement when he stated:

> In the case of important treaties, the Government will, of course, take an opportunity of submitting them to the House for discussion within this [twenty-one day] period. But as the Government cannot take upon itself to decide what may be considered important or unimportant, if there is a formal demand for discussion forwarded through the usual channels from the Opposition or any other party, time will be found for the discussion of the treaty in question.[49]

It is also possible for members of both Houses to debate a proposed treaty action by initiating a private member's statement or by making use of the parliamentary questions procedure, both written and oral.

In my view, however, the most important benefit of the Ponsonby Rule has been the timely access provided to Parliament and the public to information about recent treaties and its encouragement of greater transparency in treaty-making, albeit that not every treaty so laid is expressly approved

---

46 U.K., H.C., *Parliamentary Debates*, 5th ser., vol. 171, col. 2005 (1 April 1924).
47 H.C. Factsheet No. 14, above note 32 at 3.
48 Lord Templeman, "Treaty-Making and the British Parliament" (1991) 67 Chi.-Kent L. Rev. 459 at 466.
49 U.K., H.C., *Parliamentary Debates*, 5th ser., vol. 171, cols. 2003-2004 (1 April 1924).

by Parliament. This in fact was Ponsonby's intention in 1924 when he warned: "Resolutions expressing parliamentary approval of every treaty before ratification would be a very cumbersome form of procedure and would burden the House with a lot of unnecessary business."[50] He went on to note: "The absence of disapproval may be accepted as sanction, and publicity and opportunity for discussion and criticism are the really material and valuable elements which henceforth will be introduced."[51] The weakness of the Ponsonby process, however, is the lack of an institutionalized mechanism to ensure that a treaty laid before Parliament is given adequate and effective scrutiny.

But the Ponsonby process has undergone improvements. Since January 1997, an additional practice has developed whereby an Explanatory Memorandum (EM) is laid before Parliament for every treaty laid under the Ponsonby Rule.[52] The EMs are drafted by the government department, which has the main policy interest in the particular treaty,[53] but are cleared through the relevant legal advisor at the FCO.[54] They are signed by a minister and are intended to provide information on the treaty's contents, the rationale for the government's support for ratification, and the government's view of the treaty's benefits and burdens. EMs are also made available to the public through the FCO's website[55] and as such, they place on public record the name of the minister with primary responsibility for a treaty, the anticipated financial implications of ratification, the means required to implement the treaty, and the outcome of any discussions that have taken

---

50 U.K., H.C., *Parliamentary Debates*, 5th ser., vol. 171, cols. 2004 (1 April 1924).

51 *Ibid.*

52 The government's undertaking to provide an EM is found in the form of a Written Answer published in U.K., H.C., *Parliamentary Debates*, vol. 287, WA 9430 (16 December 1996) and U.K., H.L., *Parliamentary Debates*, vol. 576, WA 101 (16 December 1996). It was made, following an unsuccessful attempt by Lord Lester of Herne Hill QC to subject the treaty-making power to parliamentary approval through the introduction of a private member's bill to this effect: U.K., H.L., *Parliamentary Debates*, vol. 569, col. 1530 (26 February 1996). The bill was withdrawn in exchange for the government's undertaking as acknowledged in the FCO Evidence, below note 58 at para. 25.

53 Only 55 percent of EMs are drafted by the FCO: FCO Evidence, below note 58 at para. 30. This is why the FCO has prepared "Guidelines on Explanatory Memoranda for Treaties" to assist other government departments.

54 *Treaties and MOUs*, above note 21 at 9.

55 See online: www.fco.gov.uk/treaty.

place within and outside government.[56] They also provide information on the content of any reservations or declarations.

Since November 2000, the FCO has also ensured that a copy of each treaty laid under the Ponsonby Rule is also sent to the relevant departmental select committee,[57] bolstering the ability of the parliamentary committee system to initiate an inquiry by alerting them to the existence of a new treaty action under consideration. Such inquiries can involve members of the civil service, academy, and non-governmental community, as well as the general public, through a process of written submissions and witness testimony, and their utility has led to calls within the UK for the establishment of a dedicated treaty scrutiny committee. The Royal Commission on the Reform of the House of Lords reported favourably on this proposal in early 2000,[58] as did the House of Commons Procedure Committee in mid-2000,[59] after receiving a request from the Defence Committee to inquire into what some view as Parliament's "unsatisfactory role" in treaty-making.[60] In 2004 Parliament's Joint Committee on Human Rights added its voice to the call for greater treaty scrutiny, viewing "the lack of effective parliamentary scrutiny [as] particularly pressing in relation to human rights treaties."[61] To date, the British government has resisted the call for a treaty committee; however, nothing bars an existing committee from undertaking a treaty enquiry, with the Joint Committee on Human Rights showing how this may be done.[62]

---

56   See generally *Treaties and MOUs*, above note 21 at 9–11, and the sample EM at 12–14.

57   "The Ponsonby Rule," above note 32.

58   The Royal Commission recommended that the Liaison Committee (the body responsible for coordinating committee activity in the House) should consider establishing such a committee since it was "exactly the mechanism we believe is required to carry out the technical scrutiny of such treaties": *A House for the Future* (Cm. 4534) (January 2000) at paras. 8.37–8.42. The submissions in favour of a treaty scrutiny committee and the FCO Evidence in reply can be found in the appendices to this report.

59   U.K., H.C., Select Committee on Procedure, *Second Report: Parliamentary Scrutiny of Treaties*, HC 210, Session 1999-2000 (26 July 2000). The response can be found in U.K., H.C., Select Committee on Procedure, *Second Special Report: Government's Response to the Second Report of the Committee: Parliamentary Scrutiny of Treaties*, HC 990, Session 1999-2000 (22 November 2000).

60   U.K., H.C., Select Committee on Defence, *Third Report: NATO Enlargement*, HC 469, Session 1997-1998 (2 April 1998) at paras. 103–6.

61   U.K., Joint Committee on Human Rights, *Protocol No. 14 to the European Convention on Human Rights*, HL Paper 8/HC 106, Session 2004-05 (1 December 2004) at 6.

62   See U.K., Joint Committee on Human Rights, *The UN Convention on the Rights of the Child*, HL Paper 117/HC 81, Session 2002-03 (9 June 2003); U.K., Joint Committee on

D. THE AUSTRALIAN CONTRIBUTION TO AN IMPROVED TREATY-MAKING PROCESS

Like the UK, Australia has also eschewed a strict separation of powers in treaty-making, allowing for some form of parliamentary scrutiny and even a period of parliamentary approval. According to one study, the Commonwealth government sought Parliament's approval for fifty-five treaties of significance prior to ratification from 1919 to 1963.[63] Then in 1961, at the behest of Prime Minister Robert Menzies, a practice of scrutiny began, whereby all treaties were tabled in Parliament for a period of time prior to ratification.[64] In the 1970s, however, this practice gradually fell into disuse, replaced by a practice of tabling batches of treaties at six-month intervals, usually after the executive had given its consent to be bound, thus leaving no room for effective parliamentary scrutiny.[65]

In 1996, however, Australia reformed its treaty-making process through the creation of a designated parliamentary committee to which all future treaty actions must be sent before they become binding legal obligations. Known as the Joint Standing Committee on Treaties (or JSCOT), the story of its creation begins in December 1994 when a request was made to the Senate Legal and Constitutional References Committee to undertake a review of the treaty-making power. The results of this review were published in November 1995, in the form of an extensive report entitled *Trick or Treaty? Commonwealth Power to Make and Implement Treaties,*[66] which recommended improved access to treaty information, an enhanced role for

---

Human Rights, *The International Covenant on Social, Economic and Cultural Rights,* HL Paper 183/HC 1188, Session 2003-04 (20 October 2004); U.K., Joint Committee on Human Rights, *The Convention on the Elimination of Racial Discrimination,* HL Paper 88/HC 471, Session 2004-05 (16 March 2005) and U.K., Joint Committee on Human Rights, *Review of International Human Rights Instruments,* HL Paper 99/HC 264, Session 2004-05 (23 March 2005).

63 Günther Doeker, *The Treaty-Making Power in the Commonwealth of Australia* (The Hague: Martinus Nijhoff, 1966) at 138 and 257–61.

64 Anne Twomey, "International Law and the Executive" in Brian R. Opeskin & Donald R. Rothwell, eds., *International Law and Australian Federalism* (Melbourne: Melbourne University Press, 1977) at 87.

65 *Ibid.* See also Daryl Williams, "Establishing an Australian Parliamentary Treaties Committee" (1995) Public L. Rev. 275 at 278–79.

66 Online: www.aph.gov.au/senate/committee/legcon_ctte/completed_inquiries/pre1996/treaty/report/index.htm.

Parliament through the creation of a treaty committee,[67] and greater consultation with industry, civil society, and state governments. The report received a favourable response, including from the coalition government that came to power after the March 1996 election,[68] and on 2 May 1996, the minister for foreign affairs and the attorney-general made a statement to Parliament introducing reforms that would, in their words, "overcome what this Government considers to have been a democratic deficit in the way treaty-making has been carried out in the past."[69]

Under the 1996 reforms, all proposed treaty actions must, according to administrative practice rather than legislation, be tabled in Parliament at least fifteen sitting days before binding action is taken, although there is some flexibility when circumstances require a shorter or longer time period.[70] Each treaty is tabled with a National Interest Analysis (NIA), a public document prepared by the responsible line agency in consultation with the Department of Foreign Affairs and Trade (DFAT) that sets out the reasons for the proposed treaty action, its obligations and costs, and documents the consultation that has taken place.[71] The tabled treaty (and NIA) is then sent for scrutiny to JSCOT, a large all-party committee supported by a small secretariat. JSCOT is empowered to inquire into and report upon any treaty matter, whether bilateral or multilateral, and including treaties in the process of being negotiated as well as those that have already been concluded. It can accomplish this mandate through several means, including the holding of public hearings across Australia and the review of submissions from parliamentarians, non-governmental organizations, academics and industry groups, as well as individual citizens. At the completion of its inquiry,

---

67 The proposal to create a Standing Committee on Treaties was of long-standing, having been introduced in 1983 by Senator Brian Harradine (Independent) and then reintroduced in subsequent sessions: Twomey, above note 64 at 88; I. A. Shearer, "International Legal Notes" (1995) 69 Aust. L.J. 404 at 406, n12.

68 In part because the report was a reflection of the government's own policies: see Daryl Williams, "Australia's Treaty-Making Processes: The Coalition's Reform Proposals" in Philip Alston & Madelaine Chiam, eds., *Treaty-Making and Australia: Globalisation versus Sovereignty* (Sydney: Federation Press, 1995) at 192.

69 *Joint Statement by the Minister for Foreign Affairs, Alexander Downer MP, and the Attorney-General, Daryl Williams AM QC MP* (2 May 1996), online: www.dfat.gov.au/media/releases/foreign/1996/fa29.html.

70 Special arrangements can be made if a treaty is sensitive or requires urgent and immediate implementation.

71 The National Interest Analyses can be found online: www.austlii.edu.au/au/other/dfat/nia.

JSCOT prepares a report for Parliament containing its advice on whether the treaty should bind Australia and on any other issues that emerged during the review process. These reports, as well as the treaty text, the NIA, the hearing transcripts, and even the submissions received by JSCOT, are all made available to the public (and the world) through the Committee's website, thereby serving as a useful resource on a treaty's contents and consequences.[72] To bolster these reforms, Australia also created an online treaty database, providing free public access to treaty texts, their ratification records, and NIAs, as well as information on multilateral treaties under negotiation, consideration, or review by the Australian government.[73]

The reformed treaty-making process has now been in place for nine years, resulting in the examination of more than 100 treaties, the preparation of more than 60 reports,[74] and the publication of more than 30 Government Responses.[75] While some treaties so examined have been relatively bland, others have prompted substantial numbers of submissions and the holding of public hearings across Australia,[76] suggesting that, if nothing else, JSCOT has enhanced the public's awareness of treaty law. While commentators in Australia have criticized JSCOT for serving as a "tool for political management"[77] and a procedural mask where more substantive changes are needed to improve executive accountability,[78] those from abroad envy the sheer volume of treaty-making information made public through the JSCOT process, albeit that this volume can be overwhelming, absent the dedicated efforts of those within and outside Parliament interested in treaty scrutiny.

The Australian government, as one might expect, has spoken positively about the JSCOT process, concluding in a 1999 review that the typical fif-

---

72 See online: www.aph.gov.au/house/committee/jsct/index.htm.

73 The Australian Treaties Database is available online: www.info.dfat.gov.au/treaties. DFAT also supports the Australian Treaties Library maintained by the Australasian Legal Information Institute (AUSTLII) online: www.austlii.edu.au/au/other/dfat/.

74 The reports are available online: www.aph.gov.au/house/committee/jsct/report.htm.

75 These are also made available via the JSCOT website.

76 See, for example, JSCOT, *Report 61: Australia-United States Free Trade Agreement* (23 June 2004).

77 See Ann Capling & Kim Richard Nossal, "Parliament and the Democratization of Foreign Policy: The Case of Australia's Joint Standing Committee on Treaties" (2003) 36:4 Can. J. Pol. Sci. 835.

78 See Madelaine Chiam, "Evaluating Australia's Treaty-Making Process" (2004) 15 Pub. L. Rev. 265 and Hilary Charlesworth *et al.*, "Deep Anxieties: Australia and the International Legal Order" (2003) 25 Sydney L. Rev. 423 at 441–44.

teen-sitting-day period (roughly equivalent to five weeks) did not pose an obstacle to Australia's ability to undertake timely treaty action.[79] Record levels of submissions to JSCOT have, however, prompted the government to extend the scrutiny period to twenty sitting days (roughly equivalent to eight weeks) for treaties identified as being of major political, economic, or social significance and likely to attract considerable public interest and debate.[80] The government's review also concluded that the sufficiency of the scrutiny process alleviated any need for a rule requiring the parliamentary approval of treaties for ratification,[81] a proposal which was previously mooted during the deliberations of the 1988 Constitutional Commission[82] and in a private member's bill.[83] A similar proposal was also made in New Zealand by way of a private member's bill, with both proposals attracting objections on separation of powers grounds,[84] even though, as discussed later in this chapter, several countries that follow the British legal tradition already require parliamentary approval for treaty ratification.

As for the content of the scrutiny, JSCOT has examined mostly new treaty actions, although the broad interpretation it has taken of its mandate

79 Commonwealth of Australia, Attorney-General's Department. *Review of the Treaty-Making Process* (August 1999), online: law.gov.au/agd/Attorney-General/Treaty-Making%20Process.htm. See further, Glen Cranwell, "The Treaty-Making Process in Australia: A Report Card on Recent Reforms" [2001] Aust. Int'l L.J. 177.

80 Treaties are now classified as either Category A (requiring fifteen sitting days) or Category B (requiring twenty sitting days). Many bilateral treaties fall within Category A, especially "template" treaties, while Category B is for multilateral treaties and significant "one-off" bilateral treaties such as the Timor Sea Treaty.

81 1999 *Review*, above note 79 at paras. 5.1–5.8.

82 Two members of the Commission supported the view that there should be a statutory requirement to require the ratification of treaties to be conditional on either the approval of both Houses of Parliament or the disallowance by either House within a specified period: *Final Report of the Constitutional Commission*, vol. II (Canberra: Australian Government Publishing Service, 1988) at 745–46 (Professor Leslie Zines) and 749 (Sir Rupert Hamer).

83 Senator Vicki Bourne of the Australian Democrats introduced a Bill in June 1994, and again in May 1995, that would have required the executive to secure Parliament's approval to ratify a treaty. See further, Vicki Bourne, "The Implications of Requiring Parliamentary Approval of Treaties" in Alston & Chiam, *Treaty-Making and Australia*, above note 68 at 196–203.

84 See further, Mai Chen, "A Constitutional Revolution? The Role of the New Zealand Parliament in Treaty-Making" (2001) 19 N.Z.U.L. Rev. 448 and Treasa Dunworth, "International Treaty Examination: The Saga Continues" [2002] N.Z. L. Rev. 255–61. See also Allan Bracegirdle, "Domestic Procedures for International Treaty Actions: Description of New Zealand Procedures" (2003) 14 Pub. L. Rev. 28.

has allowed the examination of one treaty well after its ratification, in essence providing an audit of its implementation,[85] and the examination of another during its negotiation.[86] Some of its reports cover several treaties at once, while others focus solely on a treaty of particular importance, such as the *Rome Statute for the International Criminal Court*[87] or the Kyoto Protocol.[88] JSCOT has also examined proposed implementation legislation,[89] as well as the treaty-based subject matter of extradition law,[90] and has demonstrated on occasion that it has the powerful tool of initiative and does not work solely at the behest of executive action.

JSCOT usually concludes its review with a positive recommendation to the executive to take binding treaty action. As with other parliamentary committees, there can be dissenting reports, usually by Opposition members, but on a few very rare occasions, JSCOT has made a unanimous recommendation against the ratification of a proposed treaty action.[91] The former Attorney-General Daryl Williams has acknowledged that the unanimous conclusions of a bi-partisan committee have an impact.[92] But JSCOT's greater benefit is likely found in its more frequent criticism of the government for inadequate NIAs and insufficient consultation, and its

---

85 JSCOT, *Report 17: United Nations Convention on the Rights of the Child* (28 August 1998). This treaty has attracted considerable controversy in Australia since ratification, not least because of its role in asylum cases such as *Teoh*, above note 12. The JSCOT inquiry provided an opportunity for many Australians to be heard, as evidenced by the over 700 letters and submissions received, although some contributors believed (erroneously) that the inquiry's purpose was to facilitate Australia's withdrawal from the treaty. See further, Melinda Jones, "Myths and Facts concerning the Convention on the Rights of the Child in Australia" (1999) 5(2) A.J.H.R. 126.

86 JSCOT, *Report 14: Multilateral Agreement on Investment: Interim Report* (1 June 1998) and JSCOT, *Report 18: Multilateral Agreement on Investment: Final Report* (23 March 1999).

87 JSCOT, *Report 45: The Statute of the International Criminal Court* (14 May 2002).

88 JSCOT, *Report 38: The Kyoto Protocol – Discussion Paper* (4 April 2001).

89 JSCOT, *Report 16: OECD Convention on Combating Bribery and Draft Implementing Legislation* (2 July 1998).

90 JSCOT, *Report 40: Extradition – A Review of Australia's Law and Policy* (6 August 2001). This report has since been discussed in some detail by the Federal Court in *Hellenic Republic v. Tzatzimakis*, [2002] F.C.A. 340 at paras. 73–82 and briefly by the High Court in *Pasini v. United Mexican States*, [2002] H.C.A. 3 at para. 91.

91 JSCOT, *Report 11* (24 November 1997) concerning a proposed cooperation agreement with Kazakhstan. JSCOT's unanimous support for the International Criminal Court in *Report 45*, above note 87, is also interesting, given the division present within the governing Coalition, although the support was given with strong qualifications.

92 Williams, above note 65 at 283.

ability to make a wealth of treaty information available for public scrutiny, including departmental information. Moreover, its activities do not stop other parliamentary committees from examining a treaty action should they so desire, or be so prompted by the interest in treaties generated by the JSCOT process.

The 1996 reforms also attempted to address the "federal democratic deficit" in treaty-making, building on past attempts by the Commonwealth and the states themselves. An early example can be found in Queensland, which established a Treaties Commission from 1974 to 1977 to advise on the benefit to Queensland of existing treaties.[93] This was followed by a new era of "cooperative federalism" during the tenure of the Fraser government, as reflected in an agreement on federal–state cooperation reached with the premiers in 1977,[94] which would later evolve into an agreed statement of "Principles and Procedures for Commonwealth-State Consultation on Treaties," to be adopted by the Council of Australian Governments (COAG) in 1992[95] and then revised in 1996.[96] The goal of this statement is to ensure that the Commonwealth takes into account state views, although it is expressly confirmed that the lack of state consent does not bar treaty ratification.[97] The statement further provides for possible state representation at treaty negotiations and for the sharing of information, including departmental information through the creation of a Standing Committee on Treaties (SCOT) comprised of senior officials.[98] The revised statement also

---

93 *Treaties Commission Act 1974* (Qld.). The Act was repealed by the *Statute Law (Miscellaneous Provisions) Act 1993* (Qld.), with a note indicating that the Commission had not functioned since 1977.

94 The details of which are found in Henry Burmester, "The Australian States and Participation in the Foreign Policy Process" (1978) 9 Fed. L. Rev. 257 at 280–82.

95 COAG is the peak intergovernmental forum in Australia, comprising the prime minister, state premiers, territory chief ministers and the president of the Australian Local Government Association. It has been in existence since 1992. Further details can be obtained from its website online: www.coag.gov.au.

96 The current text is available online: www.coag.gov.au/meetings/140696/attachment_c.htm [*Principles and Procedures*].

97 *Ibid.* at para. 3.1.

98 See Williams, "Treaty-Making," above note 68 at 187–89; Cheryl Saunders, "Articles of Faith or Lucky Breaks? The Constitutional Law of International Agreements in Australia" (1995) 17 Sydney L. Rev. 150 at 162–63. Of course, some subject areas have their own mechanisms for encouraging intergovernmental consultation, with the 1992 Intergovernmental Agreement on the Environment being one example: Bill Campbell, "The Implementation of Treaties in Australia" in Opeskin & Rothwell, *International Law*, above note 64 at 149.

provides for state and territorial consultation on the development of relevant NIAs,[99] providing an opening for JSCOT, should it be inclined, to examine the NIA with a view to ensuring that such consultation has taken place.

The 1996 reforms also promised to bring into effect the idea of a "Treaties Council,"[100] bringing together the prime minister, state premiers, and chief ministers for a dedicated discussion of treaties of particular sensitivity or importance.[101] The commitment to this reform, however, is questionable given the government's own admission in its 1999 *Review of the Treaty-Making Process* that the council had met only once from 1996 to 1999, at its inaugural meeting of 1997. This is contrary to the promise to meet at least once a year.[102] No further details have been provided on the council's website of meetings since, although its members have clearly met as part of the COAG process and may have discussed treaties at this time, but then only as part of a broader intergovernmental agenda.

However, state Parliaments, with Victoria in the lead, still push for a greater role in the negotiation, scrutiny, and sometimes approval of treaties of significance to states. In 1997, the Federal-State Relations Committee (FSRC) of the Victorian Parliament recommended that Victoria establish its own treaty review committee,[103] viewing treaty-making as a subject "for which the States should have an enhanced role for the benefit of the Federation."[104] The FSRC also favoured the tabling of all treaty information in the Victorian Parliament and wanted the Commonwealth government to extend the scrutiny period so as to provide time for state consideration of future treaties. But while the Victorian government accepted the need to table treaties in the Victorian Parliament, it refused to establish a treaty committee on resource grounds, leaving the FSRC to keep an eye on treaties itself until it was disbanded in 2001.

---

99   *Principles and Procedures*, above note 96 at para. 4.2. See also Daryl Williams, "Treaties and the Parliamentary Process" (1996) 7 Pub. L. Rev. 199 at 201.

100 This idea was supported by the Australian Constitutional Convention of 1985, the Constitutional Commission of 1988, and the Senate References Committee and the Leader's Forum in 1995.

101 See Treaties Council, Council of Australian Governments www.coag.gov.au/treaties_council.htm.

102 *Principles and Procedures*, above note 96 at paras. 5.1–5.3.

103 Parliament of Victoria, Federal-State Relations Committee, *International Treaty-Making and the Role of the States* (1997) especially c. 5.

104 Federal-State Relations Committee, "Terms of Reference," *Victorian Government Gazette*, G 26, 4 July 1996, 1706–7.

In 1999 JSCOT recognized the state interest in treaty-making by con-
vening a meeting to discuss the role for "Parliaments" in treaty-making.[105]
Two proposals appeared to garner the most support: the institution of
procedures to ensure the presentation of treaty information by state executives to state Parliaments, and the creation of state and territory parliamentary treaties committees. But while some states, such as Western
Australia, support parliamentary scrutiny at the state level,[106] others, such
as Queensland, are against a Queensland treaty committee on grounds
of duplication. The Queensland premier has, however, been convinced to
periodically table in the state Parliament a schedule of treaties under negotiation, as well as all JSCOT notices regarding proposed treaty actions.[107]
It is then up to state parliamentarians, having been notified, to stimulate
a debate or inquiry about a proposed treaty. Queensland has also endorsed
the suggestion made by Professor Cheryl Saunders to require the state's
intergovernmental staff to report on treaty matters annually to a state parliamentary committee.[108]

E.   TREATY-MAKING AND THE PARLIAMENT OF CANADA

As in the UK and Australia, the power to make treaties resides in Canada
with the executive branch that represents the state abroad.[109] While claims
have been made that Canada's provinces also possess a treaty-making ca-

---

105 See JSCOT, Parliament of Australia, *Report 24: A Seminar on the Role of Parliaments in
Treaty-Making* (1999).

106 Parliament of Western Australia, Standing Committee on Constitutional Affairs,
Report 38: Report in relation to a Seminar on the Role of Parliaments in Treaty-Making
(1999).

107 Parliament of Queensland, Legal, Constitutional and Administrative Review Committee, *Report 22: The Role of the Queensland Parliament in Treaty-Making* (2000). The
tabling of the treaty text was deemed unnecessary given the existence of the Australian
Treaties Database. So far, the new process has been favourably received: Parliament of
Queensland, Legal, Constitutional and Administrative Review Committee, *Report 39:
The Role of the Queensland Parliament in Treaty-Making—Review of Tabling Procedure*
(2003).

108 Parliament of Queensland, Legal, Constitutional and Administrative Review Committee, *Report 22, ibid.* at 9.

109 A.E. Gotlieb, *Canadian Treaty-Making* (Toronto: Butterworths, 1968) at 27; Maurice
Copithorne, "Canada" in Monroe Leigh *et al.*, eds., *National Treaty Law and Practice*,
vol. 3 (Washington, DC: American Society of International Law, 2003) at 1. See also Peter W. Hogg, *Constitutional Law of Canada*, 4th ed. (Scarborough, ON: Carswell, 1997)
at §11.2.

pacity,[110] prompting the province of Quebec to enter into many treaty-like arrangements,[111] these claims have never been accepted by Ottawa[112] and are not borne out by Canadian practice.[113] Moreover, with the possible exception of France,[114] no state in the international community recognizes any competence on the part of Canada's provinces to conclude treaties.

Canada's treaty-making responsibility, much like that of the other dominions, emerged gradually. Although Confederation in 1867 marked the beginning of Canada's domestic self-governance, it was not envisaged at the time that Canada would make treaties independently from Britain. Britain retained the prerogative power to make treaties for the empire as a whole,[115] and so Canada's Constitution of 1867 contained no provision on treaty-making.[116] However, as the countries within the empire gradually acquired their full independence, so did they acquire their portion of the treaty-making power once held by the British executive, with the delegation of the Canadian portion said to be confirmed by the *Letters Patent Constituting the Office of the Governor General of Canada* of 1947.[117]

---

110 Such claims were particularly prevalent in the 1960s, bolstering claims then made by the Quebec government that led to the creation of a Quebec department of intergovernmental affairs in 1967. Quebec, however, is not the only province with a department dedicated to international affairs. Ontario, Alberta, and British Columbia are also active "internationalists," although all Canadian provinces at one time or another have made agreements with foreign states to serve their interests. See further, Gibran van Ert, "The Legal Character of Provincial Agreements with Foreign Governments" (2001) 42 C. de D. 1093.

111 It is estimated that 300 of the 550 arrangements entered into since 1967 remain in force, online: www.mri.gouv.qc.ca/en/action_internationale/ententes.

112 In 1968, the then Secretary of State for External Affairs, Paul Martin Sr., issued a background paper on *Federalism and International Relations* (Ottawa: Queen's Printer, 1968), disputing and opposing all claims to a provincial treaty-making capacity.

113 Hogg, *Constitutional Law*, above note 109 at §11.2 and §11.6; Currie, *Public International Law*, above note 25 at 208–10.

114 See Gibran van Ert, *Using International Law in Canadian Courts* (The Hague: Kluwer Law International, 2002) at 87, n163.

115 See further, Hogg, *Constitutional Law*, above note 109 at §11.2. See also Gotlieb, *Canadian Treaty-Making*, above note 109 at 6–10.

116 The closest provision on point is s. 132 of the *Constitution Act, 1867* which concerns a federal power to perform what are termed "Empire treaties"; however, this provision does not extend to treaties entered into by an independent Canada (*Labour Conventions*, above note 26 at 350) and is now viewed as obsolete.

117 Reproduced in R.S.C. 1985, App. II, No. 31. Clause 2 authorizes the Governor General "to exercise all powers and authorities lawfully belonging to [the King] in respect of Canada."

The federal government appears to guard its treaty-making power jealously, allowing no formal role for the Parliament of Canada, even though this was not always the case. From 1926 to 1966, it was the practice in Canada for all important treaties to be submitted to Parliament for approval prior to ratification; a practice initiated by Prime Minister William Lyon Mackenzie King by way of a two-part motion, the second part of which read: "This House … considers further that before His Majesty's Canadian ministers advise ratification of a treaty or convention affecting Canada, or signify acceptance of any treaty, convention or agreement involving military or economic sanctions, the approval of the Parliament of Canada should be secured."[118] While Mackenzie King acknowledged that treaty ratification was an executive act, he also stated, "Parliament should feel assured in regard to all these great obligations of an international character which involve military and economic sanctions that a government should not have the opportunity of binding Parliament in advance of its own knowledge to the obligations incurred thereby."[119] The House adopted the motion, and for the next forty years, according to Allan Gotlieb's authoritative[120] but now dated account in *Canadian Treaty-Making*, a practice developed of submitting to Parliament all treaties involving: 1) military or economic sanctions; 2) large expenditures of public funds or important financial or economic implications; 3) political considerations of a far-reaching character; and 4) obligations the performance of which will affect private rights in Canada.[121] Since the initiation of this practice took place in the same year that Canada achieved its autonomy from Britain with respect to the exercise of the treaty-making power,[122] the practice can be rightly described as being part of the *Canadian* treaty-making process since the beginning.

118 *House of Commons Debates* (21 June 1926) at 4758–59. The debate on the motion is found at 4758–800. See further, Gotlieb, *Canadian Treaty-Making*, above note 109 at 15–16.
119 *House of Commons Debates* (21 June 1926) at 4762.
120 Gotlieb was, at the time of authorship, the Assistant Under-Secretary of State for External Affairs and Legal Advisor to the Department. He would later serve as Under-Secretary of State for External Affairs (1977–81) and Ambassador of Canada to the United States (1981–89).
121 Gotlieb, *Canadian Treaty-Making*, above note 109 at 16–17.
122 The Balfour Declaration was issued at the Imperial Conference of 1926 and confirmed that no autonomous dominion could be bound by commitments incurred by the Imperial government without its consent. The question of treaty-making was specifically addressed, with the conference confirming that each dominion government had the power to negotiate, sign and ratify treaties on its own behalf. See further, Maurice

This practice, however, applied to only a small proportion of all the treaties entered into by Canada for the above time period since many of Canada's treaties were concluded by way of an exchange of notes or letters and as such, were not subject to ratification.[123] Nevertheless, for those treaties that were submitted, the practice did give Parliament a voice in relation to some treaties of significance, such as the *Canada–US Automotive Products Agreement* of 1966 (the Auto Pact),[124] and the pre-ratification timing was crucial because it meant that Parliament had a say before Canada became bound under international law. The practice, however, waned in the late-1960s, coinciding with the debate then taking place about Canada's role in the North American Aerospace Defence Command (NORAD),[125] and by 1974, it was the view of Canada's Department of External Affairs that it was up to the government of the day as to whether parliamentary approval would be sought for a proposed treaty action.[126] This continues to be the department's view[127] and as time has passed, the practice of submitting treaties to Parliament for approval has been either forgotten or aban-

---

Ollivier, ed., *The Colonial and Imperial Conferences from 1887 to 1937*, vol. 3 (Ottawa: Queen's Printer, 1954) at 150–55.

123 Gotlieb, *Canadian Treaty-Making*, above note 109 at 18. See also Anne Marie Jacomy-Millette, *Treaty Law in Canada* (Ottawa: University of Ottawa Press, 1975) at paras. 32 and 44.

124 The agreement was approved by the House of Commons on 6 May 1966 and by the Senate on 30 June 1966.

125 The 1958 Canada–US treaty establishing NORAD is subject to renewal every five years. During the 1960s, the threat of intercontinental ballistic missiles prompted the expansion of NORAD's mandate from air to aerospace defence and the creation of an extensive defence network. When questioned in Parliament about such changes, Prime Minister Pearson replied that "if such a situation developed, requiring such an important change in Canadian defence policy, ... and if Parliament was sitting, Parliament would be consulted first": *House of Commons Debates* (25 September 1967) at 2428. The NORAD agreement was renewed in 1968 during Parliament's dissolution.

126 See the excerpt from a memorandum of 11 June 1974 by the Department's Bureau of Legal Affairs reprinted in (1975) 13 Can. Y.B. Int'l Law at 366–67.

127 See the excerpts from department memoranda reprinted in (1982) 20 Can. Y.B. Int'l Law at 289–92, (1986) 24 Can. Y.B. Int'l L. at 397–402, and (2002) 40 Can. Y.B. Int'l Law at 490–92.

doned,[128] prompting the introduction of a series of private members' bills since 1999 to encourage, among other things, its reinstatement.[129] The continued demise of a parliamentary role in the making of important treaties was the Liberal government's position, as illustrated by the announcement in 2004 that there would be no parliamentary role in the conclusion of a Canada–US treaty on missile defence.[130] But according to Professor Maurice Copithorne, a former legal advisor to the Department of Foreign Affairs, "the role of Parliament as a body with which the executive consults is evolving,"[131] noting that "consultations on Canada's most important treaties now take place regularly prior to the Government taking binding action."[132] Copithorne points to the work of the House of Commons Standing Committee on Foreign Affairs and International Trade (SCFAIT),[133] and, in particular, to its examination of the proposed *Multilateral Agreement on Investment* in 1997[134] and the *Canada–US Pre-*

128 According to research undertaken by Professor Turp, then serving as a Bloc Québécois Member of Parliament, the practice stopped in the late 1960s: Daniel Turp, "Un nouveau défi démocratique: l'accentuation du rôle du parlement dans la conclusion et la mise en oeuvre des traités internationaux" [1999] CCIL Proc. at 118. As noted by both Turp (at 119) and van Ert, *Using International Law*, above note 114 at 68–69, commentary suggesting that the practice continues is suspect because of a reliance on the outdated texts of Gotlieb (above note 109) and Jacomy-Millette (above note 123).

129 Five bills were introduced by Professor Turp in 1999: *House of Commons Debates* (14 October 1999) at 113. An earlier bill requiring the tabling of treaties was introduced by Turp that spring: *House of Commons Debates* (3 May 1999) at 14601. Of the five October bills, only one proceeded to second reading, garnering support from all but the governing Liberal Party: *House of Commons Debates* (1 December 1999) at 2018–26, *House of Commons Debates* (13 April 2000) at 6127–31, and *House of Commons Debates* (8 June 2000) at 7725–31. It was later defeated by a vote of 110–151: *House of Commons Debates* (13 June 2000) at 7956–57. Similar bills were later reintroduced in the following session by Francine Lalonde, MP, the Bloc Québécois critic for foreign affairs: *House of Commons Debates* (28 March 2001) at 2440–41. The latest version was introduced as Bill C-260 by Jean-Yves Roy, MP, of the Bloc Québécois on 3 November 2004.

130 Jeff Sallot, "Missile Treaty Up to Cabinet, Graham Says" *Globe and Mail* (27 September 2004) A5.

131 Copithorne, "Canada," above note 109 at 5.

132 *Ibid.*

133 The Committee has recently adopted the acronym "FAAE" rather than "FAIT."

134 *Canada and the Multilateral Agreement on Investment: Third Report of the Standing Committee on Foreign Affairs and International Trade: First Report of the Sub-Committee on International Trade, Trade Disputes and Investment* (December 1997).

clearance Agreement in 1999,[135] as well as the practice of passing enabling legislation prior to ratifying a treaty.[136] But while there are instances where SCFAIT has examined a treaty that is in the process of being negotiated,[137] albeit treaties already in the public eye, a review of the record for the past eight years suggests that when it comes to treaty scrutiny, the usual role for SCFAIT is to review the legislation implementing a treaty, rather than a future treaty action. Moreover, the broad mandates of SCFAIT and other standing committees prompt a hit-and-miss record with respect to treaty scrutiny, given the many other matters on the agenda.[138] As for the passage of enabling legislation prior to ratification, Copithorne admits that there are "rare occasions" when this is not done, but the central point is that such occasions can occur, and have occurred—most recently with the ratification of the Kyoto Protocol. The principled rebuttal, however, to Copithorne's arguments is that Parliament is more than a body for "consultation" and as the ultimate lawmaker in a Westminster democracy, Parliament should have the opportunity to review all treaties before their ratification, whether or not enabling legislation will be required.

Parliament (and through Parliament, the public) is also not kept as well informed as it once was about the treaty-making activities of the executive branch. From its creation in 1909 until 1995, the Department of External Affairs (as it was then called) was required by statute to report annually to Parliament about its activities,[139] and from 1915 on,[140] these reports also contained an account of Canada's treaty-making activities, including a useful listing of all agreements concluded during the particular year

---

135 *Bill S-22, An Act authorizing the United States to preclear travellers and goods in Canada for entry into the United States for the purposes of customs, immigration, public health, food inspection and plant and animal health; Eighth Report of the Standing Committee on Foreign Affairs and International Trade* (May 1999).

136 Copithorne, "Canada," above note 109 at 5.

137 The only example in the past eight years, apart from the Multilateral Agreement on Investment, concerns the proposed Free Trade Area of the Americas (FTAA): *The Free Trade Area of the Americas: Towards a Hemispheric Agreement in the Canadian Interest: First Report of the Standing Committee on Foreign Affairs and International Trade: First Report of the Sub-Committee on International Trade, Trade Disputes and Investment* (October 1999).

138 The SCFAIT has issued 61 reports in the past eight years and only eight of those 61 reports concern treaties.

139 *An Act to create a Department of External Affairs* (U.K.), 8-9 Edw. VII, c. 13, s. 5, later amended to become s. 14.

140 Gotlieb, *Canadian Treaty-Making*, above note 109 at 7. The National Library of Canada record indicates that the annual reports ceased after the 1991/1992 issue.

under review.[141] But in 1995, during the passage of legislation to change the department's name and expand its mandate, the annual reporting requirement was repealed.[142] No explanation was read into the parliamentary record, and nor did any Member of Parliament ask for the reason for the repeal.[143] As a result, the Department of Foreign Affairs is no longer obliged to produce an annual public record of its treaty-making activities,[144] and while its ministers may from time to time choose to provide Parliament with a list of the treaties concluded over a specified time period, there remains no legal rule regularizing the timely provision of such information to Parliament. Only on 19 April 2005 was a political commitment made by the then Liberal government to table in Parliament "annual foreign policy updates" to "increase accountability on international affairs."[145]

It was also "the invariable practice in Canada," at least as of 1968 when Gotlieb wrote these words: "to table in Parliament all agreements, including exchanges of notes."[146] Through tabling, Parliament was kept informed of treaty obligations assumed on Canada's behalf by the federal executive, albeit after these obligations became binding under international law. But as with the practice of submitting treaties for parliamentary approval, the practice of tabling treaties has also suffered from decline and had in fact all but disappeared until criticism prompted then Foreign Minister Lloyd

---

141   *Ibid.* at 66.

142   Clause 10 of Bill C-47, *An Act to amend the Department of External Affairs Act and to make related amendments to other Acts*, which became s. 10 of *An Act to amend the Department of External Affairs Act and to make related amendments to other Acts*, S.C. 1995, c. 5, simply states: "Section 14 of the Act and the heading before it are repealed." The annual reporting requirements imposed on the Department by specific Acts such as the *Access to Information Act*, R.S.C. 1985, c. A-1 and the *Export and Import Permits Act*, R.S.C. 1985, c. E-19, remain in place.

143   See *House of Commons Debates* (4 October 1994) at 6500–5 and (9 February 1995) at 9339–48, as well as Issue No. 14 of the *Minutes of Proceedings and Evidence of the Standing Committee on Foreign Affairs and International Trade* (14–15 December 1995).

144   An annual listing of Canadian treaty activity can be found in the *Canadian Yearbook of International Law*. While useful for the Yearbook's readers, this listing does not absolve the government of its responsibility to apprise Parliament and the general public of its law-making activities.

145   "Government of Canada Releases International Policy Statement," *News Release* No. 68 (19 April 2005), online: webapps.dfait-maeci.gc.ca/MinPub/Publication.asp?Language=E&publication_id=382440.

146   Gotlieb, *Canadian Treaty-Making*, above note 109 at 18, 66. According to Jacomy-Millette, however, tabling was "not an invariable rule": *Treaty Law in Canada*, above note 123 at para. 44.

Axworthy to table dozens of ratified treaties in 1999,[147] including treaties
that were required by law to be deposited in Parliament.[148] Tabling now
occurs on an ad hoc basis at the prerogative of the executive, but often
without even the most basic details, such as the treaty's name or a précis of
its subject matter, being read into the parliamentary record. The practice
of promptly publishing all treaty texts in the Canada Treaty Series has also
been in decline and the department no longer prepares a general guide to
treaty-making,[149] as done in Britain[150] and Australia.[151] Canada has, however, followed Australia and Britain in putting some of its treaties online to
enhance public access, but unfortunately, the Canadian database contains
no memoranda or other guidance.

As for the "federal democratic deficit," Canada, like Australia, is not
without past examples of federal–provincial cooperation in treaty-making
where the circumstances have justified the involvement of one or more
provinces. There are, however, no guarantees that the federal government
will consult with the provinces about a future treaty, nor is provincial involvement in the negotiation of a significant treaty guaranteed. As a result, Canada's treaty-making process has long been identified as worthy
of change, with past studies recommending either the provincial assign-
ment of the treaty implementation power to the federal Parliament[152] or the
ratification of treaties by both Houses of Parliament, with the Senate seen

147 Turp, "Un nouveau défi démocratique," above note 128 at 128; van Ert, *Using International Law*, above note 114 at 70. Treaties that entered into force for the years 1993 to
1997 were tabled on four occasions in 1999: *House of Commons Debates* (13 April 1994)
at 13715, (12 May 1999) at 15072, (9 June 1999) at 16098, and (10 June 1999) at 16149.
148 Section 7 of the *Extradition Act*, R.S.C. 1985, c. E-23, used to require all extradition
arrangements to be laid as soon as possible before both Houses of Parliament. On 8
January 1999, Foreign Minister Axworthy belatedly deposited seven extradition treaties. Such a breach will not occur again since the requirement has now been removed,
as evident by comparing the former section 7 to the new section 8 of the *Extradition
Act*, S.C. 1999, c. 18.
149 Copithorne, "Canada," above note 109 at 4.
150 *Treaties and MOUs*, above note 21.
151 *Signed, Sealed and Delivered: Treaties and Treaty-making: An Official's Handbook*, 5th ed.
(Canberra: Department of Foreign Affairs and Trade, 2004). Australia also publishes
a Treaty Information Kit for the general public, which is made available online: www.
austlii.edu.au/au/other/dfat/reports/infokit.html.
152 *Report of the Royal Commission on Dominion-Provincial Relations* (Rowell-Sirois Commission) (Ottawa: Queen's Printer, 1940), Book II at 48.

as representing the provinces' interests.[153] A constitutional amendment was also proposed in 1972 that would require the Canadian government to consult with the provinces on treaties dealing with matters of provincial responsibility;[154] a proposal since echoed in a 2004 report by an Alberta committee of government MLAs.[155]

The provinces themselves have also considered ways to improve the treaty-making process, with Quebec taking the boldest move in 2002 by enacting legislation to require the pre-ratification approval of the Quebec National Assembly for all important international commitments intended to be made by either the Quebec or Canadian government when the subject matter of the commitment falls within an area of Quebec's responsibility.[156] The goal of the legislation, according to the minister, is to democratize the treaty process by giving a voice to the elected representatives of the citizens of Quebec,[157] but it was also intended to address long-standing concerns that the language and cultural interests of Quebec may be threatened if the federal government acts on the international stage without prior pro-vincial agreement in areas of provincial competence.[158] The Quebec law requires prior provincial parliamentary approval for all treaties requiring the passage of implementing legislation, the imposition of a tax, or the ac-ceptance of an important financial obligation, as well as treaties concerned with human rights and international trade,[159] and any other treaty that the minister feels should be approved.[160] It can also apply to the denuncia-tion and termination of a treaty,[161] but does not apply to technical treaties and treaties affecting only matters within federal jurisdiction. All treaties,

---

153 *Second Report of the [Ontario] Advisory Committee on Confederation: The Federal-Provin-cial Distribution of Powers* (Toronto: Queen's Printer, 1979) at 44.

154 Canadian Parliament, Special Joint Committee of the Senate and of the House of Commons on the Constitution of Canada. *Final Report* (Chairs: Molgat and Mac-Guigan) (Ottawa: Queen's Printer, 1972) at 68–69.

155 *Report of the MLA Committee on Strengthening Alberta's Role in Confederation* (Govern-ment of Alberta, 2004) at 46, online: www.iir.gov.ab.ca/canadian_intergovernmen-tal_relations/documents/mla_committee_report_003.pdf.

156 *An Act respecting the Ministère des Relations internationales*, R.S.Q., c. M-25.1.1, s 22.4.

157 Québec, *Débats de l'Assemblée Nationale*, 20 March 2002 at 5247 (Minister Louise Beaudoin).

158 Québec, *Débats de l'Assemblée Nationale*, 22 March 2001 at 7–8 (Premier Bernard Landry).

159 *An Act respecting the Ministère des Relations internationales*, above note 156, s. 22.2.

160 *Ibid.*, s. 22.2(4).

161 *Ibid.*, s. 22.6.

however, are required to be tabled in the provincial Parliament, with the Quebec law also requiring an explanatory note on the treaty's content and consequences, as is the practice in Britain and Australia. Once tabled, the treaty can be the subject of a motion to either approve or reject, but not amend, provided at least ten days have passed since tabling to ensure time for access and reflection.[162] The minister has also suggested that in some cases, a parliamentary commission could be established to study the proposed treaty action and invite submissions from the public.[163]

The stark problem, however, with the Quebec initiative is that it does not bind the government of Canada. The government may *choose* to seek advance provincial agreement, just as it may choose to seek parliamentary approval, but is under no legal obligation to do so. Nor is the Canadian government bound by a resolution of disapproval from a provincial legislature. Nevertheless, as a demand to address the democratic deficit in Canadian treaty-making, the Quebec law represents a bold approach, adopted by a unanimous vote of an assembly comprised of federalists and separatists, presumably because the democratic ideal of a greater role for Parliaments cuts across the political spectrum.

F. THE PARLIAMENTARY APPROVAL MODEL AND THE SOUTH AFRICAN EXPERIENCE

Several jurisdictions go further than those discussed earlier in this chapter by requiring the express approval of Parliament before the ratification of a treaty. Of those with a British legal heritage and a common law legal system, the most oft-cited example is that of the United States, where there is a constitutional requirement to involve the Senate in the making of treaties,[164] even though most treaties are considered under US law to be "executive agreements" and as such need neither Senate (nor Congressional) approval.[165] Moreover, for most of its history, the US Senate held its treaty deliberations in secret as a reaction to the public criticism it received

162 *Ibid.*, s. 22.3.
163 Québec, *Débats de l'Assemblée Nationale*, 20 March 2002 at 5248.
164 Above note 6.
165 *Third Restatement*, above note 18 at §303 and Congressional Research Service, Library of Congress, *Treaties and Other International Agreements: The Role of the United States: A Study Prepared for the Committee on Foreign Relations, United States Senate*, S. Prt. 106-71 (January 2001).

for approving the Jay Treaty in 1795,[166] a practice that continued officially until 1929, although many previous treaty discussions were leaked to the press.[167] The United States has since bolstered the role for the legislature in treaty-making by requiring the texts of executive agreements to be transmitted to Congress as soon as possible,[168] and through the passage of legislation, or "framework statutes," specifically authorizing the executive branch to conclude international agreements in certain fields, such as foreign aid, agriculture, and trade.[169]

Ireland, similarly, has a constitutional requirement to involve one of the houses of the national Parliament in treaty-making. The Irish Constitution of 1937 provides that "every international agreement to which the State becomes a party shall be laid before Dáil Éireann,"[170] but further stipulates that "the State shall not be bound by any international agreement involving a charge upon public funds unless the terms of the agreement shall have been approved by the Dáil Éireann."[171] There is thus both a tabling requirement and an approval requirement in the Irish treaty-making process, although an exception is made to both requirements for "agreements or conventions of a technical and administrative character."[172]

In a search for more recent examples, one finds parliamentary treaty approval provisions on the statute books of Antigua and Barbuda (since 1987)[173] and in the Constitutions of Namibia (as of 1990)[174] and South Af-

166 The Jay Treaty was negotiated by Chief Justice John Jay in 1794 to address the issues outstanding between the US and Britain after the American Revolutionary War. So intense was the public outcry that Jay is said to have remarked that he could have travelled the length of the country by the light of bonfires burning his effigy.
167 US Senate, "Treaties", online: www.senate.gov/artandhistory/history/common/briefing/Treaties.htm.
168 The legislation is known as the *Case-Zablocki Act* of 1972, now codified at 1 U.S.C. § 112(b). Regulations also require the State Department to provide a background statement with each text transmitted to Congress.
169 See, for example, Steve Charnovitz, "Using Framework Statutes to Facilitate U.S. Treaty Making" (2004) 98 Am. J. Int'l L. 696.
170 The Dáil Éireann is, in effect, the lower house of the Irish Parliament (the Oireachtas).
171 *Constitution of Ireland*, 1937, Arts 29.5.1 and 29.5.2°.
172 *Ibid.*, Art. 29.5.3.
173 See *Ratification of Treaties Act 1987*, No. 1 of 1987. See further, Winston Anderson, "Treaty-Making in Caribbean Law and Practice: The Question of Parliamentary Participation" (1998) 8 Carib. L. Rev. 75.
174 *Constitution of the Republic of Namibia*, 1990, art. 63(2)(e). The text of this Constitution, as well as commentary on the international law provisions, can be found in a special "Namibian Independence Edition" of the *South African Yearbook of International*

rica (as of 1993).[175] But South Africa has since modified its initial approach with the adoption, in 1996, of new constitutional provisions on the parliamentary approval of treaties, and for this reason, its experience has been chosen as worthy of further study.

Like other former dominions of the British Empire included in this study, South Africa inherited the British practice of vesting sole responsibility for the making of treaties with the national executive. Treaty-making was a prerogative power that was later given a statutory foundation in South Africa through codification in the Constitution. When South Africa proclaimed itself a republic in 1961, this codification served to confirm that the executive, and specifically the state President acting on the advice of the Cabinet, had the power to enter into treaties.[176] When further changes were made to the Constitution in 1983, including the adoption of a tri-cameral Parliament, the power to enter into and ratify treaties remained vested in the president.[177] The legislature had no role, other than the subsequent role of transforming a treaty obligation into one of domestic law through the enactment of domestic legislation.[178]

The real change to treaty-making in South Africa came about in 1994, on the day of the nation's first democratic elections, and the coming into force of first the interim Constitution,[179] and then the "final" Constitution,[180] which mandated a role for Parliament in treaty-making in advance of ratification or accession. Motivated by considerations of transparency and accountability,[181] and influenced by similar provisions adopted three years earlier in the Namibian Constitution,[182] the drafters of South Afri-

---

Law in 1989/90, later re-published as Dawid van Wyk *et al.*, eds., *Namibia: Constitutional and International Law Issues* (Pretoria: VerLoren van Themaat Centre, 1991).

175 *Constitution of the Republic of South Africa*, Act 200 of 1993, s. 231(2).

176 *Constitution of the Republic of South Africa*, Act 32 of 1961, s. 7(1)(g).

177 *Constitution of the Republic of South Africa*, Act 110 of 1983, s. 6(3)(e).

178 The accepted South African authority for this point is *Pan American World Airways v. S.A. Fire and Accident Insurance*, 1965 (3) S.A. 150 at 161(A).

179 *Constitution of the Republic of South Africa*, Act 200 of 1993 (in force 27 April 1994). See generally, Dion A. Basson, *South Africa's Interim Constitution: Text and Notes* (Kenwyn: Juta, 1994).

180 *Constitution of the Republic of South Africa*, Act 108 of 1996 (in force 4 February 1997). See generally, G.E. Devenish, *A Commentary on the South African Constitution* (Durban: Butterworths, 1998).

181 John Dugard, *International Law: A South African Perspective*, 2d ed. (Kenwyn: Juta, 2000) at 54.

182 Article 63(2)(e) of the Namibian Constitution of 1990 provides that the National Assembly shall have the power and function "to agree to the ratification of or accession to

ca's post-Apartheid constitutional order sought to ensure that all treaties of significance would be approved by Parliament before their ratification or accession, while also providing that any treaty so approved would automatically form part of South African law. The intent was to democratize the process and facilitate the incorporation of treaties into domestic law; however, a subsequent "polishing" of the draft text by the Department of Justice before it was signed into law resulted in an end product with "substantial technical deviations from the text agreed upon by the Negotiating Council."[183]

With respect to treaty approval, section 231(2) of the interim Constitution copied somewhat the wording of the Namibia Constitution by providing, "Parliament shall be competent to agree to the ratification of or accession to an international agreement negotiated and signed in terms of section 82(1)(i)," with section 82(1)(i) being the provision authorizing the President "to negotiate and sign international agreements." As for section 231(3) of the interim Constitution, it provided: "Where Parliament agrees to the ratification of or accession to an international agreement under subsection (2), such international agreement shall be binding on the Republic and shall form part of the law of the Republic, provided Parliament so expressly provides ..." The provision, however, did not specify how Parliament should indicate its express approval, which in turn led to debates as

---

international agreements which have been negotiated and signed in terms of Article 32(3)(e)," with Article 32(3)(e) providing that the president has the power to "negotiate and sign international agreements." This link to the Namibian Constitution has not gone unnoticed by South African international lawyers: see Dugard, *International Law, ibid.* at 54 and Neville Botha, "The Coming of Age of Public International Law in South Africa" (1992/93) 18 S.A.Y.B. Int'l L. 36 at 44. There was also a link between the legal advisors to each drafting process, with two of the three South African advisors to the Namibian Constituent Assembly (namely Advocate Arthur Chaskalson, later the first President of the Constitutional Court of South Africa, and Professor Marinus Wiechers of the University of South Africa) playing key roles in the drafting of the interim South African Constitution, while the third (Professor Gerhard Erasmus) contributed specifically to the drafting of the international law provisions: see Michèle Olivier, "The Status of International Law in South African Municipal Law: Section 231 of the 1993 Constitution" (1993/94) 19 S.A.Y.B. Int'l L. 1 at 2 n3, 3.

183 Olivier, "The Status of International Law," *ibid.* at 3. Olivier, then a legal advisor with the Department of Foreign Affairs and now a Professor of Law at the University of Pretoria, served as a member of the Technical Committee on Constitutional Issues, appointed by the Multi Party Negotiating Forum in May 1993 to give advice on constitutional matters to the Forum (which negotiated the transition to democracy in South Africa), and to draft on its behalf the interim Constitution.

to whether a resolution, rather than legislation, would suffice.[184] Moreover, with either interpretation, the "polished" wording from the Justice Department contradicted the intent of the Constitution's drafters since it made the incorporation of a treaty into domestic law less than automatic.[185]

But the drafters had also failed to take into account what Professor John Dugard, a recognized South African expert in international law and a technical advisor to the drafters of the 1996 Constitution, has termed "the bureaucratic mind"[186]—referring to the refusal of government departments to present treaties for parliamentary approval "until they were completely satisfied that there would be no conflict between the provisions of the treaty and domestic law."[187] This slowed down the treaty-making process considerably and made the new process cumbersome in a Parliament intent on demonstrating its commitment to a new democratic culture by making extensive use of the committee system. (This intent also means that treaties may need to be approved by several parliamentary committees before being presented for ratification).[188] As a result, when the interim Constitution was redrafted by the Constitutional Assembly, the assembly opted to return to the pre-1994 position with respect to treaty implementation, albeit with an ill-advised exception for self-executing treaties,[189] but

184 Compare John Dugard, *International Law A South African Perspective*, 1st ed. (Kenwyn: Juta, 1994) at 343 and D.J. Devine, "Some Problems Relating to Treaties in the South African Constitution and Some Suggestions for the Definitive Constitution" (1995) 20 S.A.Y.B. Int'l L. 1 at 17.

185 Olivier, "Status of International Law," above note 182 at 11. Botha writes: "[T]he draft approved by the Negotiating Council provided for automatic municipal application of treaties subject only to the constitution itself and express *exclusion* by Act of parliament": Neville Botha, "Interpreting a Treaty Endorsed Under the 1993 Constitution" (1993/1994) 19 S.A.Y.B. Int'l L. 148 at 151 (emphasis in original). For judicial confirmation that s. 231(3) does the reverse, see *Azanian Peoples Organization v. President of the Republic of South Africa*, 1996 (4) S.A. 671, 1996 (8) B.C.L.R. 1015 at paras. 26–27 (Const. Ct.).

186 Dugard, *International Law*, above note 181 at 55.

187 *Ibid.* See also Raylene Keightley, "Public International Law and the Final Constitution" (1996) 12 S.A.J.H.R. 405 at 411.

188 John Dugard, "International Law and the South African Constitution" (1997) 8 E.J.I.L. 77 at 81 n24.

189 Section 231(4) of the 1996 Constitution provides: "a self-executing provision of an agreement that has been approved by Parliament is law in the Republic unless it is inconsistent with the Constitution or an Act of Parliament," thereby presenting South African courts with the notorious difficulty, long-faced by US courts, of determining what constitutes a self-executing provision. This provision has been criticized by Dugard, *International Law*, above note 181 at 58 and Neville Botha, "Treaties after the

nevertheless retained the new role for Parliament in treaty-making at least for treaties of significance.

This new role is now mandated by section 231 of the 1996 Constitution.[190] Section 231(1) confirms that the negotiation and signature of all international agreements[191] is the responsibility of the national executive, which in turn comprises the president and Cabinet,[192] although in practice the negotiation of an agreement usually falls to the minister within whose portfolio the subject of the treaty falls.[193] Section 231(2) stipulates that an international agreement only binds the Republic of South Africa "after it has been approved by resolution in both the National Assembly and the National Council of the Provinces," but unlike under the interim Constitution, there is now an express exemption in section 231(3) for "an international agreement of a technical, administrative or executive nature, or an agreement which does not require either ratification or accession." Exempt agreements must, however, "be tabled in the Assembly and Council within a reasonable time,"[194] presumably to ensure that South Africa engages in

---

1996 Constitution: More Questions than Answers" (1997) 22 S.A.Y.B. Int'l L. 95 at 99. For an alternative view, see Michèle Olivier, "Exploring the Doctrine of Self-Execution as Enforcement Mechanism of International Obligations" (2002) S.A.Y.B. Int'l L. 99.

190 And bolstered by procedures set down by the Office of the President in chapter five of the revised *Manual on Executive Acts of the President of the Republic of South Africa* (March 1999), as cited throughout Neville Botha, "Treaty-Making in South Africa: A Reassessment" (2000) 25 S.A.Y.B. Int'l L. 69, reprinted with revisions as "South Africa" in Monroe Leigh *et al.*, eds., *National Treaty Law and Practice*, vol. 3 (Washington, DC: American Society of International Law, 2003) at 199.

191 Jurisprudence has since confirmed that the term "international agreement" in s. 231 applies to instruments "intended to create international legal rights and obligations between the parties": *Harksen v. President of the Republic of South Africa*, 2000 (2) S.A. 825, 2000 (5) B.C.L.R. 478 at para. 21 (Const. Ct). See further, JoAnn Schneeberger, "A Labyrinth of Tautology: The Meaning of the Term "International Agreement" and its Significance for South African Law and Treaty-making Practice" (2001) S.A.Y.B. Int'l L. 1.

192 Section 85 of the 1996 Constitution provides that "the executive authority of the Republic is vested in the President" and that "the President exercises the executive authority, together with the other members of the Cabinet".

193 Botha, "Treaty-Making in South Africa," above note 190 at 74. The Office of the Chief State Law Advisor (International Law) in Department of Foreign Affairs has also published a "Practical Guide and Procedures for the Conclusion of Agreements" (online: www.dfa.gov.za/department/law.doc) which requires (at 11) all international agreements to be approved by the national executive prior to signature, with this approval obtained by the signing of a Presidential Minute by the Cabinet Minister responsible for the specific subject matter of the agreement and counter-signed by the President.

194 1996 Constitution, s. 231(3).

no more secret treaties.[195] As for implementation, section 231(4) returns South Africa to the common law fold by stating explicitly that "an international agreement becomes law in the Republic when it is enacted into law by national legislation," although an exception is made for a "self-executing provision of an agreement that has been approved by Parliament."

Treaty-making in South Africa is thus a shared responsibility between the national executive and both houses of Parliament, with all bilateral treaties of significance and virtually all multilateral treaties subject to an "approval by both Houses" rule of constitutional status. Both Houses of Parliament thus have the opportunity to either approve or reject a new treaty at a stage in the process that matters in terms of that treaty's binding nature vis-à-vis South Africa, while also retaining their earlier authority for the enactment of legislation to give a treaty domestic effect. Parliament also receives an explanatory memorandum on the history, purposes, and consequences of the treaty being considered for ratification,[196] including the projected financial and other costs,[197] as well as the legal opinions from the state law advisors of the departments of justice and foreign affairs,[198] and an indication from the executive as to its intention with respect to the treaty's incorporation into domestic law.[199] Various parliamentary committees in both Houses then review the treaty, depending on its subject matter, before it is considered by each House sitting separately. The committees, and the Houses, can either accept or reject the treaty, but may also propose declarations[200] and reservations,[201] with the whole process taking from six months to a year to complete.[202]

---

195 The Apartheid government was suspected of entering into secret military agreements with Israel and Taiwan: John Dugard, "International Law and the 'Final' Constitution" (1995) 11 S.A.J.H.R. 241 at 245. Secret treaties also existed between South Africa and Transkei and Ciskei, the disclosure of which was refused by the Ministers of Internal Affairs and Law and Order: J.T. Schoombee, "A Licence for Unlawful Arrests Across the Border?" (1984) 101 S. African L.J. 713 at 713 and 720.

196 Botha, "Treaty-Making in South Africa," above note 190 at 79.

197 "Practical Guide," above note 193 at 27.

198 *Ibid.*

199 Botha, "Treaty-Making in South Africa," above note 190 at 79.

200 For an example, see the discussion of South Africa's ratification of the *African Charter on Human and Peoples' Rights* in John Dugard & Iain Currie, "Public International Law," in [1996] *Annual Survey of South African Law* 145 at 147.

201 Botha, "Treaty-Making in South Africa," above note 190 at 83, citing section 5.11 of the *Manual on Executive Acts.*

202 Schneeberger, "A Labyrinth of Tautology," above note 191 at 5.

As for agreements not subject to ratification or accession, and those of "a technical, administrative or executive nature," it is the view of the Office of the President that this exemption, although not the easiest to apply, is intended to cover agreements of "a routine nature, flowing from the daily activities of government departments."[203] These are "department-specific agreements; agreements without major political or other significance; and agreements which have no financial consequences[204] and do not affect domestic law"[205] and they are "usually bilateral."[206] As such, the Constitution tries to ensure a measure of efficiency by allowing these agreements to bypass the parliamentary approval process, while also insisting on their tabling in Parliament within a reasonable time to allow for scrutiny. But where there is doubt, according to the Office of the President, the agreement is referred to Parliament for approval pursuant to section 231(2).[207] Professor Neville Botha, however, is critical of the provision's failure to state in whose hands the determination of an agreement's nature rests given the difference between approval and tabling, describing the latter as "no more than a process of notification of a *fait accompli.*"[208] But since South Africa no longer publishes its own treaty series because of budgetary constraints,[209] the required generation of a parliamentary record through tabling may well serve a useful purpose.[210] In any event, South Africa's new procedures have not hampered its treaty-making efforts since 1994,[211]

---

203 Office of the President, *Manual on Executive Acts of the President of the Republic of South Africa*, ch. 5 (1997) as cited in Michèle Olivier, "Informal International Agreements Under the 1996 Constitution" (1997) 22 S.A.Y.B. Int'l L. 62 at 64.

204 Agreements that have financial consequence are those requiring an additional budgetary allocation from Parliament, over and above the budget that has been allocated: Schneeberger, "A Labyrinth of Tautology," above note 191 at 4. See also: "Practical Guide," above note 193 at 12–13.

205 Botha, "Treaty-Making in South Africa," above note 190 at 76, relying on the 1999 version of the *Manual on Executive Acts.*

206 Schneeberger, "A Labyrinth of Tautology," above note 191 at 5.

207 Olivier, "Informal International Agreements," above note 203 at 64; Dugard, above note 181 at 331.

208 Botha, "Treaties after the 1996 Constitution," above note 189 at 97; Botha, "Treaty-Making in South Africa," above note 190 at 77.

209 Botha, "Treaty-Making in South Africa," above note 190 at 88.

210 An annual listing of treaties concluded by South Africa can also be found in the *South African Yearbook of International Law.*

211 See, for example, the listing of treaties entered into by South Africa from 1994 to1998 in Jacqueline A. Kalley, *South Africa's Treaties in Theory and Practice 1806–1998* (Lanham, MD: Scarecrow Press, 2001) at 614–700.

with the parliamentary process applying to both bilateral and multilateral treaties of significance,[212] albeit that the vast majority of agreements concluded fall within the exemption in section 231(3).[213]

As for the federal aspect of South African treaty-making, although South Africa's nine provincial governments have no treaty-making powers,[214] Stemmet reports that "since the establishment of the new provinces, a practice has developed that provincial premiers enter into [what he terms in quotation marks] 'international agreements' on behalf of the provinces with foreign states or federal units or regions of such states," although these agreements seem more akin to contracts with foreign entities than treaties.[215] Botha also notes that "this caused considerable confusion and embarrassment to the national executive which, in terms of the Constitution is the only body authorized to negotiate and sign international agreements."[216] Nevertheless, if a proposed treaty action of the national executive should impact on the provinces, the newly established National Council of the Provinces could be used as a forum to exert influence on the national executive.[217] The council consists of ninety delegates (ten from each province),[218] who are appointed by the provincial legislature according to a formula that aims to ensure that all parties form part of the delegation and that the strength of the political party in the provincial legislature is reflected proportionally in the delegation to the council.[219] However, unless the Constitution provides otherwise, each province has only one vote in the council; a vote cast on behalf of the province by the head of its delegation.[220] In this way, it was thought that the delegation would be linked

---

212 A record of Parliament's consideration of treaties can be found in the chapters on "Public International Law" in the *Annual Survey of South African Law* for the years 1995–97. Subsequent chapters list the treaties ratified, but without reference to the parliamentary record.

213 Schneeberger, "A Labyrinth of Tautology," above note 191 at 5.

214 Dugard, "International Law and the 'Final' Constitution," above note 195 at 247. The *Manual on Executive Acts* also makes it clear that "provinces may not enter into agreements governed by international law except as agents of the national executive": Botha, Treaty-Making in South Africa," above note 190 at 95.

215 Andre Stemmet, "The Influence of Recent Constitutional Developments in South Africa on the Relationship Between International Law and Municipal Law" (1999) 33 Int'l Lawyer 47 at 68–69.

216 Botha, "Treaty-Making in South Africa," above note 190 at 95.

217 Devenish, *A Commentary*, above note 180 at 324.

218 *1996 Constitution*, s. 60.

219 *Ibid.*, s. 61 and Sch. 3, Part B.

220 *Ibid.*, s. 65(1)(a).

more to the province than to national party political interests.[221] Unfortunately, access to South African parliamentary records is limited due to the nation's financial constraints, making it difficult to verify whether this has been the case.

G. RECOMMENDATIONS

The rationale for securing a role for Parliament in treaty-making rests on the important fact that treaties are law—often permanent law—and as such, those who make the law, be they ministers or officials, should be accountable to Parliament and the public that it represents. In light of the efforts undertaken in the UK, Australia, and South Africa to enhance the role for Parliament in treaty-making, Canada's treaty-making practice stands out as outmoded and old-fashioned. Among the older countries of the Commonwealth, Canada is the only one with no requirement for some form of parliamentary involvement in the making of treaties, despite its own past practice until the 1960s. While it is not intrinsically wrong to stand alone on any matter, the experiences of other comparable states bring several recommendations for reform to mind, all with the aim of enhancing the democratic accountability, and thus legitimacy, of Canada's treaty obligations. These are also pragmatic, middle-of-the-road reforms, which do not threaten Canada's treaty negotiating capacity nor efficiency, given the experiences elsewhere.

At the negotiations stage in the treaty-making process, it is recommended that the government of Canada institutionalize a practice of providing all provincial and territorial governments with a schedule of treaties currently under negotiation, consideration, or review. Such a schedule would ensure greater opportunities for federal–provincial–territorial cooperation and improve transparency in the treaty-making process. This schedule should be provided on a quarterly or bi-annual basis, with enough information on the subject matters of the treaties for provincial governments to identify any treaty negotiations applicable to their areas of jurisdiction. The treaty schedules should also be tabled in the provincial legislatures, as is done in Queensland, thereby enabling provincial legislators to initiate a timely debate or inquiry should it be desired. The treaty schedules should also be made available to the public via posting on the

---

221 Johan de Waal, "Constitutional Law" in C.G. van der Merwe *et al.*, eds., *Introduction to the Law of South Africa* (The Hague: Kluwer Law International, 2004) at 68.

Canada Treaty Information website, as done in Australia in relation to the ongoing negotiation of multilateral treaties. For treaties of significance, the newly created Council of the Federation could serve as an additional intergovernmental forum, akin to the Australian Treaties Council, albeit with the need in Canada to extend an invitation to the federal government to participate.[222]

As for reforms applicable after the treaty has been negotiated, but before treaty ratification, several suggestions can be made, building on the experience of other Commonwealth states. Clearly, a rule requiring the tabling of all treaties in Parliament once a treaty text has been initialled or signed is useful for the provision of timely information about future treaty commitments. To ensure that there is an opportunity for effective parliamentary scrutiny, the federal executive should be required, by statute if necessary, to table in Parliament all treaties requiring ratification, accession, acceptance, or approval for at least twenty sitting days before the actual ratification takes place, thereby enabling any member of either House to call attention to the proposed treaty and stimulate public debate. An explanatory memorandum on a treaty's purposes and consequences, as well as its projected financial costs and legal implications, should also be published, as is done in one form or another in the United States, the United Kingdom, Australia, New Zealand, and South Africa. These memoranda, based on the current covering memoranda seen only by the executive, could also serve as a public record of the consultations that took place during the treaty's negotiation, including those with provincial and territorial ministers and officials, leading to an expectation and eventually a conventional requirement for such consultation. It would also be beneficial if Canada followed South Africa's example and also deposited the legal opinions from the departments of justice and foreign affairs concerning the treaty's international obligations and their intended domestic implementation.

Although a treaty so laid before Parliament could then be forwarded to the parliamentary standing committee relevant to its subject matter, as done in the UK and South Africa, it is my view that a dedicated treaty scrutiny committee, like JSCOT in Australia, is the best means to achieve both public awareness and improved accountability. A dedicated treaty committee regularizes and institutionalizes the treaty scrutiny function, provid-

222 Established at a Premiers' Meeting in December 2003, the Council comprises all thirteen of Canada's Premiers and Territorial Leaders, but not the Government of Canada. See further online: www.councilofthefederation.ca.

ing a public home for a wealth of treaty information, while ensuring that parliamentary time is given to the consideration of the proposed treaty action and its explanatory memorandum. It would also provide its members with a greater opportunity than a one-off inquiry to develop an expertise in treaties and treaty law, and puts government officials on permanent notice of a possible call from Parliament to justify the content of a memorandum in support for a treaty obligation. A treaty committee must, however, be of an adequate size and resources if it is to follow Australia's lead and carry out hearings beyond the confines of the capital, and it must be supported by a secretariat to assist with the development of a corporate memory as well as fruitful relationships with the Department of Foreign Affairs, other federal departments and provincial ministries, civil society groups, industry leaders, academics, and other non-governmental organizations. It is my view, however, that a robust treaty committee in the House of Commons, comprised of MPs from all the provinces, could also offset the need, but possibly not the political desire, for separate provincial treaty scrutiny requirements and the resulting duplication of effort. I would not, however, bar the possibility of either a federal or provincial committee embarking on an additional inquiry for specific treaties of significant public concern.

As for the need for parliamentary approval for future treaty action, whether federal or provincial, it is my view that the treaty-making process must allow for the possibility that a state will not ratify a treaty following an expression of parliamentary disapproval. All treaties need not be expressly approved by Parliament, given concerns about the cumbersome nature of such a requirement, but there should be a mechanism that enables Parliament to draw attention to a future treaty action that has strong opposition, and this mechanism should not rest on the goodwill or discretion of the executive branch. Oddly enough, such a mechanism is already in place in Canada for social security treaties,[223] and I cannot see the expansion of this legal fetter on the prerogative power of the Crown as causing great harm to Canada's treaty-making capacity. A negative resolution procedure applicable to treaties after signature but before ratification will not unduly tie the hands of the executive during treaty negotiation, and may foster a greater degree of consultation, and even cooperation, between the levels

---

223 Social security treaties are brought into force by regulation. Section 42 of the *Old Age Security Act*, R.S.C. 1985, c. O-9, requires the regulations to be laid before Parliament and enables Parliament, if it so desires, to prevent the treaty from coming into force through a negative resolution procedure.

and branches of government at the pre-signature stage. It is also a middle ground position that balances the various interests at play, admittedly sacrificing some efficiency for some accountability.

These recommendations apply to all treaties, regardless of subject matter and the number of parties, for reasons of both principle and practice. Divergent approaches can lead to unequal results, and exemptions for bilateral treaties, for example, run the risk of shielding some of the most controversial treaties from scrutiny, as evidenced by the degree of interest in the *Australia–US Free Trade Agreement*, which prompted the holding of two parliamentary inquiries. However, in response to concerns about the cumbersome nature of a one-size-fits-all approach, as applied initially in South Africa, it is worth noting that in practice, a negative resolution procedure would likely reflect a two-stream approach, with treaties of a truly technical nature being of little concern and only treaties of significance ever facing the prospect of a negative resolution. The benefit, however, of a unified approach is that the elected representatives of the public, and not the executive, determine what is a treaty of no consequence and concern.

With the increasing interdependence of the modern world, departments of foreign affairs no longer have a monopoly on law-making by treaty. Other government departments are also involved, as are officials at the provincial level, and to some extent, individuals and organizations from outside government. Courts too have assumed a greater role, having found a way to give an unimplemented treaty domestic legal significance, if not domestic legal effect. Parliament, however, remains outside the treaty-making process, only to play a role after the conclusion of a treaty and the assumption of its obligations. While the introduction of a process of scrutiny or approval is no panacea, it will provide the opportunity for dedicated parliamentarians to contribute to the treaty-making process, and in the final analysis, may serve to foster greater respect for treaty law by reducing the doubt about a treaty's democratic credentials. It would result in a public record that could be used to either counterbalance the activism of a court when Parliament is against giving domestic effect to a treaty, or bolster the decision of a court when Parliament is in favour by providing evidence of Parliament's support for a treaty's provisions. In any event, a parliamentary role in treaty-making is necessary to avoid engaging the nation in long-standing legal commitments without public scrutiny and debate.

Section B:
PARTICIPANTS OTHER THAN NATIONAL
GOVERNMENTS IN INTERNATIONAL
LAW-MAKING: CURRENT PRACTICE,
ASPIRATIONS, AND POSSIBILITIES

Labour Conventions and Comprehensive Claim Agreements: A New Model for Subfederal Participation in Canadian International Treaty-Making

GIB VAN ERT AND STEFAN MATIATION

The purpose of this chapter is to introduce a new actor to the Canadian treaty-making stage: Aboriginal governments. This purpose will immediately strike some readers as bizarre. Aboriginal peoples have been making treaties for centuries, first with each other, later with European colonists, and now with the federal, provincial, and territorial governments of Canada. There is nothing new about Aboriginal treaty-making and there should be no need to introduce Aboriginal governments as treaty-makers. Yet something new is happening. Canada has entered into a number of comprehensive claims agreements (CCAs) with Aboriginal groups since the 1970s. The most recent of these, the Nisga'a Final Agreement 1999[1] (the Nisga'a Agreement), the Tlicho Land Claims and Self-Government Agreement 2003[2] (the Tlicho Agreement), and the Labrador Inuit Land Claims Agreement 2005[3] (the Labrador Inuit Agreement) are intended to extend constitutional protection to self-government rights (collectively,

---

1 Nisga'a Final Agreement, signed on behalf of the Nisga'a Nation and the Government of British Columbia on 27 April 1999 and on behalf of the Government of Canada on 4 May 1999, and given effect by the *Nisga'a Final Agreement Act*, R.S.C. 2000, c. 7 (in force 11 May 2000; see SI/2000-38) [Nisga'a Agreement].
2 Tlicho Land Claims and Self-Government Agreement, signed on behalf of the Tlicho, the Government of the Northwest Territories and the Government of Canada on 25 August 2003, and given effect by the *Tlicho Land Claims and Self-Government Act*, R.S.C. 2005, c. 1 (in force 4 August 2005; see SI/2005-0054) [Tlicho Agreement].
3 Labrador Inuit Land Claims Agreement, signed on behalf of the Labrador Inuit Association, the Government of Newfoundland and Labrador and the Government of Canada on 21 January 2005, and given effect by the *Labrador Inuit Land Claims Agree-*

the self-government CCAs).[4] With the establishment of Aboriginal governments having law-making authority comes the prospect of Aboriginal-made laws that violate obligations binding upon the Canadian state in customary or conventional international law. At the same time, Canada must be wary of entering into international legal obligations that may infringe constitutionally entrenched Aboriginal and treaty rights, including the treaty rights described in CCAs. To meet these problems, the most recent two of the three self-government CCAs include extensive provisions governing the reception of public international law in Aboriginal law and the participation of Aboriginal governments in Canadian international treaty-making.[5]

It is in this sense that Aboriginal governments are taking a new role in Canadian treaty-making, and indeed in Canadian reception law more generally.[6] Their role is in some ways similar to that of Canadian provincial governments. But there are also important differences. Indeed, the Tlicho and Labrador Inuit model of subfederal participation in Canadian international treaty-making makes an illuminating contrast to the model established for the provinces by the *Labour Conventions* case.[7] We explore these contrasts here. We begin with a review of the constitutional framework (both written and unwritten) governing international treaty-making in Canada, including *Labour Conventions*. We then review the legal and policy

---

ment *Act*, R.S.C. 2005, c. 27 (in force 1 December 2005; see SI/2005-0117) [Labrador Inuit Agreement].

4   All these agreements include provisions stating that they are treaties and land claims agreements within the meaning of s. 35 of the *Constitution Act, 1982*: Tlicho Agreement, art. 2.1.1; Labrador Inuit Agreement, art. 2.1.1; and Nisga'a Agreement, c. 2, art. 1.

5   Throughout this chapter we use the phrase *international treaty-making* to distinguish treaty-making at the international level from treaty-making between Canadian governments and Aboriginal peoples. Similarly, we generally use *treaty* to refer to Aboriginal treaties and *international treaty* to refer to treaties made under international law.

6   Canadian Aboriginal peoples participate in international law- and policy-making in other ways not considered in this chapter. They participate as observers in a number of international fora addressing matters of interest to them. They sometimes attend international negotiations as members of Canadian delegations. They express their views on international issues through representative organizations such as the Assembly of First Nations, the Métis National Council and the Inuit Circumpolar Conference. Canadian Aboriginals are not alone in these activities. Participation in international law- and policy-making by indigenous peoples from across the globe has increased dramatically in the last twenty-five years.

7   *Attorney-General for Canada v. Attorney-General for Ontario*, [1937] A.C. 326 (J.C.P.C.) [*Labour Conventions* case].

context within which the Nisga'a, Tlicho, and Labrador Inuit Agreements were negotiated. Next, we explain and compare the international law provisions of the latter two agreements.[8] We conclude with some thoughts on the *Labour Conventions* and Aboriginal models for subfederal participation in Canadian international treaty-making.

A. THE CONSTITUTIONAL FRAMEWORK OF CANADIAN INTERNATIONAL TREATY-MAKING

The written portion of the Canadian Constitution has never had much to say about international law. When the colonies of British North America came together for the purpose of creating a federal constitution, it was not independence they sought but self-government. Phrased in international legal terms, the colonies were not to become a state. Rather, the project was to unite the colonies in a single dependency of the United Kingdom, albeit one with almost complete autonomy in internal affairs. The term *dominion* came to describe such arrangements both for Canada and other self-governing British territories. The external affairs of a dominion remained under the control of imperial authorities. They made the dominion's foreign policy and concluded treaties on the dominion's behalf. These arrangements were facilitated by a long-established feature of British constitutionalism whereby treaty-making was regarded as a purely executive act requiring no participation from the legislative branch. In the British North America Act 1867,[9] the colonists' relatively modest aspirations combined with British constitutional theory to create a constitutional document in which international law (and many other things) made little or no appearance. No provision was made for Canada's eventual accession to statehood at international law. No requirements were established for imperial consultation of the Canadian authorities on questions of foreign affairs. All that was done was to grant Parliament the legislative authority to enact laws implementing the occasional imperial treaty that might require legislative action in the dominion.[10] Reading the *BNA Act*, one is left with the impres-

---

8 As we will see, the Nisga'a Agreement does not include the elaborate reception provisions of the Tlicho and Labrador Inuit Agreements.

9 *Constitution Act, 1867* (U.K.), 30 & 31 Vict., c. 3, reprinted in R.S.C. 1985, App. II, No. 5 (formerly the *British North America Act, 1867*).

10 Section 132 provides: "The Parliament and Government of Canada shall have all Powers necessary or proper for performing the Obligations of Canada or of any Province thereof, as Part of the British Empire, towards Foreign Countries, arising under Treaties between the Empire and such Foreign Countries."

sion (rightly or wrongly) that no one contemplated the possibility that the federal and provincial governments of the new dominion might one day seek a voice in international treaty-making.

But in the aftermath of the First World War, Canada and other dominions demanded a place at the international table. This movement culminated in the *Statute of Westminster 1931*, the purpose of which was to reconcile imperial law with the international reality that Canada and the other dominions had become states.[11] In spite of that purpose, however, the statute made no amendment to Canada's written constitution in respect of treaty-making. The result was awkward. First, it was not clear, as a matter of express constitutional law, which body or bodies had inherited from Britain the power to make treaties binding on Canada at international law. Second, it was unclear where legislative authority lay to implement treaties that were not concluded by the imperial authorities and therefore did not explicitly fall within Parliament's power under section 132. These difficulties came to a head in the *Labour Conventions* case of 1937. Parliament enacted social legislation purporting to implement certain conventions of the International Labour Organization in accordance with the Labour Part of the Treaty of Versailles 1919.[12] While the substance of the legislation was clearly within provincial jurisdiction, the federal government of the day claimed that it fell within Parliament's legislative authority under section 132 of the *BNA Act* or, alternatively, under Parliament's power to legislate for the peace, order, and good government of Canada (section 91). The government of Ontario challenged this claim. It argued that the ILO treaties were not "empire treaties" of the sort contemplated by section 132 and that the peace, order, and good government power had no application here. Ontario also argued, on the basis of decided cases concerning the distribution of prerogative powers between the federal and provincial governments,[13] that the treaty-making power did not rest uniquely with the federal executive but was divided between the dominion and provincial governments according to the division of legislative powers established by sections 91 to 92 of the *BNA Act*. If so, not only was the impugned legislation unconstitutional, but the very act of concluding these treaties was *ultra vires* the

11   Reprinted in R.S.C. 1985, App. II, No. 27.
12   Can. T.S.1919 No 4.
13   See *Liquidators of Maritime Bank v. Receiver General of New Brunswick*, [1892] A.C. 437 (J.C.P.C.) and *Bonanza Creek Gold Mining Company Ltd. v. Rex*, [1916] 1 A.C. 566 (J.C.P.C.).

dominion executive because their subject matter came within provincial legislative jurisdiction.

Thus it fell to the Privy Council to say what the *BNA Act* and the *Statute of Westminster* did not. The appeal was momentous. Not only was the subject matter of the impugned legislation intensely controversial (being the Bennett Government's attempt to replicate Roosevelt's "new deal" plan to drag the country out of the Great Depression) but the questions before the board were constitutional in the highest sense of the word, implicating not only federalism concerns but also Canada's capacity as a sovereign state at international law. The importance of this decision was not lost on its author, Lord Atkin, whose biography reveals his anxiety about the case and his concern that the decision be viewed as legitimate by Canadian audiences.[14] The result was a judicial compromise of the sort commentators often see in later Supreme Court of Canada decisions such as *Re Patriation*[15] and *Re Secession of Quebec*.[16] On the question of treaty-making power, his lordship made no comment. The effect of his silence in the intervening decades has been that treaty-making power has fallen to the federal government—by constitutional usage and provincial acquiescence rather than by strict law.[17] This was a victory for the dominion. But the provinces won a crucial concession: while the power to make treaties remained, *de facto*, a federal power, authority to implement them into domestic law was governed by the ordinary division of powers set out in sections 91 to 92 of the *Constitution Act, 1867*. "In other words," said Lord Atkin, "the Dominion cannot merely by making promises to foreign countries clothe itself with legislative authority inconsistent with the constitution that gave it birth."[18]

The effects of this decision on Canadian international treaty-making practice were, and continue to be, far-reaching. If the federal government wishes to enter a treaty, and cannot comply with its terms without domestic legislation, and the required legislation falls within provincial jurisdiction, the federal government must go to the provinces and persuade them of the merits of the treaty. If they are persuaded, the provincial governments must then secure passage of the implementing legislation through their own legislatures—a step which in some cases will be almost a formality,

---

14   Geoffrey Lewis, *Lord Atkin* (Oxford: Hart, 1999) at 100–1.

15   *Re Resolution to Amend the Constitution (Patriation Reference)*, [1981] 1 S.C.R. 753.

16   [1998] 2 S.C.R. 217.

17   See Gibran van Ert, "The Legal Character of Provincial Agreements with Foreign Governments" (2001) 24 C. de D. 1093.

18   *Labour Conventions* case, above note 7 at 352.

but in others may present a real challenge. If, however, one or more provincial governments are not convinced of the desirability of the proposed treaty, the federal government may be forced to delay or even abandon Canadian adhesion to it.

This brief outline of the post–*Labour Conventions* scheme makes clear how much influence the case grants the provinces in Canadian international treaty-making. For international treaties requiring provincial implementation, *Labour Conventions* makes the provinces essential partners in the Canadian treaty-making process. While there is no formal constitutional requirement that the federal government consult the provinces before assuming new international treaty obligations, in fact such consultation must occur if the treaty in question will require provincial implementation. If such consultation does not occur, or is unsatisfactory to one or more provinces, the provinces may exercise a *de facto* veto over Canadian accession to the treaty, for there is no sense in acceding to a treaty you know you cannot perform.

But provincial influence in international treaty-making goes further. Not only is the federal government dependent on the provinces to implement certain kinds of treaties but it must also rely on their goodwill not to violate existing treaty obligations by legislation. One corollary of *Labour Conventions* (and the doctrine of parliamentary supremacy that informs it) is that provincial legislation that violates Canadian international treaty obligations is not, for that reason alone, unconstitutional. The federal government, therefore, has no legal remedy against a province that is determined to frustrate Canadian performance of federally concluded international treaties. All the federal government can do in such circumstances is negotiate a solution, either with the province or with Canada's international treaty partners.

This, then, is the *Labour Conventions* model of subfederal participation in Canadian international treaty-making. While the federal government has never challenged *Labour Conventions* in the courts (in spite of judicial encouragement to do so),[19] and while some commentators feel, counterintuitively, that the model has produced admirable compliance with international law,[20] one can readily see why the federal government would hesitate to suggest this model of subfederal participation to Aboriginal govern-

---

19 See *MacDonald v. Vapor Canada Ltd.*, [1977] 2 S.C.R. 134.
20 See Koren L. Bell, "From Laggard to Leader: Canadian Lessons on a Role for U.S. States in Making and Implementing Human Rights Treaties" (2002) 5 Yale Human

ments. And yet the emerging self-government CCA model is by no means a one-sided affair.

B. THE LEGAL AND POLICY CONTEXT OF COMPREHENSIVE CLAIMS AGREEMENTS

What makes the Aboriginal model of subfederal participation in Canadian international treaty-making as powerful, in its own way, as the *Labour Conventions* model is the legal and policy context in which Aboriginal claims to lands and resources, cultural integrity, and self-government are made. The starting point is section 35 of the *Constitution Act, 1982,* which provides in part:

(1) The existing Aboriginal and treaty rights of the Aboriginal peoples of Canada are hereby recognized and affirmed.

(2) In this Act, "Aboriginal peoples of Canada" includes the Indian, Inuit and Métis peoples of Canada.

(3) For greater certainty, in subsection (1) "treaty rights" includes rights that now exist by way of land claims agreements or may be so acquired.[21]

Case law quickly established that section 35(1) gives existing Aboriginal and treaty rights, including Aboriginal title, entrenched status under Canada's constitution.[22]

Yet section 35 gives little guidance on the nature, scope, or content of Aboriginal rights. Uncertainty regarding section 35 and the rights to which it refers is one of the themes that drives Aboriginal law- and policy-making in Canada. A second theme underlying Aboriginal law- and policy-making in Canada is reconciliation. The Supreme Court of Canada has stated on a number of occasions that the purpose of section 35 is "the

---

Rts. & Dev. L.J. 255; Jamie Cameron, "Federalism, Treaties and International Human Rights under the Canadian Constitution" (2002) 48 Wayne Law Review 1.

21 *Constitution Act, 1982,* being Schedule B to the *Canada Act 1982* (U.K.), 1982, c. 11, s. 35.

22 The Supreme Court of Canada first had occasion to consider s. 35 in the *Sparrow* case, which concerned a claim to an Aboriginal right to fish. Dickson C.J. stated: "The constitutional recognition afforded by the provision therefore gives a measure of control over government conduct and a strong check on legislative power. While it does not promise immunity from government regulation ... it does hold the Crown to a substantive promise. The government is required to bear the burden of justifying any legislation that has some negative effect on any Aboriginal right protected under s. 35(1)." *R. v. Sparrow,* [1990] 1 S.C.R. 1075 at 1110 [*Sparrow*].

reconciliation of the pre-existence of Aboriginal societies with the sovereignty of the Crown."[23] The two themes of uncertainty and reconciliation can be traced right through the legal and policy context of Aboriginal affairs in Canada to the international law provisions of the Tlicho and Labrador Inuit Agreements.

On the legal front, uncertainty regarding Aboriginal and treaty rights has given rise to a great deal of complex and novel litigation, much of which has ultimately made its way to the Supreme Court of Canada. That court has developed tests to determine when Aboriginal rights, including Aboriginal title, exist in particular circumstances, has described their nature and content on a case-by-case basis, and has provided guidance regarding what federal and provincial governments need do to carry out their activities given the existence or possible existence of Aboriginal and treaty rights. This latter point is especially significant given that, with the advent of section 35, the Crown's power unilaterally to extinguish Aboriginal and treaty rights has been eliminated. In place of this power, the Supreme Court of Canada has held that Aboriginal and treaty rights may be infringed by government action only where justified.[24] The justification analysis involves an assessment of whether a valid legislative objective is served by the infringement of the Aboriginal right or rights in question and, if so, whether the infringing action is consistent with the honour of the Crown and the fiduciary nature of the *sui generis* relationship between the Crown and the Aboriginal peoples of Canada, and minimally impairs the exercise of the right or rights.[25]

In determining whether the Crown has satisfied the minimal impairment component of the justification test, the courts generally consider whether meaningful consultations have been conducted with the affected Aboriginal group. The law respecting the Crown's duty to consult is evolving. At the moment, it appears that failure to consult may not necessarily prove fatal to the Crown's justification case. Generally speaking though, it will be a key factor in a court's decision. Already the Supreme Court of Canada has indicated that there is always a duty to consult, which in some cases may require consent, when there is an infringement of Aboriginal title.[26]

23   *R. v. Van der Peet*, [1996] 2 S.C.R. 507 at para. 31 [*Van der Peet*].
24   The justification analysis was set out by the Supreme Court of Canada in *Sparrow*, above note 22 at 1075. The Court has applied the same analysis in the context of the infringement of Aboriginal treaty rights: *R. v. Badger*, [1996] 1 S.C.R. 771.
25   *Sparrow*, *ibid.* at 1111–15.
26   See *Delgamuukw v. British Columbia*, [1997] 3 S.C.R. 1010 [*Delgamuukw*].

With its 2004 decisions in *Haida Nation v. British Columbia (Minister of Forests)*[27] and *Taku River Tlingit First Nation v. British Columbia (Project Assessment Director)*,[28] the Supreme Court of Canada has expanded consultation obligations beyond the scope of the justification test. The Court held that a duty to consult Aboriginal people and possibly to accommodate their interests arises prior to the proof or establishment of their rights "when the Crown has knowledge, real or constructive, of the potential existence of the Aboriginal right or title and contemplates conduct that might adversely affect it."[29] Governments cannot use lands and resources as they choose pending the resolution of Aboriginal claims. Rather, they must act honourably and respect the potential but unproven interests of Aboriginal peoples. Writing for the Court in *Haida Nation*, McLachlin C.J. stated: "It is a corollary of section 35 that the Crown act honourably in defining the rights it guarantees and in reconciling them with other rights and interests. This, in turn, implies a duty to consult and, if appropriate, accommodate."[30] In *Haida* and *Taku River*, the Supreme Court makes reconciliation the answer to uncertainty regarding Aboriginal rights. Note that the duty to consult described in these cases is not part of the justification test for infringing Aboriginal rights consistently with section 35. Rather, it is a stand-alone obligation derived from the concept of the honour of the Crown.

The key elements of Canadian Aboriginal law surveyed above inform the international law provisions of the Tlicho and Labrador Inuit Agreements. Existing Aboriginal and treaty rights are constitutionally entrenched. In the absence of a treaty or judicial determination, the existence, content, and scope of Aboriginal rights in any particular case is uncertain. Aboriginal and treaty rights are not absolute; they can be infringed if certain requirements are met. Consultation may be one such requirement. The fundamental principle that underlies Canadian Aboriginal law is reconcili-

27   [2004] 3 S.C.R. 511 [*Haida Nation*].
28   [2004] 3 S.C.R. 550 [*Taku River*].
29   *Haida Nation*, above note 27 at para. 35.
30   *Ibid.* at para. 20. The decisions in *Haida Nation* and *Taku River* fill a gap that existed in justification analysis. In that analysis, justification, and any required consultation, only become an issue once Aboriginal rights are proven and a *prima facie* case for infringement made. *Haida Nation* and *Taku River* stand for the proposition that a duty to consult can arise even when Aboriginal rights are unproven. For a discussion about the gap, see Patrick Macklem & Sonia Lawrence, "From Consultation to Reconciliation: Aboriginal Peoples and the Crown's Duty to Consult" (2000) 79 Can. Bar Rev. 252.

ation—"we are all here to stay"[31] and are better off working together in a respectful and responsive way to address Aboriginal interests.

On the policy front, the themes of uncertainty and reconciliation have been the impetus to resolve Aboriginal claims by negotiation. The federal government's approach to negotiation since 1982 has sought to assist Aboriginal groups attain greater political, economic, social, and cultural strength while reducing uncertainties regarding the existence, nature, scope, and content of undefined Aboriginal rights. This approach represents a contemporary revival of sorts of the treaty-making that occurred between Aboriginal and non-Aboriginal peoples from early contact to the 1920s. This revival has occurred within the framework of the federal government's comprehensive claims policy[32] and Aboriginal Self-Government Policy (the Inherent Right Policy).[33] The comprehensive claims policy began as a policy statement made in 1973 in the aftermath of *Calder v. British Columbia (Attorney-General).*[34] In that case the Supreme Court of Canada recognized Aboriginal title as a concept existing in Canadian common law. Partly in response to that, and to natural resource development pressures, the federal government signalled its willingness to negotiate Aboriginal land claims. The Inherent Right Policy was released in 1995 following the completion of the work of the Royal Commission on Aboriginal Peoples.

The first CCA negotiated under the framework of the comprehensive claims policy was the James Bay and Northern Québec Agreement 1975 (James Bay Agreement).[35] Since then, CCAs have been reached with eighteen Aboriginal groups, and negotiations continue with many more. Today, all of Canada north of 60 degrees North latitude, almost all of British Columbia, much of Quebec and Labrador, part of the Maritime Provinces,

---

31 *Delgamuukw,* above note 26 at para. 186.

32 The 1973 policy statement later became the foundation for a broader policy document: *In All Fairness: A Native Claims Policy—Comprehensive Claims* (Ottawa: Department of Indian Affairs and Northern Development [DIAND], 1981). This was revised and reissued as *Comprehensive Land Claims Policy* (Ottawa: DIAND, 1986). And again as *Federal Policy for the Settlement of Native Claims* (Ottawa: DIAND, 1998).

33 *Aboriginal Self-Government* (Ottawa: DIAND, 1995) online: www.ainc-inac.gc.ca.

34 [1973] S.C.R. 313.

35 James Bay and Northern Quebec Agreement, between the Grand Council of the Crees (of Quebec), the Northern Quebec Inuit Association, the Government of Quebec, la Société d'énergie de la Baie James, la Société de développement de la Baie James, la Commission hydro-électrique de Québec and the Government of Canada, dated 11 November 1975, as amended 12 December 1975, and given effect as of 14 July 1977 by the *James Bay and Northern Québec Native Claims Settlement Act,* R.S.C. 1976–77, c. 32.

and small parts of Saskatchewan, Manitoba, and Ontario are the subject of final CCAs or of CCA-style negotiations. Most of the CCAs concluded so far focus exclusively on land issues. They address Aboriginal ownership of a quantum of land and sometimes natural resources, priority rights to harvest wildlife and other renewable resources in a larger traditional territory, co-management of lands and resources, and funding. Typically, the Aboriginal group exchanges undefined Aboriginal rights for the rights described in their agreement.[36] Only the Nisga'a, Tlicho, and Labrador Inuit Agreements are truly comprehensive in the sense that they address, and are intended to constitutionally protect, both land and self-government rights.

For our purposes, the self-government component of these three CCAs is key. In its Inherent Right Policy, the government of Canada recognizes the inherent right of self-government as an existing Aboriginal right under section 35. This recognition is based on the view that the Aboriginal peoples of Canada "have the right to govern themselves in relation to matters that are internal to their communities, integral to their unique cultures, identities, traditions, languages and institutions, and with respect to their special relationship to their land and their resources."[37] The Inherent Right Policy can be viewed as something of a leap of faith on the part of the federal government, for the Supreme Court of Canada has not yet identified self-government as an Aboriginal right protected by section 35.[38] But the Inherent Right Policy seems also to be an attempt by the federal government to exercise some leadership and control over a situation in which litigation might otherwise (and may still) define the rules of the game.

---

36 CCAs include "certainty provisions." While earlier CCAs included provisions extinguishing Aboriginal rights in favour of those described in the agreements, the Nisga'a Agreement introduced a new approach: Nisga'a Aboriginal rights are said to be modified to take the form in which they are expressed in the Nisga'a Agreement (above note 1, at ch. 2, arts. 24–27). In the Tlicho Agreement, certainty is achieved through an agreement by the Tlicho not to assert any Aboriginal rights other than those described in the agreement (above note 2, art. 2.6).

37 Inherent Right Policy, above note 33 at 3.

38 The Supreme Court has not foreclosed the possibility that an Aboriginal right to self-government may be found. It has suggested that the test it previously identified to determine whether Aboriginal rights exist in other contexts is the appropriate one to apply to cases about the existence of a right of self-government: See *R. v. Pamajewon*, [1996] 2 S.C.R. 821 and *Mitchell v. Canada (Minister of National Revenue - M.N.R.)*, [2001] 1 S.C.R. 911. This test has been described as follows by Lamer C.J.: "in order to be an Aboriginal right an activity must be an element of a practice, custom or tradition integral to the distinctive culture of the Aboriginal group claiming the right": *Van der Peet*, above note 23 at para. 46.

The Inherent Right Policy classifies legislative powers according to three lists.[39] These lists serve as the federal government's starting point in self-government negotiations, and their influence can be clearly seen in the Nisga'a, Tlicho, and Labrador Inuit Agreements.

List 1 powers are largely internal. Matters in List 1 include: the establishment of governing structures and internal constitutions; band membership; marriage, adoption, and welfare; Aboriginal languages, cultures, and religion; education, health, and social services; policing, the administration and enforcement of Aboriginal laws, and the creation of offences normally created by local or regional governments for contravention of their laws (short of the *Criminal Code*, a List 3 item); property rights, land and natural resources management; hunting, fishing, and trapping on Aboriginal lands; taxation of members; transfer and management of group assets; housing, public works, and infrastructure; local transportation; and regulation and operation of businesses located on Aboriginal lands. In short, List 1 powers concern matters internal to Aboriginal groups, integral to their culture and essential to the operation of their governments. List 1 items make up the bulk of the law-making powers described in the Nisga'a, Tlicho, and Labrador Inuit Agreements.

List 2 powers are those that may go beyond matters integral to Aboriginal culture or strictly internal to an Aboriginal group. Although the federal government may be prepared to negotiate a measure of Aboriginal jurisdiction in these areas, primary law-making is to remain with the federal or provincial governments and their laws prevail in the event of conflict with Aboriginal laws.

List 3 powers include those "related to Canadian sovereignty, defence and external relations," including foreign policy, international treaty-making, international trade, and "other national interest powers." List 3 powers are not up for negotiation in self-government agreements.

This brings us to the role of international legal provisions in CCAs.

C. COMPREHENSIVE CLAIMS AGREEMENTS AND INTERNATIONAL LAW

The legal and policy context of CCA negotiations, described earlier in this chapter, suggests a twofold rationale for the inclusion of international legal provisions in CCAs.

---

39 Inherent Right Policy, above note 33 at 5–8.

First, the treaty rights described in CCAs encompass an array of matters that may potentially be affected by Canada's obligations under customary and conventional international law. The potential for overlap is enormous. To take a single example, an international environmental accord might create obligations for Canada which, if implemented domestically, would impact upon CCA provisions about wildlife. Since, as we have seen, Aboriginal or treaty rights protected by section 35 cannot be infringed by laws implementing Canada's international legal obligations unless the infringement can be justified, there is a real prospect that Canadian international treaty obligations may prove difficult to implement where they collide with Aboriginal rights under CCAs.

Second, Aboriginal law-makers operating under self-government CCAs might create laws within their areas of jurisdiction that conflict, whether intentionally or inadvertently, with Canada's international legal obligations. Clearly, the federal government has an interest in preventing such conflicts and ensuring Canadian compliance with international law. It is important to observe, however, that there are at least four general features of self-government CCAs that limit the risks of Aboriginal non-compliance with Canadian international legal obligations.

The first such feature is that CCAs exist within the framework of Canada's constitution, including the *Charter of Rights and Freedoms*. The *Charter* applies to Aboriginal governments and legislative bodies under the Nisga'a, Tlicho, and Labrador Inuit Agreements. Of course, section 25 of the *Constitution Act, 1982* also applies. It provides that *Charter*-guaranteed rights and freedoms shall not be construed so as to abrogate or derogate from any Aboriginal, treaty, or other rights or freedoms that pertain to the Aboriginal peoples of Canada including those recognized by the Royal Proclamation of 7 October 1763 and those existing or acquired by way of land claims agreements. Section 25 has yet to be interpreted by the Supreme Court of Canada.[40]

Second, self-government CCAs include provisions on the harmonization of laws and standards. These provisions sometimes require, and at

40 Section 25 has not received much attention from the courts so far. It is not clear whether it is best understood as "shielding" Aboriginal, treaty, or other rights from *Charter* scrutiny, as establishing a prism through which *Charter* rights must be read, or as playing a balancing role in relation to Aboriginal and *Charter* rights. For a discussion, see Jane M. Arbour, "The Protection of Aboriginal Rights within a Human Rights Regime: In Search of an Analytical Framework for Section 25 of the Canadian Charter of Rights and Freedoms" (2001) 21 Sup. Ct. L. Rev. at 3.

other times encourage, Aboriginal laws and standards to match up with their federal and provincial counterparts. For example, the Tlicho Agreement includes harmonization provisions respecting social assistance and housing[41] and education curriculum,[42] and requiring the Tlicho government to consult with government in relation to laws it enacts respecting the use, management, administration, and protection of Tlicho lands.[43]

Third, in accordance with the Inherent Right Policy, self-government CCAs include relationship of laws provisions. Self-government CCAs operate on the basis that Aboriginal government law-making powers are concurrent with those of the federal, provincial or territorial governments, as the case may be. This means that federal, provincial, or territorial laws continue to apply to Aboriginal governments and their citizens after the agreement comes into effect. Conflict of laws rules set out in each self-government CCA are used to determine when federal, provincial, territorial, or Aboriginal laws prevail in the case of conflicts or inconsistencies between them. The Tlicho Agreement, for example, provides that federal "legislation of general application," a defined term in the agreement, prevails over Tlicho laws. Tlicho laws prevail to the extent of any conflict with any other federal legislation and with territorial legislation of general application, with the exception of territorial legislation that implements Canada's international legal obligations.[44] The Labrador Inuit Agreement is based on a similar model, although its conflict of law rules are not identical to those in the Tlicho Agreement.[45] This arrangement precludes the possibility of

41   Tlicho Agreement, above note 2, art. 7.5.5.

42   *Ibid.*, art. 7.5.7.

43   *Ibid.*, art. 7.5.13.

44   *Ibid.*, art. 7.7. The definition of "legislation of general application" is found in art. 1.1.1. The term refers to legislation that does not apply only to Tlicho citizens, to the Tlicho government or to Tlicho lands.

45   It is difficult to make a general statement describing when federal, provincial or Inuit laws prevail under the Labrador Inuit Agreement. Relationship of laws provisions are included in the General Provisions chapter of the Agreement (at part 2.15 and 2.22) and in the Labrador Inuit Self-Government Chapter (ch. 17) describing the law-making powers of the Nunatsiavut government and Inuit community governments. Conflict of laws rules are set out in the Agreement for each of these powers. For example, in relation to Inuit culture and language, an area of jurisdiction that may be exercised by the Nunatsiavut government, Inuit law prevails to the extent of any conflict or inconsistency with a federal or provincial law (see all of 17.8, especially, 17.8.5). In the case of Nunatsiavut government powers in relation to health, for some matters a federal or provincial law of general application prevails in the event of conflict with an Inuit law. For others, Inuit law prevails.

a legal vacuum during the transition from the previous legal regime to the new one: until the Aboriginal government exercises its law-making powers in relation to a particular subject matter, federal and provincial or territorial laws continue to apply. Once the Aboriginal government does exercise its power, rules are used to resolve conflicts between the laws of the different orders of government.

Finally, Aboriginal treaty rights described in CCAs can be justifiably infringed in accordance with the *Sparrow* test described above. It is conceivable that a potential incident of international law non-compliance linked to Aboriginal law-making could be rectified through justified infringement.

Given these four features of self-government CCAs, one might question the need for further, specific CCA provisions addressed solely to the resolution of possible conflicts between Aboriginal laws and Canadian international obligations. No such provisions were included in the Nisga'a Agreement. That agreement does require the federal government to consult the Nisga'a government with respect to the formulation of Canada's positions in relation to international discussions or negotiations that may significantly affect Nisga'a fisheries resources,[46] migratory birds, or their habitats in Nisga'a territory.[47] But unlike the Tlicho and Labrador Inuit Agreements, the Nisga'a Agreement does not include any general provisions addressing Nisga'a participation in Canadian international treaty-making. The Nisga'a Agreement leaves conflicts between Nisga'a laws and Canada's international legal obligations to be resolved on a government-to-government basis—rather like what occurs between the federal and provincial governments under *Labour Conventions.*

The Tlicho and Labrador Inuit Agreements, by contrast, take an explicit "rules of the game" approach to the two issues: the potential for Canada's international legal obligations to infringe Aboriginal treaty rights respecting the law-making and administrative authority of Aboriginal governments, and the possibility that Aboriginal laws and actions might place Canada in a position of non-compliance with such obligations. This rules approach appears to be another attempt to reduce uncertainty in Aboriginal affairs, but in a way that respects the principle of reconciliation that is at the heart of section 35.

---

46 Nisga'a Agreement, above note 1, ch. 8, art. 115.

47 *Ibid.*, ch. 9, art. 96.

D. INTERNATIONAL LAW PROVISIONS OF THE TLICHO AGREEMENT

The Tlicho (pronounced *tlee-chon*), also known as the Dogrib, are an Aboriginal people whose traditional lands lie in a vast region roughly extending from the northern shores of Great Slave Lake to the southern reaches of Great Bear Lake, and from the boundary between Nunavut and the Northwest Territories in the East almost to the Mackenzie River Valley in the West. Prior to the Agreement, the Tlicho were covered by Treaty 11. The Tlicho Agreement creates the Tlicho government and vests it with fee simple title to a single block of land totalling about 39,000 square kilometres, including subsurface resources. The Tlicho also have priority harvesting rights and a co-management role in land use decision making in a larger settlement territory. The Tlicho government has law-making jurisdiction in relation to a number of matters corresponding more or less to the Inherent Right Policy's List 1 items described above.

The international law provisions of the Tlicho Agreement are found in Chapter 7 under part 7.13, "International Legal Obligations." The provisions of this part set out the relationship between the Tlicho government and Canada in matters of international law. Although the emphasis is on treaty-made law, the provisions of this part frequently refer more generally to an "international legal obligation" of Canada—an undefined phrase that clearly encompasses both treaty and non-treaty sources of international law. The basic structure of the Tlicho–Canada relationship may be described as follows. The Tlicho government must ensure that its laws and other exercises of power conform to Canada's obligations under international law, including but not limited to Canadian international treaty obligations. For its part, Canada must consult with the Tlicho government on certain matters that may affect Tlicho rights. Where Canada considers that a Tlicho law or other exercise of power places Canada in violation of international law, the Tlicho must either remedy the breach or, if the Tlicho government disputes the existence of the breach, submit the matter to binding arbitration.

The Tlicho government's right to consultation on international legal matters derives from two provisions of the Agreement. Section 7.13.2 provides:

> Prior to consenting to be bound by an international treaty that may affect a right of the Tlicho Government, the Tlicho First Nation or a Tlicho Citizen, flowing from the Agreement, the Government of Canada shall provide an opportunity for the Tlicho Government to make its views known with respect to the international treaty either separately or through a forum.

This section entitles the Tlicho government to a form of consultation by the federal government prior to Canada's acceptance of new international treaty obligations. The form of consultation is "an opportunity ... to make its views known ... either separately or through a forum." Significantly, the words *consult* and *consultation* are not used here. The latter word is defined by section 1.1.1 of the agreement to include notice, reasonable preparation time, the opportunity to present one's views, and full and fair consideration of them.[48] This appears to be much more consultation than is granted by section 7.13.2. The kind of international treaty to which this lesser right of consultation applies is one which "may affect a right" of the Tlicho "flowing from the Agreement." The phrase *may affect* appears to be a fairly liberal standard.

The Tlicho government's right to consultation under this section arises from international treaties that may affect "a right of the Tlicho Government, the Tlicho First Nation or a Tlicho Citizen, flowing from the Agreement." The tenor of this provision is at odds with the orthodox rule of Canadian reception law that treaties concluded by the federal government have no domestic legal effect in Canada unless implemented by legislation.[49] Section 7.13.2 suggests that the rights of the Tlicho government, the Tlicho First Nation as a body, or even a Tlicho citizen might be affected by the mere ratification of an international treaty by the federal government. It is tempting to read into this wording a recognition that the orthodox account of how treaties take effect in domestic law is something of an oversimplification.[50] It appears, however, that the wording was motivated more by consideration of the Crown's duty to consult than by reception law nice-

---

48 Section 1.1.1 provides in part:

"consultation" means

(a) the provision, to the person or group to be consulted, of notice of a matter to be decided in sufficient form and detail to allow that person or group to prepare its views on the matter;

(b) the provisions of a reasonable period of time in which the person or group to be consulted may prepare its views on the matter, and provision of an opportunity to present such views to the person or group obliged to consult; and

(c) full and fair consideration by the person or group obliged to consult of any views presented.

49 For example, *Baker v. Canada (Minister of Citizenship and Immigration)*, [1999] 2 S.C.R. 817 at para. 69; *Francis v. The Queen*, [1956] S.C.R. 618 at 621.

50 See Gibran van Ert, *Using International Law in Canadian Courts* (The Hague: Kluwer Law International, 2002) at 209–14.

ties. In any case, section 7.13.2 clearly contemplates early engagement with the Tlicho government on international treaty matters that may affect it.

The Tlicho Government's second consultation right occurs in section 7.13.5:

> The Government of Canada shall consult the Tlicho Government in the development of positions taken by Canada before an international tribunal where a law or other exercise of power of the Tlicho Government has given rise to an issue concerning the performance of an international legal obligation of Canada. Canada's positions before the international tribunal shall take into account the commitment of the Parties to the integrity of this Agreement.

This section grants the Tlicho government a right of consultation, in the defined sense of that term, in cases where a Tlicho law or other exercise of power is impugned before an international tribunal as contrary to international law. The term *international tribunal* is not defined but must be read to include any international body empowered to consider Canada's performance of its international obligations. Canada is required to consult with the Tlicho government "in the development of positions taken by Canada" before the tribunal. While this consultation does not appear to mandate any particular result, the positions Canada decides to take must "take into account the commitment of the Parties to the integrity of this Agreement."

Part 7.13 also imposes a duty on the Tlicho government to conform to Canada's international obligations. Section 7.13.3 provides,

> Where the Government of Canada informs the Tlicho Government that it considers that a law or other exercise of power of the Tlicho Government causes Canada to be unable to perform an international legal obligation, the Tlicho Government and the Government of Canada shall discuss remedial measures to enable Canada to perform the international legal obligation. Subject to 7.13.4, the Tlicho Government shall remedy the law or other exercise of power to the extent necessary to enable Canada to perform the international legal obligation.

This section gives the federal government a means of controlling internationally unlawful exercises of legislative or administrative power by the Tlicho. If a positive legislative or administrative act by the Tlicho government is viewed by the federal government as bringing Canada into violation of its international obligations, whether conventional or customary, the federal government may invoke this section to require the Tlicho to cure the defect. The section provides that the Tlicho and federal governments "shall discuss remedial measures to enable Canada to perform" its obligations, and that the Tlicho government shall take remedial action "to the extent necessary to enable Canada to perform" them. These phrases suggest that federal–Tlicho discussions are likely to result in something more subtle than a blunt instruction from Ottawa to the Tlicho to implement the treaty. Should these discussions produce a solution short of express implementation by the Tlicho government but which nevertheless permits Canada to perform its international obligation, that result will satisfy the Tlicho government's obligations under section 7.13.3.

Section 7.13.3 only applies to "a law or other exercise of power of the Tlicho Government." It does not, on its face, apply to Tlicho government failures or omissions to legislate or take other action on matters about which Canada has international legal obligations. Section 7.13.3 need not go this far because (as explained earlier) the Tlicho Agreement is based on concurrent jurisdiction. Therefore, an omission by the Tlicho government to exercise its powers to implement a treaty will not in itself result in Canada being unable to perform an international legal obligation. The federal or territorial implementing legislation will fill the gap. It is only once the Tlicho government enacts a law or otherwise exercises its power that the duty to conform arises.

Section 7.13.4 provides a means of resolving disputes that may arise where Canada and the Tlicho disagree over whether a Tlicho law or other exercise of power renders Canada unable to perform an international legal obligation. Such disputes are resolved by recourse to the mediation and arbitration provisions of chapter six of the Tlicho Agreement. First, Canada and the Tlicho go to mediation pursuant to part 6.4. This step is a mandatory precursor to arbitration: see section 6.5.1. If mediation fails to resolve the dispute, an arbitrator is appointed and an arbitration conducted pursuant to part 6.5.[51] The arbitration may give rise to two possible results:

> If the arbitrator, having taken into account all relevant reservations and exceptions available to Canada, determines that the law or other exercise of power of the Tlicho Government does not cause Canada to be unable

---

51 Sections 6.5.4 (permitting parties to the Tlicho Agreement who are not parties to the dispute to be a party to the arbitration), 6.5.5 (permitting anyone with an indirect interest in the dispute to intervene) and 6.5.10 (making arbitral awards enforceable as court orders) shall not apply: section 7.13.4.

to perform the international legal obligation, the Government of Canada shall not take any further action for this reason aimed at changing the Tlicho Government law or other exercise of power. If the arbitrator, having taken into account all relevant reservations and exceptions available to Canada, determines that the law or other exercise of power of the Tlicho Government causes Canada to be unable to perform the international legal obligation, the Tlicho Government shall remedy the law or other exercise of power to enable Canada to perform the international legal obligation.

The first notable thing about this provision is simply that it exists at all. Until the Labrador Inuit Agreement, there was nothing else like it in Canadian law. This provision establishes the prospect of an arbitrator conducting a hearing between the government of Canada and the Tlicho government on the sole question of whether a Tlicho government law or administrative action places Canada in default of an obligation imposed on it by public international law. Furthermore, section 6.5.6(f) provides that the arbitrator may refer questions of law—which this undoubtedly would be—to the Supreme Court of the Northwest Territories, with attendant appeals to the Court of Appeal for the Northwest Territories and, ultimately, the Supreme Court of Canada.

The second notable thing about section 7.13.4 is its provision concerning "all relevant reservations and exceptions available to Canada." VCLT art 2(1)(d) defines a reservation as "a unilateral statement, however phrased or named, made by a State, when signing, ratifying, accepting, approving or acceding to an international treaty, whereby it purports to exclude or to modify the legal effect of certain provisions of the treaty in their application to that State." "Exception" is not a term of art in the law of international treaties, but may be intended to refer to flexibilities built into some international treaties permitting a variety of approaches to implementation to accommodate different domestic legal settings.[52] It is unlikely that the term is intended to refer to a reservation-like exemption or exclusion from rules of customary international law, since custom rarely admits of such deviations. Section 7.13.4 requires the arbitrator (and presumably also the Supreme Court of the Northwest Territories) to take reservations and

---

52   It seems unlikely that the term *exception* is intended to refer to the state practice of attaching "statements of understanding" or "interpretive declarations" to ratified treaties, since such declarations are not intended (explicitly, at least) to create exceptions from the treaty in favour of the declaring state. Furthermore, this practice has no basis in the VCLT.

exceptions into account when determining whether a Tlicho act causes Canada to be unable to perform its international legal obligations. This implies that one possible finding available to the arbitrator (or, more likely, the court) will be that Canada may perform the international legal obligation in question by invoking any reservation it may have entered to the treaty from which the obligation derives or by asserting some other exception available to Canada under customary or conventional international law. The legal significance of such a finding is unclear. If the arbitrator or court finds that Canada can avoid an international obligation that runs contrary to a Tlicho law—thus sparing that law the consequences of non-conformity set out in the agreement—by invoking an existing reservation or exercising some other exception to the obligation, must the federal government do so? Does section 7.13.4 empower an arbitrator or court to do what no other judicial body in Canada can,[53] namely, to force the executive to exercise its foreign affairs prerogative in a judicially required way? Reception law orthodoxy suggests the answer is no. But the text of the section, viewed in light of section 35 of the *Constitution Act, 1982,* may suggest otherwise.

We have seen that section 7.13.5 requires the federal government to consult the Tlicho government in the development of Canadian positions before international tribunals in cases involving Tlicho law or administration. The final substantive provision of part 7.13 is a counterpoint to this obligation: section 7.13.6 provides:

> Notwithstanding 7.13.4 [the arbitration provision], if there is a finding of an international tribunal of non-performance of an international legal obligation of Canada attributable to a law or other exercise of power of the Tlicho Government, the Tlicho Government shall, at the request of the Government of Canada, remedy the law or action to enable Canada to perform the international legal obligation consistent with the compliance of Canada.

---

53 No such power has ever been expressly recognized and acted upon in Canada. However, in *Operation Dismantle Inc. v. Canada,* [1985] 1 S.C.R. 441 the Supreme Court of Canada made clear that the application of the *Charter* extends to the federal government's conduct of foreign affairs. It may be, therefore, that a court acting to enforce the *Charter* could order the federal government not to assume a particular treaty obligation, or not to do so without entering a *Charter*-compliant reservation. This question could itself form an entire essay and we will not pursue it here. We note, however, the obvious point that such an interpretation of the *Charter*'s ambit goes well beyond current thinking and must contend with numerous objections of high constitutional import.

Thus, if an international tribunal finds Canada in breach of international law, and this breach is attributable to a Tlicho law or power, the federal government may require the Tlicho government to remedy the breach and bring Canada into compliance with international law. The Tlicho may not have recourse to arbitration in such cases. On the face of this provision, it is up to the federal government to decide whether or not Canada's breach is attributable to the Tlicho government. There is no express provision in the Agreement on what the Tlicho may do if they dispute the federal government's view that Canada's breach is attributable to them. Judicial review of the federal government's exercise of its power under this section would presumably be available.

Section 7.13.6 does not require the Tlicho government immediately to remedy its laws or actions upon a finding of breach by an international tribunal. Rather, it must only do so "at the request of the Government of Canada." This gives the federal government the option of not complying with the decision of an international tribunal and not bringing Canada into compliance with international law. This section leaves open the possibility that the federal government may disregard the ruling of an international body and affirm a Tlicho government measure. One reason for doing so would be if the international ruling were irremediably inconsistent with the Canadian Constitution. Another reason would be to preserve Canada's domestic law until such time as Canada had exhausted whatever appeals or diplomatic remedies may be available to it to resolve the conflict at the international level.

While part 7.13 is the focus of the Tlicho Agreement's international law provisions, international law also comes up in provisions concerning amendments to the agreement,[54] Canadian taxation treaties,[55] and wildlife management.[56]

54   Section 2.10.7.
55   Section 7.5.12.
56   Sections 12.5.9 and 12.5.10 (determinations and recommendations of recommendation of the Wek'èezhìi Renewable Resources Board to be consistent with Canadian international obligations); section 12.12.1 (government to consult prior to adopting positions in relation to international agreements which may affect wildlife or wildlife habitat).

E. INTERNATIONAL LAW PROVISIONS OF THE LABRADOR INUIT AGREEMENT

The territory subject to the Labrador Inuit Agreement covers over 72,000 square kilometres of land in northeastern Labrador and over 48,000 square kilometres of ocean extending to the limit of Canada's territorial sea. The Labrador Inuit Agreement establishes two levels of government: the Nunatsiavut government and five Inuit community governments (referred to collectively in the agreement as Inuit governments). The Nunatsiavut government may make laws in such areas as education, health, child and family services, and the administration of Inuit laws, corresponding more or less to List 1 of the Inherent Right Policy. The Inuit community governments resemble municipal governments and exercise by-law powers in their jurisdictions.

International law figures even more prominently in the Labrador Inuit Agreement than in the Tlicho agreement, though the central international legal provisions of the two agreements are broadly the same. While international law references may be found in several chapters of the agreement, part 17.27, "Canada's International Legal Obligations," is the main source of reception rules. As its title suggests, this part clearly extends to all Canada's international legal obligations, whether customary or conventional. Like its parallel part in the Tlicho Agreement, part 17.27 gives the Nunatsiavut government consultation rights on matters of international law affecting rights under the Agreement and requires that Inuit governments conform to Canadian international obligations.

The general Inuit right to consultation is established by section 17.27.3. It provides that the federal government shall consult the Nunatsiavut government "either directly or through a forum" before consenting to be bound to an international agreement (defined to follow the definition of treaty in article 2 of the *Vienna Convention on the Law of Treaties 1969*)[57] that "may affect a right under the Agreement of the Nunatsiavut government, an Inuit community government or Inuit." Most of the preceding comments made about section 7.13.2 of the Tlicho Agreement apply here. For instance, here, as in the Tlicho Agreement, we find the implicit suggestion that a Canadian international treaty obligation might somehow affect domestic rights without implementation.

---

57 Can. T.S. 1980 No 37.

There are, however, two small but significant differences between the consultation provisions of the two agreements. First, since the Labrador Inuit Agreement establishes two levels of Inuit government, section 17.27.2 must identify which level is entitled to consultation. Here and throughout the Agreement, it is the Nunatsiavut government and not the Inuit community governments, or any other body, to whom federal consultation is directed. The second difference lies in the extent of the federal government's consultation obligation. The term "consult" is used in section 17.27.2 in its defined sense under section 1.1.1:

"Consult" means to provide:

(a) to the Person being consulted, notice of a matter to be decided in sufficient form and detail to allow that Person to prepare its views on the matter;

(b) a reasonable period of time in which the Person being consulted may prepare its views on the matter, and an opportunity to present its views to the Person obliged to consult; and

(c) full and fair consideration by the Person obliged to consult of any views presented.

This is notable because, as we have seen, the analogous provision of the Tlicho Agreement pointedly refrains from using the term *consult* in its defined sense. In theory, then, the Nunatsiavut government enjoys greater consultation rights on treaty matters than the Tlicho government. It seems unlikely, however, that the federal government will insist on such distinctions in practice.

A second consultation right is granted to the Nunatsiavut government by section 17.27.4:

Canada shall Consult the Nunatsiavut Government in the development of positions taken by Canada before any international tribunal where an Inuit Law or Bylaw or other exercise of power by an Inuit Government has given rise to an issue concerning the performance of an international legal obligation of Canada. Canada's positions before the international tribunal shall take into account the Agreement.

This provision is almost word-for-word the same as section 7.13.5 of the Tlicho Agreement. The main difference occurs in the last sentence which, in the Tlicho version, refers to "the commitment of the Parties to the integrity of this Agreement." It seems unlikely that the Tlicho wording creates any real disparity between the Tlicho and Nunatsiavut governments' consultation rights in such cases.

As in the Tlicho Agreement, the Nunatsiavut government's right to consultation on international treaty matters is twinned with an obligation on Inuit governments to bring their laws and exercises of power into conformity with Canada's international legal obligations. Section 17.27.5 provides:

> Canada shall provide notification to the Nunatsiavut Government where it considers that an Inuit Law or Bylaw or other exercise of power by an Inuit Government causes Canada to be unable to perform one of its international legal obligations. Subject to section 17.27.6, the Inuit Government shall remedy the Inuit Law or Bylaw or other exercise of power to the extent necessary to enable Canada to perform the international legal obligation.

This provision largely tracks the wording of section 7.13.3 of the Tlicho Agreement, with one exception. Where the Tlicho Agreement provides that the Tlicho government and Canada "shall discuss remedial measures to enable Canada to perform" its obligations, this section of the Labrador Inuit Agreement simply provides that the Inuit shall fix the problem (subject to the dispute resolution provisions described below). However, the Labrador Inuit Agreement contains a more elaborate provision to the same effect in section 17.27.10:

> If an Inuit Government is required to provide remedial action under sections 17.27.5, 17.27.8 and 17.27.9, at the request of the Nunatsiavut Government, Canada shall Consult the Nunatsiavut Government for the purpose of reaching agreement about remedial measures to be executed by the Inuit Government to enable Canada to perform such international legal obligation and Consult the Nunatsiavut Government about the ways and means Canada may employ to facilitate such remedial action by the Inuit Government.

This provision invokes the defined meaning of *consult* and therefore applies the consultation requirements described above to the process of remedying an Inuit-created breach of a Canadian international legal obligation. Whether this consultation occurs is up to the Nunatsiavut government, which may choose to request it or not. Canada must consult the Nunatsiavut government about "ways and means Canada may employ to facilitate" the required remedial action. This suggests some role for Canada in promoting or encouraging Inuit compliance. But this is a far cry from the language of "any reservations and exceptions available to Canada," found in section 7.13.4 of the Tlicho Agreement. Furthermore, unlike the reservations and exceptions provision of the Tlicho Agreement, section 17.27.10 does not occur as part of the dispute-resolution process but after it; the

Inuit obligation to conform to Canada's international obligation "as is" has already been established at this point. So whatever degree of give-and-take section 17.27.10 may provide, the end result is not open for negotiation: the Inuit government must remedy Canada's breach.

Further conformity obligations are imposed by sections 17.27.8 and 17.27.9 of the Labrador Inuit Agreement. The former provision requires Inuit governments to rectify non-conforming laws following the dispute resolution procedure described below. As is the case in section 7.13.3 of the Tlicho Agreement, section 17.27.8 does not require Inuit governments to exercise their powers to implement a Canadian treaty obligation if they choose not to do so. The section's conformity obligation is triggered by Inuit government acts not omissions. Section 17.27.9 requires Inuit governments to conform to a decision against Canada by an international tribunal "attributable to an Inuit Law or Bylaw or other exercise of power by an Inuit Government ... at the request of Canada," notwithstanding the Agreement's dispute resolution provisions. This provision is the equivalent of section 7.13.6 of the Tlicho Agreement.

Like the Tlicho Agreement, section 17.27.6 of the Labrador Inuit Agreement provides for dispute resolution in the event that the federal government and the Nunatsiavut government "disagree over whether an Inuit Law or Bylaw or other exercise of power by an Inuit government causes Canada to be unable to perform" an international legal obligation, about which Canada has notified the Nunatsiavut government under section 17.27.5. The main difference between the two agreements on this point is that the Labrador Inuit Agreement sends such disputes directly to the Federal Court. Either party may refer the dispute to that court pursuant to section 17(3)(b) of the *Federal Courts Act* RSC 1985 c. F-7, which provides:

> The Federal Court has exclusive original jurisdiction to hear and determine the following matters: ...
>
> (b) any question of law, fact or mixed law and fact that the Crown and any person have agreed in writing shall be determined by the Federal Court, the Federal Court–Trial Division or the Exchequer Court of Canada.

If the Federal Court determines that the Inuit measure does not cause Canada to be unable to perform its international legal obligation, "Canada shall take no further action ... directed at changing the Inuit Law or Bylaw or other exercise of power by the Inuit Government" (section 17.27.7). One presumes that this is subject to the federal government's right to appeal the Federal Court decision as far as the Supreme Court of Canada, if necessary. If the Inuit government loses its case in Federal Court, it shall remedy the offending measure (section 17.27.8). Again, this section must be subject to the Inuit government's right to appeal, though that is not expressly stated. By these provisions, the Federal Court is made the primary forum for dispute resolution on international conformity questions. The mediation and arbitration procedure of the Tlicho Agreement is dropped. This is surely a preferable approach for, as we noted earlier, such disputes are legal in nature and must therefore end up in court even under the Tlicho Agreement.

There is a second difference between the Tlicho and Nunatsiavut dispute-resolution schemes. The latter does not require the Federal Court to take into account "all relevant considerations including any reservations and exceptions available to Canada" (Tlicho Agreement section 7.13.4) in deciding the case. As we saw earlier, the significance of this requirement in the Tlicho Agreement is uncertain. Whatever its consequences in that Agreement, it is simply absent from the Labrador Inuit Agreement. Subject always to the ingenuity of counsel, it will seemingly not be open to an Inuit government to argue in Federal Court that the Agreement requires Canada to invoke a treaty reservation, or exercise some other exception available to it at international law, to preserve an Inuit law or exercise of power.

One final reception law provision in part 17.27 is section 17.27.11:

> Within five years from the Effective Date, if Canada and an Aboriginal group or organization enter into a treaty of a similar scope and nature as the Agreement and it includes provisions respecting international legal obligations that are different from those provided in this part, at the request of the Nunatsiavut Government, the Parties shall enter into negotiations for the purpose of amending the Agreement to reflect the new approach.

No such provision occurs in the Tlicho Agreement. The Labrador Inuit can invoke this provision in order to benefit from any improvements to international legal obligation provisions that may appear in future self-government CCAs.

Part 17.27 is not the only part of the Agreement that makes reference to international law. The matter comes up in provisions addressing wildlife and plants and specified fisheries matters,[58] wildlife harvesting tech-

---

58 Labrador Inuit Agreement, above note 3, arts. 12.14.1 and 12.14.3, and 13.14.1 and 13.14.2, respectively.

niques,[59] harvesting compensation,[60] oceans management,[61] taxation,[62] and bid criteria for federal government contracts.[63] It is notable that, in addition to its general provisions on international law, the Labrador Inuit Agreement includes more references to international law than any previous CCA. This goes to the fact that it is increasingly the case, and increasingly recognized, that Canada's international legal obligations can have an impact on Aboriginal law and policy issues, and vice versa.

F. CONCLUSION: THOUGHTS ON LABOUR CONVENTIONS AND THE ABORIGINAL MODEL

We have suggested that the compromise implicit in the Tlicho and Labrador Inuit Agreements—conformity for consultation—responds to two possible problems. The first is that Canada's international legal obligations might infringe the treaty rights of the Tlicho and Labrador Inuit. The second is that laws made and actions taken by the Tlicho or Labrador Inuit governments might place Canada in a position of non-compliance with its international legal obligations. The need to respond to these concerns has given rise to a new model for subfederal participation in Canadian international treaty-making—a model notably different than that which applies to the provinces under *Labour Conventions* and the common law.

The main difference between the two models is that the Aboriginal model does not permit the Tlicho and Labrador Inuit to enact laws in violation of international law. Whether this truly represents a concession by the Tlicho and Labrador Inuit is difficult to say. The provinces are sovereign to violate international law because the Privy Council held that Canadian legislatures, both federal and provincial, enjoy within their respective jurisdictions powers as great as those possessed by the imperial Parliament at Westminster—including the power to enact laws contrary to international law.[64] Would a court ever come to the same conclusion about an Aboriginal government in exercise of self-government powers, whether under a section 35 protected CCA or Aboriginal right of self-government (if such a right is ever recognized)? The answer to that question would depend on

---

59 *Ibid.*, arts. 12.3.4 and 12. 3.5.
60 *Ibid.*, art. 14.2.1.
61 *Ibid.*, art, 6.2.1.
62 *Ibid.*, art. 20.2.4.
63 *Ibid.*, art. 7.10.4.
64 See van Ert, above note 50 at 52–65.

the juridical nature of Aboriginal self-government in Confederation. If Aboriginal legislative bodies were merely delegates exercising law-making powers conferred to them by the federal and provincial legislatures, then the power to violate international law would almost certainly not be among the powers conferred to them. Legislatures are presumed not to intend to violate international law, and must therefore be taken as not having delegated their power to do so. Thus an Aboriginal law that violated international law could be struck down as *ultra vires*. But if Aboriginal legislative bodies were not delegates, or not merely delegates, but made laws through an inherent self-government right, the power to violate international law might conceivably be theirs. The effect of the reception law provisions of the Tlicho and Labrador Inuit Agreements is to spare us the trouble of answering these difficult questions, at least for the time being.

Though comparing the *Labour Conventions* and Aboriginal models is illuminating, the latter is not intended to replace the former. The Aboriginal model responds to similar questions but in a different context. Nevertheless, one wonders what the provinces may think of that model. In particular, might some provinces be prepared to concede their legislative power to frustrate Canadian treaty initiatives in return for guaranteed consultation and dispute resolution rights? The *Labour Conventions* case has been heavily criticized (unfairly, in the view of one of the authors)[65] and there has long been speculation that the Supreme Court of Canada might overturn it. But the Aboriginal model suggests another possibility, namely, that *Labour Conventions* might in time be displaced by federal-provincial agreements along the lines of those surveyed here. Turning the question around, one wonders how the relative merits of rules-based versus government-to-government reception schemes look from the Aboriginal perspective. The Tlicho and the Labrador Inuit have agreed to a rules-based scheme. But might some Aboriginal peoples prefer a government-to-government scheme, of the sort enjoyed by the provinces under *Labour Conventions* and by the Nisga'a under their agreement? In particular, might some Aboriginal groups view such a scheme as more consonant with their claim to an inherent right to self-government?

Throughout this chapter we have described the approach to international legal obligations in the Tlicho and Labrador Inuit Agreements as new. That is entirely apt, and yet the Aboriginal model of subfederal participation in Canadian international treaty-making has not appeared out of

---

65   *Ibid.* at 205–7.

the blue. It is the product of two bodies of Canadian legal thinking. The first is Aboriginal law, particularly since the entrenchment of Aboriginal rights in section 35 of the *Constitution Act 1982*. The second is reception law, and more specifically the interplay of international treaties and federalism. It is too soon to say whether the attempt to reconcile the potentially conflicting demands of these two areas of law in the Tlicho and Labrador Inuit agreements has succeeded. Yet it is clear that Aboriginal governments exercising self-government rights like those described in the Tlicho and Labrador Inuit Agreements are important new players in the Canadian international treaty-making process.

Table 7.1: Labour Conventions and CCAs compared

Right, duty, or power	*Labour Conventions and common law*	Tlicho Agreement	Labrador Inuit Agreement
Legislative sovereignty to violate international law.	Yes: subject to constraints of written constitution.	No: Tlicho government must bring its laws into conformity with international law at prompting of Canada (7.13.3) or as required by an arbitral award (7.13.4) or as requested by Canada following an international tribunal decision (7.13.6).	No: Inuit government must bring its laws into conformity with international law as requested by Canada (17.27.5) or as required by Federal Court (17.27.8) or as requested by Canada following an international tribunal decision (17.27.9). See also 20.2.4 (taxation).
Duty to bring laws and exercises of power into conformity with Canada's international obligations.	No: but courts interpret provincial (and federal) laws subject to the rebuttable presumption that they conform with international law.	Yes: Tlicho government shall remedy the impugned provision at prompting of Canada (7.13.3) or as required by an arbitral award (7.13.4) or as requested by Canada following an international tribunal decision (7.13.6).	Yes: Inuit government shall remedy the impugned provision as requested by Canada (17.27.5), or as required by Federal Court (17.27.8), or as requested by Canada following an international tribunal decision (17.27.9). See also 20.2.4 (taxation).

Right, duty, or power	*Labour Conventions and common law*	Tlicho Agreement	Labrador Inuit Agreement
Mandatory dispute resolution in case of disagreement over subfederal compliance with international law.	No.	Yes: disputes over compliance of Tlicho laws or other exercises of power with Canadian international obligations resolved by mediation and arbitration (7.13.4).	Yes: disputes over compliance of Inuit laws with Canadian international obligations resolved in Federal Court (17.27.6-8).
Legal right to consultation before Canada enters treaties affecting matters within subfederal jurisdiction.	No: but consultation may be necessary to assure eventual implementation of and compliance with the treaty.	Yes: Canada shall provide an opportunity for the Tlicho government to make its views known with respect to a treaty "that may affect a right ... flowing from the Agreement," either separately or through a forum (7.13.2).	Yes: Canada shall consult the Nunatsiavut government, directly or through a forum, before consenting to treaties "that may affect a right under the Agreement" (17.27.3).
Power to make Canada invoke reservations and exceptions to preserve subfederal law.	No.	Unclear: see 7.13.4, requiring arbitrator to take into account all relevant reservations and exceptions available to Canada.	Seemingly not though Canada, at request of Nunatsiavut government, shall consult about "ways and means Canada may employ to facilitate" conformity with international law (17.27.10).
Right to consultation where subfederal law impugned by an international tribunal as contrary to a Canadian international legal obligation.	No: but consultation may prove practically necessary.	Yes: Canada shall consult Tlicho government where a Tlicho law or other exercise of power has given rise to an issue concerning performance of a Canadian international obligation (7.13.5).	Yes: Canada shall consult Nunatsiavut government where an Inuit law or by-law or other exercise of power has given rise to an issue concerning performance of a Canadian international obligation (17.27.4).

Right, duty, or power	*Labour Conventions* and common law	Tlicho Agreement	Labrador Inuit Agreement
Duty to conform to decisions of international tribunals at request of Canada.	No.	Yes: Tlicho government shall remedy the impugned law or action to enable Canada to perform its obligation (7.13.6).	Yes: Inuit government shall remedy the Inuit law or by-law or other exercise of power to extent necessary for Canada to perform its obligation (17.27.9).

Fostering Compliance with International Biodiversity Law: Environmental Advocacy Groups Inside and Outside the Courtroom*

NATASHA AFFOLDER

A. INTRODUCTION

International biodiversity law is easily viewed in Canada as an exotic species of law: not only does it advance the protection of endangered species—such as the hairy-eared dwarf lemur in Madagascar, the maned three-toed sloth in Brazil, and the sandbar shark in Equatorial Guinea—but it leads to treaty negotiations in Ramsar and Rio de Janeiro. The consequence of treating this branch of law as "exotic" is perilous because it allows international biodiversity law to be regarded in Canada as something other than law—as something "to be avoided if at all possible"[1] and as something to be peppered into submissions and judgments without a principled explanation of its role in Canadian law. Indicted as being "interesting" rather than binding law in Canada,[2] international biodiversity law receives only limited consideration in recent Canadian judgments.

---

* I would like to thank Laura Track and Stephanie Case for their excellent research assistance and Gib van Ert for his helpful comments. This chapter originally appeared as "Domesticating the Exotic Species: International Biodiversity Law in Canada" (2006) 51 McGill C.J. 3. Reprint permission is gratefully acknowledged.

1 Rosalyn Higgins, *Problems and Process: International Law and How We Use It* (Oxford: Clarendon Press, 1994) at 206 (describing the treatment of international law by judges and counsel in some courts of the United Kingdom as some "exotic branch of law, to be avoided if at all possible, and to be looked upon as if unreal, of no practical application to the real world.")

2 See, for example, *MacMillan Bloedel Ltd. v. Simpson*, [1993] B.C.J. No. 3143 at para. 7 (S.C.) [*MacMillan Bloedel Ltd.*] ("In these circumstances, there is no point in dealing with the extensive submissions of the applicants, *interesting* as they were … the

The lack of engagement with international biodiversity law in Canadian judicial decisions contrasts with the proliferation of international biodiversity treaties. While a significant body of international and regional agreements now addresses habitat preservation, wildlife protection, and biological diversity, these advances on the international level often fail to be effectively translated into national law. Where international biodiversity norms fail to be implemented in Canadian law through statutes or incorporated as customary international law, internationally minded lawyers optimistically look to domestic courts as the vehicles through which international treaty and customary norms may enter the Canadian legal system.[3]

This chapter suggests that in the case of international biodiversity law, such optimism may be misplaced. An analysis of Canadian judicial decisions between 1990 and 2005 reveals an extremely limited role of the courts in internalizing international biodiversity law norms. Analysis of these judicial decisions also reveals that the majority of arguments involving international biodiversity law before Canadian courts originate in the submissions of environmental advocacy groups. Given the limited role of courts in giving effect to international biodiversity norms in domestic litigation, environmental advocacy groups attempt to foster compliance with these norms through wider campaign strategies.

In elucidating the role of Canadian environmental advocacy groups in fostering compliance with international biodiversity law, this chapter explores how international law is used by these advocacy groups both inside and outside the courtroom. It first examines the use of international biodiversity law in domestic litigation and disaggregate judicial responses to these arguments. This analysis reveals an impoverished view of international biodiversity law in Canadian courtrooms.

---

arguments relating to international agreements and resolutions, these not being expressed in Canadian law, are not relevant to this inquiry" [emphasis added]). See also *Repap New Brunswick Inc., Woodlands Division v. Pictou*, [1996] N.B.J. No. 495 at para. 12 (Q.B.T.D.) [*Repap New Brunswick v. Pictou*]. ("There is no question that there are matters of great concern at issue. There is no question that maybe they should be addressed in other forums.")

3   See Anne-Marie Slaughter, "Judicial Globalization" (2000) 40 Va. J. Int'l L. 1103 at 1103 ("National courts are the vehicles through which international treaties and customary law that have not been independently incorporated into domestic statutes enter domestic legal systems").

A richer understanding of the relevance of international law is gained by examining this litigation in the context of the wider environmental advocacy campaigns in which it is situated. International law arguments are not abandoned by environmental advocacy groups because they prove unsuccessful in court. Public interest litigation is not solely about winning, and environmental advocacy groups creatively use international law arguments outside the courtroom through public shaming devices, transnational litigation, and market-based campaigns. In these campaigns, Canada's reputation, both as a law-abiding member of the international community and as an environmental leader, is attacked. Environmental advocacy groups may strategically cite cases of judicial rejection of international law arguments as evidence that Canada refuses to implement and enforce its international obligations. In this way, courtroom failings can translate into useful fodder for shaming campaigns or appeals to international bodies. This research encourages a contextualized examination of Canadian litigation addressing international biodiversity law and a greater role for Canadian advocates and the judiciary in engaging with international biodiversity law sources in a principled manner.

B. INTERNATIONAL BIODIVERSITY LAW IN THE COURTROOM

1) The Application of International Law in Canadian Courts

Understanding the potential role for international biodiversity law in Canadian courtrooms demands an appreciation of how public international law is applied in Canadian courts. This area is not uncontested and remains rife with nuance and uncertainty, much of which is usefully explored in detail elsewhere.[4] A few central tenets of reception law require elucidation

---

4   For a "primer" on the application of International law in Canadian courts see Jutta Brunnée & Stephen J. Toope, "A Hesitant Embrace: The Application of International Law by Canadian Courts" (2002) 40 Can. Y.B. Int'l L. 3 at 9; Gibran van Ert, Using International Law in Canadian Courts (The Hague: Kluwer Law International, 2002), and Mark Freeman & Gibran van Ert, International Human Rights Law (Toronto: Irwin Law, 2004) c. 8. Examples of the growing body of academic commentary on the role of international law in Canadian courts include Anne Warner La Forest, "Domestic Application of International Law in Charter Cases: Are We There Yet?" (2004) 37 U.B.C. L. Rev. 157; Stephen J. Toope, "The Uses of Metaphor: International Law and the Supreme Court of Canada" (2001) 80 Can. Bar Rev. 534; Karen Knop, "Here and There: International Law in Domestic Courts" (2000) 32 N.Y.U. J. Int'l L. & Pol. 501; Stéphane Beaulac, "National Application of International Law: The Statutory Interpretation Perspective" (2003) 51 Can. Y.B. Int'l L. 225. In the environmental law area,

to appreciate the case discussions that follow. First, with respect to treaties, international treaties must be implemented in Canadian domestic law to be binding.[5] Further, the federalist nature of the Canadian state requires that treaties which concern matters of provincial jurisdiction may only be implemented by provincial Legislatures.[6] As treaties may be implemented in multiple ways, questions arise as to what counts as transformation.[7] Moreover, what is the status of a treaty that has been signed and ratified by Canada but not implemented by domestic statute? How does this differ from the status of a treaty that has not been ratified by Canada?

The Supreme Court has taken some steps in addressing these questions in recent cases outside the international environmental law context. Following this jurisprudence, a role for ratified (but not implemented) treaties exists where "the values reflected in the international convention may help inform the interpretation of the domestic statute."[8] This role is not uncontested.[9] Central to the approach of Canadian courts to international law sources is the presumption of legislative conformity with international law. This presumption demands that judges interpret statutes in a manner consistent with international laws that are binding on Canada. The presumption was recently articulated by Justices Iacobucci and Major in *Ordon Estate v. Grail*:

> Although international law is not binding upon Parliament or the provincial legislatures, a court must presume that legislation is intended to comply with Canada's obligations under international instruments and as

---

see Jutta Brunnée, "A Long and Winding Road: Bringing International Environmental Law into Canadian Courts" in Michael Anderson & Paolo Galizzi, eds., *International Environmental Law in National Courts* (London: British Institute of International and Comparative Law, 2002) at 45.

5   For a recent enunciation of this requirement, see *Baker v. Canada (Minister of Citizenship and Immigration)*, [1999] 2 S.C.R. 817, 174 D.L.R. (4th) 193 [*Baker*]. L'Heureux-Dubé J. makes this point at para. 69 and Iacobucci J. at para. 79.

6   *Reference Re Weekly Rest in Industrial Undertakings Act*, [1937] 1 D.L.R. 673, [1937] 1 W.W.R. 299 (J.C.P.C.). [*Labour Conventions Case*]

7   This leads courts (and commentators) to disagree as to whether certain treaties or specific treaty obligations are implemented or not. The view of the Supreme Court in *Baker* that the *Convention on the Rights of the Child* is not implemented in Canada is contested. For a discussion of what counts as treaty transformation see Brunnée & Toope, "A Hesitant Embrace," above note 4 at 22.

8   Hon. Claire L'Heureux-Dubé, "From Many Different Stones: A House of Justice" (2003) 41 Alta L. Rev. 659 at 664. See also, *Baker*, above note 5 at para. 70.

9   See *Baker*, above note 5 at paras. 79–80, Iacobucci J.

a member of the international community. In choosing among possible interpretations of a statute, the court should avoid interpretations that would put Canada in breach of such obligations.[10]

With respect to custom, Canadian courts largely appear to have accepted the view that customary international law automatically forms part of the law of Canada without the need for an explicit act of transformation.[11] This was the position of the Ontario Court of Appeal in the recent case of *Bouzari v. Iran*.[12]

These tenets of reception law frame a discussion of the limited role of international biodiversity law in Canadian courts. They also highlight the challenges for both counsel and judges in precisely clarifying the significance of an international source in Canadian law. Many treaties in the biodiversity field are not implemented by easily identifiable legislation. The absence of a *Biodiversity Convention Act* does not mean that the provisions of the *Biodiversity Convention* have not been at least partially implemented in Canadian law. Explicit implementation is not always necessary as treaty obligations can be implemented through other means, such as conformity with prior legislation.[13] Further, not all treaty provisions require implementation by statute because some operate purely at the international level (for example, provisions respecting the operation of international environmental institutions). The vital question is a results-based one. Canada as a contracting party has certain obligations under the *Biodiversity Convention*. Has Canada given effect to these obligations in Canadian law?

---

10 *Ordon Estate v. Grail*, [1998] 3 S.C.R. 437, 166 D.L.R. (4th) 193 at para 137.

11 I qualify this statement as the lack of clear affirmation of this approach by the Supreme Court of Canada leaves room for doubt in the wake of *dicta* suggesting that customary law, like treaty law, requires explicit transformation. For a discussion of the conflicting authorities on this point see Toope, "The Uses of Metaphor," above note 4 at 292; van Ert, *Using International Law*, above note 4 at 149.

12 *Bouzari v. Iran (Islamic Republic)* (2004), 71 O.R. (3d) 675 at para. 65, 243 D.L.R. (4th) 406 (C.A.). See also *Re Regina and Palacios*, (1984), 45 O.R. (2d) 269, 7 D.L.R. (4th) 112 (C.A.).

13 Irit Weiser suggests that human rights treaties are often ratified on the basis that no new legislation is required. See Irit Weiser, "Effect in Domestic Law of International Human Rights Treaties Ratified without Implementing Legislation" in Canadian Council on International Law, *The Impact of International Law on the Practice of Law in Canada: Proceedings of the 27th Annual Conference of the Canadian Council on International Law, Ottawa, 15–17 October 1997* (The Hague: Kluwer Law International, 1999) at 132.

2) Methodology: Case-Selection Criteria

Effective implementation of an international treaty offers one explanation of why a treaty might not receive judicial mention. If the *Migratory Birds Convention Act*,[14] for example, so effectively conveys the meaning, purpose, and content of the *Migratory Birds Convention* into Canadian law, little recourse would be needed to the treaty itself. One might suggest, optimistically, that the sparsity of references to international treaties in Canadian judicial decisions evidences the fact that Canada is doing such an excellent job of fully implementing its international biodiversity obligations that there is little need for consideration of these obligations by Canadian judges.

However, Canada's record of implementing its biodiversity treaty obligations is not this rigorous and the limited judicial discussion of these treaties is not likely a result of watertight treaty implementation.[15] The issue of treaty implementation informs the methodology of this research because it suggests that the quantity of judicial comment on a treaty is not necessarily significant. What matters is the quality of the engagement with an international source. This study thus offers a qualitative assessment of the judicial decisions between 1990 and 2005,[16] where judicial mention is made of one of four major biodiversity treaties: the *Biodiversity Convention*, the *Ramsar Convention*, the *World Heritage Convention*, and the *Migratory Birds Convention*.[17]

---

14 *Migratory Birds Convention Act, 1994*, S.C. 1994, c. 22.

15 See, for example, the discussion of the decade-long battle to give effect to Canada's legal obligation to introduce federal endangered species law, below at text accompanying notes 107–36.

16 This analysis is based on the author's review of the record from cases known to the author and Quicklaw searches and is current to 15 May 2005. The searches include the Quicklaw electronic databases covering federal and provincial judgments (CJ), as well as electronic databases of environmental appeal board decisions in Ontario, British Columbia, Alberta, and Quebec (AEAB, BCEA, and OEAB, and ENVQ).

17 *Convention on Biological Diversity*, 5 June 1992, 1760 U.N.T.S. 79, Can. T.S. 1993 No. 24, 31 I.L.M. 818. [*Biodiversity Convention*]; *Convention on Wetlands of International Importance Especially as Waterfowl Habitat*, 2 February 1971, 996 U.N.T.S. 245, Can. T.S. 1981 No. 9, 11 I.L.M. 963 [*Ramsar Convention*]; *Convention Concerning the Protection of the World Cultural and Natural Heritage*, 23 November 1972, 1037 U.N.T.S. 151, 27 U.S.T. 37, 11 I.L.M. 1358 [*World Heritage Convention*]; *Convention between the United States and Great Britain for the Protection of Migratory Birds*, 16 August 1916, 39 U.S. Stat. 1702, T.I.A.S. No. 628 [*Migratory Birds Convention*].

Although Canada has ratified other biodiversity treaties, this chapter does not consider those treaties that only receive judicial mention in the context of an analysis of their implementing legislation and where there is no independent engagement with the international source. For example, this study does not consider the *Agreement for the Conservation of Polar Bears,*[18] as the sole relevant case mentioning the *Agreement* is *R. v. Martin,*[19] where the court accepted that the agreement was implemented pursuant to a general implementing power in the *Export and Import Permits Act*[20] and made no independent consideration of the agreement.

Similarly, although seven Canadian cases since 1990 mention the *Convention on International Trade in Endangered Species of Wild Fauna and Flora,*[21] none address the Convention itself. Rather, the Convention is only peripherally mentioned in the context of discussion of its implementing legislation, both the *Wild Animal and Plant Protection and Regulation of International and Interprovincial Trade Act,*[22] and the *Export and Import Permits Act.*[23]

This chapter also does not consider those cases where one of the four treaties that form the subject of this inquiry is mentioned only to note the source of the domestic law obligation, and there is no independent discussion of the treaty. This eliminates from consideration many of the cases where the *Migratory Birds Convention Act* is applied (including a number of Aboriginal hunting cases) as there is no distinct consideration of the international treaty regime.

I justify these exclusions on the grounds that the goal of this research is not to measure how often the names of treaties are invoked by the courts, but the extent to which the courts are willing to discuss (even if only to reject) the use of an international instrument. With these limitations in place, a search of the case law yields nineteen references to the *Biodiversity Convention,* the *Ramsar Convention,* the *World Heritage Convention,* or the *Migratory Birds Convention.* What is significant about this result is not this

---

18   15 November 1973, Can. T.S. 1976 No. 24.

19   (1994), 72 O.A.C. 316 (C.A.).

20   R.S.C. 1970, c. E-17.

21   3 March 1973, Can. T.S. 1975 No. 32, 8249 T.IA.S. 1087.

22   S.C. 1992, c. 52. See *R. v. Deslisle* (2003), 181 B.C.A.C. 55, 2003 BCCA 196; *R. v. Kwok Shing Enterprises Ltd.* (2001), 41 C.E.L.R. (N.S.) 288, 2001 BCPC 305.

23   R.S.C. 1970, c. E-17. See *Re African Lion Safari & Game Farm Ltd. v. Kerrio* (1987), 59 O.R. (2d) 65, 37 D.L.R. (4th) 80 (C.A.); *Lechner Estate v. Canada (M.N.R.),* [1992] 2 C.T.C. 2615, 92 D.T.C. 2285 (T.C.C.).

number, but the limited and often superficial nature of the engagement with international law in these cases.

3) The Cases

The earlier doctrinal discussion of the relationship between international and Canadian law identifies some of the ambiguities, conflicts, and novel areas currently explored by Canadian courts and commentators. It does little to prepare one for the murkiness surrounding the treatment of international biodiversity law in these cases, and the absence of rigorous discussion of how international biodiversity treaties are applied in Canadian law. Of the six cases where judicial mention is made of the *Biodiversity Convention*, for example, not a single case deals with the legal status in Canada of this international treaty. Is the *Biodiversity Convention* implemented in Canadian law? Has it only partially been implemented? To what degree does it require implementation in Canadian law? Should domestic laws be interpreted to conform as far as possible with Canada's commitments under the *Biodiversity Convention* based on the presumption of conformity even if it has not been wholly implemented? A rigorous engagement with these questions eludes these cases.

Attempting to disaggregate this body of nineteen cases, I divide them into four categories of judicial response:

1. Judicial Silence;
2. Explicit Rejection of International Law as it is not Implemented in Canadian Law;
3. Judicial Uncertainty; and
4. Acceptance of International Law as a Useful Source in Interpreting Domestic Legislation.

Common to each of these categories are examples of significant judicial unease with international law sources and a reticence to apply international law as anything other than an interpretive aid for domestic statutes.

a) Judicial Silence

International biodiversity law arguments are frequently met by judicial silence. Judges may not address these arguments at all or they may expressly acknowledge that international law arguments will not be considered. Often, this refusal to consider international law is not explained.

A recent example of this lack of engagement with international biodiversity law is the 2005 decision of the Federal Court in *Pembina Institute for Appropriate Development v. Canada (Minister of Fisheries and Oceans).*[24] This case is one of a collection of cases challenging the regulatory approvals granted to Cardinal River Coals Ltd. for an open-pit coal mine project within a few kilometres of Jasper National Park. The Pembina Institute, along with other regional, provincial, and national conservation groups represented by the Sierra Legal Defence Fund (together, the Conservation Groups), sought an order to quash the project authorization and to compel the Department of Fisheries and Oceans to prepare an environmental assessment of project modifications. In their submissions, the Conservation Groups argued that the federal government's 2004 authorization of the first part of the mine should be quashed because of the mine's potential to destroy sensitive migratory bird habitat in violation of the *Migratory Birds Convention Act*. Their argument advanced a purposive interpretation of the *Migratory Birds Convention Act* reflective of Canada's commitments under the *Migratory Birds Convention* not only to protect species but also the "lands and waters on which they depend."

The Conservation Groups argued that the *Migratory Birds Convention Act* should be interpreted in a manner consistent with Canada's international obligations and an interpretation that fulfills Canada's treaty commitments should be preferred over one that does not.[25] In support of this argument, they referred to Canada's obligation under Article 8 of the *Convention on Biological Diversity* to "(d) promote the protection of ecosystems, natural habitats and the maintenance of viable populations of species in natural surroundings; and (e) promote environmentally sound and sustainable development in areas adjacent to protected areas with a view to furthering protection of these areas."[26] The Conservation Groups interpreted section 35(1) of the *Migratory Bird Regulations*[27] as prohibiting the deposit of a substance harmful to migratory birds in any waters of areas frequented by migratory birds or the authorization of such a deposit.[28] They argued that their interpretation of the provision was preferable in

24 *Pembina Institute for Appropriate Development v. Canada (Minister of Fisheries and Oceans)*, [2005] 16 C.E.L.R. (3d) 170, 2005 FC 1123 [*Pembina Institute*].

25 *Ibid.* (Memorandum of Argument of the Applicants at paras. 112–13 [Pembina Institute, MAA] (relying as authority for this point on L'Heureux-Dubé J.'s decision in *114957 Canada Ltée (Spraytech, Société d'arrosage) v. Hudson (Town of)*, [2001] 2 S.C.R. 241 at paras. 30–31, [2001] 200 D.L.R. (4th) 419, 2001 SCC 40 [*Spraytech v. Hudson*].

26 *Pembina Institute, ibid.* at para. 112; *Biodiversity Convention*, above note 17.

27 C.R.C., c. 1035.

28 Pembina Institute, MAA, above note 25 at paras. 106–9.

light of Canada's obligations under the *Convention on Biological Diversity*. In rejecting the Conservation Groups' applications, the Federal Court was entirely silent on these points of international law and the presumption of legislative conformity.[29]

In *Repap New Brunswick v. Pictou*[30] the validity of an injunction preventing certain defendants from blockading a roadway and impeding RE-PAP's logging operations was challenged. In their arguments requesting a rescission of the injunction, a group of the defendants, the Friends of Christmas Mountain, argued that the injunction against them should be rescinded as there were inaccuracies in the affidavit on which basis it was granted and because:

> there has been disregard to the Convention on Biological Diversity concluded in June of 1992 at Rio de Janeiro between Canada and many other countries. As a result there is a significant breach of international law being committed in the operations that are being carried on and therefore the court should not grant injunctive relief.[31]

Although not directly articulated in the case, the legal test for rescinding an injunction demands the court to look anew at the evidence provided in support of the Injunctive Order and to determine whether the test for an interlocutory injunction is satisfied.[32] The test involves the tripartite considerations of "a serious question to be tried," the suffering by the applicant of "irreparable injury," and finally a consideration of the "balance of convenience."[33] The Friends of Christmas Mountain argued that in weighing the "balance of convenience," the judiciary should not favour an approach which shows disregard for international law.

The court rejected this argument without discussion and rejected the application to rescind the injunction. In the words of Justice Riordon, "There is no question that there are matters of great concern at issue. There is no question that maybe they should be addressed in other forums."[34]

---

29 *Pembina Institute*, above note 24.

30 *Repap New Brunswick v. Pictou*, above note 2.

31 *Ibid.* at para. 9.

32 *Yaghi v. WMS Gaming, Inc.* (2003), 18 Alta. L.R. (4th) 280 at para. 23, [2004] 2 W.W.R. 657, 2003 ABQB 680.

33 *American Cyanamid v. Ethicon*, [1975] A.C. 396 at 399–402 (H.L.); adopted by the Supreme Court in *RJR-MacDonald v. Canada (A.G.)*, [1994] 1 S.C.R. 311, 111 D.L.R. (4th) 385.

34 *Repap New Brunswick v. Pictou*, above note 2 at para. 12.

Even putting aside the strange juxtaposition of "no question" and "maybe" in this statement, this case is unsatisfactory in its lack of precision on the international law points. What section of the *Biodiversity Convention* was violated? Was this section implemented in Canadian law? The *Biodiversity Convention* was ratified by Canada in 1992 and, at the time of the *Repap* litigation, was at least partially implemented in Canada.[35]

Wellington Centre v. P.E.I.[36] offers another example of a case where an international treaty was invoked in argument, yet its relevance was rejected without explanation. The case involves an application for judicial review of a decision approving a new waste management facility by a group of citizens living near the proposed site. The citizens' group argued that the environmental assessment and minister's report approving the disputed site were both insufficient, one of the deficiencies being a failure to mention the *Ramsar Convention*. Specifically, the applicant (Wellington Centre and Malpeque Bay Concerned Citizens Committee Inc.) asserted that the minister's approval was without jurisdiction as it was based on an environmental impact assessment "invalidated by arbitrary prior constraints and exclusions." One such exclusion was the failure to mention the significance of the *Ramsar Convention*. In dismissing the application, Justice Jenkins of the Prince Edward Island Supreme Court held that the minister's decision was not patently unreasonable, appropriate considerations were addressed, and "the consultant and the Minister had no duty to make special mention regarding the *Ramsar Convention*."[37]

This statement was not explained further. As in the case of *Repap*, a treaty was invoked with no precise reference as to which section of the treaty was of concern, nor any discussion of whether the relevant section was implemented in Canadian law. The status of the *Ramsar Convention* in Canadian law was not discussed in this case.[38]

---

35 This implementation was not by statute but through a range of non-statutory instruments including the "Canadian Biodiversity Strategy" (1995), online: Environment Canada: Canadian Biodiversity Information Network, www.cbin.ec.gc.ca/cbs.

36 *Wellington Centre and Malpeque Bay Concerned Citizens Committee v. Prince Edward Island (Minister of Environmental Resources)* (1996), 148 Nfld. & P.E.I.R. 41, 22 C.E.L.R. (N.S.) 252 (S.C.T.D.) [*Wellington Centre v. P.E.I.*].

37 *Ibid.* at para. 46.

38 For a discussion of the passive incorporation of the *Ramsar Convention* in Canadian law, see Elizabeth Brandon, "Does International Law Mean Anything to Canadian Courts" (2001) 11 J. Envtl. L. & Prac. 399 at 418–19.

b) International Law Is Not Applicable Because It Is Not Implemented in Canadian Law

Moving beyond those judgments where the rejection of international law sources goes unexplained, the cases in this section reveal a greater clarity in rejecting international treaty obligations on the basis that these obligations are not transformed into Canadian law. In *MacMillan Bloedel Ltd. v. Simpson*[39] Justice Drake of the B.C. Supreme Court heard an application to rescind an injunction prohibiting the defendants from interfering with MacMillan Bloedel's logging operations in Clayoquot Sound. The test for rescinding an injunction was not considered by the court as the motion was rejected on jurisdictional grounds. In the short oral dismissal of the motion, Justice Drake addressed the defendant's arguments "relating to international agreements and resolutions."[40] He dismissed these arguments, observing:

> In these circumstances, there is no point in dealing with the extensive submissions of the applicants, interesting as they were. However, I will simply say, as far as their merits are concerned, that the argument relating to international agreements and resolutions, these not being expressed in Canadian law, are not relevant to this inquiry.[41]

This sweeping rejection of the international law arguments of the defendants, based on the classic incantation that treaties must be implemented by statute to alter domestic law, has made absent any detailed discussion of the international agreements at issue. In appealing this decision, the applicants asserted that "Mr. Justice Drake erred in his assessment of international law"[42] in his reliance on the *Labour Conventions* case to find the international treaties inapplicable. Ms. Russow (unrepresented by counsel in these arguments) attempted to distinguish the *Labour Conventions* case, arguing that the provincial court has an obligation not to defeat a ratified treaty. She argued that by granting and extending the injunction, the court was violating this obligation by contributing to non-compliance with Canada's obligations under the *Biodiversity Convention*.

The BC Court of Appeals rejected Russow's argument and held that British Columbia courts have no jurisdiction to apply international law.

---

39 *MacMillan Bloedel Ltd.*, above note 2.
40 *Ibid.* at para. 7.
41 *Ibid.*
42 *MacMillan Bloedel v. Simpson*, [1994] B.C.J. No. 3349 at para. 6 (C.A.).

Mr. Justice Carrothers' judgment is revealing in a number of respects. He states:

> *I have not been shown and I have been quite unable to discern or identify* any pertinent or applicable principle of international law, whether developed by custom and usage, treaty or convention, or legislative or judicial determination, which falls within the judicial capacity and function of the courts of this province.[43]

This is clearly an invitation for advocates to argue points of international law with greater clarity and precision. Mr. Justice Carrothers documented his consideration of the applicant's "extensive submissions which she herself called "a lecture" rather than an argument"[44] as well as the "assemblage of material contained in the applicants' leave book, which cannot be summarized."[45]

Kohl v. Canada[46] is a case where the *Biodiversity Convention* appears to have been included in argument as a last resort. In this case, a breeder argued that an order to destroy a highland bull contravened Canada's international obligations under the *Biodiversity Convention* with respect to preservation and conservation of rare genetic resources.[47] The respondent countered with the argument that the Applicant did not have standing to represent the interest of the Highland breed and that the *Biodiversity Convention* only came into force on 22 December 1993, after the date of the decision to destroy the cattle.[48]

Rather than accept or reject these arguments as to the legal effect of the *Biodiversity Convention* in Canada, the Federal Court stated: "the legislature has specifically provided for the protection of the health of animals and, in that context, this portion of the Applicant's argument is not convincing."[49] This precluded any further discussion of the *Biodiversity Convention* and whether it is incorporated in Canadian law.

---

43 *Ibid.* at para. 7 (emphasis added).
44 *Ibid.* at para. 6.
45 *Ibid.* at para. 7.
46 *Kohl v. Canada (Department of Agriculture)* (1994), 81 F.T.R. 35, 28 Admin. L. R. (2d) 38 (T.D.), rev'd on other grounds (1995), 185 N.R. 149 (C.A.) [*Kohl v. Canada*].
47 *Ibid.* at para. 99.
48 *Ibid.* at para. 100.
49 *Ibid.* at para. 101.

c) Judicial Uncertainty

Judicial discomfort in defining the precise legal status of an international law source is not limited to treaties that Canada has ratified, such as the *Biodiversity Convention*. This unease can also be seen in cases where the principles argued may amount to customary international law. In the wake of Justice L'Heureux-Dubé's decision in *Spraytech v. Hudson*, Canadian environmental groups are repeatedly calling on the courts to apply the principle of precaution as customary international law binding on Canada.[50]

In *Western Canada Wilderness Committee v. B.C.*,[51] the Wilderness Committee sought to quash a determination by Cindy Stern, the District Manager of the Ministry of Forests, under section 41(1) the *Forest Practices Code of British Columbia Act*,[52] approving timber harvesting of a block of forest that was home to the Northern Spotted Owl, an owl species at risk of extinction. In its submissions, the Western Canada Wilderness Committee (WCWC) argued that section 41(1) of the Code should be interpreted by the court in a manner consistent with international law, specifically the precautionary principle and Canada's obligations under the *Biodiversity Convention*.[53] It submitted that Ms. Stern's failure to interpret section 41(1) of the Code in a manner consistent with these international obligations was "an error of statutory interpretation."[54] Mr. Justice Shabbits, the trial judge, found no such error.

WCWC appealed the decision and the British Columbia Court of Appeal considered the question of whether Ms. Stern's decision was patently unreasonable for failing to give effect to the precautionary principle, rendering the decision of the chambers judge incorrect. Madam Justice Prowse, writing for the appeal court, rejected the WCWC's argument that a standard of review of correctness applied as the question was one of statutory interpretation. Instead she found the "vital question" in the case to be "whether the substance of her [Ms. Stern's] decision was patently

---

50 *Spraytech v. Hudson*, above note 25 at 32 (quoting authorities supportive of the view that there may be sufficient state practice "to allow a good argument that the precautionary principle is a principle of customary international law").

51 *Western Canada Wilderness Committee v. British Columbia (Ministry of Forests, South Island Forest District)* (2002), 50 C.E.L.R. (N.S.) 56, 45 Admin. L.R. (3d) 161, 2002 BCSC 1260 [*Western Canada Wilderness Committee v. B.C. (2002)*].

52 R.S.B.C. 1996, c. 159.

53 *Western Canada Wilderness Committee v. B.C. (2002)*, above note 51 at para. 70.

54 *Ibid.* at para. 71.

unreasonable."[55] Justice Prowse observed that "while the applicability of the precautionary principle was raised before Ms. Stern, she does not state whether she took it into account in reaching her decision. The chambers judge was of the view that she did not and that her failure to do so did not constitute error."[56]

Justice Prowse noted that the precautionary principle "was not adopted in the Code."[57] She observed: "Ms. Stern did not specifically refer to the precautionary principle in her analysis," that she "may not have given full effect to the precautionary principle," but that "her decision reflects a degree of caution akin to that reflected in the precautionary principle."[58]

This decision is capable of several contradictory interpretations and leaves many questions unanswered. What is the significance of the fact that Ms. Stern's decision exhibited a degree of caution "akin to the precautionary principle"? Did Ms. Stern have a legal obligation to interpret the relevant legislation in a manner consistent with precautionary principle? Is this a suggestion that the precautionary principle does have some legal status under Canadian law? Or is this statement simply a way of explaining the absence of a more thorough engagement with the meaning of the precautionary principle in Canadian and international law.

d) International Law as an Interpretive Aid in Statutory Interpretation

Courts appeal to international biodiversity law as an aid in domestic statutory interpretation in different ways. First, a number of Canadian cases reveal that the courts are willing to consider substantive provisions of an international treaty in the interpretation of its enabling domestic statutes. A second, more expansive, use of international law sources is emerging in biodiversity cases following the approach of the Supreme Court in *Baker* and *Spraytech v. Hudson*, where international law sources are seen as useful interpretive aids outside the limited context of enabling legislation.

In a number of biodiversity cases, judges are using the *Migratory Birds Convention* with admirable clarity to interpret the *Migratory Birds Conven-*

---

55 *Western Canada Wilderness Committee v. British Columbia (Ministry of Forests, South Island Forest District)* (2003), 15 B.C.L.R. (4th) 229 at para. 33, 1 C.E.L.R. (3d) 185, 2003 BCCA 403 [*Western Canada Wilderness Committee v. B.C. (2003)*].

56 *Ibid.* at para. 74.

57 *Ibid.* at para. 80.

58 *Ibid.* at paras. 79 and 80.

tion Act.[59] In *Animal Alliance v. Canada,*[60] Justice Gibson considers both the Convention and the Act in an application for judicial review of the *Regulations Amending the Migratory Birds Regulations.*[61] The regulations create a special hunting season, during which hunters can kill overabundant species of snow geese and species not easily distinguishable from snow geese, including Ross geese. The applicants (a coalition of the Animal Alliance of Canada, the Animal Protection Institute, the Canadian Environmental Defence Fund, the Dene Nation, and Zoocheck Canada Inc.) argued that the Regulations violate the *Migratory Birds Convention* and are thus *ultra vires* the implementing legislation, the stated purpose of which is to "implement the Convention."[62] This argument was successful before the federal court, and the Regulations were found to be *ultra vires* insofar as they authorized the killing of Ross geese and other species not easily distinguishable from snow geese. In arriving at this determination, Justice Gibson discusses the relevant principles of statutory interpretation with clarity and precision. He considers the substantive language of the *Convention* in detail, noting the authority of courts "to look at the international convention underlying implementing legislation to assist interpretation, even in the absence of ambiguity on the face of the legislation."[63] In interpreting Canadian statutes, such as the *Migratory Birds Convention Act*, he acknowledges the presumption of conformity with international law.[64]

Justice Gibson's decision in *Animal Alliance* v. *Canada* stands as a rare example of a considered and clear use of international law sources in statutory interpretation. A much more limited role for the *Convention* arises in *R. v. Blackbird.*[65] This case concerns the relationship between a local band bylaw governing migratory bird hunting on a reserve and the *Migratory Birds Convention Act*. Blackbird, who has been charged with fifty-three counts of illegal hunting practices contrary to the Act, argued that the local bylaw ousts the jurisdiction of the Act as the bylaw constitutes a "complete code" regulating the hunt of migratory birds on the reserve. In

---

59 *Migratory Birds Convention Act, 1994*, above note 14.
60 *Animal Alliance of Canada v. Canada (Attorney General)*, [1999] 4 F.C. 72, 168 F.T.R. 114 (T.D.) [*Animal Alliance v. Canada*].
61 S.O.R./99-147.
62 *Animal Alliance v. Canada*, above note 60 at para. 32.
63 Ruth Sullivan, *Driedger on the Construction of Statutes*, 3d ed. (Toronto: Butterworths, 1994) at 397, cited in *Animal Alliance v. Canada, ibid.* at para. 34.
64 *Ibid.* at para. 34.
65 *R. v. Blackbird* (2005), 74 O.R. (3d) 241, 248 D.L.R. (4th) 201 (C.A).

rejecting this submission, Justice Laskin observed that as the two regimes are overlapping, but not conflicting, dual compliance is possible and the appellant could be charged under either regime. He found it particularly "significant" in arriving at this finding that the regulatory regime underlying the Act is:

> derived from a Convention and a Protocol, [and] was designed to redress a serious environmental concern in North America. I do not think that a local by-law could oust this international regime unless, at a minimum, the by-law contained clear language expressing this ouster.[66]

It is difficult to ascertain here what particular legal "significance," if any, attaches to the fact that the statute in question implements an international obligation, because a bylaw will be displaced by a statute regardless of whether it is implementing legislation or not.

A further example of reliance on the *Migratory Birds Convention* is Justice Campbell's 1999 decision in *Alberta Wilderness Assn. v. Cardinal River Coals Ltd*, an early decision in the litigation around the Cheviot Coal Mine.[67] In this case, Justice Campbell used the preamble to the Convention to justify giving a broad interpretation to the words "any other substance" used in the impugned statute, the *Migratory Birds Convention Act*. The case involved a challenge to a decision by the federal minister of the environment and the Alberta Energy and Utilities Board authorizing the construction of the mine. Based on a reading of the purpose of the Act and the Convention, Justice Campbell found "a clear intention expressed to provide wide protection to migratory birds."[68] He therefore concluded that a "similarly wide interpretation" should be given to the phrase "any substance" under the Act and that "any substance, including oil and oil wastes, is capable of being prohibited if it is 'harmful.'"[69]

4) The Practice of Environmental Appeal Boards

Despite the absence of clear authority for the proposition that environmental appeal boards can take official notice of international law, the practice of environmental appeal boards is beginning to reflect some willingness

---

66 *Ibid.* at para. 22.
67 *Alberta Wilderness Assn. v. Cardinal River Coals Ltd.* (1998), [1999] 3 F.C. 425, 165 F.T.R. 1 (T.D.) [*Alberta Wilderness Assn.*].
68 *Ibid.* at para.103.
69 *Ibid.* (emphasis in original).

to engage with international law sources in interpreting Canadian law.[70] Two cases of the British Columbia Environmental Appeal Board reflect this practice. *Resident Advisory Board v. B.C.*[71] is a 1998 decision of the B.C. Environmental Appeal Board in which both parties argued the relevance of substantive provisions of the *Biodiversity Convention*. The appellants attempted to appeal a Pesticide Use Permit issued to the Canadian Food Inspection Agency (CFIA) that authorized the use of a particular pesticide to eradicate gypsy moth populations. In support of their arguments, they submitted that the spray program contravened the *Biodiversity Convention* because it failed to respect a precautionary approach and because an environmental assessment had not been conducted, as required by article 14 of the *Biodiversity Convention* for projects likely to have an adverse impact on biological diversity.

The appellants also argued that the precautionary principle applies in Canada as customary international law and "at the very least, the precautionary principle would require CFIA and the Respondent to show that they carefully assessed the risks to health and biodiversity and chose the least destructive alternative measure to deal with the risk."[72] One of the appellants specifically referred the panel to article 14 of the Convention, which provides "that the contracting parties, as far as possible and as appropriate, shall introduce appropriate procedures requiring environmental impact assessment of its proposed projects that are likely to have significant adverse effects on biological diversity."[73]

The response of the CFIA was to refer the panel to article 8(h) of the Convention, stating the obligation of contracting parties to prevent the introduction of alien species and to "control or eradicate those alien species which threaten ecosystems, habitats or species."[74] The panel did not

---

70 For a discussion of the doctrine of official notice as it applies to administrative tribunals see Donald J.M. Brown & J.M. Evans, *Judicial Review of Administrative Action in Canada*, looseleaf (Toronto: Canvasback, 1998) at 10:8000. Van Ert, above note 4 at 37–39 discusses the practice of Canadian tribunals (although not specifically referencing environmental appeal boards) taking "judicial notice" of international law.

71 *Resident Advisory Board v. British Columbia (Ministry of Environment, Lands and Parks)*, [1998] B.C.E.A. No. 19 [*Resident Advisory Board v. B.C.*]. The appellants included the Resident Advisory Board, Sierra Club-Victoria Group, the Ecological Health Alliance, the B.C. Branch of the Allergy and Environmental Health Association, Stop Overhead Spraying, the Unitarian Church of Victoria, and Fernwood Community Association.

72 *Ibid.* at para. 52.

73 *Ibid.*

74 *Ibid.* at para. 53.

address the question of the legal status of the *Biodiversity Convention* in Canada nor offer an analysis of the substantive arguments made by the parties concerning the *Biodiversity Convention*. Without saying that it had an obligation to do so, the panel attempted to adopt an approach consistent with the *Biodiversity Convention*. The panel stated that its "very task" under domestic law is analogous to that demanded by the Convention, namely, "determining whether there is an unreasonable adverse impact in issuing a permit."[75] The panel found that "the Convention provides general principles that the contracting parties should adhere to in the conservation and sustainable use of biological diversity."[76] The panel did not address the argument that the precautionary principle is to be applied as it reflects customary international law.

The decision in *Resident Advisory Board v. B.C.* is applied and further explained in a second case before the British Columbia Environmental Appeal Board challenging the validity of a pesticide permit to eradicate gypsy moths. In *Fitzmaurice v. B.C.*, the environmental health organization appellants argued that the permit itself (and the spraying program it authorized) failed to comply with the precautionary approach of the *Biodiversity Convention*.[77] This argument is different from that in *Resident Advisory Board* where it was argued that the problem was the process by which the permit was issued. In response, the panel states that it agrees with and adopts:

> the reasoning of the Board in the 1998 Resident Advisory Board decision that the *Convention* provides general principles for the conservation and sustainable use of biological diversity, and the weighing of risk and benefits is the very kind of analysis contemplated by the Convention, and undertaken in determining whether there is an unreasonable adverse impact in issuing a permit.[78]

The board notes that it had very little evidence properly before it to undertake this task of weighing of risks and benefits and, based on the

---

75 *Ibid.* at para. 54.
76 *Ibid.*
77 *Fitzmaurice v. British Columbia (Ministry of Environment, Lands & Parks)*, [2000] B.C.E.A. No. 22 at para. 48 [*Fitzmaurice v. B.C.*].
78 *Ibid.* at para. 49. The appellants included representatives of the Ecological Health Alliance, the Sierra Club (Victoria Group), Stop Overhead Spraying Coalition, Green Party of Canada, Society Targeting Overuse of Pesticides, Society Promoting Environmental Conservation and various individuals.

limited evidence available, arrives at the following "equation": "Likely non-permanent significant decrease in non-target Lepidoptera versus trade restrictions on some forest products and nursery stock, and subsequent economic harm."[79] The panel finds that there is evidence that the use of the pesticide authorized by the permit will have an adverse effect on the environment, but to conclude that this adverse effect is "unreasonable," it must find that the "intended benefit of the proposed spray program [will] outweigh the adverse effect *in the proposed spray site.*"[80] Noting the constraints of this possible analysis, the panel concludes that "the adverse effect is not unreasonable in the circumstances of this Permit, given the limited evidence before it, and confined as it is by legislation and case law to site specific considerations."[81] The panel acknowledges that this leads to less than satisfactory results and urges the permit-holder to "seriously reconsider the requirement for 'eradication,' and contemplate an approach to the gypsy moth that uses alternative methods for control."[82]

In these two cases, the BC Environmental Appeal Board advances an approach that is consistent with the general principles of the *Biodiversity Convention.* This approach is articulated without any doctrinal discussion of the legal status of this treaty in Canada, nor any discussion of the common law presumption of legislative conformity with international law obligations. Environmental appeal boards are tasked with interpreting and applying Canadian law, including statutes that take into account principles of international law origin, such as precaution and sustainable development.[83] Even absent explicit articulation of their authority to do so, these tribunals are considering submissions founded in international law, are taking official notice of international law, and are likely to continue doing so.

---

79 *Ibid.* at para. 50. Lepidoptera is defined as "a large order of insects comprises of butterflies, moths and skippers that as adults have four broad wings and that as larvae are caterpillars" (*ibid.* at note 1).
80 *Ibid.* at para. 41 (emphasis added).
81 *Ibid.* at para. 51.
82 *Ibid.* at para. 52.
83 See, for example, Alberta's *Environmental Protection and Enhancement Act,* R.S.A. 2000, c. E-12 (ss. 2 and 38 refer to sustainable development). The Alberta Environmental Appeal Board has considered international law sources in defining sustainable development and the precautionary principle. See *Mountain View Water Services Commission (Re),* [2004] A.E.A.B.D. No. 9 at para. 195 (referring to the *Bruntland Report*); *Re Imperial Oil Ltd.,* [2002] A.E.A.B.D. No. 48 at para. 142 (referring to the *Bergen Ministerial Declaration on Sustainable Development*).

5) The Role of Environmental Advocacy Groups in Arguing International Law

The above disaggregation of judicial decisions reveals a limited engage-ment of Canadian courts with international biodiversity law. How do in-ternational biodiversity law arguments reach the court in the cases where they do feature? More often than not, international biodiversity law reaches a Canadian court because it is argued by an environmental advocacy group, acting as a plaintiff, defendant, or intervener. In well over 50 percent of the cases where these international treaties are cited, their mention can be traced back to the argument of an environmental advocacy group.

Of the six cases that explicitly refer to the *Migratory Birds Convention*, three involve environmental advocacy groups; in two cases the advocacy groups were plaintiffs advancing international law arguments,[84] and in the third the group was an intervener.[85] Of the six cases to specifically address the *Biodiversity Convention*, four involve environmental advocacy groups, three as plaintiffs,[86] and one as a defendant.[87] In each instance, arguments based on the *Biodiversity Convention* originated in the submissions of these environmental group litigants. Two cases explicitly refer to the *Ramsar Con-vention*. In one of these cases, consideration of the *Ramsar Convention* was argued by the citizen's group plaintiff.[88] In the second case, the initial men-tion of the *Ramsar Convention* is found in a report of the town's depart-ment of planning services, a department lobbied by numerous conservation groups including one of the respondents in this case, the Boundary Bay Conservation Committee.[89] Of the five cases to specifically address World Heritage Status under the *World Heritage Convention*, one case was brought by the Bow Valley Naturalists Society,[90] and another two by the Canadian

84 *Animal Alliance v. Canada*, above note 60; *Alberta Wilderness Assn.*, above note 67.

85 *Hamilton-Wentworth (Regional Municipality) v. Canada (Minister of the Environment)* (2001), 204 F.T.R. 161, 2001 FCT 381, aff'd (2001), 284 N.R. 248, 2001 FCA 347.

86 *Resident Advisory Board v. B.C.*, above note 71; *Western Canada Wilderness Committee v. B.C. (2002)*, above note 51; *Fitzmaurice v. B.C.*, above note 77.

87 *Repap New Brunswick v. Pictou*, above note 2.

88 *Wellington Centre v. P.E.I.*, above note 36.

89 *Jones v. Delta (District)* (1992), 69 B.C.L.R. (2d) 239, 92 D.L.R. (4th) 714, leave to ap-peal to S.C.C. refused, [1993] 2 S.C.R. viii, 98 D.L.R. (4th) viii.

90 *Bow Valley Naturalists Society v. Canada (Minister of Canadian Heritage)* (1999), 175 F.T.R. 122, 32 C.E.L.R. (N.S.) 84 (T.D.), aff'd [2001] 2 F.C. 461, 266 N.R. 169. (C.A.).

Parks and Wilderness Society.[91] In each of these cases, World Heritage status was raised in argument by the environmental group litigants.

The significant role of environmental advocacy groups in bringing international law sources to the attention of Canadian courts is not restricted to biodiversity treaties but exists across the field of international environmental law. In four of the six recent cases where the Supreme Court of Canada has addressed international environmental law sources, the international law arguments were brought to the Court's attention by environmental group interveners.[92] A recent study documents the Supreme Court's reliance on authorities cited by public interest interveners in its environmental law jurisprudence.[93] The significant role of environmental advocacy groups in bringing international law arguments to the attention of Canadian courts may be unique to the environmental law area. In other fields where courts have cited international law with a greater frequency, such as in human rights law, Canadian judges and counsel may be more familiar with the relevant international law, especially the major international human rights treaties.

Despite their significant role in domestic environmental litigation, little academic analysis of Canadian environmental advocacy groups exists.[94]

---

91 *Canadian Parks and Wilderness Society v. Banff National Park (Superintendent); Sunshine Village Corp. v. Canada (Minister of Canadian Heritage), (sub nom. Sunshine Village Corp. v. Canada (Minister of Environment); Sunshine Village Corp. v. Canada (Minister of Canadian Heritage))* (1996), 202 N.R. 132 (F.C.A.), leave to appeal to S.C.C. refused, [1996] S.C.C.A. No. 498; *Canadian Parks and Wilderness Society v. Canada (Minister of Heritage)*, [2003] 4 F.C. 672, 1 Admin. L.R. (4th) 103, 2003 FCA 197.

92 Jerry V. DeMarco & Michelle L. Campbell, "The Supreme Court of Canada's Progressive Use of International Environmental Law and Policy in Interpreting Domestic Legislation" (2004) 13 R.E.C.I.E.L. 320 at 330. The six Supreme Court cases examined by the authors are *R. v. Crown Zellerbach Canada Ltd.*, [1988] 1 S.C.R. 401, 49 D.L.R. (4th) 161; *Friends of the Oldman River Society v. Canada (Minister of Transport)*, [1992] 1 S.C.R. 3, 88 D.L.R. (4th) 1; *Ontario v. Canadian Pacific Ltd.*, [1995] 2 S.C.R. 1031; *R. v. Hydro-Québec*, [1997] 3 S.C.R. 213, 151 D.L.R. (4th) 32; *Spraytech v. Hudson*, above note 25; and *Imperial Oil Ltd v. Quebec (Minister of the Environment)*, [2003] 2 S.C.R. 624, 2003 SCC 58.

93 Jerry V. DeMarco, "Assessing the Impact of Public Interest Interventions on the Environmental Law Jurisprudence of the Supreme Court of Canada: A Quantitative and Qualitative Analysis" (2005) 30 Sup. Ct. L. Rev. 299.

94 For a rare discussion of the impact of Canadian environmental groups on Canadian litigation see Stewart A.G. Elgie, "Environmental Groups and the Courts: 1970–1992" in Geoffrey Thompson, Moira McConnell, & Lynne Huestis, eds., *Environmental Law and Business in Canada* (Aurora, ON: Canada Law Book Inc., 1993) at 185. For other analysis of Canadian environmental groups, see Jeremy Wilson, "Green Lobbies" in

The few Canadian studies that examine the role of domestic environmental groups in Canadian processes appear primarily in management literature, focusing on multi-stakeholder initiatives and corporate-NGO relations.[95] Details of their constituencies, membership, sources of support, and international law expertise are all largely unknown. In the United States, theoretical interest in civil society has translated into early attempts to analyze and catalogue environmental advocacy groups. Business school cases on environmental groups are emerging,[96] critical analysis of their strategic campaigns beginning,[97] and attempts to create taxonomies by which to classify non-profits are materializing.[98] Where the international–local nexus is examined, however, it is the role of local and national non-profit groups in contributing to global legal processes that attracts attention.[99]

Robert Boardman, ed., *Canadian Environmental Policy: Ecosystems, Politics and Process* (Toronto: Oxford University Press, 1992) at 109; Jerry V. DeMarco & Anne C. Bell, "The Role of Non-Governmental Organizations in Biodiversity Conservation" in Stephen Bocking, ed., *Biodiversity in Canada: Ecology Ideas and Action* (Peterborough, ON: Broadview Press, 2000) at 347; Alison Van Rooy, "The Frontiers of Influence: NGO Lobbying at the 1974 World Food Conference, The 1992 Earth Summit and Beyond" (1997) 25 World Development 93; and Andrew Fenton Cooper & J.-Stefan Fritz, "Bringing the NGOs in: UNCED and Canada's International Environmental Policy" (1992) 47 Int'l J. 796.

95   Sanjay Sharma & Irene Henriques, "Stakeholder Influences on Sustainability Practices in the Canadian Forest Products Industry" (2005) 26 Strategic Management Journal 159; Mae Burrows, "Allied Forces: Unions and Environmentalists Can Work Together for Jobs and Ecological Sustainability" (1998) 24:4 Alt. J. 18; Frances Westley & Harrie Vredenburg, "Strategic Bridging: The Collaboration Between Environmentalists and Business in the Marketing of Green Products" (1991) 27 Journal of Applied Behavioural Science 65; Patrick Fafard, "Groups, Governments and the Environment: Some Evidence from the Harmonization Initiative" in Patrick Fafard & Kathryn Harrison, eds., *Managing the Environmental Union: Intergovernmental Relations and Environmental Policy in Canada* (Kingston, ON: Institute of Intergovernmental Affairs, Saskatchewan Institute of Public Policy, 2000) at 81.

96   See, for example, Forest Reinhardt, "Environmental Defense" (2003), Harvard Business School Press online: harvardbusinessonline.hbsp.harvard.edu; Benjamin C. Esty & Aldo Sesia, Jr., "International Rivers Network and the Bujagali Dam Project (A)" (2004), Harvard Business School Press online: harvardbusinessonline.hbsp.harvard.edu.

97   Debora L. Spar & Lane T. La Mure, "The Power of Activism: Assessing the Impact of NGOs on Global Business" (2003) 45:3 California Management Review 78.

98   See, for example, P.J. Simmons, "Learning to Live with NGOs" (1998) 112 Foreign Policy 82 at 85.

99   See Margaret Keck & Kathryn Sikkink, *Activists Beyond Borders: Advocacy Networks in International Politics* (Ithaca, NY: Cornell University Press, 1998). Also, Bas Arts, *The Political Influence of Global NGOs: Case Studies on the Climate Change and Biodiversity*

In contrast, this article examines the process by which these international legal agreements are internalized in Canada.

One of the challenges of analyzing the work of Canadian environmental advocacy groups is the erroneous assumption of homogeneity of these groups. Significant differences exist between environmental advocacy groups in terms of purpose, principal activities, acceptable means of financial support, and willingness to form alliances. Significant conflict can also exist within and between these groups and treating such organizations, and the coalitions that emerge between them, as sites of uncontested opinion oversimplifies the challenges these campaigns face. Differences of opinion thus emerge, both within and between advocacy groups, over the importance to attach to international law arguments in specific campaigns or litigation.

Several public interest organizations now exist in Canada that specialize in legal issues including litigation, law reform, and legal advice. These organizations, which include the Sierra Legal Defence Fund, West Coast Environmental Law,[100] and the Canadian Environmental Law Association, appear frequently in the cases that are the subject of this study. The regular and consistent involvement of these groups allows them to build up a fluency in arguing international biodiversity sources unmatched by other counsel. In this way, a handful of international environmental law experts within the Canadian public interest environmental community are able to have a considerable impact on the international law arguments heard by Canadian courts.

A significant aspect of the work of several Canadian environmental advocacy groups is that they are active both internationally and domestically. The transnational process of forging connections between the international and local spheres is a unique contribution of environmental advocacy groups to effective biodiversity protection, yet again little analysis of this work exists. The day-to-day use of international law arguments by environmental groups in domestic litigation or campaign strategies, in

---

Conventions (Utrecht: International Books, 1998); and Rupert Taylor, ed., *Creating a Better World: Interpreting Global Civil Society*, (Bloomfield, CT: Kumarian Press, 2004).

100 West Coast Environmental Law has produced an accessible guide explaining international environmental law treaties to non-experts. Linda Nowlan & Chris Rolfe, *Kyoto, POPs and Straddling Stocks: Understanding Environmental Treaties* (Vancouver: West Coast Environmental Law, 2003).

Canada or elsewhere, has yet to be examined by scholars.[101] Canadian environmental groups are active in transnational public litigation and inform international trade dispute resolution through the submission of *amicus curiae* briefs.[102] In recent years, Canadian environmental groups have participated in international treaty negotiations as members of official Canadian delegations. The nature of the relationship between this participation and the domestic litigation employed to enforce these treaties remains to be elucidated.

A critical challenge arising from a reliance on environmental advocacy groups to bring forward international law arguments is the limited support these groups receive for this work. Fundraising for international law issues proves challenging for law-focused public interest environmental groups. These groups also suffer from the absence of a Canadian institution dedicated to promoting international environmental law domestically. Such institutions exist in the United States[103] and Britain[104] and can provide crucial support for domestic efforts to give effect to international environmental law.

B. INTERNATIONAL LAW ARGUMENTS OUTSIDE THE COURTROOM

International law arguments are employed by environmental advocacy groups in campaign strategies extending beyond the courtroom. In the wider campaigns that surround the litigation explored in the first section of this article, Canada's reputation, as both a law-abiding nation and as an international leader in issues of environmental protection, is attacked. Unhampered by the doctrinal restrictions on how international law is received by Canadian courts, environmental advocacy groups use international law arguments as a tool in these campaigns. International law is strategically

---

101 One book-length study of the techniques used by environmental NGOs to protect biodiversity makes no mention at all of using international law in domestic courts as a possible strategy. See Michael M. Gunter, Jr., *Building the Next Ark: How NGOs work to Protect Biodiversity* (Hanover, NH: Dartmouth College Press, 2004).

102 See International Institute for Sustainable Development, Amicus Curiae Submissions, "In the Arbitration under Chapter 11 of the North American Free Trade Agreement and the UNCITRAL Arbitration Rules between Methanex Corporation and United States of America" (9 March 2004), International Institute for Sustainable Development online: www.iisd.org/publications.

103 Centre for International Environmental Law (CIEL) in Washington, DC.

104 Foundation for International Environmental Law and Development (FIELD) in London, UK.

used to shame Canada; through media and public opinion campaigns, transnational litigation, and market tools. Analysis of how these strategies are used in two campaigns, the campaign for endangered species legislation in Canada and the campaign against the Cheviot Mine, reveals how environmental advocacy groups attempt to foster compliance with Canada's international legal obligations through the deployment of shame.

Shame can be a potent tool in fostering compliance with international law. A growing body of international legal theory attempts to elucidate the role of reputational concerns in explaining why nations comply with international law even absent enforcement mechanisms.[105] The following analysis of the use of shame in campaign strategies acknowledges the value of reputation in advocacy campaigns. International theorists such as Andrew Guzman focus on the external audiences affected by a country's reputation:

> Because a country's reputation has value and provides that country with benefits, a country will hesitate before comprising that reputation. A country that develops a reputation for compliance with international obligations signals to other countries that it is cooperative. This allows the state to enjoy long-term relationships with other cooperative states, provides a greater ability to make binding promises, and reduces the perceived need for monitoring and verification. On the other hand, failure to live up to one's commitments harms one's reputation and makes future commitments less credible. As a result, potential partners are less willing to offer concessions in exchange for a promised course of action.[106]

The environmental advocacy campaigns discussed in the following sections also reveal how domestic audiences are targeted in reputational attacks on Canada. Underlying these approaches are assumptions that Canada is concerned about its reputation, and that Canadians care whether Canada is perceived to be violating international law.

---

105 See Andrew T. Guzman, "A Compliance-Based Theory of International Law" (2002) 90 Cal. L. Rev.1823 at 1825; George W. Downs & Michael A. Jones, "Reputation, Compliance and International Law" (2002) 31 J. Legal Stud. 95. See also Abram Chayes & Antonia Handler Chayes, *The New Sovereignty: Compliance with International Regulatory Agreements* (Cambridge, MA: Harvard University Press, 1995) at 27; Harold Hongju Koh, "Why Do Nations Obey International Law?" (1997) 106 Yale L.J. 2599.
106 Guzman, *ibid.* at 1849–50 (footnotes omitted).

1) The Campaign for Federal Endangered Species Legislation (1992–2002)

The call for strong federal endangered species legislation emerged prior to the 1992 UNCED Conference in Rio de Janeiro and continued beyond the eventual 2002 enactment of the *Species at Risk Act*.[107] A focus on the campaign between the years 1992 and 2002 allows a detailed look at the argument advanced by environmental groups that Canada had an international legal obligation to enact federal endangered species legislation based on its Rio commitments. Specifically, once Canada ratified the 1992 *Biodiversity Convention*, Canadian environmental groups narrowed in on the obligation of contracting parties under article 8(k) to pass endangered species legislation. This international legal obligation occupied a central place in the environmental advocacy groups' domestic campaign and these groups never allowed the international legal sources of Canada's responsibility to protect endangered species to move off the agenda.

The influence of Canadian environmental groups in the political struggle to enact federal endangered species legislation waxed and waned over the course of the decade.[108] One factor contributing to the strength of the environmentalist voice was the ability of a number of considerably diverse environmental groups to unite and form a coalition (the Canadian Endangered Species Coalition). The coalition was directed by six of the major environmental groups and supported by a hundred more.

The strategies adopted by the coalition were wide-ranging—from litigation to media campaigns, to public pressure techniques, to international appeals, to consumer boycotts, to government lobbying. International law occupied a prominent place in the campaign, although its centrality differed between the litigation and the non-litigation elements of the campaign. In the court cases, international law arguments played a peripheral role, and were ultimately unsuccessful.[109] In the public, media, and government lobbying campaigns, however, international law and Canada's

---

107 S.C. 2002, c. 29.

108 For a discussion of the politics surrounding this legislation, see William Amos, Kathryn Harrison & George Hoberg, "In Search of A Minimum Winning Coalition: The Politics of Species-at-Risk Legislation in Canada" in Karen Beazley & Robert Boardman, eds., *Politics of the Wild: Canada and Endangered Species* (Don Mills, ON: Oxford University Press, 2001) 137 at 145.

109 See, for example, *Western Canada Wilderness Committee v. B.C. (2002)*, above note 51 and *Western Canada Wilderness Committee v. B.C. (2003)*, above note 55 (where the Wilderness Committee is unsuccessful at trial and on appeal in an application for judicial review of a determination made under the Forest Practices Code of British Columbia

violation of its international obligations were central and immoveable aspects of the campaign.

a) Public Opinion and the Media

International law arguments played a central role in efforts to shame Canada into introducing federal endangered species legislation. Coalition campaign materials routinely focused on the discrepancy between Canada's place as the first industrialized country to sign and ratify the *Biodiversity Convention* and Canada's reluctance to implement its treaty obligations in Canadian law. Specific references to Canada's failure to enact federal legislation to protect species at risk, despite an obligation under the *Biodiversity Convention* to do so, appeared in headlines, and in the opening sentences of reports, campaign materials, and submissions to senate committees.[110] Headlines and environmental group-sponsored ads emotively presented Canada's failure to give effect to the *Biodiversity Convention* as a deception or a lie: "Canada Lies, Endangered Species Die."[111]

Canada's internationalist reputation was repeatedly the target of attack. Sierra Legal criticized Canada's reputation as a world leader in biodiversity as false through a newspaper ad in the *International Herald Tribune* emblazoned with the headline: "Think Canada is Naturally a World Leader in Wildlife Protection: Think Again. For 10 years the Canadian Government has failed to honour its 1992 Biodiversity Convention promise to enact effective endangered species legislation."[112] An article by David Suzuki printed in the *Globe and Mail* on 22 March 2001, emphasized the same message:

Act approving timber harvesting in a block of forest home to a species of Owl, the Northern Spotted Owl, at risk of extinction).

110 See, for example, Gwen Barlee, "Presentation to the Senate Standing Committee on Energy, the Environment and Natural Resources on Bill C-5, the Species at Risk Act" (21 November 2002), online: Western Canada Wilderness Committee, www.wildernesscommittee.org/campaigns/species/sara/senate_pres.pdf; Greenpeace Canada, "Wipeout: the Liberal Government's plan for Endangered Species" (September 2001), online: Greenpeace.ca, www.greenpeace.org/raw/content/usa/press/reports/wipeout-the-liberal-governmen.pdf.

111 Greenpeace Canada, press release, "Canada Lies, Endangered Species Die" (8 November 2001), online: Greenpeace Canada, action.web.ca/home/gpc/alerts.shtml.

112 See Sierra Legal Defence Fund, media release, "Canada Guilty of Decade of Inaction After Being First Industrialized Nation to Ratify Global Conservation Pact" (10 April 2002), online: Sierra Legal Defence Fund, www.sierralegal.org/m_archive/2002/pro2_04_10.html.

Internationally, Canada still has somewhat of a boy scout reputation when it comes to the environment.... But our reputation far exceeds our track record and it has begun to fray badly.... Canada's lack of federal legislation protecting endangered species ... should be a national embarrassment.[113]

These two excerpts from the *Globe and Mail* and the *International Herald Tribune* reveal how both domestic and international audiences were targeted in these reputational attacks on Canada. Exploiting the fact that Canadians hate to be seen as less environmentally conscious than their neighbours to the South, campaigners routinely contrasted Canada's lack of federal legislation with the *Endangered Species Act*[114] in the United States. As one Greenpeace campaigner commented, "[I]f I were an endangered species I'd rather be living in the U.S."[115]

The Coalition also introduced a report card that measures the federal government and each province against the international commitment to introduce endangered species legislation. The failing "D" grade the federal government received in 1997 for failing to pass Bill C-65, the *Endangered Species Protection Act*,[116] was widely reported in Canadian newspapers.[117] Such use of the Canadian media was essential to the campaign as the public was largely unaware of the absence of federal legislation. One Pollara poll commissioned by the International Fund for Animal Welfare in May 1999 found that 66 percent of respondents thought the federal government already had a law to protect endangered species, and another 21 percent did not know whether such a law existed.[118]

Media and public awareness campaigns extended beyond Canada's borders to put international shame on Canada. At a meeting in Guadalajara, Mexico, in 2000 where conservation organizations from across North America gathered to discuss endangered species protection in the three countries, the Canadian director of the Defenders of Wildlife characterized Canada's situation as "an international embarrassment." On the subject of wildlife protection, he further lamented, "[W]e were once world leaders in

113 David Suzuki, "Our Environmental Shame" *Globe and Mail* (22 March 2001) A17.
114 *Endangered Species Act of 1973*, 16 U.S.C. §§1531–44 (2000).
115 Tzeporah Berman quoted in Malcolm Curtis, "Endangered Species Law Toothless," *Times-Colonist* (13 December 1995) 1.
116 Bill C-65, *Canada Endangered Species Protection Act*, 2d Sess., 35th Parl., 1997.
117 Allan Thompson, "Ottawa Called Flop at Saving Species" *Toronto Star* (30 September 1997) A6.
118 The results of this 1999 poll are quoted in Amos, Harrison & Hoberg, "In Search of a Minimum Winning Coalition," above note 108 at 145.

environmental protection but now we trail far behind the United States and Mexico."[119]

Reports documenting Canada's failure to uphold its obligations under the *Biodiversity Convention* also circulated at the Ancient Forest Summit meeting of 180 countries in The Hague in April 2002.[120] The campaign did not stop at shaming techniques, however, and the environmental groups leading the campaign made formal appeals to bodies outside Canada to attempt to force Canada's hand through international pressure.

b) Transnational Litigation and Foreign Appeals

i) North American Agreement on Environmental Cooperation
Canadian environmental advocacy groups are among the most committed users of the citizen enforcement process under articles 14 and 15 of the *North American Agreement on Environmental Cooperation* (NAAEC),[121] so it is not surprising that this process was used in the campaign to secure endangered species legislation. The *Biodiversity* Submission is a claim brought by the Animal Alliance of Canada, Greenpeace Canada, and the Council of Canadians.[122] The threshold requirement for claims under the citizen enforcement process is a failure to enforce domestic law. Shame was thus cast on Canada by the very suggestion it was unwilling to enforce its environmental law. The applicants faced an uphill challenge in proving that Canada's failure to enact endangered species legislation was a breach of domestic law. The CEC Secretariat had faced the question of defining domestic law in a number of previous submissions brought by Canadian environmental groups, each time rejecting international law arguments as outside the scope of its jurisdiction.

In *AAA Packaging*,[123] the secretariat refused to request a response from Canada on the basis that the international obligation in question, namely,

---

119 Defenders of Wildlife, press release, "Canada's Endangered Species at Risk" (24 March 2000), online: Defenders of Wildlife, www.defenders.org/newsroom.

120 See Sierra Legal Defence Fund, "The Lost Decade: Canada's Conservation Track Record Since Signing the 1992 Rio Convention on biological Diversity" (10 April 2002), online: Sierra Legal Defence Fund, www.sierralegal.org/reports2002.html.

121 12 and 14 September 1993, 32 I.L.M. 1480.

122 *Biodiversity* (21 July 1997), North American Commission for Environmental Cooperation SEM-97-005 (Citizen Submissions on Enforcement Matters), online: North American Commission for Environmental Cooperation, www.cec.org/citizen.index.cfm.

123 *AAA Packaging* (12 April 2001), North American Commission for Environmental Cooperation SEM-01-002 (Citizen Submissions on Enforcement Matters), online: North American Commission for Environmental Cooperation, www.cec.org/citizen.index.cfm.

the prohibition on exporting pesticides and toxic substances under article 2(3) of the NAAEC, had not been imported into Canadian domestic law. The *B.C. Logging Submission*[124] involved a challenge brought by Canadian environmental groups including the David Suzuki Foundation, Greenpeace Canada, the Sierra Club, and the B.C. Northwest Ecosystem Alliance. These groups argued that the Canadian government's practice of staying private prosecutions against logging companies brought under the *Fisheries Act*[125] was a violation of the obligation under article 6 of the NAAEC to ensure access to judicial proceedings. The secretariat dismissed this portion of the submission request on the basis that the NAAEC is not part of Canada's domestic law. *The Great Lakes Submission*[126] involved a group of eight Canadian and American NGOs alleging that the United States was failing to enforce its domestic law and two bi-national agreements, the *Great Lakes Water Quality Agreement*[127] and the *Agreement Concerning the Transboundary Movement of Hazardous Wastes.*[128] The secretariat rejected the argument that these bi-national agreements represent the "law of the nation" because they are not incorporated into the domestic law of the United States.

Attempting to steer around this discouraging body of jurisprudence, the environmental group applicants in the Biodiversity submission argued that Canada's failure to enact endangered species legislation violated its obligation under the *Biodiversity Convention* to "develop or maintain the necessary legislation and/or other regulatory provisions for the protection of threatened species and populations."[129] In an attempt to satisfy the requirement that there be a breach of Canadian domestic law, the groups focused not on the breach of the *Biodiversity Convention* itself, but the breach of the Instrument of Ratification. According to this argument, the Instrument of Ratification binds Canada under domestic law to uphold treaty obligations. The secretariat did not accept this distinction and responded that the purpose and effect

---

124 *BC Logging* (15 March 2000), North American Commission for Environmental Cooperation SEM-00-004 (Citizen Submissions on Enforcement Matters), online: North American Commission for Environmental Cooperation, www.cec.org/citizen.index.cfm.
125 R.S.C. 1985, c. F-14.
126 *Great Lakes* (28 May 1998), North American Commission for Environmental Cooperation SEM-98-003 (Citizen Submissions on Enforcement Matters), online: North American Commission for Environmental Cooperation, www.cec.org/citizen.index.cfm.
127 15 April 1972, Can. T.S. 1972 No. 12, 7312 T.I.A.S. 301.
128 28 October 1986, Can. T.S. 1986 No. 39, 11099 T.I.A.S.
129 *Biodiversity Convention*, above note 17 at art. 8(k).

of the Instrument of Ratification is to confirm Canada's international commitments regarding the Convention. It does not import those obligations into domestic law. While the argument was unsuccessful in this case, the secretariat left open the possibility of success in future cases with the statement that "in making this determination, [it] does not wish to exclude the possibility that future submissions may raise issues in respect of a Party's international obligations that would meet the criteria of 14(1)."

ii) Appeals under the Pelly Amendment

In 1999, a coalition of environmental groups led by the US environmental group Earthjustice sent a detailed letter to the secretary of the interior in the United States requesting certification of Canada pursuant to the *Pelly Amendment to the Fisherman's Protective Act of 1967*[130] for its failure to adopt endangered species legislation.[131] The letter recommended a prohibition on the importation of Canadian products into the United States until Canada passed a federal law to protect endangered species and their habitats. The letter stated that Canada was violating its commitment under the *Biodiversity Convention* and called on the United States government to pressure Canada into enacting legislation. The letter was intended as an international appeal for action, but was also aimed at shaming Canada. It was reported in a front-page story in the *Globe and Mail*:

> US environmentalists will ask their government tomorrow to enact trade sanctions against Canada because of Ottawa's failure to pass endangered-species legislation.... At the very least, the legal petition will embarrass Canada, once seen as an international leader on environmental issues, but now increasingly viewed as a laggard.[132]

---

130 *Fishermen's Protective Act* (Pelly Amendment) 22 U.S.C. § 1978 (2000).
131 Earthjustice, "Petition for Certification of Canada Pursuant to 22 U.S.C. § 1978 for Failing to Adopt Endangered Species Legislation" (22 March 1999), online: Earthjustice, www.earthjustice.org/regional/international/trade_documents/Canada%20ESA. pdf. The Pelly Amendment authorizes the President to prohibit the importation of products from countries which allow fishing operations that diminish the effectiveness of an international fishery conservation program or from countries that engage in trade or taking that diminishes the effectiveness of an international program for endangered or threatened species. For a more detailed analysis of the Pelly Amendment, see Steve Charnovitz, "Environmental Trade Sanctions and the GATT: An Analysis of the Pelly Amendment on Foreign Environmental Practices" (1994) 9 Am. U.J. Int'l. L. & Pol'y 751.
132 Anne McIlroy, "Animal Activists Push US to Punish Canada: Trade Sanctions Sought over Endangered Species" *Globe and Mail* (17 March 1999) A1.

Appeals under the Pelly Amendment also focused more specifically on the protection of individual endangered species. Following an unsuccessful attempt to secure protection for the spotted owl through litigation in Canadian courts, environmental groups turned to the Pelly certification process to request a US ban on the importation of BC wood products originating from critical spotted owl habitats. This request was a response to the failure of the environmental groups to secure adequate protection for the species through litigation in Canadian courts. In their appeal to the United States, the environmental groups cited Canada's failure to enforce its obligations under the *Biodiversity Convention*. They specifically referred to the court's decision in *Western Canada Wilderness Committee v. B.C.*[133] as "absolute authority for the proposition that laws do not exist in Canada which protect the species from extirpation caused by logging in its habitat."[134]

c) Market Pressure

Trade sanctions and consumer boycotts both feature as market tools adopted by Canadian environmental groups in campaigns to protect endangered species. In the case of campaigns to protect BC rainforests in 1995, the Friends of Clayoquot Sound petitioned US publishers to ban British Columbia's paper supplies.[135] The Western Canada Wilderness Committee used radio advertisements advising consumers to only buy lumber from second-growth trees in order to save the habitat of Canada's endangered species.[136] These strategies used both the market and the power of shame to put pressure on British Columbia and Canada. They reflect the complex, multi-faceted agenda of many environmental groups who are able to utilize a variety of economic tools in their campaigns alongside more classic strategies of litigation, media campaigns, and government lobbying.

---

133 *Western Canada Wilderness Committee v. B.C.* (2002), above note 51.
134 Canada Wilderness Committee & The Northwest Ecosystem Alliance, "Petition for Certification of Canada, pursuant to the Pelly Amendment" (24 October 2002), Western Canada Wilderness Committee online: media.wildernesscommittee.org/news/2002/10/181.php.
135 "A Yellow Environmental Campaign: US Publishers Refuse to Boycott BC's Article Suppliers" *Western Report* 10:44 (20 November 1995) 16.
136 See Western Canada Wilderness Committee, news release, "Wilderness Committee's Newest Radio Ad" (9 December 2004) Western Canada Wilderness Committee online: media.wildernesscommittee.org/news/2004/12/1062.php.

2) The Cheviot Mine Campaign

The campaign mounted against the proposed development of an open-pit coal mine a few kilometres from Jasper National Park differs from the campaign for federal endangered species legislation in a number of respects, including the involvement of a private-sector project developer. This means that the relative importance of government lobbying, transnational and domestic litigation, and public awareness strategies differs between these two campaigns. Because private companies were involved in the project, conservation groups attempted to stigmatize the companies involved as well as to shame the Canadian and Albertan governments for the approval of the project.

The history of the project has been turbulent since the decision of the federal government to approve the project in 1997. A long series of court battles have surrounded the project from 1997 to 2005, initiated by a coalition of local and national environmental groups actively campaigning to stop the mine's development, including the Pembina Institute for Appropriate Development, the Sierra Club, Nature Canada, Jasper Environmental Association, and the Alberta Wilderness Association (the Conservation Groups). The project was briefly abandoned in 2000, yet re-emerged in a revised form.

International law has featured in the campaign both in litigation and in the wider strategies which the Conservation Groups adopted to shame the Canadian and Albertan governments and the companies involved. Cardinal River Coals Ltd. (CRC), which owns the mine, put forward a project design for environmental assessment by a joint Alberta–Federal process initially in 1996. In 1997, the Joint Review Panel issued its report and recommendations, recommending that the minister of fisheries and oceans approve the project by providing CRC with the necessary regulatory approvals under the *Fisheries Act*. In October 1997 the Conservation Groups filed an application for judicial review of the Joint Review Panel's report, which was dismissed.[137] On appeal, the Appeal Division of the Federal Court set aside that ruling and ordered that the proceeding be referred back to the Trial Division for hearing on the merits.[138] The new hearing of the case was joined with a hearing of an application filed by the Conservation Groups

---

137 *Alberta Wilderness Assn. v. Canada (Minister of Fisheries and Oceans)* (1998), 152 F.T.R. 49 (T.D).

138 *Alberta Wilderness Assn. v. Canada (Minister of Fisheries and Oceans)* (1998), [1999] 1 F.C. 483, 238 N.R. 88 (C.A).

for judicial review of the minister's first project authorization pursuant to subsection 35(2) of the *Fisheries Act*.[139]

In this case, Justice Campbell found that the joint federal–provincial environmental review did not comply with the *Canadian Environmental Assessment Act*.[140] He struck down the federal authorization for the mine under the *Fisheries Act*, ruling that the minister could not issue a *Fisheries Act* approval that contravened the *Migratory Birds Convention Act Regulations*.

Justice Campbell determined that the permanent dumping of millions of tonnes of waste rock on migratory bird habitat did fall under the *Migratory Birds Convention Act*, based on a broad reading of the phrase "any other substance harmful to migratory birds" in the Act. He considered the broad purposive language in the *Migratory Birds Convention* as justification for giving a broad interpretation to language in the *Migratory Birds Convention Act*.

In 2000 CRC presented new proposals for the mine that were approved by the Joint Review Panel and accepted by the federal government. CRC modified its design again in 2002 and moved ahead with a revised project involving new undertakings and works not previously examined through the prior assessment process. The Conservation Groups, represented by Sierra Legal Defence Fund, filed two new challenges to the federal environmental assessment and authorization of the project in November 2004, which were heard by a federal court in Edmonton in June 2005. The Conservation Groups called for an environmental assessment of the project modifications and a determination that the federal government's 2004 authorization of the first part of the mine be quashed because of the mine's potential to destroy sensitive migratory bird habitat in violation of the *Migratory Birds Convention Act*. In their submissions, the groups advanced the argument that section 35(1) of the *Migratory Bird Regulations* and the *Migratory Birds Convention Act* generally should be interpreted in a manner consistent with Canada's international obligations and an interpretation that fulfills Canada's treaty commitments should be preferred over one that does not.[141] None of these international instruments and arguments was discussed by the Federal Court in its rejection of the Conservation Groups' applications.[142]

---

139 *Alberta Wilderness Assn.*, above note 67.

140 S.C. 1992, c. 37.

141 See above the text referring to notes 22–25 for a discussion of this case.

142 *Pembina Institute*, above note 24.

In the wake of the dismissal of their applications for judicial review, the Conservation Groups issued a media release on 30 September 2005 announcing their decision "to shift their campaign focus from the federal courts to the regulatory and enforcement agencies overseeing the mine, the federal and provincial endangered species provisions, and the mine's parent companies."[143] In the words of Dianne Pachal of the Sierra Club of Canada:

> Even though the approval was issued despite unresolved concerns of federal government officials, the glaringly obvious environmental harm from Cheviot likely wouldn't be rectified by pursuing it further through the courts.... Our interest in seeing that the project doesn't go past the first phase that's been approved, about one-fifth of the mine, wouldn't be addressed by the Courts.[144]

a) Public Opinion and the Media

Shaming continues to be an important weapon in the battle against the proposed mine. The Conservation Groups target tourists entering Jasper National Park, presenting them with brochures outlining the threats the mine poses to the park.[145] They argue that the Alberta government's approval of the mine amounts to a breach of Canada's obligations under the *Biodiversity Convention* and the *World Heritage Convention* as Jasper National Park is a World Heritage Site.[146] Environmental groups also capitalize on the support of the scientific community in making these arguments based on international biodiversity law.[147]

---

143 Sierra Legal Defence Fund, media release, "Conservation Groups Shift Focus in Tackling Mine Next-Door to Jasper National Park" (30 September 2005), online: Sierra Legal Defence Fund, www.sierralegal.org/news.html

144 *Ibid.*

145 Ashley Geddes, "Coalition to Lobby Tourists in Battle against Coalmine" *Edmonton Journal* (5 July 1997) A8.

146 See Dennis Hyruciuk, "Mine Foes Vow to Fight Back; Environmentalists Eye International Focus to Protest Cheviot" *Edmonton Journal* (19 June 1997) B5; Ed Struzik, "Sierra Club Opposes Cheviot Mine Project" *Edmonton Journal* (10 September 1997) B5; Alberta Wilderness Association, Pres Release, "Stop the Cheviot Mine! Legal Action Launched Over Proposed Cheviot Mine" (December 1997), online: Environmental Research and Studies Centre, www.ualberta.ca/ERSC/cheviot/protectstudy.htm.

147 A letter by a group of respected Canadian scientists, quoted in a press release of the Alberta Wilderness Association, refers to the fact that the protection of the Cheviot area falls directly under Canada's commitment to the *Network of Protected Areas* and the *Canadian Biodiversity Strategy*, above note 35, which emerged as part of the *Biodiversity Convention* See Alberta Wilderness Association Press Release, "Scientists Call for

The Sierra Club's 1997 Rio Report Card gave the Alberta government an "F" in biodiversity for considering approval of the mine in close proximity to a World Heritage Site, noting that its development would bring Canada in "clear violation" of the *Biodiversity Convention*. This grade was downgraded to an "F-" in the following year's Rio Report.[148] The Sierra Club also drew public attention to testimony by Parks Canada before the Cheviot review panel, stating the mine could jeopardize Canada's ability to meet its international obligations under the *World Heritage Convention*.[149]

The shaming argument is closely linked to the World Heritage Status of the National Park. The *World Heritage Convention* states that each participating member country has an affirmative duty to protect world heritage sites within its jurisdiction.[150] If a site is considered endangered by the World Heritage Committee, it may be included on the List of World Heritage Sites in Danger. Prompt listing of sites in danger ensures international attention for the sites, and embarrasses the governments unable (or unwilling) to protect their world heritage. Danger listing of Jasper National Park as a result of an approval of the Cheviot Mine would be a "'black eye' for Canada's image abroad."[151] As in other environmental shaming campaigns, Canada's international reputation as a world leader was also invoked in the efforts to stop the Cheviot Mine. Sam Gunsch, a director with the Canadian Parks and Wilderness Society, observed, "The prime minister has portrayed his government as a leader in environmental issues. Now the eyes of the world are on him."[152]

b) Appeal to the World Heritage Committee

The fact that Jasper National Park is a UNESCO World Heritage Site allows the network of conservation groups to raise what might otherwise have been a purely local land use issue to the international stage, placing ad-

---

Protection Instead of Mine" (April 1998), online: Environmental Research and Studies Centre, www.ualberta.ca/ERSC/cheviot/protectstudy.htm.

148 See Sierra Club of Canada, "Rio Report Card" (1998), online: Sierra Club of Canada Rio Report, www.sierraclub.ca/national/rio.

149 See "Making Mountain Park a Reality," online: Sierra Club of Canada, fanweb.ca/cheviot/index_html?main_page_name=home_reference.

150 *World Heritage Convention*, above note 17 at art. IV.

151 Ed Struzik, "UN Agency Asks Ottawa to Revoke OK for Cheviot" *Edmonton Journal* (19 March 1998) A1.

152 Ed Struzik, "Sierra Club Opposes Cheviot Mine Project" *Edmonton Journal* (10 September 1997) B5.

ditional international pressure on both the Canadian and Alberta governments involved in the mine approval process.

In March 1998 the director of the UNESCO World Heritage Committee requested that Canada's ambassador to UNESCO arrange for Canada to
consult with Alberta about reconsidering its Cheviot Mine approval. In the
letter request, the UNESCO director noted the challenges by the environmental groups in court.[153] Political responses to this "international pressure" varied from reassurance on the federal level that Ottawa is taking the
UNESCO request seriously[154] to outrage on the provincial level, expressed
by the Albertan Environment Minister Ty Lund in the media: "It really
bothers me when people from some other part of the world start telling the
people of Alberta how to operate in the province of Alberta."[155]

c) Market Pressure

It is difficult to isolate the influence of Jasper National Park's World Heritage Site designation on the development of the Cheviot Mine project. On
24 October 2000, the President and CEO of Luscar (one of the co-owners
of Cardinal River Coals Ltd.) was quoted in the media as saying that the
environmental approval process for the mine was significant in the company's decision to abandon the project, as concerns were raised that the mine
would threaten wildlife in a World Heritage Site.[156] When pressed on the
issue the next day at a press conference, however, he admitted that the environmental approval process was not the reason for indefinitely postpon-
ing the mine.[157] This contradiction suggests that in crafting their initial
explanation of the project postponement to the media, the project sponsors
were aware of the importance of appearing to be influenced by the World
Heritage Site designation of the park.

Recognizing the influence of the market, environmental groups targeted the money behind Cheviot when plans for a revised Cheviot Mine
materialized. In March 2004 environmental groups sent letters to the
mining companies responsible for the project, detailing the history of op-

153 Above note 151.
154 See Ed Struzik, "Feds to Co-operate with UN Request for Data on Project" *Edmonton
Journal* (20 March 1998) A6.
155 See Les Sillars, "This Land is Their Land: UNESCO Asks Ottawa to Revoke Approval
of Alberta's Cheviot Mine" *British Columbia Report* 9:31 (6 April 1998) 22.
156 "Mining: Coal Project Postponed Indefinitely" *Times - Colonist* (25 October 2000) D2.
157 Alberta Wilderness Association *et al.*, news release, "Indefinite Postponement of
Cheviot Mine" (25 October 2000), online: Alberta Wilderness Association, www.
albertawilderness.ca/News/News2000.html.

position to the mine and Canada's international obligation to protect Jasper as a World Heritage Site. The campaign also targeted Ontario teachers as the Ontario Teachers Pension Plan has a significant financial stake in the mine.

C. CONCLUSION

Environmental advocacy groups have a role to play both in identifying where Canada fails to give domestic effect to the obligations it assumes under ratified biodiversity treaties, and in addressing this failure. This chapter shows that despite the limited role of Canadian courts in giving effect to international biodiversity law, an important role exists for environmental advocacy groups both within and beyond the courtroom in fostering compliance with Canada's international legal commitments. Further and more profound engagement with international law sources by the Canadian judiciary can be encouraged by the clear and principled articulation of the relevance of international law in arguments before the courts.

At the same time, developments in international legal theory reveal the role of reputation in explaining why nations comply with international law. Strategies focus on shaming Canada, challenging its reputation before both international and domestic audiences, are important components of campaigns highlighting Canada's failure to live up to its international law obligations. Opportunities for further engagement with international biodiversity law are not lacking. The challenge lies in promoting greater engagement with international biodiversity law sources on the part of both counsel and the judiciary in Canada.[158] This engagement will foster familiarity with international biodiversity law, making this body of law appear not less "interesting," but perhaps less "exotic."

---

158 One step in this direction comes in the form of the new curriculum at the UBC Faculty of Law, where Transnational Law is a mandatory course for all first year students.

Section C:

THE MEDIATING LANGUAGE OF DOMESTIC
IMPLEMENTATION: THE CHALLENGES, CURRENT
AND BEST PRACTICES

A Legislative Perspective on the Interaction of International and Domestic Law

9

JOHN MARK KEYES* AND RUTH SULLIVAN

A. INTRODUCTION

Canada's form of government is based on the English model, under which domestic and international law are often thought of as, more or less, distinct legal systems. Under this model, international agreements are negotiated and ratified by the federal executive while the legislative and judicial branches have no direct role to play in the development or ratification of such agreements. Once ratified, such agreements bind Canada at international law, but they are not binding within domestic law. To operate domestically, an international agreement must either be recognized by the courts as reflecting customary international law or else it must be (or have already been) implemented through domestic legal action, typically taken by the legislative or executive branches.

This dualist position has been recognized by Canadian courts. The following pronouncement by Iacobucci J. in *Baker v. Canada* is typical: "It is a matter of well-settled law that an international convention ratified by the executive branch of government is of no force or effect within the Canadian legal system until such time as its provisions have been incorporated into domestic law by way of implementing legislation."[1] The arguments

---

*   The views expressed in this paper are those of Mr. Keyes personally and are not made on behalf of the Department of Justice.

1   *Baker v. Canada*, [1999] 2 S.C.R. 817 at para. 79 [*Baker*], citing *Capital Cities Communications Inc. v. Canadian Radio-Television Commission*, [1978] 2 S.C.R. 141 [*Capital Cities*]. Note also the recent decision of the Australian High Court in *Re Minister for Immigration and Multicultural Affairs; Ex p. Lam*, [2003] HCA 6 at para. 99 *et seq.* [*Lam*].

278 JOHN MARK KEYES AND RUTH SULLIVAN

advanced to justify this position focus on the structure of domestic government, most notably the separation of powers among the three branches of government and the division of powers between federal and provincial legislatures.

1) Separation of Powers

In Canada, as in other modern democratic states, governmental powers are divided among the legislative, executive, and judicial branches. Legislation is made by the legislature, consisting of the elected representatives of the people. The executive's power to legislate was abolished by the *Bill of Rights* of 1689, which established the law-making supremacy of Parliament.[2] Because the executive has no power to make law by itself, its ratification of an international agreement cannot in itself effect any change in domestic law.[3] If change is indeed required, then some form of implementation action must occur.

Although in principle this implementation requirement protects democratic values, the sharp distinction between the executive and legislative branches of government implicit in the separation of powers described above bears little relation to current realities. In Canada, the executive generally exercises significant control over the legislative branch through political parties. Not only does it control both the content and form of most legislation enacted by legislatures, but it also frequently arranges the delegation to itself of broad regulation-making authority, which may include the authority to implement international conventions. This state of affairs has long been criticized, most recently as the cause of the so-called democratic deficit.[4]

It is argued, with some justification, that the assumption of international obligations is a significant act of government that requires greater

---

2   Will. & Mary, 2d session, c. 2. Prerogative law-making powers in Canada have been whittled into relative insignificance through the enactment of legislation that displaces them: see John M. Keyes, *Executive Legislation* (Toronto: Butterworths, 1992) at 10. However, the Consolidated Index of Statutory Instruments published under the *Statutory Instruments Act* lists about seventy instruments issued under "Other than Statutory Authority," including the *Canadian Passport Order*, SI/81-86 and the *Reproduction of Federal Law Order*, SI/97-5.

3   The same also holds true of federal–provincial agreements: the executive has no inherent power to make laws to implement them: see *Reference re Anti-inflation Act* (1976), 68 D.L.R. (3d) 452 (S.C.C.).

4   See, for example, Peter Aucoin & Lori Turnbull, "The Democratic Deficit: Paul Martin and Parliamentary Reform" (2003) 46 Public Administration 427.

accountability to parliamentary bodies. International law is no longer confined to matters of interest only to national governments. Nowadays it is often designed to influence the rights and obligations of state subjects and to regulate their activities. This expansion of international law's focus arguably justifies a greater role for legislatures in its formulation. However, efforts to reform current practice have enjoyed limited success. Although legislative approval of the negotiation or ratification of international obligations sometimes takes place,[5] proposals to require such review and approval[6] or otherwise involve parliamentarians[7] in the negotiation and ratification process have not yet been adopted at the federal level in Canada.[8]

While criticism of the expansive role of the executive branch is warranted in some respects, it may also be overstated. The executive is no longer comprised of aristocrats with their own set of class interests who are beholden to the monarch. First ministers and their Cabinets have a democratic mandate and are accountable to the electorate not only through the legislature but also through the media and through their own consultations with subjects in the course of developing new legislation or making new regulations. A more persuasive basis for criticizing executive powers relating to international obligations is the high degree of confidentiality that the executive enjoys about its affairs through its traditional common law privileges and, more recently, under statute.[9] Arguably it is the lack of transparency and the resulting lack of accountability that makes executive treaty-making problematic.

---

5   For example, the House of Commons passed a resolution approving the ratification of the Kyoto Protocol on 12 December 2003.

6   A number of bills have been introduced in the House of Commons to provide procedures for the ratification of international agreements. The most recent, Bill C-260, 1st Sess., 38th Parl. (First Reading on 3 November 2004), would have required an "important treaty" to be approved by a resolution of the House of Commons before it is ratified and would also have required publication of ratified treaties. It would also require the federal government to consult provincial governments before negotiating or concluding a treaty in an area of provincial legislative authority. See also Joanna Harrington, "Redressing the Democratic Deficit in Treaty Law-Making: (Re-)Establishing a Role for Parliament" (2005) 50 McGill L.J 465.

7   See, for example, Michel Bissonet, "The Participation of Parliamentarians in Trade Negotiations" (2004) 27 Canadian Parliamentary Review 10.

8   Note, however, *An Act respecting the Ministère des relations international*, L.R.Q., c. M-25.1.1. Sections 22.2–22.6 (L.Q. 2002, c. 8, art. 6) provide for the tabling and approval of international agreements in the National Assembly of Quebec.

9   See the *Access to Information Act*, R.S.C. 1985, c. A-1, ss. 13–23 and 69 and the *Canada Evidence Act*, R.S.C. 1985, c. C-5, ss. 37–39.

Although attention is most often focused on the role of the legislative and executive branches in ratifying and implementing international agreements, it is important to consider the role of the courts in this context as well. The basic function of courts is to apply and enforce *domestic* law; however, their power both to decide what counts as domestic law and to interpret domestic law potentially gives them a significant role in the implementation of international law. This raises a number of questions. Are Canadian courts obliged to promote the application and enforcement of international law and, if so, on what basis? How should courts respond to agreements that have been ratified by Canada but never formally implemented? Should all agreements, regardless of subject matter, receive the same weight?

2)   Federal–Provincial Division of Powers

Another perhaps more compelling justification for the dualist position lies in the division of powers between the federal and provincial levels of government. Under the Constitution, the provinces lack the capacity to bind Canada at international law. This limitation is reflected in their lack of extraterritorial capacity. In practice, provinces are able to participate in international relations only to the extent that the federal government allows them to participate. Although they have the capacity to enter into agreements with foreign governmental bodies, the predominant view is that the power to create international law obligations belongs exclusively to the federal executive.[10]

In Canada, there is no federal power to implement international agreements entered into on behalf of Canada by the federal government. Since 1937 when the *Labour Conventions Case*[11] was decided, jurisdiction to implement international agreements has been understood to follow the division of powers established in the *Constitution Act, 1867*. Thus, Parliament may implement obligations relating to matters that fall within federal competency, including the peace, order, and good government clause, but obliga-

---

10   See Gibran van Ert, "The Legal Character of Provincial Agreements with Foreign Governments" (2001) 42 C. de D. 1093 at 1103–9. Some scholars take a contrary view: see van Ert at 1109 *et seq.* and S. Scherrer, "La pratique québecoise en matière de traités, accords et autres instruments internationaux" in *Actes de la XIe Conférence des juristes de l'État* (Cowansville, QC: Les Éditions Yvon Blais, 1992) 123.

11   [1937] 1 D.L.R. 673 (J.C.P.C.). See also Torsten Strom & Peter Finkle, "Treaty Implementation: The Canadian Game Needs Australian Rules" (1993) 25 Ottawa L. Rev. 39.

tions relating to matters that fall exclusively within provincial jurisdiction can be addressed legislatively only by the provincial legislatures. The rationale for this approach is obvious: the many important values protected by the federal distribution of powers, not the least being the integrity of civil law in Quebec, would be threatened if the federal executive could change the domestic law of Canada simply by ratifying an international convention. With the increasing expansion of international law into private law areas, the need to maintain a sharp division of powers between the federal executive and the provincial legislatures is all the more compelling.

3) Basic Principles

The constitutional framework set out above rests on three basic principles. First, ratification of an international agreement does not in itself change Canadian domestic law; if a change is necessary, it must be effected by the institutions that have domestic law-making power. Second, ratification of an international agreement does not displace the allocation of jurisdiction between federal and provincial levels grounded in the *Constitution Act, 1867*. Third, the courts have no role to play in the implementation of international agreements: they interpret and apply domestic law and have regard to international law only insofar as it sheds light on the meaning and purpose of domestic law. [12]

However well established these principles may be, their application and implications deserve close analysis, particularly in terms of the evolving roles of the legislative, executive, and judicial branches of government. In this chapter, we propose to examine them in light of the following fundamental values of democratic government:

- transparency and accountability in law-making and governmental functions, including the opportunity for participation in decisions by affected, interested parties (democracy);
- separation of powers among the legislative, executive, and judicial branches, particularly the encroachment of the latter two on the role of the legislative branch (parliamentary sovereignty);

---

12 Of course, in some instances an international agreement may codify customary international law or may be evidence of evolving customary law. A court may well point out that an agreement codifies or evidences customary law, but in doing so it is not *implementing* the agreement.

- need to preserve provincial jurisdiction from being undermined by federal treaty-making (federalism); and
- accessibility of law and coherence of the statute book (rule of law).

Section B of this chapter looks at the role international law plays in the interpretation of domestic legislation. Section C focuses on the range of strategies available to governments to implement international agreements, whether through statutes, regulations or other legal action. Section D concludes with some general comments on the role of the three branches of government in the implementation of international agreements and offers suggestions on how they might more effectively interact.

B. THE ROLE OF INTERNATIONAL LAW IN INTERPRETING DOMESTIC LEGISLATION

In this section we describe a theory of domestic interpretation that allows for reliance on international law in a variety of circumstances, justified on several grounds. Our basic assumption is that Canadian constitutional law obliges none of the branches of government when acting domestically to implement or comply with international law. The duty of legislatures is to serve the interests of their electorates. The duty of courts is to declare and apply domestic, not international, law. While courts adopt customary international law and legislatures codify that law or implement international agreements, neither is constitutionally obliged to do so. Even the executive branch, which at the federal level negotiates, signs, and ratifies international treaties, is not obliged under Canadian constitutional law to implement such treaties by introducing appropriate legislation or exercising executive powers. Of course, constitutional amendment is possible. It is also open to legislatures to impose a duty on courts or on the executive branch to implement international law. But in such cases, the duty is grounded in the particular statute and not in general constitutional law.

Because the rules governing the impact of international law within Canada are made in Canada, they could be changed in Canada. That is what some international law scholars are advocating. For example, van Ert has urged courts to enhance the role of international law within Canada by declaring the internal institutions of Canada to be subject to international law.[13] This would not limit the current power of legislatures to violate

---

13 Gibran van Ert, *Using International Law in Canadian Courts* (New York: Kluwer Law International, 2002) at 4.

that law, but it would elevate the presumption of compliance with international law to a judicial duty. What is missing is a good reason to make this change. In our view, compliance with international law is a good to be weighed against other (potentially competing) goods. There is no reason why it should automatically trump those other goods.

1) Interpretation Principles

Under the approach to interpretation adopted by the Supreme Court of Canada, "the words of an Act are to be read in their entire context."[14] This is sound advice, but the challenge is to identify, first, what constitutes context for the purposes of interpreting legislation and, second, how that context may be relied on in interpretation. By definition, the context of a legislative provision consists of anything other than the provision and in particular:

- the rest of the Act and the rest of the statute book (the *literary* context);[15]
- the common law, the *Civil Code*, Aboriginal law, international law, and the law of other jurisdictions (the *legal* context);
- relevant circumstances existing at the time the legislation was enacted (the *external* context); and
- the circumstances in which the legislation operates from time to time (the *operating* context).

Of course, how much context can be brought to bear in interpreting legislation depends partly on how much of it is known to the interpreter (this is a practical limitation) and how much of it is relevant (this limitation is legal). Assuming a given context is relevant, it must also be assigned an appropriate weight.

In addition, there is the problem of time. In all interpretation, the context in which a text was made is potentially at odds with the context in

---

14 According to Driedger's modern principle, "the words of an Act are to be read in their entire context and in their grammatical and ordinary sense harmoniously with the scheme of the Act, the object of the Act, and the intention of Parliament." As Iacobucci J. noted in *Bell ExpressVu v. Rex*, [2002] 2 S.C.R. 559 at para. 26: "Driedger's modern approach has been repeatedly cited by this Court as the preferred approach to statutory interpretation across a wide range of settings."

15 This is called the literary context because it is the context within which the conventions of legislative drafting operate, much like the conventions of poetry or the various genres of fiction. The literary context of an article in an international convention would be the rest of the convention and the body of international conventions.

which it is interpreted over time. In statutory interpretation, this potential is realized in the tension between static interpretation, which insists on the original intent of the lawmaker, and dynamic interpretation, which supports the adaptation of legal rules to changing circumstances. Implementation of an international convention may be part of a lawmaker's original intent or it may be part of the evolving context in which legislation is interpreted.

While many different types of context are relied on in statutory interpretation, in the end every use of context must be justified on one of the following grounds:

- it is a basis for inferring legislative intent;
- it is a source of domestic legal norms; and
- it contains persuasive opinion on the issue before the court.

These are not mutually exclusive categories, of course. A given contextual factor may be relevant, for example, because it both justifies adherence to a norm and offers persuasive evidence of the legislature's intention to adhere to that norm. But in our view it is important to distinguish among

- establishing legislative intent as a matter of fact on the basis of evidence;
- presuming legislative intent as a matter of law based on common law norms; or
- seeking a desirable solution based on diverse legal and academic materials.

These distinctions are important because the kind of justification offered to establish actual intent differs from that offered in support of presumed intent, as does the justification for relying on and assigning weight to comparative law materials. In the following sections of this chapter we explore these different kinds of justification under several headings. We begin with a section on legislative intent, followed by one on common law or judge-made norms. The latter section emphasizes the importance of distinguishing between the actual intent of the legislature (inferred from reading the text in context) and presumed intent (imputed to the legislature by the courts). This distinction is further explored in the next section on the role of international law in the dynamic interpretation of statute-based discretion. In the final two sections, on executive intent and comparative law, we focus on the third justification, the use of international law as a persuasive resource.

2) Legislative Intent

Our analysis of statutory interpretation takes the idea of legislative intent seriously. While it is not the only thing that matters, it is a key consideration in statutory interpretation. Under current interpretive approaches, there are two circumstances in which international law might assist in determining intent. The first is when there is reason to believe that the legislation to be interpreted was intended to codify an international law doctrine, implement an international law obligation, or impose a power or a duty on a decision-maker to consider international law.[16] The second is when there is reason to believe that international law materials formed part of the historical context in which legislation was enacted and may therefore shed light on the meaning of particular words or expressions or help infer the purpose of a particular provision.[17]

a) Intention to Implement

Ideally, the legislature's intention to implement international law or to impose a duty to consider it in exercising discretion should be signalled in the legislation itself. An intention to implement can be set out in a preamble or purpose statement.[18] A duty to consider international law when exercising discretion can be imposed in an interpretative or enabling provision.[19] However, this sort of express reference is not required.[20] The relevant intention can also be established through legislative history, for example a statement by a minister declaring that the purpose of legislation to implement a particular convention or a similar declaration in a Regulatory Impact Analysis Statement.[21] Such materials are legitimate evidence of legislative intent because they precede the enactment of the legislation and form part

16 See, for example, *National Corn Growers Association v. Canadian Import Tribunal*, [1990] 2 S.C.R. 1324 [*National Corn Growers*] and *Canada (Attorney General) v. Ward*, [1993] 2 S.C.R. 689.

17 See, for example, *R. v. Sharpe*, [2001] 1 S.C.R. 45.

18 See, for example, the preamble to the *North American Free Trade Agreement Implementation Act*, S.C 1993, c. 44.

19 See, for example, s. 7(4) of the *Postal Services Act 1975* (Cth):

> The commissioners shall exercise their powers in compliance with the Convention to the extent that it imposes obligations on Australia in relation to matters within their powers.

20 *National Corn Growers*, above note 16 at para. 73.

21 See, for example, *Animal Alliance of Canada v. Canada (Attorney General)*, [1999] 4 F.C. 72 at para. 2 (T.D.).

of the understanding on which it was made. Finally, an intention to implement can be inferred by comparing the wording of the legislative text to international law materials. Where the language of legislation tracks the language of a convention, for example, the court may legitimately infer an intention to implement.[22]

The role that international law can play in the interpretation of implementing legislation is well illustrated by the *Ward* case.[23] At the relevant time, Canada's *Immigration Act*[24] defined "Convention refugee" as a person who "by reason of a well-founded fear of persecution ... is outside the country of the person's nationality and is unable or ... unwilling to avail himself of the protection of that country." One of the issues in *Ward* was whether to qualify for refugee status, a person with dual citizenship had to be unable or unwilling to return to both countries in which he or she had citizenship. The Act was silent on this point, but the underlying Convention expressly provided in article 1(A)(2) that "in the case of a person who has more than one nationality, the term 'the country of his nationality' shall mean each of the countries of which he is a national." La Forest J. did not hesitate to adopt the Convention solution. He wrote:

> Although never incorporated into the *Immigration Act* and thus not strictly binding, paragraph 2 of Art. 1(A)(2) of the 1951 Convention infuses suitable content into the meaning of "Convention refugee" on the point.
>
> ...
>
> The fact that this Convention provision was not specifically copied into the Act does not render it irrelevant. The assessment of Convention refugee status most consistent with this theme requires consideration of the availability of protection in all countries of citizenship.
>
> This conclusion is bolstered by general rules of statutory interpretation. Section 33(2) of the *Interpretation Act*, R.S.C., 1985, c. I-21, stipulates that words in the singular include the plural. Consequently, references to "country of nationality" in the definition of "Convention refugee" in s. 2(1) of the *Immigration Act* should be read as including "countries of nationality."[25]

---

22 See, for example, *Gosselin v. Quebec (Attorney General)*, [1999] J.Q. no 1365 at paras. 365–67 (C.A.).

23 *National Corn Growers*, above note 16.

24 R.S.C. 1985, c. I-2.

25 *Canada (Attorney General) v. Ward*, above note 16 at 751–52.

In this analysis, La Forest J. relies on the underlying convention to gloss the meaning of the Act and he supports this interpretation by referring to the purpose of the international refugee protection regime. But he also, quite rightly, appeals to domestic conventions of legislative drafting and interpretation.

When a court concludes that the legislation to be interpreted was intended to give effect to an international law convention or doctrine, the court is obliged to look at the relevant international law materials, interpret them, and rely on them in interpreting Canadian law. But the following points should be noted. First, the content of the judicial duty here is not to apply international law but to give effect to the intention of the legislature. The international law materials are relevant only in so far as they cast light on domestic intentions. Second, the legislature may well intend to qualify or partly reject Canada's international obligations, as it is legally entitled to do. Given cogent evidence of such an intent, the presumption of compliance with international law is rebutted.[26] The constitutional competence to decide whether the full and unqualified implementation of international law is in the best interest of Canada or a province of Canada belongs to the legislature, not the courts.

The legislation considered by the Supreme Court of Canada in *Thomson v. Thomson*[27] illustrates the need for courts to pay close attention to the indicators of legislative intent and resist the temptation to take an all or nothing approach to implementation. The issue here was the validity of an order made under Manitoba's *Child Custody Enforcement Act*,[28] which implemented the international *Convention on the Civil Aspects of International Child Abduction*. Article 12 of the Convention provided:

> 12. Where a child has been wrongfully removed or retained ... and a period of less than one year has elapsed from the date of the wrongful removal or retention, the [judicial or administrative authority of the Contracting State where the child is] shall order the return of the child forthwith.

This obligation was qualified by article 13, which provided:

> the judicial or administrative authority of the requested State is not bound to order the return of the child if ... there is a grave risk that his or her

---

26 *Daniels v. White and the Queen*, [1968] S.C.R. 517 at 541; *Capital Cities*, above note 1 at 173.
27 [1994] 3 S.C.R. 551.
28 R.S.M. 1987, c. 360.

return would expose the child to physical or psychological harm or otherwise place the child in an intolerable situation.

Section 17 of the *Child Custody Enforcement Act* provided that "from and after December 1, 1983, the [Convention on the Civil Aspects of International Child Abduction] is in force in Manitoba and the provisions thereof are law in Manitoba." However, that is not all the Act provided. Sections 5 and 6 of the Act stated:

> 5. Notwithstanding any other provision of this Act, where a court is satisfied that a child would suffer serious harm if the child remained in or was restored to the custody of the person named in a custody order made by an extra-provincial tribunal, the court may make a custody order in respect of the child that differs from the custody order made by the extra-provincial tribunal.
>
> 6. Upon application, a court
> (a) that is satisfied that a child has been wrongfully removed to or is being wrongfully retained in Manitoba ...
>
> may do any one or more of the following:
>
> (c) make such interim custody order as the court considers is in the best interests of the child;
> (d) stay the application ...;
> (e) order a party to return the child to such place as the court considers appropriate.

In *Thomson* a Scottish court granted interim custody of a seven-month-old child to the mother and interim access rights to the father and ordered that the child remain in Scotland. When, shortly thereafter, the mother removed the child to Manitoba, the Scottish court granted permanent custody to the father. The father then applied to Manitoba's Court of Queen's Bench for the return of the child in accordance with article 12 of the Convention. The motions judge, Davidson J., found no evidence to suggest that returning the child to Scotland would create a "grave risk [of] physical or psychological harm or otherwise place the child in an intolerable situation" (article 13), nor was there evidence that the child would "suffer serious harm" (section 5). However, she thought it would be in the best interests of the child to give interim custody to the mother for a period of four months, by way of order under paragraph 6(c). This order would prevent the child from being abruptly removed from his mother's care while at the same time ensuring that she would have the custody matter dealt with before the Scottish courts in an expeditious fashion.

A majority of the Supreme Court of Canada held that there was no jurisdiction under section 6 of the Manitoba Act for an interim custody order of this sort. In considering whether an order to return the child could be refused on grounds of harm, it relied on the language of article 13 (b) of the Convention, as interpreted by courts around the world, rather than the language of section 5 of the Act, as interpreted by domestic courts. What is disturbing about the majority's analysis is its disregard for the actual intentions of the Manitoba legislature respecting these issues. Speaking for the majority, La Forest J. wrote:

> As I see it, those provisions [the provisions of the Act other than s. 17] and the Convention operate independently of one another. This result appears obvious when an application is made solely under the Convention or solely under the Act. One procedure may provide advantages that the other does not. When a particular procedure is chosen, however, it should operate independently of the other, though where the provisions of the Act are selected it may not be improper to look at the Convention in determining the attitude that should be taken by the courts, since the legislature's adoption of the Convention is indicative of the legislature's judgment that international child custody disputes are best resolved by returning the child to its habitual place of residence.[29]

It is difficult to understand the distinction drawn here between the Convention and the Act and, more particularly, how an application could be made under the Convention as opposed to the Act. The Convention does not and could not confer jurisdiction on Manitoba courts to make orders. The Convention is without legal significance in Manitoba except insofar as it is incorporated into the Act and thereby made part of Manitoba law. It follows that applications that invoke provisions of the Convention are made under the Act and in fact rely on the law of Manitoba as declared in the Act.

It is also difficult to understand why the various provisions of the Act, including those incorporated from the Convention, should operate independently of one another. Perhaps the most fundamental principle of statutory interpretation is that statutes are meant to embody coherent and internally consistent schemes to which each provision contributes in a useful way. Had the Manitoba legislature intended the Convention, once im-

---

29 Above note 27 at para. 93.

plemented, to operate independently of the Act it would have implemented the Convention in a separate Act.

Finally, it is not clear why, if the Act creates two independent schemes, the Manitoba-based scheme should be read in light of the Convention, but the latter need not be read in light of the former. La Forest J. writes that the legislature's adoption of the Convention is evidence of its judgment that international child custody disputes are best resolved in accordance with the Convention. However, this analysis ignores the other evidence of legislative intent, notably, sections 1 to 16 of the Act, the context in which the Convention was implemented and the legislative history of the enactment. Of particular concern are sections 5 and 6. The notwithstanding clause in section 5 makes it clear that, to the extent there is a conflict between the standard of child protection set out in the section and the standard set out in the Convention, the former prevails. Section 6 confers a right on interested parties to apply to the court for a variety of orders not provided for under the Convention. It is far from self-evident that the Manitoba legislature intended the discretion conferred on the court by section 6 to be displaced by the provisions of the Convention.

It would be helpful if section 6, like section 5, began with a notwithstanding clause. In the absence of such a clause, the interpreter is thrown back on other indicators of legislative intent. One such indicator is Manitoba's decision not to enact the *Uniform Act* prepared by the Uniform Law Conference of Canada to implement the Convention. The *Uniform Act* was adopted by four provinces. It includes a provision that gives paramountcy to the Convention in the event of a conflict between the Convention and other legislation. A similar clause is found in the implementing legislation of three other provinces. As La Forest J. observes, speaking of the common law provinces, only the British Columbia and Manitoba Acts do not contain such a paramountcy clause. A fair inference from these facts is that Manitoba did not intend the Convention to prevail over all other domestic legislation; rather it intended sections 1 to 16 of the Act to supplement the provisions of the Convention.

This inference is confirmed by the explanations offered by Manitoba's Attorney-General to the Standing Committee on Law Amendments, which considered the legislation in bill form. In response to questions from a committee member, the Attorney-General said:

> With respect to the point made about conflict between the Act and the Convention, it is my impression ... that in fact the bill that we're proposing gives

greater protections [to the best interests of the child] and that the Convention is a minimum. What we're doing is going beyond the Convention.

...

I don't think that there is that potential for conflict. It is always possible of course that there is some conflict that may be perceived between one section of an Act and another, but then that falls to be decided by the ordinary rules of statutory interpretation. ... It was the intention of this bill not to restrict, but to enlarge the protective mechanisms of the Convention.[30]

This indicates quite clearly that the provisions of the Convention were not intended to operate independently of the other provisions in the Act. It further indicates that the legislature was not content to simply incorporate the Convention, but wished to supplement it. As explained by the Attorney-General, the intention was "to enlarge the protective mechanisms of the Convention."

L'Heureux-Dubé J., who wrote a dissenting judgment in the case, drew attention to another indicator of legislative intent, namely, the way in which section 6 tracks the wording of the Convention. She wrote:

Both the wording of the Convention and the CCEA provide support for the complementary interpretation of the two. First the precise wording of s. 6 CCEA adopts the same terminology as that of the Convention by making reference to the wrongful removal and retention of the child, thus stressing the fact that the court's jurisdiction to make transitory orders pursuant to s. 6 is to be available regardless of whether the Convention is applicable.[31]

Finally, she drew attention to the potential conflict between giving paramount importance to the interests of children in custody matters and securing their prompt return. The Convention struck a particular balance between these interests, one that did not seem satisfactory to the Manitoba legislature, which adjusted the balance by providing additional protections for the child in sections 5 and 6. L'Heureux-Dubé J. wrote:

The emphasis placed upon prompt return in the Convention must be interpreted in light of the paramount objective of the best interests of children and in light of the express wording of the CCEA through which the

---

30 Legislative Assembly of Manitoba, Standing Committee on Law Amendments, vol. 30, no. 6 (28 June 1982) at 101.

31 Above note 27 at para. 129.

Convention was enacted in Manitoba, and should not mean return without regard for the immediate needs or circumstances of the child.[32]

In our view, the reasoning in the minority judgment is to be preferred over that of the majority because it gives appropriate weight to legislative intent.

b) External Context

In cases like *Ward*, a particular international convention is relied on in interpreting domestic legislation because the court has reason to believe that the purpose of the legislation was to implement, in part at least, the international obligations assumed by Canada upon ratifying the convention. In other cases, international law materials form part of the external context that (arguably) was present to the mind of the legislature when it enacted the legislation in question. This is certainly true of the international human rights instruments that influenced the framing of the *Charter*.

It is also possible for foreign codifying or implementing legislation to influence the interpretation of similar domestic legislation, as illustrated in *Re Canada Labour Code*.[33] In that case, to determine the meaning of a provision in Canada's *State Immunity Act*, the Supreme Court of Canada relied on case law from a number of foreign jurisdictions interpreting a comparable provision in their own immunity legislation.

3) Judge-Made Norms

In Elmer Driedger's approach to statutory interpretation, as set out in the second edition of *Construction of Statutes*, the common law presumptions of legislative intent are treated as a subcategory of legislative intent. He wrote:

> It may be convenient to regard "intention of Parliament" as composed of four elements, [including] … the presumed intention—the intention that the courts will in the absence of an indication to the contrary impute to Parliament.[34]

Driedger here explains what is not apparent from simply reading the modern principle itself, namely, that the reference to legislative intention includes presumed intent, and presumed intent in fact consists of judge-

---

32   *Ibid.* at para. 131.
33   [1992] 2 S.C.R. 50.
34   E.A. Driedger, *Construction of Statutes*, 2d ed. (Toronto: Butterworths, 1983) at 106.

made norms. These norms are applied to resolve interpretation disputes despite the absence of evidence that the legislature intended them to apply. The justification is that, in the opinion of the courts, they are important enough to warrant judicial protection against incursions by the legislative branch of government.

Of course, once a norm is established and relied on in statutory interpretation, it behooves a legislature to sit up and take notice. If the legislature knows that its silence will be interpreted in a particular way, and yet remains silent, the courts may legitimately infer that the legislature intended its legislation to be interpreted that way. In this sense, presumed intent may be considered an expression of actual legislative intent. But this analysis obscures what is most important about judge-made norms, namely, their origin. Judges make them up, and it is therefore up to judges to justify them, that is, to explain where they came from and why they should be imputed to the legislature.

Many presumptions of legislative intent are rooted in British constitutional law. As La Forest J.A. pointed out in *Estabrooks*, these are rooted in the liberal philosophy of the seventeenth century:

> Those who struggled to wrest power from the Stuart Kings and placed it in the hands of the elected representatives of the people were not of a mind to replace one despot by another. Rather they were guided by a philosophy that placed a high premium on individual liberty and private property and that philosophy continues to inform our fundamental political arrangements—our Constitution.
>
> ...
>
> With the complete realization of the implications of Parliamentary supremacy, this type of judicial approach, of course, disappeared. But the original foundations of our governmental organization remained as a legacy in a number of presumptions designed ... "as protection against interference by the state with the liberty or property of the subject."[35]

Other presumptions are rooted more specifically in Canada's constitutional experience, for example, the presumption that legislation affecting

---

35 *The Queen in Right of New Brunswick v. Estabrooks Pontiac Buick Ltd. et al.; The Queen in Right of New Brunswick v. Fisherman's Wharf Ltd. et al.* (1982), 144 D.L.R. (3d) 21 at 210–11 (N.B.C.A.).

Aboriginal peoples must be interpreted in their favour and the liberal construction of language rights.[36]

A number of well-established presumptions derive from the incorporation of customary international law into common law that took place during the eighteenth century. This category includes the presumption against the extraterritorial application of domestic law, based on the doctrine of territorial sovereignty and presumed respect for the principle of comity, which was the basis for both common law and civil law systems of private international law.[37] A good example of the incorporation process is found in the eighteenth-century case *Scrimshire v. Scrimshire*,[38] in which, for the first time, the question of the validity of a foreign marriage between two British subjects came before British courts. Under English law the marriage between the parties was valid, but under the law of France, where the marriage took place, it was null. To determine the applicable law, the court consulted some half-dozen authorities on international law. It reached the following conclusion:

> From the doctrine laid down in our books—the practice of nations—and the mischief and confusions that would arise to the subjects of every country, from a contrary doctrine, I may infer that it is the consent of all nations that it is the *jus gentium* that the solemnities of the different nations with respect to marriages should be observed, and that contracts of this kind are to be determined by the law of country where they are made. ... The *jus gentium* is the law of every country, and is obligatory on the subjects of every country. Every country takes notice of it: and the Court observing that law, in determining upon this case, cannot be said to determine

---

36 See Ruth Sullivan, *Sullivan and Driedger on the Construction of Statutes*, 4th ed. (Toronto: Butterworths, 2002) at 378 *et seq.* and 409 *et seq.*

37 The private international law of Britain was initially derived largely from the work of the Dutch scholar Huberus as published in *De Conflictu Legum*, trans. by E.G. Lorenzen, "Huber's *De Conflictu Legum*" (1919) 13 Ill. L. Rev. 375 at 401 *et seq.* Huberus explained that his system of private international law was founded on three maxims:

   1) The laws of each state have force within the limits of that government and bind all subject to it, but not beyond.

   2) All persons within the limits of a government, whether they live there permanently or temporarily, are deemed to be subjects thereof.

   3) Sovereigns will so act by way of comity that rights acquired within the limits of a government retain their force everywhere so far as they do not cause prejudice to the power or rights of such government or of its subjects.

38 (1752) 2 Hag. Con. 395, 161 E.R. 782.

English rights by the laws of France, but by the law of England of which the *jus gentium* is part.[39]

This strong statement of the principle of automatic adoption of international law is typical of the eighteenth century.[40] International law is adopted because it is universally observed by every country and the courts fear that failure to observe it would bring mischief and confusion to the subjects of a non-observing country.

Another category of presumptions derives from the judicial duty to harmonize potentially conflicting sources of law. The courts have developed a set of rules to deal with conflicts between different sources of legislation (federal/provincial, statute/regulation) and between legislation on the one hand and the entrenched constitution, the common law, and international law on the other. These rules reflect a hierarchy among the sources of law in which the entrenched constitution prevails over legislation and legislation prevails over common law, as well as international law. However, before applying these rules the courts rely on a number of harmonizing presumptions: that the legislature intends to comply with constitutional limits on its jurisdiction, that it does not intend to change the common law or derogate from the *Civil Code*, and that it does intend to comply with international law.

The first presumption, that the legislature intends to comply with constitutional limits, reflects the accepted relationship between entrenched legal norms and mere legislation and it makes good sense. Since legislatures have no capacity to exceed the limits on their jurisdiction, it would be both improper and futile for them to attempt to do so. The presumption of non-derogation from the *Civil Code* is also readily justified with reference to the role of the *Civil Code* in a civil law system.[41]

The presumption against changing the common law is more contentious. As a matter of constitutional law, validly enacted legislation prevails over the common law to the extent of any inconsistency. Given this rule, why would courts resolve legislative ambiguity in favour of the common

---

39 *Ibid.* at 790 (E.R.).
40 See, for example, *Barbuit's Caset* (1737), Cas. t. Talb. 281, 25 E.R. 777; *Roach v. Garvan* (1748), 1 Ves. Sr. 157, 27 E.R. 954; *Triquet v. Bath* (1764), 3 Burr. 1478, 97 E.R. 936.
41 For discussion, see Jean-Maurice Brisson & André Morel, "Federal Law and Civil Law: Complementarity and Dissociation," in Department of Justice, *The Harmonization of Federal Legislation with Quebec Civil Law and Canadian Bijuralism, Collection of Studies* (Ottawa: Department of Justice Canada, 1997) 213 at 217.

law? Given that the legislature does not legislate in vain, why would the courts presume an intention not to change? In responding to these questions, a distinction should be drawn between common law constitutional principles, such as the rule of law or the presumption that property will not be expropriated without compensation, and ordinary private law rules such as those governing the formation of contracts or the administration of trusts. Legislatures might be expected to defer to well-established constitutional principles, but not to common law private law. Perhaps the best justification for the presumption against changing the common law is that it creates an incentive for explicit legislative drafting so as to avoid ambiguity and ensure that change is not made surreptitiously in the case of fundamental principles or inadvertently in the case of ordinary common law.

Finally, there is the presumption of compliance with international law. Given the standard formulations of this presumption, it must be taken to apply to all obligations imposed on Canada by international law, regardless of source—whether customary law or convention—and in the case of convention-based obligations, regardless of whether the convention has been implemented. Conventions that have not been ratified obviously impose no obligations, but once ratified they are binding on Canada, whether or not they have been implemented. However, the failure to implement a convention might, in some circumstances,[42] be taken to indicate an intention not to implement.

In justifying the presumption of compliance with international law, van Ert writes:

> The normative justification for the presumption [of compliance with international law] is the principle of respect for international law. To interpret the acts of our legislatures and courts in a way that failed to respect international law or comity would impute to these bodies an unlawful or belligerent intent. Such an imputation is certainly uncharitable and usually wrong. There is also an important prescriptive justification for the presumption. Violations of international law or comity may bring inter-

---

42 This inference would not arise if there was reason to believe that the convention's obligations were already implemented by existing law. This is the case with many human rights conventions: see Irit Weiser, "Undressing the Window: Treating International Human Rights Law Meaningfully in the Canadian Commonwealth System" (2004) 37 U.B.C. L. Rev. 113 at 127 and 132 *et seq.* Arguably it is the case with the *Convention on the Rights of the Child* considered in *Baker*, above note 1, discussed below in section B(4).

national responsibility upon the state. The judiciary should therefore avoid internationally unlawful constructions of domestic law wherever possible.[43]

In our view, interpreting legislative or judicial acts in a way that violates international law or comity can be said to impute an unlawful or belligerent intent to those institutions only if one assumes that international law is binding within Canada, an assumption we reject. The second argument, that interpreting legislative or judicial acts in a way that violates international law or comity is usually wrong, is an argument about actual legislative or judicial intent, which must be based on evidence rather than presumed.

Van Ert's third argument is that violations of international law may have repercussions for the state, or possibly for its subjects. However, it is not the court's duty to avoid such repercussions. The extent to which the state or its subjects are to be put at risk through violation of international law is for the legislature to decide. Just as it is open to Canadian legislatures to derogate from *Charter* values within the limits prescribed by section 1, so it is open to Canadian legislatures to derogate from international law to whatever extent seems appropriate to secure the best interest of their electorates. And just as courts must not apply the presumption of compliance with *Charter* values so as to preclude the application of section 1, so too they must take care not to apply the presumption of compliance with international law to undermine the legislature's constitutional right and duty to consider whether compliance is in the best interest of Canada or the relevant province.[44]

We conclude that the primary justification for presuming interpretations that comply with international law is to avoid giving effect to legislative violations of international law that are surreptitious or inadvertent. In other words, the justification for presuming compliance with international law rests on much the same ground as the justification for presuming that the legislature does not intend to change the common law.

---

43 Van Ert, *Using International Law,* above note 13 at 99–100.

44 *Bell ExpressVu Limited Partnership v. Rex,* [2002] 2 S.C.R. 559 at para. 66, Iacobucci J.:

if courts were to interpret all statutes such that they conformed to the *Charter*, this would wrongly upset the dialogic balance. Every time the principle were applied, it would pre-empt judicial review on *Charter* grounds, where resort to the internal checks and balances of s. 1 may be had. In this fashion, the legislatures would be largely shorn of their constitutional power to enact reasonable limits on *Charter* rights and freedoms, which would in turn be inflated to near absolute status.

As noted above, in applying the presumption of compliance with common law, the courts distinguish between constitutional law principles and ordinary private law. A similar distinction is appropriately made between international human rights law and other areas of international law.[45] The justification for this distinction is not that international human rights law is binding on the courts, but rather that protecting human rights is an area in which courts claim inherent jurisdiction and special expertise. As asserted by Commonwealth judges in the *Bangalore Declaration*:

1. Fundamental human rights and freedoms are universal.
2. The universality of human rights derives from the moral principle of each individual's personal and equal autonomy and human dignity. That principle transcends national political systems and is in the keeping of the judiciary.[46]

Insofar as international human rights law sets out fundamental human rights and freedoms, the Canadian judiciary is obliged to give effect to it—not because international law is binding on Canadian judges, but because the judiciary is obliged to give effect to fundamental human rights within Canada.

The last category of judicial norms to be examined here includes newly emerging norms. In *Willick v. Willick*, the Supreme Court of Canada asserted that interpretations that would tend to defeat the "feminization of poverty" are to be preferred over ones that do not.[47] In *Rizzo & Rizzo Shoes Ltd. (Re)*, it asserted that interpretations that recognize the fundamental role that employment has assumed in the life of the individuals should be preferred.[48] The presumptions relied on in these cases are grounded in evolving social, cultural, and political norms, as evidenced by government reports, academic writing, and policies embodied in domestic legislation.

Another source of newly emerging legal norms is international law. This use of international law is illustrated by the reasoning of L'Heureux-Dubé J. in the *Spraytech* case.[49] The issue was whether the Town of Hudson had authority under Quebec's *Cities and Towns Act* to make a by-law

---

45   For an excellent recent analysis of this distinction, see van Ert, above note 13, c. 7.
46   As quoted by van Ert, *ibid.* at 238.
47   [1994] 3 S.C.R. 670.
48   [1998] 1 S.C.R. 27.
49   *114957 Canada Ltd (Spraytech, Société d'arrosage) v. Hudson (Town)*, [2001] 2 S.C.R. 241 [*Spraytech*].

restricting the use of pesticides to certain locations and activities.[50] Under section 410(1) of the Act, a municipal council could make by-laws to "secure peace, order, good government, health and general welfare in the territory of the municipality." The court held that this omnibus enabling authority was broad enough to authorize the pesticide by-law. In the majority reasons L'Heureux-Dubé J. wrote:

> To conclude this section on statutory authority, I note that reading s. 410(1) to permit the Town to regulate pesticide use is consistent with principles of international law and policy.
>
> ...
>
> The interpretation of By-law 270 contained in these reasons respects international law's "precautionary principle", which is defined as follows at para. 7 of the Bergen Ministerial Declaration on Sustainable Development (1990):
>
> > In order to achieve sustainable development, policies must be based on the precautionary principle. Environmental measures must anticipate, prevent and attack the causes of environmental degradation. Where there are threats of serious or irreversible damage, lack of full scientific certainty should not be used as a reason for postponing measures to prevent environmental degradation.
>
> Canada "advocated inclusion of the precautionary principle" during the Bergen Conference negotiations.
>
> ...
>
> Scholars have documented the precautionary principle's inclusion "in virtually every recently adopted treaty and policy document related to the protection and preservation of the environment."... The Supreme Court of India considers the precautionary principle to be "part of the Customary International Law."... In the context of the precautionary principle's tenets, the Town's concerns about pesticides fit well under this rubric of preventive action.[51]

This analysis illustrates how international law can be a source of domestic legal norms. The justification lies in evidence of: 1) Canada's commitment to the norm; 2) the widespread acceptance of the norm in the

---

50   R.S.Q., c. C-19, s. 410 [am. 1982, c. 64, s. 5; am. 1996, c. 2, s. 150].
51   *Spraytech*, above note 49 at 266–67.

international community; and 3) its coincidence with domestic concerns about the dangers of environmental pollution.[52]

The *Spraytech* case also illustrates a timing problem that can arise in relying on international law as a source of legal norms. Section 410 of the *Cities and Towns Act* was first enacted well before the formulation of the precautionary principle in international law. The question, then, is: To what extent is it legitimate for courts to rely on international legal norms that were not in existence when the legislation was enacted?

4) Dynamic Interpretation

The preceding question is not unique to international law norms and is best addressed in the context of Canadian law concerning the interpretation of legislative texts over time. Although this is a complex subject, two basic principles offer a helpful starting point. The first is that in interpreting all legal texts, whether entrenched constitutions or ordinary statutes, courts must mediate between the original context in which the law was made and the operating context in which the law is applied from time to time. The original context includes the law in existence when the constitution or statute was conceived—whether domestic, foreign, or international and whether hard or soft law. The operating context includes the law in existence when the constitution or statute is applied, including evolving international law, both hard and soft, and including conventions ratified after the law was enacted. Mediating between these two contexts lies at the heart of the judicial function in statutory interpretation, which is the application of more or less abstract rules conceived at one time to concrete facts occurring at another.

The second basic principle is that entrenched constitutional instruments should receive an "organic" or dynamic interpretation. This principle was most famously expressed by Lord Sankey in *Edwards* where he introduced the metaphor of a living tree.[53] Because a dynamic interpretation is called for, international law materials as they exist from time to time are an appropriate source of legal norms to be relied on in interpreting the *Charter*, both the rights and freedoms it declares[54] and the limitations it

---

52 Another emerging norm, grounded in international law, is harmonization; see, for example, the dissenting judgment of Binnie J. in *Harvard College v. Canada (Commissioner of Patents)*, [2002] 4 S.C.R. 45 at para. 12 *et seq.*

53 *Edwards v. Canada (Attorney General)*, [1930] A.C. 124 (J.C.P.C.).

54 See van Ert, *Using International Law*, above note 13 at c. 7.

accepts under section 1.[55] Even though some of these materials would not have been contemplated by the *Charter's* framers as formal sources of the law set out in the *Charter*, they form part of the operating context.

The living tree doctrine recognizes the fundamental importance of an entrenched constitution to ensure the stability of a state and the security of its subjects, coupled with the difficulty of amending it. This justification does not apply to ordinary legislation, which (in principle) can easily be amended. However, there are other grounds on which courts appropriately adopt an "organic" or dynamic approach. These grounds are sometimes formulated in terms of framers' or legislative intent. For example, when the legislature enacts a statute that is to operate for an indefinite time, particularly one that establishes institutions of governance or regulatory frameworks, it intends for those who will apply the statute to adapt it to evolving circumstance so that the statute continues to meet the legislature's original goals.

A related, but broader, basis for adopting a dynamic approach is the existence of discretion. When the legislature confers discretion on those who are to apply a statute, either directly through enabling provisions or indirectly through the use of general language or abstract terms, it intends that discretion to be exercised taking into account evolving circumstance. Otherwise there would be no reason to confer the discretion. This point is explained by McLachlin J. (as she then was) in *Tataryn v. Tataryn Estate*,[56] where the Supreme Court of Canada had to determine what provision for the testator's dependants would be "adequate, just and equitable" within the meaning of British Columbia's *Wills Variation Act*. McLachlin J. wrote:

> The language of the Act confers a broad discretion on the court. The generosity of the language suggests that the legislature was attempting to craft a formula which would permit the courts to make orders which are just in the specific circumstances and in light of contemporary standards. This, combined with the rule that a statute is always speaking ..., means that the Act must be read in light of modern values and expectations. ... The search is for contemporary justice.[57]

---

55 See, for example, L'Heureux-Dubé, J. in *R. v. Sharpe*, [2001] 1 S.C.R. 45 at para. 175 *et seq*. See also discussion by van Ert, *ibid*. at 240 *et seq*.

56 [1994] 2 S.C.R. 807.

57 *Ibid*. at 814–15.

An important source of modern values and expectations (although not the only source) is international law.

The role international law can play in dynamic interpretation is nicely illustrated by the judgment of McLachlin C.J. in *Canadian Foundation for Children Youth and the Law v. Canada*.[58] The issue there was whether section 43 of the *Criminal Code* was consistent with sections 7, 12, and 15 of the *Charter*. Section 43 provides:

> 43. Every schoolteacher, parent or person standing in the place of a parent is justified in using force by way of correction toward a pupil or child, as the case may be, who is under his care, if the force does not exceed what is reasonable under the circumstances.

Before reaching the *Charter* issues, it was necessary to determine the meaning of the rule set out in section 43 and in particular the import of the expression "reasonable under the circumstances." McLachlin C.J. wrote:

> precision on what is reasonable under the circumstances may be derived from international treaty obligations. Statutes should be construed to comply with Canada's international obligations. ... Canada's international commitments confirm that physical correction that either harms or degrades a child is unreasonable.[59]

She also emphasized the fact that "neither the *Convention on the Rights of the Child* nor the *International Covenant on Civil and Political Rights* explicitly require state parties to ban all corporal punishment of children."[60] The Conventions referred to in her judgment came into existence and were ratified long after section 43 was first enacted, yet they were legitimate indicators of the norms domestic courts could rely on in deciding what is "reasonable under the circumstances."[61]

---

58   [2004] 1 S.C.R. 76.
59   *Ibid.* at para. 31.
60   *Ibid.* at para. 33.
61   While the majority relied on international law to support their understanding of s. 43 of the *Code*, they did so selectively. As pointed out in the dissenting judgment of Arbour J., the *Convention on the Rights of the Child* establishes a Committee on the Rights of the Child. This committee has been highly critical of s. 43 of Canada's *Criminal Code*. In its 2003 report, Arbour J. notes: "[T]he Committee expressed 'deep concern' that Canada had taken 'no action to remove section 43 of the *Criminal Code*' and recommended the adoption of legislation to remove the existing authorization of the use of 'reasonable force' in disciplining children." *Ibid.* at para. 188.

The *Canadian Foundation* case illustrates the interaction between international law and the discretion conferred on interpreters by general or abstract language in a statute. In this context, it does not matter whether the court justifies its reliance on international law by appealing to the presumption of compliance or by appealing to norms whose validity and importance in domestic law is established, in part, by their recognition in international law. Things are somewhat more complicated, however, when it comes to the rule-making and decision-making discretions that are often conferred on the executive branch.

Generally speaking, the presumptions of legislative intent apply to enabling provisions that confer discretion so that, in the absence of evidence to the contrary, the powers conferred by the legislature (whether legislative or administrative) do not include the jurisdiction to violate those presumptions.[62] On this basis, regulations and decisions may be struck down as *ultra vires* because they fail to comply with international law. This approach is troubling because it does not allow for a nuanced analysis of the purpose and scope of the enabling provision. The relevance and weight of international law norms in the exercise of rule-making or decision-making discretion should be governed not by a rule—presume compliance—but rather by a pragmatic approach in which international law norms are but one of many considerations affecting the court's assessment of the purpose and scope of the delegated authority.

The reasoning of the majority in *Baker v. Canada (Minister of Citizenship and Immigration)*[63] offers an illustration of this approach. By regulations made under subsection 114(2) of the *Immigration Act*,[64] the Minister of Immigration was authorized:

> to exempt any person from any regulation made under subsection 114(1) ... where the Minister is satisfied that the person should be exempted from that regulation ... owing to the existence of compassionate or humanitarian considerations.[65]

Long after subsection 114(2) was originally enacted in 1976,[66] Canada ratified the *Convention on the Rights of the Child*, which provided (among other

---

62 See Keyes, *Executive Legislation,* above note 2 at 165 *et seq.*

63 Above note 1.

64 R.S.C. 1985, c. I-2.

65 *Immigration Regulations,* 1978, SOR/78-172, as amended by SOR/93-94.

66 S.C. 1976–77, c. 52. Note that the critical date here in terms of legislative intent is when the statutory enabling provision was enacted, not when the regulations were made.

things) that "in all actions concerning children, the best interests of the child shall be a primary consideration."[67]

The appellant, Baker, asked the minister to exempt her on humanitarian and compassionate grounds from a regulation that required her application for permanent residence to be made from outside Canada. If she were forced to leave Canada, she would be separated from her four Canadian-born children, to their detriment as well as hers. The minister rejected her request and the Federal Court dismissed her application for judicial review. However, it certified the following question as a basis for appeal:

> Given that the *Immigration Act* does not expressly incorporate the language of Canada's international obligations with respect to the International Convention on the Rights of the Child, must federal immigration authorities treat the best interests of the Canadian child as a primary consideration in assessing an applicant under s. 114(2) of the *Immigration Act?*

The appellant argued that the minister was obliged to exercise her discretion in accordance with the Convention. The minister argued that to require her discretion to be exercised in accordance with an unimplemented Convention would effectively implement the Convention, thereby undermining both the separation of powers between the executive and legislative branches of government and the division of powers between federal and provincial governments.

The majority judgment in *Baker* does not really answer the certified question nor does it directly address the issues raised by the submissions of the parties. However, some conclusions can be drawn. The majority held that the decision neglected the interests of Ms. Baker's children and this neglect was unreasonable because serving the interests of children is an important norm in Canadian law, as evidenced in several ways. L'Heureux-Dubé, J. wrote:

> In my opinion, a reasonable exercise of the power conferred by the section requires close attention to the interests and needs of children. Children's rights, and attention to their interests, are central humanitarian and compassionate values in Canadian society. Indications of children's interests as important considerations governing the manner in which H & C powers should be exercised may be found, for example, in the purposes of the

---

67 *Convention on the Rights of the Child*, Can. T.S. 1992 No. 3, art. 1.

Act, in international instruments, and in the guidelines for making H& C decisions published by the Minister herself.[68]

Later she elaborated on the significance of international instruments in constraining ministerial discretion:

> Another indicator of the importance of considering the interests of children when making a compassionate and humanitarian decision is the ratification by Canada of the Convention on the Rights of the Child, and the recognition of the importance of children's rights and the best interests of children in other international instruments ratified by Canada. International treaties and conventions are not part of Canadian law unless they have been implemented by statute....
>
> Nonetheless, the values reflected in international human rights law may help inform the contextual approach to statutory interpretation and judicial review.
>
> ...
>
> The principles of the Convention and other international instruments place special importance on protections for children and childhood, and on particular consideration of their interests, needs, and rights. They help show the values that are central in determining whether this decision was a reasonable exercise of the H & C power.[69]

As this analysis shows, the majority in *Baker* does not suggest that the minister is obliged by the Convention to give primary consideration to the best interests of the applicant's children. Nor does it rely on the presumption of compliance with international law. The *Convention on the Rights of the Child* is invoked, along with other Conventions ratified by Canada, as a justification for emphasizing the importance the minister must attach to the interests of children if the exercise of her discretion is to be reasonable. The Conventions are significant insofar as they illuminate the content and add to the weight of a norm, which the court has judged to be relevant, along with other norms, in the exercise of that discretion.

5) Executive Intent

It is axiomatic that courts must give effect to legislative intent in so far as that intent can be established. But when the legislature's intent is doubtful,

---

68   *Baker*, above note 1 at para. 67.
69   *Ibid.* at paras. 69–71.

the courts necessarily resort to other considerations to help resolve the interpretation problem. The question to be examined in this section is what notice courts may take of executive intent and what role, if any, such intent might properly play in statutory interpretation.

The issue of executive intent arises when the executive ratifies an international convention, but does not take any overt steps to implement it by introducing legislation or by exercising a delegated or prerogative power. There may be a range of explanations for this:

1) the executive considers that it is not in the best interest of the jurisdiction to implement the convention for the time being (this may particularly occur if there has been a change in government);
2) the executive is preoccupied with other matters and implementation, while desirable, is not a priority;
3) in the view of the executive, the legislature lacks jurisdiction to implement the convention and must seek implementation by other legislatures that possess the required jurisdiction; and
4) in the view of the executive, there is no need for additional implementation measures because domestic law already provides for everything undertaken by ratifying the convention.

Supposing reliable evidence of executive intent could be brought before the court,[70] should such evidence be admissible and would it be relevant? In our view, evidence of executive intent should be admissible to the same extent as evidence of legislative intent. There is no reason for courts to cling to the fiction that legislatures control the legislative agenda and the content and form of legislation. Courts should be able to take judicial notice of the real relations of power and accountability between the executive branch and the legislature.

Once those relations are acknowledged, the relevance of executive intent becomes obvious, particularly in cases where the issue is the significance of non-implementation of a ratified convention. If the executive has judged it better to avoid implementation in whole or in part or has judged it expedient to postpone implementation, the court has no business second guessing that judgment. The consequences of failure to implement is a matter for international, not domestic, law.

---

70 A major problem that arises in any attempt to rely on executive intent is that most reliable sources evidencing such intent are subject to a variety of restrictions on disclosure: see above note 9.

The analysis differs, however, when the executive branch decides that implementation is not required because the content of the ratified convention is already part of previously enacted domestic legislation. Executive opinion of this sort cannot be relied on as evidence of actual legislative intent, since it postdates the enactment of the legislation. However, the newly ratified convention is part of the operating context in which existing legislation is interpreted. Insofar as the opinion of the executive is accessible, in our view it is a legitimate to rely on it as persuasive authority in fixing the meaning or scope of particular legislation or reviewing the exercise of discretion conferred by it.

In a number of cases involving actions against Commonwealth governments, litigants have attempted to rely on conventions that have been ratified, but not expressly implemented, by invoking the doctrine of legitimate expectations. In the *Teoh* case, the High Court of Australia held that ratification by Australia of the international *Convention on the Rights of the Child* effectively evidenced the intention of the executive branch of the Australian government to be bound by the terms of the convention.[71] This approach has since been doubted by the Australian High Court[72] and was firmly rejected in *Baker*, quite rightly in our view, although not necessarily for the right reasons. Speaking for the entire court on this point, L'Heureux-Dubé emphasized that the doctrine of legitimate expectations does not create substantive rights. She wrote:

> the doctrine of legitimate expectations cannot lead to substantive rights outside the procedural domain. This doctrine, as applied in Canada, is based on the principle that the "circumstances" affecting procedural fairness take into account the promises or regular practices of administrative decision-makers, and that it will generally be unfair for them to act in contravention of representations as to procedure, or to backtrack on substantive promises without according significant procedural rights.[73]

She went on to say that ratification of the Convention did not give rise to a legitimate expectation that special procedures would be followed in addition to those normally followed in applications to the Minister under subsection 114(2) of the *Immigration Act*. Nor did it give rise to an expecta-

---

71 (1995), 183 C.L.R. 273.
72 See *Lam*, above note 1 at 97 *et seq.*
73 *Baker*, above note 1 at para. 26.

tion that the minister would apply particular criteria or reach a positive result. She wrote:

> This Convention is not, in my view, the equivalent of a government representation about how H & C applications [applications to the Minister to facilitate admission to Canada on humanitarian and compassionate grounds] will be decided, nor does it suggest that any rights beyond the [usual] participatory rights ... will be accorded. ... It is unnecessary to decide whether an international instrument ratified by Canada could, in other circumstances, give rise to a legitimate expectation.[74]

In our view, there are *no* circumstances in which the mere ratification of an international instrument, in the absence of implementation action, could fairly give rise to a legitimate expectation on the part of a citizen that the state will act in accordance with the terms of the Convention. In the first place, an expectation of compliance is far from being the sole or even the most reasonable response to the act of ratification. Under Canadian constitutional law, international conventions cannot change domestic law until they are implemented, and the executive and legislative branches have unfettered discretion whether to implement a ratified convention. As noted above, the failure to implement a ratified Convention may have several different causes, including unwillingness to implement the Convention. In these circumstances, there is no legitimate basis to expect that ratification of a Convention will have any impact on domestic law.

6) International Law as Comparative Law

In recent years, there has been considerable discussion of resort to international law for comparative law purposes. This treats international law as an inspirational resource, comparable to the foreign law of other jurisdictions, to which courts may resort in an effort to find the best solution to a given legal problem.[75] On this approach, international law is relied on as a source of good ideas and, as such, merits little weight. Stephen Toope

---

74 *Ibid.* at para. 29.
75 See, for example, Karen Knop, "Here and There: International Law in Domestic Courts" (2000) 32 N.Y.U. J. Int'l L. & Pol. 501 and Anne LaForest, "Domestic Application of International Law in Charter Cases: Are We There Yet?" (2004) 37 U.B.C. L. Rev. 157.

and Gibran van Ert object to this approach.[76] But arguably their objections target the claim that this is the primary or only use of international law in the interpretation of domestic legislation. On the analysis proposed here, reliance on international law as a source of comparison is but one approach among several.

The comparative law approach to international law is nicely illustrated in *Suresh v. Canada*,[77] in which one of the questions was whether the reference to terrorism in section 19 of the *Immigration Act* was void for vagueness. The section provided that no person may be admitted to Canada as a permanent resident if there are reasonable grounds to believe that the person has engaged in terrorism or is a member of an organization that has engaged in or might engage in terrorism. The court acknowledged that "terrorism" is a vague term, susceptible to a range of interpretations based on political or ideological considerations. In an effort to delimit the term, the court looked to a variety of international law materials, including the *International Convention for the Suppression of the Financing of Terrorism*, the *Convention on the Physical Protection of Nuclear Material*, and the *International Convention for the Suppression of Terrorist Bombings*. The Court reached the following conclusion:

> In our view, it may safely be concluded, following the International Convention for the Suppression of the Financing of Terrorism, that " terrorism" in s. 19 of the Act includes any "act intended to cause death or serious bodily injury to a civilian, or to any other person not taking an active part in the hostilities in a situation of armed conflict, when the purpose of such act, by its nature or context, is to intimidate a population, or to compel a government or an international organization to do or to abstain from doing any act." This definition catches the essence of what the world understands by "terrorism."[78]

The Convention relied on to interpret the term *terrorism* in section 19 postdates the enactment of the provision. In such a case, it is impossible to argue that the legislature intended to adopt the definition of terrorism accepted by the signatories to the Convention. Adopting the Convention's

---

76   See, for example, Stephen J. Toope, "The Use of Metaphor: International Law and the Supreme Court" (2001) Can. Bar Rev. 534 at 540; van Ert, *Using International Law*, above note 13 at 256 *et seq*.

77   2002 SCC 1.

78   *Ibid.* at para. 98.

understanding of terrorism might nonetheless be justified through appeal to a legal norm—here, possibly, the need to harmonize Canadian legislation with the legislation of other jurisdictions in the international effort to defeat terrorism. But even in the absence of such a norm, the Convention is useful, and resort to it is justified, because it offers a contained and plausible understanding of a vague term.

C. LEGISLATIVE AND ADMINISTRATIVE IMPLEMENTATION ACTION

In part B, we explored the ways in which international law can affect the interpretation of domestic legislation. In this part, we consider the types of action, both legislative and administrative, that can be taken to implement Canada's international obligations.

The threshold requirement for taking such action is to have the jurisdiction to do so. As noted above, jurisdiction to implement international agreements ratified by Canada depends on their subject-matter and follows the division of powers established by the *Constitution Act, 1867.*[79]

Many types of state action can be taken to give an international agreement domestic legal effect. Their legal effect varies considerably, as does their transparency. The following is a list of the various types, beginning with the most explicit and concluding with the most subtle:

- domestic legislation (whether primary or delegated) can provide that the agreement has effect as law (*direct implementation*);
- domestic laws can restate the provisions of the agreement (rights, prohibitions, requirements) that the agreement says are to be part of domestic law (*restatement*);
- *new powers* (legislative or administrative) can be enacted to give effect to the agreement; and
- *existing administrative powers* can be used to give effect to the agreement.

These techniques can be used separately or in combination with one another. This part reviews them and comments on their advantages and disadvantages. It also looks at some aspects of reversing implementation measures (de-implementation) when a state decides to withdraw from an agreement. Finally, a checklist for considering these techniques is provided in the appendix to this article.

---

79   (U.K.), 30 & 31 Vict., c. 3, reprinted in R.S.C. 1985, App. II, No. 5.

1) Direct Implementation by Providing That an Agreement Has Effect as Law

The most direct way to give domestic legal effect to an agreement is simply to enact that the Agreement "has the force of law." For example, section 142 of the *Canada Shipping Act, 2001* says:

> 142. (1) Subject to the reservations that Canada made and that are set out in Part 2 of Schedule 3, the International Convention on Salvage, 1989, signed at London on April 28, 1989 and set out in Part 1 of Schedule 3, is approved and *declared to have the force of law in Canada*.[80]

This language incorporates the text of the agreement into domestic law, instructing those who are bound by the domestic law to treat it as they would any other text enacted as law. This is not, however, the only language capable of conferring the force of domestic law on the text of a treaty. *Canada v. Nakane* suggests that "sanctioned" will suffice.[81] In this case, section 2 of the *Japanese Treaty Act, 1906* said simply:[82]

> 2. The convention of the 31st day of January, 1906, which is set forth in the schedule to this Act is hereby sanctioned.

Irving J. of the Full Court of British Columbia concluded:

> That seems to be a very apt and proper way of giving effect in Canada to all the terms of the Treaty. Without an Act giving effect to the Treaty there would be no binding law governing the officials of this country. The word "sanction" signifies to ratify a decree or ordinance—in an extended sense to make anything binding. In itself, it conveys the idea of authority by the person sanctioning. It is the lending of a name, an authority or an influence in order to strengthen and confirm a thing.[83]

If "sanctioned" will directly incorporate a treaty into domestic law, it appears that "approved" will not. In some countries, including Canada, there is a legislative practice in implementing legislation of providing that an agreement is "approved." The example quoted above from the *Canada Shipping Act, 2001* illustrates this. The purpose of this practice in jurisdic-

---

80 S.C. 2001, c. 26.
81 [1908] B.C.J. No. 15; 13 B.C.R. 370 (S.C.).
82 S.C. 1906-07, c. 50.
83 Above note 81 at 374–75 (B.C.R.).

tions based on the British model is not entirely clear.[84] It may be intended simply to signal legislative acceptance of the actions of the executive in concluding and ratifying the agreement. Such "approval" has no effect on the status of the agreement as a matter of international law since the power to conclude international agreements falls exclusively within the prerogatives of the executive. But it equally has no effect in terms of making the agreement part of domestic law, other than perhaps to explain why, as in the *Canada Shipping Act* example, Parliament is taking the further step of giving the treaty binding force as a matter of domestic law. The presence of additional language in this example ("declared to have the force of law") explicitly conferring this effect reinforces the conclusion that mere "approval" will not suffice.

This conclusion is also confirmed in *Pfizer Inc. v. Canada,* where the Federal Court of Appeal considered provisions "approving" the *WTO Agreement Implementation Act* and expressing the purpose of implementing it.[85] The Court rejected the argument that these had the effect of making the entire agreement part of Canadian law:

> [48] In short, Pfizer fails in its arguments. When Parliament said, in section 3 of the *WTO Agreement Implementation Act,* that the purpose of that Act was to implement the Agreement, Parliament was merely saying the obvious; it was providing for the implementation of the WTO Agreement as contained in the statute as a whole including Part II dealing with specific statutory changes. When Parliament said in section 8 of the WTO Agreement Implementation Act that it was approving the WTO Agreement, Parliament did not incorporate the WTO Agreement into federal law. Indeed, it could not, because some aspects of the WTO Agreement could only be implemented by the provinces under their constitutional legislative authority pursuant to section 92 of the *Constitution Act, 1867* [30 & 31 Vict., c. 3 (U.K.) (as am. by *Canada Act 1982,* 1982, c. 11 (U.K.), Schedule to the *Constitution Act, 1982,* Item 1) [R.S.C., 1985, Appendix II, No. 5]]. What Parliament did in approving the Agreement is to anchor the Agreement as the basis for its participation in the World Trade Organization, Canada's adherence to WTO mechanisms such as dispute settlement

---

84 J. Crawford, "The International Law Standard in the Statutes of Australia and the United Kingdom" (1979) 73 Am. J. Int'l L. 628 at 629.

85 [1999] F.C.J. No. 1122 (T.D.). See also *Council of Canadians v. Canada (Attorney General),* [2005] O.J. No. 3422 at paras. 35–36 (S.C.J.).

and the basis for implementation where adaptation through regulation or adjudication was required.[86]

Another, often complementary, way to give direct legal effect to an international agreement is to provide that it prevails over any inconsistent laws[87] or that other laws are amended so as to give effect to the agreement.[88] These sorts of provisions attempt to resolve conflicts that might arise between the existing law and the agreement. However, they do not provide any indication of where these conflicts arise. This highlights a major difficulty with giving direct legal force to an agreement: those affected by the law must identify the inconsistencies. This requires readers of the existing law to have the agreement in mind in order to verify whether there are any inconsistencies, which may itself not be an easy task given that there can be considerable debate about what constitutes an inconsistency.[89]

This question has been considered in the context of the Canadian constitutional paramountcy rule about overlapping federal and provincial legislation: in this circumstance, conflict occurs when it is impossible to comply with both the legislation of both jurisdictions.[90] A similar approach obtains when determining whether there is a conflict between primary and subordinate legislation.[91] In addition, the Supreme Court of Canada has recently revived another branch of the conflict rule, recognizing that a conflict can also arise if one piece of legislation will "frustrate the legislative purpose" of the other.[92] This standard is far more open-ended than the first branch of the test, depending on a determination of purposes that often have to be gleaned from the terms of the legislation or the context of its enactment. The task of establishing what these purposes are and how

---

86   *Ibid.* at para. 48.

87   See *Canada Shipping Act, 2001*, S.C. 2001, c. 26, s. 142(2), which reads:

> (2) In the event of an inconsistency between the Convention and this Act or the regulations, the Convention prevails to the extent of the inconsistency.

88   *International Boundary Waters Treaty Act*, R.S.C. 1985, c. I-17, s. 3:

> 3. The laws of Canada and of the provinces are hereby amended and altered so as to permit, authorize and sanction the performance of the obligations undertaken by His Majesty in and under the treaty, and so as to sanction, confer and impose the various rights, duties and disabilities intended by the treaty to be conferred or imposed or to exist within Canada.

89   See Sullivan, *Sullivan and Driedger*, above note 36 at 265–66.

90   See *Spraytech*, above note 49.

91   *Friends of Oldman River v. Canada*, [1992] 1 S.C.R. 3.

92   *Saskatchewan v. Rothmans, Benson & Hedges Inc.*, 2005 SCC 13.

particular provisions affect their attainment often leads to indeterminate, if not subjective, results, particularly in the absence of clear statements of purpose.[93] A provision that simply says that a particular law or agreement prevails over other conflicting laws invites confusion and litigation.

Direct implementation may be limited to particular provisions of an agreement. An implementing legislature need not give the force of law to all of the provisions of an agreement. As discussed later in this section, there may be other mechanisms for implementation besides the enactment of new law.[94]

Another important facet of direct implementation has to do with which languages of an agreement are authentic, a matter that is generally specified in one of its terms.[95] If these are different from the national language of the implementing jurisdiction, then many of those subject to it may have difficulty understanding it or be at a disadvantage when interpreting it. Although a translation may be available, it will not have the same status as the original, which will prevail over the translation if it does not accurately capture the original.

Legislation providing for direct implementation typically contains a preamble or purpose clause, and sometimes both, which set out contextual detail that may have a significant effect on how it is interpreted. In addition, the text of the agreement may be annexed to the implementing legislation. This is particularly useful in that it makes the text as readily available as the legislation itself. Given that the text of the agreement forms part of the law of the implementing jurisdiction, it is only reasonable that it be published in the same manner as other law. Although some texts of treaties are available online,[96] and can generally be found in official publications, such as the *Canada Treaty Series*[97] or the *United Nations Treaty Collection*,[98] general access is by no means assured since these publications are not widely available or entail substantial subscription costs.[99]

---

93 See Sullivan, *Sullivan and Driedger,* above note 36 at 230–34.

94 See below section C(6).

95 For example, the *International Space Station Agreement* specifies 6 authentic languages: see S.C. 1999, c. 35.

96 See, for example, the UN Framework Agreement on Climate Change, online: unfccc. int/not_assigned/b/items/1417.php.

97 See online: www.treaty-accord.gc.ca/Treaties_CLF/Section.asp?Page=TS.

98 See online: untreaty.un.org.

99 For example, the subscription rate for the UN Treaty Series is $60 US per month for non-profit entities, including universities and individuals, online: untreaty.un.org/ English/howtoreg.asp. However, many university law libraries offer free access to their

One consequence of direct implementation is that the agreement will be interpreted in accordance with international law principles, unless the implementing legislation provides otherwise.[100] The *Vienna Convention on the Law of Treaties* codifies these principles. Article 31 says:

> 1. A treaty shall be interpreted in good faith in accordance with the ordinary meaning to be given to the terms of the treaty in their context and in light of their object and purpose.

It also provides that subsequent agreements among the parties and "special meanings" that they intend will influence interpretation.[101] Article 32 goes on to say:

> 32. Recourse may be had to supplementary means of interpretation, including the preparatory work of the treaty and the circumstances of its conclusion, in order to confirm the meaning ... when the interpretation according to article 31:
>
> (a) leaves the meaning ambiguous or obscure; or
> (b) leads to a result which is manifestly absurd or unreasonable.

Canadian interpretation law has developed in a similar direction in recent years and reliance on the Vienna Convention as opposed to domestic interpretation law is less likely to make much difference in practice. However, Canadian courts still arguably accord greater weight to the wording of the legislation, notably through the "plain meaning" rule.[102]

---

collections, for example, the Nahum Gelber Law Library at McGill University, online: www.law.library.mcgill.ca/treaties.html.

100 *R. v. Palacios* (1984), 7 D.L.R. (4th) 112 (Ont. C.A.).

101 Vienna Convention, art. 32, subarts. 3 and 4:

> 3. There shall be taken into account, together with the context:
>
> (a) any subsequent agreement between the parties regarding the interpretation of the treaty or the application of its provisions;
> (b) any subsequent practice in the application of the treaty which establishes the agreement of the parties regarding its interpretation;
> (c) any relevant rules of international law applicable in the relations between the parties.
>
> 4. A special meaning shall be given to a term if it is established that the parties so intended.

102 See, most recently, *Will-Kare Paving & Contracting Ltd. v. Canada*, [2000] 1 S.C.R. 915 and *R. v. Daoust*, [2004] 1 S.C.R. 217.

A further potentially important consequence of direct implementation is greater judicial reliance on foreign case law in interpreting the incorporated treaty. The choice of direct implementation may signal an intention to harmonize Canadian law as much as possible with other jurisdictions that have ratified and implemented the convention. This seems to have been a factor in the majority judgment in the *Thomson* case, which considered and relied on judgments interpreting the relevant Convention from Australia and the UK.[103]

As noted above, implementing legislation may attempt to control the interpretation of directly implemented agreements through preambles and purpose clauses. Another way is through interpretation clauses such as section 5 of the *Income Tax Conventions Interpretation Act*.[104] It provides a series of definitions that apply "[n]otwithstanding the provisions of a convention or the Act giving the convention the force of law in Canada." These clauses effectively modulate the scope of the direct implementation with what amounts to a form of restatement, which is discussed later in this section.

Direct implementation is a simple and expeditious way of implementing an international agreement, but its effectiveness is far from assured. Just saying that a text has the force of law does not guarantee that those subject to it will comply with it. Most legislation is backed up with administrative and enforcement provisions, notably penal sanctions, directed toward ensuring compliance. These provisions generally have to be tailored to domestic enforcement agencies or courts and related laws. It is unlikely that an agreement can be written so as to achieve a detailed fit with the agencies, courts, and laws of all the parties to the agreement. At the very least, these have to be examined to determine whether adequate administrative and enforcement measures can be taken under existing law to ensure that the agreement is implemented in substance and not just formally. If not, then additional adjustments will be needed to domestic law and institutions. This largely explains the use of the alternative technique of restatement.

---

103 Above note 27 at 585–88, 596–97, and 599.
104 R.S.C. 1985, c. I-4.

2) Restating the Agreement in Domestic Law

This approach involves restating the terms of the agreement or enacting provisions that will otherwise accomplish what the agreement requires. It can be accomplished by either enacting a new law or amending existing laws. These laws may be either primary legislation (statutes) or delegated legislation (regulations, by-laws, rules, orders).

Restatement is not merely an exercise in copying the terms of an agreement into a piece of legislation. Words that may have a particular meaning in one context do not necessarily have the same meaning in another. The context for domestic legislation is a complex system of laws that operate together and have a bearing on each other's meaning. When an agreement is implemented through restatement, the legislation is subject to the interpretive rules of the domestic jurisdiction, as opposed to those of the Vienna Convention. Domestic legal systems are not only different from the international legal context in which an agreement is drafted, they also vary from one jurisdiction to another. Given these contextual differences, different words may be needed to achieve a meaning that will effectively implement an agreement in the domestic law of all the parties.

The purpose of implementing an international agreement heavily influences the meaning of domestic legislation. This purpose is sometimes bolstered by an interpretive provision such as section 3 of the *North American Free Trade Agreement Implementation Act*:

> 3. For greater certainty, this Act, any provision of an Act of Parliament enacted by Part II and any other federal law that implements a provision of the Agreement or fulfils an obligation of the Government of Canada under the Agreement shall be interpreted in a manner consistent with the Agreement.[105]

And as with direct implementation, there may also be provisions to say that the implementing legislation prevails over other legislation to the extent of any inconsistency.[106]

One important difference between direct implementation and restatement is that the latter makes it easier to be selective about which provisions of an agreement are being implemented. If nothing is said about a particular provision in the implementing legislation, then it is not implemented. By

---

105 S.C. 1993, c. 44.
106 See, for example, the *Income Tax Conventions Implementation Act, 1996*, S.C. 1997, c. 27, s. 5.

contrast, the direct method requires an express exclusion to accomplish this. This is not to say that such a provision will remain unimplemented, since it may be implemented in some other way besides through the enactment of new legislation. It is important to consider whether existing legislation already implements, or goes some distance towards implementing, new international agreements. If it does, there is little point in enacting duplicate provisions that will only engender confusion.

Another advantage of the restatement technique is that it allows new rights and obligations to be fitted into existing legislation so that those who already use that legislation will be able to appreciate how the new rights obligations alter existing ones. This will not only avoid conflicts, it may also make the new rights and obligations easier to understand, particularly if improvements can be made in the way they are drafted. A good example of this is the *Anti-personnel Mines Convention Implementation Act*.[107] Article 4 of the Convention states the main obligation to destroy anti-personnel mines, but the exception to this rule is found in the preceding Article 3. When the Convention was restated in the Act, the main rule was stated first in section 9 and was followed by the exception in section 10 to accord with general legislative drafting practices in Canada.[108]

3) Using Primary or Delegated Legislation

In the preceding discussion, we have noted that either primary or delegated legislation can be used to give agreements effect in law. The choice between these two turns on the significant differences between the processes for making them. Primary legislation is enacted by elected legislative bodies in accordance with procedures that allow considerable scope for public scrutiny and input. It is generally used to deal with legislative matters of some significance, as demonstrated by the guidelines that some jurisdictions have for determining what matters should be dealt with in primary legislation. For example, the Canadian Government's *Cabinet Directive on Law-Making* says:

> Matters of fundamental importance should be dealt with in a bill so that Parliamentarians have a chance to consider and debate them. The bill should establish a framework that limits the scope of regulation-making

107 S.C. 1997, c. 33.
108 See the Drafting Conventions of the Uniform Law Conference of Canada, s. 1 (logical organization) online: www.ulcc.ca.

powers to matters that are best left to subordinate law-making delegates and processes.[109]

Matters of a more technical nature, in the sense of filling in the details of a legislative scheme established by an Act, are properly left to delegated legislation.

Although it may be tempting to say that the implementation of an international agreement is a substantial matter deserving of treatment in primary legislation, this presupposes the nature of the agreement. The test for using primary legislation to implement an agreement should surely depend on whether it requires legislative measures that, in their own right, ought to be dealt with in primary legislation. The fact that this is often the case with international agreements does not mean that it is always the case. There are many examples of regulation-making powers to implement international agreements that deal with largely technical matters. For example, section 35(1) of the *Canada Shipping Act, 2001* provides general regulation-making authority to implement a variety of international shipping conventions:[110]

> 35. (1) The Governor in Council may, on the recommendation of the Minister of Transport, make regulations
>
> ...
>
> (d) implementing, in whole or in part, an international convention, protocol or resolution that is listed in Schedule 1, as amended from time to time, including regulations
>
> (i) implementing it in respect of persons, vessels or oil handling facilities to which it does not apply,
>
> (ii) establishing stricter standards than it sets out, or
>
> (iii) establishing additional or complementary standards to those it sets out if the Governor in Council is satisfied that the additional or complementary standards meet the objectives of the convention, protocol or resolution.

This Act also gives the Governor-in-Council power to amend the list of conventions in Schedule 1, but it requires that additions to the list be tabled in Parliament for referral to the appropriate committee:

---

109 Online: www.pco-bcp.gc.ca .
110 S.C. 2001, c. 26.

30. (1) The Governor in Council may, by order, add international conventions, protocols and resolutions described in subsection 29(1) to Schedule 1 or described in subsection 29(2) to Schedule 2.

(2) The Minister of Transport is to cause a copy of each order related to Schedule 1 and the Minister of Fisheries and Oceans is to cause a copy of each order related to Schedule 2, together with a description of the objectives of the convention, protocol or resolution, to be laid before each House of Parliament on any of the first 10 days on which that House is sitting after the order is made. The order stands referred to the appropriate standing committee of each House.

31. The Governor in Council may, by order, delete an international convention, protocol or resolution from Schedule 1 or 2 or amend Schedule 1 or 2 if the amendment would not, in the opinion of the Governor in Council, result in a material substantive change.

In this provision, one sees an attempt to balance parliamentary accountability against the need for flexibility in implementing these conventions.

4) Enacting Non-Legislative Powers

Often, international obligations cannot be met simply by enacting new rules: they require judicial or administrative action instead. For example, the *Mutual Legal Assistance in Criminal Matters Act*[111] implements agreements dealing with law enforcement. It recognizes that requests for enforcement must be carefully considered before they are acted upon. It makes the minister of justice responsible for the administration of the Act and confers power on the minister to examine requests for enforcement before they are placed before Canadian courts.[112]

It is also possible to shape general powers to ensure that they are exercised in a way that takes new international obligations into account. For example, subsection 35(3) of the *Citizenship Act* says:

35(3) Subsections (1) and (2) [restrictions on acquisition of property by non-Canadians] do not operate so as to authorize or permit the Lieutenant Governor in Council of a province, or such other person or authority as is designated by the Lieutenant Governor in Council thereof, to make any decision or take any action that ...

---

111 R.S.C. 1985 (4th Supp.), c. 30.
112 *Ibid.*, ss. 7–9.

(b) conflicts with any legal obligation of Canada under any international law, custom or agreement;[113]

5) Anticipatory Implementation

Legislation can be enacted in contemplation of agreements being entered into. This is particularly useful when a series of similar bilateral agreements with other countries is planned. For example, the *Mutual Legal Assistance in Criminal Matters Act* is intended to facilitate the enforcement of criminal law against persons who are outside the prosecuting jurisdiction.[114] It contains a general definition of the type of treaty it is meant to implement:

> 2. (1) In this Act,
>
> "treaty" means a treaty, convention or other international agreement that is in force, to which Canada is a party and of which the primary purpose or an important part is to provide for mutual legal assistance in criminal matters.
>
> (2) For the purposes of the definition " treaty" in subsection (1), an important part of a treaty provides for mutual legal assistance in criminal matters if the treaty contains provisions respecting all of the following matters:
>
> (a) the right of Canada, for reasons of security, sovereignty or public interest, to refuse to give effect to a request;
> (b) the restriction of mutual legal assistance to acts that, if committed in Canada, would be indictable offences;
> (c) the confidentiality of information sent by Canada to a foreign state pursuant to a request for legal assistance.

Provision can also be made to take account of possible amendments to a treaty. For example, the *Migratory Birds Convention Act, 1994* provides for changes to the list of protected birds.[115] These changes are to be incorporated textually into the Act through a ministerial order tabled in Parliament:

> 12 (2) The Minister shall, by order, amend the schedule to incorporate any amendment to the Convention as soon as is practicable after the amend-

---

113 R.S.C. 1985, c. C-29.
114 Above note 111.
115 S.C. 1994, c. 2; online: www.unhchr.ch/html/menu3/b/k2crc.htm.

ment takes effect, and table any amendment in both Houses of Parliament within fifteen sitting days after the order is made.

This provision attempts to accommodate the need for flexibility in implementing the convention with the need for legislative scrutiny. However, this provision does little more than notify members of Parliament. It does not ensure debate or offer any substantive check on the implementation of changes to the Convention.

6) Using Existing Powers

A number of cases discussed earlier in part B of this chapter clearly suggest that powers granted or recognized under existing legislation (without reference to the implementation of any international agreement) might also serve to implement obligations or international law principles when they are exercised in accordance with those obligations or principles.[116] Whether they can do so depends on the nature and breadth of the existing powers: Does the implementation action fit within the scope of the power? This question has two main dimensions:

- Does the power permit a form of action that will advance the implementation of the agreement?
- Are the purposes for which the power may be used broad enough to embrace the purposes of the agreement and its implementation?

These questions are seldom expressly articulated in the case law, but they are clearly in play. For example, in the *Baker* case discussed earlier,[117] the exemption power under subsection 114(2) of the *Immigration Act*[118] was not framed in terms of the implementation of any international agreement. Nevertheless, the Supreme Court recognized, not only that the power could be used to advance the objects of the *Convention on the Rights of the Child*, but also that the Convention had a bearing on whether the power was exercised reasonably.[119] Thus, a general power originally enacted in 1976[120] without reference to the Convention (which entered into force on 2

---

116 *Baker*, above note 1; *Spraytech*, above note 49; and *Canadian Foundation for Children, Youth and the Law v. Canada*, above note 58.

117 Above note 1, discussed above in section B(4).

118 Above note 24.

119 Above note 1 at para. 71.

120 S.C. 1976–77, c. 52.

September 1990) was capable of being used to advance the objects of the Convention.

There is no shortage of examples of the use of existing powers to implement international agreements. In the field of human rights, Irit Weiser has pointed out that international obligations "are typically adhered to on the basis that *existing laws already conform to the treaty obligations* and therefore, no new implementing legislation is required."[121] The same often occurs in relation to general regulatory matters such as those addressed by the *Canada Shipping Act*.[122] Although many of the enabling provisions of this Act are expressed in terms of implementing international agreements or instruments, there are many others that contain no such references. However, there is no obstacle to using them to implement international obligations as long as the implementation action otherwise fits within the terms of the enabling provisions.

For example, subsection 79(1) of the *Crewing Regulations*[123] was made under enabling provisions in four sections of the *Canada Shipping Act* that dealt with the certification of masters and seamen (sections 110 and 112), safety precautions (section 338), and safe navigation (section 562.1). Although none of these provisions refers to international agreements, together they confer authority to require compliance with the safety standards of the International Maritime Organization. Indeed, Canadian courts have generally recognized the propriety of regulations that incorporate, by reference, international requirements in order to achieve harmonization with the legal regimes of other countries.[124]

When an agreement requires a state party (as opposed to a member of the public) to do something, there may be no need to enact a law to implement the requirement since the state party is already bound by international law. For example, article 5, section 2 of the *Convention on the Prohibition of the Use, Stockpiling, Production and Transfer of Anti-Personnel Mines and on their Destruction* provides:

> 2. Each State Party shall make every effort to identify all areas under its jurisdiction or control in which anti-personnel mines are known or sus-

---

121 Weiser, "Undressing the Window," above note 42 at 127.

122 R.S.C. 1985, c. S-9. This Act has now been replaced by the *Canada Shipping Act, 2001*, above note 110.

123 SOR/97-390.

124 See *Reference re Manitoba Language Rights, No. 3*, [1992] 1 S.C.R. 212 and John M. Keyes, "Incorporation by Reference in Legislation" (2003) 25 Stat. L. Rev. 180.

pected to be emplaced and shall ensure as soon as possible that all anti-personnel mines in mined areas under its jurisdiction or control are perimeter-marked, monitored and protected by fencing or other means, to ensure the effective exclusion of civilians, until all anti-personnel mines contained therein have been destroyed..

This obligation was not included in the *Anti-Personnel Mines Convention Implementation Act*[125] since it entails activities that the Canadian Government can accomplish without any additional legislative authority.

The anti-personnel mines example provides an important reminder that under the Canadian Constitution many executive powers are inherent. As in other parliamentary states, the executive has the capacity to perform legal acts that all legal persons generally have, and it has prerogative powers as well. These span a range that encompasses the command of military forces, the issuance of passports, and the capacity to conclude contracts or deal with property.

Although the use of existing powers to implement international agreements simplifies the task of implementation insofar as no legislative action is required by Parliament, it is also a source of criticism that such implementation leaves too much to be determined by the executive and is therefore undemocratic. However, if there is a problem with using these powers to implement an international agreement in the absence of implementing legislation, then the problem is with the scope of the powers themselves, not with their use to implement the agreement. Would using them to advance other policy purposes raise the same objections? If not, then what is it about the implementation of international agreements that makes their use objectionable?

We would suggest that the most compelling objection is the lesser degree of transparency that often accompanies the use of existing powers, as opposed to the enactment of implementing legislation. Rather than discouraging the use of existing powers, consideration should be given to finding ways to increase the transparency of implementation when existing powers alone are used. Reporting mechanisms, such as the Departmental Reports on Plans and Priorities and the Departmental Performance Reports of the Government of Canada, could serve as a means for doing this.[126]

---

125 S.C. 1997, c. 33.
126 These reports are required as part of the annual Parliamentary Estimates process. The foreword to the *Guide for the Preparation of Departmental 2004-2005 Performance Reports* says:

It should also be borne in mind that implementation through legislative measures is hardly a panacea in terms of transparency. The enactment of legislation does not ensure that it will be administered and enforced. Additional measures are generally needed to monitor these dimensions as well. The *United Nations Framework Convention on Climate Change* and the *Kyoto Protocol* are striking examples of this. The obligations they impose on states are quite straightforward: reductions in the amount of greenhouse gases by reference to emissions in 1990.[127] Much of their detail and that of subsequent protocols has to do with measuring and reporting on emissions levels.[128]

A further issue relating to the use of existing powers is whether the executive is ever *required* to use them to implement international obligations. It is far from clear that general powers, not created for the implementation of an agreement, must be used to implement it as the discussion above of legitimate expectations demonstrates.[129] This is particularly true of delegated legislative powers, which the courts are quite reluctant to require the executive to exercise because such powers generally import a high degree of discretion, if not policy-making.[130]

7) Combining Techniques

There is no requirement to use only one technique to implement a particular agreement. In fact, most of the examples of implementation legislation discussed above rely on a combination of techniques. Direct implementation may be accompanied by legislated provisions, such as definitions, that adapt the provisions of an agreement to the specific features of the

---

Reports on plans and priorities (RPPs) and departmental performance reports (DPRs) are departments' primary instruments of accountability to Parliament and, by extension, to Canadians. It is important that they provide clear, concise, balanced, and reliable information about each department's plans to be achieved with the resources entrusted to it and how it performed against those plans. These reports also present an opportunity to engage parliamentarians and Canadians more effectively in a constructive dialogue about the future directions of the government (online: www.tbs-sct.gc.ca/rma/dpr1/04-05/guidelines/guide_e.asp).

127 Online: unfccc.int/essential_background/convention/items/2627.php.
128 See the website of the secretariat of the United Nations Framework Convention on Climate Change, online: unfccc.int/essential_background/kyoto_protocol/items/3145.php.
129 See above section B(5).
130 See John M. Keyes, "Required Rule-making: When Do You Have to Make Delegated Legislation" (2002) 15 Can. J. Admin. L. & Prac. 293.

implementing jurisdiction[131] or by regulation-making powers for carrying out the terms of the agreement.[132] And restatement legislation sometimes directly incorporates definitions from the implemented agreements.[133]

A good example of combination occurs when a domestic law is enacted to create penalties for doing things that contravene an agreement. In such a case, the text of the agreement defines the scope of the prohibited conduct, while the domestic law defines the regime used to penalize it. Section 3 of the *Geneva Conventions Act* illustrates this:

> 3. (1) Every person who, whether within or outside Canada, commits a grave breach referred to in Article 50 of Schedule I, Article 51 of Schedule II, Article 130 of Schedule III, Article 147 of Schedule IV or Article 11 or 85 of Schedule V is guilty of an indictable offence, and
>
> (a) if the grave breach causes the death of any person, is liable to imprisonment for life; and
>
> (b) in any other case, is liable to imprisonment for a term not exceeding fourteen years.[134]

By making a person "guilty of an indictable offence," this provision engages the provisions of the *Criminal Code* for the investigation and prosecution of such offences.[135] Thus, the law in this case is an amalgam of the Geneva Conventions (direct implementation) and the *Criminal Code* (statement in domestic law).

8) De-implementation

If there is some prospect that Canada may terminate or withdraw from an agreement in whole or in part, some thought should be given to how the implementing legislation will be repealed or modified. This can of course be done with another piece of legislation. However, if a more expeditious route is needed, it can be built into the implementing provisions. In addi-

---

131 See, for example, the *Foreign Missions and International Organizations Act*, S.C. 1991, c. 41 and the *Commercial Arbitration Act*, R.S.C. 1985 (2d Supp.), c. 17

132 This is done in most Canadian legislation for the implementation of tax treaties, for example, the *Income Tax Conventions Implementation Act, 2001*, S.C. 2001, c. 30.

133 For example, the *Chemical Weapons Convention Implementation Act*, S.C. 1995, c. 25 restates the terms of the Convention, but s. 2(2) gives direct legal effect to its definitions.

134 R.S.C. 1985, c. G-3.

135 The *Interpretation Act*, R.S.C. 1985, c. I-21, s. 34(2) states: "All the provisions of the *Criminal Code* relating to indictable offences apply to indictable offences created by an enactment."

tion, previous provisions can be suspended, rather than repealed, so that it is easier to reinstate them.

For example, many provisions enacted to implement the *North American Free Trade Agreement* (NAFTA) superseded but did not repeal comparable provisions enacted to implement the *US Free Trade Agreement*. In particular, implementing amendments to the *Customs Tariff*[136] did not repeal the US free trade provisions; instead, they suspended their operation for as long as the new provisions were in force. The US free trade provisions could, accordingly, be revived by repealing the NAFTA implementing provisions.

De-implementation provisions must obviously be used with a great deal of caution. They may signal to other parties a lack of commitment to the agreement and perhaps lead to questions about the good faith of a party that uses them.

D. CONCLUSIONS

In part A, we posed some questions about the roles of the legislative, executive, and judicial branches and, more particularly, whether the latter two are improperly encroaching on the legislative sphere. The legislative branch clearly has the capacity to decide whether and to what extent international obligations are implemented by or under Canadian law. However, that capacity is tempered by two realities. First, the Constitution and existing legislation, along with the interpretive principles that govern their application, provide many avenues for giving effect to international obligations. Second, legislative bodies are no more capable of dealing with all aspects of international law than they are of dealing with all aspects of the domestic laws they enact. Legislatures must rely on the executive and the courts, not only to administer laws, but also to fill in or elaborate many of the details of the law needed to allow it to operate effectively.

Courts should be praised, not criticized, for relying on international law, not only to give effect to the implementing or codifying intentions of the legislature, but also in mediating between the expressed intentions of the legislature and the contexts in which legislation must be interpreted. At the same time, it must be remembered that compliance with international law is but one of many concerns that animate judicial interpretation. Finally, courts must be responsive to indications that the legislature

---

136 R.S.C. 1985 (3d Supp.), c. 41, as amended by S.C. 1993, c. 44, s. 117(1).

intends a partial or nuanced implementation or codification of its international obligations.

As for the executive branch, its capacity to implement international law that does not require legislative change is troubling because of the lack of debate and transparency. When international law is implemented through executive action, it is often far from apparent how or to what extent implementation is taking place. More fundamentally, the executive branch has a substantial degree of control over both statutory and regulatory implementation mechanisms. However, this control is constrained by increasingly significant checks and balances. Executive action is subject to judicial review, particularly of the interpretation of domestic legislation. In addition, the executive hold on the legislative function is loosening in Canada with democratic reform of parliamentary institutions proceeding apace.[137] Finally, executive functions are subject to increasing transparency, notably through consultative processes on their domestic actions.[138] This transparency should logically extend to its international law functions as well.

Concerns about power and transparency in the implementation of international obligations should not be limited to the executive and judicial branches. The increasing interest of legislators in international law and its implications for domestic law signals a developing role for legislators.[139] We should not assume that existing parliamentary institutions and procedures are well enough equipped to take on this role and to discharge it with the transparency that is coming to be expected of the executive. This deserves to be an area of careful study over the coming years.

---

137 Note "Ethics, Responsibility, Accountability: An Action Plan for Democratic Reform," Government of Canada, Privy Council Office, 4 February 2004 (www.pco-bcp.gc.ca) and the Canadian Government's Democratic Reform website at www.pco-bcp.gc.ca/dr-rd.
138 See "Consultation Guidelines for Managers in the Federal Public Service," Government of Canada, Privy Council Office, 21 December 1992, online: www.pco-bcp.gc.c).
139 See above notes 6–8.

APPENDIX: CHECKLIST FOR DECIDING HOW TO IMPLEMENT INTERNATIONAL OBLIGATIONS

The following questions should be considered when determining how to implement international obligations:

- What result does the agreement require to be implemented?
- Does it say how the result is to be achieved?
- Does implementation require legal action?
- What existing powers are there to take this action?
- Are any new laws needed and, if so, what kind
  - statutes
  - delegated legislation
- Are any administrative powers needed?

The following criteria should be use for assessing implementation decisions:

- *Democracy*: Do those affected by implementation have enough input into decisions about implementation?
- *Transparency*: Are the implementation measures made clear to those affected?
- *Harmony with domestic law*: Are changes needed to domestic law to avoid conflicting provisions?
- *Ease of implementation*: How quickly can the implementation measures be taken?
- *Workability and effectiveness*: Will the implementation measures operate effectively in the implementing jurisdiction?
- *Harmony with law of other countries*: Will the implementation measures operate effectively with measures taken by other countries?
- *Flexibility*: How easy will it be to respond to changing circumstances (amendment or rescission of agreement)?

International Law and Statutory Interpretation: Up with Context, Down with Presumption

STÉPHANE BEAULAC[*]

A. INTRODUCTION

Since occupying centre stage after the Supreme Court of Canada 1999 decision in *Baker v. Canada (Minister of Citizenship and Immigration)*,[1] the debate in Canada about the complex questions arising from the domestic application of legal norms other than national law has given rise to a number of articles, most of which are authored by international law scholars.[2] The provenance of these articles should not be a matter for surprise, given that the interpermeability[3] of legal norms has, by definition, a non-

* The author wants to acknowledge the financial aid of the George Stellari Grants and the competent assistance of Mr. Brendan Naef and Ms. Stéphanie Garon. This paper, in a somewhat different and abridged form, also appears in the conference proceedings of "Clarity and Obscurity in Legal Language," a pluri-disciplinary event (linguistics, philosophy, law) organized in July 2005 by Anne Wagner in France.

1 [1999] 2 S.C.R. 817 [*Baker*]. These issues have also gained more attention in the United States with the Supreme Court decision in *Lawrence v. Texas*, 123 S. Ct. 2472 (2003); and *Roper v. Simmons*, 125 S. Ct. 1183 (2005). See also generally John F. Murphy, *The United States and the Rule of Law in International Affairs* (Cambridge: Cambridge University Press, 2004); and specifically, Rex D. Glensy, "Which Countries Count? *Lawrence v. Texas* and the Selection of Foreign Persuasive Authority" (2005) 45 Va. J. Int'l L. 357; and Joan Larsen, "Importing Constitutional Norms from a 'Wider Civilization': Lawrence and the Rehnquist Court's Use of Foreign and International Law in Domestic Constitutional Interpretation" (2004) 65 Ohio St. L.J. 1283.

2 See Stéphane Beaulac, "National Application of International Law: The Statutory Interpretation Perspective" (2003) 41 Can. Y.B. Int'l L. 225 at 227–28.

3 For a discussion of the "permeability" of legal norms, especially in the context of transnational law and international arbitration, see Frédéric Bachand, *L'intervention du juge*

national dimension.[4] This phenomenon has been witnessed in two different, yet intertwined, ways: first, horizontally, among national legal orders,
through comparative law[5] and transnational law;[6] second, vertically (though
avoiding a connotation of superiority), between the international legal order and the domestic legal orders, which in turn can occur 1) through the
influence of the norms in the former on the norms of the latter,[7] and 2) *vice
versa*, through the role of the norms in the latter as sources of the norms
in the former.[8] The present chapter focuses on the second category, more
particularly the vertical influence that the international may have on the
domestic.

At the outset, one must acknowledge an inherent challenge in considering this issue, namely that the narratives and logics of international law are
fundamentally different from the narratives and logics with which domestic courts are familiar. Canadian judges are not like international arbitrators
who deal with commercial litigation on a regular basis; they do not feel at

canadien avant et durant un arbitrage commercial international (Paris: L.G.D.J., 2005)
and (Cowansville: Yvon Blais, 2005) at 12–14.

4   Indeed, it goes beyond the national realm (*au-delà de la sphère nationale*).

5   See David Schneiderman, "Exchanging Constitutions: Constitutional Bricolage in
Canada" (2002) 40 Osgoode Hall L.J. 401; Jens C. Dammann, "The Role of Compara-
tive Analysis in Constitutional Adjudication" (2002) 14 St. Thomas L. Rev. 513; David
Kennedy, "New Approaches to Comparative Law: Comparativism and International
Governance" (1997) 2 Utah L. Rev. 545; and H. Patrick Glenn, "Persuasive Authority"
(1987) 32 McGill L.J. 261.

6   See Frédéric Bachand, "The 'Proof' of Foreign Normative Facts which Influence
Domestic Rules" (2005) 43 Osgoode Hall L.J. 269; Craig Scott & Robert Wai, "Tran-
snational Governance of Corporate Conduct through the Migration of Human Rights
Norms: The Potential Contribution of Transnational 'Private' Litigation" in Christian
Joerges, Inger-Johanne Sand & Gunther Teubner, eds., *Transnational Governance and
Constitutionalism* (Oxford: Hart Publishing, 2004) at 287; and Robert Wai, "Transna-
tional Liftoff and Juridical Touchdown: The Regulatory Function of Private Interna-
tional Law in an Era of Globalization" (2002) 40 Colum. J. Transnat'l L. 209.

7   For evidence that this aspect has been around for some time, see the classic piece by
Ignaz Seidl-Hohenveldern, "Transformation or Adoption of International Law into
Municipal Law" (1963) 12 I.C.L.Q. 88.

8   Indeed, domestic law is an explicit source of international law pursuant to article
38(1)(c) of the *Statute of the International Court of Justice*, 26 June 1945, U.N.T.S. 961,
entered into force 24 October 1945, which speaks of "the general principles of law
recognized by civilized nations." It is worth nothing as well that domestic case law is
a secondary source of international law under article 38(1)(d) of the *Statute* and that,
in fact, it may even act as evidence of international customs; see Anthea E. Roberts,
"Traditional and Modern Approaches to Customary International Law: A Reconciliation" (2001) 95 Am. J. Int'l L. 757.

home addressing questions of pure international law, such as the validity of treaties or the existence of customs.⁹ In fact, unless otherwise understood within the constitutional system of a country,¹⁰ domestic courts are responsible for the interpretation and application of domestic law—domestic law as such or, in certain cases, foreign law because of domestic rules of private international law¹¹—in order to settle disputes on which they have jurisdiction, be it territorial, personal, or universal jurisdiction.¹²

To put it plainly, our judges are not competent—both in the jurisdictional sense and, with all due respect, in the sense of expertise—over foreign law or over international law. Foreign decision-makers and international adjudicators are the ones competent over and versed in foreign law and international law, respectively. One hopes that, in spite of claims that we have outgrown what Stephen Toope discredited as a mere "metaphor of national sovereignty,"¹³ most private international law scholars and most

---

9   See Anne Warner La Forest, "Domestic Application of International Law in *Charter* Cases: Are We There Yet?" (2004) 37 U.B.C. L. Rev. 157 at 194: "[G]iven the rapid development of international law, the scope of international human rights law [as well as international commercial law, the present author would add], and the complexity of assessing what is custom, it is reasonable to ask whether the Court is the proper body to make such assessments" [footnotes omitted]. Case on point, see *Reference re Secession of Quebec*, [1998] 2 S.C.R. 217 at 234, where, although holding that it has jurisdiction to consider issues involving international law, the Supreme Court of Canada pointed out that it does not "purport to bind any other state or international tribunal that might subsequently consider a similar question;" (and again, *ibid.* at 276). See a similar opinion expressed also in *Suresh v. Canada (Minister of Citizenship and Immigration)*, [2002] 1 S.C.R. 3 at 38 [*Suresh*].

10 Of course, there is no objection in principle to have a national constitution providing for the direct effect of international law, as in many countries on the European continent, which means that domestic courts are mandated by the constitution to take into consideration both domestic law and international law in fulfilling their judicial function. See Francis G. Jacobs, "Introduction" in Francis G. Jacobs & Shelley Roberts, *The Effect of Treaties in Domestic Law* (London: Sweet & Maxwell, 1987) xxiii at xxiv.

11 See generally Robert Wai, "In the Name of the International: The Supreme Court of Canada and the Transformation of Canadian Private International Law" (2001) 39 Can. Y.B. Int'l L. 117.

12 See generally Malcolm N. Shaw, *International Law*, 5th ed. (Cambridge: Cambridge University Press, 2003) at 578–611; and Charles Rousseau, "L'aménagement des compétences en droit international" (1930) 37 R.G.D.I.P. 420. See also specifically Kenneth C. Randall, "Universal Jurisdiction under International Law" (1988) 66 Texas L. Rev. 785.

13 See Stephen J. Toope, "The Uses of Metaphor: International Law and the Supreme Court of Canada" (2001) 80 Can. Bar Rev. 534 at 540: "To construct the 'foreign,' one must accept the continuing influence of the dying metaphor of national sovereignty."

public international law scholars would still be forced to agree that, at the end of the day, transnational law and international law have to work within, and are in large parts tributary to, the Westphalian model of international relations,[14] at the centre of which is this *idée-force* of state sovereignty.[15] Of course, we are told that this paradigm is changing with *inter alia* the transnational and international dialogues occurring through "networks,"[16] including among the national judiciaries[17] that would connect us all, albeit through virtual reality,[18] within some kind of global village where cosmopolitanism and *mondialisation* are more than just clichés.

---

14 The so-called Westphalian model is the empirical foundation of our system of international relations whereby sovereign states exist and interact independently of each other and of any higher authority. Its name comes from the Peace of Westphalia in 1648 that ended the Thirty Years' War in Europe. According to this model, the international realm is distinct and separate from the internal realms of sovereign states, which means that "public international law exists outside and independent of national legal systems"; see John Currie, *Public International Law* (Toronto: Irwin Law, 2001) at 1. See also Stéphane Beaulac, "The Westphalian Model in Defining International Law: Challenging the Myth" (2004) 8 Australian J. Leg. History 181; and Stéphane Beaulac, "The Westphalian Legal Orthodoxy — Myth or Reality?" (2000) 2 J. History Int'l L. 148.

15 The regulation of the relations between these corporate-like entities, which govern populations on territories, remain the principal object of public international law, as originally conceptualized by the eighteenth-century author Emer de Vattel, *Le Droit des Gens; ou Principes de la loi naturelle appliqués à la conduite & aux affaires des Nations & des Souverains*, 2 vols. (London: n.b., 1758). See also Stéphane Beaulac, "Emer de Vattel and the Externalization of Sovereignty" (2003) 5 J. History Int'l L. 237.

16 See Anne-Marie Slaughter, "Governing the Global Economy Through Government Networks" in Michael Byers, ed., *The Role of Law in International Politics—Essays in International Relations and International Law* (Oxford: Oxford University Press, 2000) at 177.

17 In the now voluminous literature on this subject, see in particular Vicki C. Jackson, "Constitutional Dialogue and Human Dignity: States and Transnational Constitutional Discourse" (2004) 65 Montana L. Rev. 15; Anne-Marie Slaughter, "A Global Community of Courts" (2003) 44 Harv. Int'l L.J. 191; Christopher McCrudden, "A Common Law of Human Rights? Transnational Judicial Conversations on Constitutional Rights" (2000) 20 Oxford J. Legal Stud. 499; Claire L'Heureux-Dubé, "The Importance of Dialogue: Globalization and the International Impact on the Rehnquist Court" (1998) 34 Tulsa L.J. 15; and Anne-Marie Slaughter, "A Typology of Transjudicial Communication" (1994) 29 U. Rich. L. Rev. 99. See also the special issue of the *International Journal of Constitutional Law* in 2003, in which papers centred the discussion around the idea of "borrowing" foreign precedents.

18 One legal scholar has even explored the idea of "virtual sovereignty" in the context of international law and commercial transactions; see Karim Benyekhlef, "La souveraineté virtuelle," seminar organized by the *Chaire L.R. Wilson sur le droit des technologies de l'information et du commerce électronique*, Faculty of Law, University of Montreal, 22 March 2005.

Is Westphalia outdated and obsolete? Is sovereignty really dead? A very pragmatic and helpful way to see more clearly on these meta-theoretical claims is to refer to the hierarchy of legal norms. No doubt, where there is a conflict between a foreign or international norm, on the one hand, and a domestic norm, on the other, the answer under Canadian jurisprudence is that the latter trumps the former. This is the essence of the following excerpt from the speech of Lord Atkin in the decision by the Judicial Committee of the Privy Council in *Chung Chi Cheung v. The Queen*:[19]

> The Courts acknowledge the existence of a body of rules which nations accept amongst themselves. On any judicial issue they seek to ascertain what the relevant rule is, and, having found it, they will treat it as incorporated into domestic law, *so far as it is not inconsistent with rules enacted by statutes or finally determined by their tribunals.*[20]

How could it be otherwise?[21] This is especially the case when one takes into account, in a British-style parliamentary system like Canada's, the constitutional principles of the supremacy of Parliament and of the rule of law,[22] which *inter alia* involve the notion that the elected representatives of the people be ultimately accountable for the law they adopt and that the people are to have full knowledge and reasonable access to it.

These brief introductory remarks show how crucial questions pertaining to the domestic influence of international law bring into play the narratives and the logics of Canada's national law. Thus it is useful to distinguish the different perspectives that the study of this issue may take.[23] Interna-

---

19 [1939] A.C. 160.
20 *Ibid.* at 168 (emphasis added).
21 For a recent statement on this aspect of the interaction international/internal, see Evans J.A. of the Federal Court of Appeal in *Rahaman v. Canada (Minister of Citizenship and Immigration)*, [2002] 3 F.C. 537 at 558–59.
22 See the classic work on these issues by Albert Venn Dicey, *An Introduction to the Study of the Law of the Constitution*, 10th ed. (London: Macmillan, 1959). See also Trevor R.S. Allan, *Constitutional Justice: A Liberal Theory of the Rule of Law* (Oxford: Oxford University Press, 2001); Jeffrey Goldsworthy, *The Sovereignty of Parliament—History and Philosophy* (Oxford: Clarendon Press, 1999); and Luc B. Tremblay, *The Rule of Law, Justice, and Interpretation* (Montreal: McGill-Queen's University Press, 1997).
23 See Philip Allott, *The Health of Nations—Society and Law beyond the State* (Cambridge: Cambridge University Press, 2002) at 62, where the author expressed the view that the branches of law have their domestic realities and their international realities. Thus he distinguished international constitutional law from constitutional law, international public law from public law, international administrative law from administrative law, international economic law from economic law, international transnational law from

tional legal scholars, such as Irit Weiser,[24] Karen Knop,[25] Hugh Kindred,[26] Stephen Toope,[27] and René Provost,[28] have provided what may be called the international law perspective to the debate, with the background and the concerns of this discipline.[29] Canadian scholars in constitutional law and statutory interpretation, such as Anne La Forest,[30] Ruth Sullivan,[31] and the present author[32] (though somewhat of a "hybrid"), as well as LeBel J. of

transnational law, and international criminal law from criminal law. See also Philip Allott, "The Emerging Universal Legal System" (2001) 3 Int'l L. Forum 12.

24 Irit Weiser, "Effect in Domestic Law of International Human Rights Treaties Ratified without Implementing Legislation," in Canadian Council on International Law, ed., *The Impact of International Law on the Practice of Law in Canada—Proceedings of the 27th Annual Conference of the Canadian Council on International Law* (The Hague, London & Boston: Kluwer Law International, 1999) at 132; and Irit Weiser, "Undressing the Window: Treating International Human Rights Law Meaningfully in the Canadian Commonwealth System" (2004) 37 U.B.C. L. Rev. 113.

25 See Karen Knop, "Here and There: International Law in Domestic Courts" (2000) 32 N.Y.U. J. Int'l L. & Pol. 501.

26 See Hugh M. Kindred, "Canadians as Citizens of the International Community: Asserting Unimplemented Treaty Rights in the Courts" in Stephen G. Coughlan & Dawn Russell, eds., *Citizenship and Citizen Participation in the Administration of Justice* (Montreal: Thémis, 2002) at 263.

27 See Stephen J. Toope, "Canada and International Law" in Canadian Council on International Law, ed., The Impact of International Law on the Practice of Law in Canada—Proceedings of the 27th Annual Conference of the Canadian Council on International Law, above note 24 at 33; Stephen J. Toope, "Inside and Out: The Stories of International Law and Domestic Law" (2001) 50 U.N.B.L.J. 11.

28 Rene Provost, "Le juge mondialisé : légitimité judiciaire et droit international au Canada" in Marie-Claire Belleau & François Lacasse, eds., *Claire L'Heureux-Dubé à la Cour Suprême du Canada, 1987–2002* (Montreal: Wilson & Lafleur, 2004) at 569.

29 Stephen Toope, in a paper delivered with Jutta Brunnée at a Federal Court of Canada education seminar in January 2003, seemed to acknowledge that there are different perspectives on these questions, themselves speaking from the "standpoint of international law;" see Jutta Brunnée & Stephen J. Toope, "A Hesitant Embrace: The Application of International Law by Canadian Courts" (2002) 40 Can. Y.B. Int'l L. 3 at 39.

30 La Forest, "Domestic Application of International Law," above note 9.

31 Ruth Sullivan, *Sullivan and Driedger on the Construction of Statutes*, 4th ed. (Markham & Vancouver: Butterworths, 2002) c. 16.

32 Stéphane Beaulac, "L'interprétation de la Charte : reconsidération de l'approche téléologique et réévaluation du rôle du droit international" (2005) 27 Sup. Ct. L. Rev. (2d) 1 (selected from Gérald-A. Beaudoin & Errol P. Mendes, eds., *Canadian Charter of Rights and Freedoms*, 4th ed. (Markham, ON: LexisNexis Butterworths, 2005)); Stéphane Beaulac "Arrêtons de dire que les tribunaux au Canada sont 'liés' par le droit international" (2004) R.J.T. 359; Stéphane Beaulac, "On the Saying That 'International Law Binds Canadian Courts'" (2003) 29 C.C.I.L. Bulletin 1.

the Supreme Court of Canada (writing extrajudicially with Gloria Chao),[33] have begun to show that there are other ramifications to the issue and that there should be, indeed there already exists, a national perspective to the discourse on the domestic application of international law.

This national point of view is not completely different from, let alone opposed to, that expressed by the internationalists; it is hopefully, and most likely, complementary. Having said that, one can easily see why an analytical scheme that involves domestic reference points can prove most useful for judicial actors who work daily within the confines of the national legal order. It is therefore submitted that a statutory interpretation perspective, which is one of domestic law, is extremely relevant to issues pertaining to the national application of international law, especially as regards the use of written international norms found in treaties and their international judicial interpretations. With respect to customary international law, which is not the focus of the present discussion,[34] a similar domestic perspective is also warranted and would take into account basic domestic common law doctrines, including those dealing with how judge-made–law rules, such as *stare decisis,* as well as those concerned with the interaction of case law and statutory law.[35]

The statutory interpretation perspective on the national application of international treaty law is thus concerned with the method by which a Canadian judge, whose function requires the ascertainment of the intention of Parliament found in a legislative provision, may in doing so resort to such international norms. I have elsewhere suggested[36] that the proper approach to using the international law argument in the construction of

---

33 Louis LeBel & Gloria Chao, "The Rise of International Law in Canadian Constitutional Litigation: Fugue or Fusion? Recent Developments and Challenges in Internalizing International Law" (2002) 16 Sup. Ct. L.R. (2d) 23.

34 For more detail on the situation with regard to customs, see Stéphane Beaulac, "Customary International Law in Domestic Courts: Imbroglio, Lord Denning, *Stare Decisis*" in Chris Waters, ed., *Canada-UK Perspectives on International Law* (Leiden & Boston: Martinus Nijhoff, forthcoming 2006). See also T. Dunworth, "The Rising Tide of Customary International Law: Will New Zealand Sink or Swim? (2004) 15 Public Law 36.

35 See, on these issues, the classic piece by Frank E. Horack, Jr., "The Common Law of Legislation" (1937) 23 Iowa L. Rev. 41.

36 Stéphane Beaulac, "International Treaty Norms and Driedger's 'Modern Principle' of Statutory Interpretation" in Canadian Council on International Law, ed., *Legitimacy and Accountability in International Law—Proceedings of the 33rd Annual Conference of the Canadian Council on International Law* (Ottawa: Canadian Council of International Law, 2005) at 141.

legislation is through the "modern principle" of statutory interpretation as defined by Elmer Driedger in his book *The Construction of Statutes*.[37] This argument is further developed here. International treaty law, although not binding on our courts, must play an important role domestically through the contextual argument of statutory interpretation, which should be favoured over the use of a presumption of legislative intent.

After recalling the theoretical basis of the interaction between international law and domestic law and the parameters of Driedger's "modern approach" (section 2), the discussion focuses on the two means by which domestic courts can resort to international law, namely the presumption of legislative intent and the contextual argument of statutory interpretation (section 3). Recent case law from the Supreme Court of Canada is then analyzed to show that there is an identifiable trend in favour of considering international law as legislative context, a strategy better suited to maximize the role of such legal norms in statutory interpretation, rather than through a presumption of intent (section 4). Finally, the conclusion offers frank comments on why the idea that the presumption of conformity better serves the "cause" of the domestic use of international law is wrong.

B. COORDINATING WESTPHALIA AND DRIEDGER

The Westphalian model of international relations based on the idea of state sovereignty continues to mean that the international realm is distinct and separate from the internal realm.[38] As Karen Knop once put it: "domestic law is 'here' and international law is 'there.'"[39] Further, there is nothing inherent in the international and the national systems to bridge them, hence the need for rules to administer their relationships.[40] John Currie referred to this feature as the "international-national law interface," the

---

37 E.A. Driedger, *Construction of Statutes* (Toronto: Butterworths, 1974).

38 See Currie, *Public International Law*, above note 14 at 1, who writes: "Public international law is not so much an area or topic of the law as it is *an entire legal system, quite distinct from the national legal systems* that regulate daily life within states" (emphasis added).

39 Knop, "Here and There," above note 25 at 504.

40 Even the most unconditional advocates of the national use by courts of international law cannot but recognize the continuing and inescapable international/domestic dichotomy; see Gibran van Ert, *Using International Law in Canadian Courts* (The Hague: Kluwer Law International, 2002) at 15, where the author acknowledged that "public international law is not a subset of the internal laws of states, but a separate legal system in its own rights."

results of which "will depend on legal rules that determine, as a matter of law, how one legal system treats another."[41] Reception rules on how to bridge the international and the national realities are by nature constitutional in Canada and, with respect to international treaties, refer to the dualist theory as interpreted by the Judicial Council of the Privy Council in the *Labour Conventions* case.[42] As recently reiterated by L'Heureux-Dubé J. for the majority of the Supreme Court of Canada in *Baker*, "international treaties and conventions are not part of Canadian law unless they have been implemented by statute."[43]

Once again, it must be emphasized that the fundamental consequence of this basic theory, which continues to underlie modern international law,[44] is this: Domestic courts (such as Canadian courts) interpret and apply domestic law, and it is if, and to the extent that, legal rules allow international law to be part of domestic law—and that it has in effect become part of that domestic law—that international treaty norms may have an impact on the interpretation and application of domestic law by domestic courts. In that sense, international law can never "bind" a sovereign state like Canada, or more accurately, international law can never be "binding" *in* or *within* the domestic legal system because domestic courts are concerned with national law, not international law. What international law can do, and indeed should do when deemed appropriate, is to *influence* the interpretation and application of domestic law the degree of which will, in the words of Bill Schabas, depend largely on the extent that international law "is also part of the 'Laws of Canada.'"[45]

Now, how does Driedger's modern principle of statutory interpretation become helpful after the bridge has been crossed and we are within the Canadian domestic legal system? To begin with, one must first appreciate the unquestionable authority of this interpretative approach in the courts

---

41 Currie, *Public International Law*, above note 14 at 193.

42 *Attorney General for Canada v. Attorney General for Ontario*, [1937] A.C. 326 at 347. See also *Re Arrow River & Tributaries Slide & Boom Co. Limited v. Pigeon Timber Co.*, [1932] S.C.R. 495 at 510.

43 *Baker*, above note 1 at 861.

44 See generally Stéphane Beaulac, *The Power of Language in the Making of International Law—The Word Sovereignty in Bodin and Vattel and the Myth of Westphalia* (Leiden & Boston: Martinus Nijhoff, 2004).

45 William A. Schabas, "Twenty-Five Years of Public International Law at the Supreme Court of Canada" (2000) 79 Can. Bar Rev. 174 at 176.

of this country. It is taken from the second edition of *The Construction of Statutes* and reads as follows:[46]

> Today there is only one principle or approach, namely, the words of an Act are to be read in their entire context in their grammatical and ordinary sense harmoniously with the scheme of the Act, the object of the Act and the intention of Parliament.[47]

From its first citation in the 1984 case of *Stubart Investments Ltd. v. The Queen*[48] to the latest one of 2005 in *Castillo v. Castillo*,[49] the Supreme Court of Canada endorsed the famous excerpt some fifty-nine times.[50] Three

---

46 This part of the chapter borrows from Stéphane Beaulac & Pierre-André Côté, "Driedger's 'Modern Principle' at the Supreme Court of Canada: Interpretation, Justification, Legitimization" (2006) 40 R.J.T. 129.

47 E.A. Driedger, *Construction of Statutes*, 2d ed. (Toronto: Butterworths, 1983) at 87.

48 [1984] 1 S.C.R. 536 at 578.

49 2005 SCC 83.

50 Beside the *Stubart* case and the *Castillo* case, the other fifty-seven are: *Vachon v. Canada (Employment and Immigration Commission)*, [1985] 2 S.C.R. 417; *Canadian National v. Canada (Human Rights Commission)*, [1987] 1 S.C.R. 1114; *Thomson v. Canada (Deputy Minister of Agriculture)*, [1992] 1 S.C.R. 385; *Symes v. Canada*, [1993] 4 S.C.R. 695; *Canada v. Antosko*, [1994] 2 S.C.R. 312; *Quebec (Communauté urbaine) v. Corp. Notre-Dame de Bon-Secours*, [1994] 3 S.C.R. 3; *R. v. McIntosh*, [1995] 1 S.C.R. 686; *Friesen v. Canada*, [1995] 3 S.C.R. 103; *Schwartz v. Canada*, [1996] 1 S.C.R. 254; *Alberta (Treasury Branches) v. Canada (Minister of National Revenue*, [1996] 1 S.C.R. 963; *Verdun v. Toronto-Dominion Bank*, [1996] 3 S.C.R. 550; *2747-3174 Québec Inc. v. Quebec (Régie des permis d'alcool)*, [1996] 3 S.C.R. 919 [*Régie des permis d'alcool*]; *Royal Bank of Canada v. Sparrow Electric Corp.*, [1997] 1 S.C.R. 411; *R. v. Hydro-Québec*, [1997] 3 S.C.R. 213; *Rizzo & Rizzo Shoes Ltd. (Re)*, [1998] 1 S.C.R. 27; *R. v. Gladue*, [1999] 1 S.C.R. 688; *Winko v. British Columbia (Forensic Psychiatric Institute)*, [1999] 2 S.C.R. 625; *Best v. Best*, [1999] 2 S.C.R. 868; *Winters v. Legal Services Society*, [1999] 3 S.C.R. 160; *Francis v. Baker*, [1999] 3 S.C.R. 250; *R. v. Davis*, [1999] 3 S.C.R. 759; *65302 British Columbia Ltd. v. Canada*, [1999] 3 S.C.R. 804; *Will-Kare Paving & Contracting Ltd. v. Canada*, [2000] 1 S.C.R. 915; *R. v. Araujo*, [2000] 2 S.C.R. 992; *R. v. Sharpe*, [2001] 1 S.C.R. 45; *R. v. Ulybel Enterprises Ltd.*, [2001] 2 S.C.R. 867; *Ludco Enterprises Ltd. v. Canada*, [2001] 2 S.C.R. 1082; *Law Society of British Columbia v. Mangat*, [2001] 3 S.C.R. 113; *Chieu v. Canada (Minister of Citizenship and Immigration)*, [2002] 1 S.C.R. 84; *Sarvanis v. Canada*, [2002] 1 S.C.R. 921; *Bell ExpressVu Limited Partnership v. Rex*, [2002] 2 S.C.R. 559 [*Bell ExpressVu*]; *Lavigne v. Canada (Commissioner of Official Languages)*, [2002] 2 S.C.R. 773; *Macdonell v. Quebec (Commission d'accès à l'information)*, [2002] 3 S.C.R. 661; *R. v. Jarvis*, [2002] 3 S.C.R. 757; *Harvard College v. Canada (Commissioner of Patents)*, [2002] 4 S.C.R. 45; *Markevich v. Canada*, [2003] 1 S.C.R. 94; *Barrie Public Utilities v. Canadian Cable Television Assn.*, [2003] 1 S.C.R. 476; *C.U.P.E. v. Ontario (Minister of Labour)*, [2003] 1 S.C.R. 539; *Parry Sound (District) Social Services Administration Board v. O.P.S.E.U., Local 324*, [2003] 2 S.C.R. 157; *R. v. Blais*, [2003] 2 S.C.R.

other judgments[51] have used the third edition of *Driedger on the Construction of Statutes*[52] by Ruth Sullivan.[53]

The approach has been invoked in many different areas of the law, including human rights law,[54] criminal law,[55] family law,[56] and tax law.[57] The modern principle has also been referred to for the purpose of qualifying

---

236; *R. v. Clay,* [2003] 3 S.C.R. 735; *United Taxi Drivers' Fellowship of Southern Alberta v. Calgary (City),* [2004] 1 S.C.R. 485; *Alberta Union of Provincial Employees v. Lethbridge Community College,* [2004] 1 S.C.R. 727; *Application under s. 83.28 of the Criminal Code (Re),* [2004] 2 S.C.R. 248; *Mosanto Canada Inc. v. Ontario (Superintendent of Financial Services),* [2004] 3 S.C.R. 152; *Épiciers Unis Métro-Richelieu Inc., division "Éconogros" v. Collin,* [2004] 3 S.C.R. 257; *R. v. Clark,* [2005] 1 S.C.R. 6; *Marche v. Halifax Insurance Co.,* [2005] 1 S.C.R. 47; *Bristol-Myers Squibb Co. v. Canada (Attorney General),* [2005] 1 S.C.R. 533; *H.L. v. Canada (Attorney General),* [2005] 1 S.C.R. 401; *Canada (House of Commons) v. Vaid,* [2005] 1 S.C.R. 667; *Medovarski v. Canada (Minister of Citizenship and Immigration),* [2005] 2 S.C.R. 539; *Hilewitz v. Canada (Minister of Citizenship and Immigration),* [2005] 2 S.C.R. 706; *Montreal (City) v. 2952-1366 Quebec Inc.,* [2005] 3 S.C.R. 141; *Merk v. International Association of Bridge, Structural, Ornamental and Reinforcing Iron Workers, Local 771,* [2005] 3 S.C.R. 425; *Charlebois v. Saint John (City),* [2005] 3 S.C.R. 563; *R. v. C.D.,* 2005 SCC 78.

51 *Manulife Bank of Canada v. Conlin,* [1996] 3 S.C.R. 415; *Pointe-Claire (City) v. Quebec (Labour Court),* [1997] 1 S.C.R. 1015; *Opetchesaht Indian Band v. Canada,* [1997] 2 S.C.R. 119. There are other instances where both the second and the third editions of the work were used: see *Verdun v. Toronto-Dominion Bank,* ibid.; *Régie des permis d'alcool,* ibid.; *R. v. Gladue,* ibid.; *Winko v. British Columbia (Forensic Psychiatric Institute),* ibid.; *Best v. Best,* ibid.; *65302 British Columbia Ltd. v. Canada,* ibid.; *Chieu v. Canada (Minister of Citizenship and Immigration),* ibid.

52 R. Sullivan, *Driedger on the Construction of Statutes,* 3d ed. (Toronto & Vancouver: Butterworths, 1994) at 131–32.

53 The new version proposed by Sullivan was not nearly as popular as that from the second edition of Driedger's work. For a defence and explanation of her reformulation, see Ruth Sullivan, "Statutory Interpretation in the Supreme Court of Canada" (1998–99) 30 Ottawa L. Rev. 175.

54 *Canadian National v. Canada (Human Rights Commission),* above note 50; *Canada (House of Commons) v. Vaid,* above note 50 at para. 80, where Binnie J. for the Court even wrote: "Such interpretative principles apply *with special force* in the application of human rights laws" (emphasis added).

55 *R. v. McIntosh,* above note 50; *R. v. Gladue,* above note 50; *R. v. Davis,* above note 50; *R. v. Araujo,* above note 50; *R. v. Clark,* above note 50; *R. v. C.D.,* above note 50.

56 *Best v. Best,* above note 50; *Francis v. Baker,* above note 50.

57 *Stubart Investments Ltd. v. The Queen,* above note 48; *Symes v. Canada,* above note 50; *Canada v. Antosko,* above note 50; *Quebec (Communauté urbaine) v. Corp. Notre-Dame de Bon-Secours,* above note 50; *Friesen v. Canada,* above note 50; *Schwartz v. Canada,* above note 50; *Alberta (Treasury Branches) v. Canada (Minister of National Revenue),* above note 50; *Royal Bank of Canada v. Sparrow Electric Corp.,* above note 50; *65302 British Colombia Ltd. v. Canada,* above note 50; *Will-Kare Paving & Contracting Ltd. v.*

legislation in constitutional challenges (both *Charter*[58] cases[59] or division of powers cases[60]), as well as to interpret constitutional[61] or quasi-constitutional instruments,[62] once to help construe a contract,[63] and even, recently, to interpret *Civil Code*[64] provisions.[65] For those who may doubt the authority of Driedger's modern principle, one can point to the numerous occasions where the Supreme Court of Canada has stated that it was the "prevailing and preferred"[66] or "established"[67] approach to statutory interpretation, or that it was the "appropriate and proper"[68] or, indeed, the "traditional and correct" approach.[69] The quote is a "definite formulation,"[70] that "best captures or encapsulates"[71] the interpretative method in Canada; it has been characterized as the "starting point"[72] in considering statutes.

Canada, above note 50; *Ludco Enterprises Ltd. v. Canada*, above note 50; *R. v. Jarvis*, above note 50; *Markevich v. Canada*, above note 50.

58 *Canadian Charter of Rights and Freedoms*, Part I of the *Constitution Act, 1982*, being Schedule B of the *Canada Act 1982* (U.K.), 1982, c. 11 [*Charter*].

59 *Winko v. British Columbia (Forensic Psychiatric Institute)*, above note 50; *R. v. Sharpe*, above note 50; *R. v. Clay*, above note 50; *Application under s. 83.28 of the Criminal Code (Re)*, above note 50.

60 *R. v. Hydro-Québec*, above note 50.

61 *R. v. Blais*, above note 50.

62 *Lavigne v. Canada (Commissioner of Official Languages)*, above note 50.

63 *Manulife Bank of Canada v. Conlin*, above note 50.

64 *Civil Code of Quebec*, S.Q. 1991, c. 64.

65 *Épiciers Unis Métro-Richelieu Inc., division "Éconogros" v. Collin*, above note 50.

66 *Chieu v. Canada (Minister of Citizenship and Immigration)*, above note 50 at 102; *Sarvanis v. Canada*, above note 50 at 333; *Bell ExpressVu*, above note 50 at 580; *Alberta Union of Provincial Employees v. Lethbridge Community College*, above note 50 at 744; *Application under s. 83.28 of the Criminal Code (Re)*, above note 50 at 269; *Épiciers Unis Métro-Richelieu Inc., division "Éconogros" v. Collin*, ibid. at para. 21; *Marche v. Halifax Insurance Co.*, above note 50 at para. 54; *Bristol-Myers Squibb Co. v. Canada (Attorney General)*, above note 50 at para. 96; *H.L. v. Canada (Attorney General)*, above note 50 at para. 186.

67 *Mosanto Canada Inc. v. Ontario (Superintendent of Financial Services)*, above note 50 at para. 19.

68 *C.U.P.E. v. Ontario (Minister of Labour)*, above note 50 at 593–94; *Parry Sound (District) Social Services Administration Board v. O.P.S.E.U., Local 324*, above note 50 at 182.

69 *Lavigne v. Canada (Commissioner of Official Languages)*, above note 50 at 790; *65302 British Columbia Ltd. v. Canada*, above note 50 at 810.

70 *Bell ExpressVu*, above note 50 at 580; *Barrie Public Utilities v. Canadian Cable Television Assn.*, above note 50 at paras. 20 and 86.

71 *Rizzo & Rizzo Shoes Ltd. (Re)*, above note 50 at 41; *R. v. Sharpe*, above note 50 at 74; *Ludco Enterprises Ltd. v. Canada*, above note 50 at 1100.

72 *Barrie Public Utilities v. Canadian Cable Television Assn.*, above note 50 at para. 20; *R. v. Clay*, above note 50 at para. 55; *Montreal (City) v. 2952-1366 Quebec Inc.*, above note 50 at para. 114.

C. MAXIMIZING THE ROLE OF INTERNATIONAL LAW: CONTEXT VS. PRESUMPTION

Another way to call Driedger's modern principle is the "word-in-total-context" approach to the construction of statutes. As the author himself pointed out: "Words, when read *by themselves* in the abstract can hardly be said to have meanings."[73] Ruth Sullivan in the latest edition of *The Construction of Statutes* has further developed this idea as follows: "The meaning of a word depends on the context in which it is used. This basic principle of communication applies to all texts, including legislation."[74] The contextual elements of legislative interpretation within the word-in-total-context approach includes international law. As Ruth Sullivan put it: "Under Driedger's modern principle, the words to be interpreted must be looked at in their total context. This includes not only the Act as a whole and the statute book as a whole but also the legal context, consisting of case law, common law and *international law*."[75] Hugh Kindred is of the same opinion: "[W]here the context of the legislation includes a treaty of other international obligation, the statute should be interpreted in light of it."[76]

As it was first defended elsewhere,[77] it is submitted that treating international law as an element of context within the approach suggested by Driedger is the better strategy to maximize the chances that these legal norms, in particular treaty norms, be deemed relevant in the process of interpreting legislation in Canada. This way to resort to international law should be favoured over the presumption of conformity, according to which national legislation that is ambiguous should be read consistently with international law. This old common law canon of interpretation, inherited from Great Britain, was first formulated thus by Peter Maxwell: "[E]very statute is to be so interpreted and applied, as far as its language admits, as not to be inconsistent with the comity of nations, or with the established

---

73 E.A. Driedger, *Construction of Statutes*, above note 47 at 3 (emphasis in original).

74 Sullivan, *Sullivan and Driedger,* above note 31 at 161. See also Pierre-André Côté, *Interprétation des lois*, 3d ed. (Montreal: Thémis, 1999) at 355; and Randal N. Graham, *Statutory Interpretation—Theory and Practice* (Toronto: Emond Montgomery, 2001) at 62–63.

75 Sullivan, *ibid.* at 262 (emphasis added). See also Ruth Sullivan, "Some Implications of Plain Language Drafting" (2001) 22 Stat. L. Rev. 145 at 147–49.

76 Kindred, "Canadians as Citizens," above note 26 at 271.

77 Stéphane Beaulac, "Le droit international comme élément contextuel en interprétation des lois" (2004) 6 Can. Int'l Law. 1.

rules of international law."[78] In the English case of *Salomon v. Commissioners of Customs and Excise*,[79] Lord Diplock wrote:

> [T]here is a *prima facie* presumption that Parliament does not intend to act in breach of international law, including therein specific treaty obligations; and if one of the meanings which can reasonably be ascribed to the legislation is consonant with the treaty obligations and another or others are not, the meaning which is consonant is to be preferred.[80]

In *Corocraft v. Pan American Airways*,[81] Lord Denning went further and even spoke of the "duty of these courts to construe our legislation so as to be in conformity with international law and not in conflict with it."[82] Speaking of the presumption in terms of "duty" is an exaggeration though, especially considering that the international and national legal realities are distinct and separate.

1) Nature and Function of the Presumption of Conformity with International Law

The presumption of conformity with international law is a type of presumption of intent, the function of which is, in the words of Elmer Driedger in the first edition of *The Construction of Statutes*, "to attribute intentions to Parliament in certain circumstances, in the absence of an expression of a contrary intent."[83] When he was at the New Brunswick Court of Appeal, La Forest J.A. dwelt upon these presumptions of intent in *Re Estabrooks Pontiac Buick Ltd.*,[84] pointing out that they were originally meant to protect individual liberty and private property.[85] He further explained thus:

> If the legislation is clear, of course, the intent of the Legislature must be respected. But what these presumptions ensure is that a law that appears to

---

78 Peter B. Maxwell, *On the Interpretation of Statutes* (London: Sweet & Maxwell, 1896). See also Hersch Lauterpacht, "Is International Law a Part of the Law of England?" (1930) *Transactions Grotius Society* 51.
79 [1967] 2 Q.B. 116 (C.A.).
80 *Ibid.* at 143–44.
81 [1968] 3 W.L.R. 1273 (C.A.).
82 *Ibid.* at 1281.
83 Driedger, *Construction of Statutes*, above note 37 at 137.
84 (1982), 44 N.B.R. (2d) 201.
85 See also James A. Corry, "Administrative Law and the Interpretation of Statutes" (1936) 1 U.T.L.J. 286 at 295–97.

transgress our basic political understandings should be clearly expressed so as to invite the debate which is the lifeblood of Parliamentary democracy.[86]

A similar view was expressed by La Forest J.A., extrajudicially, in a special issue of the *Canadian Bar Review* on the *Charter*, where he associated the presumptions of legislative intent with constitutional protections, which "help to promote second thought and public debate, a debate that all recognize as an essential safeguard in a parliamentary democracy."[87] The same idea is behind the modern "dialogue metaphor" that would exist between courts and legislatures.[88]

The history of the presumptions of intent is not all positive, however. There are many cases where courts have substituted the legislative choices of legislatures with their judicial preferences.[89] Unlike the view expressed by democratically elected representatives of the people in an explicit legislative provision, the view expressed by an appointed judge in a decision involving the use of a presumption of intent does not breathe legitimacy, especially as it may frustrate the apparent legislative intention. The acceptability of this interpretative method depends on the values underlying whatever is presumed of the legislature.[90] Private property rights are considered by society as worthy of protection, thus legislation can legitimately be presumed not to encroach them;[91] fundamental rights and freedoms

---

86   *Re Estabrooks Pointiac Buick Ltd.*, above note 84 at 211.
87   Gérard V. La Forest, "The Canadian Charter of Rights and Freedoms: An Overview" (1983) 61 Can. Bar Rev. 19 at 20.
88   See Peter W. Hogg & Allison A. Bushell, "The *Charter* Dialogue Between Courts and Legislatures" (1997) 35 Osgoode Hall L.J. 75; which was endorsed by the Supreme Court of Canada in *Vriend v. Alberta*, [1998] 1 S.C.R. 493 at 565–66; and *R. c. Mills*, [1999] 3 S.C.R. 668 at 711–13. See also Christopher Manfredi & James Kelly, "Six Degrees of Dialogue: A Response to Hogg and Bushell" (1999) 37 Osgoode Hall L.J. 513; Kent Roach, "Constitutional and Common Law Dialogues Between the Supreme Court and Canadian Legislatures" (2001) 81 Can. Bar Rev. 481; and Luc B. Tremblay, "Legitimacy of Judicial Review: The Limits of Dialogue Between Courts and Legislatures" (2005) 3 Int'l J. Constitutional L. 617.
89   See John Willis, "Statutory Interpretation in a Nutshell" (1938) 16 Can. Bar Rev. 1 at 17–27.
90   See Paul Weiler, "Legal Values and Judicial Decision-Making" (1970) 48 Can. Bar Rev. 1; and Côté, *Interprétation des lois*, above note 74 at 561–62.
91   See *Attorney-General v. De Keyser's Royal Hotel Ltd.*, [1920] A.C. 508 (H.L.); *Abell v. County of York* (1921), 61 S.C.R. 345; *British Columbia Electric Railway Co. v. Public Utilities Commission of British Columbia*, [1960] S.C.R. 837; *Bayshore Shopping Centre v. Nepean (Township)*, [1972] S.C.R. 755; *Imperial Oil Ltd. v. The Queen*, [1974] S.C.R. 623; *British Columbia (Attorney General) v. Parklane Private Hospital Ltd.*, [1975] 2 S.C.R. 47;

are seen as primordial by the community, thus a court can legitimately presume that a statute is in line with them,[92] even more so since the enactment of the *Charter* in 1982 and the eventual extension of the presumption of conformity with the constitution in these cases.[93] However, as Ruth Sullivan has noted: "If the values espoused by the courts are not shared by the community, the legitimacy of the judicial vision is lost."[94]

Manitoba Fisheries Ltd. v. The Queen, [1979] 1 S.C.R. 101; *Leiriao v. Val Belair (Town)*, [1991] 3 S.C.R. 349; *Hong Kong Bank of Canada v. Wheeler Holdings Ltd.*, [1993] 1 S.C.R. 167; *Husky Oil Operations Ltd. v. Minister of National Revenue*, [1995] 3 S.C.R. 453; *Toronto Area Transit Operating Authority v. Dell Holdings Ltd.*, [1997] 1 S.C.R. 32; *Pacific National Investments Ltd. v. Victoria (City)*, [2000] 2 S.C.R. 919; and *Re Estabrooks Pontiac Buick Ltd.*, above note 84.

92 See *Shin Shim v. The King*, [1938] S.C.R. 378; *Beatty and Mackie v. Kozak*, [1958] S.C.R. 177; *Eccles v. Bourque*, [1975] 2 S.C.R. 739; *Marcotte v. Deputy Attorney General of Canada*, [1976] 1 S.C.R. 108; *R. v. Biron*, [1976] 2 S.C.R. 56; *City of Prince George v. Payne*, [1978] 1 S.C.R. 458; *R. v. Noble*, [1978] 1 S.C.R. 632; *Laidlaw v. Toronto (Metropolitan)*, [1978] 2 S.C.R. 736; *Insurance Corporation of British Columbia v. Heerspink*, [1982] 2 S.C.R. 145; *Basarabas v. The Queen*, [1982] 2 S.C.R. 730; *Costello v. City of Calgary*, [1983] 1 S.C.R. 14; *Ogg-Moss v. The Queen*, [1984] 2 S.C.R. 173; *Zurich Insurance Co. v. Ontario (Human Rights Commission)*, [1992] 2 S.C.R. 321; *British Columbia (Public Service Employee Relations Committee) v. BCGSEU*, [1999] 3 S.C.R. 3.

93 Originally, the presumption of conformity with the constitution was used in cases dealing with the division of legislative authorities, under ss. 91 and 92 of the *Constitution Act, 1867* (U.K.), 30 & 31 Vict., c. 3, thus renamed by the *Canada Act, 1982* (U.K.), 1982, c. 11. Leading cases include: *Reference re The Farm Products Marketing Act*, [1957] S.C.R. 198; *McKay v. The Queen*, [1965] S.C.R. 798; *R. v. Sommerville*, [1974] S.C.R. 387; *Nova Scotia Board of Censors v. McNeil*, [1978] 2 S.C.R. 662; *Deputy Minister of Revenue v. Rainville*, [1980] 1 S.C.R. 35; *Deloitte Haskins & Sells v. Workers' Compensation Board*, [1985] 1 S.C.R. 785; *Husky Oil Operations Ltd. v. Canada (Minister of National Revenue)*, [1995] 3 S.C.R. 453; *Reference re Firearms Act (Can.)*, [2000] 1 S.C.R. 783; *Siemens v. Manitoba (Attorney General)*, [2003] 1 S.C.R. 6; see also, generally, Joseph E. Magnet, "The Presumption of Constitutionality" (1980) 18 Osgoode Hall L.J. 87. After 1982, it was unclear whether or not the presumption of conformity with the constitution extended to *Charter* challenges: see *Manitoba (Attorney General) v. Metropolitan Stores (MTS) Ltd.*, [1987] 1 S.C.R. 110 at 125, Beetz J. It is now established that it does: see *Slaight Communications Inc. v. Davidson*, [1989] 1 S.C.R. 1038; *Schachter v. Canada*, [1992] 2 S.C.R. 679; *Canada (Attorney General) v. Mossop*, [1993] 1 S.C.R. 554; *Ontario v. Canadian Pacific Ltd.*, [1995] 2 S.C.R. 1031; *R. v. Lucas*, [1998] 1 S.C.R. 439; *Delisle v. Canada (Deputy Attorney General)*, [1999] 2 S.C.R. 989; *R. v. Mills*, above note 88; *Dunmore v. Ontario (Attorney General)*, [2001] 3 S.C.R. 1016; *Bell ExpressVu*, above note 50; see also generally, on legal interpretation, *R. v. Nova Scotia Pharmaceutical Society*, [1992] 2 S.C.R. 606, Gonthier J.

94 Sullivan, *Sullivan and Driedger*, above note 31 at 363.

Little attention has thus far been given to the legitimizing values underlying the presumption of conformity with international law.[95] *Pacta sunt servanda* with respect to international treaty law, as codified in article 26 of the *Vienna Convention on the Law of Treaties*,[96] could be one such value. More generally, the idea of good faith in the execution of international obligations, and that sovereign states should live up to their undertakings on the international plane, is central to our international law system.[97] This is an important concern, no doubt, but it is one that pertains to the international legal order, not to the domestic legal order—which are distinct and separate according to the present model of international relations.[98] Within our internal legal system, the values espoused by Canadian society that would legitimize the use of the presumption of conformity with international law appear to be less obvious.

Generally speaking, one could invoke the goals of stability and uniformity in the domestic legal system,[99] which is increasingly influenced by, and arguably modelled on, international legal norms and would gain from the formalization of such interaction.[100] In international commercial law, there are additional goals relating to the business efficacy and economic liberalism of the legal rules applicable in a region or among the different jurisdictions of trading partners.[101] Again, there are other, more subject-specific, values associated with this presumption of intent, like the allegedly increased protection of fundamental freedoms coming with the

---

95 In fact, the reasons behind the presumption of conformity with international law have always been explained, it seems, in superficial terms that refer to the common sense argument that legislatures and courts do not want to place Canada in violation of international law. See, for instance, Kindred, "Canadians as Citizens," above note 26 at 270.

96 (1969) 8 I.L.M. 679, entered into force 27 January 1980.

97 See, on good faith obligations in general, the decision of the International Court of Justice in the *Nuclear Tests* case (Australia v. France), [1986] I.C.J. Reports 253.

98 See above notes 38–39 and accompanying text.

99 See Côté, *Interprétation des lois*, above note 74 at 633–48.

100 See Bachand, *L'intervention du juge canadien*, above note 3 at 26.

101 See Robert Wai, "International Trade Agreements, Internationalist Policy Consciousness, and the Reform of Canadian Private International Law" in Canadian Council on International Law, ed., *The Measure of International Law: Effectiveness, Fairness and Validity—Proceedings of the 31st Annual Conference of the Canadian Council on International Law* (The Hague, London & New York: Kluwer Law International, 2004) at 123; Michael Whincop & Mary Keyes, *Policy and Pragmatism in the Conflict of Laws* (Aldershot, UK: Ashgate, 2001); and David Kennedy, "The International Style in Postwar Law and Policy," [1994] Utah L. Rev. 7.

bias of reading domestic law in line with international human rights law instruments.[102] Similarly, for labour relations and industrial standards, the goals pursued by the International Labour Organization[103] and its eight fundamental conventions[104] give legitimacy to the presumption of conformity in this area of the law.[105] The point here is that such legitimacy is all but automatic. Moreover, the domestic point of view on this aspect requires to consider other competing values dear to Canadians that may

---

102 See La Forest, "Domestic Application of International Law," above note 9 at 208: "In Canadian academic writing, there is often an unacknowledged preconception that international human rights law is usually more progressive than domestic human rights law." Examples include Joanna Harrington, "How Canadian Lawyers can Contribute to the Effectiveness of the UN Human Rights Committee" in Canadian Council on International Law, ed., *The Measure of International Law: Effectiveness, Fairness and Validity —Proceedings of the 31st Annual Conference of the Canadian Council on International Law, ibid.* at 132; Robert Wai, "Justice Gérard La Forest and the Internationalist Turn in Canadian Jurisprudence" in R. Johnson *et al.*, eds., *Gérard V. La Forest at the Supreme Court of Canada, 1985–1997* (Winnipeg: Faculty of Law, University of Manitoba, 2000) at 471; and William A. Schabas, *International Human Rights Law and the Canadian Charter*, 2d ed. (Toronto: Carswell, 1996) at 233–34.

103 The International Labour Organization (ILO) was established by the *Treaty of Versailles*, 28 June 1919, reprinted in Clive Parry, ed., *Consolidated Treaty Series*, vol. 225 (Dobbs Ferry, NY: Oceana Publications, 1969) at 288. It became a specialized agency within the United Nations system following the Second World War. See generally Virginia A. Leary, "Lessons from the Experience of the International Labour Organisation" in Philip Alston, ed., *The United Nations and Human Rights: A Critical Appraisal* (Oxford: Clarendon Press, 1992) at 580.

104 They are: *Convention Concerning Forced or Compulsory Labour, 1930 (ILO Convention No. 29)* 39 U.N.T.S. 55, entered into force 1 May 1932; *Convention Concerning Freedom of Association and Protection of the Right to Organise, 1948 (ILO Convention No. 87)* 68 U.N.T.S. 17, entered into force 4 July 1950; *Convention Concerning the Application of the Principles of the Right to Organise and to Bargain Collectively, 1949 (ILO Convention No. 98)* 96 U.N. T.S. 257, entered into force 18 July 1951; *Convention Concerning Equal Remuneration for Men and Women for Work of Equal Value, 1951 (ILO Convention No. 100)* 165 U.N.T.S. 303, entered into force 23 May 1953; *Convention Concerning the Abolition of Forced Labour, 1957 (ILO Convention No. 105)* 320 U.N.T.S. 291, entered into force 17 January 1959; *Convention Concerning Discrimination in Respect of Employment and Occupation, 1958 (ILO Convention No. 111)* 363 U.N.T.S. 31, entered into force 15 June 1960; *Convention Concerning Minimum Age for Admission to Employment, 1973 (ILO Convention No. 138)* 1015 U.N.T.S. 297, entered into force 16 June 1976; *Convention Concerning the Prohibition and Immediate Action for the Elimination of the Worst Forms of Child Labour, 1999 (ILO convention No. 182)* 38 I.L.M. 1207, entered into force 19 November 2000.

105 See generally Hector B. de la Cruz *et al.*, eds., *The International Labor Organization: The International Standards System and Basic Human Rights* (Boulder, CO: Westview Press, 1999).

qualify the enthusiasm for international law via a presumption of intent. First coming to mind are the values of accountability and foreseeability generally associated with the constitutional principles of the supremacy of Parliament and of the rule of law.[106] Other goals specific to the domestic legislation under scrutiny can also militate against the legitimate use of the presumption of conformity with international law.[107]

2) Preliminary Requirement of Ambiguity: Nipping International Law in the Bud

Even assuming legitimacy, there is a fatal flaw with the presumption of conformity with international law. Before courts can take into consideration such legal norms in ascertaining the intention of Parliament in the process of interpreting legislation, there must be a preliminary finding that the statutory provision at issue is ambiguous, or is otherwise problematic to construe by reason of vagueness generally or redundancy.[108] Short of fulfilling this precondition, the presumption of conformity with international law cannot become an argument of interpretation, which in turn means that the opportunity to resort to such legal norms is lost. This problem is brilliantly, be it unintentionally, highlighted in Pigeon J.'s remarks in *Daniels v. White and The Queen*,[109] often referred to as the accepted formulation in Canada of the presumption of conformity with international law:

> I wish to add that, in my view, this is a case for the application of the rule of construction that Parliament is not presumed to legislate in breach of

---

106 See above notes 21–22 and accompanying text.

107 Indeed, the values underlying an area of domestic law, like the protection of individual freedoms, may play against the use of the presumption of conformity with international law, in cases for instances where the internal piece of human rights legislation on a particular point is more generous than in the international human rights law instruments. These concerns seem to have been in the mind of Dickson C.J., dissenting in *Reference re Public Service Employees Relations Act (Alta.)*, [1987] 1 S.C.R. 313 at 349, when he wrote: "I believe that the *Charter* should generally be presumed to provide protection at least as great as that afforded by similar provisions in international human rights documents which Canada has ratified." Thus international law may influence to provide more protection, not less protection, to individual rights and freedoms enjoyed in Canada. See also La Forest, "Domestic Application of International Law," above note 9 at 211 and 218.

108 On the different problems found in statutes, see Reed Dickerson, "The Diseases of Legislative Language" (1964) 1 Harv. J. on Legis. 5; and Graham, *Statutory Interpretation*, above note 74 at 119 *et seq.*

109 [1968] S.C.R. 517.

a treaty or in any manner inconsistent with the comity of nations and the established rules of international law. It is a rule that is not often applied, because if a statute is unambiguous, its provisions must be followed even if they are contrary to international law.[110]

Pierre-André Côté noticed that this excerpt suggests that a legitimate utilisation of international law is possible if, and only if, there is a real interpretative difficulty with the statutory provision, a reasoning that involves the obsolete "plain meaning rule" (or "literal rule") of construction.[111]

In spite of *National Corn Growers Assn. v. Canada (Import Tribunal)*,[112] where Gonthier J. attempted to set aside this ambiguity requirement, the 2002 decision of the Supreme Court of Canada in *Schreiber v. Canada (Attorney General)*[113] stated that the *Daniels v. White and The Queen* excerpt indeed "sets out when international law is appropriately used to interpret domestic legislation."[114] Justice LeBel even underlined the last bit, on how the presumption of conformity *"is not often applied, because if a statute is unambiguous, its provisions must be followed even if they are contrary to international law."*[115] In the end, the international law argument was rejected: "The questions at stake fall within the purview of the domestic legislation."[116] Usually, though, the reason invoked by courts to discard the presumption of conformity and, with it, the influence of international legal norms is more explicitly linked to the conclusion that the provision at issue is clear—that is, not ambiguous.[117] In other words, if the preliminary requirement of ambiguity is not met, the international law gate is shut tight.

---

110 *Ibid.* at 541.

111 Côté, *Interprétation des lois*, above note 74 at 466–67: "Cet extrait semble suggérer que le recours au droit international n'est légitime que si le texte de la loi interne présente une difficulté d'interprétation. Il s'agit là d'une application de la «règle du sens clair des textes»."

112 [1990] 2 S.C.R. 1324 at 1371. This case is generally considered to have limited the authority of Estey J.'s statement in *Schavernoch v. Foreign Claims Commission*, [1982] 1 S.C.R. 1092 at 1098.

113 [2002] 3 S.C.R. 269 [*Schreiber*].

114 *Ibid.* at 293–94.

115 *Daniels v. White and The Queen*, above note 109 at 541 (emphasis by LeBel J. in *Schreiber, ibid.*).

116 *Schreiber, ibid.* at 294. For a similar reasoning in another case dealing with state immunity, which referred to *Schreiber*, see the decision of the Court of Appeal for Ontario in *Bouzari v. Islamic Republic of Iran* (2004), 71 O.R. (3d) 675 at 690–91.

117 Recently, the two most blatant examples in lower courts are: *Gosselin (tuteur de) c. Québec (Procureur Général)*, [2000] R.J.Q. 2973 at 3008 (S.C.); and *Ferrell v. Ontario (Attorney General)* (1997), 149 D.L.R. (4th) 335 at 339 (Ont. Ct. Gen. Div.).

On the other hand, the case law analysis that follows shows that using international law through an interpretative argument that considers such norms as contextual elements pursuant to Driedger's modern principle does not run into this problem. There is no such precondition of ambiguity before being allowed to involve international law in the process of construction. Rather, legal norms from the international order may always constitute an argument to assist in determining the intention of Parliament as regards the provision at issue, be it from ordinary statutes or from supralegislative texts like constitutional instruments (including the *Charter*).[118]

D. CASE LAW ON THE USE OF INTERNATIONAL LAW: UP WITH CONTEXT, DOWN WITH PRESUMPTION

There is an understandable temptation to think that the presumption of conformity with international law is, and shall likely remain, very much alive in this country.[119] After all, quite recently in the 1998 case of *Ordon Estate v. Grail*,[120] Iacobucci and Major JJ., after accurately describing how international law is not binding domestically, spoke as follows of this presumption of legislative intent:

> Although international law is not binding upon Parliament or the provincial legislatures, a court must presume that legislation is intended to comply with Canada's obligations under international instruments and as a member of the international community. In choosing among possible interpretations of a statute, the court should avoid interpretations that would put Canada in breach of such obligations.[121]

But in the Driedger's modern principle/post-*Baker* case era at the Supreme Court of Canada, this statement is already *passé* or, in any event, should be definitely dismissed. Along with the obsolete "plain meaning rule" (or

---

118 For more on the argument that there is no distinction in principle between statutory interpretation and the interpretation of constitutional instruments, including the *Charter*, see Beaulac, "L'interprétation de la Charte," above note 32.

119 See, for instance, Mark Freeman & Gibran van Ert, *International Human Rights Law* (Toronto: Irwin Law, 2004) at 151–59.

120 [1998] 3 S.C.R. 437. Also, *Pushpanathan v. Canada (Minister of Citizenship and Immigration)*, [1998] 1 S.C.R. 982; *Chan v. Canada (Minister of Employment and Immigration)*, [1995] 3 S.C.R. 593; *Canada (Attorney General) v. Ward*, [1993] 2 S.C.R. 689.

121 *Ordon Estate, ibid.* at 526. See also *R. v. Zingre*, [1981] 2 S.C.R. 392.

"literal rule") of interpretation,[122] the presumption of conformity with international law must indeed be buried.

1)   Understanding the Baker Case in Terms of International Law as Context

It is submitted that the majority reasons of the Supreme Court of Canada in the *Baker* decision actually signalled an intention that international law be considered by courts through the contextual argument of statutory interpretation, rather than through a presumption of conformity. This contention is based on the passage in *Baker* where L'Heureux-Dubé J., for the majority, relied on an excerpt from the third edition of *Driedger on the Construction of Statutes*,[123] where Ruth Sullivan explained the two different ways in which international legal norms may be used, namely, through a presumption of conformity and through the contextual argument of interpretation. The excerpt reads:

> First, the legislature is presumed to comply with the obligations owed by Canada as a signatory of international instruments and more generally as a member of the international community. *In choosing among possible interpretations, therefore, the courts avoid interpretations that would put Canada in breach of any of its international obligations.* Second, the legislature is presumed to respect the values and principles enshrined in international law, both customary and conventional. *These constitute a part of the legal context in which legislation is enacted and read.* In so far as possible, therefore, interpretations that reflect these values and principles are preferred.[124]

The two sentences in italic in the preceding excerpt show that Ruth Sullivan refers, first, to the presumption of conformity with international law and its role in situations of ambiguity where an interpretation that is in line with the legal norms of the international order ought to be favoured and, second, to the argument of statutory interpretation pertaining to the context of adoption and of application, in which international law falls.

What seems to be wrong with the explanation, however, is that the two ways to resort to international law involve the reasoning of an interpretative

---

122 For an impressive judicial assessment of the evolution in methods with respect to the interpretation of statutes, see the concurring set of reasons of L'Heureux-Dubé J. in *Régie des permis d'alcool*, above note 50. See also Stéphane Beaulac, "Le *Code civil* commande-t-il une interprétation distincte?" (1999) 22 Dal. L.J. 236.

123 Sullivan, *Driedger on the Construction of Statutes*, above note 52.

124 *Ibid.* at 330 (emphasis added).

presumption of intent; only the first technique relates to a presumption, the second is simply a basic argument of statutory context. It is important to dissociate the second way to resort to international law from the vocabulary of presumptions for the simple reason that the preliminary requirement of ambiguity is not applicable in this scenario. The truth of the matter is that, somewhat conversely, both techniques described by Ruth Sullivan form part of the general conception of legislative context. She noted this aspect in the latest 2002 edition, *Sullivan and Driedger on the Construction of Statutes*:

> Finally, it is helpful to notice that the presumptions of intent are merely a formal way for courts to recognize and incorporate the values that are central to the legal context in which legislation is drafted as well as read. These values necessarily and appropriately inform judicial understanding of legislation at first reading, when the reader's initial impression of meaning is formed. They also play an important role in judging the plausibility of competing interpretations.[125]

In the final analysis, she observes: "They [presumptions of intent, like the presumption of conformity with international law] are part of the 'entire context' in which legislation must be read under Driedger's modern principle."[126]

Going back to L'Heureux-Dubé J.'s reasons in *Baker*, what must be emphasized is that the reference to *Driedger on the Construction of Statutes*[127] included only the second way that international law may be used, namely the basic argument of context in statutory interpretation. Here is how the reference was made:

> Nevertheless, the values reflected in international human rights law may help inform the contextual approach to statutory interpretation and judicial review. As stated in R. Sullivan, *Driedger on the Construction of Statutes* (3rd ed. 1994), at p. 33:
>
>> [T]he legislature is presumed to respect the values and principles enshrined in international law, both customary and conventional. These constitute a part of the legal context in which legislation is

---

125 Sullivan, *Sullivan and Driedger*, above note 31, at 365.
126 *Ibid.*
127 Sullivan, *Driedger on the Construction of Statutes*, above note 52.

enacted and read. *In so far as possible, therefore, interpretations that reflect these values and principles are preferred* [emphasis added].

The important role of international human rights law as an aid in interpreting domestic law has also been emphasized in other common law countries.[128]

Put another way, the majority of the Supreme Court of Canada in *Baker* reproduced and endorsed what the author Ruth Sullivan wrote about international legal norms being part of the context of adoption and of application of domestic legislation and how this contextual element should be considered relevant by courts when appropriate. On the other hand, it must be noted, and some meaning should be given to the fact, that the first way in which international law may be utilized according to Ruth Sullivan, namely, through a presumption of legislative intent (understood in its proper sense), was not referred to, and therefore was not endorsed, in the reasons for judgment by the majority in *Baker*.

This aspect is highly significant, especially when one considers that L'Heureux-Dubé J. wrote this opinion in *Baker* and that, during her tenure at the Supreme Court of Canada,[129] she was one of the main proponents of a liberal approach to statutory interpretation in accordance with Driedger's modern principle, revolving largely around the all-inclusive concept of legislative context.[130] Thus, seeing her endorse international law as context and implicitly rejecting the presumption of conformity with international law is consistent with her, and to a large extent the Court's, general approach to statutory interpretation.[131]

---

128 *Baker*, above note 1 at 861.

129 This role was clear already in her reasons for the majority of the Supreme Court of Canada in *Hills v. Canada (Attorney General)*, [1988] 1 S.C.R. 513. See also her concurring reasons in *Régie des permis d'alcool*, above note 50.

130 See Kindred, "Canadians as Citizens," above note 26 at 270–71.

131 See Beaulac, "National Application," above note 2 at 252: "She [L'Heureux-Dubé J.] is obviously not alone anymore in openly holding that a proper interpretation and application of a statute must consider the context and purpose as well as the language of the enactment."

2) Subsequent Cases at the Supreme Court of Canada: A Return to Presumption?

A few years later, in *114957 Canada Ltée (Spraytech, Société d'arrosage) v. Hudson (Town)*,[132] L'Heureux-Dubé J. for the majority had the opportunity to reiterate and confirm her views expressed in *Baker*, that "the values reflected in international human rights law may help inform the contextual approach to statutory interpretation and judicial review,"[133] and to quote again the passage in *Driedger on the Construction of Statutes*[134] on international law as a basic contextual argument of statutory interpretation.[135] In fact, the statement in this case on using international law as context is broader than in *Baker*, as it is not limited to unimplemented treaty norms, but extends to international law in general. Here, it was the international environment law "precautionary principle" that was used to confirm the interpretation of the enabling statutory provision found in the Quebec's *Cities and Towns Act*,[136] a norm that L'Heureux-Dubé J. suggested was international customary law.[137]

This understanding of the *Baker* decision also finds support in the case of *Suresh*,[138] a unanimous decision where the Supreme Court of Canada was asked to review a ministerial decision pursuant to section 53(1)(b) of the *Immigration Act*,[139] which allowed the deportation to a country where the refugee faces serious risk of torture in exceptional cases of national security. The issue was whether such a deportation was contrary to the principles of fundamental justice under section 7 of the *Charter*, thus a typical case of constitutional challenge of government action. To assess the scope of protection against torture in Canada, the Court first referred to section 12 of the *Charter* and its case law on cruel and unusual treatment or pun-

---

132 [2001] 2 S.C.R. 241 [*Hudson*].
133 *Baker*, above note 1 at 861.
134 Sullivan, *Driedger on the Construction of Statutes*, above note 52 at 330.
135 *Hudson*, above note 132 at 266.
136 R.S.Q., c. C-19, s. 410(1).
137 *Hudson*, above note 132 at 266–67.
138 La Forest, "Domestic Application of International Law," above note 9. See also, on this case, Stéphane Beaulac, "The *Suresh* Case and Unimplemented Treaty Norms" (2002) 15 R.Q.D.I. 221.
139 R.S.C. 1985, c. I-2.

ishment,[140] including *United States v. Burns*.[141] Then the analysis moved on
to what is identified in a heading as "The International Perspective," where
the Court thus begins this part of its judgment:

> We have examined the argument that from the perspective of Canadian
> law to deport a Convention refugee to torture violates the principles of fun-
> damental justice. However, that does not end the inquiry. The provisions
> of the *Immigration Act* dealing with deportation must be considered in
> their international context: *Pushpanathan, supra, [Pushpanathan v. Canada
> (Minister of Citizenship and Immigration)*, [1998] 1 S.C.R. 982]. Similarly,
> the principles of fundamental justice expressed in s. 7 of the *Charter* and
> the limits on rights that may be justified under s. 1 of the *Charter* cannot be
> considered in isolation from the international norms which they reflect. A
> complete understanding of the Act and the *Charter* requires consideration
> of the international perspective.[142]

Such an "international perspective" involved invoking (without deciding)
that the international prohibition on torture was a peremptory norm of
customary law (that is, *jus cogens*),[143] as well as considering three international conventions: 1) the *International Covenant on Civil and Political
Right*,[144] 2) the *Convention Against Torture and Other Cruel, Inhuman or Degrading Treatment or Punishment*,[145] and 3) the *Convention Relating to the
Status of Refugees*.[146]

Concluding this part of its reasons, the Court held that international
law prohibited any deportation to face torture, even in exceptional cases
of national security. In interpreting section 7 of the *Charter* in its entire
context, therefore, this is the international legal norm that "best informs
the content of the principles of fundamental justice."[147] Other statements
in the decision show that international law was indeed used as a contextual

---

140 *Kindler v. Canada (Minister of Justice)*, [1991] 2 S.C.R. 779; *R. v. Smith*, [1987] 1 S.C.R.
    1045; and *Canada v. Schmidt*, [1987] 1 S.C.R. 500.
141 [2001] 1 S.C.R. 283.
142 *Suresh*, above note 9 at 37–38.
143 This notion is defined in art. 53 of the *Vienna Convention on the Law of Treaties*, above
    note 96. See also Lauri Hannikainen, *Peremptory Norms (Jus Cogens) in International
    Law: Historical Development, Criteria, Present Status* (Helsinki: Lakimiedliiten Kustan-
    nus, 1988).
144 (1976) 999 U.N.T.S. 171, entered into force 23 March 1976.
145 (1984) 23 I.L.M. 1027, minor changes in 24 I.L.M. 535, entered into force 26 June 1987.
146 (1951) 189 U.N.T.S. 150, entered into force 22 April 1954.
147 *Suresh*, above note 9 at 45.

argument of construction:[148] "The Canadian and international perspectives in turn inform our constitutional norms";[149] "Indeed, both domestic and international jurisprudence suggest that torture is so abhorrent that it will almost always be disproportionate to interests on the other side of the balance, even security interests."[150] A final element in the *Suresh* case indicates that international law was no more than legal context with no determinative weight, namely, the very interpretation given in the end by the Court that, according to Canadian domestic law, "in exceptional circumstances, deportation to face torture might be justified, either as a consequence of the balancing process mandated by s. 7 of the *Charter* or under s. 1."[151] Thus the legal norm against torture in the country was held to be different from that in the international legal order, less stringent in fact; it bears witness that the international law argument was given some weight, but no presumption-type of weight, let alone a determinative one.

This being so, is this identifiable trend in the case law of the Supreme Court of Canada favouring international law as context over the presumption of legislative intent interrupted, if not contradicted, by the recent decision in *Canadian Foundation for Children, Youth and the Law v. Canada (Attorney General)*?[152] The short answer is no. At issue in this case was whether section 43 of the *Criminal Code*,[153] which justifies the use of reasonable force by parents and teachers for the purpose of correcting children or pupils, unjustifiably infringed the *Charter*—either because unconstitutionally vague under section 7 of the *Charter*, because it amounts to cruel and unusual treatment or punishment under section 12, or because it is in breach of the right to equality under section 15. It was in the analysis of the first basis of the constitutional challenge that McLachlin C.J.[154] seemed to revive the presumption of conformity with international law when she

---

148 Sullivan also believes that the *Suresh* case considered international law as a basic contextual argument of statutory interpretation. See Sullivan, *Sullivan and Driedger,* above note 31 at 426: "The reliance on international law as legal context was further developed by the Supreme Court of Canada in *Suresh v. Canada (Minister of Citizenship and Immigration)*" (footnotes omitted).

149 *Suresh,* above note 9 at 45.

150 *Ibid.*

151 *Ibid.* at 46.

152 [2004] 1 S.C.R. 76 [*Canadian Foundation*].

153 R.S.C. 1985, c. C-46.

154 *Canadian Foundation,* above note 152 at 100–2, Justice Arbour's dissent included the issue of vagueness and relied on the same international law material to support the opposite conclusion; *ibid.* at 162–64.

referred to *Ordon Estate v. Grail*.[155] The international law material used was the *Convention on the Rights of the Child*,[156] the *International Covenant on Civil and Political Rights*,[157] the *Convention for the Protection of Human Rights and Fundamental Freedoms (Europe)*,[158] as well as documents by the Human Rights Committee[159] and case law by the European Court of Human Rights.[160]

Now, what must be understood is that, in spite of appearances, McLachlin C.J. did not resort to the presumption of conformity in order to assist in interpreting section 43 of the *Criminal Code* to decide the case. International law and the presumption of intent were invoked in the discussion on the void for vagueness doctrine, which must not be confused with the process of ascertaining the intention of Parliament. Specifically, the expression "reasonable under the circumstances" in the statutory provision, albeit broad at first glance, was said to have implicit limitations that "indicate what conduct risks criminal sanction and provide a principled basis for enforcement."[161] It was to apply the standard of unconstitutional vagueness, elaborated by Gonthier J. in *R. v. Nova Scotia Pharmaceutical Society*,[162] that section 43 of the *Criminal Code* was examined and that the methodology of interpretation was utilized.[163] Without needing to rigorously distinguish between the construction of statutes proper and the interpretation of legis-

---

155 Above note 120.
156 (1989) 28 I.L.M. 1448, entered into force 2 September 1990.
157 Above note 144.
158 (1955) 213 U.N.T.S. 221, entered into force 3 September 1953.
159 *Report of the Human Rights Committee*, vol. 1, UN GAOR, Fiftieth Session, Supp. No. 40 (A/50/40) (1995), at paras. 426 and 434; *Report of the Human Rights Committee*, vol. 1, UN GAOR, Fifty-fourth Session, Supp. No. 40 (A/54/40) (1999), at para. 358; and *Report of the Human Rights Committee*, vol. 1, UN GAOR, Fifty-firth Session, Supp. No. 40 (A/55/40) (2000), at paras. 306 and 429.
160 *A. v. United Kingdom* (25599/94) [1998] E.C.H.R. 85.
161 *Canadian Foundation*, above note 152 at 100.
162 Above note 93.
163 See *Canadian Foundation*, above note 152 at 97, where McLachlin C.J. borrowed from the method and precedents of statutory interpretation, indeed paraphrased Driedger's "modern principle" as follows: "To ascertain whether s. 43 meets these requirements [of unconstitutional vagueness under s. 7 of the *Charter*], we must consider its words and court decisions interpreting those words. The words of the statute must be considered in context, in their grammatical and ordinary sense, and with a view of the legislative scheme's purpose and the intention of Parliament": *Rizzo & Rizzo Shoes Ltd. (Re)*, [1998] 1 S.C.R. 27 at 40–41; *Bell ExpressVu*, above note 50 at para. 26.

lation for the purpose of the void for vagueness doctrine,[164] suffice it to note that the latter is substantially less demanding, only requiring an examination of whether the legal norm is intelligible and provides an adequate basis for legal debate and analysis.[165]

This observation, in turn, means that the role given to the presumption of conformity with international law in *Canadian Foundation* is fundamentally different from that traditionally given to this method of construction. It is not for the purpose of assisting in the determination of the meaning of a statutory provision in order to identify the legal norm applicable to settle a dispute that international law was used in this case. Pertaining to a vagueness inquiry, the hurdle was much lower than the ascertainment of the intention of Parliament in a legislative provision. Indeed, international law merely in concluding that there were implicit limitations to the expression "reasonable under the circumstances" found in section 43 of the *Criminal Code* and that, accordingly, it was not too vague to be intelligible or to provide a basis for legal debate and analysis. "Canada's international commitments confirm," the Chief Justice wrote, "that physical correction that either harms or degrades a child is unreasonable."[166]

Even if one interprets McLachlin C.J.'s reasons in *Canadian Foundation* in the way just proposed, with the suggestion that the presumption of conformity with international law has not been formally reintroduced in Canada's statutory interpretation, it would be naive and perhaps foolish not to apprehend that the pendulum may well swing back in favour of this old technique of resorting to international treaty law.[167] The *Baker* case, on its face, may not persuasively stand for the authority that international law should always be used through the basic contextual argument of statutory interpretation rather than by means of a presumption of intent. However, when one considers the details of L'Heureux-Dubé J.'s reasons in *Baker*, how she reiterated and extended the methodology to all international legal

164 For more details, see Stéphane Beaulac, "Les bases constitutionnelles de la théorie de l'imprécision : partie d'un précaire dynamique globale de la Charte" (1995) 55 R. du B. 257.

165 *R. v. Nova Scotia Pharmaceutical Society*, above note 93 at 638–40.

166 *Canadian Foundation*, above note 152 at 101.

167 One recent case at the Federal Court of Canada relied on *Canadian Foundation*, *ibid.*, in the way apprehended, that is, to support the utilisation of international law in statutory interpretation through a presumption of intent: see *Khadr v. Canada (Minister of Foreign Affairs)*, 2004 FC 1145 at para. 26.

norms for the majority in *Hudson*,[168] and that a unanimous Supreme Court of Canada agreed and went along with the idea that international law is really an element of context in *Suresh*, the argument can clearly be made that there is a trend being set in Canadian case law.[169] Up with context, down with presumption.

In any event, *Canadian Foundation* is without doubt a backward step, albeit one that is somewhat insignificant because the reasoning of presumption was borrowed to apply to a much lower interpretative hurdle, that of the void for vagueness doctrine. The real setback was *Schreiber*,[170] which chronologically postdates *Baker* and the other two judgments in *Hudson* and *Suresh*. As shown earlier in this chapter though,[171] at least LeBel J.'s reasons, by quoting from *Daniels v. White and The Queen*,[172] bring into light the fatal flaw, with the presumption of conformity with international law, namely, the requirement of ambiguity. This preliminary condition is of course an impediment to the use of international treaty law in statutory interpretation.[173] But worse, the notion of ambiguity as a finding that is necessary in order either to proceed with the complete process of statutory interpretation or with a particular method of construction[174]—be it the presumption of conformity with international law, the presumption of conformity with the *Charter*, the use parliamentary debates in statutory in-

---

168 *Hudson*, above note 132.
169 See Evans J.A.'s comments to that effect in *Rahaman v. Canada (Minister of Citizenship and Immigration)*, above note 21 at 558: "Nowadays, *there is no doubt that*, even when not incorporated by Act of Parliament into Canadian law, *international norms are part of the context within which domestic statutes are to be interpreted*: Baker v. Canada (Minister of Citizenship and Immigration), [1999] 2 S.C.R. 817 at paragraph 70. Similarly, in *Suresh v. Canada* (2002), 208 D.L.R. (4th) [1], at paragraph 59, when referring to the *Immigration Act* [R.S.C. 1985, c. I-2] the Supreme Court of Canada stated: 'A complete understanding of the Act ... requires consideration of the international perspective.' It was also said in *Suresh*, above at paragraph 60, that the reason for examining the international dimension is not to determine if Canada is in breach of its international legal obligations as such, but to use prevailing international norms to inform the interpretation of a provision of domestic law, in that case section 7 of the *Canadian Charter of Rights and Freedoms*" (emphasis added).
170 *Schreiber*, above note 113.
171 See above notes 108–17 and accompanying text.
172 Above note 109.
173 See the case law in above note 117.
174 For a recent example, see *Bell ExpressVu*, above note 50 at 581–82. Proof that this "plain meaning rule"–type of reasoning still lingers at the Supreme Court of Canada, these paragraphs were relied upon again very recently by the majority, per Binnie J., in *Bristol-Myers Squibb Co. v. Canada (Attorney General)*, [2005] 1 S.C.R. 533 at para. 43.

terpretation,[175] or other arguments—is rooted in the now obsolete rhetoric of the "plain meaning rule" (or "literal rule") of statutory interpretation.[176]

Thus along with this outdated strategy of legislative interpretation, presumptions of intent linked to an ambiguity requirement, like the presumption of conformity with international law, must definitely go.

E. CONCLUSION

Pursuant to the contemporary method of legislative interpretation that is captured in Driedger's modern principle, which enjoys unequivocal and undisputed authority in Canadian courts, and its central idea of word-in-total-context in ascertaining the intention of Parliament, legal norms of the international order must always be considered as an element of context,[177] the persuasive force of which will vary depending on the circumstances, such as the degree of incorporation of treaty norms within the Canadian legal system.[178]

This is no doubt the better strategy to maximize the domestic application of international treaty law than the use of a presumption of conformity with international law and its preliminary requirement of ambiguity. The

---

175 On this interpretative argument, see Stéphane Beaulac, "Parliamentary Debates in Statutory Interpretation: A Question of Admissibility or of Weight?" (1998) 43 McGill L.J. 287; and Stéphane Beaulac, "Recent Developments at the Supreme Court of Canada on the Use of Parliamentary Debates" (2000) 63 Sask. L. Rev. 581.

176 See Stéphane Beaulac, "Recent Developments on the Role of International Law in Canadian Statutory Interpretation" (2004) 25 Stat. L. Rev. 19 at 38–39.

177 Recent case law in lower courts that appears to endorse this strategy include: *Mack v. Canada (Attorney General)* (2001), 55 O.R. (3d) 113 at 124 (S.C.J.); and *R. v. Demers* (1999), 176 D.L.R. (4th) 741 at 765 (B.C.S.C.). Even in speaking of international law as context, however, some recent cases have managed to involve the rhetoric of the obsolete "plain meaning rule" of statutory interpretation and the ambiguity requirement; see *De Guzman v. Canada (Minister of Citizenship and Immigration)*, 2004 FC 1276 at para. 53.

178 See Beaulac, "National Application of International Law," above note 2, where the author proposes an analytical scheme of the persuasive force of international treaty norms based on their degree of incorporation within Canada's internal legal system. He writes: "Simply put, the clearer it is that the parliamentary authority intended to give effect to international law through the transformation of the convention, the more weight a court should recognize and attribute to such norms in the process of ascertaining the meaning of the statutory provision"; *ibid.* at 260. In the end, it was suggested that there are four categories of context in which fall treaty norms which, in a decreasing order of persuasive authority, are: 1) internal-immediate context; 2) internal-extended context; 3) external-immediate context; and 4) external-extended context.

idea here is to have the domestic judge in a situation where the possible influence of international law on the construction of statutes is, in a way, inescapable; at least not escapable through the subterfuge of the artificial and somewhat dishonest conclusion, at the outset of the interpretative process, that the provision is unambiguous and that it does not need to be considered in light of the legal norms of the international order.[179] As Lord Oliver of Aylmerton appositely noted in the groundbreaking decision of the House of Lords in *Pepper v. Hart*:[180] "Ingenuity can sometimes suggest ambiguity or obscurity where none exists in fact,"[181] and *vice versa* one would assume. The use of international law as an element of legislative context, pursuant to Driedger's approach to statutory interpretation, avoids this evasive feature.

That being so, what is the problem that international legal scholars in this country have with international law as context?[182] Likewise, what is the obsession with the presumption of conformity with international law?[183] The suspected answer is that there appears to be a belief that the "cause" of international law is better served if the message is sent out to the Canadian judiciary that international law is not only there to act as an argument in the process of statutory interpretation, but that judges must presumptively construe domestic law as being in line with the legal norms of the international order.[184] This argument is surely not without reminding us of the continuing claim, which is somewhat self-assertive and largely reifying, that international law is "binding" within Canada's domestic legal system,[185] which clearly show the profound divide between the international

---

179 See L'Heureux-Dubé J.'s comments to that effect in her concurring set of reasons in *Régie des permis d'alcool)*, above note 50 at 997.

180 [1993] A.C. 593.

181 *Ibid.* at 620. See also Anthony Lester, "English Judges as Law Makers," [1993] Public Law 269 at 272–75.

182 See, for instance, Brunnée & Toope, above note 29 at 41, who have a problem with always considering international law as an element of context.

183 See, most blatantly, Gibran van Ert, *Using International Law*, above note 40 at 99 *et seq.*, who managed to have a whole chapter on the presumption of conformity with international law.

184 See, for a clear illustration of this concern, Brunnée & Toope, "A Hesitant Embrace," above note 29 at 40.

185 See Provost, "Le juge mondialisé," above note 28 at 584, who accurately noted: "[Le] débat sur l'application du droit international en droit canadien [est] stérilement fixé sur la question de la force obligatoire" [footnotes omitted].

law perspective and the national law perspective on these issues.[186] Like "bindingness," the belief that international law is better off with a reasoning based on a presumption of intent is illusory, if not just plain wrong.[187]

Trite as it may seem, it is useful to remind ourselves that the function of courts, indeed no less than their constitutional mission in a British-style parliamentary democracy,[188] is to interpret and apply domestic law to settle disputes over which they have jurisdiction.[189] With respect to legal norms based on legislation, Parliament deliberates and adopts, the courts interpret and apply.[190] In this process of statutory interpretation, at the centre of which is the structural notion of legislative intent,[191] courts have at their disposal a number of methods of interpretation.[192] They include textual interpretation, teleological interpretation, historical interpretation, as well as general maxims of interpretation based on logic and several types of arguments of legislative context, be it internal or external (from the use of parliamentary debates to the use of legal norms from the international order), not to forget the more obscure pragmatic or consequential argu-

---

186 From the statutory interpretation perspective, which is a domestic law perspective, see Sullivan, *Sullivan and Driedger,* above note 31 at 421: "*Although international law is not binding on Canadian legislatures,* it is presumed that the legislation enacted both federally and provincially is meant to comply with international law generally and with Canada's international law obligations in particular" (emphasis added). See also LeBel & Chao, "The Rise of International Law," above note 33 at 62: "[I]nternational law is generally non-binding or without effective control mechanisms."

187 See also, more bluntly, Beaulac, "International Treaty Norms," above note 36, *in fine.*

188 See the classics on the subject: John Locke, *Two Treatises of Government* (London: Amen-Corner, 1690) and C.-L de S. Montesquieu, *De l'esprit des lois* (London: n.b., 1757), first published in 1748.

189 On the jurisdictional aspect, see above notes 10–12 and accompanying text.

190 See Côté, *Interprétation des lois,* above note 74 at 313. See also Ernst Freund, "Interpretation of Statutes" (1917) 65 U. Pa. L. Rev. 207.

191 In the vast literature considering and criticizing this notion, see Randal N. Graham, "Good Intentions" (2000) 12 Sup. Ct. L. Rev. (2d) 147; Gerald C. MacCallum Jr., "Legislative Intent" (1965–66) 75 Yale L.J. 754; Douglas Payne, "The Intention of the Legislature in the Interpretation of Statutes" (1956) 9 Curr. Legal Probs. 96; Harry W. Jones, "Statutory Doubts and Legislative Intention" (1940) 40 Colum. L. Rev. 957; Frank E. Horack, Jr., "In the Name of Legislative Intention" (1932) 38 West Virginia L.Q. 119; and Theodore Sedgwick, *A Treatise on the Rules which Govern the Interpretation and Construction of Statutory and Constitutional Law,* 2d ed. (New York: Baker, Voorhis, 1874) at 327 *et seq.*

192 See Willis, "Statutory Interpretation," above note 89; J.M. Kernochan, "Statutory Interpretation: An Outline of Methods," [1976] Dal. L.J. 333; and Max Radin, "A Short Way with Statutes" (1942–43) 56 Harv. L. Rev. 388.

ments like *ab absurdo* or the presumptions of intent (like the presumption of conformity with international law, with the problematic ambiguity requirement however).

The point here is not to enumerate an exhaustive list of interpretative methods. Rather, it is to emphasize how these arguments, in what I like to call the "judges' little toolbox of construction," are all available to assist in ascertaining the intention of Parliament, but none of them is obligatory or constraining. By definition, in fact, arguments of statutory interpretation are just that, arguments, which may or may not be used by a court, the mandate of which is to interpret and apply statutory provisions.[193] Not even the "rules" found in Interpretation Acts are binding on courts.[194] Instead, all of these interpretative conventions exist to guide and to justify the outcome of the process of construction.[195] The novelty with Driedger's modern principle is to say that all of them—whether falling within the broad categories commonly known as text, context and object—are equally important and may in any situation be utilized to assist in ascertaining the intention of Parliament.[196]

These general remarks go a long way to help explain why the belief that international law is more likely to play a greater role in the process of statutory interpretation if it is involved by means of a presumption of intent rather than the contextual argument is unfounded. Courts will assign the persuasive force to each of the different interpretative arguments deemed relevant in a case based on a series of factors, one of which is the general policy consideration of justice.[197] It is illusory to think that one canon of

---

193 See Frederick J. de Sloovère, "Preliminary Questions in Statutory Interpretation" (1932) 9 New York U. L.Q. Rev. 407.

194 See, for instance, the federal *Interpretation Act*, R.S.C. 1985, c. I-21, s. 3, which provides that all the rules therein apply unless provided otherwise and that common law methods of construction are still valid and applicable unless inconsistent. See also, to a similar effect, Quebec's *Interpretation Act*, R.S.Q., c. I-16, ss. 1 and 38.

195 See Pierre-André Côté, "Les règles d'interprétation des lois : des guides et des arguments" (1978) 13 R.J.T. 275 at 299. See also M.S. Amos, "The Interpretation of Statutes" (1934) 4 Cambridge L.J. 163 at 175; and Felix Frankfurter, "Some Reflexions on the Reading of Statutes" (1947) 47 Colum. L. Rev. 527 at 527–28.

196 See Sullivan, *Sullivan and Driedger*, above note 31 at 1: "The chief significance of the modern principle is its insistence on the complex, multi-dimensional character of statutory interpretation."

197 See Sullivan, *ibid.* at 3, who explained thus: "At the end of the day, after taking into account all relevant and admissible considerations, the court must adopt and interpretation that is appropriate. An appropriate interpretation is one that can be justified

interpretation will "have to" be considered and be given a determinative weight by a court.[198] Put another way, it would be most awkward to have a litigant argue in front of a judge that he or she "must" adopt the textual argument or the teleological argument or the historical argument in his or her interpretation, or that he or she "must" assign a certain weight to one or many of the different methods of interpretation. The same is true of the international law argument, which may or may not be used by a court in a particular instance, or be given more or less weight by a court depending on the circumstances. This is the true nature of statutory interpretation.[199]

In the final analysis, therefore, arguing in favour of the presumption of conformity with international law—as in arguing in favour of the "bindingness" of such legal norms[200]—based on the belief that courts will accordingly assign greater persuasive force to the argument, or will have less discretion in their judicial role, is a mistake. Considering the constitutional function of the judiciary and how the process of interpretation and application of statutes work, the international law argument based on the contextual construction of legislation pursuant to Driedger's modern principle is likely to be given as much weight (maybe more, maybe less). One thing is sure, however: Unlike the presumption of conformity, resorting to international law through the basic contextual argument will never run into the evasive feature of the ambiguity requirement; international law is thus more likely to be considered relevant, or at least an argument with which to reckon always. We all know that a bird in the hand is better than two in the bush, although at the end of the day the pair might very well be in Elmer Driedger's helping hand.

---

in terms of (a) its plausibility, that is, its compliance with the legislative text; (b) its efficacy, that is, its promotion of legislative intent; and (c) its acceptability, that is, the outcome complies with legal norms; its reasonable and just."

198 See the classic piece by Max Radin, "Statutory Interpretation" (1929–30) 43 Harv. L. Rev. 863 at 881.

199 See generally Jerzy Wróblewski, "L'interprétation en droit : théorie et idéologie" (1972) 17 Archives de Philosophie du droit 51; and Oliver Wendell Holmes, "The Theory of Legal Interpretation" (1898–99) 12 Harv. L. Rev. 417.

200 See Brunnée & Toope, "A Hesitant Embrace," above note 29 at 55.

Evidence and International and Comparative Law

11

ANNE WARNER LA FOREST

A. INTRODUCTION

> As the cases ... become more complex, we foresee that there will be an increasing need for international law evidence. The production and tendering of international law evidence in a domestic case is a challenging task.... This Court has generally relied on published documents provided by international interveners to fill this need. As issues grow in complexity, this method of evidence may not be sufficient.[1]

Since the decision in *Baker v. Canada*,[2] the Supreme Court of Canada has been engaged in a period of reflection in relation to the use of international law in its decisions.[3] In April 2002, Mr. Justice LeBel and Gloria Chao gave a paper at Osgoode Hall Law School addressing recent developments and challenges in internalizing international law.[4] At the end of that paper, the authors raised three specific challenges that accompanied the rising use of international law:

- the need to accommodate increasing numbers of parties pleading international law before the Court;

---

1   The Hon. Mr. Justice Louis LeBel & Gloria Chao, "The Rise of International Law in Canadian Constitutional Litigation: Fugue or Fusion? Recent Developments and Challenges in Internalizing International Law" (2002) 16 Sup. Ct. L.R. (2d) 23 at 61.
2   [1999] 2 S.C.R. 817.
3   Anne Warner La Forest, "Domestic Application of International Law in Charter Cases: Are We There Yet?" (2004) 37 U.B.C. L. Rev. 157 at 169.
4   LeBel & Chao, "Fugue or Fusion," above note 1.

- the need for international law evidence to respond to the increasing complexity of international law; and
- the need for new international and comparative models.[5]

There have been a number of serious efforts to respond to the last of these challenges both before and since the publication of the LeBel/Chao paper.[6] In the context of evidence, however, there has, until very recently, been little academic discussion. For many years, the most noteworthy work directly addressing the question of evidence and international law was the oft-cited and remarkable effort of Ronald St. John MacDonald, "The Relationship between International Law and Domestic Law in Canada" published in 1974.[7] In that article MacDonald expounded upon the role of judicial notice in the specific context of customary international law. More recently, Gibran van Ert has, both in his text[8] and in two recent articles,[9] relied upon judicial notice as a means to press the courts to be more vigilant in their application of international law.[10] He has "extended" MacDonald's analysis in two respects that are of interest in this article. First, he has argued that judicial notice applies to all sources of international law and

---

5   *Ibid.* at 60.
6   I note in particular the work of Irit Weiser "Undressing the Window: Treating International Human Rights Law Meaningfully in the Canadian Commonwealth System" (2004) 37 U.B.C. L. Rev. 219 and Jutta Brunnée & Stephen Toope, "A Hesitant Embrace: The Application of International Law by Canadian Courts" (2002) Can. Y.B. Int'l L. 3. Prior to the LeBel & Chao article, the relationship between international and municipal law had been the subject of much academic writing. There have also been a number of judicially based education programs through organizations such as the National Judicial Institute, the International Association of Women Judges, and the Canadian Bar Association.
7   Ronald St. John MacDonald, "The Relationship between International Law and Domestic Law in Canada" in Ronald St. J. MacDonald, Gerald L. Morris & Douglas M. Johnston, eds., *Canadian Perspectives on International Law and Organization* (Toronto: University of Toronto Press: 1974) at 88–136.
8   Gibran van Ert, *Using International Law in Canadian Courts* (Hague: Kluwer Law International, 2002) at 30–39.
9   Gibran van Ert, "Judicial Notice and Reception Theory: Thoughts on the Contribution of Ronald St. John MacDonald" (2002) Can. Y.B. Int'l L. 251; van Ert, "The Admissibility of International Legal Evidence" (March 2005) 84 Can. Bar Rev. 1.
10 Van Ert, "Judicial Notice," above note 9 at 254–55: "That Canadian judges and counsel should have some grasp of international law is not simply desirable. It is required by the doctrine of judicial notice. By this doctrine, courts and other adjudicating bodies will accept the existence of certain law or facts without requiring proof."

not simply to custom.[11] Second, he argues that the acceptance of judicial notice means that expert evidence on international law should be inadmissible, though in his most recent effort, he has refined this position somewhat in relation to customary international law.[12] In both MacDonald's and van Ert's writings, the discussion of evidence is closely tied to the discussion of reception of international law and does not address comparative law beyond characterizing it as foreign and as fact, not law.

In my view, the matter of evidence of international law and comparative law before domestic tribunals may require more than an application of the doctrine of judicial notice, and further study of the law of evidence and its application to international law and comparative law in domestic courts is required. That is the subject of this chapter. Part B of this chapter provides a foundational review of the principles underlying judicial notice and its connection to the matter of expert evidence. From this discussion, the beginning of a theory is suggested that speaks to the use of such evidence in the context of international law and comparative law. Part C will then examine these principles with reference to customary international law since the relevant case law in this area evolved in relation to this source of international law. Finally, part D will provide some brief concluding thoughts about how these principles might apply to the case of treaties and the *Charter*. Before moving directly to the undertaking at hand, I would make a few points to set the context.

First, my underlying objectives in this piece are practical and almost mirror those outlined by Ronald St. John MacDonald. Some thirty years ago he argued that there was a need for certainty in advising a client about the relationship between international law and domestic law.[13] That need continues, and it is probably right to add that the need exists not only for clients but also for judges,[14] for lawyers, and for Canadians generally. MacDonald also argued that there is a need for Canada to conform to the requirements of international law.[15] Again, in general terms, I agree with this proposition; Canada's internationalist vision is a significant part of

---

11 Van Ert, *Using International Law*, above note 8 at 33–34.
12 *Ibid.* at 39–40. See also van Ert, "Judicial Notice," above note 9 at 258. In terms of customary international law, see van Ert, "Admissibility," above note 9 at 14–15.
13 MacDonald, "Relationship between International and Domestic Law," above note 7 at 88–89.
14 As intimated by Lebel & Chao, "Fugue or Fusion," above note 1. In terms of evidence, it is also worth commenting here that the need is particularly acute at the trial level.
15 MacDonald, "Relationship between International and Domestic Law," above note 7 at 89.

our Canadian identity and that requires that our internal law generally conform to international law. I do, however, qualify that position both generally and in relation to the *Canadian Charter of Rights and Freedoms* for the simple reason that the *Charter* is also a significant aspect of our national identity and is not subsumed to any other law.[16] In this regard, it is worth stating that MacDonald's third objective was in relation to the development of a constitution.[17] That has, of course, now come to pass.

Second, there is a symbiotic relationship between one's theory of the interplay between international and municipal law and the approach one is likely to take to more procedural matters, such as evidence. To be pointed, if one is of the view that international law is binding on domestic courts, one is more likely to rely upon the doctrine of judicial notice as traditionally expounded because it is connected to the judicial duty to understand "the law of the land." One is less likely to accept the use of expert evidence because of its association with questions of fact and the proof of foreign law. In this chapter, I intend to look directly at the relationship between evidence and reception with this in mind. In a sense, the rules of evidence afford a different lens through which to examine familiar problems.

Third, it might be argued that the question of international law in relation to evidence is an esoteric exercise. However, in my view, the discussion is a useful one for a number of reasons. First, the existing academic discussion suggests that international law *must* be presented to courts through legal argument and that it is unsound for a court to refer to expert evidence in assessing international law.[18] Correspondingly, it is argued that comparative law must be treated as fact and proved through expert evidence. In my view, it is not inappropriate for courts to refer to expert evidence in relation to international law and the objective of parts B and C of this chapter is to demonstrate this point. In addition, in the current jurispru-

---

16   In La Forest, "Domestic Application," above note 3 at 160–63, I argued that the *Charter* is the supreme law of Canada and is thus not subject to international law. In my view, the *Charter* represents a unique opportunity to look forward in terms of a rights-based society and that normatively, there is value in supporting the real differences of our national community in an increasingly global world for we are not only the subjects of international human rights, we are its authors as well.

17   MacDonald, "Relationship between International and Domestic Law," above note 7 at 88–89.

18   It is suggested that if an expert is to participate in a case, he or she should be instructed as counsel: van Ert, *Using International Law*, above note 8 at 258.

dential environment, the courts are indeed looking for[19] *and* referring to expert evidence[20] and in so doing are endeavouring to apply international law in a more robust and detailed manner. As long as international law is recognized as law, the current practice should not be discouraged by focusing too narrowly on the manner in which such material comes before the courts. Finally, and perhaps most substantively, an approach that insists upon a rigid evidentiary distinction between international and comparative law is not in keeping with the practice of courts nor is it consonant with Canada's internationalist vision.

B. JUDICIAL NOTICE AND EXPERT EVIDENCE

In the *Black's Law Dictionary* definition of "judicial notice," fact and law are woven together:

> the act by which a court, in conducting a trial, or framing its decision, will, of its own motion, and without the production of evidence recognize the truth of certain facts, having a bearing on the controversy at bar, which, from their nature are not properly the subject of testimony, or which are universally regarded as established by common notoriety, e.g. the laws of state, international law, historical events, the constitution and course of nature, main geographical features, etc.[21]

In the academic treatment of judicial notice, however, there is both, in evidence texts and writings on international law, an almost immediate dichotomy drawn between judicial notice of law and judicial notice of fact, and virtually no discussion of the policy reasons underlying both.[22] In this section, I provide a short synopsis of the traditional position in relation to judicial notice of law and then reflect upon the appropriateness of this position from a policy perspective when applied to evidence of international and comparative law before domestic courts.

---

19 LeBel & Chao, "Fugue or Fusion," above note 1.

20 *Bouzari v. Iran*, [2002] O.J. No. 1624 (S.C.J), aff'd (2004), 71 O.R. (3d) 675 (C.A.), leave to appeal to the S.C.C. refused, [2004] S.C.C.A. No. 410.

21 As cited by MacDonald, "Relationship between International and Domestic Law," above note 7 at 111.

22 Materials from an evidence perspective include: Edmund M. Morgan, "Judicial Notice" (1944) 57 Harv. L.R. 269; John Sopinka, Sidney N. Lederman & Alan W. Bryant, *The Law of Evidence in Canada*, 2d ed. (Toronto: Butterworths, 1999) at 1055; Ronald J. Delisle, *Canadian Evidence Law in a Nutshell* (Scarborough, ON: Carswell, 2002).

As to the judicial notice of domestic law generally, it is postulated that there can be no proof through evidence of the laws of the land.[23] This principle is a longstanding one at common law and its rationale has been defended in terms of the role of the judge. It is the duty of judges, by virtue of their office, to know the laws of the land.[24] If judges do not know such laws, the expectation is that they are able, through their skill, to determine that law.[25] The process of the adversarial system affords counsel the opportunity through argument to provide guidance and assistance to the court. Judges are, however, free to accept or reject such material and are unrestricted in their investigation of the law and in their conclusion. On appeal, a judge's assessment of the law may be accepted or rejected until the highest court in the land determines the matter. The common law principle that there is to be judicial notice of domestic law has been supplemented through statute.[26]

Judicial notice of domestic law is thus firmly within the jurisdiction of the judge and expert evidence is inappropriate because, by definition, such evidence is limited to situations where the witness has qualifications beyond those of the court.[27] An admission of such evidence would come dangerously close to accepting the proposition that a witness can decide the penultimate issue before the court.[28] That it is the job of judges to know the domestic law applicable within their jurisdiction is as plain and simple a proposition as one can imagine in law. It is the application of judicial notice to comparative and international law that is of interest here.

---

23 The law of the land encompasses the common law, equity, and Acts of Parliament, both private and public. At common law, notice of public and private acts was to be taken but not subordinate legislation: *R. v. Evgenia Chandris (The)*, [1977] 2 S.C.R. 97; *R. v. Whalen* (1971), 4 C.C.C. (2d) 560 (N.B.S.C.A.D.).

24 John H. Wigmore, *A Treatise on the System of Evidence in Trials at Common Law* (Toronto: Canada Law Book and Boston: Little, Brown and Company, 1905) at §2572 [*Wigmore on Evidence*]. Morgan, "Judicial Notice," above note 22 at 270–72.

25 *Ibid.*

26 Judicial notice of federal acts is provided for by the *Canada Evidence Act*, R.S.C. 1985, c. C-5. See also *Statutory Instruments Act*, R.S.C. 1985, c. S-22, s. 16 (Orders in Council), *Interpretation Act*, R.S.C. 1985, c. I-26. Provincial statutes also provide for judicial notice: see for example *Evidence Act*, R.S.B.C. 1996, c. 124, s. 24(2); Judicature Act, R.S.N.B. 1973, c. J-2, s. 26 (to take judicial notice of acts, public or private). Only the Quebec legislation refers to international law but municipal law is excluded: C.c.Q., Art. 2807.

27 *R. v. Mohan*, [1994] 2 S.C.R. 9, Sopinka, *Evidence*, above note 22 at 620–22.

28 Sopinka, *Evidence, ibid.* at 634–41.

Under the traditional formulation, comparative law is treated as foreign law in the fullest sense of that term.[29] Being foreign, such law is not known to the judge and thus may not be judicially noticed.[30] Such law must be proved through an expert. This principle derives from cases in the area of conflict of laws.[31] One consequence of the firmness of this approach was that historically, with the exceptions of the Supreme Court of Canada and the Federal Court, if the law of one province was at issue in the courts of another province, that law had to be proved through expert evidence.[32] There has been some statutory relief on this point.[33]

The supposed certainty of this rule was, however, relaxed in some cases and specifically, it did not apply to some states. Wigmore indicates that while foreign law must be proved, that need not be the case where the foreign system is germane in its general features to the domestic one.[34] He accepted that reference to English law could be judicially noticed in an American court. This point can even be more readily accepted in the Canadian environment. The same approach was followed in cases relating to the law of admiralty because that law was, in effect, the law of England.[35]

Another consequence of the acceptance of the principle that comparative law cannot be judicially noticed and must be proved has been the corollary conclusion that comparative law is fact and not law.[36] I do not agree

---

29 Van Ert, *Using International Law*, above note 8 at 34–35; Sopinka, *Evidence, ibid.* at 640–41: questions of domestic law, as opposed to foreign law, are not matters on which the court will receive evidence: *R. v. Century 21 Ramos Realty Inc.* (1987), 32 C.C.C. (3d) 353, leave to appeal to S.C.C. refused (1987), 56 C.R. (3d) xxviii.

30 *Sussex Peerage Case* (1844), 11 Cl. & F. 85, 8 Jur. 793, 8 E.R. 1034: deciding that foreign law and its meaning are not matters of common knowledge and expert evidence is then required.

31 *Bondholders Securities Corp. v. Manville et al. (No. 2)*, [1935] 1 W.W.R. 452 at 457–58 (Sask. C.A.) relying on *Bremer v. Freeman* (1857), 10 Moo. P.C. 306, 14 E.R. 508; *Logan v. Lee* (1907), 39 S.C.R. 311 at 313; *Canadian Pacific Railway Co. v. Parent*, [1917] A.C. 195; *Cdn. Steamships Company Ltd. v. Watson*, [1939] S.C.R. 11. See also Jean G. Castel & Janet E. Walker, *Canadian Conflict of Laws*, 6th ed. (Toronto: Butterworths, 2005) at §§7.1–7.5.

32 *Canadian Pacific Railway Co. v. Parent, ibid.*: this is not of course because the law is not binding but because the judge is not expected to know the laws of another province; it is not law within their expertise/knowledge.

33 Castel & Walker, *Canadian Conflict of Laws*, above note 31 at §7.1.

34 Wigmore on Evidence, §690.

35 *Ibid.*, §2573 citing *Talbot v. Seaman* (1801), 1 Cranch 1 at 37; *The Scotia* (1871), 14 Wall. 170 at 188; *The New York* (1899), 175 U.S. 187.

36 Van Ert, *Using International Law*, above note 8 at 34. See also MacDonald, "Relationship between International and Domestic Law," above note 7 at 112, citing *Bondholders Securities Corp v. Manville et al. (No. 2)*, above note 31 at 457–58 (Sask. C.A.). The court

with this proposition because it makes no sense in terms of conflict of laws or otherwise. Something is not fact simply because one does not know the law and proof is required. It is still law in effect because it is the basis upon which the court will resolve the case. The question in a case of conflict of laws is which law should apply. If the court reaches the conclusion that the law of another state governs the dispute between the parties, it is no less law because the content of that law needs to be proved to the court. Brownlie accepts this point in his text on international law: "Where in a conflict of laws case, an expert gives evidence as to matters of foreign law, the method of ascertaining that law does not affect its character as law."[37] Expert evidence is required to assist the court in resolving the dispute between the parties. In cases where there is dispute in terms of the evidence, the court is able to review the law itself and to reach a conclusion as to the appropriate application of the law.

What then of international law? Black's definition accepts that there can be judicial notice of international law.[38] In his text, van Ert cites the following commentary from *Halsbury's* as the strongest authority in favour of the judicial notice of international law: "the courts take notice of every branch of English law, including international law."[39] Case authority in this regard has been described as limited.[40] It is perhaps more accurate to say that the case authority that most directly addresses judicial notice of international law is generally not of recent vintage.[41] Apart from direct authority

---

in *Bondholders* relied upon the case of *Bremer v. Freeman*, above note 31. See also Castel & Walker, *Canadian Conflict of Laws*, above note 31.

37 Ian Brownlie, *Principles of International Law*, 6th ed. (London: Oxford University Press, 2003) at 40.

38 MacDonald, "The Relationship between International Law and Domestic Law," above note 7 at 111.

39 Van Ert, *Using International Law*, above note 8 at 31, citing *Halsbury's Laws of England*, 4th ed., vol. 17 (London: Butterworths, 1977) at para. 106 and *ibid.*, vol. 18 at para. 1403.

40 See Hersch Lauterpacht, "Is International Law a Part of the Law of England?" [1939] Translations of the Grotius Society 51 at 59 n(i); van Ert, *Using International Law*, above note 8 at 31; MacDonald, "The Relationship between International and Domestic Law," above note 7 at 113.

41 *The Scotia*, above note 35; *The New York*, above note 35; *The Ship "The North"* (1906), 37 S.C.R. 385. All these cases arise in the area of admiralty. Van Ert argues that the principle should not be restricted to cases of admiralty and further that later cases and judicial practice belie this conclusion. My own view is that admiralty was in effect the law of England and was applied by other states. Thus, while properly characterized as the law of nations, it was not really much of a stretch for an English court to state that principles of admiralty law in an international sense should be judicially noticed as

on the point, the claim is made that judicial notice of international law is necessary for the proper application of the doctrine of incorporation and, to a lesser extent, the principle that domestic law should be interpreted, if possible, to be in accordance with Canada's international law obligations. Thus, the discussion of judicial notice of international law is almost inexorably tied to the question of the reception of international law within the domestic law of the state. Once received, international law is domestic law and thus judicially noticed upon the same basis as other domestic law. The cases cited in support of this argument are also not generally of recent vintage and are all ones stating that international law is the law of the land.[42] As such, the argument is that the same principles of judicial notice that apply to domestic law should apply to international law.

It is important to conclude this summary of judicial notice by stating that while there has not been much direct discussion of judicial notice of international law, the courts in Canada regularly judicially notice such material without proof.[43] In my view, it is right that the courts should be open to looking to international law. It would be a sad commentary indeed on the evolution of jurisprudence that the early insight of domestic judges—that international law should be considered in the resolution of

---

domestic law; the law of admiralty was well known to English and Canadian judges. Interestingly, these cases are also cited by Wigmore as being exceptions to the strict rule related to comparative law: see above note 35. The actual record of later direct authority is scant. Van Ert relies upon the following authority: *Post Office v. Estuary Radio Ltd.*, [1968] 2 Q.B. 740 (C.A.); *Capital Cities Communications Inc. v. C.R.T.C.*, [1978] 2 S.C.R. 141; *In Re Queensland Mercantile and Agency Company*, [1892] 1 Ch. 219 (C.A.); *Jose Pereira E Hijos S.A. v. Canada (Attorney General)*, [1997] 2 F.C. 84 (T.D.). None of these cases is a particularly strong statement for the principle relied upon. I do agree that there are numerous cases where the court is implicitly accepting the use of international law without the need for expert evidence. The real question is the basis upon which this is so and whether it prohibits the use of expert evidence. There has also been a recent case that would support the more traditional approach to judicial notice: *Lord Advocate's Reference No. 1 of 2000*, 2001 S.L.T. 507, *(sub nom. HM Advocate v. Zelter)* [2001] Scot. J. No. 84 (Scot. High Justiciary Appeal Ct.). In that case, the Scottish Court has reconfirmed the foreignness of comparative law, the character of international law as the law of the land, and the consequent inappropriateness of expert evidence of international law.

42 The classic cases relied upon are *Barbuit's Case* (1737), Cas. t. Talb. 281, 25 E.R. 777; *Triquet v. Bath* (1764), 3 Burr. 1478, 97 E.R. 936, *Lockwood v. Coysgarne* (1765), 3 Burr 1676; *Heathfield v. Chilton* (1767), 4 Burr 2015, 98 E.R. 50; *Duke of Brunswick v. The King of Hanover* (1844), 6 Beav. 1, 49 E.R. 724.

43 See for example, the cases collected below at note 45 of van Ert, "Admissibility," above note 9.

domestic disputes—should be put aside at a time when its relevance is at least as significant.[44]

Having outlined the traditional model, the question to be asked is whether it is satisfactory. Van Ert argues that it is because it supports the centrality of international law within the domestic regime. In his view, it also properly limits the scope of comparative law in hierarchical terms relative to international law. While I believe strongly in the importance of international law and the role of domestic courts in fulfilling our international obligations, the difficulty I have with this model is that it is unsatisfactory both in practical and theoretical terms.

Practically, there are two reasons why this is so. The first is that while the courts are indeed judicially noticing international law, they are also, in many cases, seeking the assistance of expert witnesses in the application of international law.[45] As the citation at the beginning of this chapter indicates, our own judges are asking for support in addressing an increasingly complex subject. I do not believe it is enough to respond to this by stating that while one can understand why a court would want this kind of material, it cannot have guidance unless it is through the argument of counsel because of the combined effect of the "doctrines" of judicial notice and incorporation. That is especially the case when the authority is decidedly aged, if not weak, and judicial notice is so clearly founded upon knowledge. Second, while there appears to be considerable certainty about the doctrine of judicial notice as applicable to comparative law, the fact of the matter is that the doctrine is supported by cases in the area of conflict of laws. The courts are judicially noticing comparative law in other cases with as much regularity as they are international law, particularly, but not exclusively, in cases involving the interpretation of the *Charter*.[46] The reality is that the

---

44   Justice Rand expressed this exact sentiment in the case of *Saint John v. Fraser-Brace Overseas*, [1958] S.C.R. 263 at 268–69.

45   *Romania (State) v. Cheng* (1997), 114 C.C.C. (3d) 289; *R. v. Finta*, [1994] 1 S.C.R. 701 at 760–64; *Bouzari v. Iran*, above note 20; *Canadian Foundation for Children, Youth and the Law v. Canada (Attorney General)* (2000), 188 D.L.R. (4th) 718 (Ont. S.C.J.), aff'd (2002), 207 D.L.R. (4th) 632 (Ont. C.A.), aff'd [2004] 1 S.C.R. 76; *Ivanov v. U.S.A.* (2003), 223 Nfld. & P.E.I.R. 33 (Nfld. S.C.T.D.), aff'd (2003), 223 Nfld. & P.E.I.R. 44 (Nfld. C.A.). United States courts regularly admit expert evidence about the content and applicability of customary international law: Harold G. Maier, "Problems of Proving International Human Rights Law in the United States Courts: The Role of Experts in Proving International Human Rights Law in Domestic Courts" (1996) 25 Ga. J. Int'l & Comp. L 205.

46   See, for example, *R .v. Parisien*, [1988] 1 S.C.R. 950.

line between international and comparative law is not as certain as it once was. And there are places in-between. How do we characterize regional organizations to which Canada is not a party but to whom the courts look regularly in assessing disputes, particularly in the area of human rights? Are we to hive this off as an exception and if so why?

Theoretically, the model is also unsatisfactory because it entrenches an approach established in another time and place that may no longer be appropriate, especially, but not exclusively, in relation to the *Charter*. The relevant question is what policies should underline the concept of judicial notice in terms of international law. I would respond by saying that reference should be made to both Canada's international perspective and the objectives of evidence law.

Canada has an internationalist vision.[47] This has at least two consequences. The first is the established principle that Canada should fulfil its international law obligations both in terms of custom and convention. Courts have assisted in this "harmonization" through the doctrine of incorporation and interpretation. I would underscore the importance of this by stating that decisions of the courts become sources of international law. The second is that there is much to be said in favour of an approach that, in making decisions (especially constitutional ones), courts should be able to turn to the approaches and assessment of issues beyond our borders. We are increasingly part of the world.[48] The positive project then is one where international law and, I would argue, comparative law are critical to our development and to resolving increasingly interconnected problems; it is appropriate to refer to both in the interpretation of our law.

If one accepts this project, then the existing model is problematic in two important respects. First, while in theory the traditional approach to

---

47 A recent expression of this is found in the 5 October 2004 Speech from the Throne: "In today's world, effective international engagement is needed to advance national aspirations. Now that time and distance have lost their isolating effect, it is no longer possible to separate domestic and international policies. Canada's internationalism is a real advantage, but we must find new ways to express it if we are to effectively assert our interests and project our values in a changing world."

48 Harold H. Koh, "Agora: The United States Constitution and International Law: International Law as Part of our Law" (2004) 98 A.J.I.L. 43. See also Justice Stephen Breyer, "Keynote Address" (2003) 97 A.S.I.L. Proc. 265 at 267. And see the Hon. Claire L'Heureux-Dubé, "From Many Different Stones: A House of Justice" (2003) 41 Alta. L. Rev. 659; Anne-Marie Slaughter, "A Typology of Transjudicial Communication" (1994) 29 U. Rich. L. Rev. 99; David Kennedy, "New Approaches to Comparative Law: Comparativism and International Governance" (1997) Utah L. Rev. 545.

judicial notice encourages the courts to apply international law, the manner in which it does must be clearly understood. While it may in fact be helping with respect to admissibility, it may be counterproductive to the objective of using international law in another sense. The concern I have with the traditional model is that, if rigidly adhered to, it may in fact result in the courts being less willing to apply international law. Justice LeBel has clearly suggested that the current approach may not always be adequate to the complexity of the issues before the court. This concern would be especially present at the trial level. The obvious and reasonable questions that can be asked are why should courts not have the benefit of expert guidance? And why must courts be restricted to legal argument? Second, the current approach makes it difficult to refer to comparative law when it is precisely comparative examples that may be closer to the ground in terms of the specific issues that are before the court. I would agree, and have argued, that there is a distinction to be drawn between international and comparative law because the former may be binding upon Canada.[49] However, I do not see that the battle of hierarchy needs to be played out at the level of evidence before the court in the rigid manner propounded by the traditional approach to judicial notice.

There are also evidentiary policies that must be considered and that have been essentially ignored in the international discussion of this question. As noted, international lawyers write about the subject of judicial notice as connected to the issue of reception. Fundamentally, however, evidence is a tool that supports a court in its decision-making process. If one leaves aside the dichotomy between fact and law to look more closely at what underlies judicial notice as an evidentiary principle, one will find that it is at base connected to the efficient utilization of knowledge.[50] There is judicial notice of facts of common notoriety because, if facts are commonly known, it saves the process time and costs. Increasingly, there is also reference to legislative and historical facts that are capable of immediate and accurate demonstration by resorting to readily acceptable sources of indisputable accuracy.[51]

---

49   La Forest, "Domestic Application," above note 3 at 185.
50   Ron Delisle & Don Stuart, *Evidence: Principles and Problems*, 6th ed. (Toronto: Carswell, 2001) at 211, citing the *Advisory Committee's Note to Rule 201 of the United States Federal Rules of Evidence* as follows: "The judicial process cannot construct every case from scratch, like Descartes creating a world based on the postulate *Cognito, ergo, sum*."
51   Sopinka, *Evidence*, above note 22 at 1058–65.

From this evidentiary perspective, the problem with the current model is that it is putting the cart before the horse. One cannot say that judges do not have knowledge of international law and then in the same breath say that the doctrine of judicial notice requires that knowledge. The principle has force where there is either such knowledge or it can be easily obtained by reference to basic texts.

In my view, any approach that is adopted and applied should be conscious of the desirability of referring to international and comparative law and the underlying need for knowledge. What is also required is an approach that is flexible. To fulfil the internationalist vision, courts must be able to refer to international law and comparative law without proof. To require proof would necessarily reduce the number of cases in which international and comparative law is part of the analysis and this would not be a positive outcome given Canada's internationalist vision. That said, to the extent that there is limited knowledge of international and comparative law and expert evidence is not allowed, the less likely it is that international and comparative law will be applied in a robust and detailed manner.

When should there be expert evidence? Stated simply, my argument is that this is a matter to be left to the discretion of the court. I would expect that where international and comparative material is referred to and utilized by the court in a manner that is merely interpretive, there would not generally be a need for expert evidence because, in such circumstances, the courts are interpreting the law of Canada and are simply looking either for guidance and assistance with a new problem or are trying to ensure that Canadian law is applied in accordance with Canada's international law obligations.[52] Where, however, as in the case of conflict of laws, international law is directly applicable to the issues before the court and the court is not able to obtain sufficiently clear guidance from readily accessible and credible sources, the court should be able to hear and refer to expert evidence. As has been outlined earlier in the context of comparative law, the fact that there is expert evidence does not mean that international law thereby loses its character as law. Judges are free to accept or reject such material and are unrestricted in their investigation of the law and in their conclusion. On appeal, the judge's assessment is not entitled to deference; it may be accepted or rejected until the Supreme Court of Canada reaches a deter-

---

52 While appropriate as a general rule, there may be situations where the court might find that expert evidence would be of assistance in such cases: see, for example, *Reference re: Bill 7 respecting the criminal justice system for young persons*, [2003] Q.J. No. 2850 (C.A.).

mination. It might finally be added that in the context of international law, the pronouncements of jurists, like those of learned writers, are useful in setting out practices and principles, though they are themselves subsidiary sources of international law.[53] In the next section, this argument is refined with specific reference to customary international law.

C. EVIDENCE AND CUSTOMARY INTERNATIONAL LAW

As noted in the introduction, the traditional approach to judicial notice in the context of international law finds its roots in the case law relating to customary international law. And, as also noted in the introduction, there is to some extent a symbiotic relationship between reception and evidence. As such, it is appropriate to discuss customary international law in terms of the principles outlined in the previous part of this chapter.

The test for establishing the existence of a principle of customary international law has been described as straightforward.[54] It is twofold and involves an objective and a subjective element.[55] First, the courts must be shown *evidence* of a general though not universal degree of state practice, and second, there must be a determination that states conceive themselves as being under a legal obligation to act in accordance with that principle. This latter subjective element is described as *opinio juris*.[56]

There is general academic support for the proposition that in terms of reception, custom should be directly incorporated into the law of Canada.[57] This is to say that it should be binding and part of the law of Canada unless it is in direct conflict with domestic law. It is also to say that in the case of custom, the courts rather than Parliament should be the ones to determine the existence of a principle of customary international law. This "monist" position has much to do with the connection between custom and the common law in the development of international law. This connection is not surprising; just as the law in England in its earliest stage was largely common law rather than statute, the law of nations in its earliest stages was primarily custom rather than treaty. Custom developed in much the

---

53 *R. v. Finta*, above note 45 at 762.

54 Van Ert, *Using International Law*, above note 8 at 20.

55 *North Sea Continental Shelf Case*, [1969] I.C.J. 3 at paras. 73–77.

56 La Forest, "Domestic Application," above note 3 at 192.

57 See, for example, Brunnée & Toope, "A Hesitant Embrace," above note 6 at 50; Stephen Toope, "Inside and Out: The State of International Law and Domestic Law" (2001) 50 U.N.B.L.J. 11 at 21; William Schabas, "Twenty-five Years of Public International Law at the Supreme Court of Canada" (2000) 79 Can. Bar Rev. 174 at 182.

same way as the common law, through experience and evolving consensus rather than through explicit agreement. In a number of eighteenth- and nineteenth-century English decisions, this connection was made explicit; Lord Mansfield and others stated that the law of nations was part of the common law of England.[58] In an international case, Lord Moore stated that custom was tied to the great stream of the common law.[59] The position in English law was applied in a number of Canadian cases.[60] Incorporation has remained the position in England though there were considerable challenges to that position beginning in the twentieth century.[61] Any doubt, however, ended with the decision in *Trendex Corp. v. The Central Bank of Nigeria*.[62] Similar monist positions are expressed in Australian and American authority.[63]

In terms of evidence, the test outlined at the outset of this section suggests that evidence is necessary to establish custom. However, if custom is indeed the law of the land, then the argument in favour of judicial notice, as traditionally understood, is a strong one. It is a near perfect syllogism. If custom is the law of the land, and the law of the land is to be judicially noticed, then custom should be judicially noticed. Van Ert states this argument very well as follows:

> Customary international law must be noticed by Canadian courts to give effect to the doctrine of incorporation (whereby customary international

---

58 *Barbuit's Case*, above note 42; *Triquet v. Bath*, above note 42 at 1480–81 (Burr.) and at 937–38 (E.R.); *Heathfield v. Chilton*, above note 42 at 2016 (Burr.) and at 51 (E.R.); *Duke of Brunswick v. The King of Hanover*, above note 42 at 45 (Beav.) and at 741 (E.R.); *Emperor of Austria v. Day and Kossuth* (1861), 2 Giff. 628 at 678, 66 E.R. 263 at 282. See also *Blackstone's Commentaries on the Law of England*.

59 *The Lotus*, [1927] P.C.I.J. Series A, No. 10 at 75.

60 *The Ship "The North" v. The King*, above note 41 (1906); *Dunbar and Sullivan Dredging Co. v. The Ship "Milwaukee"* (1907), 11 Ex. C.R. 179 at 188; *Re Power of the Corporation of the City of Ottawa and the Corporation of the Village of Rockliffe Park to Levy Rates on Foreign Legations and High Commissioners' Residences*, [1943] S.C.R. 208; *Reference as to Whether Members of the Military or Naval Forces of the United States of America are Exempt From Criminal Proceedings in Canadian Courts*, [1943] S.C.R. 483; *Saint John v. Fraser-Brace Overseas*, above note 44.

61 MacDonald, "Relationship between International and Domestic Law," above note 7, discussing *R. v. Keyn (The Franconia)* (1876), 2 Ex. D. 63; *Chung Chi Cheung v. The King*, [1939] A.C. 160 (P.C.). In favour he cites *West Rand Central Mining Co. v. The King*, [1905] 2 K.B. 391.

62 [1977] 1 Q.B. 529 (C.A.). See also *Congreso del Partido*, [1983] 1 A.C. 244 (H.L.).

63 *Mabo v. Queensland (No. 2)* (1992), 175 C.L.R. 1 (H.C.A.) and *Paquete Habana* (1900), 175 U.S. 677, 20 Su. Ct. 290.

law is incorporated into the common law). Incorporation means that customary international law and the common law are one. Thus, a failure to take judicial notice of international custom is also a failure to take judicial notice of the common law.[64]

A necessary corollary to this argument is that expert evidence must be excluded because to state otherwise is to usurp the role of the court. While there is limited direct judicial pronouncement to this effect,[65] the application of judicial notice seems to have been adopted in a number of early decisions.[66] In *The North*,[67] the Supreme Court of Canada stated that the right of hot pursuit, being part of the law of nations, was properly judicially noticed and acted upon. Furthermore, it is also the position articulated in *Trendex*[68] by both Lord Denning and Lord Stephenson and most recently in the Scottish *Ploughshares*[69] case.

In juxtaposition to the clarity of the material just outlined, it is also almost universally acknowledged that the Supreme Court of Canada has vacillated on the status of custom; there has been no clear statement that the monist approach should apply to custom.[70] Stephen Toope has pointed out that the Supreme Court of Canada has not, since the *Charter*, clarified whether custom is merely compelling or binding.[71] More recently, writing

---

64 Van Ert, *Using International Law*, above note 8 at 33–34. See also above note 10. As noted in above note 12, van Ert has refined this position somewhat in terms of customary international law.

65 MacDonald, "Relationship between International and Domestic Law," above note 7 at 113, citing Lauterpacht, "Is International Law Part of the Law of England?" above note 40 at 59: "While judicial practice supports the position that international law is judicially noticed, it is difficult to trace judicial pronouncements." Van Ert states that *Halsbury's Laws of England*, vol. 17, 4th ed., above note 39 at para. 100, is the best authority for the proposition.

66 See *Triquet v. Bath*, above note 42. See also *The Scotia*, above note 35 at 188; *The New York*, above note 35. A more recent example referred to by van Ert is *Jose Pereira E Hijos S.A. v. Canada (Attorney General)*, above note 41.

67 Above note 41.

68 Above note 62.

69 *Lord Advocate's Reference No. 1 of 2000*, above note 41.

70 Cases that have been critiqued on this basis include: *Re Newfoundland Continental Shelf*, [1984] 1 S.C.R. 86; *Reference re Succession of Quebec*, [1998] 2 S.C.R. 217; *114957 Canada Ltee (Spraytech Société d'arrosage) v. Hudson (Town)*, [2001] 2 S.C.R. 241; *Suresh v. Canada (Minister of Citizenship and Immigration)*, [2002] 1 S.C.R. 3.

71 Toope, "Inside and Out," above note 57 at 21. He further states that it was only prior to 1943 that the courts were fairly consistent in favouring the monist approach. The apex of the adoptionist approach involved two cases of sovereign immunity. See also

with Jutta Brunnée, Toope has said that custom should be directly applicable but that it is currently unclear:

> Customary international law should be directly applicable—it is part of Canadian law. This means that Canadian courts, to the extent possible, should strive to interpret both statutes and the common law to be consistent with Canada's obligations under customary international law. However, the approach of senior Canadian courts to customary international law is utterly unclear.[72]

William Schabas has also decried the failure of the Supreme Court of Canada to take the opportunity to apply customary international law.[73] And van Ert, while arguing forcefully that custom, like the common law, does, in Canadian jurisprudence, form part of the law of the land, acknowledges that the courts have not been clear in this regard.[74] One notable exception is *Bouzari v. Iran*,[75] a case discussed at the end of this part. It is also apparent that the courts are increasingly referring to expert evidence in relation to international law, *Bouzari* being a most prominent example.[76] Courts then are ambivalent about incorporation of custom and are looking for expert evidence. Is there a reason for this?

In another article addressing the domestic implementation of international human rights law, I questioned the continued appropriateness of the monist approach to customary international law.[77] I did so on two bases: the recent evolution of international customary law; and, the propriety of domestic courts assessing when something has become a custom. The first of these points is directly at issue in the present context.[78]

In terms of this first point, the argument is that from an evolutionary perspective, custom, in its earliest stages evolved relatively slowly and was closely connected to the development of the common law. As law in

---

Stephen Toope, "The Uses of Metaphor: International Law and the Supreme Court of Canada" (2001) 80 Can. Bar Rev. 534 and John Currie, *Public International Law* (Toronto: Irwin Law, 2001) at 201.

72 Brunnée & Toope, "A Hesitant Embrace," above note 6 at 50.

73 Schabas, "Twenty-Five Years," above note 57 at 182.

74 Van Ert, *Using International Law*, above note 8 at 21 and 149.

75 Above note 20.

76 *Ibid.*

77 La Forest, "Domestic Application," above note 3 at 191–94.

78 I continue to have concerns with respect to the role of Canadian courts in determining the existence of customary international law principles especially where based upon treaties that have not been transformed.

the domestic context has moved from a primary focus upon the common law, to legislation and administrative regulation, a parallel development has occurred internationally. International law has evolved from a set of customary understandings between states (especially in relation to such matters as sovereign immunity, the law of the sea, and the laws of war), to the development of treaties, to the establishment of international organizations addressing many complex aspects of the relations between states. This evolution has been particularly evident in both domestic and international law since the end of the Second World War.

The cases to which academics refer in supporting the monist approach are almost entirely in the areas of sovereign immunity, the law of the sea, and the laws of war, and almost all pre-date or end roughly after the end of the Second World War. State practice, or the law of nations, had evolved quite slowly and was not foreign to the domestic law of England. It was thus not difficult for Lord Mansfield to say, in the domestic context, that the law of nations was part of the law of England and for Lord Moore, in the international context, to say that custom was tied to the great stream of the common law. Correspondingly, in evidentiary terms, it was not difficult to rely upon the doctrine of judicial notice as traditionally expounded because the law was known or could be easily accessed and assessed.

The assessment of custom is now far more complex and is not so easily known. It is said to require an extensive summary of the practice of nations.[79] Contemporary international law touches virtually every facet of life and many matters that would previously have not been considered international. Custom today does not only include slowly evolving practices, but may involve inquiring whether a treaty has become custom. And it is no longer simply a matter of looking to state practice. Such diverse sources as United Nations General Assembly Resolutions, the writings of publicists, the statements of international agencies, and the comments and decisions of expert bodies set up under the terms of treaties must also be examined.[80] International tribunals themselves acknowledge that the assessment of custom is a difficult matter.[81] It may reasonably be asked, then, whether the assessment of custom appropriately falls within the parameters of judicial notice. I would suggest that it does not and might go some

---

79   *R. v. Finta*, above note 45 at 773.

80   Brunnée & Toope, "A Hesitant Embrace," above note 6 at 12–13.

81   *Delimitation of the Maritime Boundary in the Gulf of Maine Area (Canada v. United States)*, [1984] I.C.J. 246 at para. 111.

way to explaining the reluctance of senior courts to clarify the position in relation to custom.[82] Reviewing Justice LeBel's comment at the outset of this article, there is strong reason to believe that courts are not comfortable with the traditional approach. If one accepts this argument, it becomes apparent that holding steadfast to the doctrine of judicial notice in its most traditional sense may in fact not result in the application of international law. Perhaps we should return to the test for custom as expounded at the outset of this section; that is, that there be sufficient evidence presented of a general though not universal practice.

It is useful to highlight the preceding discussion by referring directly to two cases addressing a fairly similar question: *Trendex*—the decision described as providing the clearest statement to the effect that custom is incorporated into domestic law; and *Bouzari*—a recent Canadian case in which reference was made to expert evidence.

In *Trendex*, the court was faced with the task of assessing whether there had been a change in the scope of the international customary principle relating to sovereign immunity. Specifically, the court was asked whether there was exception to sovereign immunity in the case of commercial activity. In terms of the approach to assessment of custom, Lord Denning had this to say:

> Like all rules of international law, this rule [the doctrine of state immunity] is said to arise out of the consensus of the civilised nationals of the world. All nations agree upon it. So it is part of the law of nations. To my mind, this notion of consensus is a fiction... Yet this does not mean that there is no rule of international law upon the subject. It only means that we differ as to what that rule is. Each country delimits for itself the bounds of sovereign immunity.... *It is I think for the courts of this country to define the rule as best they can, seeking guidance from the decisions of the courts of other countries, from the jurists who have studied the problem, from treaties and conventions and, above all, defining the rule in terms which are consonant with justice rather than adverse to it* (emphasis added).[83]

---

82 Brunnée & Toope, "A Hesitant Embrace," above note 6 at 15–16: "Indeed, we suspect that the fluidity of custom and the challenges involved in determining whether a norm has acquired customary law status go a long way toward explaining the reluctance of senior Canadian courts to apply customary law."
83 Above note 62 at 552.

The actual assessment involved reference to the following materials: Hersch Lauterpacht's "The Problem of Jurisdictional Immunities of Foreign States"; the 1952 "Tate" letter; and, a "valuable collection of recent decisions in which the courts of Belgium, Holland, the German Federal Republic, the United States of America *and others* granted only restrictive immunity."[84]

After reviewing this material, Lord Denning concluded as follows:

> Seeing this great cloud of witnesses, I would ask: is there not here sufficient evidence to show that the rule of international law has changed? What more is needed? Are we to wait until every country save England recognises the change? ... "We must take the current when it serves, or lose our ventures" (*Julius Caesar*, Act IV, Sc. III).[85]

Unless the custom at issue in a case is relatively straightforward and can be easily assessed by reference to standard materials, I do not find this a particularly compelling standard of assessment. In this regard, it is noteworthy that the case addressed sovereign immunity and none of the materials examined were particularly complex; all were European or American.

The case of *Bouzari v. Iran*[86] also addresses the scope of sovereign immunity. There, the plaintiff had been tortured in Iran and sought to take a civil action against that state in the province of Ontario. The *State Immunity Act*[87] imposes limitations upon the ability to sue a foreign state in a Canadian court. The plaintiff argued that the prohibition against torture was a principle *of jus cogens* and that an exception should be read into the Act to permit a civil action for damages for torture against a foreign state. Justice Swinton relied on the Federal Court of Appeal decision in *Suresh*,[88] stating that customary rules of international law are directly incorporated into Canadian domestic law unless ousted by contrary legislation. However, in contrast to the approach in *Trendex*, she also allowed expert evidence and stated that "such experts can assist the court in determining the applicable international law by setting out the relevant sources and describing the

---

84   *Ibid.* at 555–56; Hersch Lauterpacht, "The Problem of Jurisdictional Immunities of Foreign States" (1951) 28 Brit. Y.B. Int'l L. 220.

85   Above note 62 at 556.

86   Above note 20.

87   R.S.C. 1985, c. S-18.

88   *Suresh v. Canada (Minister of Citizenship and Immigration)* (2000), 183 D.L.R. (4th) 629 at 659 (F.C.A.). On appeal, the Supreme Court of Canada (above note 70) did not state this principle.

general principles of law accepted in the international community."[89] In the result, she determined that the legislation at issue, the *State Immunity Act*, codified the law of state immunity in Canada and that any further exception would be for Parliament.[90] Based upon her assessment of the expert evidence before her, she also determined that the legislation in its current form was consistent with both customary international law respecting state immunity and Canada's treaty obligations; no international undertaking or rule of customary international law required Canada to provide a civil remedy for acts of torture that took place outside of Canada.[91] The Court of Appeal upheld this decision and leave to the Supreme Court of Canada has been refused.[92]

I agree with the approach taken in *Bouzari*. It is apparent that judicial notice may well be an incomplete tool. If, in fact, the reason courts are not applying custom relates to its complexity, then how can the doctrine of judicial notice be appropriate? If custom is to be directly applicable, then it should be known with some certainty. Is it petulant to argue that the position, with respect to custom as part of the law of the land, might be more compelling if there was greater certainty about when something is indeed custom? In other words, instead of coupling reception with judicial notice, why not frame the argument in different terms. Specifically, if we accept that custom should be the law of the land but that courts are not applying it because there is uncertainty as to when something is in fact custom, then I would think it counterproductive to state that judges must decide these matters on their own, because it is for them to know the law as part of their role. Would it not make greater sense to have clarity and certainty that something is understood to be a custom before applying it as law? This is completely consonant with both international and evidentiary policy.

One shortcoming of such an approach that I can see is that if there is expert evidence in relation to international law, it may be incorrectly considered to be fact rather than law. Indeed, the uncertainty of how to treat such evidence makes an appearance in the Court of Appeal decision in *Bouzari*:

> However, the more fundamental question is whether Canada has the international law obligation contended for by the appellant. After careful con-

---

89 Above note 20 at para. 37 (S.C.J.).
90 *Ibid.* at para. 41 (S.C.J.).
91 *Ibid.* at para. 42 (S.C.J.).
92 *Ibid.*

sideration, the motion judge concluded that it does not. She analyzed this first as a matter of treaty law and then of customary international law. In both contexts, she relies on the expert evidence of Professor Greenwood concerning the scope of Canada's international law obligations. She preferred this evidence to that of Professor Morgan because she found Professor Greenwood to be more helpful on the issue she had to decide, namely, the current state of international law.... *While the motion judge's acceptance of Professor Greenwood's opinion over that of Professor Morgan is not a finding of fact by a trial judge, it is a finding based on the evidence she heard and is therefore owed a certain deference in this court. I would depart from it only if there were good reason to do so, and, having examined the transcript, I can find none. Indeed, for the reason she gave, I agree with her reliance on Professor Greenwood's evidence* (emphasis added).[93]

It is clear that the Court of Appeal has recognized that the assessment of international law is not a matter of fact and is careful to state that it *agrees* with the conclusion of Justice Swinton. I think that this is right. As stated earlier, the fact that there is evidence about international or comparative law does not mean it is fact. It is still law. However, in my view, the deference to be afforded to a lower court should not differ from that generally afforded to any decision of law. The purpose of expert evidence of international law must be to assist the court in making a decision; it is not to turn over the penultimate decision to Professor Greenwood or any other expert, for such individuals are themselves subsidiary sources of international law.

D. CONCLUSION

The purpose of this chapter has been to provide a foundational review of judicial notice, its connection to expert evidence, and its application to domestic, comparative, and international law. As noted, the jurisprudence in this area directly addressing international law is strongly connected to the early evolution of customary international law and its reception into domestic law. Under this approach, customary international law is judicially noticed because it is also domestic law. I have tried to argue that the approach established by this authority may no longer be appropriate to the current context, in large part, because custom is increasingly complex and not easily accessible or assessed as being domestic law. The claim is thus

---

93 *Ibid.* at 691 (C.A.).

made that a more flexible approach may be desirable. There is no doubt that international law is relevant in our modern world and there is no question that international law is law and that proof thereof should not be required. However, the argument has been made that expert evidence may in fact assist the court in its role of harmonizing international and domestic law. It has also been argued that the courts should be more open to the review of international and comparative law in assessing increasingly interconnected problems. That, however, does not end the discussion in terms of evidence. Further work is required in terms of treaties and the *Charter*. In this conclusion, I very briefly consider these matters.

A review of how treaties become part of Canadian law discloses a paradigm similar to that explored in relation to customary international law. Historically, and under current jurisprudence, Canada has operated on the basis of a fairly narrow "dualist" model. Specifically, while the executive has the authority to enter into treaties, the treaties must be constitutionally transformed (or explicitly implemented) into domestic law by the appropriate legislative branch[94] before they are considered to be binding by the judicial branch.[95] More recently, it has been held that where a treaty has been legislatively transformed, the court is to interpret the treaty in accordance with the underlying treaty.[96] This development is a positive one because it results in a more cohesive relationship between national and international law in cases where a treaty has been ratified by the executive and transformed by the appropriate legislative branch. Within this framework, judicial notice, as traditionally expounded, would seem to be appropriate because a treaty that has been legislatively transformed is the law of the land. While I have argued that this is a matter that should be left to the discretion of the court, it should be expected that in most cases expert evidence would be excluded.

---

94 This refers to the division of powers between the federal and provincial governments in sections 91 and 92 of the *Constitution Act*, 1867 (U.K.), 30 & 31 Vict., c. 3, reprinted in R.S.C. 1985, App. II, No 5. While the federal executive may ratify a treaty, the government with authority over the subject matter of the treaty has the authority to enact the legislation: *Attorney-General for Canada v. Attorney-General for Ontario*, [1937] A.C. 326 (J.C.P.C.).

95 *Francis v. R.*, [1956] S.C.R. 618; *Capital Cities Communications Inc. v. C.R.T.C.*, above note 41. See also *Thomson v. Thomson*, [1994] 3 S.C.R. 551 at 611–12.

96 See *National Corn Growers Association v. Canada (Import Tribunal)*, [1990] 2 S.C.R. 1324, *Canada (Attorney General) v. Ward*, [1993] 2 S.C.R. 689, and *Pushpanathan v. Canada (Minister of Citizenship and Immigration)*, [1998] 1 S.C.R. 982.

The framework, as described however, is deceptively simple. As Toope and Brunnée state: "Beneath the surface of this straightforward [approach] … lies an array of twists and turns that make the domestic application of treaties complex territory to navigate."[97] For example, entirely apart from the fact that transformation through legislation can take many forms,[98] the executive increasingly enters into treaties upon the basis of prior conformity with Canadian law and policy.[99] Courts, however, have held firmly to the position that such treaties are not part of Canadian law unless implemented by statute.[100] Academics have argued forcefully that treaties ratified by Canada on this basis should be considered as implicitly implemented for purposes of domestic law and subject to the same interpretive principles as other international obligations that are part of Canadian law.[101] They argue that the courts approach to prior conformity is overly restrictive.[102]

---

97 Brunnée & Toope, "A Hesitant Embrace," above note 6 at 20–21.

98 See, for example, Gibran van Ert, "What is Treaty Implementation" in *Legitimacy and Accountability in International Law*, (2004) *Proceedings of the 33rd Annual Conference of the C.C.I.L.* at 168–69, and Elisabeth Eid & Hoori Hamboyan, "Implementation by Canada of its International Human Rights Treaty Obligations: Making Sense out of the Nonsensical" in *Legitimacy and Accountability in International Law*, (2004) Proceedings of the 33rd Annual Conference of C.C.I.L. 175 at 178–82.

99 Weiser, "Undressing the Window," above note 6 at 127. See also Eid & Hamboyan, "Implementation by Canada," *ibid*. at 182.

100 *Baker v. Canada (Minister of Citizenship and Immigration)*, above note 2, *Ahani v. Canada (Attorney General)* (2002), 58 O.R. (3d) 107 (C.A.), *Suresh v. Canada*, above note 70. There is also a judicial canon of interpretation to the effect that the court should interpret domestic law in accordance with Canada's international obligations subject to the sovereign right to legislate in violation of international law: see *Daniels v. White*, [1968] S.C.R. 517; *Zingre v. The Queen*, [1981] 2 S.C.R. 392, *Schreiber v. Canada (Attorney General)*, [2002] 3 S.C.R. 269, and Ruth Sullivan, *Driedger on the Construction of Statutes*, 3d ed. (Markham: Butterworths, 1994) at 330. Under the *Vienna Convention on the Law of Treaties*, 23 May 1969, 1155 U.N.T.S. 331, Can. T.S. 1980 No. 37 Art. 27: A party may not invoke the provisions of its internal law as justification for failure to perform a treaty. Even in this case, there is concern that too wide an application of the principle has the impact of undermining the requirement that treaties be transformed. It has been observed that courts are increasingly inclined to approach unimplemented treaties as relevant and persuasive and are not distinguishing between treaties that are binding on Canada and ones that are not: Brunnée & Toope, "A Hesitant Embrace," above note 6 at 51–52.

101 See, for example, Brunnée & Toope, *ibid*. at 26–27; J. Currie, *Public International Law*, above note 71 at 209; van Ert, "Treaty Implementation," above note 98 at 167.

102 Brunée & Toope, "A Hesitant Embrace," above note 6 at 26 and van Ert, "Treaty Implementation," above note 98 at 167.

What does this mean in terms of judicial notice and evidence? While judicial notice may be appropriate in the case of explicit transformation, it is far less clear that judicial notice is a complete tool in the case of implicit transformation. Even if one agrees that a more expansive approach to implicit implementation is desirable on the basis that it is more consistent with respect for Canada's international law obligations, a question arises as to the assessment of prior conformity. This is not presently a matter capable of immediate and accurate demonstration by reference to acceptable sources of indisputable accuracy.[103] There are proposals suggesting that there should be a public record of the legislation, policies, and programs that are relied upon to assert compliance[104] but in the absence of such a record, it seems somewhat questionable to expect a court to fulfil this role through the principle of judicial notice. Again, it is not unreasonable to argue that part of the courts' reluctance to adopt a more expansive approach to implementation can be explained by the uncertainty as to the effect of the treaty provisions in domestic law.[105]

In drafting the *Charter*, there was certainly reference to existing international, regional, and comparative human rights documents, many of which Canada is not party to.[106] And, in entering into new human rights treaties and obligations, the executive has relied upon prior conformity, using the *Charter* and jurisprudence thereunder.[107] It is difficult to argue, however, that the *Charter* was intended to directly transform and incorporate specific international law obligations.[108] In my view, the courts have rightly taken the approach that international law is "relevant and persua-

---

103 See Eid & Hamboyan, "Implementation by Canada," above note 98 at 187. "[L]itigants and judges have difficulty determining what specific legislation and policies were relied upon that showed pre-exisiting compliance." See also van Ert, "Treaty Implementation," above note 98 at 171.

104 Eid & Hamboyan, "Implementation by Canada," above note 98 at 187. See also Weiser, "Undressing the Window," above note 6 at 144.

105 There are of course other reasons why courts may be reluctant to take an expansive approach: see Stéphane Beaulac, "International Treaty Norms and Dreidger's 'Modern' Principal of Statutory Interpretation" in *Legitimacy and Accountability in International Law*, (2004) Proceedings of the 33rd Annual Conference of C.C.I.L. 141 at 147–50.

106 Anne F. Bayefsky, *International Human Rights Law: Use in Canadian Charter of Rights and Freedoms Litigation* (Toronto: Butterworths, 1992) at 33–49.

107 Eid & Hamboyan, "Implementation by Canada," above note 98 at 182.

108 La Forest, "Domestic Implementation," above note 3 at 187.

sive." They have looked to international and comparative law for guidance and assistance when faced with problems of *Charter* interpretation.[109]

I have stated earlier in this paper that the courts should be open to international and comparative law and that when such material is referred to and utilized in a manner that is merely interpretive, there would not generally be a need to refer to expert evidence. Given this, one might expect that the conclusion should be that, in the context of the *Charter*, there is little need for expert evidence. However, I believe the matter to be more nuanced than this. In another article, I argued that where the court chooses to rely upon international and comparative law in a significant way, the court should engage in a more detailed and thorough analysis of that law.[110] As also noted in this paper, when international or comparative law is directly applicable to the issues before the court and the court is not able to obtain sufficiently clear guidance from readily accessible sources, the court should be able to rely upon expert evidence. In short, expert evidence should be used as a procedural tool to allow the court to fulfil its decision-making role.

Leaving aside the procedural question of evidence and international and comparative law, my argument, more generally, has been that the courts should refer to international and comparative law, but, in so doing, they must take a fuller measure of its meaning before relying upon it.[111] The means by which this should come to pass includes, of course ,judicial education. It is certainly also important that counsel become more knowledgeable in understanding and arguing international and comparative law. The simple argument in this article is that at present, expert evidence too can have a role to play and should not be excluded on the basis of a traditional analysis that does not serve current needs.

---

109 *Ibid.* at 170.
110 *Ibid.* at 195–96: "As with any source of law that is raised, international and comparative law must be examined fully if it is to form the basis of a decision."
111 *Ibid.* at 217.

Part Three:

CASE STUDIES

Section A:
THE SPECIAL CASE OF IMPLEMENTING HUMAN
RIGHTS TREATIES WHOSE STANDARDS EVOLVE
DOMESTICALLY AND INTERNATIONALLY:
CURRENT PRACTICE AND REFORM

12

Making a Difference: The Canadian Duty to Consult and Emerging International Norms Respecting Consultation with Indigenous Peoples

STEFAN MATIATION AND JOSÉE BOUDREAU[*]

A. INTRODUCTION

Consultation with Indigenous[1] peoples has become a matter of high priority over the past few years in Canada and internationally. The topic arises in relation to a variety of issues, including: access to Indigenous knowledge, innovations, and practices; land use and natural resource development decision-making; the delivery of health care and conduct of research on human subjects; legislation and policy-making generally; and the relocation of communities. This chapter focuses on consultation with Indigenous groups in the context of land and natural resource development

---

[*] The authors would like to take this opportunity to express special thanks for the comments and support provided by their fellow colleagues, including Richard Boivin and Sylvia Batt. The opinions expressed in this article are solely those of the authors and do not represent the views of the Department of Justice or the government of Canada. Any errors or omissions are solely those of the authors.

[1] In keeping with international practice, the term *Indigenous* is used in the chapter when referring to Indigenous peoples or individuals in general. The international community has not elaborated a widely accepted definition for this term. However, certain elements may be relevant, such as self-identification as Indigenous, distinctive cultural and social characteristics, historic continuity with prior inhabitants of a region, etc. (For a discussion, see Benedict Kingsbury, "Indigenous Peoples in International Law: A Constructivist Approach to the Asian Controversy" (1998) 92 Am. J. Int'l Law 414). For the purposes of this chapter, it is sufficient to say that the term includes the Aboriginal peoples of Canada. *Aboriginal peoples* (or groups, communities, people, individuals) is the term used when referring to the Canadian context. Pursuant to s. 35(2) of the *Constitution Act, 1982*, the Aboriginal peoples of Canada include the "Indian, Inuit and Métis peoples of Canada."

decision-making. More and more, Indigenous groups are insisting that they be consulted and that their interests be accommodated when governments and private industry are planning activities that could have an impact on them.

Two questions are addressed in this chapter: 1) Do states have any obligations under international law to consult with Indigenous communities before making land or natural resource development decisions that affect them, and if so, when? 2) What observations can be made about the law and experience in Canada respecting consultation with aboriginal communities that could inform efforts at the international level or in other countries to develop, clarify, or fulfil such obligations?

The approach taken to consultation with Indigenous groups as a matter of international law is still imprecise. This should come as no surprise given the fact that a widely accepted elaboration of Indigenous land and resource rights, or of the circumstances in which consultations with Indigenous communities may be required, has not yet achieved international consensus. Meanwhile, consultation is a preoccupation in Canada in light of ongoing treaty negotiations and current uncertainty regarding the existence of specific Aboriginal rights, including Aboriginal title, in some parts of the country. The recent *Haida* and *Taku River* judgments from the Supreme Court of Canada have given further impetus to the view that a consultative approach should be embraced in the field of Aboriginal affairs as a matter of good public policy, transformative governance, and astute risk management. Consultation is at the heart of the principle that underlies Aboriginal law in Canada—the reconciliation of Aboriginal and non-Aboriginal Canadians for the benefit and enrichment of both.[2]

A framework for consultations with Aboriginal people can be identified in Canadian law and experience. Drawing out general observations about this framework may be useful to members of the international community, including other countries, intergovernmental organizations, relevant treaty bodies, Indigenous groups, and industry, when they grapple with consultation issues and challenges.

---

2   John Borrows, a leading academic in the field of Aboriginal law in Canada, is a champion of the reconciliation theme. See, for example, John Borrows, *Recovering Canada: The Resurgence of Indigenous Law* (Toronto: University of Toronto, 2002).

B. CONSULTATION UNDER INTERNATIONAL LAW

1) Framing the Discussion

Over the course of the last twenty-five years or so, Indigenous people have emerged as one of the most important "non-state" actors in the international system.[3] Despite the considerable success they have had in making their voices heard at the international level, a widely accepted elaboration of their rights at international law has not yet occurred. Instead, Indigenous rights and issues are addressed piecemeal in a few instruments, by different treaty bodies and through various processes. The lack of a widely accepted elaboration—a declaration endorsed by the members of the United Nations or a widely ratified international convention, for example—does not mean that international norms respecting international Indigenous rights are not evolving. Some commentators argue that such norms have already emerged and are part of customary international law—the body of international law derived from state practice that is undertaken on the basis of a widely held view that such practice is governed by internationally recognized rules.[4] Although there continues to be room for debate about the status at international law of rights claimed by Indigenous groups, like Mr. Jones—an everyman bewildered by social change in Bob Dylan's "Ballad of a Thin Man"—it cannot be denied by international participants that "something is happening" even if they "don't know what it is"[5] in relation to the process of international norm-creation respecting Indigenous rights.

Something is clearly happening in relation to the topic of consultation with Indigenous peoples in connection with land and natural resource de-

---

3   Although it is true that Indigenous peoples are more "present" in international fora than they probably ever have been, consideration of Indigenous peoples has been a preoccupation of international law scholars before. Prof. Anaya traces the changes in the way that Indigenous peoples were viewed by international law scholars from the early days of international law theory to the early-twentieth century when the state sovereignty-based approach to international law really took hold. Basically, the "international law status" of Indigenous peoples declined in the eyes of international law commentators over the course of that period: James Anaya, *Indigenous Peoples in International Law*, 2d ed. (New York: Oxford University Press, 2004). See also Felix Cohen, "The Spanish Origin of Indian Rights in the Law of the United States" (1942) 31 Geo. L.J. 1; and for a discussion of the matter from the perspective of British imperial law, see Russel Barsh, "Indigenous Rights and the *Lex Loci* in British Imperial Law" in Kerry Wilkins, ed., *Advancing Aboriginal Claims* (Saskatoon: Purich, 2004).

4   For argument in favour of the proposition that Indigenous rights are part of customary international law, see Anaya, *Indigenous Peoples, ibid.*

5   Bob Dylan, "Ballad of a Thin Man," copyright 1965.

velopment activities. Certain terms are used in the context of Indigenous issues in a variety of places in the international system with a regularity and consistency that suggests they are taking hold as principles carrying some level of force, or at least, that their level of force is ripe for investigation. Consultation is one such term. It comes up in a number of contexts that have significance for international law creation.

Before turning to a discussion of those contexts, we wish to make a few comments about terminology. The terms *consultation, participation,* and *free, prior and informed consent* (FPIC) are sometimes used interchangeably in materials addressing the issue of Indigenous involvement in decision-making. Of these terms, FPIC is the most controversial because it seems to signal that Indigenous versus non-Indigenous relations are a zero sum game in which there is always a winner and a loser.[6] For many Indigenous people this has been the experience to date. It is therefore not surprising when they react with skepticism to calls for relationship-building rather than the adoption of absolute standards. However, the point of a consultative approach is to overcome the problems of a zero sum game, and instead give Indigenous peoples a key or even controlling role in developments that are important to their communities.

"FPIC" is sometimes used as an expression of the appropriate standard of Indigenous involvement with respect to land-use decisions. Under this standard it is not enough to consult with Indigenous peoples about natural resource development projects that will affect them; they have a right of FPIC.[7] States generally resist the notion that Indigenous groups have a

---

6 It is interesting to note that FPIC appears to have roots outside of the Indigenous rights debate. It is a term that is familiar to those working in the medical field, where it is generally regarded as a prerequisite to research on human subjects or to medical investigations or treatment of patients. It is also used in the environmental field in the context of a state's control over the transportation of hazardous materials into its territory (for example, the *Rotterdam Convention on the Prior Informed Consent Procedure for Certain Hazardous Chemicals and Pesticides in International Trade,* online: www.pic. int) or of genetic resources out of its territory (the *Convention on Biological Diversity* [CBD], discussed further below). The origins of FPIC are briefly discussed in Anne Perrault, "Facilitating Prior Informed Consent in the Context of Genetic Resources and Traditional Knowledge" (2004) 4 Sustainable Dev. L. & Pol'y 21. Although beyond the scope of this chapter, it may be informative to review sources from the medical and environmental fields describing what is required in order to satisfy an FPIC standard.

7 See Fergus MacKay, "Indigenous Peoples' Right to Free, Prior and Informed Consent and the World Bank's Extractive Industries Review" (2004) 4 Sustainable Dev. L. & Pol'y 43. Also, see the statement made by the Indian Law Resource Centre at the UN Permanent Forum on Indigenous Issues (PFII) international seminar on the "method-

consent-based veto on development in all cases. This may be because they regard it as contrary to the principle of state sovereignty and potentially contrary to the theory that national governments represent all of their citizens and must have the authority to balance competing interests for the greater good of the country as a whole.[8]

The different views regarding the question of a right of FPIC are illustrated in the debate that has followed the publication of the final report of the World Bank-commissioned *Extractive Industries Review* in December 2003, and subsequent release of the Bank's response to that document. One of the conclusions arrived at by the author of the review is that "Indigenous peoples and other affected parties have the right to participate in decision-making and to give their free, prior and informed consent throughout each phase of a project cycle."[9] World Bank management has declined to endorse the concept of a right to FPIC. Instead, the Bank intends to respect the principle of "free, prior and informed consultation" when considering whether to finance development projects.[10] The Bank

---

ologies of free, prior and informed consent and Indigenous peoples," held in January 2005 (UN Doc. PFII/2004/WS.2/6). Similarly, the PFII does not distinguish among FPIC, consultation, and participation. Rather, it collapses all the terms and promotes the view that Indigenous peoples have a right to FPIC with respect to development decisions that affect them. See *Report of the International Workshop on Methodologies Regarding Free, Prior and Informed Consent and Indigenous Peoples, FPIC Workshop*, UN Doc. E.C.19/2005/3, 17 February 2005. The documents referred to in these footnotes from the FPIC Workshop are online: www.un.org/esa/socdev/unpfii.

8 See *Statement by the Observer Delegation of Canada on Agenda Item 5: Examples of applications of the principle of FPIC at the national and international levels, FPIC Workshop*, UN Doc. PFII/2005/WS.2/17/Add.1, esp. para. 17. As is mentioned in the next part of this chapter, the Supreme Court of Canada has come out against the notion of an Indigenous veto on development.

9 *Striking a Better Balance—The World Bank Group and Extractive Industries: Final Report of the Extractive Industries Review*, vol. 1 (December 2003) at 21 [*EIR Report*].

10 *EIR Report*, World Bank Management Response (17 September 2004). At p. 7, the Bank states: "We fully support the importance of protecting the rights of those who are affected by (extractive industry (EI)) projects that the (World Bank Group (WBG)) supports. The Bank Group will only support EI projects that have the broad support of affected communities (including Indigenous Peoples communities). This does not mean a veto power for individuals or any group, but it does mean that the Bank Group requires a process of free, prior and informed consultation with affected communities that leads to broad support by them of the project."

For a critique of the World Bank's approach, see Fergus MacKay, "Indigenous Peoples' Right," above note 7. A motion calling on the World Bank to adopt the recommendations in the *EIR Report* was adopted at the World Conservation Congress in

takes a similar approach in its revamped policy on the financing of projects affecting Indigenous people.[11]

Suggesting that FPIC is the only appropriate standard in every situation in which land-use decisions are at stake may have the effect of increasing the resistance of states to the elaboration of principles and best practices that could otherwise be beneficial to all interested parties, including Indigenous groups. The insistence on a consent-based approach may also have the effect of either narrowing the category of situations in which the desirability of Indigenous involvement is acknowledged, or of reducing FPIC to a lower standard than may be called for in particular situations when consent is a justifiable requirement.

Of course, both the sovereignty and national interest rationales for resistance to a general FPIC standard can be abused. A growing interest among treaty bodies and a general increase at the international level in attention paid to the topic of consultation with Indigenous groups is therefore important. If this heightened attention becomes fixated on the notion of a right of FPIC as veto, momentum may stall short of the point at which consultative approaches that admit of different standards based on the circumstances can be more firmly established in international law and better enforced and operationalized.

The following examination of the manner in which consultation/participation/FPIC is referred to in international instruments and fora suggests that the approach taken by the international community to the matter is more flexible than a "pure" right of FPIC demands. The better approach is to recognize that these terms each have different meanings, and evoke different standards, even while they all convey the idea of Indigenous involvement in decision-making that affects their interests.

Although it can be difficult to distinguish clearly between these terms in every situation, each generally refers to a different level of involvement along a spectrum. At one end of the spectrum, sitting just beside "no involvement at all" is perhaps a level of minimal public engagement through information-sharing: receiving information through a public notice posted in a news periodical, for example. At the other end lies an effective right

November 2004 (RECWCC3.082), online: www.iucn.org/congress/members/submitted_motions.htm.

11   The World Bank's *Revised Draft Operational Policy on Indigenous Peoples* (OP 4.10) online: wbln0018.worldbank.org/Institutional/Manuals/OpManual.nsf/ B52929624EB2A3538525672E00775F66/0F7D6F3F04DD70398525672C007D08ED? OpenDocument.

to say no: at the extreme, the unilateral and unqualified power to veto a natural resource development proposal. Various levels of participation and consultation range in the middle of the spectrum, encompassing an invitation to participate in a public forum, to "mere" consultation, to "meaningful" and more "meaningful consultation." Different levels of Indigenous involvement may be required depending on the circumstances.[12]

2) Consultation in International Instruments and Treaty Body Views

This section describes how the topic of consultation with Indigenous peoples in relation to land-use decisions that affect them is addressed in international treaties, by international human rights treaty bodies that have taken an interest in Indigenous issues,[13] and in the UN draft declaration on the rights of Indigenous peoples. It is an overview of key binding and non-binding elements of the international system that are relevant to the question of whether a customary international law norm or principle has taken shape to the effect that states have a general obligation, under international law, to consult with Indigenous communities before making land or natural resource development decisions that affect them. Neither taken alone nor taken together do these elements answer that question.[14] However, they do show that there is considerable momentum behind the idea.

a) *International Labour Organization Convention 169*

International Labour Organization Convention 169 Concerning Indigenous and Tribal Peoples in Independent Countries, 1989 (Convention 169) is currently the only international treaty that specifically and comprehensively describes Indigenous rights. To date, it has been ratified by seventeen

---

12   The "spectrum" view represents the approach that has been taken by the Supreme Court of Canada (see *Delgamuukw v. British Columbia*, [1997] 3 S.C.R. 1010 [*Delgamuukw*] and *Haida Nation v. British Columbia (Minister of Forests)*, 2004 SCC 73 [*Haida*], for example).

13   Decisions or "views" of international human rights treaty bodies are not legally enforceable in states' parties. However, because they are authoritative interpretations of the extent of international treaty obligations that contribute to the development of international human rights law, they carry significant weight and can give rise to domestic and international political pressure for their implementation by states' parties.

14   A more extensive review of approaches taken to consultation issues in relevant countries and domestic courts, and of relevant international resolutions, guidelines, reports, commentaries, and other materials, would be required to arrive at a more determinative answer. A useful comparative and international law overview is provided in Siegfried Wiessner, "Rights and Status of Indigenous Peoples: A Global Comparative and International Legal Analysis" (1999)12 Harv. Hum. Rts. J. 57.

countries.[15] For these countries, most of which are in Latin America, the Convention clearly has created an international law obligation to consult with Indigenous groups in certain circumstances.

The central themes of Convention 169 are consultation and participation.[16] Article 6 is the most important article in this regard as it appears in the general provisions section of the Convention and guides the interpretation and implementation of the rest of the instrument:

> 1. In applying the provisions of the Convention, governments shall:
>
> (a) consult the peoples concerned, through appropriate procedures and in particular through their representative institutions, whenever consideration is being given to legislative or administrative measures which may affect them directly;
>
> (b) establish means by which these peoples can freely participate, to at least the same extent as other sectors of the population, at all levels of decision-making in elective institutions and administrative and other bodies responsible for policies and programmes which concern them;
>
> (c) establish means for the full development of these peoples' own institutions and initiatives, and in appropriate cases provide the resources necessary for this purpose.
>
> 2. The consultations carried out in application of this Convention shall be undertaken, in good faith and in a form appropriate to the circumstances, with the objective of achieving agreement or consent to the proposed measures.[17]

The lands and resources articles of the Convention are infused with the consultation and participation themes. Indigenous involvement is required if governments are to live up to those articles addressing the identification

---

15 Convention 169 was adopted on 27 June 1989 by the General Conference of the International Labour Organisation at its seventy-sixth session, and entered into force 5 September 1991 [Convention 169]. Argentina, Bolivia, Brazil, Colombia, Costa Rica, Denmark, Dominica, Ecuador, Fiji, Guatemala, Honduras, Mexico, Netherlands, Norway, Paraguay, Peru, and Venezuela have ratified Convention 169.

16 Contribution of the ILO to the *International Workshop on Free, Prior and Informed Consent and Indigenous Peoples*, UN Doc. PFII/2005/WS.2.4 at para. 2 [Contribution of the ILO].

17 Convention 169, above note 15, art. 6. For a discussion of Convention 169, see Lee Swepston, "A New Step in the International Law on Indigenous and Tribal Peoples" (1991)15 Okla. City U.L. Rev. 677.

of Indigenous lands and the safeguarding of lands owned, possessed, or traditionally used by Indigenous groups, and recognizing the importance of those lands for Indigenous cultures and spiritual values.[18] In addition, the Convention describes a right of Indigenous peoples to participate in the use, management, and conservation of natural resources on their lands, and, in cases in which the state owns natural resources, to be consulted regarding possible impacts of development projects, to participate in the benefits of such projects, and to be compensated for any harm caused.[19] The Convention also provides that customary procedures established by Indigenous peoples for the transmission of land rights among themselves should be respected and that they should be consulted whenever consideration is being given to the alienation of their lands.[20]

It is noteworthy that in the context of lands and resources, Convention 169 only refers to a consent requirement in relation to relocation of Indigenous people.[21] In keeping with this, the International Labour Organization (ILO) has clarified that the fact that participation obligations are found in Convention 169:

> ... does not mean, however, that a lack of consent will be sufficient grounds under the Convention to block a development programme or project. The Convention requires that procedures be in place whereby Indigenous and tribal peoples have a realistic chance of affecting the outcome—it does not require that their consent to the proposed measures is necessary.[22]

What is required by Convention 169 has been considered on occasion by ILO supervisory bodies that are available to monitor compliance with the organization's conventions. Of the various supervisory and complaints mechanisms established by the ILO constitution, Convention 169 has been addressed by three: examination of state reports, "representations," and "interpretations."[23] The representation mechanism is the most relevant

---

18   Convention 169, *ibid.*, arts. 13 and 14.
19   *Ibid.*, art. 15.
20   *Ibid.*, 17.
21   *Ibid.*, 16(2).
22   Contribution of the ILO, above note 16 at para. 12.
23   States parties must report to the ILO regarding their implementation of Convention 169 every five years. These reports are reviewed by a Committee of Experts that issues an annual report containing its observations and recommendations about them. The committee has addressed Convention 169 in its reports. The "interpretation" tool permits members of the ILO who are in doubt as to the meaning of particular provisions of an ILO convention or other ILO instrument to request the ILO to communicate its

to this discussion.[24] It is a mechanism through which complaints can be made alleging violations of ILO conventions by state parties.[25] Decisions respecting representations are not binding on the governments they are addressed to, but they do carry political and moral weight.

A number of representations have been submitted alleging violations of Convention 169. Those which have addressed its lands and resources provisions, have included a focus on issues of consultation. For example, the tripartite committee examining a representation against Peru found that decisions involving legislative or administrative measures that may affect the land ownership of certain Indigenous peoples must be taken in consultation with them.[26] In a proceeding involving Bolivia, the committee requested that the government conduct consultations, prior to granting logging concessions, as well as environmental, cultural, social, and spiritual impact studies, jointly with the peoples concerned.[27]

---

opinion. The office has no binding authority to interpret these conventions, but it can provide its opinion. To date, one interpretation has been requested regarding Convention 169, but it did not address a question relevant to the topic of consultation with Indigenous groups.

24 The ILO has a tripartite structure consisting of government, employers, and workers' representatives. Indigenous groups do not have a formal position within the ILO structure, but can participate in ILO meetings and other activities as representatives of governments, employers, or workers, or as representatives of NGOs recognized on the ILO's Special List of NGOs. They can also send information to the ILO through employer or worker organizations, or can send information themselves. The representations referred to in this paper were made on behalf of Indigenous peoples by labour organizations.

25 Pursuant to art. 24 of the ILO constitution, representations can be made by employers' and workers' organizations who think that a state has failed to observe a ratified convention. A tripartite committee of the governing body is set up to examine the matter; its conclusions are considered and, if accepted, adopted by the governing body. Reports of tripartite committees are made available to the public and their recommendations are followed up by the Committee of Experts in the context of its ongoing dialogue with governments through the ILO's state report procedure.

26 Report of the committee set up to examine the representation alleging non-observance by Peru of the Indigenous and Tribal People's Convention, 1989 (No. 169), made under art. 24 of the ILO constitution by the General Confederation of Workers of Peru (CGTP), submitted 17 July 1997. For an analysis of the utility of Convention 169 in the context of oil exploration in Bolivia, see Laurie Sargeant, "The Indigenous Peoples of Bolivia's Amazon Basin Region and ILO Convention No. 169: Real Rights or Rhetoric?" (1998) 29 Inter-Am. L. Rev. 451.

27 Report of the committee set up to examine the representation alleging non-observance by Bolivia of the Indigenous and Tribal People's Convention, 1989 (No. 169), made

The impact of extensive petroleum exploitation undertaken without community involvement on Indigenous peoples and their lands was the basis for a representation against Ecuador. When it authorized the extraction of these resources, the government of Ecuador had taken the position that consultations were not required because the resources at issue were, under Ecuadorian law, owned by the state. The committee noted that balancing national development interests with local community concerns can be difficult, "particularly when differing interests and points of view are at stake such as the economic and development interests represented by the hydrocarbon deposits and the cultural, spiritual, social, and economic interests of the Indigenous peoples situated in the zones where those deposits are found."[28] However, the committee emphasized that consultation is at the core of Convention 169. Even when compelling national economic development interests are at stake and ownership of the resources are not at issue, a party to the convention must consider the impacts on any Indigenous communities that may be affected, by engaging them in the decision-making process, and mitigate those impacts.

On the basis that the concept of consultation includes "establishing a genuine dialogue between both parties characterized by communication and understanding, mutual respect, good faith and the sincere wish to reach a common accord,"[29] the committee describes a few elements of a good consultation process, including: consultation should occur before decisions are made; it should involve more than making information about a project available; and it should be conducted with the true representatives of the community (or with the community as a whole).[30]

Canada has not ratified Convention 169 and is therefore not bound by it or subject to its compliance mechanisms. Nevertheless, the Convention has had an impact in ways that are relevant to Canada. Outside of the framework of the ILO, no international body has the authority to issue

under art. 24 of the ILO constitution by the Bolivian Central of Workers (COB), submitted 28 February 1998.

28 Report of the committee set up to examine the representation alleging non-observance by Ecuador of the Indigenous and Tribal Peoples Convention, 1989 (No. 169), made under art. 24 of the ILO constitution by the Confederacion Ecuatoriana de Organizaciones Sindicales Libres (CEOSL), submitted 2000, para. 36. For a discussion of the report and others made by ILO tripartite committees, see David Baluarte, "Balancing Indigenous Rights and a State's Right to Develop in Latin America" (2004) 4 Sustainable Dev. L. & Pol'y 9.

29 Report of the committee, *ibid.* at para. 38.

30 *Ibid.*

determinative interpretations of ILO conventions.[31] However, since it is the most comprehensive iteration of Indigenous rights currently available in final form, Convention 169 has informed the approach taken to Indigenous rights in domestic legislation,[32] the resolution of civil strife,[33] the decisions of domestic courts in countries that have ratified it,[34] the development of policies relevant to international development,[35] and the preparation of the UN and OAS draft declarations on the rights of Indigenous peoples.[36]

Convention 169 is also referred to in the reports and other documents prepared by some treaty bodies, such as the Committee on the Elimination of Racial Discrimination[37] and the Inter-American Commission on Human Rights, which have suggested that it is an expression of customary

31 In countries that have a monist approach to international treaties—where simple ratification of a treaty makes it part of domestic law—domestic courts can interpret and apply ILO conventions that have been ratified by that country. An example of a monist country is Denmark, whose Supreme Court considered Convention 169 in domestic litigation arising from the relocation of an Inuit community in Greenland. Information about the 27 November 2003 ruling can be obtained online: www.inuit.org/index. asp?lang=eng&num=218. In contrast, Canada is dualist with respect to international treaties. In order to become part of Canadian domestic law, international treaties that Canada has ratified must generally be implemented domestically through legislation.

32 Philippines' *Indigenous Peoples Rights Act*, October 1997, Republic Act 8371.

33 Guatemala—Maya, Garifuna, and Xinca Indigenous peoples, *Agreement on Identity and Rights of Indigenous Peoples*, 31 March 1995, online: www.usip.org/library/pa/guatemala/guat_950331.html.

34 For example, see Sentencia SU-039 febrero 3 de 1997 (Corte Constitucional) 655 (Colom.), a Colombian case that recognized the need for consultation in connection with the protection of Indigenous peoples' lands. The following elements of active and effective consultation were identified by the court: 1) full disclosure regarding proposed projects; 2) full disclosure of possible effects; 3) opportunity to freely and privately discuss the proposed project within the community or among authorized representatives; 4) the opportunity to have their concerns heard; and 5) a real effort to reach agreement with the Indigenous community (quoted in S. James Anaya and Robert A. Williams, Jr., "The Protection of Indigenous Peoples' Rights over Lands and Natural Resources Under the Inter-American Human Rights System" (2001) Harv. Hum. Rts. J. 33 at 81.)

35 World Bank, *Revised Draft Operational Policy on Indigenous Peoples*, above note 11.

36 The lands and resources provisions in the UN *Draft Declaration on the Rights of Indigenous Peoples* and OAS *Proposed Declaration on the Rights of Indigenous Peoples*, which are discussed later in the chapter, draw partly on Convention 169.

37 In its concluding observations on state reports, the committee appears to have a practice of considering whether countries with Indigenous populations have ratified Convention 169, and if so, whether they comply with it. See, for example, the *Concluding Observations of the Committee concerning Finland*, UN Doc. CERD/C/63/CO/5, 22 August 2003 at para. 12, where the committee encourages Finland to adhere to the Convention.

international law respecting international Indigenous rights.[38] Although states that have not ratified the Convention might challenge this view, it is certainly an important document that has played a role in promoting a consultative and participatory framework to address Indigenous issues.[39]

b) The Inter-American Human Rights System

The Inter-American human rights system is fertile ground for the elaboration of international Indigenous rights. Both the Inter-American Commission on Human Rights (the Commission) and the Inter-American Court on Human Rights (the IA Court) have taken an interest in Indigenous issues. Together with the fact that many Latin American countries have ratified ILO Convention 169 and that the history of Indigenous peoples in the Americas is broadly comparable, the attention these treaty bodies have paid to Indigenous issues, and the impact this has had on domestic law and policy in the region, bolsters arguments that a regional set of customary international Indigenous rights norms have taken hold among the countries in the Inter-American human rights system.[40]

The Commission can investigate rights complaints that are put to it by individuals living in OAS member countries. It has the authority to issue reports setting out its conclusions and recommendations concerning alleged violations of the *American Declaration on the Rights and Duties of Man* (the American Declaration) or of the *Inter-American Convention on Human Rights* (the American Convention).[41] These reports carry political and moral weight at the domestic and international levels, but are not binding.

The Commission can refer a complaint by an individual to the IA Court for its determination if the country against which the complaint is made is an OAS member that is also a party to the American Convention, and

38 See, for example, Inter-American Commission on Human Rights Report (IACHR); *Mary and Carrie Dann v. United States*, Report 75/02, 27 December 2002 [*Dann Report*].

39 Convention 169 has some shortcomings that have made it unpopular even with some Indigenous people. For example, it does not address the right to self-determination, a cornerstone of contemporary positions on Indigenous rights.

40 Anaya & Williams, above note 34, writing before the decisions in the cases discussed in this section, added credence to the argument. The impact of the IACHR and IA Court attention to Indigenous rights issues in the Americas is shown by the increasing use of the friendly settlement mechanism available to parties with disputes before the Commission. Friendly settlements are essentially negotiated agreements brokered by the IACHR—a consultative approach to dispute resolution.

41 American Declaration, adopted by the ninth International Conference of American States, 1948 [American Declaration]; American Convention, adopted 22 November 1969, in force 18 July 1978 [American Convention].

has accepted the jurisdiction of the IA Court. Once a proceeding has been elevated to that level, the Commission takes the lead, with the assistance of the claimant, in presenting the complaint to the Court. The IA Court has the authority to issue judgments that are binding under international law on countries that are subject to its jurisdiction.

Canada is a member of the OAS, but is not a party to the American Convention.[42] Accordingly, it can be the subject of individual complaints to the Commission based on alleged violations of the American Declaration, but is not subject to the jurisdiction of the IA Court. However, there is a significant fluidity between interpretations of the Declaration and the Convention. Both the Commission and the IA Court have expressed the view that the American Declaration must be interpreted in light of developments in the field of international human rights law since the American Declaration was adopted in 1948, including developments in the interpretation of the American Convention.[43]

Neither the American Convention nor the American Declaration contains articles referring to Indigenous peoples specifically. However, the Commission and the IA Court have each considered whether these instruments protect Indigenous property rights. Their approach to this issue is relevant to an analysis of the status of an "Inter-American consultation principle."

Both instruments describe a right to property, but in different terms. Article 21 of the American Convention provides:

1. Everyone has the right to the use and enjoyment of his property. The law may subordinate such use and enjoyment to the interest of society.

---

42 The Senate Standing Committee on Human Rights recently considered why Canada has not ratified the IACHR. It issued a report in May 2003 titled *Enhancing Canada's Role in the OAS—Canadian Adherence to the American Convention on Human Rights*, which includes a recommendation that "the Government of Canada take all necessary action to ratify the *American Convention on Human Rights*, with a view to achieving ratification by 18 July 2008, which is the thirtieth anniversary of the entry into force of the American Convention. Ratification of the Convention would be incomplete if it did not include a declaration that Canada recognizes the jurisdiction of the Court on all matters relating to the interpretation or application of the *American Convention*." The report includes some discussion of the reasons why Canada has not adhered so far.

43 See *Dann Report*, above note 38 at para. 96, and IA Court, *Interpretation of the American Declaration of the Rights and Duties of Man Within the Framework of Article 64 of the American Convention on Human Rights*, Advisory Opinion OC-10/89 of July 14, 1989, Inter-Am. Ct. H. R. (Ser. A) No. 10 (1989) at para. 37.

2. No one shall be deprived of his property except upon payment of just compensation, for reasons of public utility or social interest, and in cases and according to the forms established by law.
3. Usury and other forms of exploitation of man by man shall be prohibited by law.[44]

Article XXIII of the American Declaration provides:

Every person has the right to own such private property as meets the essential needs of decent living and helps to maintain the dignity of the individual and of the home.[45]

The IA Court has concluded that article 21 of the American Convention protects a right to Indigenous communal property. The same conclusion has been reached by the Commission with respect to Article XXIII of the American Declaration, despite the differences between the two texts.

In its judgment in the *Case of the Mayagna (Sumo) Awas Tingni Community v. Nicaragua* (the *Awas Tingni* judgment), the first and, to date, sole decision by the IA Court concerning a complaint by an Indigenous group, the Court concludes that "through an evolutionary interpretation of international instruments for the protection of human rights, taking into account applicable norms of interpretation," article 21 of the American Convention protects the right to property in a sense which includes Indigenous communal property.[46] The Court identifies some characteristics of the concept of communal Indigenous property, including: ownership is centred on the group or community, and property is not merely a matter of possession—the close tie that Indigenous groups have to their lands is regarded as a fundamental basis of their cultures, spiritual life, integrity, and economic survival.[47] The Court goes on to conclude that Nicaragua must adopt measures to protect Indigenous use and enjoyment of their property, in particular through demarcation and titling of their territory.[48]

---

44 American Convention, above note 41, art. 21.
45 American Declaration, above note 41, art. XXIII.
46 Inter-American Court of Human Rights, *Case of the Mayagna (Sumo) Community of Awas Tingni v. Nicaragua*, Inter-Am. C.H.R. Series C, No. 79 (31 August 2001) at para. 148 [*Awas Tingni* judgment]. The Court has now addressed Indigenous communal property in a second case: *Case Communidad Indigena Yakey Axa v. Paraguary*, Inter-Am. C.H.R. Series C, No. 125 (17 June 2005) [Spanish only].
47 *Ibid.* at para. 149.
48 *Ibid.* at para. 173(3).

Although the *Awas Tingni* judgment is focused on demarcation and titling of lands, a consultation component is incorporated in the Court's order that Nicaragua "officially delimit, demarcate, and title the lands belonging to the Awas Tingni Community within a maximum period of 15 months, with the full participation of, and considering the customary law, values, usage, and customs of, the Community."[49]

It is possible that a consultation requirement could play a larger role in a future decision of the IA Court. Although the Court's conclusion that article 21 protects Indigenous communal property is based on its interpretation of developments in the field of international Indigenous rights, its finding that Nicaragua must demarcate and title the traditional lands of the Awas Tingni Community flows, in large part, from Nicaraguan domestic law, which contemplates the establishment of a procedure to do so. Had it complied with its own domestic law, Nicaragua may not have fallen short of its international law obligation to protect the use and enjoyment of the Indigenous communal property at issue. The *Awas Tingni* judgment does not mean that a program of demarcation and titling is the only way that the enjoyment of Indigenous communal property can be protected under the American Convention.[50] On the contrary, it appears that consultation, including the negotiation of interim agreements, could constitute another option. In some cases, consultative processes might be used to address Indigenous interests and allow economic development projects to proceed before Indigenous lands are fully "demarcated and titled."[51]

However, the right to communal property is subject to the second sentence of article 21(1): "The law may subordinate the use and enjoyment of property to the interest of society," (but any deprivation of property must satisfy Article 21(2) addressing issues of compensation, public purpose and rule of law). The notion that the right to property can be subordinated to the

49 *Ibid.* at para. 164.
50 The concept of "demarcation and titling" was not invented by the IA Court. Besides being found in Nicaraguan domestic law, it is a concept referred to in at least one prior report of the Inter-American Commission (see Inter-American Commission on Human Rights, *Yanomani v. Brazil*, Resolution no. 12/85 (Case no. 7615), 5 March 1985), and in international boundary disputes adjudicated by the International Court of Justice (see International Court of Justice, *Case Concerning the Land and Maritime Boundary between Cameroon and Nigeria*, no. 94, 10 October 2002.)
51 For a discussion of the use of negotiated agreements in Canada that was filed with the IA Court in connection with the *Awas Tingni* case, see Patrick Macklem & Ed Morgan, "Indigenous Rights in the Inter-American System: The Amicus Brief of the Assembly of First Nations in *Awas Tingni v. Nicaragua*" (2000) 22 Hum. Rts. Q. 569.

interests of society is not dissimilar to the principle found in Canadian law that aboriginal rights can be justifiably infringed in accordance with applicable legal principles.[52] This qualification seems to eliminate the possibility that the right to property in the American Convention includes a veto on activities impacting an individual or communal property interest.[53]

The Commission has also addressed Indigenous land issues in a number of its reports. In two recent cases, *Mary and Carrie Dann v. United States* (the *Dann* report) and *Maya Indigenous Communities of the Toledo District v. Belize* (the *Toledo District* report), the Commission considered Article XXIII of the American Declaration.[54] In both cases, the Commission concluded that despite the differences of wording between Article XXIII of the American Declaration and article 21 of the American Convention, the former protects Indigenous communal property in essentially the same manner as the latter.

The *Dann* report concerns a complaint by two members of the Western Shoshone tribe that they were deprived of property rights in their ancestral territory. The United States argued that the Western Shoshone lost any interest in these lands by 1872 as a result of encroachment by non-Native Americans, and that this determination was properly made in 1966 through fair proceedings before the US Indian Claims Commission (ICC), a quasi-judicial body that the United States had established to adjudicate Indian land claim issues.[55]

The *Dann* report is focused primarily on the procedural question of whether the Western Shoshone claim was properly addressed through the ICC process. In this regard, Article XVIII of the American Declaration provides:

> Every person may resort to the courts to ensure respect for his legal rights. There should likewise be available to him a simple, brief procedure whereby

52 See *R. v. Sparrow*, [1990] 1 S.C.R. 1075 [*Sparrow*].

53 The American Declaration includes a general limitation clause: "The rights of man are limited by the rights of others, by the security of all, and by the just demands of the general welfare and the advancement of democracy." American Declaration, above note 41, art. XXVIII.

54 *Dann Report*, above note 38. Inter-American Commission on Human Rights, *Maya Indigenous Communities of the Toledo District v. Belize*, Report no. 96/03, 24 October 2003 [*Toledo District Report*]. Neither the United States nor Belize is a party to the American Convention so these cases were considered on the basis of the American Declaration.

55 *Dann Report, ibid.* at para. 3.

the courts will protect him from acts of authority that, to his prejudice, violate any fundamental constitutional rights.[56]

The Commission concluded that the ICC procedure fell short of the requirements of the American Declaration. The Commission reached this conclusion on the basis of its view that, at a minimum, Article XXIII and XVIII require that a State making any determination of the extent to which Indigenous claimants retain an interest in land, hinges on a review of whether that interest was relinquished with "fully informed and mutual consent on the part of the [I]ndigenous community as a whole."[57] In the Commission's opinion, this "requires ... that all of the members of the community are fully and accurately informed of the nature and consequences of the process and provided with an effective opportunity to participate individually or as collectives."[58] The Commission concluded that this was not done *via* the ICC process because only one band of the Western Shoshone people was involved. Even the consultations conducted with this group were not, in the Commission's view, adequate.

The *Toledo District* report concerns a claim by Mayan Indigenous communities that the grant of logging and oil concessions by Belize violated a number of articles of the American Declaration, including Article XXIII on the right to property. Belize has a land titles system, but has no mechanism to recognize or protect Indigenous land rights. Nevertheless, in practice, the Government of Belize permits a wide degree of self-government by Indigenous groups in certain parts of the country, including the Toledo District, in relation to the holding and transfer of Indigenous traditional lands. In the Commission's view, an Indigenous communal property interest could be demonstrated by the Maya through their customary laws, practices, and activities in relation to their traditional lands, all engaged in without objection by Belize.[59] On this basis, the Commission concluded that the failure of Belize to take effective measures to recognize the communal property right to the lands traditionally occupied and used by the Maya constitutes a violation of Article XXIII. It recommended that Belize:

> Adopt in its domestic law, and through fully informed consultations with the Maya people, the legislative, administrative, and any other measures

---

56   American Declaration, above note 41, art. XVIII.
57   *Dann Report*, above note 38 at para. 140.
58   *Ibid.*
59   *Toledo District Report*, above note 54 at paras. 121–34.

necessary to delimit, demarcate and title or otherwise clarify and protect the territory in which the Maya people have a communal property right, in accordance with their customary land use practices, and without detriment to other Indigenous communities.[60]

As in the *Awas Tingni* judgment, demarcation and titling are offered as options for the clarification and protection of traditional territory. The Commission calls on Belize to undertake necessary reforms based on a consultative approach.

In addition, the Commission observes that an element to the protection of Indigenous property rights is "the requirement that States undertake effective and fully informed consultations with Indigenous communities regarding acts or decisions that may affect their traditional territories."[61] In *Dann* and *Awas Tingni*, this applied to the act of determining the boundaries of Indigenous lands. In *Toledo District*, the Commission takes the view that it also applies to other decisions by the state that may impact on Indigenous lands and their communities, such as the approval of land or resource development projects.

A number of principles can be drawn from the approaches taken by the IA Court and the Commission to Indigenous land and natural resource issues in the Inter-American human rights context:

(1) The right to property set out in both the American Declaration and the American Convention protects Indigenous peoples' property in at least equal measure to other forms of property. This protection is not absolute and does not appear to include a veto on development.

(2) If domestic law recognizes Indigenous communal property, effective measures must be taken to protect that property, which may include effective participatory mechanisms.

(3) Any domestic legal procedures to determine the existence of Indigenous communal property, or to recognize and protect such property must be fair and effective and, in the view of the Commission, be undertaken on the basis of "fully informed consultations," if not "fully informed and mutual consent" with the Indigenous group concerned, which may require consultations with Indigenous collectives and with Indigenous individuals.

---

60 *Ibid.* at para. 190.
61 *Ibid.* at para. 141.

(4) Where domestic law lacks effective legislative, administrative, and other measures to recognize, clarify, and protect Indigenous communal property, such measures should be adopted, again through fully informed consultations with the Indigenous peoples concerned.

(5) Indigenous communities should be consulted regarding any act or decision that may affect their lands, including those concerning land and resource development projects.

(6) The American Declaration and American Convention are flexible human rights instruments, and their interpretation by the IA Court and by the Commission can be expected to evolve to address changing circumstances and expectations, novel situations and problems, and international and domestic developments relevant to the concept of Indigenous rights. The words of the instruments will not be interpreted narrowly.

It can be expected that over the course of the next few years, these principles will be further elaborated and refined by the IA Court and the Commission, whose dockets are dominated by Indigenous rights complaints. Indeed, the Commission is considering the merits of a human rights complaint by an Indigenous group from Ecuador that directly raises the question of whether the group had a right to be consulted about a petroleum project on their traditional lands, is expected later this year. The matter may then proceed to the IA Court in 2006.[62]

c) The International Human Rights Covenants

Although a right to property is not found in the *International Covenant on Civil and Political Rights* (ICCPR),[63] the Human Rights Committee (the Committee) has addressed Indigenous land rights issues as a cultural matter in the context of its interpretation of article 27 of the ICCPR. Consultation is a focus of the Committee in its observations concerning complaints it receives from Indigenous individuals pursuant to the mechanism established by the Optional Protocol to the ICCPR. [64]

---

62 See IACHR, *The Kichwa Peoples of Sarayaku v. Ecuador*, Admissibility, Report no. 64/04.

63 ICCPR, adopted and opened for signature by UN General Assembly resolution 2200 A (XXI) of 16 December 1966, in force 23 March 1976 [ICCPR].

64 Canada is a party to both the ICCPR and the Optional Protocol. A number of complaints have been submitted by Aboriginal people pursuant to the Optional Protocol alleging that Canada has violated art. 27. Besides individual complaints, the committee considers the reports that states parties must submit pursuant to the ICCPR at regular intervals. The committee is interested in hearing how states address Indig-

Article 27 provides:

In those States in which ethnic, religious or linguistic minorities exist, persons belonging to such minorities shall not be denied the right, in community with the other members of their group to enjoy their own culture, to profess and practice their own religion, or to use their own language.[65]

In paragraph 7 of its general comment on this article, the Committee observes that "culture manifests itself in many forms, including a particular way of life associated with the use of land resources, especially in the case of Indigenous peoples." It goes on to state that the right may include traditional activities such as hunting or fishing. Further, the enjoyment of those rights may require "positive legal measures of protection and measures to ensure the effective participation of members of minority communities in decisions which affect them."[66]

The Committee is guided by its general comment when it considers complaints by Indigenous individuals. In the observations it has issued in relation to these complaints, the Committee has indicated that not every impact on land-based Indigenous activities will constitute a violation of article 27.[67] A critical issue, in the Committee's opinion, is whether a State has taken effective measures to involve Indigenous peoples in decisions that affect their land-based cultural activities. In cases in which a state can show that effective consultations were conducted, the Committee has concluded that impacts are minimal and fall short of a violation of article 27.[68]

The Committee's general approach to Indigenous complaints, therefore, appears to embrace the notion that national governments have to be able to balance various competing interests, but with respect for a rights-based bottom line. For example, the Committee has stated:

---

enous peoples' issues. Committee observations are not binding in domestic courts but they carry significant political and moral weight.

65 ICCPR, above note 63, art. 27.

66 Human Rights Committee General Comment no. 23, *The Rights of Minorities (art. 27)*, UN Doc. CCPR/C/21/Rev.1/Add.6, adopted 8 April 1994 at para. 7.

67 See *Lansmann v. Finland* (511/1992), ICCPR, CCPR/C/52/D/511/1992 (26 October 1994) [*Lansmann*] and *Aarela and Makkalajarui v. Finland* (779/1997) ICCPR, CCPR/C/73/D/779/1997 (24 October 2001).

68 See *ibid.* and *Mahuika v. New Zealand* (547/1993) ICCPR, CCPR/C/70/D/547/1993 (27 October 2000) [*Mahuika*].

A State may understandably wish to encourage development or allow economic activity by enterprise. The scope of its freedom to do so is not to be assessed by reference to a margin of appreciation, but by reference to the obligations it has undertaken in article 27. Article 27 requires that a member of a minority shall not be denied his right to enjoy his own culture. Thus, measures whose impact amount to a denial of the right will not be compatible with the obligations under Article 27. However, measures that have a certain limited impact on the way of life of persons belonging to a minority will not necessarily amount to a denial of the right under Article 27.[69]

In determining whether the right to enjoy one's culture is actually denied, the Committee will consider whether the members of the minority in question were given opportunities to participate in the decision-making process related to the measures that the complaint relates to, and whether the minority will continue to be able to benefit from its traditional economy.[70]

Key principles identified by the Committee in its consideration of the article 27 aspects of the land and resource interests of Indigenous peoples include the following: 1) although governments must be able to balance competing considerations in the national interest, they must ensure that proposed land or resource development projects do not deny the right of Indigenous people to enjoy the cultural elements of their relationship with their lands and resources (which could presumably be very broad); 2) in order to ensure that this is done, affected Indigenous people should be involved in the decision-making process; and 3) at the end of the day, the Indigenous people should be able to benefit from their traditional cultural activities and economies after the project is undertaken.

Besides article 27 of the ICCPR, Common Article 1 of the ICCPR and the International Covenant on Economic, Social and Cultural Rights (IC-ESCR) are relevant to consideration of the existence of an obligation to consult with Indigenous groups.[71] Common Article 1 describes the right to self-determination of peoples as follows:

---

69 *Lansmann*, above note 67 at para. 9.4.

70 *Mahuika*, above note 68 at para. 9.5.

71 Neither the Human Rights Committee (HRC) nor the Committee on Economic, Social and Cultural Rights (CESCR) has the ability to consider individual complaints alleging violations by States of Common Article 1. The HRC does not have the mandate to consider complaints by groups under the Optional Protocol, as discussed in its observations in *Ominayak v. Canada*, UN GAOR, 45th Sess., Supp. no. 40, Annex 9, at 27, UN Doc. A/45/40 (1990), and an individual complaints mechanism does not exist

All peoples have the right of self-determination. By virtue of that right they freely determine their political status and freely pursue their economic, social and cultural development.

Although Indigenous claims to self-determination, based on Common Article 1, are certainly a challenge to the view that the state is the dominant body to which allegiance is owed and identity defined, they do not necessarily include a complete rejection of its role.[72] Kingsbury notes: "Most of the groups participating in the international Indigenous peoples movement ... expect to continue in an enduring relationship with the State in which they presently live."[73] This is reflected in the deliberations at the tenth session of the Working Group of states on the Draft Declaration (WGDD) when some states and Indigenous representatives agreed that Indigenous peoples have a right of self-determination, but that this right does not impair the territorial integrity or political independence of states.[74]

---

for the ICESCR, although the UN has established a working group to look into options for one. Nevertheless, both committees look to states to report on their approach to the right to self-determination in their state reports. The HRC has asked Canada to explain how it understands the right in relation to Indigenous peoples (UN Doc. CCPR/C/79/Add.105, 7 April 1999) at para. 7.

72 In a book published in 1979, Crawford suggested that "since 1945 there has been no more divisive an issue among international law writers than the question whether there exists a legal right or principle of self-determination of peoples, and if so, its impact on the notion of State sovereignty" (James Crawford, *The Creation of States in International Law* (Oxford: Clarendon Press, 1979)). Although the principle is now firmly established in international law, it is not always clear who the "peoples" are that the right refers to, or what the right entails. In its decision in *Québec Secession Reference* the Supreme Court of Canada did not offer a definition of "peoples." The Court did say that a right to self-determination does not necessarily imply a right to secede. The right to self-determination of a people may be satisfied when they are able to participate in the democratic process and in government institutions and structures in the same measure as other individuals and groups in the society at issue (See *Reference Re: Secession of Québec*, [1998] 2 S.C.R. 217).

73 Benedict Kingsbury, "Reconciling Five Competing Conceptual Structures of Indigenous Peoples' Claims in International and Comparative Law" (2001) 34 N.Y.U. J. Int'l L. & Pol. 189 at 221.

74 This qualification is elaborated in the UN *Declaration on Principles of International law Concerning Friendly Relations and Co-operation among States in Accordance with the Charter of the United Nations*, UNGA Res. 2625 (XXV), UN GAOR, 25th Sess., Supp. no. 28, at 121, UN Doc. A/8028 (1971), adopted by consensus on 24 October 1970, and arguably reflects the principles set out in art. 2 of the UN *Charter*. For a summary of the tenth session, see: *Report* of the working group established in accordance with

Although the precise meaning of the right of self-determination of Indigenous peoples is uncertain, it can be said that it is increasingly becoming more widely accepted internationally that Indigenous peoples have this right in some form. Anaya argues that the right to self-determination establishes a broad norm favouring Indigenous participation in all decisions that affect them.[75] Whether or not the right is sufficiently developed in relation to Indigenous peoples to draw that conclusion, at a minimum increasing acceptance that it exists provides additional support for a participatory approach to Indigenous peoples' issues.

d) The *Convention on the Elimination of All Forms of Racial Discrimination*

The *Convention on the Elimination of all Forms of Racial Discrimination* (CERD)[76] does not contain any provisions specifically addressing Indigenous peoples or the topic of consultations, but it does apply to them, and the Committee on the Elimination of Racial Discrimination (the CERD Committee) has shown an interest in Indigenous issues.[77] In its general recommendation on Indigenous peoples, the CERD Committee calls upon states to: "Ensure that members of Indigenous peoples have equal rights in respect to effective participation in public life and that no decisions directly relating to their rights and interests are taken without their informed consent."[78] The Committee's general recommendations are not binding on states, but indicate how the experts on the Committee view the provisions of CERD and what matters the Committee will take into account when it reviews state reports, materials submitted to it under its "early warning"

Commission on Human Rights resolution 1995/32 of 3 March 1995 at its tenth session, E/CN.4/2005/89, 28 February 2005.

75 Anaya, *Indigenous Peoples,* above note 3 at 153–56. Anaya describes the right to self-determination as the foundational right upon which other international Indigenous rights norms are based.

76 Opened for signature on 21 December 1965, entered into force 4 January 1969. The parties to CERD, including Canada, condemn "any distinction, exclusion, restriction or preference based on race, colour, descent, or national or ethnic origin which has the purpose of nullifying or impairing the recognition, enjoyment or exercise, on an equal footing, of human rights and fundamental freedoms in the political, economic, social, cultural or any other field of public life" (art. 1). CERD includes exceptions for discrimination between citizens and non-citizens and for "special measures taken for the sole purpose of securing adequate advancement of certain racial or ethnic groups."

77 See generally CERD Committee, General Recommendation XXIII, "Indigenous Peoples," 18 August 1997, UN Doc. A/52/18, annex V.

78 *Ibid.* at para. 4(d).

system to assess alleged human rights violations, and complaints submitted to it by individuals.

e) The *Convention on Biological Diversity*

The *Convention on Biological Diversity* (the CBD) is one of the most widely ratified international conventions, with 188 state parties. It includes three objectives: "the conservation of biological diversity, the sustainable use of its components, and the fair and equitable sharing of the benefits arising out of the utilization of genetic resources."[79] The CBD is significant for Indigenous peoples because, to date, it is the only widely ratified treaty that includes provisions describing obligations owed specifically to them.

The relationship between Indigenous knowledge, innovations, and practices (also referred to as "traditional knowledge" or "TK") and the conservation of biological diversity is recognized in the preamble to the CBD.[80] More importantly, article 8j of the Convention provides that each party shall, "as far as possible and as appropriate":

> Subject to its national legislation, respect, preserve and maintain knowledge innovations and practices of Indigenous and local communities embodying traditional lifestyles relevant for the conservation and sustainable use of biological diversity and promote their wider application with the approval and involvement of the holders of such knowledge, innovations and practices and encourage the equitable sharing of the benefits arising from the utilization of such knowledge, innovations and practices.[81]

The CBD's provisions on access and benefit-sharing in relation to genetic resources are also relevant to Indigenous peoples.[82] The attention of the parties to the CBD is currently focused on these provisions. "Mega-biodiverse" countries, which are predominantly developing nations along a band near the equator that are particularly rich in biodiversity (and therefore plant and animal genetic resources), are concerned that researchers and companies based primarily in certain developed countries have been able to exploit genetic resources for biotechnology innovations without sharing the financial or technological benefits with the countries from which the resources originate. As a result, the parties to the CBD are considering

---

79 CBD, above note 6, art. 1. All the documents related to the CBD, including those referred to in these footnotes, are online: www.biodiv.org.

80 *Ibid.* at preambular para. 12.

81 *Ibid.*, art. 8j. Arts. 10(c) and 17 also address traditional knowledge issues.

82 *Ibid.*, art. 15.

whether to elaborate and negotiate an international regime on access and benefit-sharing that would address developing country concerns without placing a chill on biotechnology research and development.[83]

In many cases, plant and animal genetic resources only attract the attention of researchers and companies because they are used by Indigenous peoples as medicines or other products. Traditional knowledge associated with genetic resources has therefore been included in the access and benefit-sharing negotiations. Indigenous groups argue that they have a right to FPIC with respect to access to traditional knowledge[84] and with respect to access to genetic resources found on their lands.[85] The CBD has therefore become another international venue where consultation with Indigenous peoples in connection with land and resource matters is at issue.

Over time, Conference of the Parties (COP) decisions have increasingly acceded to the link advocated by Indigenous peoples between FPIC and traditional knowledge.[86] A similar process may well occur in relation to access to genetic resources on Indigenous lands, although, to date, COP decisions that refer to land-use issues carefully avoid recognition of an unqualified right to FPIC as veto.[87] COP decisions have no immediate effect on international law, but over time may be interpreted as demonstrating, once again, international acceptance that there is a special connection between

---

83 For an overview of the issue, see Sabrina Safrin, "Hyperownership in a Time of Biotechnological Promise: The International Conflict to Control the Building Blocks of Life" (2004) 98 Am. J. Int'l Law 641.

84 The terms *approval and involvement* in CBD art. 8j and *prior informed consent (PIC)* in CBD art. 15 have been conflated. PIC is emerging as the preferred term of Indigenous participants, and increasingly, the working term in CBD documents.

85 This has been done on the basis of the links that have been made by Indigenous participants, which are increasingly reflected in CBD documents, between protection of traditional knowledge and respect for land and resource rights.

86 See, for example, the latest COP decision on *Article 8j and Related Provisions*: UN Doc. UNEP/CBD/COP/7/21, Annex, Decision VII/16, as compared to earlier COP decisions which repeated the "approval and involvement" phrase from art. 8j.

87 See the *Bonn Guidelines on Access to Genetic Resources and Fair and Equitable Sharing of the Benefits Arising out of their Utilization* at para. 31 (UN Doc. UNEP/CBD/COP/6/20, Annex I, Decision VI/24), the *Guidelines on Biodiversity and Tourism Development* at para. 56 (UN Doc. UNEP/CBD/COP/7/21, Annex, Decision VII/14), and the *Akwé Kon: Voluntary Guidelines for the Conduct of Cultural, Environmental and Social Impact Assessments regarding Developments Proposed to Take Place on, or which are likely to Impact on, Sacred Sites and on Lands and Waters Traditionally Occupied or Used by Indigenous and Local Communities* at para. 53 (UN Doc. UNEP/CBD/COP/7/21, Annex, Decision VII/16).

Indigenous peoples, their traditional knowledge, and their lands and that this special connection should be recognized in rights terms and respected through consultation measures. Further, based on developments to date, it can be anticipated that the states participating in the access and benefit-sharing negotiations will eventually find it necessary to decide whether they agree that Indigenous peoples have a right to FPIC (or to some level of consultation) in relation both to access to their traditional knowledge and to access to genetic resources found on their lands. The working documents that have been generated to date to guide the negotiations signal an awareness that these issues will have to be confronted.[88] Indigenous representatives participating in the process will promote an outcome that accommodates the interests of Indigenous communities.[89]

f) The UN Draft Declaration on the Rights of Indigenous Peoples

Other than ILO Convention 169, the most comprehensive elaboration of Indigenous rights is found in the draft texts that are the basis for the negotiation of declarations on the rights of Indigenous peoples at the UN and OAS. If they are ever adopted, these declarations will occupy a central position in the articulation of international Indigenous rights. Even in their current draft form, the declarations that are the basis for the UN and OAS work have been referred to as sources of relevant principles of international law,[90] including by Justice Binnie of the Supreme Court of Canada in his concurring reasons in *Mitchell v. Canada (Minister of National Revenue).*[91]

In the working groups that have been established under the auspices of the UN and the OAS to elaborate declarations on a Indigenous rights, a wide range of issues are being addressed, such as the right of Indigenous peoples to self-determination, the nature and scope of collective rights, and the elaboration of Indigenous rights to lands, resources, and cultural integ-

---

88 See COP Decision: UN Doc. UNEP/CBD/COP/7/21, Annex, Decision VII/19 and the *Report of the Third Session of the Working Group on Access and Benefit Sharing*, UN Doc. UNEP/CBD/WG-ABS/3/7, Annex 1.

89 Indigenous people have been permitted to participate in the WGABS as observers. This gives them the opportunity to make interventions during formal sessions and to lobby state officials in the corridors. See COP Decision: UN Doc. UNEP/CBD/COP/5/23, Annex III, Decision V/26 and UN Doc. UNEP/CBD/COP/7/21, Annex Decision VII/19.

90 See *Dann Report*, above note 38 at paras. 128–30; *Toledo District Report* above note 54 at para. 117, and "*Awas Tingni* Judgment, Concurring Opinion of Judge Sergio Garcia Ramirez," reprinted in (2002) 19 Ariz. J. Int'l & Comp. L. 449 at paras. 8 and 9.

91 [2001] 1 S.C.R. 911 at paras. 81–83. Binnie J. also refers to Convention 169 in the same paragraphs.

rity. Both working groups are conducting their negotiations on the basis of texts drafted by experts. Although there are differences between them, for the most part the two texts cover broadly the same ground. Since they are similar, the following comments focus on the UN draft Declaration on the rights of Indigenous peoples (the draft Declaration).

In 1995, the UN Commission on Human Rights (CHR) established the ad hoc, open-ended Working Group of states on the Draft Declaration (WGDD), and gave it the responsibility to elaborate a declaration on Indigenous rights for eventual adoption by the UN General Assembly. At its first meeting, the WGDD agreed to use the draft Declaration as the basis for its work. Indigenous representatives participate actively and in significant numbers in WGDD sessions.

The initial ten-year mandate of the WGDD came to a close at the end of 2004 without a consensus text. The CHR subsequently adopted a resolution to extend the mandate of the WGDD for an additional ten working days.[92] At the end of this extended mandate the Chairperson-Rapporteur released a report that includes his proposal for a compromise text of the declaration.[93] It is expected that the Chair's text will be considered for adoption at the first session of the new UN Human Rights Council in June 2006. It would then be trasmitted to the UN General Assembly for its consideration at the 2006 session.

Like ILO Convention 169, the draft Declaration is infused with the themes of Indigenous participation and consultation. This is reinforced by the reiteration in the draft text of common Article 1 of the ICESCR and ICCPR as a right of Indigenous peoples to self-determination.[94] Further, in relation to consultation and land use issues specifically, the draft Declaration includes the following preambulary paragraph:

---

92 Resolution on the Working group of the Commission on Human Rights to elaborate a draft declaration in accordance with para. 5 of General Assembly resolution 49/214 of 23 December 1994, UN Doc. E/CN.4/2005/L.61. During its initial ten-year mandate, the working group generally met once a year for a two week (or roughly ten-day) formal session. In some years additional informal sessions were held.

93 The Chair's text can be found in the report of the working group established in accordance with the Commission on Human Rights regulation, 1995/32 of 3 March 1995 on its eleventh session, UN Doc. E/CN.4/2006/79, 22 March 2006.

94 Draft Declaration on the Rights of Indigenous Peoples, UN Doc. E/CN.4/sub.2/ RES/1994/45, art. 3.

Convinced that control by Indigenous peoples over developments affecting them and their lands, territories and resources will enable them to maintain and strengthen their institutions, cultures and traditions, and to promote their development in accordance with their aspirations and needs.[95]

Building on that paragraph, the body of the draft Declaration includes articles referring to the rights of Indigenous peoples to maintain and develop their political, economic, and social systems;[96] to maintain and strengthen their distinctive spiritual relationship with their lands and resources;[97] to own, develop, control, and use their lands;[98] and, most relevant to this chapter, to determine and develop priorities and strategies for the development of their lands and resources, "including the right to require that states obtain their free and informed consent prior to the approval of any project affecting their lands and resources."[99]

In WGDD sessions, states have shown discomfort with the reference to a right of FPIC. In an effort to find a compromise, New Zealand tabled an amended text of the draft Declaration at the tenth session of the WGDD. Among other things, the alternative text proposes using the phrase *"seek* their free and informed consent" instead of *"obtain* their free and informed consent" as a way around states' concern about the recognition of an Indigenous veto.[100]

It is possible that, despite best efforts from WGDD participants, the UN General Assembly will never adopt a declaration on the rights of Indigenous peoples. However, it is inconceivable at this point that a consensus text, or even a text that is adopted by a vote, will not include significant emphasis on the themes of consultation and participation of Indigenous peoples in relation to a range of issues, including lands and resources. Given the central role the draft Declaration has played in debate about international Indigenous rights, this is a strong indication of the direction that the international community is taking on the topic of consultation. The fact that the document has been in the works for so long and has

---

95 *Ibid.* preambulary para. 8.
96 *Ibid.*, art. 21.
97 *Ibid.*, art. 25.
98 *Ibid.*, art. 26.
99 *Ibid.*, art. 30.
100 The alternative text carries UN Doc. E/CN.4/2004/WG.15/CRP.1. It was tabled on behalf of Denmark, Finland, Iceland, New Zealand, Norway, Sweden, and Switzerland. The Chairperson-Rapporteur has recommended that the WGDD keep the original word *obtain* (Report, tenth session, above note 93 at para. 35).

been given so much attention and effort by many states (particularly those whose Indigenous peoples share similar experiences of colonization), and that its iteration has involved considerable Indigenous participation, will help give a UN declaration on Indigenous rights, if adopted, that much more weight as a statement of customary international law norms, even though it will not be a treaty.

g) Indigenous Participation in International Fora

While the substantive content of relevant international instruments and the standard-setting activities of various international bodies must be the focus of a review of the status and trends regarding the emergence of a consultation principle, the mere fact that many venues have been established at the international level in the last fifteen years or so that permit the expression of Indigenous peoples' perspectives is itself an indication that states recognize that those perspectives should be heard and considered.[101] The growth in opportunities for the expression of Indigenous voices internationally does not necessarily translate into an international consultation principle or right. Indeed, in keeping with their intergovernmental nature, states retain decision-making authority in these venues, including the authority to discontinue them or to block Indigenous participation. Nevertheless, it is fair to say that state acceptance, and even encouragement, of Indigenous participation in international venues addressing issues relevant to their land and resource claims is relevant to an analysis of the status of a consultation principle at the international level.

In the speech he delivered on the last day of the first session of the UN Permanent Forum on Indigenous Issues in May 2002, the secretary-general of the UN proclaimed to the world's Indigenous peoples, "You have a home at the United Nations."[102] While this welcome has only recently been extended, Indigenous participation at the international level is already making a difference. Indigenous participation must make a difference within the countries in which Indigenous people live too. The second part

---

101 Indigenous people participate in the international deliberations that take place in the following venues, among others, in significant numbers: the WGIP, the PFII, the WGDD, and the OAS Working Group on a Draft Declaration on the Rights of Indigenous Peoples, the World Summit on the Information Society, the World Intellectual Property Organization Intergovernmental Committee on Genetic Resources, Traditional Knowledge and Folklore, and the CBD Working Groups on Article 8j and Related Provisions and on Access and Benefit Sharing.

102 Quote found at website of the UN Permanent Forum on Indigenous Issues online: www.un.org/esa/socdev/unpfii/documents/doc_first_session1.htm.

of this chapter will describe how the topic of consultation with Indigenous peoples in the context of land and natural resource development, is addressed in Canadian law and policy.

C. CONSULTATION UNDER CANADIAN LAW

1) Overview

At the same time that consultation with Indigenous peoples has been taking on importance at the international level, consultation with Aboriginal peoples has become a legal and policy priority in Canada. Since Aboriginal and treaty rights were recognized and affirmed in section 35 of the *Constitution Act, 1982*, governments, Aboriginal groups, and the courts have struggled to define those rights and give meaning to this provision.[103] Section 35 has been interpreted by the Supreme Court of Canada both as a strong measure of protection for Aboriginal and treaty rights and as a means of reconciling the prior occupation of North America by Aboriginal peoples with the exercise of sovereignty by the Crown.[104] Although the jurisprudence on Aboriginal law has evolved rapidly over the last two decades, the courts have only defined the existence of specific Aboriginal rights in a limited number of circumstances.[105]

The evolving nature of Aboriginal law, together with the fact that a majority of Aboriginal groups have yet to conclude land claims agreements with the federal government that would clarify and define their rights,[106]

---

103 *Constitution Act, 1982*, being Schedule B to the Canada Act 1982 (U.K.), 1982, c. 11. Section 35(1) reads as follows: "The existing Aboriginal and treaty rights of the aboriginal peoples of Canada are hereby recognized and affirmed."

104 *Sparrow*, above note 52 and *Delgamuukw*, above note 12.

105 The courts have yet to rule on the existence of a specific instance of Aboriginal title in Canada, although there are ongoing trials on the issue. Some examples of ongoing trials where Aboriginal groups are claiming the existence of Aboriginal title: *The Council of the Haida Nation et al. v. Her Majesty the Queen in Right of the Province of British Columbia and the Attorney General of Canada*, Action No. L020662, Vancouver Registry; *Roger William et al. v. Her Majesty the Queen in Right of the Province of British Columbia and the Attorney General of Canada*, Action no. 900913, Victoria Registry.

106 The 1973 Supreme Court decision in *Calder v. British Columbia (Attorney General)*, [1973] S.C.R. 313, also marked an important turning point in Aboriginal law and policy by holding that Aboriginal title to land was still available in Canada. That decision precipitated the adoption of the Comprehensive Land Claims policy aimed at the settlement of Aboriginal land claims, based on the assertion of continuing Aboriginal title to lands and natural resources, where no treaties were previously signed. While some comprehensive land claims agreements have been concluded with First Nations,

means that there is uncertainty regarding what specific Aboriginal rights are constitutionally recognized. This uncertainty underlies the current emphasis being placed on consultations among Aboriginal groups, governments, and private industry.[107]

In the recent decisions of *Haida Nation v. British Columbia (Minister of Forests)*[108] and *Taku River Tlingit First Nation v. British Columbia (Project Assessment Director)*,[109] the Supreme Court of Canada confirmed that governments have a legal obligation to consult with Aboriginal peoples prior to the proof or establishment of their rights before land and resource development is permitted in areas where Aboriginal rights are disputed. For the first time, the Court held that consultation is grounded in the honour of the Crown and is a key element to the implementation of the principle of reconciliation that underpins section 35.[110] More recently in *Mikisew Cree First Nation v. Canada (Minister of Canadian Heritage)*, the Supreme Court held that the honour of the Crown is also at stake in the implementation of historic treaties, which implies a duty to consult with the First Nation signatories of those treaties when the Crown is "taking up" land, which it has a right to do pursuant to Treaty 8 and other historic treaties concluded in Western Canada, for purposes that may include resource development.[111]

---

the federal government, in coordination with provinces, is still engaged in treaty negotiations with First Nations across Canada. See *Comprehensive Claims Policy and Status of Claims*, February 2003, online: www.ainc-inac.gc.ca/ps/clm/brieft_e.html.

107 Notably, Aboriginal groups are more and more seeking injunctions to prevent developments from proceeding, and are seeking to have governmental decisions quashed on the basis that they were not adequately consulted in applications for judicial review. For example, see *Blaney et al. v. British Columbia (Minister of Agriculture, Food and Fisheries) et al.*, 2004 BCSC 1764 ; *Musqueam Indian Band v. British Columbia (Minister of Sustainable Resource Management)*, 2005 BCCA 128; *Chief Apsassin v. British Columbia (Oil and Gas Commission)*, 2004 BCCA 286.

108 *Haida*, above note 12.

109 2004 SCC 74 [*Taku River*].

110 *Haida*, above note 12 at paras. 16–17; *Taku River, ibid.* at para. 24.

111 2005 SCC 69 [*Mikisew Cree*]. At issue in *Mikisew Cree* was an approval for the construction of a winter road in Wood Buffalo National Park in the vicinity of the First Nation's reserve in the Treaty 8 area. Treaty 8 provides that hunting, fishing, and trapping rights are guaranteed in the land surrendered under the treaty "saving and excepting such tracts as may be required or taken up from time to time for settlement, mining or other purposes." The issue was whether the Crown had a legal obligation to consult prior to "taking up" land. The Supreme Court held that when the Crown exercises its treaty right to "take up" land, it has a duty to act honourably, which requires the Crown to consult with First Nations whose rights under the treaty would be adversely affected.

This part of the chapter provides a brief overview of the early elaboration of the "duty to consult" in Canadian law, followed by a more detailed
discussion of *Haida* and *Taku River*. Key observations about the framework
for consultations in Canada are made, with a view to informing developments on the international stage.

2) The "Duty to Consult" in Canadian Law

Any discussion of consultation in Canadian law must begin with section
35(1) of the *Constitution Act, 1982,* which states that "the existing aboriginal
and treaty rights of the aboriginal peoples of Canada are hereby recognized
and affirmed."[112] This recognition and affirmation has brought about fundamental changes to the legal landscape in the Aboriginal area. Aboriginal
peoples have often turned to the courts to resolve outstanding issues in the
absence of a clear, comprehensive, and cohesive federal Aboriginal policy.
The legal framework developed since 1982 has contributed a great deal to
reshaping the federal government's relationship with Aboriginal peoples
and the direction of Canadian Aboriginal policy initiatives. It is through
the interpretation of section 35, starting with the 1990 *Sparrow* decision,
that the Supreme Court of Canada introduced the element of consultation,
now a key issue in Canadian Aboriginal law and policy.

a) The *Sparrow* Duty to Consult: Limits of a Model Based on Established Rights

The *Sparrow* case provided the Supreme Court of Canada with its first
opportunity to examine and interpret section 35. Simply put, the section
was held to be a limitation on the discretion of governments to adopt and
implement policies and legislation that restrict the exercise of Aboriginal
rights.[113] Prior to 1982, those rights were not constitutionally recognized
and they could be unilaterally extinguished or limited by Parliament.[114] In

112 See above note 103.
113 See *Sparrow*, above note 52 at 1109 where the Court writes: "Yet, we find that the words
     'recognition and affirmation' incorporate the fiduciary relationship referred to earlier
     and so import some restraint on the exercise of sovereign power. ... These powers
     must, however, now be read together with s. 35(1). In other words, federal power must
     be reconciled with federal duty and the best way to achieve that reconciliation is to
     demand the justification of any government regulation that infringes upon or denies
     aboriginal rights."
114 For a discussion on the extinguishment of Aboriginal rights, see Peter W. Hogg, *Con-
     stitutional Law of Canada*, 3d ed., vol. 1, looseleaf (Toronto: Carswell, 1992) at 27–28.

Sparrow, the Supreme Court of Canada stated that this was no longer the case.

The Supreme Court of Canada also held that Aboriginal rights are not absolute and can be limited or infringed if the infringement is justified.[115] Once an Aboriginal group has established the existence of an Aboriginal right and of a *prima facie* infringement of that right, the Crown must justify the infringement by demonstrating that: 1) the government action at issue serves a valid legislative objective; and 2) if so, the action is consistent with the honour of the Crown and the fiduciary nature of the Crown–Aboriginal relationship.[116] One consideration identified by the Court in connection with the second element of the analysis is whether there was adequate consultation. Whether or not consultation with the affected Aboriginal group took place prior to the infringement is one factor courts may consider in determining whether the infringement is justified.[117] Other considerations may include minimal impairment of the right and, in a situation of land expropriation, whether there was adequate compensation given to an affected Aboriginal group.[118] The Supreme Court of Canada did not conclude that an infringement of an Aboriginal right can never be justified when there has not been appropriate consultation: consultation is an important, but not mandatory, element of the justification framework.

This justification framework provides a foundation for the reconciliation of section 35 rights with the exercise of Crown sovereign powers.[119]

---

115 *Sparrow*, above note 52 at 1109.

116 See *Sparrow, ibid.* at 1110, where the Court writes: "The government is required to bear the burden of justifying any legislation that has some negative effect on any aboriginal right protected under s. 35(1)." See also at 1113–14.

117 The Court writes: "Within the analysis of justification, there are further questions to be addressed, depending on the circumstances of the inquiry. These include the questions of whether there has been as little infringement as possible in order to effect the desired result; whether, in a situation of expropriation, fair compensation is available; and, whether the aboriginal group in question has been consulted with respect to the conservation measure being implemented. The aboriginal peoples, with their history of conservation-consciousness and interdependence with natural resources, would surely be expected, at the least, to be informed regarding the determination of an appropriate scheme for the regulation of the fisheries." See *ibid.* at 1119.

118 *Ibid.*

119 The justification framework is similar in purpose and structure to the Supreme Court's s. 1 *Charter* analysis. See *R. v. Oakes*, [1986] 1 S.C.R. 103, where the Supreme Court of Canada prescribed a standard of justification for all *Charter* rights. For a discussion on s. 1 of the *Charter*, see Hogg, *Constitutional Law of Canada*, above note 114 at c. 35.

Reconciliation is the basis for requiring that government actions that interfere with Aboriginal rights must be justified.

> Rights that are recognized and affirmed are not absolute. Federal legislative powers continue, including, of course, the right to legislate with respect to Indians pursuant to s. 91(24) of the Constitution Act, 1867. These powers must, however, now be read together with s. 35(1). In other words, *federal power must be reconciled with federal duty and the best way to achieve that reconciliation is to demand the justification of any government regulation that infringes upon or denies aboriginal rights* (emphasis added).[120]

In determining whether there has been a reconciliation of Aboriginal interests with the Crown's responsibility to govern, the courts must assess whether the honour of the Crown has been upheld. In the context of consultation, this means that the specific Aboriginal rights that exist must be seriously considered and addressed appropriately.

The case law emanating from the Supreme Court of Canada following the *Sparrow* decision confirmed the "duty to consult" as part of the justification framework and clarified the nature and scope of consultation.[121] In *R. v. Badger*, the Court held that the justification framework also applies to infringements of Aboriginal treaty rights and that consultation is one factor to consider when determining if such infringements are justified.[122]

The Supreme Court of Canada also appeared to expand upon the element of consultation in the *Delgamuukw* decision by suggesting that there is *always* a duty to consult in the context of an infringement of Aboriginal title. For the majority of the Court, Lamer C.J. states:

> First, aboriginal title encompasses within it a right to choose to what end a piece of land can be put. The aboriginal right to fish for food, by contrast, does not contain within it the same discretionary component. This aspect of aboriginal title suggests that the fiduciary relationship between the Crown and aboriginal peoples may be satisfied by the involvement of aboriginal peoples in decisions taken with respect to their lands. *There is always a duty of consultation.* Whether the aboriginal group has been consulted is relevant to determining whether the infringement of aboriginal title is justified, in the same way that the Crown's failure to consult an

---

120 *Sparrow,* above note 52 at 1119.
121 See *R. v. Badger,* [1996] 1 S.C.R. 771; *Delgamuukw,* above note 12; *R. v. Marshall,* [1999] 3 S.C.R. 456, additional reasons at [1999] 3 S.C.R. 533.
122 *Badger, ibid.* at paras. 85 and 96–97.

aboriginal group with respect to the terms by which reserve land is leased may breach fiduciary duty at common law: *Guerin* (emphais added).[123]

While *Sparrow* indicated that consultation is only one factor to be examined by the courts in relation to infringements of Aboriginal and treaty rights, *Delgamuukw* suggests that consultation is always required in order for the Crown to be able to justify infringements of Aboriginal title.

The *Delgamuukw* decision also introduced the notion of a "spectrum" of consultation. That is, the nature and scope of the "duty to consult" will vary with the circumstances. For the majority, Lamer C.J. writes:

> In occasional cases, when the breach is less serious or relatively minor, it will be no more than a duty to discuss important decisions that will be taken with respect to lands held pursuant to aboriginal title. Of course, even in these rare cases when the minimum acceptable standard is consultation, this consultation must be in good faith, and with the intention of substantially addressing the concerns of the aboriginal peoples whose lands are at issue. In most cases, it will be significantly deeper than mere consultation. Some cases may even require the full consent of an aboriginal nation, particularly when provinces enact hunting and fishing regulations to aboriginal lands.[124]

Various lower and appeal courts also provided additional guidance on what is meant by a "duty to consult" within the justification context.[125]

Beyond its statements in *Sparrow* and *Delgamuukw*, the Supreme Court of Canada provided relatively little guidance on the "duty to consult" prior to the *Haida* and *Taku River* decisions. In the earlier decisions, the Court only discussed consultation in the context of "established" or "proven" section 35 rights. This resulted in a practical difficulty for determining when consultation is legally required, both from the government and the Aborig-

---

123 Above note 12 at para. 168.
124 *Ibid.*
125 For example, in *Halfway River First Nation v. British Columbia (Ministry of Forests)*, [1999] 4 C.N.L.R. 1 at para. 161, the British Columbia Court of Appeal held that consultation is a reciprocal "two-way street" in relation to which all parties, including Aboriginal groups, must act reasonably. In that decision, the Court also stated that the Crown must ensure that Aboriginal groups "are provided with all necessary information" at an appropriate time in the consultation process so that "they have an opportunity to express their interests and concerns" with a particular government activity in an informed manner (at para. 160).

inal perspectives, in light of uncertainty regarding which rights claimed by Aboriginal groups are constitutionally protected.

Pursuant to the framework set out in *Sparrow*, the requirement for the Crown to justify infringements, including providing proof of prior consultation, arises only after an Aboriginal group has proven the existence of a section 35 right and a *prima facie* infringement. This meant that in order for the Crown to demonstrate that appropriate consultation has taken place, it needed to be undertaken before the infringing activity occurred. That is, consultation had to be conducted prior to the infringement and prior to the establishment of the Aboriginal right, but the legal obligation to consult did not arise until after the determination of the existence of rights was completed and a *prima facie* case made regarding their infringement. However, the courts have only ruled on the existence of specific Aboriginal rights in a few cases and have yet to rule on the existence of an instance of Aboriginal title. Further, only a minority of Aboriginal groups have signed comprehensive claims agreements with the federal government. The Crown found itself with a case-sensitive legal duty that had to be satisfied before it actually crystallized from a legal perspective.

The consultation obligation, as defined in *Sparrow*, was also unsatisfactory from the Aboriginal perspective. The fact that the justification framework did not legally require governments to consult prior to engaging in measures that could impact on potential constitutional rights made it difficult for Aboriginal people to protect their interests in anticipation of a government activity that might infringe claimed but unproven rights. Aboriginal groups strongly criticized the requirement that they prove their rights in court, a long and costly process, before the Crown was legally obligated to consult.[126]

The "consultation dilemma" emerging out of the *Sparrow* framework was put to the test in *Haida* and *Taku River*.

b) The "New" Duty to Consult: The *Haida/Taku River* Innovation

The central issue in *Haida* and *Taku River* was whether governments and private industry are legally obligated to consult with Aboriginal groups where decisions could affect their unproven but potential rights.

---

126 For a discussion of the unsatisfactory nature of the *Sparrow* duty to consult that foreshadowed, to an extent, the direction the Supreme Court eventually took in *Haida* and *Taku River*, see Patrick Macklem & Sonia Lawrence, "From Consultation to Reconciliation: Aboriginal Peoples and the Crown's Duty to Consult" (2000) 79 Can. Bar Rev. 252.

In *Taku River*, the respondent, Redfern Resources Ltd., sought approval to reopen a mine, which would involve, among other things, building a road over lands to which the Taku River Tlingit First Nation claimed Aboriginal rights and title. Following a process of consultation, established under the British Columbia *Environmental Assessment Act*, in which the Tlingit participated, Redfern's application to reopen the mine was approved and the ministers issued a project approval certificate that provided for the construction of the road, subject to conditions. The Tlingit filed a petition for judicial review of that decision on the basis that the construction of the road would interfere with their asserted Aboriginal rights and title and that the conditions imposed were not sufficient to protect their interests.

The *Haida* case concerned a judicial review application by the Haida Nation of provincial decisions to renew and transfer a Tree Farm Licence to Weyerhaeuser Co. Ltd. over an area where the Haida claimed Aboriginal rights and title. The Haida sought to set aside both the transfer of the Licence to Weyerhaeuser and the minister's decision to replace Tree Farm Licence 39.

Both the Taku River Tlingit and the Haida Nation argued that the BC Government failed to sufficiently consult them before issuing the approvals. In far-reaching decisions, the British Columbia Court of Appeal held that governments have a legally enforceable fiduciary and constitutional duty to consult with an Aboriginal group and to seek workable accommodations prior to the establishment of an Aboriginal right. In their turn, the Supreme Court of Canada ruled in unanimous decisions that the federal and provincial governments have a legal duty to consult, and possibly accommodate, when the Crown has knowledge of the potential existence of an Aboriginal right or title and contemplates conduct that might adversely affect it.[127] The Supreme Court of Canada clearly rejects the view that governments do not have a legally enforceable duty to consult with Aboriginal groups prior to the proof of section 35 rights. In order to achieve reconciliation, and preserve land and resources pending the resolution of claims, it may be necessary to consult and possibly accommodate section 35 rights before they are proven.

---

127 *Haida*, above note 12 at para. 35; *Taku River*, above note 109 at para. 21. The SCC dismissed the province of British Columbia's appeal in *Haida* and found that the provincial government had not adequately consulted and accommodated the Haida Nation. The SCC allowed the province's appeal in *Taku River* and found that the BC government had fulfilled its obligation and adequately consulted and accommodated.

The source of the obligation to consult, described in *Taku River* and *Haida*, is the honour of the Crown. Writing for the Court in the *Taku River* decision, McLachlin C.J. states:

> As discussed in the companion case of *Haida*, *supra*, the principle of the honour of the Crown grounds the Crown's duty to consult and if indicated accommodate Aboriginal peoples, even prior to proof of asserted Aboriginal rights and title. The duty of honour derives from the Crown's assertion of sovereignty in the face of prior Aboriginal occupation. It has been enshrined in s. 35(1) of the *Constitution Act, 1982*, which recognizes and affirms existing Aboriginal rights and titles.... In all its dealings with Aboriginal peoples, the Crown must act honourably, in accordance with its historical and future relationship with the Aboriginal peoples in question. The Crown's honour cannot be interpreted narrowly or technically, but must be given full effect in order to promote the process of reconciliation mandated by s. 35(1).[128]

Reconciliation is a central theme underlying the Supreme Court of Canada's findings on consultation. As a result of the *Haida* and *Taku River* decisions, governments cannot use lands and resources as they choose, pending the final resolution of Aboriginal claims. Rather, they must act honourably and respect the potential but unproven interests of Aboriginal peoples. Underlying the requirement that the Crown must act honourably and in good faith is the need to reconcile the prior occupation of the land by Aboriginal peoples with "the reality of Crown sovereignty."[129] McLachlin C.J. states: "It is a corollary of section 35 that the Crown act honourably in defining the rights it guarantees and in reconciling them with other rights and interest. This, in turn, implies a duty to consult and, if appropriate, accommodate."[130] Reconciliation is defined as a process flowing from the constitutional recognition of rights in section 35. As such, limiting consultation to the situation where those rights have been proven, and not when

---

128 *Taku, ibid.* at para. 24.
129 *Ibid.* at para. 26. The Supreme Court of Canada decision in *Mikisew Cree* subsequently confirmed the importance of reconciliation. Writing for the Court, Binnie J. begins his reasons by stating: "The fundamental objective of the modern law of aboriginal and treaty rights is the reconciliation of aboriginal peoples and non-aboriginal peoples and their respective claims, interest and ambitions."
130 *Haida*, above note 12 at para. 20.

they have been claimed to exist, would render the reconciliation process meaningless.[131]

Having described reconciliation as a guiding principle of the Crown's duty to consult with Aboriginal peoples, the Supreme Court of Canada goes on to set out more specific criteria for the fulfilment of this duty. First, the Court states that the duty to consult "arises when the Crown has knowledge, real or constructive, of the potential existence of the Aboriginal right or title and contemplates conduct that might adversely affect it."[132] The difficulty in identifying potential Aboriginal rights and possible infringement is recognized: the Court states that Aboriginal groups must "outline their claims with clarity, focussing on the scope and nature of the Aboriginal rights they assert and on the alleged infringements."[133] Where treaty rights are at issue, the Supreme Court stated in *Mikisew Cree* that, as a party to a treaty, the Crown will "always have notice of its content."[134]

Second, the Supreme Court of Canada confirms that the content of the duty to consult varies with the circumstances. The scope of consultation will be "proportionate to a preliminary assessment of the strength of the case supporting the existence of the right or title, and to the seriousness of the potential adverse effect."[135]

Third, the Supreme Court of Canada clarified that consultation does not give Aboriginal groups a veto over what can be done with land pending final proof of a claim.[136] Rather, the consultation process described by the Court involves a balancing of societal interests. In all cases, as a matter of honour, the Crown must act in good faith and undertake meaningful consultation.

---

131 See *ibid.* at para. 33, where the Court writes: "To limit reconciliation to the post-proof sphere risks treating reconciliation as a distant, legalistic goal, devoid of the 'meaningful content' mandated by the 'solemn commitment' made by the Crown in recognizing and affirming Aboriginal rights and title": *Sparrow*, above note 52 at 1108. "It also risks unfortunate consequences. When the distant goal of proof is finally reached, the Aboriginal peoples may find their land and resources changed and denuded. This is not reconciliation. Nor is it honourable."
132 *Haida*, above note 12 at para. 35; *Taku River*, above note 109 at para. 25.
133 *Haida, ibid.* at para. 36.
134 *Mikisew Cree*, above note 111 at para. 34.
135 *Haida*, above note 12 at para. 39; *Taku River*, above note 109 at para. 29. The Supreme Court of Canada confirmed the concept of a spectrum of duties in *Mikisew Cree, ibid.* at paras. 62–63.
136 *Haida, ibid.* at para. 48. See also *Mikisew Cree, ibid.* at para. 66.

The Supreme Court of Canada also held that the duty to consult only falls on governments and does not apply to third parties, such as private industry.[137] The Crown can delegate procedural aspects of consultation to third-party industry proponents but always remains legally responsible for the fulfilment of the duty to consult.[138]

By holding that governments have a legal duty to consult with Aboriginal groups prior to the proof or establishment of rights, the *Taku River* and *Haida* decisions have addressed the outstanding consultation dilemma flowing from the *Sparrow* justification framework. Aboriginal groups have hailed the *Haida* and *Taku River* decisions as a major victory for the recognition of their interests. Governments can no longer "cavalierly run roughshod" over lands where Aboriginal peoples have outstanding claims to lands and resources without first consulting with the Aboriginal groups making those claims.[139] Further, the process of treaty implementation also requires that the Crown act honourably and consult with treaty rights holders when "taking up" land pursuant to historic treaties.[140] Clearly, the imposition of a legal duty to consult in the context of unproven claims of Aboriginal rights is intended to improve the framework within which governments make decisions in the context of land and resource development.

---

137 In *Haida*, the BCCA held that on the basis of a constructive trust fiduciary duty, third party industry may have an enforceable and legal duty to consult with Aboriginal groups if their proposed action will result in a *prima facie* infringement of asserted s. 35 rights. The Court stated that Weyerhaeuser, the third party at issue in this case, had such an obligation because of its knowledge of the Haida's claim, its knowledge of the provincial Crown's fiduciary duty and also because it should have been aware of the Crown's breach of that duty. See *Haida Nation v. British Columbia (Minister of Forests)*, [2002] 2 C.N.L.R. 121 (27 February 2002); additional reasons, 2002 BCCA 462 (19 August 2002).

138 *Haida*, above note 12 at para. 53.

139 *Ibid.* at para. 27.

140 See *Mikisew Cree*, above note 111 at para. 59. It is worth noting that the duty to consult is defined in *Mikisew Cree* as a "procedural right" stemming from the treaty itself. Binnie J. states at para. 57: "As stated from the outset, the honour of the Crown infuses every treaty and the performance of every treaty obligation. Treaty 8 therefore gives rise to Mikisew procedural rights (e.g., consultation) as well as substantive rights (e.g., hunting, fishing and trapping rights)."

3) The Canadian Experience: A Focus on Meaningful Processes of Consultation

a) Consultation Is Challenging

The "duty to consult" is now entrenched in Canadian law. The challenge is for federal, provincial, and territorial governments to live up to this new standard. This challenge is not a small one.

Even before *Haida* and *Taku River*, governments were engaged in consultations with Aboriginal peoples in the context of various initiatives on a policy basis and for strategic reasons. Although practices have varied and been inconsistent, it has been widely recognized for some time that consultation with Aboriginal people is key to promoting a better understanding of government initiatives, to making informed and appropriate decisions, and generating support for proposed activities. Consultation is an important factor in developing good working relationships between governments and Aboriginal groups. In addition, there are many instances in which Canada has assumed treaty obligations, usually in the form of a comprehensive claims agreement, to consult or obtain the consent of Aboriginal groups in specific circumstances.[141] More pragmatically, consultation has long been a means through which governments manage legal risks. Although governments have become increasingly aware of the importance of discussing planned activities with Aboriginal peoples, there is still a long way to go before consultation is carried out on a systematic basis in Canada.

Industry proponents have also been involved in consulting with Aboriginal peoples in relation to land and resource development projects. Even though *Haida* has confirmed that industry does not have a legal duty to consult, proponents understand that if they wish their projects to pro-

---

141 For example, the *Sahtu Dene and Metis Comprehensive Land Claim Agreement* (1993) states at s. 9.2.1, dealing with the Norman Wells Proven Area: "Government shall consult with the Sahtu Tribal Council with respect to those matters to be discussed with Esso or other parties on any amendment, renegotiation or renewal of the Proven Area Agreement or any new agreement for the development of the Proven Area and shall keep the Sahtu Tribal Council fully informed of the progress of such negotiations." In the definitions section of the agreement, *consultation* is defined as: "(a) the provision, to the party to be consulted, of notice of a matter to be decided in sufficient form and detail to allow that party to prepare its views on the matter; (b) the provision of a reasonable period of time in which the party to be consulted may prepare its views on the matter, and provision of an opportunity to present such views to the party obliged to consult; and (c) full and fair consideration by the party obliged to consult of any views presented." Online: www.ainc-inac.gc.ca/pr/agr/sahtu/sahmet_e.pdf.

ceed smoothly they need the support of affected Aboriginal communities. Industry is also keenly aware that failure by governments to appropriately consult with Aboriginal groups can have significant consequences for them. The courts have shown that they are capable and willing to quash approvals and permits, grant injunctions, and delay projects to ensure that governments fulfil their duty to consult with the Aboriginal groups involved.[142] In order to foster mutual respect, reduce the risk to investments, and have something to show to the courts if litigation occurs, industry players "should develop their own strategies to be proactively involved with the Aboriginal community."[143] While there may always be some who regard consultation with Aboriginal groups as an obstacle to Canada's economic growth, the better view is that the legal obligation to consult, articulated in *Haida* and *Taku River*, will help establish a stronger investment climate in parts of Canada that are subject to Aboriginal claims. By providing a viable and beneficial alternative to costly litigation, parties may avoid delays or possible abandonment of projects.

Consultation also poses challenges for Aboriginal peoples. Their communities must deal with the substantial capacity and human resource pressures created by an intensive consultation atmosphere in which they may be contacted by officials from a variety of departments in different levels of government on many issues. While some communities have been

---

142 See *Musqueam Indian Band v. British Columbia (Minister of Sustainable Resource Management)*, above note 107, where the British Columbia Court of Appeal allowed the Musqueam Indian Band's appeal and found that the consultation by the province had occurred too late in the process of selling lands. The BCCA ordered a two-year suspension of the sale to allow the provincial Crown to conduct proper consultation with the Musqueam. See also *Première nation de Betsiamites v. Canada (Procureur général)*, [2005] J.Q. no 8173, where the Québec Superior Court granted a safeguard order to cease logging on land to which the Innu First Nation of Betsiamites claim Aboriginal rights and title on the basis that no consultation was done by the province prior to granting the logging permits in 1997 when it had knowledge of those claims. The Québec Court of Appeal subsequently overturned the Superior Court's decision to grant the safeguard order. (*Kruger v. Première nation des Betsiamites et al.*, No. 500-09-015771-058, 28 April 2006). Further, in allowing the appeal in *Mikisew Cree*, the Supreme Court of Canada quashed the minister's approval for the construction of the winter road.

143 See Deborah M.I. Szatylo, "Recognition and Reconciliation: An Alberta Fact or Fiction?" (Spring 2002) 1 Indigenous L.J. 201 at 217 and 234–35 for a discussion on the duty to consult in Alberta and the impact on the oil and gas industry. Note that this article was written and published before the SCC decisions in *Haida* and *Taku River*.

involved in consultative processes for many years, others are only just start-ing to grapple with the new reality.[144]

b) Flexibility of Consultation: Continuum of Approaches

One of the more important lessons learned from Canada's experience is that consultation is not a "one size fits all" proposition. Rather, flexibility and adaptability is critical to successful and meaningful consultation pro-cesses for all concerned. A consultation that is sensitive to the culture and traditions of Aboriginal groups, and that is tailored to the specific circum-stances at issue, is more likely to result in outcomes that meet the objec-tives of all parties involved.

i)   A Focus on Aboriginal Cultures and Traditions

It is important that consultation processes be capable of adaptation to the circumstances of different Aboriginal communities. The Aboriginal popu-lation in Canada includes a considerable diversity of cultures, traditions, experiences, and lifestyles. How consultations are conducted, and with, whom will need to be tailored to the community involved. This is expressed in the guiding principles in the British Columbia *Provincial Policy for Con-sultation with First Nations* (the BC Policy), which states that "consultation processes should be clearly defined to the First Nations in question."[145] The ability of government entities to adapt consultation processes to reflect the specific cultures and traditions of the Aboriginal groups they intend to en-gage with is key to conducting successful and meaningful consultations.

---

144 Collecting and sharing the experience of Aboriginal communities that have already been engaged in consultative processes would be valuable not only for other Aborigi-nal communities in Canada, but also for Indigenous peoples worldwide. This is hap-pening to some extent. For example, some Aboriginal people from Canada participate in international meetings and negotiations, together with Indigenous people from other parts of the globe. They share experiences and apply what they learn when they return to their home communities and activities.

145 See online: www.gov.bc.ca/tno/down/consultation_policy_fn.pdf at p. 10 of the docu-ment [BC Policy]. Canada can also learn from New Zealand's consultation policy, which states: "When consulting with Mäori you need an understanding and aware-ness of the Mäori culture, and to be prepared to observe Mäori protocol and beliefs. Consulting may involve participating in ceremonies, such as formal welcomes, as well as respecting the traditions, beliefs, and values of the Mäori world." See New Zealand Department of Justice, *A Guide for Consultation with Mäori*, at 3.6. Online: www. justice.govt.nz/pubs/reports/1998/maori_consultation/process.html.

ii) Tailoring Consultation to the Circumstances
The nature and scope of consultation is also dependent on the Aboriginal interest at play and the particular activity contemplated by governments. As discussed above, *Haida* and *Taku River* confirm that the "content of the duty to consult and accommodate varies with the circumstances"[146] and is proportionate to the strength of the case supporting the claimed Aboriginal interest and the potential impact of the government activity or project.

The Supreme Court of Canada has explained that the appropriate level of consultation is to be determined by reference to a spectrum of possibilities, taking into account the nature of the situation. At one end of that spectrum, where the Aboriginal claim is relatively weak and the potential impact of the activity is minor, consultation may be limited to giving notice, disclosing information and discussing issues with the Aboriginal group concerned. At the other end of the spectrum, where a strong case for an Aboriginal claim exists and the potential impact on Aboriginal interest is severe, deeper consultation may be required. This may entail giving an Aboriginal group the opportunity to make submissions to the decision-maker, to formally participate in the decision-making process, and to receive written reasons from the decision-maker demonstrating how their concerns were addressed.[147]

The ability to adapt consultation processes to various circumstances is key to the approach taken by Canadian courts to the issue of government consultation with Aboriginal peoples. This is illustrated in the Supreme Court of Canada's *Haida* decision:

> Every case must be approached individually. Each must also be approached flexibly, since the level of consultation required may change as the process goes on and new information comes to light. The controlling question in all situations is what is required to maintain the honour of the Crown and to effect reconciliation between the Crown and Aboriginal peoples with respect to the interests at stake.[148]

Along these lines, the BC Policy incorporates the following guiding principle:

> While the nature and scope of consultation may vary, the fundamental principles of consultation are the same for all aboriginal interests con-

---

146 *Haida*, above note 12 at para. 39.
147 *Ibid.* at paras. 43–44.
148 *Ibid.* at para. 45.

templated by this Policy. Consultation efforts should be made diligently and meaningfully, and with the intention of fully considering aboriginal interests. Where a sound claim of aboriginal rights and/or title is made out, consultation efforts must attempt to address and/or accommodate a First Nation's concerns relating to the impact of proposed activities on the aboriginal interests that it identifies or of which the Crown is otherwise aware. *In practical terms, this means the quality of consultation is of primary importance, and the soundness of the claim will dictate the scope and depth of required consultation* (emphasis in original).[149]

The need for flexible consultation processes is also important in light of the complexity sometimes associated with statutory and regulatory approvals sought by industry in the context of land and resource development projects. For example, "mega projects" often involve a number of levels of government and a complex web of statutory and regulatory requirements, as well as environmental assessment processes.[150] The involvement of quasi-judicial and regulatory bodies can add to the challenges, partly because ambiguities can arise regarding their ability to discharge the Crown's legal duty to consult. Flexibility in the regulatory framework is necessary to ensure that the consultation requirement can be fulfilled and the Aboriginal interests addressed.

c) Balancing Interests

In *Haida* and *Taku River*, the Supreme Court of Canada defined consultation in terms of a process of information sharing and balancing of interests that may lead to the accommodation of Aboriginal concerns.[151] Information obtained during the consultation process may require that steps be taken to minimize the effects that a proposed activity would have on Aboriginal

---

149 BC Policy, above note 145 at 18.
150 Canada's North is currently the focus of mega-project attention with plans to develop the Mackenzie Delta oil and gas reserves and to construct a pipeline linking them with Alberta's infrastructure, which involves the investment of hundreds of millions of dollars on the part of industry. It may also result in billions in additional revenues for governments and should create significant employment and revenue sharing opportunities for affected Aboriginal communities. There is considerable pressure to proceed with such projects. The complexity involved in these projects is increased when a requirement to consult with Aboriginal peoples arises.
151 See *Haida*, above note 12 at para. 47, where the Court writes: "Thus the effect of good faith consultation may be to reveal a duty to accommodate." See also *Mikisew Cree*, above note 111 at para. 64, where the Court writes: "The duty here has both informational and response components."

interests in lands and resources. Accommodation is defined as "seeking compromise in an attempt to harmonize conflicting interests" and may oblige the Crown to make changes to its proposed action or to amend Crown policy.[152]

However, it is significant that the Court specifically states that accommodation does not mean that Aboriginal people have a veto on government decision-making, and does not require that parties come to an agreement on the nature of the accommodation.[153] Also important in *Haida* and *Taku River* is the idea that Aboriginal groups may not "frustrate the Crown's reasonable good faith attempts, nor should they take unreasonable positions to thwart government from making decisions."[154]

The idea of balancing Aboriginal and other Canadian interests is consistent with the fact that Aboriginal rights that are recognized under section 35 are not absolute. It is also in line with the purpose of the justification framework of effecting a reconciliation of Aboriginal concerns with the exercise of Crown sovereignty. The balancing of interests approach is not intended to undermine Aboriginal rights. On the contrary, in some cases a fair balance may only be achieved when every effort is made to accommodate the Aboriginal interests above all else, or by making a project contingent on Aboriginal participation. The focus of the Canadian approach to consultation is on the establishment of a meaningful process of consultation that is appropriate to the particular circumstances. Each situation must be approached individually to ensure that the honour of the Crown is upheld and that reconciliation of Aboriginal and Crown interests is achieved.

d) Observations about Consultation in Canadian Law

A number of important observations can be made regarding elements of the conceptual and legal framework for the duty to consult with Aboriginal peoples under Canadian law.

---

152 *Haida, ibid.* at para. 49.
153 See *ibid.* at paras. 48–49, where the Court writes: "This process does not give Aboriginal groups a veto over what can be done with land pending final proof of the claim. The Aboriginal 'consent' spoken of in *Delgamuukw* is appropriate only in cases of established rights, and then by no means in every case. Rather, what is required is a process of balancing of interests, of give and take. ... A commitment to the process does not require a duty to agree. But it does require good faith efforts to understand each other's concerns and move to address them." See also *Mikisew Cree*, above note 111 at para. 66.
154 *Haida, ibid.* at para. 42.

1) Governments and industry can always consult as a matter of good policy and good business. However, the legal recognition of a consultation obligation places Indigenous peoples in a stronger position, and tends to encourage the implementation of better practices and the application of higher standards. The emergence of consultation principles under international law will have greatest impact if implemented in domestic legal systems.

2) Paradoxically, uncertainty regarding the existence, definition or scope of Indigenous rights, when combined with a clear legal obligation to consult, creates conditions that favour the carrying out of complete and fair consultations in which governments and proponents work to substantially accommodate Indigenous interests.

3) Consultation is both a procedural obligation that compels governments (and industry by extension) to engage Indigenous groups, and a substantive obligation that requires that Indigenous peoples' interests and concerns be articulated, addressed, and where appropriate, accommodated.

4) The principle of reconciliation of Indigenous and non-Indigenous citizens can be a solid foundation for meaningful consultations if it is based on respect for the cultural integrity and diversity of Indigenous communities.

5) The depth of consultations will depend on such factors as the nature of the proposed activity, the circumstances and activities of the Indigenous group concerned, the possible impacts on the group, and the nature of their interests. Although Indigenous communities are unlikely to have an absolute veto on development projects, in some cases consent will be the only practical standard, and sometimes may even be legally required.

6) Consultation is a matter of honour. Accordingly, meaningful consultations should be established that are directed at the good faith consideration of Indigenous interests.

(7) The success of consultations carried out by governments or industry is linked to the ability to fashion processes that are flexible. This requires respect for the Indigenous group concerned, including its cultures and traditions, and the ability to modify processes to suit the specific circumstances associated with the projects or activities at issue.

The foregoing observations about the conceptual and legal framework that underpins the duty to consult in Canada may be informative for other domestic and international contexts. The Canadian framework is already reflected to varying degrees in the laws and practices of other countries, in the policies of intergovernmental organizations, in the decisions and observations of some treaty bodies, in the practices of "good corporate citizens," and in the positions advocated for on behalf of Indigenous peoples.

D. CONCLUSION

The topic of consultation with Indigenous peoples regarding decisions about land and resource development projects has become a matter of high priority in Canada and internationally in the last few years. It is a good time to assess how the topic is addressed under international and Canadian law.

The situations in which, as a matter of international law, an obligation to consult with Indigenous peoples in relation to land and natural resource developments clearly exists are few: ILO Convention 169 is the only international treaty that addresses the topic of Indigenous land and natural resource rights and the themes of consultation and participation in a direct and comprehensive fashion, and it has not been widely ratified. However, the foregoing overview suggests that the importance of Indigenous involvement is increasingly recognized. Whether a consultation principle is emerging as a matter of customary international law requires an analysis of state practice, which is beyond the scope of this chapter. However, it can at least be said that there appears to be growing recognition internationally that consultation with Indigenous groups makes good moral and practical sense in some situations—or more strongly, ought to be undertaken at times. As a result, it is increasingly common for major natural resource development projects to include consultations or negotiations with affected Indigenous peoples, reflecting both government and industry awareness that working with Indigenous communities is the better way to go.[155] In many cases, however, a consultative approach is still the exception rather than the rule.[156]

---

155 Recent examples include agreements in Chile and Colombia regarding dam projects, and Canada's Voisey's Bay project. For a relevant discussion, see Stefan Matiation, "Impact Benefits Agreements Between Mining Companies and Aboriginal Communities in Canada: A Model for Natural Resource Developments Affecting Indigenous Groups in Latin America?" (2002) 7 Great Plains Nat. Resources J. 204.

156 Natural resource companies with their head office or with operations in Canada often have significant experience working with Aboriginal communities in Canada. It is fair to compare their activities here with their approach to local community interests in connection with their operations in other countries, as is sometimes done, and to demand high standards from them. Mining giant BHP Billiton was the focus of this

Since this is an evolving issue, the conceptual and legal framework that would give a consultation norm or principle more purchase remains underdeveloped. Two UN bodies have recently begun work to try to address this problem. In connection with its standard-setting activities, the UN Working Group on Indigenous Populations (WGIP) has started to elaborate a legal commentary on "the principle of free, prior and informed consent of Indigenous peoples in relation to development affecting their lands and natural resources."[157] Meanwhile, in January 2005, the UN Permanent Forum on Indigenous Issues (PFII) held an international workshop on "methodologies regarding free, prior and informed consent and Indigenous peoples" for the benefit of UN agencies that work on issues relevant to Indigenous peoples.[158] Neither the WGIP nor the PFII activities can themselves produce a legally binding output, but they do help to generate discussion about consultation issues.

Canadian government officials and a few experts from the Aboriginal community in Canada made statements at the PFII workshop describing how various forms of negotiated agreements and consultations are used in

---

kind of attention. NGOs compared its Ekati diamond mine in Northwest Territories and Tintaya copper mine in Peru. Impact benefits agreements and an environmental agreement were used by the company in connection with Ekati to address local Aboriginal interests, but not at Tintaya. Earlier in 2005, the company did negotiate impact and benefits agreements with local communities affected by the Tintaya operation. For information, see José de Echave & Cesar Mosquera, *Reactivation of Mining in the South and Behaviour of Canadian Companies in Peru: A Community Consultation* (December 1996), online: www.embcbc.miningwatch.org/emcbc/international/cooperac.htm, and Ken Traynor, "A Tale of Two Standards" (Sept.-Dec. 2001) 26:4 CELA Intervenor (Newsletter)online: www.cela.ca, and "Peru Communities, Copper Mine Reach Historic Agreement" (21 December 2004) Oxfam America, online: www.oxfamamerica. org/newsandpublications/news_updates/Tintayaagreement.

157 The decision to undertake the work was made at the 21st session of the WGIP. See *Report of the WGIP on its 21st Session*, UN Doc. E/CN.4/Sub.2/2003/22, 11 August 2003. A preliminary working paper on the topic has been prepared (UN Doc. E/CN.4/Sub.2/ AC.4/2004/4, 8 July 2004). Whether the work will be completed is an open question. A number of countries argue that the WGIP has become redundant since the PFII was established and have begun to vote against the annual UN Commission on Human Rights resolution that keeps it alive.

158 As noted above, many of the materials submitted by participants in the workshop, including many UN agencies, some organizations representing Indigenous interests and Canada are available on the website of the PFII: www.un.org/esa/socdev/unpfii. The PFII seminar followed a review undertaken by the UN Inter-Agency Support Group on Indigenous Issues to identify whether and how Indigenous participation is integrated into the relevant policies of UN agencies (UN Doc. E/C.19/2004/11, 12 March 2004).

Canada.[159] In Canada, governments, industry, and Aboriginal groups have accumulated a significant amount of experience in Aboriginal consultation issues over the years. This began before *Haida* and *Taku River*, but these judgments have brought greater focus to the issue. They provide a broader legal justification for the common-sense notion that Aboriginal involvement is good practice. Developments in international law are beginning to do the same on a regional and global scale but a conceptual and legal framework for a consultative approach is less developed at the international level than it is in Canadian law. While the Canadian framework for consultations has arisen in a particular context in which Aboriginal and treaty rights are constitutionally protected, this does not mean that many of the principles that can be drawn from that framework cannot contribute to international standard setting.

Although Canada is not alone among states in addressing consultation with Indigenous communities, and may not even be the "best" at it, the idea of putting its most helpful insights forward on this topic is in keeping with the activist call to make a difference.[160] At the same time, Canada can learn from the manner in which the topic of consultation is being addressed at the international level.[161] Besides the fact that various treaty bodies are providing informative commentary about consultation issues and requirements that it can draw upon for its own domestic law- and policy-making, Canada can take strength from the fact that the international community faces the challenge of developing methodologies for land and

---

159 *Ibid.* See: *Statement by the Observer Delegation of Canada on Agenda Item 5*, above note 8, and *Statement by Observer Delegation of Canada on Agenda Item 1*, UN Doc. PFII/2005/WS.2/17/Add.2, 17 January 2005. A list of participants can be found on the PFII website.

160 This call is included in *A Role of Pride and Influence in the World—Canada's International Policy Statement* (2005). In his forward to the document, former Prime Minister Martin provided the following answer to the question, Why is the time right for foreign policy review?: "[W]e want to make a real difference in halting and preventing conflict and improving human welfare around the world. This may sound naively altruistic, but it's not. Rather, it's a doctrine of activism that over the decades has forged our nation's international character—and will serve us even better in today's changing world." The statement is online: www.dfait-maeci.gc.ca/cip-pic/IPS/IPS-Overview.pdf.

161 Canadian Supreme Court decisions respecting Aboriginal rights have influenced important decisions in other countries. For example, see Australia (*Mabo v. Queensland* (No. 2) (1992), 175 C.L.R. 1 (H.C.A.)), Malaysia (*Adong bin Kuwau and Ors v. Kerajaan Negeri Johor and Anor*, [1997] 1 M.L.J. 418), and South Africa, but more in the lower court decision than in that of the constitutional court (*Alexkor Ltd. v. Richtersveld Community*, CCT19/03).

natural resource development that balance competing interests, while fully respecting Indigenous peoples and their rights and claims. The existence of a framework in Canadian law that makes it necessary for governments and industry to work closely with Aboriginal peoples is not a burden, but an opportunity to demonstrate leadership and vision both at home and abroad.

Implementation by Canada of Its International Human Rights Treaty Obligations: Making Sense Out of the Nonsensical

13

ELISABETH EID AND HOORI HAMBOYAN*

A. INTRODUCTION

Domestic implementation of international human rights law is an intriguing and complex topic. The complexity, with respect to Canada, stems from a variety of reasons, including the following:

- Canada's approach to the domestic effect of international law is generally considered a "hybrid approach";[1]
- the responsibility for implementing human rights falls not only on the federal government but also on the provinces and territories;
- the usual method of implementing human rights treaties is to rely on existing legislation and policies; and
- there is a lack of a clear and consistent jurisprudential approach regarding the relationship between international human rights law

---

*   The views expressed in this chapter are those of the authors and do not necessarily reflect the position of the Department of Justice or Government of Canada. An earlier version of this paper was presented at the 2004 annual meeting of the Canadian Council of International Law and published in the proceedings of that meeting.

1   By "hybrid approach" we are referring to Canada's dualist method with respect to the domestic effect of international treaties but monist approach towards customary international law (these terms are explained later in the chapter). Note, however, that according to Brunnée & Toope, the status of customary international law within Canadian law is ambiguous. They write that Canadian courts have actually vacillated on its application, that is, it is not always treated as if it applies directly. Jutta Brunnée & Stephen Toope, "A Hesitant Embrace: The Application of International Law by Canadian Courts" (2002) 40 Can. Y.B. Int'l L. 3 at 42–44.

and domestic law, including: the *Canadian Charter of Rights and Freedoms,* ordinary laws, and administrative action.

Given the substantial volume of academic writings on the topic of domestic implementation of international human rights law,[2] this chapter focuses on and provides a critical analysis of the usual Canadian method of ratifying human rights treaties on the basis of existing legislation and programs, as opposed to passing specific implementing legislation. This paper first provides an overview of the terminology used, and often confused, in this area. It then briefly describes and provides examples of the various methods that are employed to implement treaties. Consideration is given to whether these different methods result in varying degrees of weight being attributed to the provisions of international treaties in domestic law. The chapter then examines more particularly the situation of human rights treaties, which are generally ratified on the basis of existing legislation, policies, and programs. It contemplates the implications of this practice, which some authors refer to as "implicit transformation,"[3] "passive incorporation,"[4] or "co-option."[5]

Finally, this paper examines implementation issues that arise after treaty adherence, particularly because of the impact of human rights monitoring mechanisms, such as the treaty reporting process. The important role played by the provinces and territories in implementing Canada's human rights treaty obligations is emphasized.

---

2   See generally Brunnée & Toope, "A Hesitant Embrace," *ibid.* See also Irit Weiser, "Undressing the Window: A Proposal for Making International Human Rights Law Meaningful in the Canadian Commonwealth System" (2004) 37:1 U.B.C. L. Rev. 113; Elizabeth Brandon, "Does International Law Mean Anything in Canadian Courts?" (2002) 11 J. Env. L. & Prac. 399; Anne Warner La Forest, "Domestic Application of International Law in *Charter* Cases: Are We There Yet?" (2004) 37:1 U.B.C. L. Rev. 157; Anne F. Bayefsky, "International Human Rights Law in Canadian Courts" in Irwin Cotler & F. Pearl Eliadis, eds., *International Human Rights Law: Theory and Practice* (Montreal: The Canadian Human Rights Foundation, 1992) at 115; Stéphane Beaulac, "Recent Developments on the Role of International Law in Canadian Statutory Interpretation" (2004) 25:1 Stat. L. Rev. 19; William Schabas, *International Human Rights Law and the Canadian Charter,* 2d ed. (Toronto: Thompson Canada Limited, 1996); and Gibran van Ert, *Using International Law in Canadian Courts* (The Hague: Kluwer Law International, 2002).

3   Brunnée & Toope, "A Hesitant Embrace," *ibid.* at 51.

4   Brandon, "Does International Law Mean Anything," above note 2 at 5–6, 7–8, and 15–17.

5   This term has been suggested by Gibran van Ert to describe the situation where legislation that originally had no implementing function is later "coopted" by the executive as implementing legislation. Van Ert, *Using International Law,* above note 2.

B. STRUGGLING THROUGH THE TERMINOLOGY

The term *implementation*, in relation to treaties, is used by academics, practitioners, the judiciary, and human rights treaty bodies in a variety of different ways. It is probably most commonly used as a synonym for "transformation," that is, "the positive act by which an international norm is made part of the domestic legal order in a dualist regime."[6] However, it is also used in a much broader sense, particularly in the context of the human rights treaty reporting process, to refer to legislation, programs, and policies that attest to Canada's compliance with its treaty obligations.[7] Implementation is often used interchangeably with "incorporation," where a treaty in whole or in part is replicated in a domestic statute or regulation. Many authors have criticized the use of incorporation to mean implementation because incorporation also refers to the "theory whereby [customary] international law enters the Canadian legal order immediately, i.e. without legislative or executive action."[8] Nevertheless, the literature and case law are replete with examples of the former use of the term.[9]

For the purposes of this paper, we will employ the term *implementation* in its broad sense as including both "explicit implementation" and "implicit implementation."[10] The term *explicit implementation* means that there has been a definite legislative act that has transformed the international treaty provision into a domestic statute or regulation. The phrase "implicit implementation" refers to legislation, programs, and policies that have been relied upon by the government to confirm pre-existing compliance with a human rights treaty upon ratification. This method constitutes

---

6   Van Ert, *Using International Law, ibid.* at 51.

7   The main human rights treaties require states parties to submit periodic reports on the legislative, judicial or other measures which have been adopted to give effect to the provisions of the treaty. See, for example, art. 18 of the *Convention on the Elimination of All Forms of Discrimination against Women*, 18 December 1979, Can. T.S. No. 31, entered into force 3 September 1981, ratified by Canada on 10 December 1981.

8   *Ibid.* at 50.

9   See, for example, *R. v. Zundel*, [1992] 2 S.C.R. 731 at 811; *Suresh v. Canada (Minister of Citizenship and Immigration)*, [2002] 1 S.C.R. 3 at paras. 60, 104 and 105; *Baker v. Canada (Minister of Citizenship and Immigration)*, [1999] 2 S.C.R. 817 at para. 78. All cases found online: Supreme Court of Canada homepage, www.scc-csc.gc.ca/Welcome/index_e.asp. See also Mark A. Luz, "NAFTA, Investment and the Constitution of Canada Will the Watertight Compartments Spring a Leak?" (2000–1) 32 Ottawa Law R. 35 at para. 79.

10 We have borrowed these descriptors from Brunnée & Toope, "A Hesitant Embrace," above note 1 at 51.

the general Canadian approach to implementation of human rights treaties, which tend to be ratified on the basis that domestic law is already in
compliance with the obligations in the treaty. As a result, no additional
implementing legislation is required.

C. EXPLICIT IMPLEMENTATION TECHNIQUES

There are numerous techniques employed to explicitly transform treaty
provisions into domestic law. The following discussion only identifies a
few of them.[11]

1) Full Implementation

This technique entails giving the full text of the treaty the "force of law" in
Canada through a provision in domestic legislation. The text of the treaty is
also often attached and published as a schedule to the implementing Act.[12]
For example, section 449.1 of the *Canada Shipping Act*[13] provides as follows:

> s. 449.1(1) Subject to such reservations as Canada may make, the Inter-
> national Convention on Salvage, 1989 … and set out in Schedule V, is ap-
> proved and declared to have the force of law in Canada …
>
> (2) In the event of an inconsistency between the Convention and this Act or
> the regulations, the Convention prevails to the extent of the inconsistency.

This technique gives the precise terms of the treaty the force of law in
Canada. Although there is a provision of a domestic statute that gives legal
force to the treaty, this technique most closely approximates direct application of the treaty in domestic law.

Another example of "full implementation" occurs where the provisions
of the treaty are essentially reproduced into the body of a statute or regulation, usually with some minor modification. This method is often accompanied with a preamble or purpose clause explaining that the legislation
is implementing the treaty.[14] An example of this method is found in the

---

11   For a more detailed discussion, see Brandon, "Does International Law Mean Any-
     thing," above note 2 and Keyes, "Drafting Laws," below note 12.
12   John Mark Keyes, "Drafting Laws to Implement International Agreements," presenta-
     tion to lawyers in the Department of Justice, 13 January 2003, Ottawa.
13   *Canada Shipping Act*, R.S.C. 1985, c. S-9, ss. 449.1(1) and 449.1(2).
14   This method is differentiated from simple reference in the preamble of a statute,
     discussed below.

Anti-Personnel Mines Convention Implementation Act,[15] where the purpose was to implement the *Convention on the Prohibition of the Use, Stockpiling, Production and Transfer of Anti-Personnel Mines and on their destruction.*[16]

2) Partial Implementation

During a review of the provisions of a treaty by government officials, it may be determined that domestic law and policy already fulfil and can be said to "implement" certain provisions of the treaty. However, other provisions of the same treaty may require implementing legislation to ensure compliance. For example, prior to Canada's ratification of the *Convention against Torture and Other Cruel, Inhuman or Degrading Treatment or Punishment*[17] (*Convention against Torture*), a new offence of "torture" was added to the *Criminal Code*, along with a definition of "torture" that uses the same language as the *Convention against Torture.*[18]

A further example of partial implementation is the inclusion of certain provisions of the *Convention Relating to the Status of Refugees* (Refugee Convention)[19] and the *Convention against Torture* in the *Immigration and Refugee Protection Act* (IRPA).[20] For instance, subsection 97(1) of the Act defines a person "in need of protection" as including "a person whose removal to their country ... of nationality ... would subject them personally ... (a) to a danger, believed on substantial grounds to exist, of torture within the meaning of Article 1 of the *Convention against Torture.*"[21] Article 1 of the *Convention against Torture*, which defines "torture," is attached as a schedule to the IRPA.

---

15 S.C. 1997, c. 33, online: Department of Justice laws.justice.gc.ca/en/A-11.5/1946.html.

16 *Convention on the Prohibition of the Use, Stockpiling, Production and Transfer of Anti-Personnel Mines and on their destruction*, online: International Committee of the Red Cross www.icrc.org/ihl.nsf/0/d111fff4b9c85b0f41256585003caec3?OpenDocument.

17 *Convention against Torture and Other Cruel, Inhuman or Degrading Treatment or Punishment*, GA Resolution 39/46 of 10 December 1984, online: Office of the High Commissioner for Human Rights www.unhchr.ch/html/menu3/b/h_cat39.htm.

18 See Multiculturalism and Citizenship Canada, *Outlawing an Ancient Evil: Torture—Initial Report of Canada* (Ottawa: Multiculturalism and Citizenship Canada, 1989) at para. 10. See also *Criminal Law Amendment Act (Torture)*, S.C. 1987, c. 13.

19 *Convention relating to the Status of Refugees*, GA Resolution 429 (V) of 14 December 1950, online: Office of the High Commissioner for Human Rights www.unhchr.ch/html/menu3/b/o_c_ref.htm.

20 *Immigration and Refugee Protection Act*, R.S.C. 2001, c. 27 online: Department of Justice laws.justice.gc.ca/en/I-2.5/index.html [*IRPA*].

21 *Ibid.* at s. 97(1).

Where legislation is passed explicitly implementing in whole or in part the provisions of a treaty, the analytical framework that needs to be adopted has been quite clearly articulated by the Supreme Court of Canada. When the purpose of the given Act is to implement a treaty provision, the courts must adopt an interpretation consistent with Canada's obligations under the treaty.[22] In order to determine the scope and content of Canada's treaty obligations, resort may be had to the international rules of treaty interpretation as set out in the *Vienna Convention on the Law of Treaties* (Vienna Convention).[23] These rules require that a treaty be interpreted in good faith in accordance with the ordinary meaning given to the terms of the treaty in light of its object and purpose[24] as well as any other instruments or state practice that establishes states' interpretation of the treaty.[25]

Explicit implementation of international treaty provisions into domestic legislation has the important advantage of enhancing transparency, accessibility, and understanding of the treaty norm amongst Parliamentarians, litigants, the courts, and officials responsible for the administration of the legislation. In such cases, it is clear that the executive and Parliament intended to transform treaty provisions into domestic law.

3) Reference to a Treaty in Domestic Legislation as an Interpretive Aid

In some statutes, reference is made to a treaty in a preamble or purposes clause. The reference may state that the provisions of the statute should, to the extent possible, be interpreted in a manner consistent with the treaty. An example of this is found in the "objectives and application," section 3 of IRPA:[26]

> (2) The objectives of this Act with respect to refugees are ...
>
> (b) to fulfil Canada's international legal obligations with respect to refugees and affirm Canada's commitment to international efforts to provide assistance to those in need of resettlement;
>
> ...
>
> (3) This Act is to be construed and applied in a manner that ...

22 *Pushpanathan v. Canada (Minister of Citizenship and Immigration)*, [1998] 1 S.C.R. 1222; [1998] S.C.J. No. 77 at para. 51.
23 Can. T.S. 1980 No. 37 arts. 31–32.
24 *Ibid.*, art. 31(1).
25 *Ibid.*, art. 31(2).
26 Above note 20.

(f) complies with international human rights instruments to which Canada is signatory.

Some authors argue that reference to a treaty in a preamble can be construed as explicit implementation of the treaty provisions in domestic law.[27] Others assert that such reference does not constitute explicit implementation but should be determinative in the interpretation of domestic legislation.[28] In our view, simple reference in a preamble or purposes section that a domestic statute should be interpreted in light of Canada's treaty obligations, does not explicitly implement the treaty provisions into domestic law. Rather, Parliament's intention was to interpret the statute to the extent possible in a manner that complies with Canada's treaty obligations but not to actually incorporate the precise provisions of the treaty into domestic law.[29] If particular provisions of the legislation are inconsistent with the treaty, the domestic provisions prevail over the international treaty norm.

In this section, we have described different drafting techniques used to explicitly implement in full or in part treaty provisions or to expressly indicate that the domestic statute is to be interpreted in a manner consistent with the treaty. We will now describe the process Canada generally employs for the ratification of human rights treaties, and its implications for implementation of Canada's human rights obligations.

D. CANADA'S PROCESS FOR ADHERENCE TO HUMAN RIGHT TREATIES

Prior to adherence to an international human rights treaty, Department of Justice officials carefully examine the provisions of the treaty and determine whether existing federal laws and policies already conform to the treaty obligations.[30] State obligations under human rights treaties are often

---

27 Schabas, *International Human Rights Law,* above note 2 at 22–23.

28 See generally Brunnée & Toope, "A Hesitant Embrace," above note 1.

29 Note that in *Guzman v. Canada (Minister of Citizenship and Immigration),* 2004 FC 1276, Klein J. held at para. 53 that s. 3(3)(f) of *IRPA* does not incorporate international human rights conventions as part of domestic law, or state that they override the plain words of the statute. Rather it codifies the common law principle of statutory interpretation that domestic law should be interpreted to reflect the values contained in international human rights conventions to which Canada has ascribed.

30 This section is largely borrowed from Irit Weiser & Elisabeth Eid, "Interaction between International and Domestic Human Rights Law: A Canadian Perspective" (Paper presented at the Sino-Canadian International Conference on the Ratification and Implementation of Human Rights Covenants, October 2001) [unpublished] at 16.

already covered by the *Canadian Charter of Rights and Freedoms*, federal, provincial, and territorial human rights legislation, and other legislation and policies. If there are inconsistencies, officials determine whether new legislation should be adopted or if existing legislation should be amended to ensure that Canada is in compliance with the treaty prior to adherence.

Alternatively, should there be any inconsistencies between existing domestic legislation and the given international treaty, officials may consider the option of entering a reservation prior to consenting to the agreement. For example, before the ratification of the *Convention on the Rights of the Child*, two potential conflicts were discovered when compared with relevant domestic legislation. As a result, a decision was made to enter two reservations to the Convention.[31]

Should gaps be found in the existing domestic legislation in light of the treaty obligations, relevant legislation may be amended. For example, article 1 of the *Optional Protocol to the Convention on the Rights of the Child on the Involvement of Children in Armed Conflict* states:

> States Parties shall take all feasible measures to ensure that members of their armed forces who have not attained the age of 18 years do not take a direct part in hostilities.[32]

In reviewing the Optional Protocol, it was determined that although the government already had a policy prohibiting the deployment of individuals under eighteen to places where there might be armed combat, Canada would amend its *National Defence Act* to entrench into law the Canadian Forces' policy.[33]

It should be emphasized that many provisions of human rights treaties fall within provincial and territorial jurisdiction. In such cases, a similar review is conducted at the provincial and territorial levels. Provinces and territories may also decide that new legislation is required or that provisions of existing legislation require amendment. They may also determine that a reservation or statement of understanding is needed.

---

31 *Convention on the Rights of the Child*, online: United Nations Office of the High Commissioner for Human Rights www.unhchr.ch/html/menu3/b/treaty15_asp.htm.

32 *Optional Protocol to the Convention on the Rights of the Child on the Involvement of Children in Armed Conflict*, A/RES/54/263 of 25 May 2000, online: Office of the High Commissioner for Human Rights www.unhchr.ch/html/menu2/6/protocolchild.htm.

33 Canada, *Optional Protocol to the Convention on the Rights of the Child on the Involvement of Children in Armed Conflict: First Report of Canada* (Ottawa: Canadian Heritage, September 2004) at para. 4.

Federal-provincial-territorial discussions of possible Canadian adherence to a treaty take place during meetings of the Continuing Committee of Officials on Human Rights. The latter committee currently meets face-to-face twice per year and holds monthly conference calls to discuss various international human rights issues, including treaty ratification. The formal support of the provinces and territories is sought by the federal government prior to the ratification of a human rights treaty that impacts on matters under provincial jurisdiction.

If new federal, provincial, or territorial legislation is required for a particular treaty provision, it will be passed prior to ratification. In such instances, parliamentarians may be apprised of the need for specific implementing legislation to bring Canada into compliance with a treaty prior to ratification. However, in many instances no explicit implementing legislation is required and the human rights treaty is ratified on the basis of existing legislation and policies as demonstrating compliance.

After adherence, the human rights treaty may be tabled in Parliament for the information of parliamentarians. The decision whether to table a treaty in Parliament is done on a case-by-case basis and there is no uniform approach to informing parliamentarians. In 2002, the Quebec government passed legislation requiring that the National Assembly approve any important international commitment the federal government intends to assume.[34] An explanatory note respecting the content and effects of the international commitment must also be tabled. Since human rights treaties have been determined to be "important international commitments," they are therefore laid before the National Assembly for approval prior to adherence by Canada. While there was some concern that this requirement would result in delay, to date, it has not had an adverse impact on the human rights treaty adherence process.

E. CRITICAL ANALYSIS OF "IMPLICIT IMPLEMENTATION"

It should be emphasized at the outset, that there is generally no obligation in human rights treaties for states to pass explicit implementing legislation. Rather, the obligation is to ensure that the state, upon adherence, is in compliance with the treaty, which obligation may be met through a variety of legislative, policy, and administrative measures.

---

34   Bill 52, *An Act to amend the Act respecting the Ministère des Relations internationales Act and other legislative provisions,* 2d Sess., 36th Leg., Quebec, 2001 (assented to 9 May 2002) s. 22.1.

Further, even if there were a desire to pass specific implementing legislation for a human rights treaty, given that the subject matters of such treaties often fall under both federal and provincial jurisdiction, it will often be the case that legislation passed by a single legislative body would not be sufficient to give effect to all of the provisions of the treaty. For example, the *Convention on the Rights of the Child* contains provisions relating to education and health for children as well as other provisions that pertain to matters under federal jurisdiction. All jurisdictions are required to take measures to fulfil Canada's obligations under the Convention.

One of the main benefits of reliance on existing legislation, policies, and programs for compliance with or "as having implemented" Canada's human rights treaty obligations, is to avoid duplication of the same or similar norms through explicit implementation of the treaty provision. For example, the *Convention on the Rights of the Child* requires that states parties recognize, *inter alia,* that every child has the "inherent right to life,"[35] the "right to freedom of expression,"[36] and "freedom of thought, conscience and religion."[37] At the time of Canada's ratification of the Convention, these rights already existed for children under the *Canadian Charter of Rights and Freedoms.*[38] Moreover, reliance on existing legislation ensures that legislation is drafted in a manner and with concepts that are readily understood in Canadian law. Certain terminology used in international agreements is not employed in domestic legislation. Furthermore, several human rights treaty provisions require states parties to implement obligations through measures other than legislation. For example, article 19(2) of the *Convention on the Rights of the Child* states that measures to protect children from physical and mental violence "should, as appropriate, include effective procedures for the establishment of social programmes to provides necessary support for the child."[39] Similarly, article 10 of the *Convention against Torture* requires states parties to ensure that education and information regarding the prohibition against torture are included in the training of law enforcement personnel. Finally, reliance on existing

---

35 *Convention on the Rights of the Child,* Assembly resolution 44/25 of 20 November 1989, online: Office of the High Commissioner for Human Rights www.unhchr.ch/html/menu2/6/crc/treaties/crc.htm at art. 6.

36 *Ibid.,* art. 13.

37 *Ibid.,* art. 14.

38 *Canadian Charter of Rights and Freedoms,* Part I of the *Constitution Act, 1982,* being Schedule B to the *Canada Act 1982* (U.K.), 1982, c. 11.

39 Above note 35 at art. 19(2).

legislation, policies, and programs as having implemented Canada's human rights treaty obligations, avoids the often difficult and lengthy process of passing legislation through Parliament.

On the other hand, there are problems associated with reliance on pre-existing legislation, programs, and policies for conformity with treaty obligations. Disadvantages include the current lack of a clear analytical approach on the part of the judiciary respecting the domestic effect of treaties that have not been explicitly implemented; the absence of a public record listing the legislation, programs, and policies that were relied upon for the purposes of treaty adherence; and the lack of parliamentary involvement in the treaty adherence process. Each of these problems will be discussed in turn.

1) The Lack of a Principled Analytical Approach

Contrary to the Supreme Court of Canada's relatively straightforward approach with respect to explicitly implemented treaty provisions, the Court's approach to human rights treaties that have been ratified on the basis of existing legislation and policies is much more tentative.[40] The Court has held that international human rights treaties serve as an important source for informing [but not determining] interpretations of the *Charter*, ordinary legislation, policies, and administrative action. However, Canadian courts generally view such treaties as "unimplemented," given the absence of explicit implementing legislation,[41] and do not acknowledge that these treaties may have been "implicitly implemented." The courts also rarely draw distinctions between binding and non-binding instruments and seem to employ either in a manner that will support the result they want to achieve. Moreover, the international treaty interpretation rules are rarely applied and there is often little discussion respecting the content and scope of international norms.[42]

To be fair to the Court, the rigour of its reasoning depends to a great extent upon the quality of the pleadings it receives by the litigants that appear before it. The purpose of this chapter is not to critique the Court but to call upon those knowledgeable about international human rights law to better inform the legal community, which can in turn enlighten the judiciary.

---

40 Weiser, "Undressing the Window," above note 2 at 132.
41 Brunnée & Toope, "A Hesitant Embrace," above note 1 at 51.
42 Weiser, "Undressing the Window," above note 2 at 132.

Several authors argue that the same presumption of conformity of domestic legislation with international treaties should apply both to treaties ratified by Canada on the basis of existing legislation as well as those explicitly implemented.[43] Brunnée and Toope assert that "courts must search for compatible interpretation of domestic law with Canada's international obligations."[44] However, they note that federal and provincial legislatures maintain control over domestic law, since the presumption only applies "where possible" and legislatures may decide to enact provisions inconsistent with Canada's obligations.[45] In such cases, Canada would arguably be in contravention of its international obligations as a matter of international law, but the inconsistent provision would apply as a matter of domestic law.

Irit Weiser agrees that the presumption of conformity should apply to ordinary legislation, absent clear legislative intention to the contrary.[46] If the government becomes concerned about the evolution in the interpretation of the provisions of the international treaty and its relation to domestic law, the government has the opportunity to re-enact the legislation and clearly identify that it is to prevail over the international obligation.[47] However, with respect to constitutional provisions, Weiser maintains that while the international treaty provisions should be highly persuasive, there should not be an automatic presumption of conformity.[48] If the presumption of conformity applied to the *Charter* for example, then interpretations of *Charter* provisions would be *required* to be consistent with international human rights treaties. Given the supremacy of the *Charter*, Parliament could not legislate (without employing the override clause if applicable) in a contrary manner. Precluding the ability of Parliament to legislate in a manner contradictory to a given international instrument would be inappropriate since adherence to a treaty is an executive act that does not require Parliament's consent.[49] Weiser further notes that the courts are obliged to consider treaty obligations as highly relevant and persuasive sources for the interpretation of the *Charter*, but are not *bound* to interpret the *Charter* in a manner consistent with a treaty provision.

---

43   Brunnée & Toope, "A Hesitant Embrace," above note 1 at 51; van Ert, *Using International Law*, above note 2 at 99.
44   Brunnée & Toope, *ibid.* at 52.
45   *Ibid.*
46   Weiser, "Undressing the Window," above note 2 at 147.
47   *Ibid.*
48   *Ibid.* at 148.
49   *Ibid.*

2) Absence of Public Record of Implementing Legislation

Under the current practice, there is no public record of the legislation, policies, and programs that were relied upon to assert compliance with the human rights treaty at the time of its ratification. With the passage of time, government officials responsible for interpreting and applying legislation that was relied upon for compliance with Canada's treaty obligations may not know of this reliance or the assertion that such legislation demonstrated compliance with the treaty. The absence of explicit implementing legislation means that officials may not see the relationship with the treaty nor the need to interpret the domestic legislation in a manner consistent with its provisions. Similarly, litigants and judges have difficulty determining what specific legislation and policies were relied upon that showed pre-existing compliance with Canada's human rights treaty obligations. This problem could be remedied to a certain degree, if upon ratification, a statement were prepared listing the domestic statutes, regulations, and policies that were relied upon as asserting conformity with the treaty. Such a statement could be tabled in Parliament along with the treaty.

3) Absence of Parliamentary Involvement

Another problem area, particularly where there is no need for any new legislation, is the often complete absence of parliamentary involvement in the process. It is the executive branch that determines when a treaty may be ratified on the basis of existing legislation, policies, and programs without specific implementing legislation. While there may be a clear executive intention to rely on existing legislation for the purposes of implementing the treaty, it is difficult to attribute such intention to Parliament.

The usual absence of Parliament's involvement in the human rights treaty adherence process underlies repeated concerns, often expressed by the judiciary, that to accept such treaties as "implemented" in domestic law means giving the executive the power to affect the interpretation of domestic law without parliamentary sanction. Such concerns were articulated in Iacobucci J.'s dissent in *Baker v. Canada*:

> In my view, one should proceed with caution in deciding matters of this nature, lest we adversely affect the balance maintained by our Parliamentary tradition, or inadvertently grant the executive the power to bind citizens without the necessity of involving the legislative branch. I do not share my colleague's confidence that the Court's precedent in *Captial Cit-*

ies, supra, survives intact following the adoption of a principle of law which permits reference to an unincorporated convention during the process of statutory interpretation. Instead, the result will be that the appellant is able to achieve indirectly what cannot be achieved directly, namely, to give force and effect within the domestic legal system to international obligations undertaken by the executive alone that have yet to be subject to the democratic will of Parliament.[50]

Although this commentary has been criticized by international law academics,[51] it reflects an existing unease in the judiciary that needs to be addressed. Moreover, as Irit Weiser notes, "the absence of a Parliamentary role in treaty ratification reduces public awareness of Canada's international commitments and works to minimize international law's influence in subsequent court disputes."[52] Most European countries involve their Parliaments, albeit to varying degrees, in the treaty-adherence process. Commonwealth countries such as Australia and New Zealand have introduced reforms that permit greater parliamentary scrutiny and participation in the treaty-adherence process. As a general rule, treaties are tabled before their respective Parliaments for a set period of time to allow for debate, prior to any binding action taken by the executive. As was mentioned earlier, Quebec has adopted a similar procedure.[53] While there are a variety of models that could be adopted for Parliament, at a minimum, human rights treaties should be tabled upon adherence for the information of parliamentarians. This process should be accompanied with a statement of the purpose and contents of the treaty, along with a list of the federal legislation relied upon for the purposes of adherence. Serious consideration should be given to further measures that would enhance the role for parliamentarians in the process.

4) The Role of the Treaty-Reporting Process in Ensuring Ongoing Compliance and Implementation

Pursuant to the main UN human rights treaties that Canada has ratified or acceded to, states parties are required to submit periodic reports of their

---

50   *Baker v. Canada,* above note 9 at 80.
51   Brunnée & Toope, "A Hesitant Embrace," above note 1 at 41.
52   Weiser, "Undressing the Window: Treating International Human Rights Law Meaningfully in the Canadian Commonwealth System" (September 2002) [unpublished, archived at the Department of Justice, Human Rights Law Section] at 66.
53   Note that Quebec's process did not alter the existing law and practise with respect to treaty ratification at the federal level.

compliance with their treaty obligations to specific monitoring bodies. This is a continuing obligation, which clearly suggests that implementation of international human rights obligations is an ongoing requirement post-adherence. For example, article 18 of the *Convention on the Elimination of Discrimination against Women* (CEDAW) requires states' parties to submit to the CEDAW Committee "a report on the legislative, judicial, administrative or other measures which they have adopted to give effect to the provisions of the ... Convention and on the progress made in this respect."[54] There is a requirement for an initial report and then subsequent reports at regular intervals.[55] Interestingly, the treaties recognize that full compliance with treaty obligations may pose challenges for states' parties and that the latter are asked in their reports to identify factors and difficulties they experience in their ability to fulfil their obligations under the treaty.[56] In this regard, interpretations of treaty provisions by treaty bodies may result in changes to the scope or meaning of a state's obligations that were unanticipated at the time of adherence and result in difficulties in states meeting their obligations.

The drafting of Canada's report to human rights treaty-monitoring bodies is a resource-intensive exercise involving officials from numerous federal departments and the provinces and territories. While the process is sometimes criticized as an ineffective public relations exercise, whereby federal, provincial, and territorial governments list a wide range of legislation, programs, and policies in relation to treaty obligations, the review does require officials to turn their minds to the obligations under the treaty and the extent of Canadian compliance. Canada's first reports under the treaties may reflect most closely the legislation, programs, and policies relied upon for the purposes of adherence, although there is no conscious intention to do so. Subsequent reports contain additional measures that Canada has adopted, some of which may have intentionally been adopted with the treaty in mind, while others are mentioned because they are relevant to the treaty obligation, but may have been developed for other policy reasons.

After the report is submitted to the relevant human rights treaty body, Canada will be asked to present its report orally and to respond to questions from the members of the treaty body or committee. Non-governmental organizations often prepare their own reports respecting the extent of

---

54   Above note 7.
55   *Ibid.* at art. 18(1)(a) & (b).
56   See, for example, *ibid.* at art. 18(2).

Canada's compliance with its human rights treaty obligations. The committee will often use information received from non-governmental organizations in devising questions to pose to the Canadian delegation as well as in formulating their recommendations or "concluding observations." The concluding observations are examined and given due consideration by relevant federal, provincial, and territorial officials. At the federal level, interdepartmental meetings are generally held to discuss the concluding observations shortly after they are issued and at subsequent intervals during the reporting period. Some recommendations are capable of implementation while others pose significant difficulties for governments. The concluding observations form the focus of Canada's subsequent report to the respective treaty body.

The treaty-reporting process represents a forum for dialogue, influenced by the participation of non-governmental organizations, between Canada and the treaty body respecting the implementation by Canada of its obligations under the treaty. Although the process has been the subject of much criticism, it does serve an important function, particularly in the absence of explicit implementing legislation, of reminding government officials of Canada's international human rights obligations and the government's continuing obligation to ensure that domestic legislation, policies, and programs are in compliance with such obligations.

One of the difficulties in fulfiling this continuing obligation is the current absence of a process in the government for the systematic review of proposed legislation and policies for consistency with human rights treaty obligations post-adherence. Rather, such review occurs on an ad hoc basis, when concerns are identified by Department of Justice counsel. Given that government lawyers are typically less familiar with international human rights law than they are with the *Charter*, it is possible that issues respecting consistency with international human rights obligations are not identified prior to enactment of legislation.[57] In this regard, we are continuing our efforts to train Justice lawyers with respect to international human rights law, as well as enhance internal mechanisms for the review of proposed legislation.

---

57 Also, pursuant to s. 4.1 of the *Department of Justice Act*, R.S.C. 1985, c. J-2, the Minister of Justice is required to examine every regulation and proposed government bill for consistency with the *Canadian Charter of Rights and Freedoms*. This statutory requirement serves to ensure scrutiny of proposed legislation for consistency with the *Charter*.

F. CONCLUSION

The objective of this chapter is to make some sense out of the complex and often confusing subject of the implementation of international human rights treaties in the Canadian system. Human rights treaties are generally ratified on the basis of existing legislation, policies, and programs since specific implementing legislation is usually not required for compliance with the treaty. Despite reliance on existing legislation for compliance, Canadian courts continue to view such treaties as "unimplemented" in domestic law and accordingly struggle with the degree of weight that should be accorded to them in relation to domestic law. This characterization of these treaties stands in stark contrast to the position Canada takes before international human rights treaty bodies, wherein Canada asserts that it has taken a wide range of legislative and administrative measures to implement its obligations. This apparent contradiction has been rightly criticized by academics. We have argued here, as have others before us, that the concept of "implementation" should be broadly construed so as to encompass human rights treaties that are ratified on the basis of existing legislation. If this understanding is generally accepted, it will hopefully result in greater coherence between Canada's international and domestic positions. We agree that the presumption of conformity with human rights treaties should apply "where possible" with respect to the interpretation of domestic legislation. Parliament still may deviate from its treaty obligations expressly through legislation.

Much work remains to be done to ensure greater awareness of Canada's international human rights treaty obligations and their effect on domestic legislation and policies. This is a task that falls to all those knowledgeable about international human rights law, whether in academia, the government, private practice, Parliament, or the judiciary.

The Domestic Application of International Human Rights Law in Canada: The Role of Canada's National Human Rights Institutions

LINDA C. REIF[*]

A. INTRODUCTION

In recent years, the international community has increasingly highlighted the need for states to strengthen their domestic laws and mechanisms in order to fulfil their international human rights obligations. In particular, international bodies have promoted the establishment and strengthening of National Human Rights Institutions (NHRIs).

In the Canadian context, the relationship between international human rights law and Canadian domestic law has drawn much attention over the same timespan. Yet, scholars have focused on the roles of the executive and judiciary in scrutinizing Canada's implementation of, and compliance with, its international human rights obligations.[1] In contrast, the complementary roles of NHRIs in this project have been generally overlooked.

[*] The author wishes to thank Leonard G. Magawa (LL.M. candidate, Faculty of Law, University of Alberta) for his research assistance. She is also grateful to Mary Marshall, Patricia Paradis, Joanna Harrington, Elizabeth Eid, Gibran van Ert, and Hugo Cyr for their comments on an earlier draft of this paper.
[1] From a growing body of work see, for example, Gibran van Ert, *Using International Law in Canadian Courts* (The Hague: Kluwer Law International, 2002); Jutta Brunnée & Stephen J. Toope, "A Hesitant Embrace: Baker and the Application of International Law by Canadian Courts" in David Dyzenhaus, ed., *The Unity of Public Law* (Oxford: Hart, 2004) at 357; Irit Weiser, "Undressing the Window: Treating International Human Rights Law Meaningfully in the Canadian Commonwealth System" (2004) 37 U.B.C. L. Rev. 113; Anne Warner La Forest, "Domestic Application of International Law in Charter Cases: Are We There Yet?" (2004) 37 U.B.C. L. Rev. 157; Stephen J. Toope, "The Uses of Metaphor: International Law and the Supreme Court of Canada" (2001)

468 LINDA C. REIF

This chapter defines NHRIs, provides a description of NHRIs around the world, examines international law standards on the establishment and structure of NHRIs, and describes the methods by which NHRIs can act as mechanisms for the domestic application of international human rights law. It moves on to explore NHRIs in Canada; their structures and legal frameworks, the extent to which they satisfy international standards for NHRIs, and their roles in the application of international human rights law in the Canadian domestic legal system. I argue that some NHRIs in Canada do not fully conform with international standards on NHRIs. I further argue that although Canadian NHRIs currently play a relatively modest role in the domestic application of international human rights law, they do apply these norms receptively, and serve as another valuable route for the domestic diffusion of Canada's international human rights obligations. Further, the framework and operation of NHRIs in Canada could be enhanced through the establishment of new NHRIs, reform of existing NHRIs, and an increased use of the methods by which some Canadian NHRIs already use international human rights norms in their work.

B. NATIONAL HUMAN RIGHTS INSTITUTIONS (NHRIs)

1) Defining NHRIs

The United Nations (UN) has defined an NHRI as "a body which is established by a Government under the constitution, or by law or decree, the functions of which are specifically designed in terms of the promotion and protection of human rights."[2] Courts, tribunals, and government departments dealing with human rights matters are excluded from this definition.[3] Rather, NHRIs are non-judicial state mechanisms for the domestic promotion and protection of human rights.[4] The main types of NHRIs

---

80 Can. Bar Rev. 534; Stephen J. Toope, "Inside and Out: The Stories of International Law and Domestic Law" (2001) 50 U.N.B.L.J. 11.

2   United Nations Centre for Human Rights, *National Human Rights Institutions: A Handbook on the Establishment and Strengthening of National Institutions for the Promotion and Protection of Human Rights*, Professional Training Series No. 4, UN Doc. HR/P/PT 4 (1995) at 6.

3   *National Human Rights Institutions: A Handbook, ibid.* at 6.

4   On NHRIs see, for example, Linda C. Reif, *The Ombudsman, Good Governance and the International Human Rights System* (Leiden: Martinus Nijhoff, 2004); Linda C. Reif, "Building Democratic Institutions: The Role of National Human Rights Institutions in Good Governance and Human Rights Protection" (2000) 13 Harv. Hum. Rts. J. 1; Kamal Hossain *et al.*, eds., *Human Rights Commissions and Ombudsman Offices: National*

are human rights commissions, ombudsmän, hybrids (human rights om-budsman/commissioner), and specialized institutions.⁵ While the classical ombudsman does not have an express human rights mandate, a number of ombudsmän do, in practice, engage in some work that involves human rights issues and the application of human rights norms. Also, the UN considers that the ombudsman falls within its NHRI definition.⁶ In federal states, such as Canada, NHRIs may be found at the provincial or state levels of governance.

One characteristic of NHRIs, however, is that many do not have the power to issue legally binding decisions to enforce their determinations; instead, their powers are recommendatory, advisory, and sometimes prosecutory in nature. Some NHRIs are empowered to take cases to human rights tribunals, boards of inquiry, or the courts for binding determination of complaints or for interpretation of legal issues, and a few can even go to court for enforcement of their own recommendations or can issue their own orders for compliance. The "soft" power exercised by these institutions distinguishes them from the courts, but this relative lack of direct enforcement power is compensated for by their flexible and varied powers and their ability to act creatively over a longer time frame.⁷ Some NHRIs are given the power to launch own-motion investigations, which enable NHRIs to act proactively, especially with respect to vulnerable persons; for example, children and prisoners.⁸ Given their mandates and powers, NHRIs can also address systemic human rights issues effectively. Further, NHRIs are accessible to the public and do not have the same financial barriers to access compared with the courts.

In addition to the application of domestic law (including human rights law), NHRIs may be able to use the international human rights law obligations of the state in their work and, thus, act as a mechanism for the domes-

---

Experiences throughout the World (The Hague: Kluwer Law International, 2000); Anne Gallagher, "Making Human Rights Treaty Obligations a Reality: Working With New Actors and Partners" in Philip Alston & James Crawford, eds., *The Future of UN Human Rights Treaty Monitoring* (Cambridge: Cambridge University Press, 2000) at 201.

5   The Swedish word *ombudsman* means representative and is considered gender-neutral in Swedish. The plural form is ombudsmän. As both women and men hold the office of ombudsman, the pronouns used in this paper reflect this fact.

6   *National Human Rights Institutions: A Handbook*, above note 2 at 6.

7   See Carolyn Evans, "Human Rights Commissions and Religious Conflict in the Asia-Pacific Region" (2004) 53 I.C.L.Q. 713 at 720–21.

8   See Gallagher, "Making Human Rights Treaty Obligations a Reality," above note 4 at 214.

tic application of the state's international human rights obligations. NHRIs may also be able to use other international human rights instruments in their work. Given that economic, social, and cultural rights are often non-justiciable at the domestic level, NHRIs, with their broad mandates and flexible powers, can contribute to the domestic application of economic, social, and cultural rights.[9] NHRIs can also monitor their state's compliance with its international human rights obligations.[10] Further, the work of NHRIs can be used by international and domestic actors to help determine the state's level of compliance with its international obligations.[11]

2) The Human Rights Commission

With a multi-member format, human rights commissions are given express and varied human rights protection and promotion functions. A human rights commission may be established by constitutional provision, legislation or, occasionally, by executive order, and its members may be appointed by the legislative or executive branches. Each commission will have a different set of functions, including some or all of the following: human rights research and education; providing advice to government on human rights law and policy, including the ratification of human rights treaties and the passage of domestic legislation; inspection of state facilities where individuals are confined involuntarily; monitoring state compliance with its international and domestic human rights obligations; publication of annual and special reports; and the investigation of public complaints. However, a few commissions only have advisory functions and do not have the power to investigate complaints.

Commissions may have jurisdiction over complaints against the public and/or private sectors. Commissions also vary in the scope of the human rights they are empowered to protect and promote. Some commissions have jurisdiction only over matters involving discrimination, while others have a broader jurisdiction over various civil and political rights, and even over economic, social, and cultural rights. According to Gallagher, "[t]he

---

9   See Barbara von Tigerstrom, "Implementing Economic, Social and Cultural Rights: The Role of National Human Rights Institutions" in Isfahan Merali and Valerie Oosterveld, eds., *Giving Meaning to Economic, Social, and Cultural Rights* (Philadelphia: University of Pennsylvania Press, 2001) 139 at 153–54; Gallagher, *ibid.*

10 Gallagher, *ibid.* at 216; Reif, *Ombudsman, International Human Rights*, above note 4 at 123.

11 Gallagher, *ibid.*

majority of independent human rights commissions are explicitly assigned a monitoring role *vis-à-vis* international human rights treaties."[12]
One example is Australia's Human Rights and Equal Opportunity Commission Its founding legislation lists numerous human rights treaties and
declarations upon which the commission is to base its activities and take
complaints about human rights breaches by the federal government and
private actors.[13] The commissions that have the power to investigate, on
receipt of a complaint or on own-motion, typically have strong powers of
investigation, attempt to settle the complaint using conciliation or mediation and, after an investigation, issue recommendations. Some commissions have the power to refer an unresolved complaint to a human rights
tribunal or the courts for an enforceable decision and the commission may
act as "prosecutor" of the case either on behalf of the complainant or in its
own name, and some can intervene or appear as *amicus curiae* in human
rights cases, obtain declaratory judgments on human rights statutes, apply
to the courts for directions and orders, and issue orders for compliance
with its determinations.

Human rights commissions of this complexion have been established
in the post–World War II period.[14] The number of new human rights commissions has increased markedly since the 1990s, especially in developing
countries.[15] Although human rights commissions are located around the

---

12   *Ibid.* at 211.

13   *Human Rights and Equal Opportunity Commission Act 1986*, Act No. 125 of 1986, ss. 3,
     11, 46C(4), 47, Schs. 1–5, plus racial and sex discrimination and native title legislation
     online: www.hreoc.gov.au. See also Aboriginal and Torres Strait Islander Social Justice
     Commissioner.

14   France's *Commission nationale consultative des droit de l'homme* was established in
     1947, but its initial mandate was directed toward "the codification of international law
     and the definition of the rights and duties of states and human rights," online: www.
     commission-droits-homme.fr. Today, the *Commission nationale* is an advisory com-
     mission. The first Canadian human rights legislation was passed in Ontario (1944)
     and Saskatchewan (1947). Commissions were established later, starting with Ontario's
     1958 Anti-Discrimination Commission (no complaints-handling function) followed by
     the 1961 Human Rights Commission. See R. Brian Howe & David Johnson, *Restrain-
     ing Equality: Human Rights Commissions in Canada* (Toronto: University of Toronto
     Press, 2000) at 6–9 and 12; Walter Tarnopolsky, "The Iron Hand in the Velvet Glove:
     Administration and Enforcement of Human Rights Legislation in Canada" (1968) 46
     Can. Bar Rev. 565 at 571.

15   For human rights commissions see Reif, *Ombudsman, International Human Rights*,
     above note 4 at 83–84.

world, as discussed later in the chapter, the hybrid human rights ombudsman is preferred in Latin America and in Central and Eastern Europe.

3) The Classical Ombudsman

An ombudsman, usually established by constitutional provision and/or
legislation, is mandated to monitor government administration in order
to improve its performance in terms of legality, fairness, and accountability to the public.[16] Many ombudsmän around the world are appointed by
the legislature, but in some countries the ombudsman is appointed by the
executive power.

An ombudsman is given the powers to: investigate, in an impartial
manner, public complaints of illegal or unfair government administration,
make recommendations to remedy any illegality or injustice that may be
uncovered, and publicize the findings in annual and special reports and
before the legislature. Many ombudsmän also have the power to launch
own-motion investigations. Classical ombudsmän are given jurisdiction
over public-sector entities and, in some cases, this extends to universities,
hospitals, etc.; but the vast majority do not have jurisdiction over private-
sector conduct.[17] Most ombudsmän have strong powers of investigation
and a number have been given the duty of inspecting institutions where
individuals are involuntarily detained.[18]

Most ombudsmän not only investigate cases of administrative illegality
but can also take broader criteria into consideration in scrutinizing administrative conduct such as injustice, unfairness, or "wrong" behaviour. As
the Supreme Court of Canada has stated, "[t]he powers granted to the Om-

---

16 See *ibid.* at 1–4 and 12–19. See, for example, *Human Rights Commissions and Ombudsman Offices*, above note 4; Roy Gregory & Philip Giddings, eds., *Righting Wrongs: The
Ombudsman in Six Continents* (Amsterdam: IOS Press, 2000); Linda C. Reif, ed., *The
International Ombudsman Anthology: Selected Writings From the International Ombudsman Institute* (The Hague: Kluwer Law International, 1999).

17 But see New South Wales Ombudsman with jurisdiction over child abuse cases in the
private sector; Katrina Del Villar, "Who Guards the Guardians? Recent Developments
Concerning the Jurisdiction and the Accountability of Ombudsmen in Australia"
(2002) 6 Int'l Omb. Y.B. 3.

18 A 1991 survey of national and subnational ombudsmän found that 86.8 percent had
inspection powers, with many of these in Europe, Udo Kempf & Marco Mille, "The Role
and Function of the Ombudsman: Personalized Parliamentary Control in Forty-Eight
Different States" in *International Ombudsman Anthology*, above note 16, 195 at 213.

budsman allow him to address administrative problems that the courts, the legislature, and the executive cannot effectively resolve."[19] The ombudsman dates back to 1809, established in Sweden.[20] It spread outside Scandinavia starting in the 1960s.[21] Today, there are numerous classical ombudsmän at the national and subnational levels of government in Western Europe, North America, the Caribbean, Africa, Asia, and the Pacific region.[22]

4) Hybrid Institutions: The Human Rights Ombudsman (Commissioner, Attorney)

While some countries have established separate human rights commissions and ombudsmän, a growing number of states have combined the two concepts into one hybrid institution. With a long wave of democratization of states starting in the 1970s, and accelerating in the late 1980s with the fall of Communism and the collapse of military dictatorships in Latin America, the new governments in these nations saw the need to restructure their state institutions and improve human rights protections afforded by the state. In looking to improve government accountability and human rights protection, these governments established hybrid institutions with one office-holder, called a human rights ombudsman, human rights commissioner, human rights attorney, or defender of the people (*defensor del pueblo*).[23]

Portugal and Spain started this trend in the 1970s, with the Portuguese *Provedor de Justiça* (Provider of Justice) and Spain's *Defensor del Pueblo*.[24] The *defensor del pueblo* model has been influential in the establishment of human rights ombudsmän in many Latin American states in the past twenty years.[25] In the post-Communist period, most Central and Eastern European nations have established human rights ombudsmän.[26]

---

19   *British Columbia Development Corporation* v. *Friedmann*, [1985] 1 W.W.R. 193 at 206 (S.C.C.).

20   Reif, *Ombudsman, International Human Rights*, above note 4 at 4–6.

21   *Ibid.* Today, the ombudsmän in Sweden, Finland, and Norway all have express human rights protection functions.

22   While many are formally called "ombudsman," other representative titles are used, for example, Commissioner for Public Administration (United Kingdom), *Protecteur du citoyen* (Protector of the Citizen, Quebec).

23   Reif, *Ombudsman, International Human Rights*, above note 4 at 87–89.

24   *Ibid.* at 141–42 and 145–49.

25   *Ibid.* at 187–205.

26   *Ibid.* at 155–68.

Other human rights ombudsmän are found in Western Europe and are being set up in Africa, Asia, the Caribbean, and the Pacific region.[27] Human
rights ombudsmän have also been the favoured type of NHRI established
or strengthened in postconflict peace-building processes of the past twenty
years.[28] In another recent development, a number of states have turned
their classical ombudsman into a human rights ombudsman, such as in
Finland, Norway, Jamaica, Ghana, and Tanzania.[29]

Human rights ombudsmän differ in their powers and functions, with
some having more aspects of the human rights commission and others
more of the ombudsman model. Human rights ombudsmän are always
given the power to investigate complaints that public authorities have violated human rights or have committed maladministration, and many can
start own-motion investigations. However, only a handful of human rights
ombudsmän have also been given jurisdiction over complaints against
private-sector entities.[30] A number of human rights ombudsmän are empowered to look to international human rights law obligations of the state,
either by express designation in their governing laws or, indirectly, by en-
shrinement of the institution in the constitution as a procedural mechanism to uphold constitutional human rights provisions that refer to the
international law obligations of the state. Some human rights ombudsmän
address economic, social, cultural, and third-generation rights in their
work.[31] Many human rights ombudsmän also have stronger powers. For
example, some have the power to go to constitutional or other courts to
determine legal and constitutional issues pertaining to an investigation,
others can ensure legal aid funding for litigation or can provide legal advice, and still others can even go to court for a judicial order to enforce their
own recommendations.[32] Many human rights ombudsmän also have other
functions, such as human rights research and education.

---

27 *Ibid.* at 152–55, 205–12, 224–31, 234–37, 245, and 249–52.
28 *Ibid.* at 253–87. See El Salvador, Guatemala, Bosnia-Herzegovina, Kosovo, and East
    Timor. But see Northern Ireland and Ireland human rights commissions (1998 Good
    Friday Agreement), and Afghan Human Rights Commission (2001 Bonn Agreement).
29 *Ibid.* at 138–41, 209–12, and 225–31.
30 *Ibid.* at 402.
31 *Ibid.*
32 *Ibid.* at 403–4. The hybrid Ghana Commission on Human Rights and Administrative
    Justice and the Tanzania Commission on Human Rights and Good Governance have
    the power to go to court for orders to enforce their recommendations, *ibid.* at 227–31.

5) Specialized Institutions for the Protection and Promotion of Human Rights

There are also NHRIs that are designed to protect a specific area of human rights that is seen to need special attention. These NHRIs can be found at national and subnational levels of governance, appointed by the legislative or executive power, and have differing degrees of independence and powers.

One example is the ombudsman or commissioner for children.[33] These are found predominantly in some European countries, some Australian and US states, and New Zealand.[34] As will be discussed later, a growing number of Canadian provinces have created children's advocates. In most of the European states and New Zealand the legislation gives the children's ombudsmän the duty to work to apply the United Nations *Convention on the Rights of the Child* (CRC) in the domestic legal system and in their work.[35] Another example of a specialized institution is the ombudsman/commissioner for the protection of ethnic minorities or Indigenous peoples.[36]

C. THE UN AND NHRIs

Various international organizations recognize the importance of NHRIs in human rights protection and promotion, including the domestic implementation of international human rights law.[37] The following discussion will focus on the UN system.

The UN has supported the development of NHRIs since its inception.[38] The UN has paid greater attention to the establishment and strengthening of NHRIs since the 1990s, exemplified by the 1993 Vienna and 1995

33 *Ibid.* at 289–331.
34 *Ibid.* at 313–25.
35 *Ibid.* at 313–23; [1992] Can. T.S. No. 3. For example, New Zealand broadened the mandate of its children's commissioner in 2003, including the CRC in a schedule to the Act (for reference purposes only), requiring the commissioner to have regard to the CRC in her work and *inter alia* raise awareness and understanding of the CRC, monitor the application of the CRC by government departments, and present reports to courts when the proceeding relates to the CRC at request of the court or lawyers involved, *Children's Commissioner Act 2003*, S.N.Z. 2003, no. 121, ss. 3(c), 11, 12(1), 13, Sch. 2; online: www.occ.org.nz.
36 *Ibid.* at 36–38. On indigenous commissioners see Australia's Aboriginal and Torres Strait Islander Social Justice Commissioner, above note 13, and Alberta's Métis Settlements Ombudsman, below note 135.
37 *Ibid.* at 89–94, 172–86, and 216–17.
38 *Ibid.* at 95. On the UN and NHRIs see, for example, Sonia Cardenas, "Emerging Global Actors: The United Nations and National Human Rights Institutions" (2003) 9

Beijing Conference Declarations,[39] Commission on Human Rights resolutions,[40] General Assembly resolutions,[41] the work of the Office of the UN High Commissioner for Human Rights and the Secretary-General,[42] the development of the Paris Principles, and documents issued by UN human rights treaty committees.

1) Paris Principles

The "Principles Relating to the Status of National Institutions" (Paris Principles) were issued in 1991 and adopted by the UN Commission on Human Rights in 1992 and the General Assembly in 1993.[43] They list the essential requirements for NHRIs as follows: a broad mandate established in the constitution or by legislation; a pluralist representation of society in the choice of commission members; competence to promote and protect human rights; adequate funding to provide independence from government; and a variety of responsibilities, such as submitting reports and proposals on human rights matters, promoting the harmonization of national legislation with the state's international obligations, encouraging the state to become bound by international human rights instruments and ensuring their domestic implementation, contributing to state reports submitted to UN bodies, and engaging in research and public education and information.[44]

The Paris Principles, however, are based on the paradigm of a human rights commission and do not fully take into account the evolution of hybrid institutions or that some classical ombudsmän, in practice, investigate cases with human rights aspects.[45] In addition, the Paris Principles are criticized for considering that the power to investigate is only an op-

---

Global Governance 23; Gallagher, "Making Human Rights Treaty Obligations a Reality," above note 4 at 201.

39   United Nations World Conference on Human Rights, Vienna Declaration and Programme of Action (June 25, 1993), UN Doc. A/CONF.157/24, (1993) 32 I.L.M. 1663, paras. 36, 67–69, 74, and 83–85; Fourth World Conference on Women, Report of the Fourth World Conference on Women, A/CONF.177/20 (Oct. 17, 1995) (1996) 35 I.L.M. 405, c. I, res. I, annex II, para. 230(e) (include women's rights in NHRI work).

40   Reif, *Ombudsman, International Human Rights*, above note 4 at 98.

41   *Ibid.*

42   *Ibid.*

43   UN G.A. Res. 134, UN GAOR, 48th Sess., 85th mtg., UN Doc. A/RES/48/134 (1993), rep. in *National Human Rights Institutions: A Handbook*, above note 2 at 37–38 (Paris Principles).

44   *Ibid.*

45   Reif, *Ombudsman, International Human Rights*, above note 4 at 96.

tional NHRI function.[46] Also, the Paris Principles provide little detail on NHRI independence. While an argument has been made that the Paris Principles form part of customary international law, I disagree with this position.[47] The Paris Principles have been used as a template by a number of UN entities but, as noted later, UN treaty bodies only began to refer to them more recently. The Principles have not been replicated in other international instruments and the many NHRIs created around the world vary considerably in their mandates, powers, and independence. Nonetheless, the Paris Principles are critically important guidelines for states in structuring NHRIs.

2) UN Treaty Committees and NHRIs

The main UN human rights treaties have committees that monitor state parties' implementation of, and compliance with, their treaty obligations; Canada is a party to all of these human rights treaties.[48] At least since the early 1990s, the UN treaty committees have made references to the presence and strength of NHRIs in their Concluding Observations on periodic state reports submitted pursuant to the state's treaty obligations although, for the most part, references to the Paris Principles have only appeared since the late 1990s.[49] These Concluding Observations praise states for establishing a NHRI, make suggestions for strengthening a NHRI, or recommending that a NHRI be established. Some treaty committees have issued General Comments that support the establishment of NHRIs and

---

46 *Ibid.* at 96–97; Paris Principles, above note 43, "Additional principles concerning the status of commissions with quasi-jurisdictional competence." In practice, the power to investigate complaints is always given to classical and human rights ombudsmän and to many human rights commissions.

47 Canadian Association of Statutory Human Rights Agencies, *The Government of British Columbia's Draft Human Rights Code Amendment Act Bill 53* (September 2002) at 6.

48 For example, *International Covenant on Civil and Political Rights*, Annex to UN G.A. Res. 2200A, UN GAOR, 21st Sess., Supp. No. 16 at 52, UN Doc. A/16316; *International Covenant on Economic, Social and Cultural Rights*, Annex to UN G.A. Res. 2200A, UN GAOR, 21st Sess., Supp. No. 16 at 49, UN Doc. A/16316; *Convention on the Rights of the Child*, above note 35; *Convention on the Elimination of All Forms of Discrimination Against Women*, (1979) 1249 U.N.T.S. 135, [1982] Can. T.S. No. 31; *Convention on the Elimination of All Forms of Racial Discrimination*, (1966) 660 U.N.T.S. 195, [1970] Can. T.S. No. 28; *Convention Against Torture and Other Cruel, Inhuman or Degrading Treatment or Punishment* (1984), 1465 U.N.T.S. 85, [1987] Can. T.S. No. 36.

49 Reif, *Ombudsman, International Human Rights*, above note 4 at 96–99 and 117–20.

may specify powers and functions that should be granted to the NHRI, with several based on the Paris Principles.

In 1993, the Committee on the Elimination of Racial Discrimination issued General Comment No. 17 on the establishment of NHRIs to facilitate implementation of the *International Convention on the Elimination of all Forms of Racial Discrimination* (ICERD), which recommended that state parties establish national commissions or other bodies, taking into account the Paris Principles, and giving them functions in working to eliminate discrimination and assist the government in preparing its state report.[50] In 2002, the Committee issued General Comment No. 28, which followed up on the UN Durban Conference on Racism, recommending that NHRIs assist their state in complying with their ICERD reporting obligations and closely monitor the state's responses to the committee's Concluding Observations and recommendations.[51]

The Committee on Economic, Social, and Cultural Rights of the *International Covenant on Economic, Social, and Cultural Rights* (ICESCR) issued General Comment No. 10 in 1998 on the role of NHRIs in protecting economic, social, and cultural rights.[52] The Committee called upon ICESCR state parties to include appropriate attention to economic, social, and cultural rights in the mandates of all NHRIs,[53] stating:

> [N]ational institutions have a potentially crucial role to play in promoting and ensuring the indivisibility and interdependence of all human rights. Unfortunately, this role has too often either not been accorded to the institution or has been neglected or given a low priority by it. It is therefore essential that full attention be given to economic, social and cultural rights in all of the relevant activities of these institutions.[54]

The Committee also indicated that the entire range of NHRI activities can include attention to economic, social, and cultural rights.[55] The Committee has also issued general comments on the ICESCR rights to health, food,

---

50 Committee on the Elimination of Racial Discrimination, General Comment No. 17 (25 March 1993); Paris Principles, above note 43.

51 Committee on the Elimination of Racial Discrimination, General Comment No. 28 (19 March 2002), para. 2(a).

52 Committee on Economic, Social and Cultural Rights, General Comment No. 10, UN Doc. E/C.12/1998/25 (3 December 1998).

53 *Ibid.*, para. 4.

54 *Ibid.*, para. 3.

55 *Ibid.*

and water that state that human rights commissions and ombudsmän should be permitted to address violations of these rights.[56]

The Committee on the Rights of the Child issued General Comment No. 2 in 2002 on the role of independent NHRIs in the protection and promotion of the rights of the child, calling on all CRC parties to establish independent NHRIs for the protection of children's rights (for example, ombudsman/commissioner for children) to promote and monitor the implementation of the CRC, and specifying the functions and attributes that these children's NHRIs should enjoy.[57] The Committee stated that it "considers the establishment of such bodies to fall within the commitment made by States parties upon ratification to ensure the implementation of the Convention."[58] The Committee also stated that these NHRIs should be established in accordance with the Paris Principles but, in contrast to the weak content of the Paris Principles on NHRI investigatory powers, the committee specified that NHRIs covering children's rights must have the power to investigate individual complaints, including those made by or on behalf of children.[59] The General Comment recognized that it may not be financially feasible for states with limited resources to establish a children's NHRI in addition to a general NHRI, and allows in these cases for a general NHRI to be developed that includes within its mandate a dedicated focus on children's rights.[60]

In 2004, the Human Rights Committee issued General Comment No. 31 on the Nature of the General Legal Obligation Imposed on States Parties to the *International Covenant on Civil and Political Rights* (ICCPR).[61] Addressing ICCPR article 2(3), which requires state parties to ensure

---

56 Committee on Economic, Social and Cultural Rights, General Comment No. 12, UN Doc. E/C.12/1999/5 (12 March 1999), at para. 32 (food); Committee on Economic, Social and Cultural Rights, General Comment No. 14, UN Doc. E/C.12/2000/4 (4 July 2000), at para. 59 (health); Committee on Economic, Social and Cultural Rights, General Comment No. 15, UN Doc. E/C.12/2002/11 (20 January 2003), at para. 55 (water).

57 UN Committee on the Rights of the Child, General Comment No. 2, UN Doc. CRC/GC/2002/2 (4 October 2002), at paras. 2 and 7; Reif, *Ombudsman, International Human Rights*, above note 4 at 297–98, and 330–31.

58 General Comment No. 2, *ibid.*, at para. 1. See also UN Committee on the Rights of the Child, General Comment No. 5, General measures of implementation of the Convention on the Rights of the Child (arts. 4, 42 and 44, para. 6), UN Doc. CRC/GC/2003/5 (27 November 2003), para. 65 (independent human rights institutions).

59 General Comment No. 2, *ibid.*, at paras. 4 and 13; Paris Principles, above note 43.

60 General Comment No. 2, *ibid.*, at para. 6.

61 UN Doc. CCPR/C/21/Rev.1/Add.13 (26 May 2004).

that individuals have accessible and effective remedies to uphold their IC-CPR rights through judicial, administrative, and legislative authorities, the Committee stated that administrative mechanisms are required to implement the obligation to investigate human rights breach allegations promptly, thoroughly, and effectively through independent and impartial bodies, and that NHRIs with the appropriate powers can contribute to the fulfilment of this obligation.[62]

3) UN Human Rights Instruments and NHRIs

A few international human rights instruments make specific reference to NHRIs. As noted above, there are the Paris Principles and the Vienna and Beijing Conference declarations. Also, the *UN Guidelines for the Prevention of Juvenile Delinquency* (Riyadh Guidelines) stipulate that states should consider the establishment of an ombudsman or similar independent body to ensure that the status, rights, and interests of young persons are upheld, and to supervise implementation of the Riyadh Guidelines, the *UN Standard Minimum Rules for the Administration of Juvenile Justice* (Beijing Rules), and the *UN Rules for the Protection of Juveniles Deprived of Their Liberty.*[63]

More recently, the *Optional Protocol to the Convention against Torture and other Cruel, Inhuman or Degrading Treatment or Punishment*, adopted on 18 December 2002, but not in force as of 29 June 2005, sets up a "system of regular visits undertaken by independent international and national bodies to places where people are deprived of their liberty in order to prevent torture and other cruel, inhuman or degrading treatment or punishment."[64] Canada has not yet signed the Protocol. Each state party is required to set up, designate, or maintain at the domestic level one or several independent visiting bodies (the "national preventive mechanism") to carry out these visits, giving due consideration to the Paris Principles, and each state party shall allow visits by the national preventive mechan-

---

62 *Ibid.* at para. 15.
63 *UN Guidelines for the Prevention of Juvenile Delinquency* (Riyadh Guidelines), UN G.A. Res. 45/112 (14 December 1990); *UN Standard Minimum Rules for the Administration of Juvenile Justice* (Beijing Rules), UN G.A. Res. 40/33 (29 November 1985); *UN Rules for the Protection of Juveniles Deprived of Their Liberty*, UN G.A. Res. 45/113 (14 December 1990).
64 *Optional Protocol to the Convention against Torture and other Cruel, Inhuman or Degrading Treatment or Punishment*, adopted 18 December 2002, art. 1 (2003) 42 I.L.M. 26. As of 29 June 2005 there were thirty-seven signatures and ten parties, with twenty ratifications required for entry into force.

ism to places of detention in accordance with the Protocol.[65] The purpose of the visits is to strengthen, if needed, the protection of persons in places of detention.[66] The Protocol requires *inter alia* that the national preventive mechanisms have functional independence, powers of access, and the powers to regularly examine persons deprived of their liberty, make recommendations to the authorities taking relevant UN norms into consideration, and submit observations and proposals concerning existing or draft legislation.[67] The express reference to the Paris Principles in the Protocol indicates that existing or new NHRIs could be designated as "visiting bodies." Evans and Haenni-Dale state that "[i]t is difficult to predict what forms of national preventive mechanisms will be considered appropriate and they will vary from country to country. Some may have a single Human Rights Commission or Ombudsman's Office which already enjoys most or all of the visiting capacities required. Others will not, but will have an extensive patchwork of bodies operating in different sectors that, in combination, produce an appropriate overall coverage."[68] Federal states may have to look to the designation of both federal and provincial bodies.

D. METHODS BY WHICH NHRIs ACT AS MECHANISMS FOR THE DOMESTIC APPLICATION OF INTERNATIONAL HUMAN RIGHTS LAW

1) Overview

The ability of NHRIs to use international human rights norms in their work depends on factors such as: the mandate and jurisdiction of the NHRI; the extent to which the state has become bound by human rights treaties; whether its international human rights obligations have been given domestic effect; and the receptiveness of the NHRI to using international human rights law.[69] Clearly, human rights commissions, hybrids, and some specialized institutions—NHRIs with express human rights mandates—can act as domestic mechanisms for the protection and promotion of human rights. These NHRIs may even have the mandate to carry out their work,

---

65 *Ibid.*, arts. 3, 4(1) and 17–23; Paris Principles, above note 43.

66 *Ibid.*, art. 4(1).

67 *Ibid.*, arts. 18(1), 19, & 20.

68 Malcolm D. Evans & Claudine Haenni-Dale, "Preventing Torture? The Development of the Optional Protocol to the UN Convention Against Torture" (2004) 4 H.R. L. Rev. 19 at 53.

69 Reif, *Ombudsman, International Human Rights*, above note 4 at 105.

taking into account the international human rights obligations of the state. However, all NHRIs—including classical ombudsmän—can rely on international human rights norms in various ways in their activities. With classical ombudsmän, the number of cases involving human rights issues is often a low percentage of the total—but some of the investigations that do involve human rights are important and high profile. A classical ombudsman will have more possibilities for encountering human rights issues in complaints investigation if the institution has jurisdiction over sensitive areas, such as the military, police, prisons, and immigration departments. Examples of classical ombudsmän that have dealt with investigations involving human rights issues, and have used domestic and international human rights norms in their investigations, include: ombudsmän in Western European nations such as Norway, Denmark, Iceland, the Netherlands, France, and Ireland;[70] ombudsmän in several Caribbean nations;[71] the ombudsmän of New Zealand;[72] and, as discussed later, ombudsmän in some Canadian provinces. Further, classical ombudsmän do receive and resolve some complaints involving economic, social, and cultural rights norms.[73]

2) Use of Internalized Treaty and Customary International Law Obligations

NHRIs can use treaty or customary international human rights law obligations directly through the medium of domestic law when treaty or customary international law obligations of the state have been automatically adopted in the domestic legal system or transformed into domestic law through legislation. Whether international human rights law obligations of the state can be considered to be part of the domestic legal system depends upon whether the state follows a monist or dualist approach to the international law source.[74] For example, where the state follows a dualist approach to treaties (for example, Canada), the treaty obligation needs to be transformed into domestic law before it will be considered part of domestic

---

70   *Ibid.* at 86–87, 108–9, and 142–45; Emily O'Reilly, "Protecting Rights and Freedoms" (2003) 7 Int. Omb. Y.B. 24.

71   Reif, *Ombudsman, International Human Rights, ibid.* at 185.

72   A. Satyanand, "The Ombudsman Concept and Human Rights Protection," *I.O.I. Occasional Paper* No. 68 (Edmonton: International Ombudsman Institute, January 1999).

73   For example, New Zealand (complaints by social welfare beneficiaries), Satyanand, *ibid.* at 5; Ireland (care of elderly in nursing homes), O'Reilly, above note 70 at 29–30; Canada, below text accompanying notes 187–207.

74   See van Ert, *Using International Law in Canadian Courts*, above note 1 at 50–51.

law.[75] Treaty provisions can be implemented through a variety of mechanisms, such as express incorporation in constitutional or statutory language or amendment of existing statutes. Alternatively, the government may consider that existing domestic law already complies with the new treaty obligations, as does the Canadian government with respect to a number of human rights treaties entered into by Canada.[76]

Human rights commissions and hybrid NHRIs can apply the state's internalized international human rights obligations if the constitution, their foundational legislation, or other statute law implements these norms. For example, many human rights ombudsmän use international human rights obligations of the state that have been internalized in domestic law.[77] In their investigations, classical ombudsmän can use constitutional or statutory provisions that implement international human rights obligations as a standard to determine the legality and fairness of administrative conduct.[78] Based on the position of the Canadian government and international law scholars that many Canadian human rights treaty obligations are "implicitly implemented" in domestic law through the prior conformity of Canadian statute law or through the *Canadian Charter of Rights and Freedoms*, it can be argued that the relevant laws are actually implementing statutes and Canadian NHRIs must interpret and apply them as such.[79]

Thus, in using domestic law that implements international human rights law obligations of the state, the NHRI serves as a non-judicial mechanism for the further internal application of international human rights obligations.

---

75 *Ibid.* "Canada is a hybrid jurisdiction: monist in respect of customary international law, and dualist in respect of treaties." But see Brunnée & Toope, "A Hesitant Embrace," above note 1 at 381: "the approach of senior Canadian courts to customary international law is utterly unclear."

76 For example, Weiser, "Undressing the Window," above note 1 at 127.

77 Reif, *Ombudsman, International Human Rights*, above note 4 at 106–7, 138–41,145–69, 192–212, 225–37, and 260–84.

78 *Ibid.* at 106; Reif, "Building Democratic Institutions," above note 4 at 19.

79 For example, Brunnée & Toope, "A Hesitant Embrace," above note 1 at 369 and 382; Mark Freeman & Gibran van Ert, *International Human Rights Law* (Toronto: Irwin Law, 2004) at 166–68. See also presumption of legislative intent, below text accompanying note 85, and *Pusphanathan v. Canada (Minister of Citizenship and Immigration)* (1998), 160 D.L.R. (4th) 193 (S.C.C.) (interpretation of implementing statute must be consistent with the treaty obligation, use rules of treaty interpretation to assist in construing meaning of statute).

3)   Use of Unimplemented Treaty Obligations and Other International Instruments

NHRIs can also use unimplemented treaty obligations of the state or other international instruments (for example, "soft law") in a variety of ways. First, as noted by Gallagher, NHRIs with express human rights mandates must use unimplemented human rights treaty obligations of the state in all their activities if their foundational legislation directs them to apply these treaties, with the result that:

> [t]he inclusion of references to international human rights treaties in the mandate of a national institution is of special significance in relation to countries which follow the "non self-executing" theory of treaty law. In such instances, the national institution may be able to cover, at least partially, the gap which is often left by state parties failing to pass the necessary incorporating legislation.[80]

Second, it is possible for a NHRI to use unimplemented treaty obligations of the state and other international instruments as interpretive guidance in construing constitutional or statute law that is relevant to their investigations or other activities, for example, research and public education.[81] Further, with respect to NHRIs that can scrutinize administrative conduct, where an administrative authority can exercise discretion in making a determination, the NHRI can recommend that such discretion should be exercised in accordance with the state's international human rights law obligations, even if they are unimplemented.[82] The ability of a NHRI to use international norms in this manner depends upon whether there is permissive domestic law. For example, in their investigations the ombudsmän in Iceland and Norway have used unimplemented international human rights treaties to aid in the interpretation of domestic law.[83] In Canada, the situation is more complex. In contrast to the views of the federal government and scholars, the courts have taken a more conservative view on whether human rights treaty obligations of Canada have been implemented in domestic legislation.[84] Also, whether or not a treaty

---

80   Gallagher, "Making Human Rights Treaty Obligations a Reality," above note 4 at 210–11 (footnotes omitted).
81   Reif, *Ombudsman, International Human Rights*, above note 4 at 108–10.
82   *Ibid.*
83   *Ibid.* at 108–9.
84   Above note 79.

obligation has been implemented in domestic law, Canadian courts should apply the presumption of legislative intent to act consistently with Canada's international law obligations, so that domestic law should, if possible, be construed in conformity with Canada's international law obligations.[85] In practice, the Supreme Court of Canada has used human rights treaty obligations of Canada, which the Court considers have not been implemented in the domestic legal system, only as persuasive sources for interpretive guidance or context in the elaboration of the meaning of Canadian *Charter*[86] and statutory provisions.[87] Thus, Canadian NHRIs may follow the approach of the Supreme Court of Canada and use what the Court considers to be unimplemented human rights treaty obligations of Canada as persuasive aids in construing the *Charter* and domestic statutes that are relevant in the resolution of an investigation or other NHRI activity.[88]

Third, classical or human rights ombudsmän can use unimplemented treaty law obligations of the state and other international instruments to construe the broader and more flexible ombudsman standards of fairness and justice as applied to a particular case.[89] Even if administrative authorities are in technical compliance with domestic law, if there is a gap between the contents of the international law obligations and domestic law/policy with the international law providing better protection, then the ombudsman can point out that the administrative conduct may still breach broader standards of fair and equitable conduct reflected in the international law. At a minimum, the international obligations or norms can be used as guiding principles for domestic administrative authorities, and if the international instrument is an unimplemented treaty obligation there is a much stronger argument for NHRI reliance on the treaty.[90]

Fourth, those NHRIs that have a mandate to recommend changes to domestic laws and policies can use international human rights obligations

85   Freeman & van Ert, *International Human Rights Law*, above note 79 at 151–59; Brunnée & Toope, "A Hesitant Embrace," above note 1 at 382.

86   For example, *Reference re Public Service Employee Relations Act (Alberta)*, [1987] 1 S.C.R. 313, Dickson C.J. in dissent; *Slaight Communications Inc. v. Davidson*, [1989] 1 S.C.R. 1038 and numerous subsequent cases discussed in La Forest, "Domestic Application of International Law," above note 1.

87   For example, *Baker v. Canada (Minister of Citizenship and Immigration)*, [1999] 2 S.C.R. 817 [*Baker*]; *Canadian Foundation for Children, Youth and the Law v. Canada*, [2004] 1 S.C.R. 76.

88   Reif, *Ombudsman, International Human Rights*, above note 4 at 110.

89   *Ibid.* at 104, and 110; Reif, "Building Democratic Institutions," above note 4 at 21.

90   See Brunnée & Toope, "A Hesitant Embrace," above note 1.

of the state as standards for recommending domestic law reform and to highlight the gap between the state's international obligations and the contents of its domestic law.[91] A NHRI may also assist in the treaty implementation process through the provision of advice on statute drafting.

Fifth, even where a state is not bound by a human rights treaty or there is only evolving customary international law on point as evidenced by soft law, a NHRI can still use these international law instruments as informal sources of guidance for what are "best practices" or fair and just conduct on the part of the government.[92] This approach can certainly be used by the ombudsman empowered to scrutinize administrative conduct according to broader standards of justice and equity. Whether other NHRIs can use international human rights law in this manner will depend upon their legislative framework and mandate.

E. Nhris IN CANADA: THE CURRENT ENVIRONMENT

1)   Human Rights Commissions

In Canada, there are human rights commissions at the federal level and in every province and territory except British Columbia (BC) and Nunavut, all established between 1961 and 2004.[93] In 2003, the BC government abolished its commission and created a Human Rights Tribunal that accepts,

---

91   Reif, *Ombudsman, International Human Rights*, above note 4 at 111.

92   *Ibid.* at 111–12. See Brunnée & Toope, "A Hesitant Embrace," above note 1 at 383: "[w]e argue that these non-binding norms ... should be treated as potentially relevant and persuasive sources for the interpretation of domestic law. Courts may, and in cases of particularly compelling norms *should*, draw upon such norms for interpretive purposes, but they are not strictly speaking required to do so"; Freeman & van Ert, *International Human Rights Law*, above note 79 at 158, "there are good reasons not to apply the presumption of conformity to non-binding international instruments."

93   *Canadian Human Rights Act*, R.S.C. 1985, c. H-6; *Employment Equity Act*, S.C. 1995, c. 44; Yukon: *Human Rights Act*, R.S.Y. 2002, c. 116; NWT: *Human Rights Act*, S.N.W.T. 2002, c. 18 (in force 2004); Alberta: *Human Rights, Citizenship and Multiculturalism Act*, R.S.A. 2000, c. H-14; *Alberta Bill of Rights*, R.S.A. 2000, c. A-14 (no connection to Alberta's human rights commission); *The Saskatchewan Human Rights Code*, S.S. 1979, c. S-24.1; Manitoba: *The Human Rights Code*, C.C.S.M., c. H175; *Quebec Charter of Human Rights and Freedoms*, R.S.Q. c. C-12; Ontario: *Human Rights Code*, R.S.O. 1990, c. H.19; Nova Scotia: *Human Rights Act*, R.S.N.S. 1989, c. 214.; New Brunswick: *Human Rights Act*, R.S.N.B. 1973, c. H-11; Prince Edward Island: *Human Rights Act*, R.S.P.E.I. 1988, c. H-12; Newfoundland and Labrador: *Human Rights Code*, R.S.N.L. 1990, c. H-14.

mediates, and adjudicates discrimination complaints against persons.[94] Similarly, Nunavut's new human rights statute envisages a tribunal without a commission.[95]

Most of the human rights commissions have jurisdiction only over antidiscrimination matters.[96] However, the Saskatchewan, Yukon, and Quebec human rights commissions have broader jurisdictional mandates. The Saskatchewan legislation also has a bill of rights containing political freedoms (rights to freedom of religion and conscience, expression, assembly, and association) and the right of qualified persons to vote.[97] The Saskatchewan Human Rights Commission's complaint-handling function covers both discrimination and the other rights, although the vast majority of complaints involve discrimination, its other human rights functions also cover all rights in the legislation.[98] The Yukon Human Rights Commission legislation also has a bill of rights containing the same political freedoms and a right to property.[99] However, the functions of the Yukon Commission are essentially tied to equality and the elimination of discrimination through education, research, and the investigation of complaints.[100] Unique in Canada, the *Quebec Charter of Human Rights and Freedoms* includes a catalogue of civil, political, judicial, economic, and social rights in addition to antidiscrimination provisions.[101] Quebec's Human Rights and Youth Rights Commission (*Commission des droits de la personne et des droits de la jeunesse*), *inter alia*, promotes and upholds the principles in the *Quebec Charter* and the Commission's functions relating to public information, education, research, and advice, and recommendations concerning provincial laws that are contrary to the *Quebec Charter* cover the full range of rights in the *Quebec Charter*.[102] However, its investigatory functions cover only matters of discrimination and harassment, and alleged violations of

---

94 *Human Rights Code*, R.S.B.C. 1996, c. 210.

95 *Human Rights Act*, S. Nun. 2003, c. 12 (in force 5 November 2004).

96 See sexual harassment, hate messages, and employment equity falling within broad statutory definitions of discrimination.

97 *The Saskatchewan Human Rights Code*, above note 93, ss. 4–8 (Bill of Rights), ss. 9–15 (non-discrimination provisions).

98 *Ibid.*, ss. 25(b), (d), (f), (g), 27(1), (4), and 27.1(2)(c).

99 *Human Rights Act* (Yukon), above note 93, ss. 3–7.

100 *Ibid.*, ss. 16 and 20–26.

101 *Quebec Charter*, above note 93, ss. 1–48. However, many of the economic and social rights are limited "to the extent provided by law."

102 *Ibid.*, ss. 57 and 71(4), (5)–(8).

the right of aged or disabled persons against exploitation found in section 48 of the *Charter* (an economic and social right).[103]

Only the legislation supporting the Yukon, Northwest Territories (NWT), Manitoba, Ontario, and Prince Edward Island (PEI) commissions expressly refer to international human rights law, especially the *Universal Declaration of Human Rights* (UDHR), and Canada's international obligations.[104]

While most of the human rights commissions are appointed by the executive branch and report to a minister who in turn reports to the legislature, a few commissions are appointed by the legislature although they may still have some ties to the executive, and several, which are executive appointments, report to the legislature directly.[105]

Most human rights commissions in Canada have various combinations of human rights research, statute review, public information and education, and annual reporting functions, but these are often confined to equality and non-discrimination matters.[106] All commissions have the

---

103   *Ibid.*, s. 71(1), (9).

104   *Human Rights Act* (Yukon), above note 93, s. 1(1)(c) states that an objective of the Act is to promote recognition of the dignity, worth and equal rights of humans, principles underlying the *Charter*, the UDHR and other international and national undertakings that Canada honours; *Human Rights Act* (NWT), above note 93, Preamble, refers to equality of rights in accordance with the UDHR, and that it is of vital importance to promote respect for and observance of human rights in the NWT, including *Charter* rights and "rights and freedoms protected under international human rights instruments"; *The Human Rights Code* (Manitoba), above note 93, Preamble, refers to the UDHR, the *Charter* and other international and domestic undertakings honoured by Canada; *Human Rights Code* (Ontario), above note 93, Preamble, refers to the UDHR; *Human Rights Act* (PEI), above note 93, Preamble, refers to UDHR and that the original human rights legislation was passed in response to the UDHR. See UDHR, UN G.A. Res. 217(III), UN GAOR, 3d Sess., Supp. No. 13 at 71, UN Doc. A/810 (1948).

105   *Human Rights Act* (Yukon), *ibid.*, ss. 16–17 (appointed by and accountable to legislature); *Quebec Charter*, above note 93, s. 58 (appointed by legislature upon the motion of the premier); *Human Rights Act* (PEI), *ibid.*, ss. 16(2) & 17 (appointed by legislature on recommendation of legislative committee, but responsible to Minister); Canadian Human Rights Commission, appointed by executive, reporting to Parliament, *Canadian Human Rights Act*, above note 93, ss. 26(1) and 61; NWT Human Rights Commission, appointed by Commissioner on recommendation of legislature, responsible and reporting to legislature, *Human Rights Act* (NWT), *ibid.*, ss. 16, 19, and 21. But see Alberta Human Rights Commission, appointed by executive and reporting to the minister, with no legislative provision that report shall be forwarded to legislature, *Human Rights, Citizenship and Multiculturalism Act*, above note 93, s. 19.

106   But see *Saskatchewan Human Rights Code*, above note 93, s. 25(b), (d), (f), and (g) (promotion, information, education, research covering the broader provisions of the legislation); *Quebec Charter*, *ibid.*, s. 71(4), (5)–(8) (public information and education,

power to receive complaints from persons, with a majority of commissions given the power to launch own-motion investigations.[107] Complaints can be made against private- and public-sector entities. Once an admissible complaint is investigated and cannot be settled informally, it usually can be referred to a human rights tribunal, panel, or board of inquiry for a binding determination.[108]

The problems encountered by Canadian human rights commissions—such as insufficient funding, heavy caseloads, substantial delay in processing complaints, and under-utilization of own-motion investigation, research, and education functions—have led to criticism from sources including commissioned reports,[109] some provincial ombudsmän,[110] Can-

---

research and publications, advice and recommendations on laws contrary to *Charter*, receive and examine suggestions, recommendations, etc. on human rights made by interested persons, cooperation with other human rights organizations, all extending to full range of rights in *Quebec Charter*); Alberta's *Human Rights, Citizenship and Multiculturalism Act, ibid.*, s. 16(1)(b) (multiculturalism promotion duties); Nova Scotia's *Human Rights Act*, above note 93, s. 24(1)(c), (d), (f) (research, advice, cooperation with and assistance to those involved with human rights on human rights in general); Newfoundland's *Human Rights Code*, above note 93, s. 18(d)–(f) (advisory work, cooperation with those concerned with human rights covering human rights in general); *Human Rights Act* (NWT), *ibid.*, ss. 22(d), 22(3) (research, education programs on human rights); *Canadian Human Rights Act, ibid.*, ss. 27(1)(f), 61(2) (human rights studies and reports). The BC Human Rights Tribunal does not have such powers, and the responsible minister is tasked with research, public information, and education on the *Human Rights Code*, above note 94, ss. 5–6.

107 For example, the commissions in Alberta, Saskatchewan, Manitoba, Ontario, Quebec, Nova Scotia, and NWT, and the Canadian Human Rights Commission have own-motion investigatory powers.

108 But see BC Human Rights Tribunal format, which has no investigations phase.

109 For example, Canadian Human Rights Act Review Panel, *Promoting Equality: A New Vision*, The Report of the Canadian Human Rights Act Review Panel (Ottawa: Department of Justice, 2000); Saskatchewan Human Rights Commission, *Renewing the Vision: Human Rights in Saskatchewan* (Regina, SK: The Commission, 1996); Ontario Human Rights Code Review Task Force, *Achieving Equality: A Report on Human Rights Reform* (Toronto: Ministry of Citizenship,1992) [Cornish Report], and other earlier reports on Ontario's Human Rights Commission discussed in M. K. Joachim, "Reform of the Ontario Human Rights Commission" (1999–2000) 13 Can. J. Admin. L. & Prac. 51 at 83–89; New Brunswick Human Rights Commission, *Towards a World Family. A Report and Recommendations Respecting Human Rights in New Brunswick* (Fredericton, NB: Department of Labour,1989) [Ferris Report].

110 See, for example, Ombudsman Ontario, *2002–2003 Annual Report* at 5, 11, Ombudsman Ontario, *1998–1999 Annual Report* at 4; Manitoba and Nova Scotia Ombudsman reports discussed in David Johnson & R. Brian Howe, "Human Rights Commissions in Canada: Reform or Reinvention in a Time of Restraint?" (1997) 12 C.J.L.S. 1 at 15.

ada's Auditor General,[111] the Supreme Court of Canada,[112] and academic commentators.[113]

2) Ombudsman and Related Specialized Institutions

Commencing in 1967, classical ombudsmän have been established in every Canadian province except for PEI, and in the Yukon.[114] They are typically appointed as officers of the legislature with substantial legislative in-

---

111   Auditor General of Canada, *Annual Report* (September 1998) at paras. 10.8–10.123 (Canadian Human Rights Commission).

112   *Blencoe v. British Columbia (Human Rights Commission)*, [2000] 2 S.C.R. 307, 190 D.L.R. (4th) 513. While the majority found that the commission's delay of over two years in processing the complaint did not breach either s. 7 of the *Charter* or administrative law principles, the majority stated at para. 135, Bastarache J.: "I am very concerned with the lack of efficiency of the Commission and its lack of commitment to deal more expeditiously with complaints. Lack of resources cannot explain every delay ... nor can it justify inordinate delay where it is found to exist. The fact that most human rights commissions experience serious delays will not justify breaches of the principles of natural justice in appropriate cases."

113   See, for example, Howe & Johnson, *Restraining Equality: Human Rights Commissions in Canada*, above note 14; Robert E. Hawkins, "Reputational Review III: Delay, Disrepute and Human Rights Commissions" (1999–2000) 25 Queen's L.J. 599; Joachim, "Reform of the Ontario Human Rights Commission," above note 109; Johnson & Howe, "Human Rights Commissions in Canada: Reform or Reinvention in a Time of Restraint?" above note 110; R. Brian Howe & David Johnson, "Variations in Enforcing Equality: A Study of Provincial Human Rights Funding" (1995) 38 Can. Pub. Admin. 242; Gavin A. Anderson, "Filling the '*Charter* Gap?' Human Rights Codes in the Private Sector" (1995) 33 Osgoode Hall L.J. 749; R. Brian Howe & Malcolm J. Andrade, "The Reputation of Human Rights Commissions in Canada" (1994) 9 C.J.L.S. 1.

114   Alberta: *Ombudsman Act*, R.S.A. 2000, c. O-8; British Columbia: *Ombudsman Act*, R.S.B.C. 1996, c. 340; Manitoba: *Ombudsman Act*, C.C.S.M., c. O45; New Brunswick: *Ombudsman Act*, R.S.N.B. 1973, c. O-5; Newfoundland and Labrador: *Citizens' Representative Act*, S.N.L. 2001, c. C-14.1 (Newfoundland government terminated office of ombudsman from 1992–2001); Nova Scotia: *Ombudsman Act*, R.S.N.S 1989, c. 327; Ontario: *Ombudsman Act*, R.S.O. 1990, c. O.6; Quebec: *Public Protector Act*, R.S.Q., c. P-32; Saskatchewan: *Ombudsman and Children's Advocate Act*, R.S.S. 1978, c. O-4; Yukon: *Ombudsman Act*, R.S.Y. 2002, c. 163. See generally Jacques Meunier, "The Special Relations of the Canadian Provincial Ombudsmen with the Courts and Quasi-Judicial Authorities" in *International Ombudsman Anthology*, above note 16 at 491; Mary A. Marshall & Linda C. Reif, "The Ombudsman: Maladministration and Alternative Dispute Resolution" (1995) 34 Alta. L. Rev. 215; Stephen Owen, "The Expanding Role of the Ombudsman in the Administrative State" (1990) 40 U.T.L.J. 670. The ombudsmän in Manitoba, New Brunswick, and the Yukon are also responsible for privacy and freedom of information.

volvement and are accountable to the legislature.[115] Canadian ombudsmän impartially investigate conduct relating to public administration on the grounds of illegality, improper discrimination, various procedural unfairness criteria, and other wrong or unjust conduct standards, they also make recommendations for change, report to the legislature in specific cases if no action is taken by the administration, and report to the legislature in annual and special reports.[116] All have the power to investigate on receipt of a complaint, most can initiate own-motion investigations, and all have strong powers of investigation.[117] The ombudsmän can make numerous types of recommendations, for example, changes to provincial laws, practices, and decisions. There are variations among the ombudsmän over the extent of public sector entities under their jurisdiction.[118]

---

115 Most are appointed by the Lieutenant-Governor-in-Council on the recommendation or resolution of the legislature, but see Quebec: appointment by the legislature on the motion of the premier; and Nova Scotia: appointment by the Governor-in-Council.

116 But see Manitoba and Newfoundland Ombudsmän (cannot report to legislature in specific cases, only in annual report).

117 But see Yukon Ombudsman (no own-motion investigative power). In some provinces, the legislature, legislative committees and/or ministers can refer complaints to the ombudsman.

118 For example, Yukon ombudsman (jurisdiction over municipalities and Yukon First Nations by invitation, public schools, colleges, hospitals, local/regional health authorities, and professional and occupational association professional bodies); BC Ombudsman (for example, municipalities, schools, and school boards, universities, colleges, hospitals, regional health boards, governing bodies of professional associations); Manitoba Ombudsman (municipal governments); Alberta Ombudsman (listed professional bodies); Nova Scotia Ombudsman (municipalities, colleges, school boards, hospitals, child welfare agencies and licensed facilities, nursing homes, and seniors' residential care facilities); New Brunswick Ombudsman (municipalities, provincial boards of education, district parent advisory boards, adult education and training institutions, and regional health authorities); Newfoundland (for example, university, college, health care corporations, and school boards). Montreal and Quebec City have municipal ombudsmän.

There are specialized commissioners at the federal level for official languages,[119] privacy,[120] freedom of information,[121] RCMP conduct,[122] and federal correctional institutions.[123] These institutions have differing levels of independence and powers. There is also the Canadian Defence Forces ombudsman (government department executive ombudsman with no legislative support),[124] the Communications Security Establishment (CSE)

---

119 *Official Languages Act*, R.S.C. 1985, c. 31 (4th Supp.), Parts IX-X online: www.ocol-clo. gc.ca. The Official Languages Commissioner, appointed by commission under the Great Seal after approval of the appointment by Parliament and reporting to Parliament: investigates complaints about official languages issues in federal government administration and makes recommendations; can intervene in court adjudicative proceedings involving official languages matters; monitors compliance with the legislation by the federal administration; monitors the development of new laws affecting language rights; and has promotion and education roles.

120 *Privacy Act*, R.S.C. 1985, c. P-21, ss. 53–68 online: www.privcom.gc.ca. The Privacy Commissioner, appointed by the Governor-in-Council by commission under the Great Seal after approval of the appointment by Parliament and reporting to Parliament: conducts audits and investigates complaints (from persons or on own-motion) concerning personal information held by the federal government and the private sector (the latter under separate legislation); and conducts research and public education.

121 *Access to Information Act*, R.S.C. 1985, c. A-1, ss. 30–66 online: infocom.gc.ca. The Information Commissioner, appointed by the Governor-in-Council after approval of the appointment by Parliament and reporting to Parliament: investigates complaints from persons or on own-motion about denial of rights under the legislation against federal government institutions and makes recommendations (the Federal Court can review the matter after the Commissioner has finished an investigation and the commissioner can appear on behalf of the complainant or as a party).

122 *Royal Canadian Mounted Police Act*, R.S.C. 1985, c. R-10, Parts VI–VII online: www. cpc-cpp.gc.ca. The RCMP Public Complaints Commissioner, appointed by the Governor-in-Council and reporting to the minister who in turn has annual report laid before Parliament: reviews public complaints against the RCMP after an internal RCMP investigation into the matter does not satisfy the complainant; can ask the RCMP to reinvestigate, initiate own investigation, or hold a public hearing; and make recommendations.

123 *Corrections and Conditional Release Act*, S.C. 1992, c. 20, Part III online: www.oci-bec. gc.ca. The Correctional Investigator, appointed by the Governor-in-Council and reporting to the minister who in turn has the annual report tabled in Parliament: investigates complaints on receipt of a complaint by federal offenders, or on own-motion, about the conduct of federal corrections officials and makes recommendations; and undertakes systemic reviews and makes recommendations concerning Correctional Services' policies and procedures concerning individual complaints.

124 Reif, *Ombudsman, International Human Rights*, above note 4 at 42–43; online: www. ombudsman.forces.gc.ca. Based on ministerial directives and appointed by the minister of defence, the ombudsman investigates 1) complaints against the Canadian Forces

Commissioner, and the Military Police Complaints Commission.[125] Overall, these entities provide for spotty coverage of federal public administration. Areas of federal administration that can impact the public negatively are not monitored by an ombudsman, for example, taxation and immigration/refugee matters. While there have been a number of initiatives over the years to establish a federal classical ombudsman, they have been unsuccessful to date.[126]

3) Specialized Institutions for Children and First Nations in Canada

While the children's ombudsman model has not been adopted in Canada, the provinces of Alberta, Saskatchewan, Manitoba, Newfoundland, and New Brunswick have Children and Youth Advocates, and BC has an Office for Children and Youth.[127] In Quebec, the provincial human rights commission has a second role as the commission for the rights of children and

---

(CF) and the Department of National Defence(DND) from current and former members of the CF and DND and their immediate family members, or 2) on own-motion.

125 CSE Commissioner, Part V.1 of the *National Defence Act*, R.S.C. 1985, c. N-5, and the *Security of Information Act*, R.S.C. 1985, c. O-5, s. 15, is appointed by and reports to the minister of national defence, who in turn reports to Parliament. The CSE Commissioner reviews the operations of the CSE and their compliance with law, investigates complaints about the legality of CSE activities, and carries out duties under the "public interest defence" provisions in the *Security of Information Act*. See online: csec-ccst. gc.ca/. The Military Police Complaints Commission, established under Part IV of the *National Defence Act*, appointed by Governor-in-Council, 1) investigates complaints about the conduct of military police in the exercise of their policing duties or interference in or obstruction of MP investigations by Forces or DND personnel, 2) reports and makes recommendations to the Forces, the deputy minister, and minister of defence. See online: www.mpcc-cppm.gc.ca.

126 See Donald C. Rowat, "Federal Ombudsman Would Reduce Democratic Deficit" (May 2004) Policy Options 46; Ombudsman Ontario, *A Federal Ombudsman for Canada: A Discussion Paper*, from the Canadian Ombudsman Association (1999); Stephen Owen, "Proposal for a Canadian Federal Ombudsman Office" (1992) 10 Omb. J. 5.

127 *Child, Youth and Family Enhancement Act*, R.S.A. 2000, c. C-12 (Alberta Child and Youth Advocate); *The Ombudsman and Children's Advocate Act*, above note 114 (Saskatchewan Children's Advocate); *The Child and Family Services Act*, C.C.S.M., c. C80 (Manitoba Children's Advocate); *Child and Youth Advocate Act*, S.N.L. 2001, c. C-12.01 (Newfoundland); *Child and Youth Advocate Act*, S.N.B. 2004, c. C-2.5 (in force 1 April 2005); *Office for Children and Youth Act*, S.B.C. 2002, c. 50; Reif, *Ombudsman, International Human Rights*, above note 4 at 326–28. As of mid-2005, the New Brunswick government was in the process of passing amending legislation that may limit the statute's reach, and a Child and Youth Advocate had not yet been appointed.

youth.[128] In March 2005, the Ontario government announced that it will introduce legislation to create an independent Child Advocate to replace its Office of Child and Family Service Advocacy.[129]

Each institution has a different set of functions, including some or all of the following: giving advice to government, research and education, the investigation of complaints, the making of recommendations, the use of ADR to resolve disputes, and the representation of minors before the courts and tribunals.[130] The advocates in Saskatchewan, Manitoba, Newfoundland, and New Brunswick are officers of the legislature, while the others operate under executive authority. The advocates in Saskatchewan, Newfoundland, and New Brunswick do have public education, research, and advocacy roles that cover the rights and interests of minors in general. The advocates in Alberta and Manitoba have narrower mandates over minors (child welfare, adoption, child prostitution) and the BC office does not have independent investigatory powers.[131] The Quebec Commission protects children's rights in the implementation of provincial youth protection and youth criminal justice legislation, provides public information/education, undertakes research concerning the protection of the rights of children, and makes recommendations to government ministers concerning children's rights.[132] Also, the provincial ombudsmän in BC and Nova Scotia have dedicated teams for matters concerning minors. However, none of the provincial statutes establishing children's institutions make any references to the CRC, a treaty Canada ratified in 1991.[133]

The concept of an ombudsman for First Nations is slowly evolving, although First Nations need to consider whether the concept is workable in

---

128 See Reif, *ibid.* at 325–26.
129 Ontario Ministry of Children and Youth Services, *News Release: McGuinty Government Moves to Make Ontario's Child Advocate Independent* (8 March 2005). For the Office of Child and Family Service Advocacy see *Child and Family Services Act*, R.S.O. 1990, c. C-11, s. 102.
130 Reif, *Ombudsman, International Human Rights*, above note 4 at 325–28.
131 The BC Officer for Children and Youth, an executive appointment, can conduct an investigation only at the request of the attorney general and can only advocate on behalf of individual minors in extraordinary circumstances. It has jurisdiction over child welfare, adoption, mental health, addiction, and youth justice services, *Office for Children and Youth Act*, above note 127, ss. 3(2)(c), 6.
132 See online: www.cdpdj.qc.ca.
133 Above note 35.

their particular cultural environment.[134] A Métis Settlements ombudsman was established in Alberta in 2003—appointed by the Alberta minister of Aboriginal affairs and northern development—to investigate complaints about the settlements' management or leadership.[135]

F. INTERNATIONAL LAW AND Nhris: THE STATE OF Nhris IN CANADA

The foregoing survey of NHRIs in Canada illustrates that our NHRIs are relatively conservative and somewhat dated in terms of jurisdiction and orientation toward international human rights law compared to the rapidly changing environment of NHRIs in other countries. Further, the structure and mandates of some Canadian NHRIs may not live up to the Paris Principles and the UN treaty committee comments on NHRIs.[136]

1) Human Rights Commissions

Only a minority of human rights commissions have statutes that refer to Canada's international human rights obligations, and, of those that do, most references are placed only in the preamble of the legislation. Unsuccessful proposals for change have been made periodically. For example, the 1989 *Ferris Report* recommended that a New Brunswick *Charter of Rights* be enacted containing civil, political, economic, social, cultural, and environmental rights based on Canada's international obligations, and monitored by the provincial human rights commission.[137] The Canadian Human Rights Commission has proposed that international human rights treaties be incorporated in its legislation and that it be given an express role in monitoring Canada's compliance with its international human rights obligations.[138] The 2000 Review Panel Report on the Canadian Human Rights Commission, however, only recommended that references to the various international agreements that Canada has entered into that refer

---

134 See Lisa Statt Foy, "A First Nations Ombudsman: Some Considerations" (2003) 7 Int. Omb. Y.B. 76.

135 Métis Settlements Ombudsman, *1st Annual Report* (1 April 2003–31 March 2004) at 5–6. See also Yukon Ombudsman, above note 118.

136 See above text accompanying notes 43–62. This is ironic given that the Canadian Human Rights Commission stated that it played a major role in getting the UN to adopt the Paris Principles, Canadian Human Rights Commission, *Annual Report 2003* at 38–39.

137 Ferris Report, above note 109, recs. 2.1–2.5, 2.9, 2.12, and 3.4.

138 Canadian Human Rights Commission, *Annual Report 2000* at 3, 16–17, 22.

to equality and discrimination be inserted in the preamble of the legislation.[139] In comparison, for example, Australia's federal human rights commission has an extensive listing of international human rights treaties and
declarations in the body of its governing legislation.[140]

Human rights commissions in Canada—with the exceptions of those
in Quebec and, to a lesser extent, Saskatchewan and the Yukon—have relatively narrow subject matter jurisdictions and investigatory mandates when
compared with various human rights commissions and hybrid NHRIs in
other countries. Most are purely antidiscrimination commissions. Only a
few have jurisdiction over additional civil and political rights, and each
to differing degrees. Although some provincial commissions can examine discrimination based on socially related grounds, with the exception
of Quebec, economic and social rights do not fall within the mandates
of commissions in Canada.[141] Thus, for the most part, the broad range of
first- and second-generation human rights can only be addressed indirectly
through the prism of a discrimination complaint.

The Paris Principles state that the mandate of a NHRI should be as
broad as possible.[142] In its 1999 Concluding Observations to Canada's
periodic report under the ICCPR, the UN Human Rights Committee was
concerned that gaps remained between the protection required by the IC-
CPR and that afforded by the *Charter* and domestic human rights legislation, recommending that "consideration be given to the establishment of
a public body responsible for overseeing implementation of the Covenant
and for reporting on any deficiencies."[143] The Human Rights Committee's
2004 General Comment No. 31 further supports this recommendation.[144]
With respect to economic, social, and cultural rights, the UN Committee
on Economic, Social, and Cultural Rights has repeatedly recommended
that these rights be given more explicit recognition in Canadian federal,
provincial, and territorial human rights legislation.[145] This Committee also

---

139 2000 Review Panel Report, above note 109, rec. 1.
140 Above note 13.
141 For example, social origin, source of income, receipt of public assistance. See proposal
    that discrimination on the basis of "social condition" be added to its legislation in
    Canadian Human Rights Commission, *Annual Report 2003* at 52.
142 Paris Principles, above note 43, "Competence and Responsibilities," s. 2.
143 Concluding Observations of the Human Rights Committee: Canada, UN Doc. CCPR/
    C/79/Add.105 (7 April 1999), para. 10.
144 See above notes 61–62.
145 Concluding Observations of the Committee on Economic, Social and Cultural Rights:
    Canada, UN Doc. E/C.12/1993/5 (3 June 1993) at para. 25; Concluding Observations of

encouraged the federal government to take steps to ensure that ICESCR rights are enforceable in the provinces/territories through legislation or policy measures and "the establishment of independent and appropriate monitoring and adjudication mechanisms."[146] The 2000 Review Panel decided that it would not recommend the addition of social and economic rights to the Canadian Human Rights Commission legislation, but it did recommend that the Commission should have the duty to monitor and report to Parliament and the UN Human Rights Committee on the federal government's compliance with international human rights treaties that might be included in its legislation.[147]

A minority of human rights commissions are appointed by or have other ties to the legislature—the majority are appointed by and usually accountable to the executive branch. The activities of commissions often require them to criticize their appointers and the executive, and many are dependent on the executive for their budgets. The Paris Principles are silent on whether NHRIs must be appointed by the legislature or can be executive appointments. However, the principles do state that appointment of the NHRIs' members should involve input from diverse elements of civil society involved in human rights and NHRIs should be adequately funded to ensure their independence from government.[148] A few commissions in Canada have recently called for more independence through closer attachment to the legislative branch in terms of appointment, reporting responsibility, and budget.[149] Nevertheless, commissions that are appointed by and have other ties to the executive branch have suboptimal levels of independence.

---

the Committee on Economic, Social and Cultural Rights: Canada, UN Doc. E/C.12/1/ Add.31 (10 December 1998) at para. 51.

146 1998 Concluding Observations, *ibid.* at para. 52. However, provincial/territorial juris diction comes into play.

147 2000 Review Panel Report, above note 109, rec. 130 (also noting that provincial/territorial commissions, in consultation with the Canadian Human Rights Commission, might wish to comment on matters within their jurisdiction). Currently there are no references to human rights instruments in the Canadian Human Rights Commission legislation, see report's recommendations on this point, above note 139.

148 Paris Principles, above note 43, "Composition and guarantees of independence and pluralism," ss. 1–2.

149 For example, "The Quebec Commission des droits de la personne et des droits de la jeunesse proposes an update of the Charter of Human Rights and Freedoms," press release (20 November 2003) at 2; New Brunswick Human Rights Commission, *2003–2004 Annual Report* at 2; Canadian Human Rights Commission, *Annual Report 2003* at 54.

2) Ombudsmän

Looking at ombudsmän in Canada, there is still no federal ombudsman to cover the entire federal administration. Our provincial classical ombudsmän do not have an express mandate to investigate human rights complaints against their governments although, as discussed further later in this chapter, a number of their investigations do involve human rights issues and a few actually use international human rights norms. Provincial ombudsmän have good levels of independence from the executive branch, given that most are appointed by, and all are accountable to, the legislature. However, provincial ombudsmän do not always have jurisdiction over all areas of government administration—provincial and municipal police forces are typically excluded from their purview.[150]

3) Children's Institutions

Although dedicated institutions for children are now established in seven provinces and will be established in an eighth, and there are several ombudsmän with a focus on children, there is no children's ombudsman or similar institution at the federal level or in the other provinces and territories. As noted, none of the statutes establishing children's institutions make any express reference to the CRC and none give these institutions an official mandate to work to implement or monitor CRC rights in Canada although, as discussed later, a few do so in practice. This contrasts with children's ombudsmän legislation in Europe and New Zealand.[151]

A majority of children's institutions are legislative appointments, although the remainder are appointed by and accountable to the executive branch, which is problematic for their independence.[152] In 2003, the UN Committee on the Rights of the Child noted that a number of provinces

---

150 This is not invariably the case with ombudsman; see, for example, New South Wales and Commonwealth Ombudsmän in Australia, and Netherlands Ombudsmän (jurisdiction covers police), and Boise Community Ombudsman (specialized police ombudsman). See Del Villar, "Who Guards the Guardians?" above note 17 at 6–10; Reif, *Ombudsman, International Human Rights*, above note 4 at 33–34. But see police complaints commissions.

151 See above note 35.

152 See, for example, Alberta Children's Advocate, (2000–2001) *Annual Report* at 3, stating that for the institution to be truly independent and to be seen as independent it should become an office of the Legislative Assembly and not be responsible to the Minister. The recent amendments to the institution in the *Child, Youth and Family Enhancement Act*, above note 127, maintained the *status quo*.

have an "Ombudsman for Children" but conveyed its concern that "not all of them are adequately empowered to exercise their tasks as fully independent national human rights institutions in accordance with the [Paris Principles]."[153] The Committee noted the lack of a children's ombudsman at the federal level.[154] In its Concluding Observations, the Committee recommended that Canada:

> ... establish at the federal level an ombudsman's office responsible for children's rights and ensure appropriate funding for its effective functioning ... that such offices be established in the provinces that have not done so, as well as in the three territories where a high proportion of vulnerable children live. In this respect, the Committee recommends that the State party take fully into account the Paris Principles and the Committee's general comment No. 2 on the role of national human rights institutions.[155]

Also, the Manitoba and Quebec children's institutions, which have mandates only over departments directly addressing minors, have publicly called for their jurisdiction to be expanded to cover more government departments.[156]

4) NHRIs and Funding

A perennial issue for all types of Canadian NHRIs has been government underfunding. As recent examples, the Saskatchewan Human Rights Commission states that cuts to its budget have resulted in a reduction of its public education and outreach activities, the Manitoba Child Advocate has indicated that it has funding challenges, the Canadian Human Rights Commission needs more resources for human rights promotional and educational activities, and the BC Ombudsman stopped processing complaints against municipalities and professional associations for several

---

153 UN Committee on the Rights of the Child, Concluding Observations: Canada, UN Doc. CRC/C/15/Add.215 (27 October 2003) at para. 14. The committee noted that eight provinces had these institutions, but this may have encompassed ombudsmän with children's sections.

154 *Ibid.*

155 *Ibid.* at para. 15.

156 Manitoba Children's Advocate, *2001–2002 Annual Report* at 13–14; Manitoba Children's Advocate, *2004–2005 Annual Report* at 30 (also calling for the power to issue special reports); Quebec Commission, press release, above note 149 at 2.

years due to severe budget cuts.[157] As noted above, the Paris Principles require that a NHRI be given adequate funding in order to be independent of
government. Thus, those governments in Canada that provide insufficient
budgets for their NHRIs are diverging from the Paris Principles and may
be prejudicing the independence of these NHRIs by forcing them to cir-
cumscribe the scope of their legislated activities.[158]

G. USE OF INTERNATIONAL HUMAN RIGHTS LAW BY CANADIAN NHRIs

In this section I explore the use of international human rights norms in
the recent work of Canadian NHRIs, focusing on human rights commissions, ombudsmän, and children's institutions.[159] These NHRIs do play
a role in the domestic application of international human rights law, although to date it is a relatively modest one.

1) Human Rights Commissions

In examining human rights commissions, I address their mandates as
NHRIs but I do not explore the quasi-judicial decisions of associated human rights tribunals. However, it should be noted that at least several of
these tribunals (notably Quebec's) in some decisions do use international
human rights norms, including economic, social, and cultural rights in
interpreting equality and non-discrimination legislative provisions.[160]

---

157 Saskatchewan Human Rights Commission, *2002–2003 Annual Report* at 3; Manitoba
    Children's Advocate, *2004–2005 Annual Report* at 30; Canadian Human Rights Com-
    mission, *Annual Report 2001* at 7; Ombudsman of BC, *Annual Report 2004* at 5.
158 Saskatchewan Human Rights Commission, *2002–2003 Annual Report* at 3 (citing Paris
    Principles to point to importance of sufficient funding to ensure independence from
    government).
159 My research methodology involved scrutinizing NHRI websites and available annual/
    special reports, covering primarily the 2000–4 period. My research did not extend to
    interviews with NHRI personnel that might possibly unearth more information on the
    use of international human rights law in the activities of NHRIs.
160 See UN Committee on Economic, Social and Cultural Rights, Concluding Observa-
    tions of the Committee on Economic, Social and Cultural Rights: Canada, UN Doc.
    E/C.12/1/Add.31 (10 December 1998) at para. 6 (Quebec Human Rights Tribunal has
    taken ICESCR into account some decisions when construing the *Quebec Charter*);
    Lysiane Clément-Major, *International Human Rights Standards: The Québec Perspec-
    tive* (Montreal: Quebec Commission des droits de la personne et des droits de la
    jeunesse,2000) at 5–8: "Since its creation, it is on a regular basis that the Quebec
    Human Rights Tribunal refers to various international documents in order to define

Human rights commissions in Canada clearly contribute to the implementation and application of Canada's international human rights obligations concerning non-discrimination and equality through their complaint-handling and other functions. Domestic human rights law is the predominant legal source relied on in their activities, although human rights commissions do make occasional reference to or use of international human rights law in their work. This is seen in their policy, research, educational activities, and in some arguments made before human rights tribunals.[161]

Some commissions centre public education initiatives on the anniversary of the UDHR and other notable dates.[162] Some have website information containing references or links to international human rights law sources and provide brochures and human rights educational materials for both adults and children that refer to international human rights law.[163] The need to follow up on the agreements reached at the UN Durban Conference against Racism by creating a national plan to fight racism has been

---

the right to equality and the various prohibited grounds. Its reasoning for doing so is: either because the preparatory work referred to international standards, or because of the similarity of wording, or, more generally, on the assumption that Quebec is not supposed to legislate in a manner which would be contrary to its international engagements." *Ibid.* at 6. See also Manitoba Human Rights Adjudication Decision, *Morriseau v. Paisley Park* (12 December 2000), online: www.gov.mb.ca/hrc/english/publications/ morriseau.html (UDHR art. 10, CRC Preamble, art. 24 in a claim of family status and gender discrimination concerning breastfeeding in a store).

161 The Supreme Court of Canada considers human rights legislation to be quasi-constitutional in nature for the purposes of statutory interpretation, which would suggest that international human rights law can be used to aid in its interpretation, although the courts, in practice, rarely use international norms in this fashion, Freeman & van Ert, *International Human Rights Law*, above note 79 at 202–4.

162 For example, Yukon Human Rights Commission, *2003–2004 Annual Report* at 8 (celebrating UDHR anniversary and Day for Elimination of Racial Discrimination).

163 Yukon Commission online: www.yhrc.yk.ca (link to UDHR, *Human Rights Resources for Children and Adults* with international human rights law/institutional websites); Saskatchewan Human Rights Commission, *Erasing Racism* (March 2003 rev.) at 2 (role of international law such as UDHR and Convention on the Elimination of all Forms of Racial Discrimination in development of Canadian laws), online: www. gov.sk.ca/shrc/; Manitoba Human Rights Commission, *Human Rights in the School* (by Judy Burch) (1991), online: www.gov.mb.ca/hrc/ (references to UDHR, CRC, UN Declaration on the Rights of the Child); New Brunswick Human Rights Commission, *2003–2004 Annual Report* at 12; Canadian Human Rights Commission online: www. chrc-ccdp.ca (links to international human rights instruments, etc.); PEI Human Rights Commission online: www.gov.pe.ca/humanrights/ (links to international human rights instruments,etc.).

noted.[164] Commissions have intervened in human rights cases before the courts, making arguments based on Canada's international human rights obligations.[165] Commissions also provide information on discrimination and equality rights in their province for Canada's state reports, submitted periodically to UN human rights treaty bodies.[166]

Given the limitations of the Canadian *Charter* and the judiciary in protecting economic and social rights, human rights commissions in Canada have begun to explore how within their existing mandates they can become more involved in protecting and promoting economic, social, and cultural rights and in implementing relevant treaty obligations of Canada.[167] Beyond the argument that "social condition" should be added as a covered ground of discrimination in human rights legislation, it is also argued that more proactive measures on economic and social rights pursuant to the commissions' public policy and education mandates can be taken, including review of government and private programs to ensure they are respectful of social and economic rights, research and education on social and economic issues, policy development in areas related to socioeconomic interests and ensuring that policy development in all areas is consistent with and recognizes Canada's international human rights commitments.[168] It is argued that "[r]elying on the interpretive presumption in *Slaight Communications* and *Baker*, human rights legislation can be interpreted, and administrative discretion can be exercised, in a manner that is most consistent with international human rights norms."[169]

---

164 Saskatchewan Human Rights Commission, *2001–2002 Annual Report* at 6.

165 For example, *Gosselin v. Quebec (Attorney-General)*, [2002] 4 S.C.R. 429 (ICESCR), Canadian Human Rights Commission, *Annual Report 2001* at 8; *Canadian Foundation for Children, Youth and the Law v. Canada* (CRC), above note 87.

166 For example, New Brunswick Human Rights Commission, *2003–2004 Annual Report* at 12; New Brunswick Human Rights Commission, *2000–2001 Annual Report* at 17; Canadian Human Rights Commission, *Annual Report 2003* at 40; *International Human Rights Standards: The Québec Perspective*, above note 160 at 4–5 (Quebec Commission); Ontario Human Rights Commission, *2003–2004 Annual Report* at 9; Ontario Human Rights Commission, *2002–2003 Annual Report* at 20; Ontario Human Rights Commission, *2001–2002 Annual Report* at 17; PEI Human Rights Commission, *2000–2001 Annual Report* at 3.

167 Ontario Human Rights Commission, *Human Rights Commissions and Economic and Social Rights*, Research Paper (2001) (not a commission-approved policy statement); Ontario Human Rights Commission, *2001–2002 Annual Report* at 17–18.

168 *Human Rights Commissions and Economic and Social Rights, ibid.* at 43–44.

169 *Ibid.* at 43. *Baker*, above note 87; *Slaight Communications*, above note 86.

The Ontario, Quebec, and federal human rights commissions provide examples of commissions that do use international human rights law in their activities. Their methods vary—including direct use of human rights treaty obligations, without concern whether these treaties have been domestically implemented, reliance on the jurisprudence of the Supreme Court of Canada, and use of the statutory interpretation presumption that the legislature does not intend to violate Canada's international law obligations.

a) Ontario Human Rights Commission

The Ontario Commission has made commitments to monitor relevant UN treaties and human rights decisions, and to ensure that Canada's international obligations are integrated into all new policy work.[170] The former has been accomplished through comments on Canada's periodic reports to UN and ILO treaty bodies and by participating in initiatives to explore how Canada can meet its international obligations.[171] The latter commitment is implemented in the commission's policy development and education initiatives. For example, "[i]nternational standards have been incorporated directly into Commission policies that deal with rights that are explicitly protected under the Code."[172] International human rights law has been applied in a number of its policy reports on topics such as age discrimination, intersectionality of rights, accessibility issues, and racism.[173] In a statement of policy on female genital mutilation (FGM), the Commission surveys

---

170 Ontario Human Rights Commission, *2002–2003 Annual Report* at 42–43; Ontario Human Rights Commission, *2001–2002 Annual Report* at 33.

171 Ontario Human Rights Commission, *2002–2003 Annual Report* at 42–43; Ontario Human Rights Commission, *2000–2001 Annual Report* at 26. See, for example, *The Government of British Columbia's Draft Human Rights Code Amendment Act Bill 53*, above note 47.

172 *Human Rights Commissions and Economic and Social Rights*, above note 167 at 34.

173 Ontario Human Rights Commission, *2002–2003 Annual Report* at 42. See, for example, Ontario Human Rights Commission, *Education and Disability: Human Rights Issues in Ontario's Education System*, Consultation Paper (Toronto: The Commission, 2002) at 3, 5 (CRC arts. 23, 28, 29; *Declaration on the Rights of Disabled Persons*, UN G.A. Res. 3447 (XXX) (9 December 1975)); Ontario Human Rights Commission, *An Intersectional Approach to Discrimination: Addressing Multiple Grounds in Human Rights Claims*, Discussion Paper (Toronto: The Commission, 2001) at 7, 14–15 (UDHR; European Court of Human Rights jurisprudence; UN Human Rights Committee, *Lovelace v. Canada*, Communication No. 24/1977, UN Doc. CCPR/C//13/D/24/1977); Ontario Human Rights Commission, *Time For Action: Advancing Human Rights for Older Ontarians* (Toronto: The Commission, 2001) at 37 (ICESCR; UN Committee on Economic, Social and Cultural Rights, General Comment No. 6: the Economic, Social and Cultural Rights of Older Persons, UN Doc. E/C.12/1995/16/Rev.1).

numerous international human rights treaties and instruments on elimination of discrimination against women, children's rights, and health
rights.[174] It concludes by stating, "[b]ecause FGM is gender-specific discrimination, internationally condemned and proscribed in international
instruments to which Canada is a party, the Province of Ontario would
be in compliance with its obligations by taking steps to eradicate this
practice."[175] This use of international human rights law in public reports
extends to social and economic rights, as well as soft law and treaty law
that is not binding on Canada, and is not rigidly concerned about whether
Canada's treaty obligations have been explicitly implemented by domestic
legislation. International human rights law also appears to have been used
as guidance in interpreting the human rights legislation and Canadian
Charter rights, based on Supreme Court of Canada jurisprudence.

b)   Quebec Commission des droits de la personne et des droits de la jeunesse

The Quebec Commission states that international human rights instruments are very influential in their activities:

> For instance, in its various studies and reports, the Commission frequently
> refers to international standards in defining and promoting the human
> rights and freedoms guaranteed by the [Quebec] Charter. The Commis-
> sion has also invoked International Standards before the tribunals.
>
> According to the Commission, such a recourse to international docu-
> ments is justified considering that Quebec should not legislate in a man-
> ner which would be incompatible with its international commitments.
> Hence, the laws and, therefore [Quebec] Charter, should be constructed
> in a manner compatible with them. Also, from a historic point of view, the
> elaboration and the adoption of the [Quebec] Charter was very influenced
> by the existing international standards.[176]

As an example, the Quebec Commission has a number of publications that
either use international human rights law in the elaboration of the law on

---

174   Ontario Human Rights Commission, *Human Rights Policy in Ontario*, 3d ed. (Toronto:
    CCH Canadian, 2001) at 122–30 (female genital mutilation: UDHR; ICCPR; ICESCR;
    regional treaties, *UN Convention on the Elimination of All Forms of Discrimination
    Against Women*, above note 48; *UN Declaration on the Elimination of Violence Against
    Women*, UN Doc. A/Res/48/104 (20 December 1993); CRC; Vienna Conference Declar-
    ation and Programme of Action, above note 39).

175   *Human Rights Policy in Ontario, ibid.* at 129–30.

176   *International Human Rights Standards: The Québec Perspective*, above note 160 at 4.

a topic (for example, poverty, freedom of religion, and children's rights) or are devoted to an international human rights law area.[177] The international human rights addressed include economic, social, and cultural rights, in addition to civil and political rights. In using international norms, the Commission indicates that it is relying on the presumption of legislative intent to comply with Canada's international obligations.

c) Canadian Human Rights Commission

The Canadian Human Rights Commission states that it "has played an important role in ensuring Canada implements its international human rights obligations domestically."[178] While this undoubtedly takes place through their investigations of discrimination, the role of the Canadian Human Rights Commission in domestic human rights implementation in other respects is more limited. The Commission does contribute to the compilation of Canada's reports to UN treaty bodies and has met with UN human rights Special Rapporteurs.[179] It has referred to international human rights norms in some annual and public reports.[180] The authors of a recent public report were requested to review the situation of the Innu *inter alia* in relation to Canada's international human rights commitments.[181]

---

177 Quebec Commission des droits de la personne et des droits de la jeunesse, *Poverty is the Most Pressing Issue in Today's Quebec* (Montreal: The Commission, 2000) (ICE-SCR); *Religious Pluralism in Québec: A Social and Ethical Challenge* (Montreal: The Commission, 1995) at 11, 16, 27, 34 (ICCPR, Human Rights Committee General Comment, CRC); *Corporal Punishment as a Means of Correcting Children* (Montreal: The Commission, 1998) (CRC, CRC Committee documents, European Ct. HR jurisprudence); *The Convention on the Rights of the Child After 10 Years—From Promises to Reality* (Montreal: The Commission, 2000); *International Human Rights Standards: The Québec Perspective, ibid.*

178 Canadian Human Rights Commission, *Annual Report 2003* at 38.

179 *Ibid.* at 40.

180 Canadian Human Rights Commission, *Annual Report 2000* at 9–10 (living conditions of Innu: CRC, ICESCR), 14 (jailing women in male institutions: *UN Standard Minimum Rules for the Treatment of Prisoners*, UN ECOSOC Res. 663 C (XXIV) (July 31, 1957, UN ECOSOC Res. 2076 (LXII) (13 May 1977)); Canadian Human Rights Commission, *Annual Report 2001* at 6 (detention provisions in new immigration/refugee legislation: UDHR, ICCPR, UN Refugee Convention); Canadian Human Rights Commission, *Protecting Their Rights: A Systemic Review of Human Rights in Correctional Services for Federally Sentenced Women* (December 2003) at 65 (UDHR, UN Standard Minimum Rules for the Treatment of Prisoners applied by a Correctional Services audit).

181 Constance Backhouse & Donald McRae, *Report to the Canadian Human Rights Commission on the Treatment of the Innu of Labrador by the Government of Canada* (26 March 2002) at 1 and 43–46.

506 LINDA C. REIF

The report applied the ICCPR and ICESCR common provisions on self-determination, the CRC and, as context for the interpretation of the Covenants, the UN *Draft Declaration on the Rights of Indigenous Peoples*.[182] The treaties were applied directly, with the report stating that Canada's CRC international law obligations were an appropriate standard for judging Canada's conduct towards Innu children, concluding that the government was at risk of violating its ICCPR, ICESCR, CRC, and *Draft Declaration* international obligations, and emphasizing that "Canada is obliged under the [CRC] to have the well-being and best interests of the children as a primary consideration."[183]

However, the Canadian Human Rights Commission has recognized that over time, due in part to funding constraints, it has given up most of its preventive activities such as education, where international human rights law can more easily be used, and devotes most of its efforts to the investigation and adjudication of human rights complaints.[184] Yet the Canadian Human Rights Commission does provide substantial international technical assistance in the establishment and strengthening of NHRIs in developing countries.[185] The Commission has proposed that some matters, such as systemic human rights issues, should be dealt with through information, ADR, special reports to Parliament, or public inquiries, rather than through the formal complaint process.[186]

---

182 *Ibid.* at 43–45; *UN Draft Declaration on the Rights of Indigenous Peoples*, UN Doc. E/CN.4/Sub.2/1994/2/Add.1 (20 April 1994).

183 *Ibid.* at 46. See *Baker*, above note 87 (SCC considers CRC to be an unimplemented treaty obligation of Canada).

184 Canadian Human Rights Commission, *Annual Report 2003* at 46.

185 Canadian Human Rights Commission, *Annual Report 2003* at 38–39. See Sonia Cardenas, "Transgovernmental Activism: Canada's Role in Promoting National Human Rights Commissions" (2003) 25 H.R.Q. 775. See 2000 Review Panel Report, above note 109, recs. 26–27, calling for legislative authorization to enable the Commission to continue to enter into these assistance projects, but recommending that they be funded by the government departments requesting such foreign assistance and not by the Commission.

186 Canadian Human Rights Commission, *Annual Report 2003* at 46–47; Canadian Human Rights Commission, *Annual Report 2004* at 33–36. The 2000 Review Panel Report recommended that the complaint-processing function be removed from the Commission's mandate, complainants be given direct access to the Tribunal, and the Commission be given stronger human rights education and promotion roles backed up by sufficient resources, *ibid.*, recs. 23–24 and 28–29.

2) Provincial Ombudsmän

Provincial ombudsmän in Canada certainly investigate numerous complaints about government administration that raise civil, political, economic, and social rights issues. For example, complaints and investigations often concern correctional institutions, children's services, and income and housing assistance. These complaints often involve vulnerable populations. Although most ombudsman reports do not make reference to international human rights law, relying on domestic law including *Canadian Charter* rights, the ombudsmän in BC, Ontario, Manitoba, and Quebec have used international human rights law in their investigations and resulting reports. This tends to occur in investigations involving the treatment of children and correctional facility inmates. The ombudsmän appear to apply both treaty obligations that are not explicitly implemented and non-binding soft law directly, typically to determine the broader ombudsman standards of fairness, and often underlining the fact that the treaty obligations are binding on Canada.

a) BC Ombudsman

The BC Ombudsman has engaged in initiatives to promote the CRC in domestic law, such as assisting the government in preparing the province's response to the federal government supporting the CRC, providing information on the CRC in some annual reports, and disseminating information on children's rights.[187] The BC Ombudsman states that:

> [t]he Ombudsman's Office relies on provisions in the [CRC] … as a tool in investigating complaints about any public service to children and youth. This Office has a longstanding tradition of promoting the rights articulated in the [CRC]. Canada is a signatory to the [CRC], and it has been cited by the Supreme Court of Canada, although it lacks the force of law.[188]

Further, the BC Ombudsman applies international law and UN treaties, instruments, and resolutions in some investigations.[189] A few own-motion reports have used the CRC to support the protection of minors in their

---

187 Reif, *Ombudsman, International Human Rights*, above note 4 at 305. The BC Ombudsman has a child and youth team and used to have a deputy ombudsman for Children and Youth.

188 Ombudsman of British Columbia, *2002 Annual Report* at 31. The language "lacking the force of law" may refer to the Supreme Court of Canada holding in *Baker*, above note 87, that the CRC has not been implemented in Canadian domestic law.

189 *Ibid.*

encounters with the provincial administration.[190] For example, the public report on Doukhobor children dealt with the infringement of the human rights of these children who were forcibly separated from their parents by the provincial government in the 1950s because of their parents' religious beliefs and confined in institutions where they were physically and emotionally mistreated.[191] This report recognized that the CRC was not in existence at the time the events occurred, but still applied the unimplemented CRC, retrospectively, as a guide to the rights infringed, and in order to elucidate the broader standards of fairness and justice found in the ombudsman mandate.[192] The report uses the CRC extensively in support of its investigation findings, conclusions, and recommendations, including the recommendation that standards consistent with the CRC be used by all places of confinement.[193] The CRC rights cited include economic and social rights of the child in addition to a variety of civil, political, and protective rights. In a more recent own-motion investigation into correctional facilities, the BC Ombudsman cited the UN *Standard Minimum Rules for the Treatment of Prisoners.*[194]

b) Saskatchewan Ombudsman

The Saskatchewan Ombudsman has stated that the institution is increasingly relying on rights-based documents, including those to which Canada is committed.[195] For example, in 2002 the Saskatchewan ombudsman published a special report on prison conditions in provincial correctional centres.[196] The report refers to the treaty obligations of Canada under the ICCPR with respect to the rights of inmates under international law.[197]

---

190 Ombudsman of British Columbia, *Abuse of Deaf Students at Jericho Hill School*, Public Report No. 32 (November 1993); Ombudsman of British Columbia, *Building Respect: A Review of Youth Custody Centres in British Columbia*, Public Report No. 34 (June 1994); Ombudsman of British Columbia, *Righting the Wrong: The Confinement of the Sons of Doukhobor Children*, Public Report No. 38 (April 1999).

191 *Righting the Wrong, ibid.*

192 *Ibid.* See above notes 87 and 183.

193 *Ibid.*, arts. 3, 8, 9, 12–14, 19, 20, 25, 29, 31, 32, and 39 of the CRC were used. See also Ombudsman of British Columbia, *Annual Report 2004* at 25–26.

194 Ombudsman of British Columbia, *2002 Annual Report* at 13; *UN Standard Minimum Rules for the Treatment of Prisoners*, above note 180.

195 Saskatchewan ombudsman, *2002 Annual Report* at 6.

196 Ombudsman of Saskatchewan, *Locked Out: A Review of Inmate Services and Conditions of Custody in Saskatchewan Correctional Centres* (Special Report, October 2002).

197 For example, one of the themes of the report is that inmates are entitled to be treated with respect and dignity, supported by an express reference to the ICCPR and Can-

The report makes extensive use of provisions of the *UN Standard Minimum Rules for the Treatment of Prisoners* as the main legal standard in the investigation, applying them to many aspects of living conditions in the centres, and leading to numerous recommendations for change.[198] The report states that the UN Standard Minimum Rules "were approved by the United Nations Economic and Social Council as an authoritative guide to meeting binding treaty standards. As such, compliance with the Standard Minimum Rules should not be considered optional but minimal."[199] The international human rights norms applied in the ombudsman's special report cover not only civil rights, but also a range of social rights.[200] The ombudsman justified applying international human rights law in treaty and non-binding form to the investigation based on the broader standard of fairness given to the ombudsman in her foundational legislation.[201] She stated "[a]lthough these agreements have no force in a court of law, Canada is a signatory to the agreements and Corrections can therefore be expected to comply."[202] Thus, the Saskatchewan Ombudsman directly applied treaty obligations of Canada and other soft international human rights instruments to construe the broader ombudsman standard of fairness.[203]

c) Ontario, Manitoba, and Quebec Ombudsmän

A recent own-motion investigation, conducted by the Ontario Ombudsman, into over-crowding in provincial correctional facilities producing "triple bunking" and reduced outdoor access, relied on the *UN Standard*

---

ada's treaty obligations, *ibid.*, executive summary at 4. One of the guiding principles of the report is that "[i]nmates retain all of the rights, both domestic and international, of free citizens except those rights that are necessarily limited as a result of incarceration," *ibid.* at x and 185. With respect to exercise when in segregation, "inmates have a right under article 10 of the International Covenant on Civil and Political Rights to be treated 'with humanity and with respect for the inherent dignity of the human person,'" *ibid.* at 132.

198 *UN Standard Minimum Rules for the Treatment of Prisoners*, above note 180. For example, on privacy, air, and lighting quality, cleanliness, temperature control, laundry and bedding, daytime activities, meals, showers, exercise, visitors, relations between inmates and staff, educational programs, segregation, and double-bunking. *Locked Out*, above note 196 at 16–17, 19–25, 27, 47, 132–33, and 146.

199 *Locked Out, ibid.* at 16–17, 132, and 146.

200 *Ibid.* at 65; UDHR, above note 104, art. 25 (includes a right to medical care).

201 *Locked Out, ibid.* at 194.

202 *Ibid.* at 195.

203 *Ibid.* at 194–95.

Minimum Rules for the Treatment of Prisoners.[204] The Manitoba Ombudsman referred to the CRC in an own-motion investigation on the designation and use of a correctional facility as a "place of safety" for youth under the provincial child and family services legislation.[205] In concluding that the conduct was unacceptable, the Ombudsman relied partly on international law, stating that the conduct "may well be contrary to International law. The [CRC] of which Canada is a party, protects against the arbitrary detention and imprisonment of a child."[206] The Quebec *Protecteur* has also used the UN *Standard Minimum Rules for the Treatment of Prisoners* in an investigation against the correctional authorities involving the quality of health care provided to an ill inmate in solitary confinement.[207]

3) Provincial Children's Institutions

The CRC contains not only civil and political rights for children, but also economic, social, cultural, and protective rights. As noted earlier, the Supreme Court of Canada has held that the CRC is an unimplemented treaty obligation of Canada, although it can be argued that the CRC has been implicitly implemented in various federal and provincial statutes.[208] Although there are no references to the CRC or other international human rights obligations of Canada affecting minors in the framework legislation of the provincial institutions for children and youth, the children's institutions in Saskatchewan, Newfoundland, Manitoba, and Quebec do make reference to and use the CRC in their work, even though they recognize that it is not considered by the courts to be implemented into domestic law.

a) Saskatchewan Children's Advocate

The past Saskatchewan Children's Advocate was a strong proponent of the CRC, using it a variety of ways. She stated that among her activities, she "advocates for the rights of children to be respected and valued as identified

---

204 Above note 180; Ombudsman Ontario, *2002–2003 Annual Report* at 25. See actions taken by Ontario government in response to report, Ombudsman Ontario, *2003-2004 Annual Report* at 35.

205 Ombudsman of Manitoba, *2002 Annual Report* at 49–50.

206 *Ibid.* at 50.

207 Protecteur du citoyen, *2001–2002 Annual Report* at 78: "the directive on health care and the *Standard Minimum Rules for the Treatment of Prisoners* adopted by the United Nations and ratified by Canada, require that prisoners in solitary confinement be visited daily by medical personnel."

208 See *Baker*, above note 87. For arguments on implementation, see above note 79.

in the [CRC],"[209] noting that Canada is a signatory to the CRC and "Saskatchewan has affirmed these rights."[210] She has also stated that the CRC "becomes an advocacy tool and a visionary document used to promote increased voice for and protection of children. There continues to be a lack of awareness of the Convention and of the rights of children in particular."[211]

Recent annual reports of the Saskatchewan Children's Advocate make various references to the CRC and the Concluding Observations of the Committee on the Rights of the Child in response to Canada's periodic reports.[212] For example, the views of children are taken into account in the work of the advocate based on article 12 of the CRC.[213] The CRC is used as a guide for the advocate's public education activities; for example, educational materials for children and adults describe the history of international children's rights, discuss the CRC contents in detail but in terms understandable to minors, and provide CRC-learning games.[214] Educational material states that the: "[CRC] is not considered to be "Canadian Law"; however, when a country ratifies an international convention, it means they are agreeing to reflect the principles of the Convention in their country's legislation, policies and programs."[215]

b) Newfoundland Child and Youth Advocate

In its first annual report, the Newfoundland Child and Youth Advocate states that, in addition to its prime function of advancing the rights and interests of children and youth, the institution "took into consideration the

---

209 See online: www.saskcao.ca; *The Ombudsman and Children's Advocate Act*, above note 114.

210 Saskatchewan Children's Advocate, *2004 Annual Report* at 10.

211 *Ibid.*

212 Saskatchewan Children's Advocate, *2003 Annual Report* at 8 (committee's observations on establishment of independent children's ombudsmän in Canada); Saskatchewan Children's Advocate, *2004 Annual Report* at 10, 13, 26, 28 (committee's recommendations on strengthening and centralizing its mechanism to integrate and analyze data on minors, use of data to formulate and evaluate laws, policies, etc., for the implementation and monitoring of the CRC, reference to CRC art. 12, measures to implement CRC rights for Aboriginal children); see above note 35.

213 Saskatchewan Children's Advocate, *2002 Annual Report* at 7: "We believe, in accordance with Article 12 of the [CRC], that the child's views must be given due weight in accordance with the age and maturity of the child." See also *2004 Annual Report, ibid.* at 28.

214 See online: www.saskcao.ca; RAP (Rights Advocacy Project) with brochures, Concepts and Extended Learning Activities (for teachers, youth group leaders) at 5–6 (history and contents of CRC), plus learning activities (for example, "Rights Bingo").

215 RAP, Concepts and Extended Learning Activities, *ibid.* at 6.

[CRC], to which Canada is a signatory partner … it was determined that the Office of the Child and Youth Advocate would operate from a rights-based perspective and use the [CRC] as a basis for its advocacy services."[216] The annual report also included the text of the CRC in child-friendly language and public educational materials, such as brochures and children's projects, that make reference to the CRC.[217]

c) Manitoba, Quebec, and BC Institutions for Children

The Manitoba Children's Advocate also uses the CRC as a cornerstone of her activities, ideas, and principles.[218] The Quebec commission applied for and obtained intervener status on its own behalf and on behalf of the Canadian Council of Provincial Child and Youth Advocates in *Canadian Foundation for Children, Youth and the Law v. Canada* before the Supreme Court of Canada, to argue that section 43 of the *Criminal Code* (permitting reasonable corrective force against a pupil or child) did not respect the principles of the CRC.[219] However, in a more conservative reading of the CRC, the BC Child and Youth Officer states that the vision of their office reflects the values of the CRC, which "affirms the joint responsibilities of families, communities and governments for children and youth."[220]

H. CONCLUSION: REFORM PROPOSALS FOR NHRIs IN CANADA

Despite the regular criticism from both UN treaty bodies and some NHRIs themselves, about the limited effectiveness of Canadian NHRIs in terms of both the Paris Principles criteria and the NHRIs' ability to implement Canada's international human rights obligations, for the most part governments have not acted. The structures of NHRIs in Canada are dated when

---

216 Newfoundland and Labrador Child and Youth Advocate, *Annual Report 2002–2003* at 2; *Child and Youth Advocate Act*, above note 127; see online: www.childandyouthadvocate.nl.ca.

217 *Annual Report 2002–2003, ibid.* at 20; adult brochure (according to *Charter* and CRC, all children and youth have same rights and freedoms as adults), information on calendar project for kids (explains CRC and indicates child participation in advocacy encouraged by CRC), see online: www.childandyouthadvocate.nl.ca.

218 Manitoba Children's Advocate, *2004–2005 Annual Report* at 12. See also weblink to the *UN Declaration on the Rights of the Child*, online: www.childrensadvocate.mb.ca.

219 Above note 87 (the SCC found that s. 43 did not violate the *Charter* but, through statutory interpretation, narrowed the application of s. 43); Saskatchewan Children's Advocate, *Corporal Punishment and Saskatchewan Children* (February 2005) 1:1 Perspectives at 2.

220 BC Child and Youth Officer, *2003–2004 Annual Report* at 2.

one surveys the variety of NHRIs that have evolved around the world in the past twenty-five years, such as human rights commissions and human rights ombudsmän, with broad mandates to work with a variety of international and domestic human rights norms, and children's ombudsmän with express mandates to apply the CRC in their work. Further, while some NHRIs in Canada currently use and apply international human rights law in their work, including Canada's human rights treaty obligations, and can do so more flexibly and broadly compared to the courts, this practice is relatively limited compared to the proportion of their work that is based on domestic law.

While it is hard to be optimistic about prospects for federal and provincial government action to strengthen NHRIs in Canada and improve their abilities to use international human rights law, there are a number of suggestions that can be made, and some of these ideas have already been proposed by review bodies and some of the NHRIs.

Although ombudsmän have good levels of independence, many human rights commissions and children's institutions are executive appointments with the limitations this entails in terms of freedom of action and budget-setting. These NHRIs should be given greater independence from the executive through means such as appointment by, and accountability to, the legislature, and reduced ministerial control over their budgets. Further, all Canadian NHRIs need to be assured of adequate funding for reasons of independence, pursuant to the Paris Principles, and to enable them to engage in their full range of mandated activities, including those that may be more conducive to the use of international human rights law (for example, own-motion investigations, research, policy development, and education).

As discussed earlier, many human rights commissions and children's institutions in Canada have relatively narrow subject-matter jurisdiction. Consideration should be given, for example, to giving human rights commissions a broader range of civil, political, economic, social, and cultural rights to work with, based on Canada's human rights treaty obligations in the ICCPR, ICESCR, and CRC.[221] One option would make all of these additional rights applicable to all activities of a commission, including

---

221 See, for example, Human Rights Committee, General Comment No. 31, above note 61; Human Rights Committee, 1999 Concluding Observations, above note 143; Committee on Economic, Social and Cultural Rights, General Comments No. 10, 12, 14, 15, above notes 52, 56; Committee on Economic, Social and Cultural Rights, 1993 and 1998 Concluding Observations, above note 145.

complaints-handling. However, this alternative is not likely to be palatable to many governments in Canada at the present time. Another option is to limit a commission's investigatory functions to equality and discrimination matters (or the complaints-handling function could be given over entirely to the relevant human rights tribunal), and attach the expanded rights mandate to the human rights promotion activities of the commissions (research, policy development, education, public inquiries, etc.). Further, with the exception of the discrimination provisions that apply to both public and private actors, the enlarged human rights protection and/or promotion activities could be applied purely to public sector conduct given the focus in human rights treaties on state obligation to respect rights. Similarly, children's institutions should be given jurisdiction over all government administrative conduct, not just the few departments that expressly affect children. Consideration should also be given to expanding provincial ombudsman jurisdiction to cover complaints against the police, similar to the jurisdiction of the Australian North South Wales or Commonwealth ombudsmän.[222]

More explicit and expansive reference should be made to the international human rights treaty obligations of Canada in the body of federal and provincial/territorial human rights commission legislation, and not just in a statutory preamble. The founding legislation of all children's institutions in Canada should contain an express reference to the CRC and require the institution to apply or have reference to the CRC in all of its activities.[223] If such references are added to NHRI legislation, human rights commissions and children's institutions could also be given the duty to monitor and report on the level of their government's compliance with the human rights obligations of Canada listed in their legislation.[224]

Based on these changes, human rights commissions and children's institutions would be given an enhanced role in monitoring and reporting on Canada's compliance with its human rights treaty obligations. Also, given the general non-justiciability of economic, social, and cultural rights in Canada, this would improve on the limited means by which these rights are currently implemented and applied internally through the activities of

---

222 Above note 150.

223 For example, New Zealand children's commissioner legislation, above note 35.

224 See, for example, above text accompanying note 147 (could also include examination of government compliance with UN treaty committee Concluding Observations issued in response to Canada's periodic reports).

NHRIs, as described above. Further, if a protocol to the ICESCR permitting individual complaints to the Committee on Economic, Social and Cultural Rights is adopted in the future and Canada subsequently contemplates signature and ratification, improved domestic NHRIs and other mechanisms for implementing these rights will become necessary in order to avoid a flood of complaints to the committee.

More immediately, Canada is faced with the decision whether to sign the *Optional Protocol to the Convention against Torture.* If Canada decides to proceed, then "national preventive mechanisms" to visit and inspect places of detention must be designated taking federal–provincial jurisdiction into account.[225] Rather than establish new institutions with the associated costs, it would be more sensible to use existing institutions, such as our human rights commissions or ombudsmän. In Europe, for example, a number of ombudsmän have powers to inspect places of detention.[226] While our provincial ombudsmän currently do not have these powers, they already undertake numerous investigations against correctional authorities, so it would be relatively easy and cost-effective to amend ombudsman legislation to provide for inspection powers over provincial correctional facilities as preventive mechanisms under the Protocol.[227] On the federal level, in the current institutional environment, either the Correctional Investigator or the Canadian Human Rights Commission could be designated as the national preventive mechanism for federal facilities with the appropriate legislative amendments.[228]

Looking at gaps in NHRI coverage, the federal government and those provinces and territories without children's institutions need to establish children's ombudsmän or advocates that comply with the Paris Principles, have investigatory powers, cover all government administration, and are given an express mandate to apply the CRC.[229] A children's section in an ombudsman office or a children's branch attached to a human rights commission (as in Quebec) likely do not live up to the criteria for children's

225 Above text accompanying notes 64–68.
226 Above note 18.
227 Only PEI, NWT, and Nunavut do not have an ombudsman. In these provinces, for the preventive mechanisms, the human rights commission legislation could be amended, ombudsmän could be established, or other institutions could be used.
228 Above notes 93 and 123.
229 See UN Committee on the Rights of the Child, 2003: Concluding Observations and General Comment No. 2 on National Human Rights Institutions, above notes 153–55 and 57.

NHRIs laid down by the UN Committee on the Rights of the Child.[230] As the committee has implicitly indicated, wealthier countries such as Canada have the resources to establish discrete institutions for children, and the committee has expressly called for children's ombudsmän to be established in the remaining provinces and territories and at the federal level.[231]

Ombudsmän need to be established in PEI, NWT, and Nunavut. Finally, Canada needs a federal ombudsman—appointed by and accountable to Parliament with jurisdiction over the full federal public administration. Several of the existing federal commissioners could be merged into such an ombudsman institution (for example, RCMP and corrections), as could the Defence Forces Ombudsman, which would give it greater independence. A comparative example is Australia's Commonwealth and Defence Force Ombudsman.[232] As demonstrated earlier in this paper, classical ombudsmän in Canada do investigate complaints with human rights issues and occasionally use international human rights law in their resolution. This would also likely be the case with a federal ombudsman, especially if it has jurisdiction over federal corrections, defence, and immigration/refugee matters.[233] A more provocative alternative would be to establish a federal human rights ombudsman that would have the power to investigate complaints of poor administration and human rights breaches by the federal public administration. Given that most of the Scandinavian countries, the birthplaces of the ombudsman concept, have turned their classical ombudsmän into hybrid human rights ombudsmän, this is not a radical idea.[234] In particular, this would be an alternative to reforming the Canadian Human Rights Commission along the lines mentioned in the preceding paragraphs, although provisions to avoid conflict of jurisdictions would have to be included.[235]

---

230 UN Committee on the Rights of the Child, General Comment No. 2 on National Human Rights Institutions, *ibid*.

231 Above text accompanying note 155 (that is, the Committee on the Rights of the Child does not appear to be making allowances for less wealthy sub-national governments located in a wealthy state).

232 See online: www.comb.gov.au.

233 A federal ombudsman of this type could also act as a "national preventive mechanism" under the *Protocol to the Convention against Torture*, above text accompanying notes 64–68 and 225–27.

234 Above text accompanying note 29.

235 See Reif, *Ombudsman, International Human Rights*, above note 4 at 102–3.

Yet, even if little or no material legislative reform occurs in Canada, it has been shown in this chapter that some Canadian NHRIs—human rights commissions, ombudsman, and children's institutions—already occasionally apply Canada's human rights treaty obligations and other international instruments in their educational, research, policy, and investigatory activities. When this occurs, Canadian NHRI use of international human rights law is not uniform and is sometimes more receptive to the application of unimplemented treaty obligations of Canada compared to the attitude of the judiciary. The different approaches of Canadian NHRIs to the domestic application of international human rights law include using treaty obligations that are not explicitly implemented and international soft law to interpret domestic law or give meaning to broader ombudsman standards of fairness used to scrutinize administrative conduct. Indeed, NHRI interest in applying Canada's international human rights obligations seems to have increased in recent years. These approaches should be encouraged and developed in all NHRIs in Canada.

Section B:

SUBSTANTIVE DOMESTIC LAW AND THE IMPLEMENTATION OF INTERNATIONAL LAW

15

Domestic Implementation of Canada's
International Human Rights Obligations

DONALD J. FLEMING AND JOHN P. McEVOY

A. INTRODUCTION

Two malingering influences define the present approach to domestic implementation of Canada's international human rights obligations: the concept of federalism as reflected in the *Labour Conventions* case[1] and the dated "Cold War" political stance that economic, social, and cultural rights are less justiciable than civil and political rights. These influences must be addressed in a fresh manner if individuals—and collectivities of Canadians—are to realize the benefits of Canada's international human rights obligations and if Canada is to achieve recognition as a country in full compliance with those obligations. Critical to a new approach is acceptance that international human rights obligations not only bind the honour of the Crown but, in many instances, are also more than just conventional international law; they are customary international law.

In this chapter, we examine the implementation of Canada's obligations under the International Covenants—the *International Covenant on Civil and Political Rights* and the *International Covenant on Economic, Social and Cultural Rights*—both of which were ratified after federal–provincial consultation and with the unanimous consent of the federal and provincial governments. The focus of this chapter is not on the mechanics of implementation but on the weaknesses in the attitude to implementation. Part B reviews the traditional Canadian approaches to international hu-

---

1 *Attorney-General of Canada v. Attorney-General of Ontario (Labour Conventions)*, [1937] A.C. 326 (J.C.P.C.), on appeal from [1936] S.C.R. 461.

man rights law while Part C focuses on implementation within Canada of the two international covenants pertaining to civil and political rights and economic, social and cultural rights, respectively. In Part D, we present a new approach to implementation of international human rights obligations—at least, a new attitude with legal consequences.

B. CONSTRAINTS OF THE PAST

The *Labour Conventions* case established the present approach to domestic "implementation" of Canada's obligations at international law. The case is so pivotal to Canadian perceptions of the relationship between international and national law that we must begin our analysis with it. In the last year of his mandate, Prime Minister R.B. Bennett proposed a "New Deal" to Canadians that presented such a dramatic shift in social policy he did not consult in advance with either his Cabinet colleagues or his provincial counterparts.[2] Included in the New Deal package were three legislative advances, all grounded in Conventions of the International Labour Organization (ILO): 1) *The Weekly Rest in Industrial Undertakings Act*[3] to implement the 1921 *Convention concerning the Application of the Weekly Rest in Industrial Undertakings*,[4] ratified by Canada on 21 March 1935; 2) *The Minimum Wages Act*[5] to implement the *Convention concerning the Creation of Minimum Wage-Fixing Machinery*[6] ratified by Canada on 25 April 1935; and 3) *The Limitation of Hours of Work Act*[7] to implement the *Convention Limiting the Hours of Work in Industrial Undertakings to Eight in the Day and Forty-Eight in the Week*[8] ratified by Canada on 21 March 1935. This New Deal legislation did not stop the inevitable defeat of the Bennett government in the general election of 14 October 1935 and the return of Mackenzie King

---

2   See Richard Simeon & Ian Robinson, *State, Society, and the Development of Canadian Federalism* (Toronto: University of Toronto Press, 1990) at 78–80.
3   S.C. 1935, c. 14 (Royal Assent 4 April 1935)(in force three months after Royal Assent).
4   *C14 Weekly Rest (Industry) Convention, 1921* adopted 17 November 1921 and entered in force 19 June 1923.
5   S.C. 1935, c. 44 (Royal Assent 28 June 1935)(in force upon assent except for provisions establishing the machinery to fix minimum wages and identification of rateable trades that came into force on Proclamation).
6   *C26 Minimum Wage-Fixing Machinery Convention, 1928* adopted 16 June 1928 and entered into force on 14 June 1930.
7   S.C. 1935, c. 63 (Royal Assent 5 July 1935)(entered into force three months after assent).
8   *C1 Hours of Work (Industry) Convention, 1919* adopted 28 November 1919 and entered into force 13 June 1921.

to the Prime Minister's Office. Using the federal reference power, the King government quickly referred the question of the validity of the legislation to the Supreme Court on 31 October 1935.

The six-member Supreme Court panel divided equally on the reference. Duff C.J.C. (Davis and Kerwin JJ., concurring) concluded that the three statutes were valid. He grounded this conclusion, in part, on the characterization for constitutional purposes of the "matter" of an international treaty to which Canada is a state party as the "international unit"; such treaty being, therefore, outside the scope of exclusive federal implementation authority under the imperial treaty provision, section 132 of the *Constitution Act, 1867*. By this analysis, any such matter is subject to the exclusive jurisdiction of Parliament under the section 91 "Peace, Order and Good Government" power regardless of its nominal allocation as a matter within exclusive federal or provincial legislative jurisdiction. Thus, when a matter within exclusive provincial legislative jurisdiction (such as hours of work or a minimum wage in the provincial marketplace) becomes the subject of an international treaty, it is thereby transformed into a matter of international concern beyond provincial legislative competence for the purposes of the *Constitution Act, 1867*. In separate opinions, Rinfret, Cannon, and Crocket JJ. each applied a literal interpretation of section 132 to restrict its scope to imperial treaties and rejected the metamorphosis reasoning of Duff C.J.C., that is, that a matter of local concern became a matter of international concern by the process of treaty-making.

On appeal, the Privy Council maintained the integrity of the original Confederation bargain. Lord Atkin rejected both the progressive interpretation of section 132 and the shifting characterization for constitutional purposes of treaty matters. Reasserting the strict "watertight compartments" approach to the distribution of legislative jurisdiction, Lord Atkin affirmed: "[T]he Dominion cannot, merely by making promises to foreign countries, clothe itself with legislative authority inconsistent with the constitution which gave it birth."[9]

The reasoning of the Privy Council is limited to the issue of legislative jurisdiction to implement the international obligations undertaken. Lord Atkin expressly reserved any opinion on the mechanics of treaty formation. In argument, counsel for the provinces had stressed the role of provincial ministries to advise the Crown on the formation of international obligations within provincial legislative jurisdiction; a position summa-

---

9   Above note 1 at 352 (A.C.).

rized by Lord Atkin as "[t]hat the Canadian Government had no executive authority to make any such treaty as was alleged."[10] Put more forcefully by counsel for Ontario: "Ontario has a right to enter into an agreement with another part of the British Empire or with a foreign State. So far as legislative and executive authority are concerned the Governor-General and the Lieutenant-Governors of the Provinces, and the Dominion Parliament and the Provincial Legislatures are equal in status. The *Treaty of Versailles* is binding on Ontario as part of the British Empire."[11] To this position, Lord Atkin merely stated:

> Counsel did not suggest any doubt as to the international status which Canada had now attained, involving her competence to enter into international treaties as an international juristic person. Questions were raised both generally as to how the executive power was to be exercised to bind Canada, whether it must be exercised in the name of the King, and whether the prerogative right of making treaties in respect of Canada was now vested in the Governor-General in Council, or his Ministers, whether by constitutional usage or otherwise, and specifically in relation to the draft conventions as to the interpretation of the various paragraphs in art. 405 of the *Treaty of Versailles*, and as to the effect of the time limits expressed both in art. 405 and in the conventions themselves. Their Lordships mention these points for the purpose of making it clear that they express no opinion upon them.[12]

The provincial assertion of a direct role in treaty-formation did not end with *Labour Conventions*. It is, however, an assertion that the federal government has never accepted. Instead, the federal government adopted a strategy of avoidance. It developed the "umbrella agreement" approach by which provinces, such as Quebec and New Brunswick, are authorized to enter into agreements directly with countries such as France and to provide provincial representation in Canadian delegations. This practical compromise maintains the position of federal exclusiveness while rejecting provincial pretensions to attend international conferences as of right.[13]

---

10   *Ibid.* at 342.

11   *Ibid.* at 333.

12   *Ibid.* at 349.

13   See generally Peter W. Hogg, *Constitutional Law of Canada*, looseleaf (Toronto: Carswell, 2001) at c. 11.6. Professor Hogg acknowledges that the Letters Patent constituting the office of governor general, which delegates Royal Prerogative powers in relation to Canada, may be interpreted as delegating only those powers linked to federal classes

On the international plane, it is the federal government that represents the sovereign "international unit." As Peter Hogg notes, sovereign provincial international units would be recognized if the Constitution expressed a provincial treaty-making capacity.[14]

The *Labour Conventions* case is also instructive for the selection of the three ILO conventions in issue. It will be recalled that the federal government ratified these international human rights obligations without consulting the provinces. By the end of 1934, the Bennett government could have selected any of forty-four ILO conventions for implementation. Why these three? It may be because provincial legislation, in at least some measure, already regulated maximum hours of work, minimum wages, and weekly days of rest. For example, the old Factories Acts of Ontario,[15] Manitoba,[16] Saskatchewan,[17] and British Columbia[18] regulated maximum hours of work (specifically for young girls and women); provinces such as Nova Scotia,[19] Ontario,[20] Manitoba,[21] Saskatchewan,[22] and British Columbia[23] regulated minimum wages; and provinces such as Quebec,[24] Ontario,[25] Manitoba,[26] and Saskatchewan[27] regulated weekly days of rest—a matter previously regulated by provincial *Lord's Day Acts* but held invalid as criminal law in *Attorney-General for Ontario v. Hamilton Street Railway Company*[28] (1903). The rights declared in the three ILO Conventions were not new but had been recognized as minimum standards of social conduct in the decades

---

of subjects under the *Constitution Act, 1867*, s. 91. Professor Hogg is clear (at c. 11.2) that "the federal government does in fact exercise exclusive treaty-making powers."

14   *Ibid.*

15   *The Factory, Shop and Office Act*, R.S.O. 1897, c. 256, ss. 32–35.

16   *The Fair Wage Act, 1916*, S.M. 1916, c. 121, s. 7 (re: both minimum wage and maximum hours of work).

17   *The Factories Act*, R.S.S. 1920, c. 176, s. 11.

18   *Factories Act*, R.S.B.C. 1924, c. 84, s. 16.

19   *The Minimum Wages for Women Act, 1920*, S.N.S. 1920, c. 9.

20   *The Minimum Wage Act*, S.O. 1920, c. 87 (re: women and girls only).

21   Above note 16.

22   *The Minimum Wage Act*, R.S.S. 1920, c. 186.

23   *Minimum Wage Act*, S.B.C. 1918, c. 56.

24   *Act to provide for one day of rest each week for employees in certain industries*, S.Q. 1918, c. 53 (hotels, restaurants, and clubs).

25   *One Day's Rest in Seven Act*, S.O. 1922, c. 93 (hotel, restaurants, and clubs).

26   *The One Day's Rest in Seven Act*, S.M. 1928, c. 45.

27   *The One Day's Rest in Seven Act*, S.S. 1930, c. 81, s. 1 (general scope; not limited to hotels, restaurants, clubs).

28   [1903] A.C. 524 (J.C.P.C.).

preceding the 1935 federal implementing legislation. These were basic economic and social rights already protected by provincial legislation.

In addition to the impact of the *Labour Conventions* case, a second negative influence is the characterization of economic, social, and cultural rights as lesser rights than their civil and political cousins—that economic, social, and cultural rights are "second generation," that is, more aspirations than rights. This influence is a relic of the Cold War divide between capitalist and socialist states. Yet, the 1948 *Universal Declaration of Human Rights* proclaims all its rights as "*a common standard of achievement for all peoples and all nations, to the end that every individual and every organ of society ... by progressive measures, national and international, to secure their universal and effective recognition and observance*" (emphasis added). Whether it be the article 18 "right to freedom of thought, conscience and religion" or the article 25 "right to a standard of living adequate for ... health and well-being," all human rights are subject to the same limitation clause expressed in article 29: "such limitations as are determined by law solely for the purpose of securing due recognition and respect for the rights and freedoms of others and of meeting the just requirements of morality, public order and the general welfare in a democratic society." Defining limitations on the exercise of human rights is the prerogative of the state in the exercise of its sovereign power to regulate its citizens and others within its territory, but such limitations must be consistent with the Universal Declaration. By the same token, and using the Hohfeldian jural correlatives of "right" and "duty,"[29] where the right resides with the individual, the duty resides with the state.

Where the Universal Declaration drew no clear distinction between the types of rights (both being expressed as "a common standard of achievement"), the two Covenants[30] are distinguished by the recognition in only the CESCR of a financial constraint on state support for the full realization of the rights. The *International Covenant on Economic, Social and Cultural Rights* article 2(1) expresses the undertaking of each state to support full implementation "to the maximum of its available resources, with a view to achieving progressively the full realization of the rights recognized in the present Covenant by all appropriate means, including, particularly, the

---

29   Wesley N. Hohfeld, *Fundamental Legal Conceptions*, ed. by Walter W. Cook (New Haven and London: Yale University Press, 1919) at 35–64.

30   The *International Covenant on Civil and Political Rights* (CCPR) and the *International Covenant on Economic, Social and Cultural Rights* (CESCR).

adoption of legislative measures." As the committee observed in General Comment 3: The Nature of States Parties Obligations (fifth session, 1990),[31] article 2(1) imposes obligations of result and obligations of conduct. The principal obligation of result is to achieve progressively the full realization of Covenant rights. Obligations of conduct relate to the undertaking to take steps to the maximum of available resources and by "all appropriate means, including particularly the adoption of legislative measures," a phrase which the committee observes must be interpreted in its natural sense to include the recognition of justiciable rights ("judicial remedies") within the domestic legal order.[32] Thus, ultimately, both civil and political rights and economic, social, and cultural rights should be fully justiciable.

In Canada, this has yet to be fully achieved.

C. IMPLEMENTING THE COVENANTS

In 1967, the federal government commenced the ratification process in respect of both the *International Covenant on Civil and Political Rights* (CCPR) and the *International Covenant on Economic, Social and Cultural Rights* (CESCR) when it invited the provinces to review their own legislation for conformity to protected rights and to indicate whether they would undertake to ensure conformity where needed. Following lengthy debates and delays, the federal government received permission from each provincial government to ratify the conventions in December 1975 at the Federal–Provincial Ministerial Conference on Human Rights.[33] At that meeting, the federal and provincial governments agreed to proposals grounded in the principle of "concertation" (advanced by Quebec) involving federal–provincial and interprovincial cooperation. The proposals ("modalities and mechanisms") provide *inter alia* for consultation on issues of substance, consultation on the composition of Canadian delegations and provincial participation, an opportunity for provincial response (oral or written) to criticism by a Covenant committee, and participation in the Canadian delegation presenting

---

31 Published in E/1991/23.

32 *Ibid.* at para. 5. Within the Covenants regimes, the CCPR but not the CESCR, through its Optional Protocol, permits individual access to an international forum by means of a complaint. A mirror protocol to the CESCR is under consideration.

33 See Philippe LeBlanc, "Canada's Experience with United Nations Human Rights Treaties," *The Agenda for Change Series: Perspectives on UN Reform*, No. 3 (Ottawa: Canadian Committee for the 50th Anniversary of the United Nations, 1994).

that response.[34] In 1988, the federal and provincial ministers approved the "Mandate of the Continuing Committee of Officials on Human Rights" to facilitate "consultation and collaboration" in the implementation of Canada's international human rights obligations.[35]

1) Implementing the *International Covenant on Civil and Political Rights*

Following the 1975 Federal–Provincial Ministerial Conference on Human Rights, Canada ratified the CCPR on 19 May 1976 and it came into force for Canada on 19 August 1976; specifically, it came into force in relation to federal Canada and each of the provinces and territories. Implementation of the Covenant did not pose particularly difficult issues. Many of the civil and political rights it recognizes were already well grounded in federal substantive and procedural criminal law and reflected in the *Canadian Bill of Rights, 1960*. For the purposes of implementation, the provinces benefited from the foresight of the framers of the Constitution in conferring on Parliament exclusive legislative jurisdiction in relation to criminal law and procedure. The path to implementation was eased by the principles given effect in federal criminal law jurisdiction and mirrored procedurally in provincial legislation for the prosecution of provincial regulatory offences.

Some of the CCPR rights became constitutionally entrenched in Canada with the *Canadian Charter of Rights and Freedoms*. It is that instrument, along with the earlier federal, provincial, and territorial human rights codes, on which Canada, the provinces, and territories largely rely in Canada's article 40 country reports to the Human Rights Committee. The *Fifth Report of Canada Covering the Period January 1995–April 2004*[36] confirms that the principal concerns are not necessarily at the core of state interaction with individuals in traditional areas of civil and political rights (except in relation to the antiterrorism legislation) but have shifted to what might be considered the economic and social issues of gender equality (under article 2), homelessness, and poverty (under article 6 "right to life"). In

---

34 *Ibid.*, reproduced in App. A, "Modalities and Mechanisms" approved at the Federal–Provincial Conference on Human Rights, 11–12 December 1975.

35 *Ibid.*, reproduced in App. B, "Mandate of the Continuing Committee of Officials on Human Rights" approved at the Federal–Provincial–Territorial Conference on Human Rights, 27 September 1988.

36 *Fifth Report of Canada Covering the Period January 1995–April 2004* (Ottawa: Minister of Public Works and Government Services Canada, 2004).

a General Comment, the committee has confirmed its view that the right to life is to be interpreted beyond a strictly civil and political scope:[37]

> The expression "inherent right to life" cannot properly be understood in a restrictive manner, and the protection of this right requires that States adopt positive measures. In this connection, the Committee considers that it would be desirable for States parties to take all possible measures to reduce infant mortality and to increase life expectancy, especially in adopting measures to eliminate malnutrition and epidemics.

The individual complaint mechanism under the Optional Protocol has proved in practice a modestly utilized means of seeking redress by those claiming a violation of a Covenant right by federal, provincial, or territorial governments. Of the sixty-four complaints against Canada at the time of writing this chapter, the committee has denied forty-four as inadmissible, dismissed nine after a determination on the merits, and found violations in only ten—the latest being *Mansour Ahani v. Canada*.[38] In *Ahani*, the committee found a violation of the article 7 right not to be subjected to torture because Canada had deported the complainant, a former member of the Iranian security services, before appeal proceedings had been completed, including consideration of the complaint by the committee itself.[39]

Five successful complaints have been, at least to some extent, remedied by legislative, constitutional, or judicial reforms. These complaints presented a variety of challenges: that is, the right to culture, language, and community in the context of the right to live on an Indian reserve (*Lovelace*);[40] minority language rights (*Ballantyne, Davidson and McIntyre*);[41] undue delay in a criminal appeal (*Pinkney*);[42] and extradition in the face of a

---

37   Human Rights Committee, General Comment No. 6: The Right to Life, art. 6 (30/04/82).
38   Communication No. 1051/2002; committee decision dated 15 June 2004.
39   The deportation followed refusal by the Supreme Court of Canada to grant leave to appeal: *Ahani v. Canada (Minister of Citizenship and Immigration)*, [2002] S.C.C.A. No. 62.
40   *Lovelace v. Canada*, Communication No. 24/1977; committee decision dated 30 July 1981. Federal *Indian Act* subsequently amended to conform to equality right.
41   *Ballantyne and Davidson and McIntyre v. Canada*, Communication No. 359/1989 and 385/1989; committee decision dated 5 May 1993. Quebec authorities modified the *Charter of the French Language*.
42   *Pinkney v. Canada*, Communication No. 24/1977; committee decision dated 29 October 1981. The Supreme Court of Canada addressed the right to trial within a reasonable time in *R. v. Askov*, [1990] 2 S.C.R. 1199.

possible death penalty as constituting cruel and unusual punishment or extradition as a means to impede a further appeal (*Ng* and *Judge*).[43]

Some successful complaints have not been fully or finally addressed. In *Waldman v. Canada*,[44] the committee found that Ontario's policy of funding Roman Catholic schools but not other religious groups, specifically Jewish schools, constituted discrimination. Though other provinces have addressed this discrimination,[45] Ontario has failed to conform to its international human rights obligation—its then minister of education responded to the committee finding by asserting that Ontario has no intention of changing its funding system and that position has generally held firm.[46] In *Omninayak and the Lubicon Lake Band v. Canada*,[47] the committee found a violation of the rights of an Aboriginal community per article 27 because the federal and Alberta governments had acted to expropriate and sell traditional lands that had not been ceded to the Crown. Though Canadian jurisprudence and government policies have since improved the position of Aboriginal groups seeking control over traditional territories,[48] the Lubicon have seen little actual improvement. They have won several court battles against companies that exercised economic rights over Lubicon claimed land, and have entered into some agreements with the federal government. But the Alberta government continues to refuse recognition of the land claims and has recently offered for sale a large parcel of tim-

---

43   *Ng v. Canada*, Communication No. 469/1991); committee decision dated 7 January 1991. *Judge v. Canada*, Communication No. 829/1998; committee decision dated 20 October 2003.

44   Communication No. 694/1996; committee decision dated 5 November 1999. For a discussion of this complaint and its aftermath, see John McEvoy, "Denominational Schools and Minority Rights: *Hogan v. Attorney General of Newfoundland*" (2001) 12 N.J.C.L. 449–66. This article also discusses the companion complaint in *Tadman v. Canada*, Communication No. 694/1996; committee decision dated 3 November 1999.

45   Quebec and Newfoundland and Labrador negotiated constitutional changes with the federal government to either secularize the entire school system or to fund all religious schools where numbers warrant.

46   "Ontario's Catholic School Funding Violates Rights: UN" *National Post* (6 November 1999) A10. In 2001, the Ontario government announced a limited tax credit for parents with children attending fee-paying schools. See "Equity in Education Tax Credit—Discussion Paper" (Ontario: Ministry of Finance, 30 August 2001). The tax credit was implemented under *The Right Choices for Equity in Education Act (Budget Measures), 2003*, S.O. 2003, c. 5 but then cancelled with effect from 1 January 2003 pursuant to the *Fiscal Responsibility Act, 2003*, S.O. 2003, c. 7.

47   Communication No. 167/1984; committee decision dated 10 May 1990.

48   *Delgamuukw v. British Columbia*, [1997] 3 S.C.R. 1010.

ber land, including an area claimed by the Lubicon.[49] A critical feature in these lingering complaints is the non-fulfilment by provincial officials of their responsibilities to respect the international human rights obligations to which their governments have committed themselves. As with the complaint in *Waldman*, the Lubicon complaint has been submitted and proceeded against Canada as the state actor in international law. But this identification of the respondent state should not and does not provide real cover for provincial governments.

Civil and political rights enjoy a status atop the perceived (but false) hierarchy of rights. As Canadian courts have confirmed repeatedly, financial considerations do not alone justify infringement of *Charter* rights: "[b]udgetary considerations in and of themselves cannot normally be invoked as a free-standing pressing and substantial objective for the purposes of s. 1 of the *Charter*."[50] Financial considerations do come into play in fashioning the appropriate remedy: "This Court has held, and rightly so, that budgetary considerations cannot be used to justify a violation under s. 1. However, such considerations are clearly relevant once a violation which does not survive s. 1 has been established, s. 52 is determined to have been engaged and the Court turns its attention to what action should be taken thereunder."[51] As will be seen, the Court revisited consideration of financial constraints in *Newfoundland (Treasury Board) v. N.A.P.E.*[52] discussed in the section that follows.

2) Implementing the *International Covenant on Economic, Social, and Cultural Rights*

As with the CCPR, Canada submitted its instrument of ratification of the CESCR on 19 May 1976 and the Covenant came into force for Canada three months later (per article 27(2)) on 19 August 1976. In contrast to civil and political rights, implementation of economic, social, and cultural rights has been more problematic for Canada.

The *Canadian Bill of Rights, 1960* is a civil and political rights document. Unless coverage is found in the section 1(a) right to life and security of the person, the bill does not protect economic, social, and cultural rights. But this does not mean that such rights are alien to Canadian legal tradi-

---

49 *Edmonton Journal* (1 and 4 February, 2005).
50 *Nova Scotia (Workers' Compensation Board) v. Martin*, [2003] 2 S.C.R. 504 at para. 109.
51 *Schachter v. Canada*, [1992] 2 S.C.R. 679 at 709, Lamer C.J.C.
52 [2004] 3 S.C.R. 381.

tions. Indeed, the historical evidence is just the opposite. Economic, social, and cultural rights, as legally binding obligations, did not begin with the Universal Declaration and the CESCR, but were merely codified and affirmed by these important instruments. For example, the recognition of "social condition" as a prohibited ground of discrimination under the federal and provincial human rights codes provides a means to challenge the inadequate provision of services generally available to the public but does not constitute more than an indirect recognition of the economic rights of the CESCR. The Quebec *Charter of Human Rights and Freedoms*[53] goes further than other provincial codes in expressly recognizing economic and social rights (articles 39 to 48) but limits the protection of those rights by permitting subsequent legislative derogation.[54]

Other Canadian federal and provincial legislation recognized and implemented similar rights long before the United Nations and its Universal Declaration and CESCR came into existence. Consider, for example, various rights applicable in the labour setting set out in articles 7 (the right to fair wages and to "safe and healthy working conditions") and 8 (the right to form and join trade unions) of the CESCR. The existence of these rights had been socially and politically accepted in Canada since at least the late-nineteenth century and into the early years of the twentieth century.

Rights to fair wages and safe working conditions and to form and join trade unions found early legislative expression, though it was not applicable to all workers when first enacted. Instead, these rights developed progressively from initial legislation to protect discrete and vulnerable groups, such as youth (defined as males under eighteen years of age), young girls, and women, to general coverage in subsequent years. For example, the 1920 Ontario *Minimum Wage Act*, section 2(d)[55] defined "employee" as "every female person in any trade or occupation in Ontario who works for wages." This early legislative focus on women (and on children) derived from the practical reality of early unionization in male-dominated sectors of the economy. In 1872, the Canadian Parliament finally recognized the legality of trade

---

53 R.S.Q., c. C-12.
54 *Ibid.*, art. 52: "No provision of any Act, even subsequent to the Charter, may derogate from sections 1 to 38, except so far as provided by those sections, unless such Act expressly states that it applies despite the Charter." The economic and social rights provisions of the *Charter*, being arts. 39–48, are not within the scope of this non-derogation clause.
55 S.O. 1920, c. 87. See also *The Minimum Wages for Women Act, 1920*, S.N.S. 1920, c. 9.

unionism in the *Trade Unions Act*,[56] which provided that a registered trade union is not an unlawful restraint of trade and by enacting the *Criminal Law Amendment Act*[57] to permit peaceful picketing. In the 1930s, provincial legislation in Quebec, Ontario, Alberta, Nova Scotia, Saskatchewan, and New Brunswick[58] provided a form of negotiated industry-wide standards for minimum wages and maximum hours of work. Today, and since formal provincial statutory recognition in 1937,[59] the right of employees to form and join trade unions is well entrenched in the Canadian legal order.

The same is true of the right of every worker to safe and healthy working conditions. Modelled on earlier English legislation, the preamble to the 1884 Ontario *Factories Act*[60] identifies as one of its purposes the "safety, health and well-being of operatives employed in and about factories and like places." The Act provided enforcement through a scheme of inspections coupled with prosecutions for breach of its standards. By 1897, legislation provided the same protections to persons employed in factories and in other places of business.[61] Over time, these two enactments were repealed and replaced by statutes the titles of which reflect the further expansion of this protection of the social right to safe working conditions—the *Factory, Shop and Office Building Act* (1914);[62] the *Industrial Safety Act* (1964);[63] and finally to the now familiar *Occupational Health and Safety Act* (1978).[64] The legislative experience in other provinces generally mirrored that of Ontario so that today, occupational health and safety legislation exists in all provinces and territories and at the federal level.[65]

---

56 S.C. 1872, c. 30.

57 S.C. 1872, c. 31. Now *Criminal Code*, s. 423.

58 *Collective Labour Agreements Extension Act*, S.Q. 1934, c. 56; *Industrial Standards Act*, S.O. 1935, c. 56; *The Industrial Standards Act*, S.A. 1935, c. 47; *The Industrial Standards Act*, 1936, S.N.S. 1936, c. 3; *The Industrial Standards Act, 1937*, S.S. 1937, c. 90 and *The Industrial Standards Act*, S.N.B. 1939, c. 57.

59 For example, *Trade Union Act*, S.N.S. 1937, c. 6; *Strikes and Lockouts Prevention Act*, S.M. 1937, c. 40; *Freedom of Trade Union Association Act*, S.A. 1937, c. 75.

60 S.O. 1884, c. 39.

61 *Protection of Persons Employed in Factories Act*, R.S.O. 1897, c. 256 and *Protection of Persons Employed in Places of Business other than Factories Act*, R.S.O. 1897, c. 257.

62 R.S.O. 1914, c. 229.

63 S.O. 1964, c. 45.

64 S.O. 1978, c. 83.

65 For example, *An Act respecting Industrial Accidents and Occupational Diseases*, R.S.Q., c. A-3.001; *Occupational Health and Safety Act*, R.S.O. 1990, c. O.1 as amended; *Occupational Health and Safety Act*, R.S.P.E.I. 1988, c. O-1 as amended and the *Canada Labour Code*.

The legislative record demonstrates that most CESCR labour-related rights have a long and honoured history of progressive recognition and acceptance in Canadian society and were firmly established in federal and provincial law prior to the ratification of the Covenant. Other labour-related rights, with a less specific legislative history, are nevertheless grounded in long-established principles. The article 7 right to "just and favourable conditions of work" including the "equal remuneration for work of equal value" is of more recent Canadian vintage but obviously represents a specific application of the right to equality.

Recently, in *Newfoundland (Treasury Board) v. N.A.P.E.*,[66] the Supreme Court considered the interplay of the right to pay equity and financial constraints on the implementation of that right in the context of equality rights as guaranteed by the *Canadian Charter of Rights and Freedoms*. Having agreed to pay equity for female health care workers in 1988, the government of Newfoundland and Labrador enacted legislation in 1991 to defer payment of equity adjustments and to extinguish the adjustments then due. Binnie J., for the Court, did not find it necessary to respond to the provincial argument that the *Charter* section 15(1) equality rights do not include a specific right to pay equity. Instead, focusing analysis on the legislation in issue, Binnie J. applied the *Law*[67] approach to conclude that the legislation clearly and unequivocally discriminated on the basis of sex: "The Act froze wage scales in the male-dominated jobs as well as in the female-dominated jobs, but the men were already paid money for value whereas the women were not."[68] The real issue before the Court centred on the *Charter* section 1 justification analysis.

Simply stated, the issue became whether severe financial constraints are sufficient to justify a breach of the constitutional right to equality. Binnie J. answered in the affirmative—at least in the context of the financial constraints evidenced in this case. He accepted that a budgetary deficit of $130 million, which the government and Legislative Assembly struggled to address, justified legislative choices on social priorities (that is, hospital beds versus salary adjustments) that adversely impacted on *Charter* rights: "At some point, a financial crisis can attain a dimension that elected governments must be accorded significant scope to take remedial measures, even if the measures taken have an adverse effect on a *Charter* right, sub-

---

66   Above note 52.
67   *Law v. Canada (Minister of Employment and Immigration)*, [1999] 1 S.C.R. 497.
68   Above note 52 at para. 50.

ject, of course, to the measures being proportional both to the fiscal crisis and to their impact on the affected *Charter* interests."[69]

This approach is generally consistent with the approach that equality rights are not of the same order as *Charter* rights in relation to which the state enacts limitations in its role as "singular antagonist," such as the legal rights on arrest or imprisonment. With equality, the state acts as "mediator" between competing groups in society with the result that *Charter* section 1 analysis is applied in a more deferential manner.[70] It is with this view that Binnie J. summarized the Court's position:[71]

> courts will continue to look with strong scepticism at attempts to justify infringements of *Charter* rights on the basis of budgetary constraints. To do otherwise would devalue the *Charter* because there are always budgetary constraints and there are always other pressing government priorities. Nevertheless, the courts cannot close their eyes to the periodic occurrence of financial emergencies when measures must be taken to juggle priorities to see a government through the crisis. It cannot be said that in weighing a delay in the timetable for implementing pay equity against the closing of hundreds of hospital beds, as here, a government is engaged in an exercise "whose sole purpose is financial." The weighing exercise has as much to do with social values as it has to do with dollars. In the present case, the "potential impact" is $24 million, amounting to more than 10 percent of the projected budgetary deficit for 1991–92. The delayed implementation of pay equity is an extremely serious matter, but so too (for example) is the layoff of 1,300 permanent, 350 part-time and 350 seasonal employees, and the deprivation to the public of the services they provided.

The Court deferred to the legislative choice concerning the competing social values. It must be stressed, however, that the financial exigency considered in *N.A.P.E.* was accepted as severe and not in the nature of deficits usually incurred by governments in furtherance of macro-economic policies.

The continuing impact of the perceived distinction between orders of rights in Canada is illustrated by domestic implementation of the CESCR article 11(1) "right to an adequate standard of living ... and to the continuous improvement of living conditions." Provincial social assistance or family income security legislation is decidedly grounded in attitudes more in

---

69 *Ibid.* at para. 64.

70 *Irwin Toy v. Quebec (Attorney General)*, [1989] 1 S.C.R. 927.

71 Above note 52 at para. 72.

keeping with nineteenth-century poor laws. Contemporary legislation is not rights-based; it conveys a sense of reluctant benefaction rather than a duty or obligation of the state—yet, the very existence of such legislation since at least the nineteenth century confirms the acceptance of that duty or obligation of the state. For example, in New Brunswick a person may apply for income assistance to the maximum amount established by law and has a right to appeal a decision to deny assistance or the amount of assistance granted as insufficient or inappropriate—subject of course to the income assistance limits established by law.[72] An appeal is determined at first instance by a government employee designated by the minister and on further appeal by an independent board the members of which are appointed by the Lieutenant-Governor-in-Council. Thus, the legislative scheme recognizes in each qualified applicant a defined legal right to income assistance and in the province a corresponding duty or obligation to provide that assistance. The appeal mechanism just described for New Brunswick is consistent with the conditional obligation established under the former *Canada Assistance Plan*,[73] an obligation which the federal government became notorious for deleting when it enacted the *Federal–Provincial Fiscal Arrangements Act*.[74] The appeal mechanism is not uniform across Canada; for example, in Alberta, the minister appoints members of the appeal panel whose decision is then declared final.[75]

The real issue pertaining to the right to an adequate standard of living lies not with the eligibility requirements or appeal structures but with the adequacy of available income security benefits. Again, in New Brunswick, the maximum amounts have remained unchanged since 1997, notwith-

---

72 *Family Income Security Act*, S.N.B. 1994, c. F-2.01 and N.B. Reg. 95-61, s. 15.

73 R.S.C. 1985. c. C-1. The Supreme Court of Canada recognized public interest standing to challenge provincial compliance with national standards under CAP in *Finlay v. Canada (Minister of Finance)*, [1986] 2 S.C.R. 607.

74 R.S.C. 1985, c. F-8 as amended by S.C. 1995, c. 17. See Part V Canada Health and Social Transfer. The deletion of such detailed provisions may reflect a concern that a court may characterize the legislation as "in relation to" a matter of provincial legislative jurisdiction rather than as an exercise of the federal spending power. Consider: *Attorney-General of Canada v. Attorney-General of Ontario (The Employment and Social Insurance Act)*, [1937] A.C. 355 (J.C.P.C.) and *Winterhaven Stables v. Canada (Attorney General)* (1988), 53 D.L.R. (4th) 413 (Alta. C.A.), leave to appeal to S.C.C.denied (1989), 95 A.R. 236.

75 *Social Development Act*, R.S.A. 2000, c. S-12, s. 28. Judicial review would be available assuming that an applicant for income security benefits could afford legal counsel or benefited from *pro bono* representation.

standing an increase of approximately 15.6 percent in the Consumer Price Index (CPI). The situation is not much better in other provinces. For example, Ontario benefits increased by about 3.1 percent between 2000 and 2004, a period in which the CPI increased approximately 13.6 percent.[76] This situation is inconsistent with the full realization and acceptance of a right in individuals and a duty or obligation on the province.

On the constitutional plane, many scholars and advocates find a right to an adequate standard of living in the *Charter* section 7 "right to life, liberty and security of the person." In *Irwin Toy*,[77] the joint reasons for the decision of Dickson C.J.C. and Lamer and Wilson JJ. famously declined to decide whether the right includes economic security:

> The intentional exclusion of property from s. 7, and the substitution therefor of "security of the person" has, in our estimation, a dual effect. First, it leads to a general inference that economic rights as generally encompassed by the term "property" are not within the perimeters of the s. 7 guarantee. This is not to declare, however, that no right with an economic component can fall within "security of the person." Lower courts have found that the rubric of "economic rights" embraces a broad spectrum of interests, ranging from such rights, included in various international covenants, as rights to social security, equal pay for equal work, adequate food, clothing and shelter, to traditional property—contract rights. To exclude all of these at this early moment in the history of *Charter* interpretation seems to us to be precipitous. We do not, at this moment, choose to pronounce upon whether those economic rights fundamental to human life or survival are to be treated as though they are of the same ilk as corporate-commercial economic rights. In so stating, we find the second effect of the inclusion of "security of the *person*" to be that a corporation's economic rights find no constitutional protection in that section.

The inclusion of a right to economic security would certainly be consistent with the approach of the Human Rights Committee as expressed in its General Comment 6 on the CCPR.[78] As further expressed by John D. Whyte, "[T]here seems to be no compelling reason to view security of the

---

76 *Ontario Works Act, 1997*, S.O. 1997, c. 25; Ont. Reg. 165/99 s. 4 and Ont. Reg. 417/04, s. 1.

77 Above note 70 at para. 95.

78 Human Rights Committee, General Comment 6, Article 6 (Sixteenth session, 1982), Compilation of General Comments and General Recommendations Adopted by Human Rights Treaty Bodies, U.N. Doc. HRI/GEN/1/Rev.6 at 127 (2003).

person as exhaustively defined by reference to privacy and bodily integrity and not encompassing economic aspects of personhood."[79]

Charter litigation alleging breach of section 7, in the poverty law context, have generally not been successful as courts have held such claims not justiciable and not within the scope of the interests protected. For example, courts have rejected under *Charter* section 7 a claim concerning eviction from public housing,[80] a claim for protection of nursing home residents from alleged inadequate care,[81] a claim for an additional allowance to permit extended home care in lieu of institutional care,[82] and, most significantly, a claim concerning the adequacy of social assistance benefits.[83] In the latter case, O'Driscoll J. concluded: "In my view, section 7 does not provide the Applicants with any legal right to minimal social assistance. The Legislature could repeal the social assistance statutes (FBA and GWAA); there is no question that the Lieutenant-Governor-in-Council is empowered to increase and/or decrease the rates of social assistance."[84] The Supreme Court of Canada recently considered this issue, also in the context of the adequacy of income security benefits.

Gosselin v. Quebec (Attorney General)[85] provided the Supreme Court with the opportunity to determine the constitutional validity of a Quebec social assistance program that provided young adults under thirty years of age with a level of basic assistance approximately one-third of that provided to adults over age thirty, but that provided a further income supplement for participation in job training, community work, or educational programs. The most that a recipient could receive under this program amounted to only 55 percent of the poverty level for a single person. Ms. Gosselin commenced a class action suit challenging the validity of this social benefits program and claiming compensation for recipients under age thirty—a claim worth approximately $389 million. All levels of court rejected this claim as well as an alleged violation of equality rights. The trial judge con-

79 John D. Whyte, "Fundamental Justice: The Scope and Application of Section 7 of the *Charter*" (1983) 13 Man. L.J. 455 at 474.

80 *Bernard v. Dartmouth Housing Authority* (1988), 53 D.L.R. (4th) 81 (N.S.C.A.).

81 *Ontario Nursing Home Assn. v. Ontario* (1990), 72 D.L.R. (4th) 166 (Ont. H.C.J.).

82 *Fernandes v. Manitoba (Director of Social Services (Winnipeg Central))* (1992), 93 D.L.R. (4th) 402 (Man. C.A.).

83 *Masse v. Ontario (Ministry of Community and Social Services)* (1996), 134 D.L.R. (4th) 20 (Ont. Ct. Gen. Div.), motion for leave to appeal to Ontario Court of Appeal refused, [1996] O.J. No. 1526 (C.A.).

84 *Ibid.* at 42 (D.L.R.).

85 [2002] 4 S.C.R. 429.

cluded that section 7 of the *Charter* does not include protection of economic interests and does not include a right to freedom from poverty.[86] The three-member panel of the Quebec Court of Appeal also found that the life, liberty, and security of the person interests protected by section 7 do not include the interest claimed in this matter.[87] The Supreme Court majority, per McLachlin C.J.C. (Gonthier, Iacobucci, Major, and Binnie JJ. concurring), found no violation of *Charter* equality rights because of the absence of proof of discrimination (due to the absence of a historic disadvantage of young adults as a group) and because, rather than being arbitrary and stereotypical as claimed by Gosselin, the program responded to the needs of the subject group. More importantly for present purposes, the majority rejected the *Charter* section 7 claim.

McLachlin C.J.C., for the majority, agreed with Bastarache J., in dissent, that the section 7 interests serve as negative rights to protect against state action in the context of the justice system—that is, in the enforcement of the law.[88] Characterizing as "premature" Bastarache J.'s conclusion that section 7 is limited to the process of adjudication, McLachlin C.J.C. found it necessary to address the scope of section 7 interests more generally.[89] She applied a literal interpretation of section 7 that emphasized the word *deprive* as an internal modifier on the scope of the interests protected and rejected interpretation of section 7 as imposing a positive obligation on the state (which led her to express disagreement with the dissenting reasons of Arbour J. on this point):[90]

> Even if s. 7 could be read to encompass economic rights, a further hurdle emerges. Section 7 speaks of the right not to be deprived of life, liberty and security of the person, except in accordance with the principles of fundamental justice. Nothing in the jurisprudence thus far suggests that s. 7 places a positive obligation on the state to ensure that each person enjoys life, liberty or security of the person. Rather, s. 7 has been interpreted as restricting the state's ability to deprive people of these. Such a deprivation does not exist in the case at bar.
>
> One day s. 7 may be interpreted to include positive obligations. To evoke Lord Sankey's celebrated phrase in *Edwards v. Attorney-General for*

---

86 [1992] R.J.Q. 1647 (Sup. Ct.).
87 [1999] R.J.Q. 1033 (C.A.).
88 Above note 85 at para. 77.
89 *Ibid.* at para. 78.
90 *Ibid.* at paras. 81–83.

Canada, [1930] A.C. 124 (P.C.), at p. 136, the Canadian Charter must be viewed as "a living tree capable of growth and expansion within its natural limits": see Reference re Provincial Electoral Boundaries (Sask.), [1991] 2 S.C.R. 158, at p. 180, per McLachlin J. It would be a mistake to regard s. 7 as frozen, or its content as having been exhaustively defined in previous cases. In this connection, LeBel J.'s words in Blencoe, supra, at para. 188 are apposite:

> We must remember though that s. 7 expresses some of the basic values of the Charter. It is certainly true that we must avoid collapsing the contents of the Charter and perhaps of Canadian law into a flexible and complex provision like s. 7. But its importance is such for the definition of substantive and procedural guarantees in Canadian law that it would be dangerous to freeze the development of this part of the law. The full impact of s. 7 will remain difficult to foresee and assess for a long while yet. Our Court should be alive to the need to safeguard a degree of flexibility in the interpretation and evolution of s. 7 of the Charter.

> The question therefore is not whether s. 7 has ever been—or will ever be—recognized as creating positive rights. Rather, the question is whether the present circumstances warrant a novel application of s. 7 as the basis for a positive state obligation to guarantee adequate living standards.

> I conclude that they do not. With due respect for the views of my colleague Arbour J., I do not believe that there is sufficient evidence in this case to support the proposed interpretation of s. 7. I leave open the possibility that a positive obligation to sustain life, liberty, or security of the person may be made out in special circumstances. However, this is not such a case. The impugned program contained compensatory "workfare" provisions and the evidence of actual hardship is wanting. The frail platform provided by the facts of this case cannot support the weight of a positive state obligation of citizen support.

In relation to the claimed breach of art. 45 of the Quebec *Charter*, the majority agreed with the courts below that, coupled with article 52, which permits derogation of economic and social rights:[91]

> s. 45 requires only that the government be able to point to measures of the appropriate kind, without having to defend the wisdom of its enactments.

---

91 *Ibid.* at paras. 93–94.

This interpretation is also consistent with the respective institutional competence of courts and legislatures when it comes to enacting and fine-tuning basic social policy.

For these reasons, I am unable to accept the view that s. 45 invites courts to review the adequacy of Quebec's social assistance regime.

It is important to observe that the Supreme Court did not foreclose the possibility that section 7 of the *Charter* protects the right of every person to an adequate standard of living within the meaning of CESCR article 11; but, at the very least, we are not there yet. The key rests with acceptance of the *Charter* as imposing positive obligations on the state, a position accepted by Arbour J. in *Gosselin*:[92]

> Clearly, positive rights are not at odds with the purpose of the *Charter*. Indeed, the *Charter* compels the state to act positively to ensure the protection of a significant number of rights, including, as I mentioned earlier (at para. 320), the protection of the right to vote (s. 3), the right to an interpreter in penal proceedings (s. 14), and the right of minority English- or French-speaking Canadians to have their children educated in their first language (s. 23). Positive rights are not an exception to the usual application of the *Charter*, but an inherent part of its structure. The *Charter* as a whole can be said to have a positive purpose in that at least some of its constituent parts do.

It is important to note, however, that existence of a right does not necessitate constitutional entrenchment. Rights exist at various legal levels—from the Constitution to statutes and regulations to the common law. What is of significance is acceptance and implementation of the right.

D. THE WAY FORWARD

Implementation of Canada's international human rights obligations is not a matter for federal Canada alone. Consistent with the 1975 *Modalities and Mechanisms* document approved by responsible ministers at the Federal–Provincial Conference on Human Rights, provincial and territorial governments consent to ratification by Canada of international human rights obligations and individually undertake to affect compliance with these ob-

---

92   *Ibid.* at para. 348.

ligations.[93] Yet, as discussed earlier in this chapter, full compliance is not always realized and, as with the negative reaction of Ontario to the Human Rights Committee decision in *Waldman*, at times a government in Canada will ignore an existing international human rights obligation. Federal responses to such provincial refusals (for example, in *Waldman* and those raised by the CESCR Committee) routinely assert the challenges of federalism. Those responses attempt to explain that Canada's treaty obligations cannot be honoured in parts of the country because the constitutional power to implement them lies with provinces that are reluctant to do so.[94]

International law recognizes Canada as a sovereign unit. It accepts that the federal government is the sole entity that can enter into treaty obligations. Both notions coincide with Canadian constitutional law—that is, that the provincial and federal Crowns are sovereign entities within their respective constitutional powers and that the federal government holds the sole authority to ratify or accede to treaties. The *Vienna Convention on the Law of Treaties*[95] article 26 expresses the principle of *pacta sunt servanda*: "Every treaty in force is binding upon the parties to it and must be performed by them in good faith." However, it is wrong, in our view, to consider that only federal Canada is obliged to international human rights obligations to which the provinces have agreed to bind themselves. In such cases, the provinces (and territories) are also subject to the *pacta sunt servanda* principle.

As the provincial and federal Crowns share an equal status insofar as the Constitution allocates areas of exclusive rights of governance to those entities, sovereignty within Canada is divided. In 1892, the Judicial Committee of the Privy Council in *Liquidators of the Maritime Bank v. New Brunswick* rejected the excessively centrist views of early federal officials who considered the provinces as somewhat lesser entities.[96] That decision specifically determined that a provincial lieutenant governor serves not as a delegate of the governor general but as an equal representative of the Crown in relation to the classes of subjects of provincial legislative juris-

---

93   The one exception is Canada's ratification of the *Convention on the Rights of the Child*, which Alberta initially rejected. Shortly afterward, however, the Alberta premier sent a letter to the prime minister accepting that treaty and its obligations, but modelled closely on a treaty ratification containing a questionable reservation.

94   Federal Government Responses to Issues (10 June 1998). See online: www.canadian-socialresearch.net/uncan.htm.

95   United Nations, Treaty Series, vol. 1155, at 331 (entered into force on 27 January 1980).

96   [1892] A.C. 437.

diction: "A Lieutenant Governor … is as much the representative of Her Majesty for all purposes of provincial government as the Governor General … is for all purposes of Dominion government."[97]

When the decision to assume international human rights obligations by treaty ratification arises from the conjoint consents of the federal and provincial crowns, it binds all of Canada and invokes legal obligations from both the provincial and federal bodies charged with implementing those obligations. In conveying that consent to the international community, the federal Crown acts on behalf of all the provincial Crowns that have agreed to assume those obligations. The critical point is that the obligations undertaken do not lie at the federal level alone. Instead, they are shared with the provinces.

Two definitions in the *State Immunity Act*[98] confirm the previous jurisprudence that, in an international sense, sovereignty applies to the provinces and territories of Canada. The definition of *foreign state* extends to:

a) any sovereign or other head of the foreign state or of any political subdivision of the foreign state while acting as such in a public capacity,

b) any government of the foreign state or of any political subdivision of the foreign state, including any of its departments, and any agency of the foreign state, and

c) any political subdivision of the foreign state.[99]

The second relevant definition is that of "political subdivision," which is expressed to include "a province, state or other like political subdivision of a foreign state that is a federal state."[100] As provinces enjoy such sovereignty, they must be obliged to adhere to their freely undertaken international human rights obligations.

In Canadian Aboriginal law, the honour of the Crown is frequently invoked to justify compliance with undertakings ("treaties") between local representatives of the Crown and the Aboriginal peoples of Canada. The Crown is presumed to act in good faith. The Supreme Court of Canada affirmed the function of the honour of the Crown in *R. v. Marshall*.[101] In that case, Binnie J. for the majority approved the statement of Gwynne J. in *Province of Ontario v. Dominion of Canada and Province of Quebec; In re Indian*

---

97 *Ibid.* at 443.
98 R.S.C. 1985, c. S-18.
99 *Ibid.*, s. 2.
100 *Ibid.*
101 [1999] 3 S.C.R. 456.

Claims: "that the terms and conditions expressed in those instruments as to be performed by or on behalf of the Crown, have always been regarded as involving a trust graciously assumed by the Crown to the fulfilment of which with the Indians the faith and honour of the Crown is pledged, and which trust has always been most faithfully fulfilled as a treaty obligation of the Crown."[102] Surely, the Crown that engages with Aboriginal peoples is the same Crown which engages with foreign sovereigns. As such, it is beyond question that provinces are bound to implement their international human rights obligations.

Our governments have struggled with the problem of ensuring the enforcement of international human rights obligations arising from treaties that the federal government has ratified after obtaining the agreement of the provinces. At times, political and diplomatic negotiations between governments have failed to ensure full compliance with those obligations. Should any government—provincial or federal—steadfastly refuse to respect the international human rights obligations it has accepted, they should be referred to our courts. The courts can achieve a legal resolution by employing the customary and conventional rules of international law governing treaty obligations and state responsibility to resolve the breach. Those rules complement the constitutional notions of "sovereignty" that are reflected in the *Labour Conventions* case and affirmed consistently throughout Canadian constitutional jurisprudence.

The concept of state sovereignty—that is, the notion that all states are formally equal in the eyes of the law—constitutes the foundation of international law. It is reflected in article 2.1 of the *Charter of the United Nations* and reconfirmed in the 1970 *Declaration on Friendly Relations*.[103] Canadian constitutional law coincides with the international legal notion of sovereignty in that both the federal and provincial governments enjoy equality of legal authority over their respective heads of jurisdiction within the parameters set by the Constitution; that is, they enjoy the powers to prescribe (to create binding laws), to adjudicate (to settle disputes), and to enforce (to coerce individuals and entities to obey the law or punish them for violating the law). However, once a state or a government agrees to an international

---

102 (1895), 25 S.C.R. 434 at 511–12.

103 *Declaration on Principles of International Law Concerning Friendly Relations and Co-operation among States in Accordance with the Charter of the United Nations*, UNGA Res. 2625 (XXV), UN GAOR, 25th Sess., Supp. No. 28, at 121, UN Doc. A/8028 (1971), adopted by consensus on 24 October 1970.

obligation and, as part of that obligation, to permit an international body to adjudicate disputes arising from it, the state is bound to implement the obligation and defer to the findings of the international adjudicative body. The Permanent Court of International Justice, in its Advisory Opinion concerning *Polish Nationals in Danzig*,[104] is a commonly quoted reference employed to demonstrate a basic customary rule of international law: once states assume an international legal obligation, they are expected to adhere to it. That advisory opinion even provides that no state can "adduce ... its own Constitution with a view to eroding obligations incumbent upon it under international law or treaties in force."[105] The first rule embodied, in the term *pacta sunt servanda*, is codified in article 26 of the *Vienna Convention on the Law of Treaties*.[106] The second rule, prohibiting a state from invoking its internal law to evade treaty obligations, is codified in article 27 of that treaty.

Canadian courts should accept the jurisdiction to employ the rules of international law to enforce international human rights obligations only when negotiations with the sovereign in breach of the obligation (either provincial or federal) have clearly failed. The party alleging a breach of an international obligation should have the right to invoke the jurisdiction of Canadian courts in order to ensure the non-existence of federal–provincial complicity to ignore the obligation. Both provincial and federal Crowns should have the right to invoke the jurisdiction of Canadian courts to ensure that each entity respects the same obligations.

Some commentators and courts consider that permitting domestic legal action to ensure international human rights compliance threatens to undermine the notion of parliamentary sovereignty. This is unfounded, as it would not arise unless a federal or provincial sovereign had violated the obligation it had made to other Canadian sovereigns. The legal action would not be to review the merits of the international adjudication but to ensure that the federal–provincial agreement to accept the international legal obligation is respected.

If a provincial or federal government believes that it should not adhere to an international human rights obligation it has assumed, it remains free to reject the obligation by withdrawing from the agreement. A province would do so by withdrawing from the federal–provincial accord that

---

104 (1931), Advisory Opinion, P.C.I.J. (Ser A/B) No. 42.
105 *Ibid.* at 24.
106 Above note 95.

prompted the federal government to ratify the treaty and the federal government would do so by formally withdrawing from the treaty obligation. Such occurrences should be rare—just as governments seldom rely on the *Charter* section 33 "notwithstanding" clause.

A second approach is to recognize that Canada's international human rights obligations are not only conventional in nature. Instead, as noted above in relation to both civil and political rights and economic, social and cultural rights, such rights were not created by the CCPR and the CESCR nor are they created by the 1948 Universal Declaration. These rights are of longstanding and universal acceptance. They have been given expression and affirmation in the Universal Declaration and the two International Covenants but must also be considered as customary international law. In *Mack et al. v. Canada (Attorney General)*,[107] the Ontario Court of Appeal confirmed the dismissal of a class action seeking damages and other remedies for discrimination suffered by Chinese immigrants to Canada in the relation to the "head tax" imposed by federal legislation in the late nineteenth and early twentieth centuries.[108] The claimants grounded their action, in part, on an alleged breach of pre-1947 customary international law prohibiting racial discrimination. Citing Ian Brownlie, the court accepted that customary international law depends on satisfaction of two elements: 1) sufficient state practice; and 2) acceptance of that practice as legally binding.[109] In *Mack*, the claimants failed to establish either element but the court, considering the situation if they had succeeded, observed that a critical limitation on incorporation of customary international law into the domestic legal order is the primacy given to both inconsistent legislation and judicial decisions.[110] Thus, subject to that limitation and recognizing the developed sense of both recognition and binding acceptance of international human rights post-1947, individual Canadians may find their courts willing to declare that Canada, a province, or a territory (as appropriate) is in breach of an international human right under customary international law. The logic of *Mack* certainly leaves that option open.

---

107 (2002), 60 O.R. (3d) 737.

108 *The Chinese Immigration Act, 1885,* S.C. 1885, c. 71; *The Chinese Immigration Act, 1923,* S.C. 1923, c. 38.

109 Ian Brownlie, *Principles of Public International Law,* 5th ed. (Oxford: Clarendon Press, 1998) at 4–7.

110 Above note 107 at para. 32, again quoting Brownlie, *Principles of Public International Law, ibid.* at 42.

To succeed, claimants before Canadian courts must have access to lawyers and judges with knowledge or, at least, exposure to international law. That may be more the exception than the rule, given the optional nature of international law courses in Canadian law faculties. To date, courts have been receptive to the use of the International Covenants to aid in the interpretation of *Charter* rights.[111] They may be receptive to the invitation to do more.

The Standing Senate Committee on Human Rights issued a report in December 2001. The report records the realization by committee members: "that one of the major issues needing to be addressed is the gap that has developed between our willingness to participate in human rights instruments at the international level and our commitment to ensuring that the obligations contained in these instruments are fully effective within this country."[112] Among its recommendations is that the federal *Human Rights Code* express its connection to Canada's international human rights obligations, a recommendation easily appropriate for provincial human rights codes as well.

The way ahead is not certain; crucial to progress is recognition and acceptance of the obligation to implement Canada's international human rights obligations at all levels of government. If not achieved voluntarily through implementation of the International Covenants and other obligations, the time for a different tack may be nigh—that Canada's international human rights obligations are not just conventional but are grounded in customary international law. We think counsel for Ontario in the *Labour Conventions* case expressed it well when arguing before the Privy Council that "[t]he *Treaty of Versailles* is binding on Ontario"; so are Canada's international human rights obligations.

---

111 *R. v. Advance Cutting & Coring Ltd.*, [2001] 3 S.C.R. 209 at para. 12:
This Court has regularly made reference to and relied upon the aforementioned international documents in interpreting fundamental freedoms in the *Charter*. As stated in *Canadian Egg Marketing Agency v. Richardson*, [1998] 3 S.C.R. 157 at para. 57, "the development of international human rights [is] an important influence leading to an entrenched guarantee of rights and freedoms in this country."
112 Hon. R. Andreychuk, "Chair's Forward," in Standing Senate Committee on Human Rights, *Promises to Keep: Implementing Canada's Human Rights Obligations* (Ottawa: The Committee, 2001) at para. 3.

16

The Role of International Treaties in the Interpretation of Canadian Intellectual Property Statutes

DANIEL J. GERVAIS

A. INTRODUCTION

The relationship between international and domestic intellectual property norms is growing in both scope and depth. In scope, first: the number of areas that are regulated by international norms has grown rapidly in the recent past. Since 1995, the Agreement on Trade-Related Aspects of Intellectual Property Rights (TRIPS),[1] a part of the Uruguay Round package administered by the World Trade Organization (WTO), imposes minimum standards concerning almost all intellectual property rights, including copyrights, patents, trademarks, confidential information, and designs.[2] In depth: TRIPS language is generally much more precise than that of previous treaties. For example, while article 9 of the Paris Convention[3]—a World Intellectual Property Organization (WIPO)-administered instrument—only includes a "wish" that member countries provide for seizure of infring-

---

1   *Agreement Establishing the World Trade Organization, Annex 1C: Agreement on Trade-Related Aspects of Intellectual Property Rights,* 15 April 1994, 1869 U.N.T.S. 299, 33 I.L.M. 81 (being Annex 1C of the *Marrakesh Agreement Establishing the World Trade Organization,* 1867 U.N.T.S. 3; 33 I.L.M. 1125). [TRIPS Agreement].
2   This incorporation of intellectual property rules, which had traditionally been developed and administered by the World Intellectual Property Organization (WIPO), a specialized agency of the United Nations, into the trade realm may set a precedent for other norm-making activity at the WTO in areas such as labour or environmental standards. See Jagdish Bhagwati, *In Defense of Globalization* (Oxford: Oxford University Press, 2004) at 182–85.
3   *Paris Convention for the Protection of Industrial Property,* 20 March 1883, 828 U.N.T.S. 305, most recently revised 14 July 1967 [Paris Convention].

ing goods at the point of importation, articles 51 to 59 of TRIPS provide an extremely detailed procedure that must be made available to rights-holders, including strict maximum time periods, to obtain a similar remedy.

As well, and perhaps because of these changes, and the fact that WTO agreements are "enforceable" between WTO members, courts (in particular the Canadian Supreme Court) and litigants are taking a closer look at TRIPS and other intellectual property instruments.[4] The impact of international norms has now moved beyond classic doctrines of ensuring compatibility between national and international law wherever possible. Recent decisions are informed by policy analyses of the need for uniformity of trade rules and their impact on Canadian innovation and business.

This short chapter, after a statement of the classical doctrine of reliance on international treaties as a subsidiary source of law, will look at the most salient recent cases and provide an analysis of the ongoing changes in the use and importance of international intellectual property norms in Canadian jurisprudence. The purpose of the chapter is thus twofold. First, it will attempt to demonstrate that the way in which international norms are now being used by Canadian courts at the appellate level has changed and is increasingly "trade-related" and policy-based. Put differently, the main use of international norms is not (or not only) to interpret statutes in light of international norms, but rather to apply Canadian norms in ways that mirror international developments and are conducive to a better trade environment. Second, it will draw the practitioner's attention to the importance of relying on international norms before Canadian courts, and on the consequences of increasing reliance on those norms, in particular by the Supreme Court. The last part of the chapter will also offer some thoughts on the potential influence that Canadian courts could play in the interpretation of international norms.

B. THE CLASSIC PRINCIPLE

The classical exposition of how international treaties are to be applied by courts when interpreting national laws was stated very adroitly by my colleague Professor Ruth Sullivan:

---

4   Under the WTO dispute-settlement system. See *Agreement Establishing the World Trade Organization: Annex 2* 15 April 1994, 1869 U.N.T.S. 40:33 I.L.M. 1226. See also online: www.wto.org/english/tratop_e/dispu_e/dispu_e.htm and Daniel Gervais, *The TRIPS Agreement: Drafting History and Analysis*, 2d ed. (London: Sweet & Maxwell, 2003) at 3 and 337–45.

the legislature is presumed to respect the values and principles enshrined in international law, both customary and conventional. These constitute a part of the legal context in which legislation is enacted and read. In so far as possible, therefore, an interpretation that reflects these values and principles is preferred.[5]

Customary and conventional international law norms should, in principle, be used as part of the legal context in such a way as to maximize the degree of compatibility between the (domestic) statutory norm and the international one, unless the language of the statute is unambiguously incompatible.[6] The relevant international norms are those by which Canada is bound, either because they are contained in a treaty to which Canada is party or by a rule of customary law. In the former case, the *Vienna Convention on the Law of Treaties*[7] is, of course, a useful reference. In the latter, article 38(1) of the *Statute of the International Court of Justice*[8] offers a starting point.[9]

---

5   Ruth Sullivan, *Sullivan and Driedger on the Construction of Statutes*, 4th ed. (Toronto: Butterworths, 2002) at 422.

6   The subsidiary nature of international norms was emphasized, for example, in *Daniels v. White*, [1968] S.C.R. 517, where the Court stated (at para. 65):

> [P]arliament is not presumed to legislate in breach of a treaty or in any manner inconsistent with the comity of nations and the established rules of international law. It is a rule that is not often applied, because if a statute is unambiguous its provisions must be followed, even if they are contrary to international law. ... [T]he plain words of a statute could not be disregarded in order to observe the comity of nations and the established rules of international law. However, the principle of construction was recognized as applicable in a proper case.

7   *Vienna Convention on the Law of Treaties*, 23 May 1969, 1155 U.N.T.S. 331. See in particular arts. 11–15.

8   *Statute of the International Court of Justice*, 26 June 1945, 59 Stat. 1055, 1060, T.S. No. 993, art. 38, para. 1(b). See also *Reference re Newfoundland Continental Shelf*, [1984] 1 S.C.R. 86.

9   The sources are:
   a.   international conventions, whether general or particular, establishing rules expressly recognized by the contesting states;
   b.   international custom, as evidence of a general practice accepted as law;
   c.   the general principles of law recognized by civilized nations;
   d.   subject to the provisions of article 59, judicial decisions, and the teachings of the most highly qualified publicists of the various nations, as subsidiary means for the determination of rules of law.

There is no need to belabour this well-documented point here.

There are a number of decisions by the Supreme Court of Canada that explicate how the principle should be applied. Among them of course is *Pushpanathan v. Canada (Minister of Employment & Immigration).*[10] The question in that case was whether a determination of exclusion, under article 1F(C) of the *Convention Relating to the Status of Refugees*[11] by the United Nations High Commissioner for Refugees, affected how Canada should decide a claim for refugee status. Bastarache J. explained the linkage as follows:

> Since the purpose of the Act incorporating Article 1F(C) is to implement the underlying Convention, the Court must adopt an interpretation consistent with Canada's obligations under the Convention. The wording of the Convention and the rules of treaty interpretation will therefore be applied to determine the meaning of Article 1F(C) in domestic law.[12]

Referring to its decision in *Canada (Attorney General) v. Ward*[13] and the Vienna Convention, the Court then noted that in the Court of Appeal:

> In deciding on the relative weight to be accorded the various interpretative sources made available under the Vienna Convention, Strayer J.A. found that the terms "purposes and principles of the United Nations" were relatively clear. He was also of the opinion that the *travaux préparatoires* were confused, ambiguous, or unrepresentative, and therefore, "completely unhelpful". The UNHCR Handbook, which was accepted as a valid source under Article 31(3)(b) of the Vienna Convention, was considered "far from emphatic" as to the meaning of Article 1F(c). Finally, the categorization of the purpose of the Convention as a "'human rights' instrument" did not favour the applicant."[14]

The Supreme Court overturned the Court of Appeal, finding it had erred in dismissing the objects and purposes of the treaty and in according virtually no weight to the indications provided in the *travaux préparatoires*. It also noted that the "starting point of the interpretative exercise is, first, to define the purpose of the Convention as a whole, and, second, the purpose and place of Article 1(C) within that scheme."[15]

10   [1998] 1 S.C.R. 982 [*Pushpanathan*].
11   *Convention Relating to the Status of Refugees, 28 July 1951,* 189 U.N.T.S. 150.
12   *Pushpanathan, ibid.* at para. 51.
13   [1993] 2 S.C.R. 689.
14   *Pushpanathan,* above note 10 at para. 55.
15   *Ibid.* at para. 56.

Three years later, in *R. v. Sharpe,*[16] the Court applied the United Nations' *Convention on the Rights of the Child.*[17] Bastarache J.[18] noted that the "protection of children from harm is a universally accepted goal. While this Court has recognized that, generally, international norms are not binding without legislative implementation, they are relevant sources for interpreting rights domestically; ... In *Slaight Communications,*[19] this Court explained that a balancing of competing interests must be informed by Canada's international obligations."

Let us turn now to how this principle has surfaced in recent intellectual property decisions.

C. APPLICATION OF INTERNATIONAL NORMS IN INTELLECTUAL PROPERTY CASES

1) Supreme Court of Canada

Since 1875[20] and until 2000, there had been relatively few intellectual property cases heard by the Supreme Court. In recent years, however, leave to appeal was granted in several cases, which will be the focus of the following pages. In almost every one of those recent decisions the Supreme Court relied on international intellectual property norms.

The first case that should be mentioned in this context is *Harvard College v. Canada (Commissioner of Patents),*[21] where, in a 5–4 decision, the Court found that higher life forms, such as plants or animals, could not be patented in Canada. To be patentable in Canada, an invention must be a "new and useful art, process, machine, manufacture or composition of matter."[22] Because plants and animals are neither processes nor machines, and because it is difficult to consider them as "manufactures," the central question before the Court was whether life forms are "compositions of matter." Life, the majority stated, could not be defined "only" as a composition of matter, because life transcends matter. The Court concluded that

---

16 [2001] 1 S.C.R. 45 [*Sharpe*].

17 *Convention on the Rights of the Child,* 20 November 1989, 1577 U.N.T.S. 3.

18 *Sharpe,* above note 16 at paras. 175 & 176. Bastarache J. wrote an opinion on behalf of L'Heureux-Dubé, Gonthier JJ., and himself that concurred in the result with the majority, but on different grounds.

19 *Slaight Communications v. Davidson,* [1989] 1 S.C.R. 1038 at 1056–57.

20 The year the Court was established.

21 [2002] 4 S.C.R. 45 [*Harvard College*].

22 *Patent Act,* R.S.C. 1985, c. P-4, s. 2.

higher life forms did not fit the statutory definition of patentable material contained in the Act.[23] However, the Court allowed the patent on the process used to produce the modified gene.[24]

The majority decision relied on international norms according to the classic principle discussed above. Bastarache J., writing the majority opinion, said:

> [T]he respondent refers to the World Trade Organization's *Agreement on Trade Related Aspects of Intellectual Property Rights* (TRIPS), and the *North American Free Trade Agreement* (NAFTA), which both contain an article whereby members may "exclude from patentability" certain subject matter, including plants and animals other than micro-organisms. The respondent argues that it is apparent from this provision that plants and animals are considered patentable, unless specifically excluded from patentability. I see little merit to this argument since the *status quo* position in Canada is that higher life forms are not a patentable subject matter, regardless of the fact that there is no explicit exclusion in the *Patent Act*. In my view, the fact that there is a specific exception in TRIPS and NAFTA for plants and animals does however demonstrate that the distinction between higher and lower life forms is widely accepted as valid.[25]

The minority decision went much further and used both international norms and the policy context to support an expansion of patentability of biotechnological inventions. Binnie J. noted:

> Intellectual property has global mobility, and states have worked diligently to harmonize their patent, copyright and trademark regimes. In this context, the Commissioner's approach to this case sounds a highly discordant note. Intellectual property was the subject matter of such influential agreements as the *International Convention for the Protection of Industrial Property (Paris Convention)* as early as 1883. International rules governing patents were strengthened by the *European Patent Convention* in 1973, and, more recently, the World Trade Organization *Agreement on Trade-Related Aspects of Intellectual Property Rights* (TRIPS) in 1994. Copyright was the subject of the *Berne Convention for the Protection of Literary and Artistic*

---

23   *Ibid.*
24   Known as an "oncogene" because it promoted cancer in mice bearing the modified gene.
25   *Harvard College,* above note 21 at para. 205.

Works[26] in 1886, revised by the *Berlin Convention of 1908* and the *Rome Convention* of 1928. ... The mobility of capital and technology makes it desirable that comparable jurisdictions with comparable intellectual property legislation arrive (to the extent permitted by the specifics of their own laws) at similar legal results.[27]

Arguably, the minority is relying on international norms to make "policy statements." To state that "the mobility of capital and technology makes it desirable that comparable jurisdictions with comparable intellectual property legislation arrive (to the extent permitted by the specifics of their own laws) at similar legal results" certainly appears to go beyond the classic principle of compatibility of domestic statutes with "black-letter" international norms and in fact calls for the uniformity of (trade) rules in response to globalization. From a trade perspective, the minority opinion also logically adopts an instrumentalist/utilitarian view of intellectual property: intellectual property is neither a human right[28] nor a property right, but an instrument designed to maximize creativity and innovation (or the commercial development thereof) without imposing unduly high welfare costs. This view would be confirmed two years later in a copyright case,[29] the same year as *Monsanto Canada Inc. v. Schmeiser,*[30] a patent case in which the Court "clarified" *Harvard* by stating: first, that while a plant (a higher life form) per se could not be patented, biotechnologically engi-

---

26 *Berne Convention for the Protection of Literary and Artistic Works,*1886, 828 U.N.T.S. 221. As revised until 1971. [*Berne Convention*] [footnote inserted by the author].

27 *Harvard College,* above note 21 at paras. 12–13.

28 See, for example, art. 27(2) of the *Universal Declaration of Human Rights:* "(2) Everyone has the right to the protection of the moral and material interests resulting from any scientific, literary or artistic production of which he is the author."

29 Such a view was expressed even more clearly in 2000 in *Théberge v. Galeries d'art du Petit Champlain Inc.,* [2002] 2 S.C.R. 336 at paras. 30–31 [*Théberge*]:

> The *Copyright Act* is usually presented as a balance between promoting the public interest in the encouragement and dissemination of works of the arts and intellect and obtaining a just reward for the creator (or, more accurately, to prevent someone other than the creator from appropriating whatever benefits may be generated).... The proper balance among these and other public policy objectives lies not only in recognizing the creator's rights but in giving due weight to their limited nature. In crassly economic terms it would be as inefficient to overcompensate artists and authors for the right of reproduction as it would be self-defeating to undercompensate them.

> The case is discussed below.

30 [2004] 1 S.C.R. 902.

neered cells of the plant could be; and second, that growing a plant containing the modified genetic sequence would infringe the patent. In practical terms, though formally unpatentable, higher life forms can thus be protected by patent by applying a broad infringement doctrine to patents protecting individual cells. The trend to use international treaty norms is apparent also in *Monsanto*, but more along the lines of the classic principle. In her dissent, Arbour J. actually used TRIPS to *limit* patent protection:

> In *Harvard College, supra*, both the majority and the minority called for Parliament's intervention on the issue of patenting higher life forms. As things stand, my conclusion on the scope of Monsanto's patent claims that is determinative of both validity and infringing use is not contrary to art. 27(1) of *TRIPS* whereby Canada has agreed to make patents available for any invention without discrimination as to the field of technology. My conclusion does not violate, and indeed is supported by art. 27(3)(b) of *TRIPS* ... Allowing gene and cell claims to extend patent protection to plants would render this provision of *TRIPS* meaningless. To find that possession of plants, as the embodiment of a gene or cell claim, constitute a "use" of that claim would have the same effect as patenting the plant. Therefore, my conclusion on both the scope of the claims and the scope of use is consistent with Canada's international obligations under *TRIPS*.[31]

International treaty norms were also mentioned in a number of copyright cases. The first recent Supreme Court case to rely substantially on such norms was *Théberge v. Galeries d'art du Petit Champlain Inc.*[32] The Court had to decide whether transferring the ink from a poster onto a canvas (a process known as "canvas-backing") constituted an infringement of Quebec painter Claude Théberge's copyright in the underlying artistic work (a painting). Writing for the majority this time,[33] Binnie J. opens with a clear reference to international intellectual property norms and the desirability of uniformity of rules among Canada's trading partners:

> Canada has adhered to the *Berne Convention for the Protection of Literary and Artistic Works* (1886) and subsequent revisions and additions, and other international treaties on the subject including the *Universal Copyright Convention* (1952). In light of the globalization of the so-called "cultural industries," it is desirable, within the limits permitted by our own

---

31   *Ibid.* at paras. 164 and 166–67.

32   See *Théberge*, above note 29.

33   As noted above, in *Harvard College* he wrote the dissenting opinion.

legislation, to harmonize our interpretation of copyright protection with other like-minded jurisdictions.

In *Théberge*, the Court uses international treaty norms for two reasons, namely: 1) to interpret the statute in a way that is in conformity with applicable treaties (the classic approach); and 2) to ensure uniformity, basically because globalization of economic and trade relations makes uniformity desirable. In other words, there are two different reasons to rely on the TRIPS Agreement and other intellectual property instruments. First, there is a normative argument of keeping Canada as much as possible from infringing its multilateral commitments. Second, there's a desire to increase economic "predictability," thereby making it easier for Canadian companies to compete internationally.

This was confirmed by *Society of Composers, Authors & Music Publishers of Canada v. Canadian Assn. of Internet Providers.*[34] The case dealt with the liability of Internet Service Providers (ISPs) for music transmitted over the Internet by their subscribers. ISPs usually have no control over such content and the Court indeed found that they were the wrong target for music authors who wanted to get paid for music transmissions. The analytical framework adopted by the Court includes a detailed comparative analysis and is testimony to the fact that recourse to international treaties is not motivated only by normative concerns. Nor was the Court trying to rely on customary law by admixing international and foreign (domestic) norms. Its purpose was to identify "global policy trends." In the words of Binnie J.:

> In the United States, unlike Canada, detailed legislation has now been enacted to deal specifically with the liability of Internet intermediaries ... Australia has enacted its *Copyright Amendment (Digital Agenda) Act 2000* ... The European Commission has issued a number of directives, as will be discussed. Parliament's response to the *World Intellectual Property Organization's (WIPO) Copyright Treaty*, 1996, ("WCT") and the *Performances and Phonograms Treaty*, 1996,[35] remains to be seen. In the meantime, the courts must struggle to transpose a *Copyright Act* designed to implement the *Berne Convention for the Protection of Literary and Artistic Works* of 1886,[36] as revised in Berlin in 1908, and subsequent piecemeal amend-

---

34 [2004] 2 S.C.R. 427 [*SOCAN v. CAIP*].

35 1996, 36 I.L.M. 76 [WPPT].

36 See *Berne Convention*, above note 26.

ments, to the information age, and to technologies undreamt of by those early legislators.[37]

In trying to interpret provisions of the Canadian Act, the Court (both the majority opinion by Binnie J. and LeBel J.'s partial dissent) refers to the *WIPO Copyright Treaty* (WCT), a treaty that Canada had signed but not ratified and that was not in force at the time of the facts under consideration:[38]

> Canada is a signatory but not yet a party to the WIPO Copyright Treaty. This treaty responded to the development of the Internet and other on-demand telecommunications technology. Article 8 provides that:
>
> > ... authors of literary and artistic works shall enjoy the exclusive right of authorizing any communication to the public of their works, by wire or wireless means, including the making available to the public of their works in such a way that members of the public may access these works from a place and at a time individually chosen by them.
> >
> > ...
>
> The "making available" right is generally exercised at the point of transmission. This does not deny the interest of the country of reception but avoids, as a matter of policy, a "layering" of royalty obligations in different countries that are parties to the WCT.[39]

The Court also considered European and other foreign legislation. The majority's reliance on the WCT was clearly not strictly normative (the treaty was not ratified in Canada). Together with the laws of our major foreign partners, it was seen as a sign of "things to come." The partial dissent by LeBel J. also uses the WCT and WPPT, apparently in keeping with the classical recourse to international treaty norms. However, because the two trea-

---

37 *SOCAN v. CAIP*, at para. 43.

38 1996, 36 I.L.M. 65 [WCT]. Clearly, the government does not consider itself bound by the WCT at this stage. In a statement issued jointly by the ministers of heritage and industry in March 2005 (*Government Statement on Proposals for Copyright Reform*, online at: www.pch.gc.ca/progs/ac-ca/progs/pda-cpb/reform/statement_e.cfm), the government notes that it intends to table a bill precisely to implement the WCT and a sister treaty, the WPPT.

39 *SOCAN v. CAIP*, above note 34 at paras. 65–66.

ties were neither in force at the time[40] nor ratified by Canada,[41] this required some additional justification. In discussing whether Canadian copyright law should apply to music transmissions outside Canada,[42] LeBel J. stated:

> Article 5 of the Berne Convention calls for the territorial treatment of copyright; however, the Berne Convention does not specifically address the communication of works over the Internet.[43] Canada is a signatory to the WCT, but it is not yet party to the treaty; it has yet to ratify it. The Board refused to interpret the Act in light of the WCT because the WCT is "not binding in Canada since it has been signed but not ratified by the Canadian Government" (at p. 448). I disagree. Although Canada has not ratified the treaty, this does not mean that it should not be considered as an aid in interpreting the Act.
>
> ... As McLachlin C.J. recently held, even though international norms are generally not binding without domestic implementation, they are relevant in interpreting domestic legislation: see R. v. Sharpe ..., at para. 175. Parliament is presumed not to legislate in breach of a treaty, the comity of nations and the principles of international law. This rule of construction is well established: see Daniels v. White .... Although the Copyright Act has not yet been amended to reflect the signing of the WCT, I believe this canon of interpretation is equally applicable to the case at bar.[44]

The rule of construction referred to by LeBel J. is well established. It was usually applied, however, to treaties both in force and ratified or acceded to by Canada, which was not the case with the WCT. LeBel J.'s reliance on *Sharpe* is also debatable.[45] In that case, when the Court stated that "generally, international treaty norms are not binding without legislative implementation, they are relevant sources for interpreting rights domestically," it was not referring to norms not yet in force.[46]

---

40 The WCT came into force on 6 March 2002 and the WPPT on 20 May 2002. The tariff filed by SOCAN that was the object of the *SOCAN v. CAIP* litigation covered the years 1996, 1997, and 1998.

41 Which is still the case as of this writing.

42 That is, whether an Internet communication occurs in Canada. See *SOCAN v. CAIP*, above note 34 at para. 134.

43 Indeed. The Convention was last revised in 1971.

44 *SOCAN v. CAIP*, above note 34 at paras. 148–50.

45 See above note 16 and accompanying text.

46 Though of course Canada has signed the WCT, which may produce effects under international law.

A final Supreme Court case that deserves to be mentioned here is *CCH Canadian Ltd. v. Law Society of Upper Canada*.[47] The Court had to decide *inter alia* whether reported judicial decisions were protected by copyright and whether photocopying of those decisions and other materials by patrons of the Law Society's Great Library, or by the staff of library on behalf of LSUC members not physically present in the library, constituted an infringement of that copyright. On the first question, there is little doubt that the text of a judicial decision itself is "original"[48] enough to be protected by copyright. However, the rights belong to the Crown.[49] Private legal publishers of judicial decision were arguing that they held a *separate* copyright stemming from their original formatting of the text, the addition of keywords, headnotes, etc. To succeed, the publishers had to convince the Court that those additions and changes were themselves "original." Because the notion of originality is not defined in the *Copyright Act*,[50] the Court relied on international treaties. Interestingly, those treaties do not explicitly define the notion, but the *travaux préparatoires* offer a significant degree of guidance.[51] In the words of the chief justice:

> The idea of "intellectual creation" was implicit in the notion of literary or artistic work under the *Berne Convention for the Protection of Literary and Artistic Works* (1886), to which Canada adhered in 1923, and which served as the precursor to Canada's first *Copyright Act*, adopted in 1924. ... Professor Ricketson has indicated that in adopting a sweat of the brow or industriousness approach to deciding what is original, common law countries such as England have "depart[ed] from the spirit, if not the letter, of the [Berne] Convention" since works that have taken time, labour or money to

---

47 [2004] 1 S.C.R. 339 [*CCH*].
48 Originality is the fundamental condition for a work to be protected by copyright, both in Canada and internationally. See generally, Daniel Gervais, *La notion d'œuvre dans la Convention de Berne et en droit comparé* (Genève: Librairie Droz, 1998). The second fundamental condition is that the work must either belong to the category of literary or artistic works or be a compilation.
49 *Copyright Act.*, R.S.C. 1985, c- C-42, s. 12.
50 *Ibid.* See Daniel Gervais, "Feist Goes Global: A Comparative Analysis of the Notion of Originality in Copyright Law" (2002–3) 49 J. Copyright Soc'y USA 949.
51 See Sam Ricketson, "The Boundaries of Copyright: Its Proper Limitations and Exceptions: International Conventions and Treaties" (1999) I.P.Q. 56; Daniel Gervais, "The Compatibility of 'Skill & Labour' with the Berne Convention and the TRIPS Agreement" (2004) 2 Eur. I.P. Rev. 75; and, Gervais, *La notion d'œuvre*, above note 48.

produce but are not truly artistic or literary intellectual creations are accorded copyright protection.[52]

Applying the Berne Convention principles, the Court concluded that publishers could get copyright protection for certain aspects of the headnotes, but not for mechanical or intellectually trivial exercises such as formatting.

TRIPS incorporated, by reference, the normative content of the Berne Convention.[53] TRIPS added new norms to the Berne Convention (and hence was known as a "Berne-plus" agreement), but not a definition of originality. As rightly noted by the chief justice, however, there is a definition implicit in Berne, and Canada is bound by this implicit definition.

It may be useful to compare the approach chosen by the Supreme Court in *CCH* with the approach taken by two WTO dispute-settlement panels. In a 2000 decision in a dispute between the United States and the European Union, a WTO panel[54] considered whether an exception contained in section 110(5) of the US *Copyright Act*[55] was compatible with the TRIPS Agreement and, because of its incorporation into TRIPS, also with the Berne Convention. The exception in question, a victory for the powerful lobby of bars, hotels, and restaurants, exempted from the payment of music royalties[56] almost all hotels, bars, restaurants, and smaller food stores in the United States. To be justifiable under Berne and TRIPS, the United States had to show that the exemption was covered by an exception contained in those instruments. However, because there was no specific exception that applied, the United States could only rely on a provision of Berne (and now TRIPS) known as the "three-step test." That test[57] is a "filter" for small exceptions not otherwise provided for in Berne. One of the questions that the WTO panel had to decide in interpreting the three-step test was whether the Berne *travaux préparatoires*, including a reference to "understandings"

---

52   *CCH*, above note 47 at para. 19.

53   Namely, arts. 1 to 21—except arts. 6*bis* and 10(3), which deal with moral rights. TRIPS Article 9(1). See also Daniel Gervais, *TRIPS Agreement*, above note 4 at 123–32.

54   United States – Section 110(5) of the US Copyright Act: Report of the Panel, WTO document WT/DS160/R of 15 June 2000.

55   17 U.S.C.

56   In this case the right to perform music "in public," that is, within the establishments, which often use loudspeakers to play radio or recorded music. In Canada, those uses would typically be licensed by SOCAN, which represents authors of music and lyrics.

57   Contained in *Berne Convention*, above note 26, art. 9(2), and TRIPS Agreement, above note 1, art. 13.

about the meaning of certain provisions, were binding also in a TRIPS context. The panel concluded that the entire *"acquis"* of Berne, including the *travaux*, had been made part of TRIPS, not just the text of the Convention itself.[58] The panel also found that a statement contained in the general report of a conference at which the Berne Convention had been revised could constitute an "agreement" as defined by article 31(2)(a) of the *Vienna Convention*.[59]

Another WTO panel, in a dispute concerning the Canadian *Patent Act*, was called upon to interpret article 30 of TRIPS, which applies the language of the Berne three-step test to patents.[60] That panel also referred to the history of the test in the Berne Convention. It thus seems that the Supreme Court's reference to the Berne *acquis* (though somewhat indirectly) and its conclusions on the notion of originality are both compatible with that *acquis*[61] and with WTO practice.

2) Federal Court of Canada

International intellectual property treaties were mentioned in most of the appellate decisions that led to the Supreme Court decisions discussed in the previous section. We will leave those aside for the purposes of this chapter. There are, however, a number of other Federal Court decisions that relied directly on international treaty norms and that are worth mentioning here. In two cases, the court relied fairly heavily on international norms. In two other cases, it was very reluctant to do so.

---

58   WTO document WT/DS160/R of 15 June 2000 at paras. 6.62–6.63.

59   *Ibid.* at para. 6.53.

60   The case is *Canada—Patent Protection of Pharmaceutical Products*, 17 March 2000, WTO document WT/DS114/R [*Canada—Patent Protection*]. Canada amended its *Patent Act* twice in response to decisions by the WTO Dispute-Settlement Body (DSB) that found the Act incompatible with the Agreement. Apart from the *Canada—Patent Protection* decision, which dealt with the so-called stockpiling exception that allowed generic drug manufacturers to begin manufacturing a patented molecule up to six months prior to the expiry of the patent (ss. 55.2(2) and (3) of the *Patent Act* were repealed by 2001, c. 10, s. 2(1)), another decision, *Canada—Term of Patent Protection*, doc. WT/DS170/AB/R of 12 October 2000, dealt with the term of protection of patents at the time of entry into force of TRIPS. S. 45, which was found to be in violation of TRIPS, was repealed and substituted by 2001, c. 10, s.1.

61   See Daniel Gervais, "Canadian Copyright Law Post CCH" (2004) 18 I.P.J. 131.

In *Tele-Direct (Publications) Inc. v. American Business Information Inc.,*[62] the Federal Court had to decide whether a telephone directory was a "compilation" for the purposes of the *Copyright Act.* Décary, J.A., explained his decision as follows:

> The definition of "compilation" must be interpreted in relation to the context in which it was introduced. Simply put, it was introduced as a result of the signature of the North American Free Trade Agreement[63] and with the specific purpose of implementing it. It is therefore but natural when attempting to interpret the new definition to seek guidance in the very words of the relevant provision of NAFTA which the amendment intends to implement.
>
> ...
>
> I do not wish to be interpreted as saying that Canadian courts, when interpreting these provisions, should move away from following the Anglo-Canadian trend. I am only suggesting that where feasible without departing from fundamental principles, Canadian courts should not hesitate to adopt an interpretation that satisfies both the Anglo-Canadian standards and the American standards where, as here, it appears that the wording of Article 1705 of NAFTA and, by extension, of the added definition of "compilation" in the Canadian Copyright Act, tracks to a certain extent the wording of the definition of "compilation" found in the United States Copyrights Act.[64]

The court was thus using international norms both to find the meaning of statutory terms and to ensure a certain degree of harmony with United States law and practice in the wake of NAFTA, though not as explicitly as the Supreme Court in *Théberge* or in the *Harvard* dissent. Interestingly, the court also found that Canada's acceptance of NAFTA should inform the intended meaning of certain provisions of the *Copyright Act*[65] even where the Act was not amended by the implementing legislation.

---

62   [1998] 2 F.C. 22 (C.A.), leave to appeal to S.C.C. refused, [1997] S.C.C.A. No. 660 (21 May 1998) [*Tele-Direct*].

63   *North American Free Trade Agreement Between the Government of Canada, The Government of the United Mexican States and the Government of the United States of America*, 17 December 1992, Can. T.S. 1994 No. 2 [NAFTA].

64   *Tele-Direct*, above note 62 at paras. 14–18 (footnotes omitted).

65   See *North American Free Trade Agreement Implementation Act*, S.C. 1993, c. 44, 53(2).

Another example worth mentioning in this context is *Baker Petrolite Corp. v. Canwell Enviro-Industries Ltd.*[66] The Federal Court of Appeal had to interpret whether the notion of novelty in patent law[67] had changed since the 1993 amendments[68] that defined a novelty-defeating disclosure as one that renders the subject matter of the invention "accessible to the public." While the application of this criterion is fairly straightforward in the case of, for example, a scientific or trade publication clearly describing the invention, it is less clear whether a disclosure takes place when the invention (or a product embodying or resulting from the use of the invention) is sold or simply "used in public." In *Baker Petrolite* the court concluded that if a sale or use in public allows a "person skilled in the art" to understand all the essential elements of the invention without adding his or her own ingenuity, then that sale or use defeats the novelty and thus makes it impossible to obtain the patent—unless the disclosure takes place within the "grace period" of twelve months provided for in section 28.2 of the *Patent Act*. Litigants in the case based a considerable part of their argument on international and foreign norms and this is reflected in the decision. In trying to discern Parliament's intention, the court used both an international treaty and comparative tools, referring to the *European Patent Convention* of 1973 and the *North American Free Trade Agreement, 1992.*[69]

In two cases involving an international pharmaceutical company, the Federal Court had to decide whether and, if so, to what extent it could directly rely on international intellectual property treaties. First, in *Pfizer Inc. v. R.*,[70] the well-known pharmaceutical company was seeking relief by relying directly on article 33 of the TRIPS Agreement. The basis for the relief claimed was a minimum term of protection for all patents of not less than twenty years from the filing date of the patent application. Prior to TRIPS, Canada granted patents a term of seventeen years from the date of issue of the patent. In its initial implementation of TRIPS, Canada only applied the twenty-year term to patents filed on or after 1989. Because TRIPS entered

---

66 2002 FCA 158.

67 According to s.2 of the *Patent Act* (see above note 22 and accompanying text), to be patented in Canada an invention must be new. In most cases, this means that the invention must not have been disclosed "more than one year before the filing date by the applicant, or by a person who obtained knowledge, directly or indirectly, from the applicant" (*Patent Act*, s. 28.2(1)(a)).

68 S. C. 1993, c. 15, s. 33. The amendments entered into force in 1996.

69 Above note 63.

70 [1999] 4 F.C. 441 (T.D.)

into force on 1 January 1995, there were still many patents in force then granted prior to 1989 and to which the shorter term applied. In the case at bar, Pfizer's patent had been granted in October 1980.

The conclusion reached in the case is of little practical importance because Canada amended the *Patent Act* after it was found to be in violation of article 33 by the WTO.[71] However, the decision is interesting to the extent that the court refused to "reinterpret" the Act in a way that was compatible with TRIPS article 33. In fact, not only did the court not follow the broad policy approach adopted in a number of Supreme Court decisions, but the decision also seems conservative even when analyzed against the backdrop of the classic principle of statutory interpretation.

Relying on the *WTO Implementation Act*,[72] the government claimed that "the aggregate effect of [the Act] is to bar any person from commencing any type of legal action under either the Act itself or the underlying WTO Agreement without the consent of the Attorney General."[73] It asked the court to conclude that the plaintiffs' action was barred because the attorney general's consent had not been given in the case. The court examined the detailed implementation of WTO rules and TRIPS in particular. It then concluded that TRIPS per se did not form part of Canadian law:

> The central issue in this case is whether Parliament, in enacting the *WTO Implementation Act*, gave legal effect or translated into federal law that Agreement as a whole and, in particular, its annexed *TRIPS Agreement* or section 33 thereof.... In my view, much guidance to answer the central question considered here is derived from the recent Supreme Court of Canada judgment in *Re British Columbia (Attorney General) v. Canada (Attorney General); An Act respecting the Vancouver Island Railway*.[74] ... I have come to the conclusion it is plain and obvious that Parliament did not legislate into federal domestic law the *WTO Agreement* and, in particular, section 33 of the *TRIPS Agreement*, which is essential to the success of Pfizer's declaration. Parliament, in my view, manifestly indicated its intention as to how it was implementing the *WTO Agreement* and its annexed *TRIPS Agreement* or any part thereof.[75]

---

71 See above note 60.

72 *World Trade Organization Agreement Implementation Act*, S.C. 1994, c. 47.

73 *Pfizer Inc. v. R*, above note 70, at para. 11.

74 [1994] 2 S.C.R. 41.

75 *Pfizer Inc. v. R.*, above note 70 at paras. 36–45.

Then in *Pfizer Canada Inc. v. Canada (Attorney General),*[76] the Canadian subsidiary of the same multinational company was trying to get the Federal Court to interpret the notion of "filing date" for patent application, in light of applicable international treaties. Strayer J.A. was not convinced:

> I am of the view that there is no need to resort to these instruments in this case. I base this conclusion on the long-established jurisprudence that while Parliament is presumed not to intend to legislate contrary to international treaties or general principles of international law, this is only a presumption: where the legislation is clear one need not and should not look to international law.... The appellants nevertheless say this principle has been modified by the Supreme Court in *National Corn Growers Assn. v. Canada (Canadian Import Tribunal).*[77] They take that case to mean that "international treaties are always a proper aid to be used to interpret domestic legislation." But in that case Gonthier J. put it thus:
>
> > If the convention may be used on the correct principle that the statute is intended to implement the convention then, it follows, the latter becomes a proper aid to interpretation, and, more especially, may reveal a latent ambiguity in the text of the statute even if this was 'clear in itself' [at 1371–72].
> >
> > ...
>
> The other important international obligation invoked by the appellants is found in article 4.B of the Paris Convention.... [T]he Paris Convention does not, as I understand it, confer immediate enforceability in Canada of a patent applied for or obtained in another member country.[78]

Here again we see that the Court is strikingly less enthusiastic about the application of international norms.

3) Analysis

The Federal Court of Appeal has been more reluctant to use international treaties to interpret and, *a fortiori*, reinterpret, existing intellectual property statutes than the Supreme Court, looking instead at the intention expressed by Parliament in the implementing legislation (if any). However, the type of action launched by Pfizer is likely the first of many. The two

---

76 2003 FCA 138, leave to appeal to S.C.C. refused (2003), 27 C.P.R. (4th) vi.
77 [1990] 2 S.C.R. 1324.
78 *Pfizer Canada Inc. v. Canada (Attorney General),* above note 76 at paras. 20–24.

Pfizer cases dealt with patent law, but similar conclusions can be drawn with respect to copyright, trademarks, and any other intellectual property rights governed by international treaties and, in particular, TRIPS.[79] As the area of intellectual property is regulated ever more deeply and broadly by international norms,[80] and the policy flexibility left for individual nations is proportionally reduced, the number of cases in which a provision of a domestic intellectual property statute or other legal rule[81] can be tested against an international norm will increase. The boundaries of the classical doctrine (interpreting the statute with a view to ensuring maximum compatibility with applicable international norms[82]) may be redefined to encompass broader policy issues, including an analysis of the economic and trade-related considerations that undergird the instrumentalist view of intellectual property[83] adopted by the Supreme Court, one which seems

---

79 These would include, in addition to those already mentioned, industrial designs, layout of computer chips, geographical indications, and confidential information, in particular clinical test information submitted to obtain marketing approval (see art. 39 of the TRIPS Agreement).

80 See Daniel Gervais, "The Internationalization of Intellectual Property: Challenges from the Very Old and the Very New" (2002) 12 Fordham I.P. Media & Ent. L.J. 929.

81 Because "intellectual property" as defined in TRIPS includes confidential information (see *ibid.*), one could also apply this reasoning to common law (or civil law) doctrines protecting trade secrets and other forms of secret commercial information from misappropriation and/or unfair competition.

82 See above notes 5-7 and accompanying text.

83 The concept of utilitarianism deals with the maximisation of the good to society. It is linked to the writings of Jeremy Bentham and John Stuart Mill. Instrumentalism assesses actions in relation to their objective. Thus, actions are tools to achieve certain goals. The instrumentalist utilitarianism view is to see law as an instrument to achieve the greatest good for society. Thus, intellectual property is useful because it encourages creativity and encourages people to share their creations with others thus benefiting society as a whole. The utilitarian rationale for intellectual property rights has been described as follows:

> The utilitarian argument is that intellectual property rights provide incentives to produce new intellectual objects. By assigning property rights to creators, an incentive is in place for people to undertake the expense and time to invent new products or develop new ideas. If intellectual property protection is removed, the argument goes, then there will be no incentive to produce intellectual objects because people will be free to copy the object without compensating the creator. The utilitarian argument weighs the long-term development of the society against the short-term drawback of assigning exclusive production rights to a creator [footnote omitted].

Robert L. Ostergard, Jr., "Intellectual Property: A Universal Human Right?" (1999) 21 *Hum. Rts. Q.* 156 at 162. See also Stephen R. Munzer, *A Theory of Property* (New York: Cambridge University Press, 1990).

fully consistent with the TRIPS approach.[84] In parallel, private litigants can be expected to use international norms to convince national courts to reinterpret intellectual property norms and standards. Indeed, it now behoves Canadian practitioners to use international norms wherever possible to convince courts of the interpretation of the statute or legal doctrine favourable to their clients' interests.[85] The policy direction indicated by Parliament, and adopted by the Supreme Court, of minimizing differences between Canada and its main trading partners in areas that may negatively affect trade in informational goods and services or goods whose value is essentially derived from their ideational content is certain to take on greater prominence in the coming years. This approach is arguably supported by

---

84   Graeme Dinwoodie & Rochelle Dreyfuss, "International Intellectual Property Law and the Public Domain of Science" (2004) 7 J. Int'l Econ. L. 431 at 447–48:

The [TRIPS] Agreement, as an instrument of intellectual property law, must strike a balance between sufficient levels of protection to stimulate the desired social and commercial activity undertaken by first-comers, and sufficient limits on those rights to ensure the maximum socially useful exploitation of that activity. It partly achieves this balance substantively by allocating rights as between private and public interests, that is, between producers and users of intellectual property. But TRIPS, like any international agreement, must also deal with issues such as sovereignty, diversity, and legitimacy that pervade international relations. It must accordingly allocate power between supranational and national institutions, between national and international laws. In the TRIPS context, that allocation has the additional effect of giving member states an important role in striking the producer/user balance of intellectual property law.

This debate goes beyond intellectual property proper. It is related to the question of the public funding of scientific research. Proponents of greater public funding argue that it would increase access to scientific research (and that would increase the pace of innovation) while allowing research efforts to be devoted to orphan or tropical diseases, areas where the profit motive may not be sufficient to warrant efforts by private laboratories.

Empirical data is still being developed and the validity of the thesis has not (yet) been conclusively demonstrated. For a survey of arguments, see John C. Low, "Finding the Right Tool for the Job: Adequate Protection for Research Tool Patents in a Global Market?" (2005) 27 Hous. J. Int'l L. 345. For a more theoretical analysis, see Keith E. Maskus & Jerome H. Reichman, "The Globalization of Private Knowledge Goods and the Privatization of Global Public Goods" (2004) 7 J. Int'l Econ. L. 279.

85   See Louis LeBel & Gloria Chao, "The Rise of International Law in Canadian Constitutional Litigation: Fugue or Fusion? Recent Developments and Challenges in Internalizing International Law" (2002)16 Sup. Ct. L.Rev (2d) 23; Stéphane Beaulac, "On the Saying That 'International Law Binds Canadian Courts'" (2003) 29:3 Canadian Council on International Law Bulletin 1; and Gib van Ert, "International law does bind Canadian courts: a reply" (2004) 30:1 Canadian Council International Law Bulletin 1.

the assumption that rational, public-minded government will seek to minimize the transaction costs of international cooperation.[86]

Although the approach taken by the Federal Court of Appeal is not uniform, it seems that the road ahead, as mapped by the Supreme Court, is clear. Beyond the need for uniform trade and trade-related rules, one could discern an attempt to apply intellectual property statutes so as to maximize the innovation potential of Canadians and Canadian enterprises. That is particularly true of the strong *Harvard College* dissent and of the opinions penned by the chief justice in *Monsanto* and *CCH*. These considerations led the Supreme Court to a different set of conclusions in the two other copyright decisions, namely *Théberge* and *SOCAN v. CAIP*, where the statute was interpreted more narrowly and where the interest of Canadians was perceived to be to allow use of copyright content without authorization and/ or limiting the reach of the author's exclusive rights in favour of "balance."

In the five Supreme Court decisions since 2002 examined earlier in the chapter, a constant has been the reference to international intellectual property instruments not only, as in traditional jurisprudence, to interpret the relevant statute(s), but also to determine the underlying policy objectives. Those decisions show that intellectual property is not an end in itself. Copyright is not there to "protect" authors (or other owners of copyright), but to maximize the creation, production, and dissemination of knowledge and access thereto. Patents are there as part of a broader social contract to "incentivize" and promote access to innovation. To put it differently, protection of intellectual property rights is not an end but a means to achieving that end. This implies that the level of protection must be properly calibrated.

That conclusion seems consonant with the displacement of intellectual property negotiations. Those rules were initially developed in a "pure" circle of intellectual property, epitomized by the Paris and Berne Conventions, both housed in the World Intellectual Property Organization (WIPO).[87] At the international level, norm-setting activity moved in 1986 to the GATT, and the set of norms that emerged at the end of that process was incorporated into a new instrument, the TRIPS Agreement, at the inception of the WTO on 1 January 1995.[88] The pragmatic, instrumentalist approach of

---

86 See John K. Setear, "An Iterative Perspective on Treaties: A Synthesis of International Relations Theory and International Law" (1996) 37 Harv. Int'l L.J. 139 at 174.

87 See online: www.wipo.int.

88 TRIPS Agreement, above note 1 at para. 3.

trade law, the principal objective of which is not there to "protect" property or traders but to maximize legitimate trade (which includes a degree of protection for goods and persons, but only to the extent necessary), has infused intellectual property with a new approach, and one that the Supreme Court seems to have embraced fully.[89]

Practitioners of intellectual property would be well advised to take account of the approach chosen by the Supreme Court, one that reflects the transfer of jurisdiction in intellectual property to the domain of trade rules. Claiming a right as ordinary "property" that "deserves" on Lockean grounds, or as a human right, might fall on deaf ears. The path laid down by the Supreme Court emphasizes the need to show the social welfare impacts of protection—and the related search for "balance." If that is not the way Parliament intended intellectual property statutes to be interpreted and applied, it would have to say so in upcoming legislative amendments.

A few thoughts, before concluding, on whether the appropriation of international treaty norms by Canadian courts, and in particular the Supreme Court, might be a two-way street. Increasingly, courts in various countries are called upon to interpret TRIPS or other international instruments. In two cases dealing with the "three-step test,"[90] the WTO adopted dispute-settlement reports that interpreted certain TRIPS provisions[91] as including the *travaux préparatoires* of another instrument, the Berne Convention, which was incorporated into TRIPS. Yet, since 1995, out of nearly three hundred cases filed under the *WTO Dispute-Settlement Understanding (DSU)*,[92] only seven TRIPS cases led to a decision by a panel and two by the appellate body. This leaves large parts of TRIPS, including dozens

---

89 There would be much more to say on the property-based vs. instrumentalist theories of intellectual property of course. For our purposes, it seems fair to say that the lobbies that pushed for moving of international intellectual property norms in the trade arena could be expected to live with the pragmatism of trade rules, rather than defend pre-trade views based on property, theft, and piracy.

90 The test, borrowed by TRIPS drafters from art. 9(2) of the Berne Convention, limits exceptions to exclusive rights to cases that serve a special policy purpose, do not interfere with normal commercial exploitation, and do not unreasonably prejudice the legitimate interests of rights-holders. TRIPS Agreement, above note 1, arts. 13, 26(2) and 30, respectively.

91 World Trade Organization, *United-States-Section 110(5) of the US Copyright Act*, Report of the Panel, 15 June 2000, WTO Document WT/DS160/R; *Canada—Patent Protection*, above note 60.

92 Above note 4.

of provisions of other conventions incorporated in TRIPS by reference,[93] to be interpreted.

As national courts are increasingly called upon to provide interpretations of those norms to determine the compatibility of their own legislation, a national layer of jurisprudence of international intellectual property rules may emerge. As Professor Dinwoodie noted in that respect:

> In the classical system, national courts had very little role to play in the construction of international intellectual property law. Litigation involved national rights…. National courts are, however, beginning to tackle multinational cases and thus contribute to the creation of international norms.[94]

D. CONCLUSION

Canadian courts are occasionally called upon to interpret statutes in light of relevant international norms. According to the classical doctrine of statutory interpretation, courts should try to ensure compatibility between domestic statutes and (binding) international norms wherever possible. This was true also of cases involving intellectual property rights.

In recent years, however, under the impulsion of the Supreme Court, international norms have taken on a different hue. Beyond a simple compatibility analysis, the Supreme Court and, in a few cases, lower courts as well have signalled the desirability of ensuring compatibility and uniformity of rules governing trade with our main trading partners. Since 1995, that includes intellectual property norms contained in the WTO TRIPS Agreement. The analysis is informed by a perceived need to maintain and enhance Canada's competitiveness and innovation, while not hampering the free flow of information and knowledge. Those are seen as competing objectives in maximizing general welfare. The view may be characterized as instrumentalist.

---

93 Arts. 1–21 (minus 6*bis* and 10(3)) of the Berne Convention (Paris Act, 1971) and its Appendix (minus art. IV(3)); arts. 1-12 and 19 of the Paris Convention; arts. 2–7 (minus 6(3)), 12 and 16(3) of the *Treaty on Intellectual Property in Respect of Integrated Circuits* (known as the "Washington Treaty"). See arts. 2(1), 9(1), and 35 of the TRIPS Agreement, above note 1.

94 Graeme Dinwoodie, "The International Property Law System: New Actors, New Institutions, New Sources" in *Proceedings of the 98th Annual Meeting of the American Society of International Law* (2004) at 216. A symposium on that theme was held at the Chicago-Kent Program in Intellectual Property Law in October 2001. Papers were published in (2002) 77 Chi.-Kent L. Rev.

In parallel, litigants have begun to use international norms to buttress arguments in favour of one interpretation or another of Canadian intellectual property statutes. In certain cases, litigants asked courts, unsuccessfully, to impose obligations on the federal government that had not been expressly implemented in domestic legislation. In a number of cases already decided, and in many more to come, international norms constitute a strong support for interpreting or reinterpreting extant rules. Given the increasing internationalization of rules and globalization of economic relations, that trend is likely to increase rapidly in the coming years.

17

The Effect of International Conventional Criminal Law on Domestic Legislative Initiatives since 1990

DOUG BREITHAUPT[*]

A. INTRODUCTION

Any discussion of the relationship between international and domestic law would be incomplete without an examination of the relationship that exists in the criminal law domain. This chapter is principally concerned with the effect that international conventional criminal law has had on domestic legislative initiatives since 1990. It looks at the role of criminal law in Canada; it examines the remarkable growth of international conventional criminal law since 1990; it highlights the added impetus for the development of criminal law at the global, regional, and national levels in support of a new global consensus on collective security; and it explains Canada's role in support of the development and implementation of international conventional criminal law.

The growth of international conventional criminal law since 1990 has been considerable and has had an undeniable impact on domestic criminal law in Canada. This growth continues unabated because criminal law issues are at the forefront of international, regional, and domestic agendas, and the influence of international conventional criminal law on domestic criminal law is likely to take on an increased importance in coming years. Canada has an opportunity to shape that growth in the future, as it has in the past.

---

[*]   The views expressed by the author in this paper do not necessarily represent the views and the position of the Department of Justice of Canada.

There is a common understanding—both in Canada and internationally—that criminal law can be used as an effective means to forge international cooperation to combat common threats, as well as to advance shared interests, such as respect for the rule of law, democracy, and human rights.

For government criminal law policy-makers, addressing policy from a global and domestic perspective has become part of the way of doing business. For Parliament, the provinces and territories, the courts, non-governmental organizations, and the public at large, international criminal law issues are also becoming increasingly relevant. This development is consistent with the traditional role of criminal law in Canada, although the scope of criminal law in Canada has been expanded considerably as a result of international initiatives.

B. THE ROLE OF CRIMINAL LAW IN CANADA

Pursuant to section 91(27) of the *Constitution Act, 1867*, the Parliament of Canada has the responsibility for making criminal law in Canada.

The criminal law has a public character and is a statement of public policy. At its root, the state seeks to prosecute and punish an accused person for conduct that Parliament has decided, on behalf of Canadian society, to be serious, harmful, and deserving of being dealt with through the criminal law process and attracting criminal law sanctions, including possible imprisonment.

The purpose of sentencing (after a finding of guilt for a criminal offence) is to "contribute, along with crime prevention initiatives, to respect for the law and the maintenance of a just, peaceful and safe society by imposing just sanctions."[1] Of the various sentencing objectives, many are community-oriented. For example, these objectives include denunciation of the criminal conduct (as an affront to the community), general deterrence (to discourage others from engaging in criminal behaviour), reparations for harm done to the community, and promoting a sense of responsibility in offenders by their acknowledgment of harm caused by them to the community.[2]

In 1982, in *The Criminal Law in Canadian Society*, the government of Canada outlined its views about the purpose of the criminal law in Canada:

---

1 Section 718 of the *Criminal Code*, R.S.C. 1985, c. C-46, as amended.
2 *Ibid.*

[T]he criminal law has, and should continue to have, two major purposes:

1. preservation of the peace, prevention of crime, protection of the public—security goals; and
2. equity, fairness, guarantees for the rights and liberties of the individual against the powers of the state, and the provision of a fitting response by society to wrongdoing—justice goals.[3]

C. THE GROWTH OF INTERNATIONAL CRIMINAL LAW SINCE 1990

International law derives its source content from international conventions and customs, the general principles of law recognized by civilized nations, and the writings of distinguished publicists.[4] In the case of international criminal law, however, given the need to respect the principle of legality, only the first three of these sources apply.[5]

International criminal law has been described as "the law that governs international crimes."[6] International crimes are proscribed conducts resulting principally from conventional international law, but they may also be based on customary international law.[7] *Jus cogens* (or universal international) crimes are said to include the following: aggression; genocide; crimes against humanity; war crimes; piracy; slavery and slave-related practices; and torture.[8] These crimes are described as affecting "the interests of the world community as a whole because they threaten the peace and security of humankind and because they shock the conscience of humanity."[9]

However, it is largely through the multilateral treaty-making process that states develop binding international criminal law; the development and implementation of international conventional criminal law will be the

---

3 Canada, *The Criminal Law in Canadian Society* (Ottawa: Department of Justice, 1982) at 40. This document provided background information about the criminal law review and, among other things, offered a formal statement about the appropriate scope, purpose, and principles of the criminal law.

4 Article 38 of the *Statute of the International Court of Justice.*

5 M. Cherif Bassiouni, "The Sources and Content of International Criminal Law: A Theoretical Framework" in M.C. Bassiouni, ed., *International Criminal Law*, 2d ed., vol. 1: *Crimes* (Ardsley, NY: Transnational, 1999) at 4.

6 Kriangsak Kittichaisaree, *International Criminal Law* (Oxford: Oxford University Press, 2001) at 3.

7 For a discussion of the sources of substantive international criminal law, see Bassiouni, above note 5 at 31–33.

8 *Ibid.* at 41.

9 *Ibid.* at 42.

focus of this chapter. States assume international obligations when they ratify or accede to international criminal law or related conventions. Such conventions call upon states parties to criminalize in their own laws certain agreed-upon conduct. In negotiating and in implementing such conventions, states have made the calculation that it would be advantageous collectively for them to criminalize such behaviour in their national legislation and, invariably, they also agree in the same conventions to various international cooperation measures in respect of that conduct, such as the provision of extradition and mutual legal assistance.

At this juncture, international criminal law and the international legal regime rely on six modalities of interstate cooperation in penal matters: extradition, mutual legal assistance in penal matters, transfer of prisoners, seizure and forfeiture of illicit proceeds of crime, recognition of foreign penal judgments, and transfer of penal proceedings.[10]

International criminal law is by no means a new phenomenon. Indeed, M. Cherif Bassiouni has listed 274 major criminal law instruments applicable to 25 international crimes that had been entered into between 1815 and 1996, most of which had been in place by 1990.[11] That said, the growth of international conventional criminal law and the large number of significant developments in this field since 1990 have been quite dramatic.

Various factors can be offered to explain this development, including the impact of globalization, the end of the Cold War, and the increase in the number of democratic states, as well as the influence of international organizations. This phenomenon will also be studied by reviewing developments and initiatives in relation to particular subject matter.

1) Globalization

Globalization has had the effect of transforming the world into a "global village." Improvements in such areas as communications, the transfer of funds, transportation, and travel have given rise to the globalization of the world economy. These same advances, however, are also well suited to, and create opportunities for, criminals who seek to use them for their own benefit.

It is well understood by states that international and transnational crime can only be effectively addressed through international cooperation. This

---

10   *Ibid.* at 5.
11   M. Cherif Bassiouni, *International Criminal Law Conventions and their Penal Provisions* (Irvington-on-Hudson, NY: Transnational, 1997) at 20 and 45–78.

cooperation is often accomplished through the development of international and domestic criminal law. Since 1990, criminal law has increasingly been called upon as a means to further international cooperation to battle threats, such as terrorism, organized crime, corruption, and cybercrime.

2) The End of the Cold War and the Increase of Democracies

The fall of the Berlin Wall on 9 November 1989 marked the end of the Cold War. This development led to the creation of a number of states in transition in Central and Eastern Europe that had formerly been part of the Soviet Union. As nascent democracies, these states set about to establish new institutions and governance structures. They also became prey to criminal elements. More generally, the end of the Cold War put an end to protracted Cold War geopolitical struggles and freed up individual states around the world, as well as the international community at large, to take an increased interest in and to energize their efforts to address rule of law, governance, and crime issues through the development of international conventional criminal law. Indeed, an interesting fact to note is that since 1990 the number of democracies around the world has nearly doubled.[12]

The importance of the phenomenon of globalization and the end of the Cold War as factors explaining the development of international conventional criminal law appears to be reflected in UN General Assembly Resolution 46/152 (18 December 1991), which created the UN crime prevention and criminal justice program. The resolution indicates that the General Assembly was alarmed by "the scope of criminality and by the dangers posed to the welfare of all nations by the rising incidence of crime generally and by the many forms of crime that have international dimensions," as well as by "the high cost of crime ... especially in its new and transnational forms."[13] The very first principle of the statement of principles in the resolution read as follows:

> 1. We recognize that the world is experiencing very important changes resulting in a political climate conducive to democracy, to international cooperation, to more widespread enjoyment of basic human rights and fundamental freedoms, and to the realization of the aspirations of all nations to economic development and social welfare. Notwithstanding these developments, the world today is still beset by violence and other forms of

---

12 See online: www.un.org/millennium/sg/report/ch3.htm at para. 192.
13 UN GA Resolution 46/152 of 18 December 1991.

serious crime. These phenomena, wherever they occur, constitute a threat
to the maintenance of the rule of law.[14]

3)   International Organizations

There is a growing web of international conventional criminal law, which
owes its genesis to a wide variety of international organizations and initiatives. As Canada is a member state of many of these organizations, Canada
has both the opportunity and the obligation to participate in their activities.

These international organizations have been created on a functional or
regional basis because like-minded states have seen the need and utility
of having such forums within which they can work together to address
matters of common concern, promote shared values, and forge closer cooperation. In part, the creation of such organizations, and of special subject-
specific working groups within such organizations, has been in response
to developments that states believe need to be addressed collectively. An additional factor to take into account is that once these organizations (and the
working groups) are established, they begin to take on a life of their own
and consequently generate new initiatives as a means of sustaining their
further existence. Political commitments made in relation to various subject matters within these organizations can and often do ultimately lead to
the negotiation of international criminal law conventions.

The focus of the ensuing discussion will necessarily be trained upon
those global, regional, and other international organizations within which
Canada is a member or has a special relationship. These are many in number and, therefore, this survey will be representative rather than exhaustive. Attention will be given to their activities since 1990, where criminal
law issues have played a particularly prominent role.

The UN has been very active in the development of international law, including international criminal law. International criminal law and related
conventions have been developed under the auspices of various UN bodies,
including the International Maritime Organization, the International Civil
Aviation Organization, the International Atomic Energy Agency (IAEA),
the UN Office on Drugs and Crime, as well as by ad hoc committees of the
UN General Assembly (UN GA).

As mentioned, on 18 December 1991, the UN GA adopted Resolution
46/152, which approved the statement of principles and the program of ac-

---

14   *Ibid.*

tion for the UN Crime Prevention and Criminal Justice Program. Whereas the first principle of the statement of principles focused on security goals (that is, the threat posed by crime to the maintenance of the rule of law), the second principle called attention to justice goals:

> 1. We believe that justice based on the rule of law is the pillar on which civilized society rests. We seek to improve its quality. A humane and efficient criminal justice system can be an instrument of equity, constructive social change and social justice, protecting basic values and peoples' inalienable rights. Every right of the individual should enjoy the protection of the law against violation, a process in which the criminal justice system plays an essential role.[15]

The statement of principles also observed that the growing international nature of crime required new and sufficient responses and that the international dimensions of many criminal offences highlighted the urgent need for states to build linkages to permit mutual legal assistance and extradition. Principle 7 conceptualized the ultimate objective of such a program:

> 7. We also recognize that democracy and a better quality of life can flourish only in a context of peace and security for all. Crime poses a threat to stability and to a safe environment. Crime prevention and criminal justice, with due regard to the observance of human rights, is thus a direct contribution to the maintenance of peace and security.[16]

The UN International Drug Control Program (UNDCP), established in 1991, was renamed the UN Office on Drugs and Crime (UNODC) in 2002. Among other things, the UNODC is tasked with strengthening international action against drugs, crime, and terrorism.[17] More generally, the UNODC Crime Program is responsible for crime prevention, criminal justice, and criminal law reform and has numerous functions, including promoting internationally recognized criminal justice standards and norms, as well as Global Programs against Corruption, Trafficking in Human Beings, and Transnational Organized Crime.[18] The UN Commission on Crime Prevention and Criminal Justice, established in 1992, is the

---

15   *Ibid.* This approach reflected in the initial two principles is reminiscent of the purpose of the criminal law as espoused in *The Criminal Law in Canadian Society*, above note 3.
16   *Ibid.*
17   See online: www.unodc.org/unodc/about.html.
18   See online: www.unodc.org/unodc/en/crime_cicp.html.

forum within which UN member states discuss ways to address crime and adopt resolutions that are often ultimately endorsed by the UN GA.[19]

Every five years since 1955, the international community has gathered together at UN congresses on crime prevention and criminal justice to set down standards, norms, and guidelines in criminal justice. These norms and standards have largely formed the foundation upon which UN work in the area of criminal justice rests; they have played a key role in the development of international principles; and they have been reflected in subsequent UN treaties.[20]

The 10th UN Congress on the Prevention of Crime and the Treatment of Offenders, held in Vienna from April 10 to 17, 2000, adopted the *Vienna Declaration on Crime and Criminal Justice: Meeting the Challenges of the Twenty-First Century*, which was subsequently endorsed by the UN GA, through Resolution 55/59 (4 December 2000). Plans of action for the implementation of the Vienna Declaration were subsequently developed, calling for national and international actions in the following areas:

- transnational organized crime;
- corruption;
- trafficking in persons;
- smuggling of migrants;
- illicit manufacturing of and trafficking in firearms, their parts and components, and ammunition;
- money-laundering;
- terrorism;
- crime prevention;
- witnesses and victims of crime;
- prison overcrowding and alternatives to incarceration;
- high-technology and computer-related crime;
- juvenile justice;
- the special needs of women in the criminal justice system;
- standards and norms; and

---

19   See online: www.unodc.org/en/crime_cicp_commission.html. The commission had been preceded by the Committee on Crime Prevention and Control, which had a narrower focus.

20   UN, *Fifty Years of United Nations Congresses on Crime Prevention and Criminal Justice: Past Accomplishments and Future Prospects, Report of the Secretary General of the Congress*, A/CONF.203/15 (24 March 2005) at 9–12.

- restorative justice.[21]

The Group of Eight (G8) addresses a wide range of international economic, political, and security issues. Following the 1995 Summit, held in Halifax, a group of experts worked to examine ways to fight international crime more effectively. The following year the fruits of their efforts—*Forty Recommendations to Combat International Crime*—were approved by heads of state at the G8 Summit in Lyon, France. Thereafter, subgroups were established to look at subject-specific issues. In October 2001, the decision was taken in Rome to combine meetings of the G8 Lyon Group (fighting international crime) with the new Roma Group (fighting international terrorism).[22] G8 justice ministers meet annually. At their 2004 meeting, for example, justice ministers focused on terrorism, border and transportation safety, cybercrime, and fighting corruption.[23]

The Financial Action Task Force (FATF) is an intergovernmental body that was established in 1989 at the G8 Summit. It is charged with developing and promoting policies to combat money-laundering and terrorist financing. In 1990, the FATF set out its list of *Forty Recommendations* for a comprehensive plan of action against money-laundering, which was revised in 1996 and updated in 2003. In October 2001, the FATF developed *Eight Special Recommendations on Terrorist Financing*. FATF countries are committed to multilateral monitoring and peer review. Canada is a member.[24]

With thirty-four participating member states (including Canada as of 1990), the Organization of American States (OAS) promotes, among other things, democracy, human rights, and peace and security. In the criminal law area since 1990, it has adopted treaties dealing with matters, such as terrorism, torture, corruption, forced disappearance of persons, firearms, and mutual legal assistance in criminal matters, but it also addresses other matters, including drugs and trafficking in persons.[25] In April 2004, ministers of justice addressed diverse topics, including hemispheric cooperation against transnational organized crime and against terrorism, mutual legal assistance in criminal matters and extradition, cybercrime, corrup-

---

21 UN GA Res. 56/261.

22 See online: www.usdoj.gov/ag/events/g82004/g8_background.html.

23 See online: www.usdoj.gov/ag/events/g82004/index.html.

24 See online: www1.oecd.org/fatf/AboutFATF_en.htm. A *Ninth Special Recommendation on Terrorist Financing* was adopted in 2004.

25 See online: www.oas.org/main/main.asp?sLang=E&sLink=../../documents/eng/oasinbrief.asp.

tion, trafficking in persons, especially women and children, and violence against women.[26]

The Organization for Economic Co-operation and Development (OECD) is an intergovernmental organization composed of thirty member countries (including Canada) that share a commitment to democracy and to a market economy.[27] Although primarily an economic and social policy forum, the OECD has also addressed criminal law matters through the *Convention on Combating Bribery of Foreign Public Officials in International Business Transactions*, which entered into force in 1999.

Founded in 1949, the Council of Europe (COE) includes forty-six member states and five official observer countries.[28] The COE was established to defend human rights, parliamentary democracy, and the rule of law. Since 1990, it has developed a number of international criminal law conventions, including treaties on terrorism, corruption, cybercrime, trafficking in human beings, proceeds of crime, torture, protection of the environment through criminal law, mutual legal assistance, and transfer of sentenced persons.

Canada also takes an active role in meetings of other international organizations and initiatives that discuss criminal law matters, such as the Commonwealth, the Organization for Security and Cooperation in Europe, Asia–Pacific Economic Cooperation, La Francophonie, and the Global Forum on Fighting Corruption and Safeguarding Integrity. There are also bilateral mechanisms, such as the Canada–US Cross-Border Crime Forum.

4) International Criminal Law Conventions Since 1990

Since 1990, there have been important and considerable advances in the development of international conventional criminal law, as evidenced by the broad range and the significant nature of international criminal law conventions that have been adopted. This section will survey recent international criminal law conventions grouped under a number of important subject areas and will focus on those conventions to which Canada has or could become a state party.

---

26   OAS Summits began in 1994. See OAS General Assembly Resolution 2040 (XXXIV-0/04) online: www.oas.org/main/main.asp?sLang=E&sLink=../../documents/eng/structure.asp.

27   See online: www.oecd.org/about/0,2337,en_2649_201185_1_1_1_1_1,00.html.

28   See online: www.coe.int/T/e/Com/about_coe/. Canada was granted official observer status in 1996.

a) Genocide, Crimes against Humanity, and War Crimes

Although initially mandated in the *Treaty of Versailles* in 1919, efforts to develop an international criminal court (ICC) took on renewed momentum in 1989 when the issue was put back on the agenda of the UN GA. In 1992, the UN GA requested the International Law Commission (ILC) to give priority attention to drafting a statute for an ICC. By 1994, the ILC presented a draft statute to the UN GA which thereafter established the Ad Hoc Committee on the Establishment of an ICC. On 17 July 1998, the *Rome Statute of the International Criminal Court* (Rome Statute) was adopted by 120 countries. It came into force on 1 July 2002.[29]

The ICC is the first international permanent court to have jurisdiction over genocide, crimes against humanity, and war crimes. In addition to the Rome Statute, texts of the *Elements of Crimes and of Rules of Procedure and Evidence* have been developed for the ICC.

Since 1990, other developments have included the adoption of the *Statute of the International Tribunal for the Former Yugoslavia* (1993) and the *Statute of the International Tribunal for Rwanda* (1994). On 16 January 2002, the UN signed an agreement with Sierra Leone to set up a Special Court for Sierra Leone.

b) Terrorism

The UN developed a number of major counterterrorism conventions or protocols between 1963 and the present, with more than half of them having been developed since 1988.[30] In addition, other antiterrorism conventions have been developed in regional organizations, such as the *Inter-American*

---

29 See online: www.dfait-maeci.gc.ca/foreign_policy/icc/history-en.asp.

30 These are: the *Protocol for the Suppression of Unlawful Acts of Violence at Airports Serving International Civil Aviation, supplementary to the Convention for the Suppression of Unlawful Acts against the Safety of Civil Aviation* (1988); the *Convention for the Suppression of Unlawful Acts against the Safety of Maritime Navigation* (1988); the *Protocol for the Suppression of Unlawful Acts against the Safety of Fixed Platforms Located on the Continental Shelf* (1988); the *International Convention for the Suppression of Terrorist Bombings* (1997); the *International Convention for the Suppression of the Financing of Terrorism* (1999). In addition, in 2005, negotiations were concluded on the *International Convention for the Suppression of Acts of Nuclear Terrorism*, on amendments to strengthen the *Convention on the Physical Protection of Nuclear Material* and on amendments to the *Convention for the Suppression of Unlawful Acts Against the Safety of Maritime Navigation, 1988* and to the *Protocol for the Suppression of Unlawful Acts Against the Safety of Fixed Platforms Located on the Continental Shelf, 1988*. See online: www.iaea.org/NewsCenter/PressReleases/2005/prn200503.html and www.imo.org/Conventions/mainframe.asp?topic_id=259&doc_id=686, respectively.

Convention against Terrorism (2002), the *Council of Europe Convention on the Prevention of Terrorism* (2005), and the *Council of Europe Convention on Laundering, Search, Seizure, and Confiscation of the Proceeds from Crime and on the Financing of Terrorism* (2005).

There has also been a number of UN Security Council (UNSC) Resolutions on this subject,[31] most notably UNSC Resolution 1373 of 28 September 2001, which directed states to take further action against terrorism, including addressing terrorist financing. UNSC Resolution 1373 also established the Counter Terrorism Committee (CTC) that is charged with monitoring the implementation of this resolution by member states, which are required to report to the CTC.[32]

c) Transnational Organized Crime

There have been many recent, and significant, developments in international efforts to combat transnational organized crime. The *UN Convention against Transnational Organized Crime* was adopted on 15 November 2000 and entered into force on 29 September 2003. In addition, three protocols to the convention were also negotiated, namely: the *Protocol to Prevent, Suppress and Punish Trafficking in Persons, Especially Women and Children, supplementing the UN Convention against Transnational Organized Crime* (entered into force on 25 December 2003); the *Protocol against the Smuggling of Migrants by Land, Sea and Air, supplementing the UN Convention against Transnational Organized Crime* (entered into force on 28 January 2004); and the *Protocol against the Illicit Manufacturing of and Trafficking in Firearms, Their Parts and Components and Ammunition, supplementing the UN Convention against Transnational Organized Crime* (entered into force on 3 July 2005). Other recent developments have included the *Inter-American Convention against the Illicit Manufacturing of and Trafficking in Firearms, Ammunition, Explosives and Other Related Materials* (1997) and the *Council of Europe Convention on Action against Trafficking in Human Beings* (2005).

d) Corruption

International anticorruption initiatives began in earnest in about 1995. Since then, major international anticorruption conventions have been developed, including the *Inter-American Convention against Corruption*, the

---

31   See online: www.un.org/terrorism/sc.htm; and, for example, UNSC resolutions 1267, 1373, 1540, 1566, and 1624.

32   In addition to the UN Security Council Counter Terrorism Committee, there is also the 1540 Committee, the 1267 Committee and the 1566 Working Group.

Convention on Combating Bribery of Foreign Public Officials in International Business Transactions, the Council of Europe *Criminal Law Convention on Corruption* and the *Additional Protocol to the Criminal Law Convention on Corruption* and the *United Nations Convention against Corruption.* The *United Nations Convention against Transnational Organized Crime* also includes provisions on corruption. Follow-up mechanisms exist to evaluate the implementation by states parties of the obligations contemplated by each of these conventions.

e) Cybercrime
The Council of Europe adopted the Convention on cybercrime, which entered into force on 1 July 2004. Subsequently, the Council of Europe developed the *Additional Protocol to the Convention on cybercrime, concerning the criminalisation of acts of a racist and xenophobic nature committed through computer systems.* In addition, the Commonwealth has developed a Model Law on Computer and Computer Related Crime and discussions of these issues are also taking place in other organizations, such as in the UN, G8, APEC, and the OAS.

f) Drugs
The most significant global treaties in this field pre-date 1990, with the most recent major global convention being the *United Nations Convention against Illicit Traffic in Narcotic Drugs and Psychotropic Substances, 1988.* International convention activity has also taken place at the regional level, notably at the Council of Europe, with the *Agreement on illicit traffic by sea, implementing Article 17 of the United Nations Convention against illicit traffic in narcotic drugs and psychotropic substances* (1995). Much activity has also taken place in the OAS.

g) Other
There have been a number of other global and regional conventions pertaining to other subjects that have been developed since 1990, including, for example, the *Convention on the Safety of United Nations and Associated Personnel* (entered into force in 1999) and its Optional Protocol (adopted in 2005), as well as the *Optional Protocol to the Convention on the Rights of the Child on the sale of children, child prostitution and child pornography* (entered into force in 2002).

5) A New Consensus on Collective Security

Notwithstanding the accelerated pace of international conventional criminal law development over the past fifteen years, very recent efforts towards promoting a new consensus on collective security are likely to result in providing an added impetus for an even greater role in the future for the criminal law at the global, regional, and national levels.

On 2 December 2004, the UN High-Level Panel on Threats, Challenges, and Change (HLP) issued its report called *A More Secure World: Our Shared Responsibility*. In it the HLP noted a paradigm shift in the nature of collective security between the worlds of 1945 and 2005. It described the new security climate in the following way:

> The attacks of 11 September 2001 revealed that States, as well as collective security institutions, have failed to keep pace with changes in the nature of threats. The technological revolution that has radically changed the worlds of communication, information-processing, health and transportation has eroded borders, altered migration and allowed individuals the world over to share information at a speed inconceivable two decades ago. Such changes have brought many benefits but also great potential for harm. Smaller and smaller numbers of people are able to inflict greater and greater amounts of damage, without the support of any State. A new threat, transnational organized crime, undermines the rule of law within and across borders. Technologies designed to improve daily life can be transformed into instruments of aggression. We have yet to fully understand the impact of these changes, but they herald a fundamentally different security climate—one whose unique opportunities for cooperation are matched by an unprecedented scope for destruction.[33]

Whereas in 1945 at the time of the founding of the UN, the notion of collective security was centred on state security and was concerned with military aggression by states against other states, the security threats of today and of tomorrow, in the view of the HLP, stem also from non-state actors, deal with human security in addition to state security, and include the spread and possible use of weapons of mass destruction (WMD), terrorism, and transnational organized crime. The HLP identified six "clusters" of threats: economic and social threats (for example, poverty, infectious diseases, and environmental degradation); interstate conflict; internal conflict (for example, civil war, genocide, and other large-scale atrocities); nuclear, radiological, chemical, and biological weapons; terrorism and transnational

---

33 *A More Secure World: Our Shared Responsibility*, UN GA Doc. A/59/565 of 2 December 2004 at 19.

organized crime.[34] In the face of these threats, it is increasingly recognized, more than ever, that no state acting alone can successfully address them.

The nature of these threats and their magnitude elevate them to a global level. For example, the World Bank estimates that the attacks of 9/11 increased the number of people living in poverty by 10 million and cost the world economy more than $80 billion.[35] The detonation of a simple nuclear device in a major city could result in as many as 1 million deaths; it could have an adverse impact of at least $1 trillion on international commerce, employment, and travel; and it could have devastating effects on international security, democratic governance, and civil rights.[36] Drug trafficking is also a genuine threat, with major security implications. It has a global retail trade between $300 billion and $500 billion per year, which threatens state authority, economic development, and the rule of law.[37] Further, it is estimated that in 2000, between $500 billion and $1.5 trillion were laundered by organized crime.[38]

These threats can be interconnected, mutually reinforcing, and demand concerted action. To counter them, it is argued that a new comprehensive collective security system must be put in place.[39] The criminal law can be used, at the global, regional, and national levels, to facilitate international cooperation to combat these common threats and to promote shared interests, such as respect for the rule of law, democracy, and human rights.

On 21 March 2005, in response to the HLP report, the UN Secretary-General issued his own report entitled *In Larger Freedom: Towards Development, Security and Human Rights for All*. This report fully endorses the work of the HLP and, in emphasizing the need for collective action, organizes its comments and recommendations, in part, under three themes: freedom from want, freedom from fear, and freedom to live in dignity.

Under the freedom from fear theme, the report urges a new security consensus against threats to international peace and security to be accom-

---

34 *Ibid.* at 12.

35 *Ibid.* at 19.

36 *Ibid.* at 39.

37 *Ibid.* at 49. The UN also estimates that more than 700,000 people, mostly women and children, are trafficked annually worldwide, generating annual profits estimated at $10 billion. Department of Justice, "Trafficking in Persons: a Brief Description" *Backgrounder* (12 May 2005), online: canada.justice.gc.ca/en/news/nr/2005/doc_31486.html.

38 *Ibid.* at 51.

39 *Ibid.* at 21.

panied by state action, much of which would engage the criminal law.[40] It also emphasizes the interrelationship of the threats and the diverse adverse effects generated by criminal activity. For example, in addressing the threat posed by organized crime, the report makes the following observation:

> The threat of terrorism is closely linked to that of organized crime, which is growing and affects the security of all States. Organized crime contributes to State weakness, impedes economic growth, fuels many civil wars, regularly undermines United Nations peacebuilding efforts and provides financing mechanisms to terrorist groups. Organized criminal groups are also heavily involved in the illegal smuggling of migrants and trafficking in firearms.[41]

Under the freedom to live in dignity theme, the report supports the promotion of the rule of law, democracy, and human rights. In respect of the rule of law, the report encourages member states to cooperate fully with the ICC and with other international or mixed war crimes tribunals[42] and highlights the need to increase state participation in multilateral conventions.

The report defines the role of states as having the responsibility:

> ... to guarantee the rights of their citizens, to protect them from crime, violence and aggression, and to provide the framework of freedom under law in which individuals can prosper and society can develop. If States are fragile, the peoples of the world will not enjoy the security, development and justice that are their right. Therefore, one of the challenges of the millennium is to ensure that all States are strong enough to meet the many challenges they face.[43]

The central thesis focuses on the relationship between security, development, and human rights:

---

40   Recommendations include the development of comprehensive strategies to address the threats; a further strengthening of the *Biological and Toxin Weapons Convention*; developing legally binding instruments to regulate small arms and light weapons; implementing a comprehensive UN counterterrorism strategy, including urgently concluding a convention on nuclear terrorism and a comprehensive convention on terrorism; and states becoming parties to all relevant conventions on corruption and organized crime: UN GA, *In Larger Freedom: Towards Development, Security and Human Rights for All*, UN Doc. A/59/2005 of 21 March 2005, at 57–58.

41   *Ibid.* at 27.

42   *Ibid.* at 36.

43   *Ibid.* at 6.

Not only are development, security and human rights all imperative; they also reinforce each other. This relationship has only been strengthened in our era of rapid technological advances, increasing economic interdependence, globalization and dramatic geopolitical change. While poverty and denial of human rights may not be said to "cause" civil war, terrorism or organized crime, they all greatly increase the risk of instability and violence. Similarly, war and atrocities are far from the only reasons that countries are trapped in poverty, but they undoubtedly set back development. Again, catastrophic terrorism on one side of the globe, for example an attack against a major financial centre in a rich country, could affect the development prospects of millions on the other by causing a major economic downturn and plunging millions into poverty. And countries which are well governed and respect the human rights of their citizens are better placed to avoid the horrors of conflict and to overcome the obstacles to development.

...

Accordingly, we will not enjoy development without security, we will not enjoy security without development, and we will not enjoy either without respect for human rights. Unless all these causes are advanced, none will succeed.[44]

The criminal law plays an important role in this security, development, and human rights equation.[45] In this respect, one should not underestimate the significant role that an effective criminal justice system may play in support of the rule of law. This connection has been articulated recently in the following way:

While there has been considerable evolution in the concept of the rule of law in recent years and substantial debate about the importance of the rule of law on development, there has been little progress in understanding the key role that the criminal justice system has in establishing, maintaining and strengthening the rule of law. There must be recognition of the fact that the criminal justice system is the soft underbelly of the rule of law. While the concept of the rule of law is undeniably broader, unless the central role of the criminal justice system is recognized and approached

---

44 *Ibid.* at 5–6.

45 This point was also made by Antonio Maria Costa at the United Nations Commission on Crime Prevention and Criminal Justice (14th Session) on 23 May 2005, at 6. See online at: www.unodc.org/unodc/en/speech_2005-05-23_1.html.

as a main pillar of the entire edifice, there is a great risk that the measures proposed and attempted will not produce the desired results. The time has come to move away from misconceptions and, in some cases, apprehensions regarding adverse effects of programmes to strengthen law enforcement and the criminal justice system as a whole. If such apprehensions were ever justified, they have certainly ceased to have any basis in the current political environment. The time has also come to invest in building and strengthening institutions of the criminal justice system and to do so in an integrated, coordinated and sustainable manner as part and parcel of both the development and security agendas of the international community.[46]

In September 2005, world leaders committed themselves to working towards this new security consensus.[47] Also at the 2005 World Summit, member states were encouraged to sign and ratify thirty-two multilateral treaties, which were identified as being particularly important in being able to assist the world community in responding to these global challenges.[48] Of the treaties identified, almost half of them were either international criminal law conventions or were international conventions that included criminal law matters.[49]

---

46 *Fifty Years of United Nations,* above note 20 at 14.
47 See UN GA Doc. A/60/L.1 at 21 & 22.
48 See UN, press release L/T/4387 (20 May 2005) at 2–4.
49 These included the *Convention on the Prevention and Punishment of Genocide;* the *Convention against Torture and Other Cruel, Inhuman or Degrading Treatment or Punishment; Optional Protocol to the Convention against Torture and Other Cruel, Inhuman or Degrading Treatment or Punishment; Optional Protocol to the Convention of the Rights of the Child on the involvement of children in armed conflict; Optional Protocol to the Convention on the Rights of the Child on the sale of children, child prostitution and child pornography; Rome Statute of the International Criminal Court; Convention on the Safety of United Nations and Associated Personnel; International Convention for the Suppression of Terrorist Bombings; International Convention for the Suppression of the Financing of Terrorism: International Convention for the Suppression of Acts of Nuclear Terrorism; United Nations Convention against Transnational Organized Crime; Protocol to Prevent, Suppress and Punish Trafficking in Persons, Especially Women and Children, supplementing the United Nations Convention against Transnational Organized Crime; Protocol against the Smuggling of Migrants by Land, Sea and Air, supplementing the United Nations Convention against Transnational Organized Crime; Protocol against the Illicit Manufacturing of and Trafficking in Firearms, Their parts and Components and Ammunition, supplementing the United Nations Convention against Transnational Organized Crime; United Nations Convention against Corruption;* and the *United Nations Convention on the Law of the Sea,* online: untreaty.un.org/English/TreatyEvent2005/List.asp. Ninety-nine states took

6) Canada's Role in the Development and Implementation of International Criminal Law

a) Introduction

The Canadian government has an interest in, and a responsibility for, the protection of Canadian society from threats, whether domestic, transnational, or international. Effectively addressing these threats requires domestic and international action. Canada's membership in many international organizations provides Canada with an opportunity to advance its values internationally and creates considerable impetus for action. Recent political and policy commitments serve to illustrate the abundance of and high profile given to criminal law policy issues on the national and international agenda. They point to enhanced Canadian participation and interest in domestic and international criminal law policy.

The National Security Strategy of April 2004 included domestic, Canada–US, Canada–US and Mexican, and multilateral initiatives as action items. The chapter devoted to international security emphasized the need for Canada to continue to play an important role in countering international terrorism, preventing the proliferation of WMDs, defusing key intra- and interstate conflicts and expanding capacity-building efforts to assist in developing failed and failing states.[50]

On 19 April 2005, the government of Canada released its International Policy Statement. This statement echoed the views of the HLP and the report of the secretary-general, *In Larger Freedom*, in its description of the challenges and threats facing Canada and the world. The statement adopted the position that Canada's task is to promote collective action at both the regional and global level.[51] According to the statement, "Canada's continued success depends on the joint pursuit of democracy, human rights and the rule of law"[52] and Canada should secure its own interests by creating a more stable and prosperous world, which in turn is dependent upon effective multilateral governance.

---

265 actions to approve international treaties on this occasion and the *International Convention for the Suppression of Nuclear Terrorism* received 82 signatures, online: www.un.org/apps/news/story.asp?NewsID=15898&Cr=world&Cr1=summit.

50 Privy Council Office, *Securing an Open Society: Canada's National Security Policy* (April 2004) at 51.

51 Canada. *Canada's International Policy Statement: A Role of Pride and Influence in the World: Overview* (2005) at 1, online: www.dfait-maeci.gc.ca/cip-pic/IPS/IPS-Overview.pdf.

52 *Ibid.* at 4.

In charting the directions for Canada to take in the future, the statement groups various priorities and key initiatives under broad themes. In "Revitalizing Our North American Partnership," the security focus is on protecting North America from twenty-first century threats (for example, terrorism) and implementing the National Security Policy. In "Making a Difference Globally," among other things, the statement aims at building a more secure world by countering terrorism (for example, full implementation of international conventions on terrorism and terrorism financing); stabilizing failed and fragile states by promoting good governance, human rights, democracy, and the rule of law; and combating the proliferation of WMDs.

Political commitments continue to be made at multilateral meetings of heads of state and government, which concern criminal law matters. Examples include communiqués, declarations, and action plans agreed to at summits within the G8, the Commonwealth, the OAS, APEC, as well as at bilateral and trilateral summits, which cover topics ranging from renewing commitments to fundamental political values to addressing specific threats, such as terrorism, corruption, small arms and light weapons, and the proliferation of WMDs. It is interesting to note, for example, that the Joint Declaration of the Canada-European Union Summit (19 June 2005) included a commitment for Canada and the European Union to work together to promote support for *In Larger Freedom*.[53]

Of particular importance to North America was the announcement by the prime minister of Canada and the presidents of the United States and Mexico of the *Security and Prosperity Partnership of North America*, in Waco, Texas, on 23 March 2005. This agreement proposes cooperation in a number of areas, including cross-border law enforcement, maritime and aviation security, and critical infrastructure protection.[54]

b) Government Policy-Makers

Government policy-makers are living this reality. Indeed, Justice Canada policy-makers in the criminal law area play a wide range of roles: from assisting directly in the development of international criminal law and criminal justice policy, including: negotiating international criminal law conventions with their colleagues from the Department of Foreign Affairs and International Trade; preparing the legislative proposals designed to

---

53 See online: www.pm.gc.ca/eng/news.asp?id=514.
54 See online: www.fac-aec.gc.ca/spp/spp-menu-en.asp.

implement international criminal law obligations for Canada; participating in the work of international follow-up mechanisms; contributing to Canada's international reporting on implementation efforts and on the state of Canadian legal and operational frameworks; and engaging in technical assistance and capacity-building efforts.

To be effective and comprehensive, action plans designed in Canada to address various issues often call for a mix of domestic and international components or approaches. In the criminal law area, legislative and other initiatives may be dictated by a need to deal with threats or may involve criminal law issues that have an international and transnational, as well as a domestic, dimension. In addition, effective solutions may often require approaches that address both domestic and international (or transnational) aspects of the issue. It would be difficult to conceive of comprehensive strategies to be employed by Canada, for example, to address comprehensively matters such as terrorism without taking into account international and comparative law approaches.

The *Anti-terrorism Act*[55] was developed, in part, to enable Canada to ratify the *International Convention for the Suppression of Terrorist Bombings*, the *International Convention for the Suppression of the Financing of Terrorism*, the *Convention on the Safety of United Nations and Associated Personnel* and to comply with UNSC Resolution 1373. As well, it allowed Canada to comply broadly with the FATF *Special Recommendations on Terrorist Financing*. It is also worth noting that the first part of the definition of "terrorist activity" in paragraph 83.01(1)(a) of the *Criminal Code* (Part 1 of the *Anti-terrorism Act*) is tied to a number of offences referred to in section 7 of the *Criminal Code* that implement named UN counterterrorism conventions and protocols. This branch of the definition applies to activities that stem from the implementation of these conventions, covering hijacking, terrorist financing, and terrorist bombings, for example. The Act also serves as an effective legislative answer to Canada's specific and more general international obligations in this area, including even to political commitments made long after the coming into force of the Act.

As another example, the Action Plan against Racism announced on 21 March 2005 that it includes a large combination of measures to address the issue, one of which related to the signing the Council of Europe's *Additional Protocol to the Convention on cybercrime, concerning the criminalisa-*

---

55 S.C. 2001, c. 41, as amended.

tion of acts of a racist and xenophobic nature committed through computer systems.[56]

As well, on 12 May 2005, the minister of justice tabled amendments to the *Criminal Code* (Bill C-49) in an effort to create new offences directed at prohibiting trafficking in persons, as a first deliverable of a strategy against human trafficking. As the backgrounder document indicates: "Canada recognizes that human trafficking is a global problem and, in keeping with international standards, is focusing on internationally-recognized key objectives: the prevention of trafficking; the protection of victims; and the prosecution of traffickers. The proposed reforms to the *Criminal Code* will help Canada to achieve these objectives."[57] Bill C-49 received Royal Assent on 25 November 2005.[58]

Significant advances have been made since about 1990 in developing and modernizing Canadian legislation to support interstate cooperation in criminal matters. The new *Extradition Act*,[59] which was granted Royal Assent in 1999, repealed and replaced the former *Extradition Act* and *Fugitive Offenders Act*. Among other things, the legislation was designed to streamline the extradition process, while ensuring continued fairness. The *Mutual Legal Assistance in Criminal Matters Act* was given Royal Assent in 1988.[60] The *International Transfer of Offenders Act*, which was given Royal Assent in 2004,[61] repealed and replaced the former *Transfer of Offenders Act*. Legislation to create a new part in the *Criminal Code* dealing with proceeds of crime was given Royal Assent in 1988.[62] Since then, there has been a series of legislative initiatives addressing proceeds of crime and money-laundering. The *Proceeds of Crime (Money Laundering) Act*, which received Royal Assent in 2000,[63] created the Financial Transactions and Reports Analysis Centre (FINTRAC), which serves as Canada's financial intelligence unit and can enter into arrangements with foreign financial intelligence units. This legislation was subsequently amended, through

---

56   See online: www.canadianheritage.gc.ca/newsroom/news_e.cfm?Action=Display&code=4No331E.

57   See online: canada.justice.gc.ca/en/news/nr/2005/doc_31486.html.

58   See online: www.parl.gc.ca/38/1/parlbus/chambus/house/bills/government/C-49/C-49_4/C-49_cover-E.html.

59   S.C. 1999, c. 18.

60   R.S.C. 1985, c. 30 (4th Supp.).

61   S.C. 2004, c. 21.

62   S.C. 1988, c. 51.

63   S.C. 2000, c. 17.

the *Anti-terrorism Act*, to become the *Proceeds of Crime (Money Laundering) and Terrorist Financing Act*. The *Seized Property Management Act* received Royal Assent in 1993.[64] Among other things, the Act permits the attorney general of Canada, under certain circumstances, to enter into reciprocal sharing agreements with foreign governments.

In addition, there has been legislative change that has addressed issues of extraterritorial prosecutorial jurisdiction.[65] These matters often arise when Canada creates new offences pursuant to international criminal law or other conventions, but this is not always the case.

Other examples of legislative proposals to implement international obligations and thereby permit Canada to be able to ratify international criminal law and other related conventions include the *Antarctic Environmental Protection Act*, [66] the *Corruption of Foreign Public Officials* Act,[67] the *Crimes Against Humanity and War Crimes Act*,[68] and the 2005 amendments to the *Criminal Code and the Cultural Property Export and Import Act* contained in Bill S-37, which received Royal Assent on 25 November 2005.[69]

As a related issue, in developing criminal law policy, attention is also paid to the importance of comparative law. There may be instances where, for example, other states have implemented international criminal law conventions before Canada or have developed novel criminal law legislation to address issues of common concern, and domestic policy-makers take an interest in such efforts. Similarly, policy-makers from other countries often take an interest in Canadian legislative initiatives.

c) Parliament

Parliament is the body responsible for the creation of criminal law in Canada. Thus, any legislative proposals prepared to implement international criminal law obligations must be approved by Parliament in order to take effect. Parliamentarians, quite understandably, take an interest in such matters. For example, bearing in mind a political commitment by countries to ratify the *Convention on Combating Bribery of Foreign Public*

---

64 S.C. 1993, c. 37.

65 See, for example, ss. 7(2.3)–7(2.34) of the *Criminal Code*, which gives Canada jurisdiction to prosecute some offences under certain circumstances when committed at the international space station.

66 S.C. 2003, c. 20.

67 S.C. 1998, c. 34.

68 S.C. 2000, c. 24.

69 See online: www.parl.gc.ca/38/1/parlbus/chambus/house/bills/government/S-37/S-37_4/S-37_cover-E.html.

Officials in International Business Transactions before the end of 1998, Parliament expedited the passage of the legislation to enact the *Corruption of Foreign Public Officials Act* to permit Canada to meet this deadline. In addition, the Senate amended the bill to call for an annual report to Parliament on the enforcement of the Act, as well as on the implementation of the convention by states parties to the convention. Also of note, the international dimension of the *Anti-terrorism Act* has been of particular interest to parliamentarians in their review of the Act.

International experts and officials of public international organizations appear as witnesses before parliamentary committees. As well, private members' bills have been presented in recent years, and have been the subject of debate, which propose expanding the role of Parliament in the treaty-making and implementation process.[70] Further, parliamentarians are often generally interested in comparative law information and parliamentary committees can travel on fact-finding missions.

d)   Provincial and Territorial Governments

Mechanisms are in place for consultations by federal officials with the provinces and territories concerning international criminal law initiatives. Where Canada wishes to sign and ratify an international criminal law treaty, this may have provincial and territorial implications. While the making of the criminal law in Canada, as mentioned, is the sole preserve of the Parliament of Canada, generally provincial attorneys general are responsible for the prosecutions of *Criminal Code* offences in the provinces. Frequently, offences that implement international obligations have a concurrent prosecutorial jurisdiction, so that either the attorney general of Canada or the provincial attorneys general may prosecute.[71] As well, some corruption conventions contain provisions unrelated to the criminal law (for example, preventive measures), and the assistance of the provinces and territories is often sought in completing reports by Canada to international organizations on the implementation of these convention obligations within the country as a whole.

---

70   A recent example was Bill C-260, introduced on 3 November 2004 by Mr. Roy, MP, online: www.parl.gc.ca/38/1/parlbus/chambus/house/bills/private/C-260/C-260_1/C-260_cover-E.html.

71   See, for example, ss. 2(c)–(f) of the *Criminal Code*.

e) The Courts

The courts play a role in interpreting the laws of Canada, including the criminal laws. In conducting this task, the courts may have recourse to international law materials. There can also sometimes be an ongoing dialogue between the courts and Parliament. In this regard, for example, the interpretation by the Supreme Court of Canada of the former *Criminal Code* war crimes provisions in *R. v. Finta*[72] ultimately led in part to the introduction of the *Crimes Against Humanity and War Crimes Act*. Crimes that are legislated as a result of Canada's implementation of international criminal law obligations are prosecuted in Canada before the courts.

f) Civil society

Given that criminal law matters are of interest to civil society in Canada and elsewhere, non-governmental organizations and individuals may hold views on various international and domestic initiatives in this area. Members of civil society and non-government organizations in Canada can sometimes play a role in the activities of international follow-up mechanisms, including providing their own views concerning the effectiveness of efforts by Canada in implementing international criminal law conventions. They also appear as witnesses before Parliament during its examination of international issues and for its consideration of legislative initiatives and they may organize seminars or conferences on international criminal law issues. As well, the federal government may partner with non-governmental organizations to promote international initiatives.[73] In addition, consultations take place with civil society.[74]

g) Canadian Accomplishments

Canada can point to a large number of successes or accomplishments in relation to the development and implementation of international criminal law and criminal justice policy. These include the following:

- Canada has long played a leading role in supporting the development of criminal justice norms and standards within the UN commission and the UN congresses, and has spearheaded resolutions on various topics, including the development of *Basic Principles on the*

---

72 [1994] 1 S.C.R. 701.

73 The government of Canada worked with various non-governmental organizations, for example, in its campaign to promote the ratification of the Rome Statute.

74 For example, a consultation document on the proposed United Nations Instrument against Corruption was prepared and was updated after each negotiating session.

Use of Restorative Justice Programmes in Criminal Matters; Guidelines for the Prevention of Crime; Guidelines on Justice for Child Victims and Witnesses of Crime; and *Model Strategies and Practical Measures on the Elimination of Violence against Women in the Field of Crime Prevention and Criminal Justice.*

- Canada played a major role in the negotiations of the Rome Statute, leading a group of states during the preparatory committees and chairing the Committee of the Whole during the diplomatic conference.

- Canada was the first country in the world to adopt comprehensive legislation to implement its obligations under the Rome Statute and Canada's *Crimes Against Humanity and War Crimes Act* has served as a model for other countries. In addition, Canada has been very active in promoting the ratification of the Rome Statute by other countries and helped develop a manual for the ratification and implementation of the Rome Statute.

- The government of Canada also contributed to the development of the *Legislative Guide for the Implementation of the United Nations Convention against Transnational Organized Crime.*

- Canada has ratified almost all of the major UN conventions and protocols against terrorism and was the first state to ratify the *Inter-American Convention against Terrorism.*

- Canada's *Anti-terrorism Act* has been used as a model by other states and by the Commonwealth in the development of the *Commonwealth Model Legislative Provisions on Measures to Combat Terrorism.*

- Canada is a world leader in fighting cybercrime. Canada played a lead role in the negotiation of the Council of Europe convention and protocol, has signed both, and has been training developing countries in the establishment of legislative frameworks to deal with cybercrime.

- Canada is a state party to the *Inter-American Convention against Corruption,* the *United Nations Convention against Transnational Organized Crime,* the *Convention on Combating Bribery of Foreign Public Officials in International Business Transactions* (triggering the latter convention's entry into force) and has signed the *United Nations Convention against Corruption.*

- As well, Canada has played a lead role within the OAS in promoting the establishment of a secure electronic network on mutual legal assistance in criminal matters within the hemisphere.

F. FUTURE TRENDS AND CHALLENGES

At the 11th UN Congress on Crime Prevention and Criminal Justice (April 2005), there were calls among some states for new UN conventions on cybercrime and on money-laundering, although some other states opposed such calls.[75] At the 2005 World Summit, leaders agreed to undertake efforts to conclude a comprehensive convention on international terrorism.[76]

The action plans flowing from international organizations may be expected to be pursued, in addition to various bilateral and trilateral action plans. New initiatives can be anticipated to combat, for example, terrorism, transnational organized crime, proliferation, cybercrime, money laundering, and corruption. Follow-up mechanisms will commence and continue their work.

According to the secretary-general's report to the 11th UN Congress, the way forward is for the international community to proceed with a strategy that incorporates multiple elements and actions, with the objective of realizing improved international regulatory frameworks, having sufficient compliance by the international community with such frameworks, and achieving enhanced cooperation among states as well as effective coordination among international agencies. Capacity-building to promote and institutionalize respect for the rule of law, with particular emphasis on countries in transition, is also believed to be an essential part of an effective strategy to address new forms of threats to human security.[77]

The challenge will be to keep pace with these developments, in a continually evolving world, and to ensure, to the extent possible, that each initiative is meaningful and fits with Canadian values. Although there needs to be a continuing assessment of the adequacy of existing instruments, ideally, such evaluations should take into account implementation efforts on the part of states parties and should allow adequate time to pass in order to be able to make these assessments meaningful and effective. Where genuine gaps are discovered, efforts should be undertaken to close them. Capacity-building efforts, including those directed at assisting states to participate fully in international criminal law conventions, will continue to take on added importance.

In the near future, the international community will explore new uses for the criminal law in grappling with new and deadly global threats. In the

---

75   Above note 45 at 2.
76   See online: www.un.org/summit2005/.
77   *Fifty Years of United Nations,* above note 20 at 14.

years to come, the connection between effective criminal justice systems, the rule of law, and global security should become increasingly apparent and justice ministries will likely be called upon more often to provide technical assistance.

G. CONCLUSION

This chapter has surveyed to some extent the growth of international conventional criminal law since 1990 and has observed the significant and undeniable impact that such growth has had on domestic legislative initiatives. Criminal law issues are at the forefront of international, regional, and domestic agendas.

As we have seen, government criminal law policy-makers are becoming increasingly accustomed to addressing policy from a global and domestic perspective. Further, for Parliament, the courts, non-governmental organizations, and the public at large, international criminal law issues are also very relevant. International criminal law should not be seen as a mere theoretical and esoteric construct, but should be seen as grounded in practical reality and having very real consequences.

Canada is a developed country with a sophisticated criminal justice system and criminal law framework. It is committed to human rights, democracy, and the rule of law; it has a bilingual and bijural character; and it has considerable international experience in addressing criminal law issues in different settings, given its membership in many international organizations. Moreover, seeking consensus and working cooperatively, whether interdepartmentally with the provinces and territories or internationally, is part of the culture of the Canadian government—as is the understanding of the need to address criminal law policy issues, bearing in mind domestic and international perspectives. Canada has played, and should continue to play, an important role in international criminal law activities in the future, advancing Canadian values and seeking effective international instruments.

In 1982, at the time of launching the criminal law review in Canada, it is interesting to see that *The Criminal Law in Canadian Society*, in its assessment of the pressures and trends with respect to future policy, failed to note activities related to the development of international conventional criminal law and their possible impact on domestic criminal law.

In today's world, and in the foreseeable future, there would be no such oversight, since international conventional criminal law and related initiatives, and their impact on domestic criminal law in Canada, are expected to become even more pronounced. However, while this phenomenon is ever-present and continues to take on added importance in an ever-shrinking and interconnected world, this development is consistent with the traditional role of the criminal law in Canada as articulated in *The Criminal Law in Canadian Society* (that is, including both security and justice goals), although the scope of the criminal law in Canada (for example, playing a role in global collective security efforts) has been expanded considerably as a result of international initiatives.

18

"If Commerce, Why Not Torture?"
An Examination of Further Limiting State Immunity with Torture as a Case Study

MAURICE COPITHORNE[*]

A. INTRODUCTION

This chapter[1] will begin with a description of the changing attitude towards torture and similar serious crimes and the impact it has had. A description of the legal status of torture at international law and jurisprudence follows, as does a discussion of international immunities and, particularly, state immunities. Then there will be a description of existing criminal and civil remedies followed by two emerging but still controversial concepts: *jus cogens* and universal jurisdiction. Finally, the chapter will look at Canadian legislation and jurisprudence.

B. THE CHANGING ATTITUDE TOWARDS TORTURE

As massive, egregious violence has grown over the past twenty-five years, particularly against civilians, the cry for accountability and the end of impunity has become an important theme in international discourse. The responses, limited or reluctant in some cases, have included the:

- establishment of international ad hoc tribunals, such as those for Yugoslavia and Rwanda;

---

[*] The author wishes to thank Hilary Thomson (Law 2) Faculty of Law, University of British Columbia, for her research and preliminary drafting assistance.

[1] The quotation in the title is paraphrased from Harold Koh, "Transnational Public Law Litigation" (1991) 100 Yale L.J. 2347 at 2365. Koh queries, "If contracts, why not torture?"

- increased invocation of the concept of universal jurisdiction, as in the "Princeton Principles on Universal Jurisdiction," and its adoption in varying forms by some jurisdictions;[2]
- emergence of the concept of "serious crimes" as in the *Statute of the International Criminal Court* (ICC);
- growing demand that state and personal immunities be restricted, as in the *Pinochet* judgment;[3] and
- growing willingness of domestic courts to address these issues leading to occasional judgments, separate opinions, and dissents that have given currency to the concepts just mentioned.

There is considerable literature on these developments and it is growing quickly.[4] This chapter will take a narrow view and advance the argument that the time has come for governments to adopt activist agendas in this regard. In particular, it will use the debate over torture to suggest that traditional immunities should no longer be allowed to stand in the way of criminal accountability or of redress.

2) The Move towards Accountability

In examining the law of immunity in relation to torture, it is useful to consider the historical developments that led to the increased demands for accountability. The First World War produced the first major rumblings in the international community demanding accountability for the acts of a sovereign. In a brutal war characterized by the use of mustard gas and atrocities against civilians, the Allies declared their intent in the *Treaty of Versailles* to prosecute Kaiser Wilhelm II.[5] However, the Kaiser, who had

---

2   This was a Princeton University Project that in January 2001 brought together a group of scholars and jurists to make a first effort at articulating, in a systematic way, the concept of universal jurisdiction. The resulting principles remain very much the centre of the ongoing discourse of the concept.

3   There were three iterations of the seminal and much-discussed decision of the House of Lords involving the request by a Spanish magistrate to have the former Chilean dictator extradited to Spain to stand trial for various crimes against Spanish nationals in Chile. An excellent discussion of the intricacies can be found in Hazel Fox, *The Law of State Immunity* (Oxford: Oxford University Press, 2002) at 343–447 and 538–40.

4   At this early stage it would be appropriate for the author to acknowledge the importance for anyone working in this field of the recent treatise by Fox, *Law of State Immunity, ibid.*

5   *Treaty of Versailles*, 28 June 1919, 225 C.T.S. 195, art. 227.

fled to the Netherlands, escaped trial when that country refused to extradite him.[6]

There were also provisions in the 1920 *Treaty of Sèvres* to try those responsible for the 1915 Armenian genocide; but these came to naught when the provisions were left out of the subsequent 1923 *Treaty of Lausanne*.[7] The Armenian genocide marked the first use of the term "crimes against humanity" in a 1915 declaration by France, Great Britain, and Russia denouncing the massacre.[8]

Following the Second World War, the Nuremburg and Tokyo International Tribunals were set up by the 1945 *London Charter* to deal with certain offences against peace, war crimes, and crimes against humanity that had taken place during the war.[9] The 1949 Geneva Convention system was based on "the principle that persons not actively engaged in warfare should be treated humanely."[10] The Conventions included an obligation upon states in the face of grave breaches of them:

> Each High Contracting Party shall be under the obligation to search for persons alleged to have committed or to have ordered to be committed, such grave breaches, and shall bring such persons, regardless of their nationality, before its own courts. It may also, if it prefers, and in accordance with the provisions of its own legislation, hand such persons over for trial to another High Contracting Party concerned, provided such High Contracting Party has made out a *prima facie* case.[11]

---

6 Peter Burns, "The *Convention against Torture* and Diminishing Immunity" in *The Changing Face of International Criminal Law* (Vancouver: International Centre for Criminal Law Reform and Criminal Justice Policy, 2001) 149 at 150; M. Cherif Bassiouni, "World War I, the War to End All Wars and the Birth of a Handicapped International Criminal Justice System" (2002) 30 Denv. J. Int'l L. & Pol'y 244.

7 Burns, *Convention against Torture, ibid.*

8 Kriangsak Kittichaisaree, *International Criminal Law* (Oxford: Oxford University Press, 2001) at 85.

9 Burns, *Convention against Torture*, above note 6 at 150–51.

10 Malcolm S. Shaw, *International Law*, 5th ed. (Cambridge: Cambridge University Press, 2003) at 1055.

11 *Geneva Convention for the amelioration of the condition of the wounded in Armed Forces in the field*, 12 August 1949, C.T.S. 1965 No. 20, 75 U.N.T.S. 31; *Geneva Convention for the amelioration of the condition of wounded, sick and shipwrecked members of Armed Forces at sea*, 12 August, 1949, C.T.S. 1965 No. 20, 75 U.N.T.S. 85. *Geneva Convention relative to the treatment of prisoners of war*, 12 August 1949, C.T.S. 1965 No. 20, 75 U.N.T.S. 135 [Geneva Convention]; *Geneva Convention relative to the protection of civilian persons in time of war*, 12 August 1949, C.T.S. 1965 No. 20, 75 U.N.T.S. 287. See also Burns, *Convention against Torture*, above note 6 at 151.

The *Geneva Convention relative to the Treatment of Prisoners of War* explicitly lists "torture or inhuman treatment" as a grave breach.[12]

In the past few decades, there has been a growing intolerance for state immunity as it relates to crimes against humanity, including torture. There has been an increased demand for accountability of leaders and a rising recognition of the cost of giving states or state officials impunity for these crimes. Even the word "impunity," once a neutral piece of legal terminology, has gained a negative connotation for an absence of accountability.

3) The Campaign against Impunity

The invoking of immunity in cases of serious crimes and, in particular, torture began to attract greater recognition in the 1990s. In 1997 impunity was defined by the UN Sub-Commission on the Prevention of Discrimination and Protection of Minorities' Rapporteur, Louis Joinet, as "[t]he impossibility, *de jure or de facto*, of bringing the perpetrators of human rights violations to account, whether criminal, civil, administrative or disciplinary proceedings, since they are not subject to any inquiry that might lead to them being accused, arrested, tried and if found guilty, convicted."[13] By the mid-1990s the term "impunity" was appearing increasingly in legal literature.[14] The word entered daily language after the *Pinochet* decision; the French newspaper *Le Monde* declared that the limitation of Pinochet's immunity marked the end of an age of impunity and the transition to an age of illegality for dictators.[15]

The Joinet Report charted the origins of the "campaign against impunity" and concluded that it had reached a stage where the "international community realized the importance of combating impunity."[16] Attached to

---

12   Geneva Convention, *ibid.*, art. 130.
13   Louis Joinet, "The Administration of Justice and the Human Rights of Detainees: Question of Perpetrators of Human Rights Violations (Civil and Political), Revised Final Report," UN ESC 49th Sess. UN Doc. E/CN.4/Sub.2/1997/Rev.1 [Joinet Report]. Quoted in Geneviève Jacques, *Beyond Impunity: An Ecumenical Approach to Truth, Justice and Reconciliations* (Geneva: WCC Publications, 2000) at 3.
14   *Hein On-line*, Database Search; see, for example, Stephen Macedo, ed., *Universal Jurisdiction: National Courts and the Prosecution of Serious Crimes under International Law* (Philadelphia: University of Pennsylvania Press, 2004) at 195.
15   Jacques, *Beyond Impunity*, above note 13 at 5.
16   Joinet Report, above note 13 at 3.

this report was the *Set of Principles for the Protection and Promotion of Human Rights through Action to Combat Impunity* (Joinet Principles).[17]

C. THE LEGAL STATUS OF TORTURE

1) Torture as an International Crime

Torture is widely recognized as a crime against humanity.[18] It was first placed on the international agenda in the *Universal Declaration of Human Rights* where it is declared that "no one shall be subjected to torture of the cruel, inhuman or degrading treatment or punishment."[19] In 1975 the UN General Assembly adopted the *Declaration on the Protection of All Persons from Being Subjected to Torture and Other Cruel, Inhuman or Degrading Treatment or Punishment*.[20] Seven years later, the UN General Assembly adopted the *Convention against Torture*.[21] Article 1 of the Convention defines torture as:

> any act by which severe pain or suffering, whether physical or mental, is intentionally inflicted on a person for such purposes as obtaining from him or a third person information or a confession, punishing him for an act he or a third person has committed or is suspected of having committed, or intimidating or coercing him or a third person, or for any reason based on discrimination of any kind, when such pain or suffering is in-

---

17 *Ibid.*, annex 2.

18 Shaw, *International Law*, above note 10 at 596. Torture may also be a self-standing offence. In 1998, the International Criminal Tribunal for the Former Yugoslavia (ICTY) adopted the definition from the *Convention against Torture* and noted that torture was prohibited by peremptory norms of international law and was *jus cogens*. The adoption of this definition, now generally accepted, has meant that torture is not only a crime within the context of crimes against humanity but also is a self-standing offence. This distinction between torture as a crime against humanity perpetrated by the state and as an incident of "individual criminal responsibility" was affirmed by the ICTY in *Prosecutor v. Kunarac et al.* (2002) Case No. IT-96-23 & 23/1-A at para. 489. For a further discussion of torture as a crime against humanity or as a self-standing offence, see Steven R. Ratner & Jason Abrams, *Accountability for Human Rights Atrocities in International Law: Beyond the Nuremberg Legacy*, 2d ed. (Oxford: Oxford University Press, 2001) at 72 and 117–20. For the purposes of this chapter, torture will be discussed in the context of crimes against humanity.

19 *Universal Declaration of Human Rights*, art. 5, GA Res. 217A (III) (10 December 1948).

20 GA Res. 3452, 30 UN GAOR Supp. (No. 34) at 91, UN Doc. A/1034 (1975).

21 *Convention against Torture and Other Cruel, Inhuman or Degrading Treatment or Punishment*. 10 December 1984, 1465 U.N.T.S. 85, C.T.S. 1987 No. 36 (entered into force 26 June 1987) [*Convention against Torture*].

flicted by or at the instigation of or with the consent or acquiescence of a public official or other person acting in an official capacity. It does not include pain or suffering arising only from, inherent in or incidental to lawful sanctions.

It is clear that this article is referring to acts endorsed or at least tolerated by the state. The Convention also provides that "[n]o exceptional circumstances whatsoever, whether a state of war or a threat of war, internal political in stability or any other public emergency, may be invoked as a justification of torture."[22] The Convention further specifies that an order from a superior officer or a public authority may not be invoked as a justification of torture.[23]

There has also been some withdrawal by the courts from the *de facto* recognition of torture as legitimate state conduct. In the landmark *Filartiga* case, a US judge declared that the "torturer has become like the pirate or slave trader before him, *hostis humani generis*, an enemy of all mankind."[24] The European Court of Human Rights noted in *Aksoy v. Turkey* that the European Convention for the Protection of Human Rights and Fundamental Freedoms "prohibits in absolute terms torture or inhuman or degrading treatment or punishment." The court declared that no exceptions or derogations were permissible.[25] In a very recent House of Lords judgment, Lord Bingham declared:

> the English common law has regarded torture and its fruits with abhorrence for over 500 years, and that abhorrence is now shared by over 140 countries which have acceded to the Torture Convention. I am startled, even a little dismayed, at the suggestion (and the acceptance by the Court of Appeal majority) that this deeply-rooted tradition and an international obligation solemnly and explicitly undertaken can be overridden by a statute and a procedural rule which make no mention of torture at all.[26]

---

22 *Ibid.*
23 *Ibid.*
24 *Filartiga v. Pena-Irala*, 630 F.2d 876 (2d. Cir 1980) [*Filartiga*].
25 *Aksoy v. Turkey*, [1996] E.C.H.R. 68 at para. 72.
26 *A (FC) and others (FC) v. Secretary of State for the Home Department (Respondent)* (2004); *A and others v. Secretary of State for the Home Department (Respondent) (Conjoined Appeals)*, [2005] UKHL 71 at para. 51.

2) Torture as an Act of State

The idea that torture cannot be an official act was raised in the United States in the case of *Princz v. Federal Republic of Germany*, in which an American Holocaust survivor sought to obtain damages from Germany for his treatment in Nazi concentration camps during the Second World War.[27] Although the applicant lost in the District of Columbia Court of Appeal, Judge Patricia Wald issued her well-known dissent stating:

> I believe that Germany's treatment of Princz violated *jus cogens* norms of the law of nations, and that by engaging in such conduct, Germany implicitly waived its immunity from suit within the meaning of § 1605(a)(1) of the FSIA.... *Jus cogens* norms are by definition non-derogable and thus when a state thumbs its nose at such a norm, in effect overriding the collective will of the entire international community, the state cannot be performing a sovereign act entitled to immunity.[28]

Two years later, the 9th Circuit Court of Appeal seemed open to considering the same question about whether immunity applied to *jus cogens* crimes in *Siderman*. However, the case was settled out of court. In 1997, in *Prefecture of Voiotia v. Federal Republic of Germany*, a Greek court dealt with claims by applicants over atrocities committed in Greece by the German Reich.[29] The court held that states could not claim immunity for *jus cogens* crimes and that illegal acts cannot be considered official acts.[30] In *Pinochet*, three judges "found that torture and conspiracy to torture could not be part of a head of state's official functions."[31] In 2000, the *Gerechtstof* Amsterdam court ruled in *Bouterse* that torture could not be considered "one of the official duties of a head of state."[32] As such, they denied im-

---

27 *Hugo Princz v. Federal Republic of Germany*, 26 F.3d 1166 (D.C. Cir. 1994) [*Princz*]. For a further discussion, see Bederman, "Dead Man's Hand," below note 71 at 258–70.

28 *Princz, ibid.* at 1178–82. See also *In re: Estate of Ferdinand Marcos Human Rights Litigation*, 25 F.3d 1467 at 1470–72 (9th Cir. 1994).

29 *Prefecture of Voiotia v. Federal Republic of Germany*, Case No. 11/2000, Decision of 4 May 2000 (Areios Pagos [Hellenic Supreme Court]), summarized in (2001) 95 A.J.I.L. 198.

30 See also Kerstin Bartsch & Björn Elberling "*Jus Cogens v. State Immunity*, Round 2," 4 Germ. L.J. 5, online: www.germanlawjournal.com/article.php?id=271#fuss16.

31 As summed up by Naomi Roht-Arriaza in *The Pinochet Effect: Transnational Justice in the Age of Human Rights* (Philadelphia: University of Pennsylvania Press, 2005) at 57.

32 Translation quoted in Wirth, "Immunity for Core Crimes," below note 74 at 885 (translation no longer available online).

munity to Bouterse *in absentia* for the torture of political dissidents committed while he was the head of state of Suriname. Finally, the US Senate Judiciary Committee in its report on the *Torture Victim Protection Act* of 1991 declared that "no state commits torture as a matter of public policy."[33] In *Bouzari*, the Appeal Court relied largely on the *State Immunity Act* (SIA) to refuse to reach such a conclusion.[34]

D. IMMUNITY

1) Personal and State Immunities

To begin with it must be recalled that absolute immunity was not without its skeptics as far back as Sir Robert Phillimore and Chief Justice Marshall, who both declined to endorse an absolute immunity that disregarded the nature of the act.[35] In the last century, Sir Hersch Lauterpacht argued cogently that traditional international law did not imply total and absolute immunity, a view shared by Mr. Justice Laskin, in dissent, in the 1971 state immunity case, *Democratic Republic of the Congo v. Venne*, before the Canadian Supreme Court.[36] In 1954, Professor Elihu Lauterpacht, commenting on the work of the International Law Commission (ILC) on the law of diplomatic intercourse and immunities, stated: "Immunity from jurisdiction amounts in practice to immunity from the rule of law; it amounts to a denial of a legal remedy whether the injured party is (as in the field of civil jurisdictions) a private person or whether (as in the realm of exemption from criminal process) it is the community at large."[37]

Two types of immunities may be involved in the defence of prosecutions for serious crimes: personal immunity (*rationae personae*) and state immunity (*rationae materiae*).[38] Personal immunity, generally viewed as part of customary international law, covers all acts of state officials dur-

---

33   Quoted in Fox, *Law of State Immunity*, above note 3 at 214.

34   *Bouzari v. Iran (Islamic Republic)*, [2002] O.J. No. 1624 (S.C.J.), aff'd (2004), 243 D.L.R. (4th) 406, 71 O.R. (3d) 675 (C.A.) leave to appeal to S.C.C. refused (2005), 122 C.R.R. (2d) 376n [*Bouzari*].

35   Referred to in H.L. Molot & M.L. Jewett, "The State Immunity Act of Canada" (1982) 20 Can.Y.B. Int'l Law at 84–85.

36   *Ibid.* at 85; *Congo (République démocratique) v. Venne*, [1971] S.C.R. 997.

37   Quoted in J. Craig Barker, *The Abuse of Diplomatic Privileges and Immunities: A Necessary Evil?* (Aldershot: Dartmouth, 1996) at 189.

38   Shaw, *International Law*, above note 10 at 638–46 and 655–59; Mark W. Janis, *An Introduction to International Law* (New York: Aspen, 2003) at 347–62; John Currie, *Public International Law* (Toronto: Irwin Law, 2001) at 316–52.

ing the period they are in office. Personal immunity has been successfully invoked as a defence even for acts committed before coming into office.[39] However, in *Pinochet*, the House of Lords made a break with tradition, declaring that personal immunity expires once the individual leaves office.[40] In contrast, state immunity protects states and individuals only for official acts, that is, those attributable to the state. While the scope of state immunity is narrower, it does not expire. The challenge with regard to state immunity lies in determining what qualifies as an official act of the state, or on behalf of the *"jure imperii,"* and what qualifies as a non-official, private act or *"jure gestionis."*[41]

With the emergence in the 1950s of state-owned manufacturing, trading, and transportation companies, chiefly in Eastern Europe and China, state immunity became a widespread issue in contexts that, until then, had been largely non-governmental activity. The application of immunity in such circumstances virtually eliminated the prospect for the settling of disputes through third-party processes and, moreover, created an uneven playing field between public and private commercial enterprises. The argument arose that state-owned enterprises engaged in commercial activities should not benefit from the traditional concept of absolute state immunity. This approach became known as the "restrictive" theory or doctrine of state immunity. Gradually, through legislation and jurisprudence, the restrictive theory came to be widely applied in Europe and North America.[42]

---

39 In *Democratic Republic of Congo v. Belgium* (judgment of 14 February 2002, ICJ Reports 2002, online: www.icj-cij.org/icjwww/idocket/iCOBE/icobejudgment/icobe_ijudgment_toc.htm) [*Democratic Republic of Congo*], the International Court of Justice declared that "the functions of a Minister of Foreign Affairs are such that, throughout his or her office, he or she when abroad enjoys full immunity from criminal jurisdiction or inviolability. That immunity and that inviolability protect the individual concerned against any act of authority of another State which would hinder him or her in the performance of his or her duties. In this respect no distinction can be drawn between acts performed by a Minister for Foreign Affairs in an 'official' capacity, and those claimed to have been performed in a 'private capacity,' or, for that matter, between acts performed before the person assumed office."

40 *R. v. Bow Street Metropolitan Stipendiary Magistrate, ex parte Pinochet Ugarte (No. 2)*, [1999] ICHRL 3 [*Pinochet No. 2*]. For a quite different approach, see Dapo Akande, "International Law Immunities and the International Criminal Court" (2004) 98 A.J.I.L. 407 at 415.

41 Bryan A. Garner, *Black's Law Dictionary*, 8th ed. (St. Paul, MN: Thomson/West, 2004), online: ecarswell.westlaw.com.

42 *Dralle v. Republic of Czechoslovakia* (1950), 17 I.L.R. 155; *The Empire of Iran* (1963), 45 I.L.R. 57, *Victory Transport Inc. v. Comisaria General de Abasteciementos y Transportes*

In 1971 the Canadian Supreme Court rejected the restrictive approach,[43] but in the 1982 *State Immunity Act*, Parliament adopted it.[44] In the United States, the restrictive immunity approach had been officially endorsed much earlier through the Tate Letter process introduced in 1952,[45] which was later adopted in *The Foreign State Immunity Act* (FSIA).[46] The UN General Assembly has recently endorsed the restrictive approach in the adoption without a vote, of *The Convention on Jurisdictional Immunities of States and their Property*, in November 2004.[47] This Convention declares that states parties cannot invoke immunity in cases arising out of commercial transactions as well as in certain other circumstances, not relevant here.[48]

The adoption of the Convention clearly reflects a trend towards a narrowing of the concept of absolute immunity.[49] Allowing states to resort to legal process in disputed commercial matters would seem to counter one of the procedural arguments, that states do not have the ability or capacity to investigate overseas transactions. As pointed out by Koh, "If private litigants could conduct massive overseas discovery and adduce probative facts regarding a foreign state's commercial conduct, what rendered them incompetent to do the same with regard to a foreign state's heinous treatment of its own citizens?"[50]

2) Waivers of Immunity

Some commentators have suggested that certain acts might be seen as implied waivers of immunity by the state concerned, particularly in those

---

(1964), 35 I.L.R. 110. For a discussion of the restrictive *doctrine* to immunity, see the many references in Fox, *Law of State Immunity*, above note 3; Shaw, *International Law*, above note 10 at 628–31; and Robert Wai, "The Commercial Activity Exception to Sovereign Immunity and the Boundaries of Contemporary International Legalism" in Craig Scott, ed., *Torture as Tort* (Portland, OR: Hart, 2001) at 216.

43 *Gouvernement de la République démocratique du Congo c. Venne*, [1971] S.C.R. 997, 22 D.L.R. (3d) 669 [*Congo*].

44 S.C. 1980–81–82–83, c. 95, art. 5.

45 (1952) 26 Department of State Bulletin 984.

46 28 U.S.C. 1602.

47 UN Res. 59/38. For a detailed treatment of the Convention, see David Stewart, "The U.N. Convention on Jurisdictional Immunities of States and their Property" (2005) 99 A.J.I.L. 1 at 194.

48 C6 59th Sess. 13th Mtg. UN Doc. A/C.6/59/SR.13 (2004) at 5, art. 11.

49 *Ibid.*

50 Koh, "Transnational Public Law Litigation," above note 1 at 2366.

cases, such as the United States and Canada, that have immunity legislation providing for waiver.[51] There is also some jurisprudence on this matter. In *Prefecture of Voiotia v. Federal Republic of Germany*, the court held that Germany's conduct as an occupying state amounted to a waiver of immunity in subsequent claims for damages. As noted earlier in this chapter, Judge Wald stated that the defendant state had implicitly waived its immunity from suit within the meaning of the FSIA.

3) International Statutes Limiting Immunities

The statutes of both the International Criminal Tribunal for Rwanda (ICTR) and the International Criminal Tribunal for the former Yugoslavia (ICTY) contain identical wording removing immunity for certain offences, including war crimes, genocide, and crimes against humanity: "The official position of any accused person, whether as head of state or government or as a responsible government official, shall not relieve such person of criminal responsibility nor mitigate punishment."[52] The ICC statute states: "Official capacity as a head of state or government a member of a government or Parliament an elected representative or a government official shall in no way exempt a person from criminal responsibility under the statute."[53]

---

51 In Canada, the *State Immunity Act*, R.S.C. 1985, c. S-18, s. 4 states that immunity is waived only when the state explicitly submits to the jurisdiction, initiates the proceedings, or intervenes or takes steps in the proceedings other than in cases where it does so to claim immunity, or in ignorance of facts entitling it to immunity. The US s. 1605(1)(a) *et seq.* of the *Foreign Sovereign Immunities Act of 1976*, above note 46, stipulates: "A foreign state shall not be immune from the jurisdiction of courts of the United States or of the States in any case (1) in which the foreign state has waived its immunity either explicitly or by implication, notwithstanding any withdrawal of the waiver which the foreign state may purport to effect except in accordance with the terms of the waiver."

52 *Statute of the International Criminal Tribunal for the Former Yugoslavia*, art. 7(2), S.C. Res. 808, UN SCOR, 48th Sess., 3175th Mtg. UN Doc. S/RES/808 (1993); *Statute of the International Criminal Tribunal for Rwanda*, art. 6(2), S.C. Res. 955, UN SCOR, 49th Sess., 3453d Mtg., Annex, UN Doc. S/RES/955 (1994). See also Macedo, *Universal Jurisdiction*, above note 14 at 32.

53 ICC Statute, art. 27.

E. REMEDIES

1) Civil Remedies

The updated *Set of Principles to Combat Impunity* identified a clear need for civil remedies. As well, in 2005 the United Nations High Commissioner for Human Rights, the UN Committee against Torture, the Special Rapporteur of the Commission on the Question of Torture, and the Board of Trustees of the UN Voluntary Fund for Victims of Torture reiterated the need for a civil remedy for human rights violations. In a joint statement these bodies reminded states parties of their obligations under the *Convention against Torture* to ensure fair and adequate compensation, and noted the "right to sue for compensation, including civil compensation, which can be based on universal jurisdiction."[54] Article 14 of the *Convention against Torture* states:

> (1) Each State Party shall ensure in its legal system that the victim of an act of torture obtains redress and has an enforceable right to fair and adequate compensation, including the means for as full rehabilitation as possible. In the event of the death of the victim as a result of torture, his dependents shall be entitled to compensation.

> (2) Nothing in this article shall affect any right of the victim or other persons to compensation, which might exist under international law.

Arguing in favour of a purposive interpretation, some have suggested that this provision places an obligation on states to ensure that there is a civil remedy available, even for torture committed abroad.[55] Combined with the fact that the Convention allows no justification for allowing torture, this could be interpreted as requiring states to limit immunities on torture.

Both civil and criminal remedies are beginning to exist in other countries. In the United States, there are civil remedies for both aliens and US citizens through the *Alien Tort Claims Act* (ATCA) and the *Torture Victim Prevention Act* (TVPA).[56] The ATCA simply states: "[D]istrict courts shall have original jurisdiction of any civil action by an alien for a tort only, com-

---

54   United Nations, *Joint Statement on the Occasion of the United Nations International Day in Support of Victims of Torture*, 26 June 2005.

55   Andrew Byrnes, "Civil Remedies for Torture Committed Abroad: An Obligation under the Convention Against Torture?" in Scott, *Torture as Tort*, above note 42.

56   *Alien Tort Claims Act of 1789*, 28 U.S.C. 1350 [*ATCA*]; *Torture Victim Prevention Act of 1991*, 28 U.S.C. 1350 [*TVPA*].

mitted in violation of the law of nations or a treaty of the United States." In *Filartiga*, a non-US citizen successfully sued her husband's non-US torturer for acts committed outside the United States.[57] The ATCA has been used to sue commanders who were not the direct perpetrators of the crime, under the doctrine of "command responsibility."[58] The TVPA extends the rights set out in the ATCA to US citizens but is limited to torture and extrajudicial killings. The *Anti-Terrorist Act* of 1996 goes further in removing state immunity, in the case of certain designated states, and by further action in 1998 permits execution of judgments even against diplomatic and consular property of the defendant state.[59]

2) Criminal Remedies

States are also becoming involved in criminal remedies. Belgium has made several attempts in this regard. In September 2005, Belgium utilized a 1993 law establishing the right to exercise jurisdiction over violations of the *Geneva Convention on the Conduct of War* to issue an arrest warrant for the former leader of Chad, Hissene Habre, for acts committed during his rule of Chad.[60] Spain claimed jurisdiction in a case involving a military officer from Argentina and alleged crimes committed in Argentina against, among others, Spanish nationals in the 1970s "Dirty War." The officer, arrested while visiting Spain, is currently serving a 640-year sentence in Spain.[61] In October 2005 a Spanish judge issued arrest warrants for three American soldiers charged with firing on a hotel in Iraq in 2003, killing a Spanish journalist.[62] In issuing the warrant, the judge said there was a possible "crime against the international community."[63]

---

57 *Filartiga*, above note 24.
58 *Xuncax et al. v. Gramajo*, 886 F. Supp. 162 (D Mass 1995). See also Valerie Oosterveld & Alejanda C. Flah, "Holding Leaders Liable for Torture by Others: Command Responsibility and *Respondeat Superior* as Frameworks for Derivative Civil Liberties" in Scott, *Torture as Tort*, above note 42.
59 For a discussion on the *Anti-Terrorist Act*, see Fox, *Law of State Immunity*, above note 3 at 214.
60 Associated Press, "Belgium Seeks Arrest of Chad's Ex-Leader" *New York Times* (29 September 2005).
61 Renwick McLean, "Spain Sentences Argentine for 'Dirty War' Crimes" *International Herald Tribune* (20 April 2005), online: www.iht.com/articles/2005/04/19/news/spain.php.
62 Renwick McLean, "Three U.S. Soldiers Face Arrest in Spain" *International Herald Tribune* (20 October 2005), online: www.iht.com/articles/2005/10/19/news/spain.php.
63 *Ibid.*

The application of laws allowing civil and criminal charges for serious crimes committed extraterritorially are still not common, and some continue to be fine-tuned.[64] However, the exercise of extraterritorial jurisdiction over serious crimes does appear to be a growing trend, particularly in Europe.

F.   INTERNATIONAL PRINCIPLES

1)   *Jus Cogens*

The tenet of *jus cogens* reflects the view that there are "certain overriding principles of international law" from which there can be no deviation.[65] These principles are "based upon an acceptance of fundamental and superior values within the system and in some respects are akin to the notion of public order or public policy in domestic legal orders."[66] *Jus cogens* norms are those that are "so fundamental to the international community of states as a whole that the rule constitutes a basis for the community's legal system."[67] States cannot derogate from *jus cogens* norms and they cannot be avoided through treaty or custom.

This tenet emerged largely as a response to the atrocities that took place in the Second World War. The first use of the term in a legal document seems to have been the 1969 *Vienna Convention on the Law of Treaties*.[68] The Vienna Convention uses the term "peremptory norm" interchangeably with *jus cogens* and defines it as one from which "no derogation is permitted." A rule that violates a peremptory norm is invalid. Article 53 of the Vienna Convention states that a "treaty is void if, at the time of its conclusion, it conflicts with a peremptory norm of general international

---

64   In May 2003, in response to strident objections from some countries, the Belgian government made changes to the law to allow it to "block complaints against citizens of countries it judges to have a fair and functioning judicial system by referring the cases to the authorities there" (Paul Meller, "Now Belgian Official Faces Charges" *International Herald Tribune* (21 June 2003), online: www.iht.com/articles/2003/06/21/belge_ed3__0.php). For a review of developments with regard to Belgium's *War Crimes Statute*, see Steven R. Ratner, "Belgium's War Crimes Statute: A Postmortem" (editorial comment) (2003) 97 Am. J. Int'l L. 888.

65   Ian Brownlie, *Principles of International Law*, 6th ed. (Oxford: Oxford University Press, 2003) at 489.

66   Shaw, *International Law*, above note 10 at 117.

67   Janis, *An Introduction to International Law*, above note 38 at 65.

68   *Ibid.* at 64; *Vienna Convention on the Law of Treaties*, 22 May 1969, C.T.S. 1980 No. 37, 1155 U.N.T.S. 331.

law." Article 64 states that an existing treaty that violates a newly emergent peremptory norm is also void.

Although there is no definitive list of crimes that have acquired this status, and indeed even to try to create such a list is bound to be controversial, there have been certain relevant statements by writers and judges. It is widely accepted by writers that torture, like piracy, slavery, genocide, and other crimes against humanity, has achieved the status of *jus cogens*.[69] In the 1998 ICTY *Furundzija* case, the court held that "the prohibition on torture is a peremptory norm or *jus cogens*."[70] In *Siderman de Blake v. Republic of Argentine*, the 9th Circuit US Court of Appeal reversed and remanded a lower court decision that the US *Foreign Sovereign Immunity Act* applied to *jus cogens* crimes.[71] Judge Fletcher, for the court, held that torture was *jus cogens*, stating that "the crack of the whip, the clamp of the thumb screw, the crush of the iron maiden, and, in these more efficient modern times, the shock of the electric cattle prod are forms of torture that the international order will not tolerate."[72]

Some decisions declare that state immunity may not extend to *jus cogens* crimes, such as torture.[73] In *Pinochet*, the House of Lords affirmed that sovereign immunity did not apply to *jus cogens* crimes, including torture.[74] In *Jones*, the UK Court of Appeal held that the 1978 *State Immunity Act* did not automatically entitle state officials to immunity for acts of torture.[75]

2) Universal Jurisdiction

As will be seen, certain courts have found torture to be one of the crimes subject to universal jurisdiction. This is certainly one of the most beguil-

---

69 Shaw, *International Law*, above note 10 at 303; Brownlie, *Principles of International Law*, above note 65 at 489.

70 *Prosecutor v. Anton Furundzija*, ICTY, 10 December 1998 at para. 144.

71 965 F.2d 699 at 717 (9th Cir. 1992) [*Siderman*]. For a further discussion, see David J. Bederman, "Dead Man's Hand: Reshuffling Foreign Sovereign Immunities in U.S. Human Rights Litigation" (1995/96) 25 Ga. J. Int'l & Comp. L. 255 at 270–81.

72 *Siderman, ibid.*, quoted in Janis, *Introduction to International Law*, above note 38 at 66.

73 Diane Orentlicher, "Promotion and Protection of Human Rights: Impunity; Report of the Independent Expert to Update the Set of Principles to Combat Impunity," UN ESCOR, 61st Sess. UN Doc. E/CN.4/1005/102 at 14 and 26 [Report of the Independent Expert]; *Pinochet No. 2*, above note 40; *Jones v. Saudi Arabia et al.* [2004] EWCA Civil 1394 [*Jones*].

74 See also Stephen Wirth, "Immunity for Core Crimes: The ICJ's Judgements in the *Congo v. Belgium* Case" (2002) 13 Eur. J. Int'l L. 877 at 884.

75 Above note 51.

ing concepts to be invoked in the campaign against impunity. Its definition remains to be pinned down; its proponents sometimes understate its complexity. Bassiouni and Hall have each discussed this concept in detail.[76] The Princeton Principles, for their part, define it as follows:

> For purposes of these Principles, universal jurisdiction is criminal jurisdiction based solely on the nature of the crime, without regard to where the crime was committed, the nationality of the alleged or convicted perpetrator, the nationality of the victim, or any other connection to the state exercising such jurisdiction.[77]

In the commentary associated with the principles, their drafters set out some of the questions they faced, such as how firmly universal jurisdiction is established in international law and whether the time is ripe to bring greater clarity to the concept.[78] In the end, the principles are declared to be "written so as to both clarify the current law of universal jurisdiction and encourage its further development."[79]

There was significant concern among the drafters for abuse of the concept through its use to pursue politically motivated prosecutions. A requirement that the accused had to be physically in the territory of the enforcing state was discussed. However, the commentary makes clear the drafters' view that this was an open question.[80]

The Joinet Principles foresaw domestic courts playing an important role in combating impunity. This is reflected in the complementarity provisions of the Rome Statute establishing the ICC, which state the ICC may exercise jurisdiction only in cases where the state is unwilling or unable to prosecute itself.[81] The Joinet Principles included a provision that "the

---

76   See Bassiouni's article, "The History of Universal Jurisdiction and Its Place in International Law" in Macedo, *Universal Jurisdiction*, above note 14 at 41; Christopher K. Hall, "Contemporary Universal Jurisdiction" in Morten Bergsmo, ed., *Human Rights and Criminal Justice for the Downtrodden* (Leiden: Brill Academic Publishers, 2003) at 111.

77   Stephen Macedo, ed., *The Princeton Principles on Universal Declaration* (Princeton, NJ: Princeton University, Program in Law and Public Affairs, 2001) at 29. These principles can also be found in Macedo, *Universal Jurisdiction, ibid.* at 21.

78   *Princeton Principles, ibid.* at 40.

79   *Ibid.*

80   *Ibid.* at 43.

81   Article 17 of the *Rome Statute of the International Criminal Court*, 17 July 1998, 2187 U.N.T.S. 90 (entered into force 1 July 2002) states:

> Having regard to paragraph 10 of the Preamble and article 1, the Court shall determine that a case is inadmissible where:

jurisdiction of foreign courts may be exercised by virtue either of a universal jurisdiction clause contained in a treaty in force or of a provision of domestic law establishing a rule of extraterritorial jurisdiction for serious crimes under international law."[82] Principle 22 said:

> ... in the absence of a ratification making it possible to apply a universal jurisdiction clause to the country where the violation was committed, States may take practical measures in their domestic legislation to establish extraterritorial jurisdiction over serious crimes committed under international law outside their territory, which by their nature fall not only within the scope of domestic law but also of an international punitive system which disregards the concept of frontiers.

The intent of this provision is clear; states may enact domestic legislation to assume jurisdiction over serious crimes wherever they occur. In fact, states have been doing so for many years with regard to other matters. For example, the civil law system provides for the right of states to claim jurisdiction over offences by their own nationals, wherever the offences occur.

In 2004, the UN Human Rights Commission passed a resolution reaffirming "the duty of all States to put an end to impunity" and commissioned an updated version of the Joinet Principles. [83] These were prepared by Independent Expert Diane Orentlicher and were intended to clarify the previous version and also to reflect the current state of international law and practice.[84] In reference to domestic courts, the Orentlicher Report

---

    (a) The case is being investigated or prosecuted by a State which has jurisdiction over it, unless the State is unwilling or unable genuinely to carry out the investigation or prosecution;

    (b) The case has been investigated by a State which has jurisdiction over it and the State has decided not to prosecute the person concerned, unless the decision resulted from the unwillingness or inability of the State genuinely to prosecute.

    Complementarity with national courts is also mentioned in the preamble and art. 1. See also Akande, "International Law Immunities," above note 40 at 407–33; and Bruce Broomhall, *International Justice and the International Criminal Court: Between Sovereignty and the Rule of Law* (Oxford: Oxford University Press, 2003) at 86–93.

82 Principle 19, "Set of Principles for the Protection and Promotion of Human Rights Through Action to Combat Impunity" Annex II of E/CN.4/Sub.2/1997/Rev.1 [1997 Set of Principles].

83 UN Human Rights Commission (UNHCR) Resolution 2004/72 (21 April 2004) UN Doc. E/CN.4/RES/2004/72, online: ap.ohchr.org/documents/E/CHR/resolutions/E-CN_4-RES-2004-72.doc.

84 Report of the Independent Expert, above note 73.

mentions *Furundzija*, commenting that the decision recognizes "the right of every State to prosecute and punish the authors of international crimes such as torture."[85] The Orentlicher Principle 21 now calls for states to take measures:

> ... including the adoption or amendment of *internal legislation*, that are necessary to enable their courts to exercise *universal jurisdiction* over serious crimes under international law in accordance with applicable principles of customary and treaty law (emphasis added).

Although the sections related to universal jurisdiction in the 1997 report had proved controversial,[86] the updated Principle 21 does not depend solely on a universal jurisdiction clause, but rather looks to an "extradite or prosecute" provision found in certain treaties. Principle 21 notes:

> States must ensure that they fully implement any legal obligations they have assumed to institute criminal proceedings against persons with respect to whom there is credible evidence of individual responsibility for serious crimes under international law if they do not extradite the person or transfer them for prosecution before an international or internationalized tribunal.

Additionally, the updated Principle 22 calls for states to "enforce safeguards against any abuse of rules such as those pertaining to ... amnesty [and] official immunities ... that foster or contribute to impunity."

In the accompanying report, the independent expert notes: "States should undertake measures necessary to enable their courts to exercise universal jurisdiction to the extent permitted by international law."[87] Principle 34(1) reaffirms the importance of "a readily available, prompt and effective remedy in the form of criminal, civil, administrative or disciplinary proceedings."[88] The independent expert believed this principle "reflects a well-established rule of international human rights law."[89]

---

85 *Ibid.* at 25.

86 The American Association of Jurists' criticism of Principle 22 is set out in E/CN.4/1998/NGO/20.

87 Report of the Independent Expert, above note 73 at 16.

88 Diane Orentlicher, "Set of Principles for the Protection and Promotion of Human Rights Through Action to Combat Impunity" UN Doc. E/CN.4/1005/102/Add. 1 at 17 (2004) [updated Set of Principles].

89 Report of the Independent Expert, above note 73 at 16.

The ICTY, in *Furundzija*, recognized the right of states to exercise universal jurisdiction over torture.[90] The House of Lords, in *Pinochet*, found that the crime of torture was "subject to universal jurisdiction," and the International Court of Justice in *Democratic Republic of the Congo v. Belgium* concluded "that international law allows the exercise of universal jurisdiction over war crimes and crimes against humanity."[91]

G. CANADIAN LEGISLATION AND JURISPRUDENCE

Canadian courts are not following suit yet. In the recent case of *Bouzari v. Iran (Islamic Republic)* Bouzari and his wife and children sought to sue Iran for his torture in Iran before he became a Canadian citizen.[92] The court held that it was barred by section 3 of the *State Immunity Act* which provides blanket immunity, aside from explicit exceptions, stating that "[e]xcept as provided by this Act, a foreign state is immune from the jurisdiction of any court in Canada."[93] This judgment was upheld on appeal and the Supreme Court declined to review the case.

With regard to the argument that the Torture Convention obliged Canada to provide a civil remedy for victims of torture, the court accepted expert evidence that states' parties had not so interpreted their obligation under the Convention and that, with regard to comments made in the *Pinochet* case about such an obligation, these applied only in criminal cases. Finally, with regard to confirming torture as a *jus cogens* crime, the Court accepted this proposition but was not prepared to accept the argument that that being the case, states' parties to the *Convention against Torture* had an obligation to provide a civil remedy even for offences occurring outside of Canada. The court also noted that experts for both sides in this case took the position that the prohibition of torture was indeed a *jus cogens* norm. However, it concluded that "there is no principle of customary international law which provides an exception from state immunity where an act of torture has been committed outside the forum, even for acts contrary to *jus cogens*."[94]

---

90 *Prosecutor v. Furundzija*, Case No. IT-95-17/1-T, on 10 December 1998 at para. 156 [*Furundzija*].

91 *Regina v. Bow Street Metropolitan Stipendiary Magistrate and Others, ex parte Pinochet Ugarte* (1999), [2000] A.C. 147 [*Pinochet No. 3*]; *Democratic Republic of Congo*, above note 39. See Report of the Independent Expert, above note 73 at 22, 25–26.

92 *Bouzari*, above note 34.

93 *Ibid.* at para. 2 (S.C.J.).

94 *Ibid.* at para. 63.

While both ministers and officials in Canada have publicly expressed support for the universality of human rights as a general principle, Canada has not extended its jurisdiction to crimes against humanity that occur outside of Canada. Canada has reportedly objected to the extraterritorial application of US law to provide compensation for alleged human rights abuses by Canadian companies abroad.[95]

It should be noted that Canada has, in fact, legislated with regard to a number of offences that occur abroad. The *Criminal Code* now contains assertions of jurisdiction for certain extraterritorial acts including offences committed on aircraft registered in Canada, hostage-taking of or by a Canadian citizen, terrorism committed by a resident or citizen, terrorism committed against a Canadian citizen or Canada, and sexual offences against children committed by a Canadian citizen.[96] Prior to the adoption of the United Nations *Law of the Seas Convention*, Canada enacted the *Arctic Waters Pollution Prevention Act*, which regulated pollution within 100 nautical miles of shore, before such jurisdiction was adopted in Article 234 of the 1982 Convention.[97]

The *Crimes against Humanity and War Crimes Act* also makes the offences of genocide, a crime against humanity, and a war crime committed outside Canada indictable in this country.[98] The Act includes provisions that allow a military commander or "superior," defined as a "person of authority," to be charged under the Act even if he or she did not directly commit the offence.[99] In late 2005 a Toronto man was the first person charged

---

95 Madelaine Drohan, "Alien Torts: U.S. Resolve, Our Hypocrisy" *Globe and Mail* (5 July 2004). Drohan's article discusses a US case where Talisman Energy, a Canadian company, was being sued under the *Alien Tort Claims Act*. Talisman's "accusers claim it aided and abetted the Sudanese government's campaign of ethnic cleansing in southern Sudan during its four-year stay .... In making his case to the Supreme Court, US Solicitor-General Theodore Olson stated that the Canadian government had complained to the United States about its companies (that is, Talisman Energy) being subject to US law. A spokesman at Foreign Affairs Canada confirmed that Canada had objected, and would continue to object, to such lawsuits. The basis of the complaint, said the spokesman, was the extraterritorial application of the US law. He cited the 1996 Helms-Burton legislation as another example, among other things, that penalized foreign firms, including Canadians, for profiting from property expropriated by President Fidel Castro in Cuba."

96 *Criminal Code*, R.S.C. 1985, c. C-46, s. 7.

97 *Arctic Waters Pollution Act*, R.S.C. 1970, (1st Supp.), c. 2; *United Nations Convention on the Law of the Sea*, 10 December 1982, 33 I.L.M. 1309, 1833 U.N.T.S. 3. (1994).

98 *Crimes Against Humanity and War Crimes Act*, S.C. 2000, c. 24, s. 6. *Note*: the United States has similar legislation, *The War Crimes Act of 1996*, 18 U.S.C. § 2441.

99 *Crimes Against Humanity and War Crimes Act, ibid.*, ss. 5 and 7.

under the Act, accused of crimes against humanity during the Rwandan genocide.[100] Additionally, the Royal Canadian Mounted Police (RCMP) is reportedly investigating more than 100 other "war crimes" cases.[101] Most of the focus of this program has been to bar entry to Canada of potential war criminals. According to the report, 385 alleged war criminals were barred from entering Canada through visa denials and other measures between April 2004 and March 2005.

However, visa denial and deportation, while convenient, does not address the underlying issue of accountability for serious crimes abroad. Perhaps there needs to be further Canadian statutory limitations of immunity available to individuals and states charged with offences defined by the ICC statute as "serious crimes." With regard to civil remedies, it may be necessary for Parliament to incorporate another exception in the *State Immunity Act.*

H. CONCLUSION

Continuing efforts of victims of torture to take their torturers to court demonstrate a growing demand for accountability, and this probably means a change in the application of the traditional state immunity regime in such cases.[102] It is hard, indeed, to explain to a victim of torture that states no longer enjoy immunity for commercial transactions, and yet gross violators of human rights continue to benefit from it. In the words of Professor Koskenniemi: "International law's energy and hope lies in its ability to articulate existing transformative commitment in the language of rights and duties and thereby to give voice to those who are otherwise routinely excluded."[103]

The issue of redress and reparation for victims of torture is becoming a more widely discussed issue. In most cases, justice is simply not available to the victims in the countries where they were tortured. Some commenta-

100 Sean Gordon, "T.O. Man Accused of Genocide" *Toronto Star* (20 October 2005) A1.

101 Canada, "Canada's Program on Crimes against Humanity and War Crimes: Eighth Annual Report, 2004–2005," online: www.cbsa.gc.ca/general/enforcement/annual/wc-cg2005-e.html#modern; see also Stewart Bell, "RCMP Probing 100 War-Crimes Cases: Investigation Involves 25 Countries" *Vancouver Sun* (4 November 2004).

102 Examples of victims taking their torturers to court include the US *Siderman* case (above note 71), the UK *Jones* case (above note 73), and the Canadian *Bouzari* case (above note 34).

103 Martti Koskenniemi, *The Gentle Civilizer of Nations: The Rise and Fall of International Law 1870-1960* (Cambridge: Cambridge University Press, 2001) at 516–17.

tors speak of a complementarity relationship between national and international jurisdictions. There will be a growing body of serious offences coming before national or international courts, and the need to address impunity as a matter of public policy will only increase.

Those with policy concerns may be reluctant to provide precedents for other states to claim jurisdiction over Canadians for committing acts within Canada that were lawful in this country. Such a risk is likely to be substantially reduced by the use of some precision in the definitions in the categorization of such offences.

There is also the issue of an obligation to exercise jurisdiction, in contrast to the right to exercise jurisdiction. It is clear that governments shy away from the creation of obligations. There is little evidence, so far, that states take seriously the clear wording to this effect, for example, in the Genocide Convention and in the *Convention against Torture*. Article 14 of the UN *Convention against Torture* articulates an obligation to ensure that "the victim of an act of torture obtains redress and has an enforceable right to fair and adequate compensation including the means for as full rehabilitation as possible." However, the *Bouzari* judgment suggests the courts are not ready to go alone, at least just yet.

Another approach may lie among the ideas that have come forward recently to limit the application of state immunities. These include a more rigorous and consistent interpretation *jure imperii* of a characterization of serious crimes as involving implicit waivers of state immunity, and the introduction of a hierarchical approach with *jus cogens* "trumping" state immunity.

It remains to be seen if and how the government of Canada as well as Canadian courts will fulfill their part in the process of combating impunity. Assertions of extraterritorial jurisdiction over torture have now been recognized through a series of judgments, which may come to form a rule of customary international law. The pressure will only increase upon states to assert jurisdiction, at least in cases of the most serious crimes—whether or not they occurred within the boundaries of the state concerned.

19

Implementation of International Humanitarian and Related International Law in Canada

OONAGH E. FITZGERALD[*]

A. INTRODUCTION AND OVERVIEW

Sometimes we treat international humanitarian law, also known as the law of armed conflict, as though it is something new we are just discovering. Despite man's long history of brutality and inhumanity, rules to protect individuals from the consequences of war and rules that limit the means and methods of warfare have existed since antiquity, surviving the middle ages and being further developed in modern times. The instruments of the nineteenth and twentieth centuries are only the latest treaties on this issue. Indeed, the humanitarian ideals and concepts that have been formalized in legal instruments transcend various cultural traditions and make the rules and principles of international humanitarian law timeless.

This chapter examines how international humanitarian law and related fields of international law are implemented into domestic law, and how international humanitarian law is relevant to the practice of law within the

---

* The original presentation from which this paper is derived was prepared for the Organization of American States Law Days (October 2005), with the generous and expert assistance of John McManus, Ruth Barr, Johanne Levasseur, Clare Barry, Doug Breithaupt, and Michel Bourbonnière of the Department of Justice Canada; Sabine Nolke and John F.G. Hannaford of the Legal Bureau, Foreign Affairs Canada; L.Col.Blaise Cathcart and Capt.Tony Farris of the Office of the Judge Advocate General, Canadian Forces. The author also gratefully acknowledges the assistance of Tania Nesrallah, Administrative Assistant to the Special Advisor International Law. The views expressed are those of the author alone, and do not represent the position of the Department of Justice.

government of Canada. Domestic implementation is a multi-dimensional task shared by a number of departments and agencies of the federal government, and in preparing this chapter I had assistance from colleagues at the Department of Foreign Affairs, the Office of the Judge Advocate General, and throughout the Department of Justice.

It needs to be stated at the outset that the purpose of the chapter is modest: simply to provide an overview of implementation issues relating to humanitarian law within the federal government, without providing any definitive answers or interpretations regarding the many challenging and contested issues facing practitioners today. The chapter begins by describing international humanitarian law generally and outlining other related fields of international law. It then explains in broad terms how international humanitarian law is implemented in Canada, and how the practice of international humanitarian law and other related fields of international law are distributed at the federal level in Canada between the Department of Justice, the Canadian Forces, and the Department of Foreign Affairs. The chapter considers the types of legal issues that these institutions deal with and how they work cooperatively to find policy and operational solutions. It also describes the Canadian National Committee for Humanitarian Law, which links these three institutions with the Canadian Red Cross and several other federal departments in a steering committee for the implementation and broader dissemination of international humanitarian law in Canada. The chapter notes the new challenges facing international humanitarian law but provides no solutions, leaving the field open to all who are interested to engage in finding answers and concludes by suggesting that continued interdepartmental, intergovernmental, and international cooperation will help drive the quest for solutions.

B. WHAT IS MEANT BY INTERNATIONAL HUMANITARIAN LAW?

This chapter focuses on domestic implementation of international humanitarian law, specifically *jus in bello* (law applicable during war), but by necessity it also touches on somewhat related international law areas such as *jus ad bellum* (law concerning use of force), aspects of arms control, and international human rights law. International humanitarian law is concerned with *jus in bello*, itself a vast domain, encompassing international law rules to protect victims of armed conflict and limit the methods of conflict. It aims to find a balance between military necessity and humanitarian considerations.

Although international humanitarian law has been specified in numerous international conventions, it remains founded in customary law, as expressed in the famous Marten's Clause: "[I]n cases not covered by international agreements, civilians and combatants remain under the protection and authority of the principles of international law derived from established custom, from the principles of humanity and from the dictates of public conscience."[1] The International Committee of the Red Cross has recently completed and published a massive study and compendium of customary international humanitarian law.

The treaty law relevant to international humanitarian law consists primarily of the "Law of Geneva," aimed at the protection of victims of armed conflict, and the "Law of the Hague," aimed at the actual conduct of hostilities. With respect to the former class, the key conventions protecting the victims of armed conflict are: the 1864 *Geneva Convention for the Amelioration of the Condition of the Wounded in Armies in the Field* (the first Red Cross Convention); and the Geneva Conventions of 1949 for the protection of war victims and the Additional Protocols to these Conventions of 1977.

With respect to the latter class, international humanitarian law encompasses a long series of international conventions that limit the methods of warfare and regulate the conduct of hostilities. This includes the Law of the Hague,[2] as well as many other international conventions on conventional weapons, nuclear weapons, biological weapons, chemical weapons, and landmines.[3]

Breaches of international humanitarian law are the subject matter of trials before the international criminal tribunals.[4] Such breaches may also be considered by the UN General Assembly and the Security Council, the International Court of Justice, as well as national courts and legislative bodies.

---

1 Originally from the 1899 *Hague Convention II*, and incorporated into numerous subsequent international instruments, including art. 1 of *Protocol Additional I* 1977 to the Geneva Conventions, 1949.

2 Starting with the 1868 *St-Petersburg Declaration Renouncing the Use in Time of War, of Explosive Projectiles Under 400 Grammes Weight*; the *Hague Regulations* of 1899 and 1907, the 1925 *Protocol prohibiting use in war of asphyxiating poisonous or other gases and bacteriological methods of warfare*.

3 For example, the 1980 *Convention on Certain Conventional Weapons* and the 1997 *Convention on the Prohibition of the Use, Stockpiling, Production and Transfer of Anti-Personnel Mines and on their Destruction*.

4 The International Criminal Tribunal for former Yugoslavia, International Criminal Tribunal for Rwanda, International Criminal Court, and the Ad Hoc Criminal Tribunal for Sierra Leone.

C. WHAT ARE SOME OF THE RELATED FIELDS OF INTERNATIONAL LAW?

While international humanitarian law is *lex specialis*, and in some contexts can operate independently of other areas of international and domestic law, it is important to recognize that, with the growth of international law, increasingly we find there are areas of potential overlap and interconnection. In particular, questions are now being asked about the possible application of international human rights law in situations of armed conflict. There are overlapping concepts and sometimes little or no inconsistency in applying both international humanitarian law and international human rights law to a situation, as the International Court of Justice has recently suggested. The language of common article 3 of the Geneva Conventions, 1949, may provide an umbrella under which some fundamental human rights norms, such as the prohibition against torture and genocide and basic due process principles, can shelter.[5] The following are some of the

---

5   *Article 3.* In the case of armed conflict not of an international character occurring in the territory of one of the High Contracting Parties, each party to the conflict shall be bound to apply, as a minimum, the following provisions:

1. Persons taking no active part in the hostilities, including members of armed forces who have laid down their arms and those placed hors de combat by sickness, wounds, detention, or any other cause, shall in all circumstances be treated humanely, without any adverse distinction founded on race, colour, religion or faith, sex, birth or wealth, or any other similar criteria.

To this end the following acts are and shall remain prohibited at any time and in any place whatsoever with respect to the above-mentioned persons:

 (a) Violence to life and person, in particular murder of all kinds, mutilation, cruel treatment and torture;
 (b) Taking of hostages;
 (c) Outrages upon personal dignity, in particular, humiliating and degrading treatment;
 (d) The passing of sentences and the carrying out of executions without previous judgment pronounced by a regularly constituted court affording all the judicial guarantees which are recognized as indispensable by civilized peoples.

2. The wounded and sick shall be collected and cared for.

An impartial humanitarian body, such as the International Committee of the Red Cross, may offer its services to the Parties to the conflict.

The Parties to the conflict should further endeavour to bring into force, by means of special agreements, all or part of the other provisions of the present Convention.

The application of the preceding provisions shall not affect the legal status of the Parties to the conflict.

more obvious human rights instruments with a potential connection to international humanitarian law: the *Universal Declaration of Human Rights,* 1948, the *International Covenant on Civil and Political Rights,* 1966, the *Convention on the Prevention and Punishment of the Crime of Genocide,* 1948, the *Convention against Torture,* 1987, the *Convention on the Elimination of all Forms of Racial Discrimination,* 1966, the *Convention on the Elimination of all Forms of Discrimination against Women,* 1979, the *Convention on the Rights of the Child,* and its *Optional Protocol on the Involvement of Children in Armed Conflict,* 2000.[6]

A broad view of international humanitarian law would also include the law related to displaced persons and refugees, embodied *inter alia* in the 1951 UN *Convention on the Status of Refugees.* The third category of law that this author would argue is relevant to consideration of international humanitarian law is the law pertaining to use of force (*jus ad bellum*). This includes the *Charter of the United Nations,* specifically the prohibition on resort to use of force except for self-defence or collective defence; customary international law on self-defence; the role of the UN Security Council in maintaining international peace and security; and relevant jurisprudence of the International Court of Justice.

D. HOW DOES INTERNATIONAL HUMANITARIAN LAW BECOME PART OF DOMESTIC LAW?

The usual and surest way that international humanitarian law becomes part of Canadian domestic law is through explicit statutory enactment. The *Geneva Conventions Act*[7] implements some of Canada's obligations under the Geneva Conventions, 1949. For example, 7(1) makes every prisoner of war subject to the *Code of Service Discipline,* as defined in section 2 of the *National Defence Act,*[8] and every prisoner of war who is alleged to have committed an offence under section 3(1) is deemed to have been subject to the *Code of Service Discipline* at the time of the alleged offence.

---

6   The recent advisory opinion of the International Court of Justice asserted that certain key international human rights obligations applied in a situation governed also by Geneva Convention IV: UN General Assembly reference regarding the *Legal Consequences of the Construction of a Wall in the Occupied Palestinian Territory* (ICJ Advisory Opinion of 9 July 2004).

7   R.S.C. 1985, c. G-3.

8   R.S.C. 1985, c. N-5.

The *Crimes Against Humanity and War Crimes Act,*[9] the *Mutual Legal Assistance in Criminal Matters Act,*[10] and the *Extradition Act,*[11] among other Acts, implement Canada's obligations under multilateral and bilateral treaties—as well as the Rome Statute establishing the International Criminal Court, the Geneva Conventions, the Genocide Convention, and the UN Security Council Resolution 827 creating the International Criminal Tribunal for the former Yugoslavia (ICTY), and Resolution 955 establishing the International Criminal Tribunal for Rwanda (ICTR).

Domestic courts may also recognize principles of international humanitarian law as part of customary international law. Canadian courts have confirmed that customary international law is incorporated as part of the common law of Canada.[12] Also, the UK House of Lords in the *Pinochet* case[13] considered whether the protection of state immunity was available to a former head of state for acts of torture committed when in power. The *Crimes Against Humanity and War Crimes Act* section 4(3), in defining "crimes against humanity," makes express reference to customary international law ("being criminal according to the general principles of law recognized by the community of nations"). While clear in principle, specific instances of the interplay between customary international law and statutory law may be complex and contested.

E. FEDERAL DEPARTMENTS' ROLES IN INTERNATIONAL HUMANITARIAN LAW AND RELATED INTERNATIONAL LAW

The three lead federal offices for matters of international humanitarian law and related areas of international law are the Legal Bureau of the Department of Foreign Affairs, the Office of the Judge Advocate General at the Depart-

---

9 S.C.2000, c. 24.
10 R.S. 1985 (4th Supp.), c. 30.
11 S.C. 1999, c. 18.
12 Gib van Ert, "International Law Does Bind Canadian Courts: A Reply" (Spring 2004) 30:1 Canadian Council on International Law Bulletin, referring to *The Ship "North" v. The King* (1906), 37 S.C.R. 385; *Re Foreign Legations (sub nom. Reference Re: Powers of Ottawa (City) and Rockcliff Park)*, [1943] S.C.R. 208 (notably the reasons of Duff C.J.); *Saint John (City) v. Fraser-Brace Overseas*, [1958] S.C.R. 263; *Re Regina and Palacios* (1984), 45 O.R. (2d) 269 (C.A.); and *Bouzari v. Iran*, [2002] O.J. No. 1624 (S.C.J.), aff'd (2004), 71 O.R. (3d) 71, leave to appeal to S.C.C. refused, [2004] S.C.C.A. No. 410. See also *Triquet v. Bath* (1764), 3 Burr. 1478, 97 E.R. 936; *Trendtex Trading v. Bank of Nigeria*, [1977] Q.B. 529 (C.A.); and *I Congreso del Partido*, [1983] 1 A.C. 244 (H.L.).
13 *In Re Pinochet* (1999), [1999] UKHL 1, [2000] 1 A.C. 119, [1999] 1 All E.R. 577.

ment of National Defence, and the Department of Justice. First, the Legal Bureau at the Department of Foreign Affairs provides legal and policy advice to the minister of foreign affairs and the government of Canada on matters of international law and international humanitarian law. With other relevant departments, the Legal Bureau represents Canada in the development and negotiation of new instruments of international humanitarian law. With the attorney general of Canada, the Legal Bureau represents Canada before the International Court of Justice and other international tribunals to advocate Canada's position on relevant principles of international humanitarian law, and it facilitates cooperation with international criminal tribunals.

The judge advocate general and the Office of Judge Advocate General provide legal advice to the government of Canada, the minister of national defence, and the chief of defence staff on military law, including international humanitarian law and military justice. They provide operational legal advice on the application of international humanitarian law, other international laws, and domestic law to all Canadian Forces operations, facilitate cooperation with international criminal tribunals, and provide training in the law of armed conflict to members of the Canadian Forces.

The Department of Justice[14] provides operational legal advice and legal policy advice to federal departments and the government of Canada on matters of domestic and international law relevant to international humanitarian law. Justice officials prepare federal legislation and ensure the quality of federal regulations as needed to implement Canada's international humanitarian law obligations. Crown counsel litigate on behalf of the federal Crown (and Canada) cases involving questions of domestic or international law relevant to international humanitarian law. They prosecute war crimes and crimes against humanity, process extradition and mutual legal assistance requests, and facilitate cooperation with international criminal tribunals, as well as with other states, in dealing with breaches of international humanitarian law.

There are a number of other federal departments and agencies that play important, specialized roles in the implementation of Canada's international humanitarian law obligations. The Department of Citizenship

---

14 In the federal government of Canada the functions of the attorney general and justice ministry have been the responsibility of one department, and traditionally, one Cabinet minister serves as minister of justice and attorney general of Canada. Part 3 of the *Federal Accountability Act*, Bill C-2, enacts the *Director of Public Prosecutions Act*, providing for a director of public prosecutions to perform the functions of the deputy attorney general.

and Immigration Canada identifies persons suspected of war crimes or crimes against humanity for purposes of excluding them from Canadian immigration processes and from the refugee determination process, consistent with article 1F(a) of the 1951 UN *Convention Relating to the Status of Refugees*. Royal Canadian Mounted Police investigate allegations that persons living in Canada participated in conflict-related offences including war crimes, for purposes of prosecution in Canada or before foreign or international tribunals. Legal counsel at the Privy Council Office (which is the central agency that coordinates all federal departments) obtain comprehensive international humanitarian law and related international and domestic law advice from Foreign Affairs, the Office of the Judge Advocate General, and Justice, in order to provide the prime minister with synthesized international humanitarian law advice as needed in the exercise of the Crown Prerogative of national defence and international relations.

F. WHAT KINDS OF ISSUES ARISE IN GOVERNMENT LAW PRACTICE?

There are a wide variety of international humanitarian law issues that arise for governments in the post–Cold War, post–9/11 setting. While some of these are specific to the expertise of one department, many of the more complex questions require collaboration across several government departments to arrive at a comprehensive legal analysis. International peacekeeping and peace enforcement, international travel of former and current foreign heads of state, immigration and refugee claims, extradition requests, and requests for mutual legal assistance in criminal matters can all give rise to issues of international humanitarian law:

- prosecuting an alleged war criminal found in Canada, or where prosecution is unlikely to succeed, defending the government's decision to strip an alleged war criminal of citizenship and removal of suspected war criminals from Canada;[15]
- assisting a foreign government or international tribunal in gathering evidence or in obtaining the extradition of a person, for the pur-

---

15 On 19 October 2005, the RCMP "A" Division (National Capital Region) War Crimes Section arrested Rwandan Désiré Munyaneza on seven charges under the *Crimes Against Humanity and War Crimes Act*, including two counts of genocide, two counts of crimes against humanity, and three counts of war crimes. Revocation of citizenship proceedings were taken against Helmut Oberlander. *Mugesera v. Canada (Minister of Citizenship and Immigration)*, [2005] 2 S.C.R. 100 [*Mugesera*] involved proceedings to remove from Canada a person suspected of inciting genocide.

poses of prosecution or sentencing, either before a foreign criminal court or an international tribunal for war crimes or crimes against humanity;[16]

- advising on anticipated entry to Canada of a (former or current) foreign official who is the subject of allegations of having committed war crimes or crimes against humanity—this could arise if Canada is hosting a large multilateral meeting and security concerns arise with respect to anticipated foreign participants or members of their entourage;
- advising on the application of the *Immigration and Refugee Protection Act*[17] and relevant provisions of the 1951 Geneva *Convention Relating to the Status of Refugees* in a particular case;
- advising on how to effectively implement international humanitarian law obligations into domestic law, given domestic and international jurisprudence;[18]
- presenting Canada's position on the distinction between *jus in bello* and *jus ad bellum* in legal cases involving persons claiming refugee status on the basis of the alleged illegality of a conflict in which they are expected to participate;[19]
- presenting and defending Canada's record in relation to human rights Conventions before UN treaty bodies;[20]
- inquiring into and presenting Canada's position with respect to individual complaints brought before UN treaty bodies;[21]
- defending Canada before the International Court of Justice against allegations of breach of international humanitarian law and other international legal obligations;[22]

---

16 The prosecution before the ICTY of Dragoljub Ojdanic, a former colonel general in the Yugoslav Army for alleged war crimes would be an example.

17 S.C. 2001, c. 27.

18 *R. v. Finta*, [1994] 1 S.C.R. 701; *Mugesera*, above note 15.

19 This issue arose in the case of a US army deserter, Jeremy Hinzman, claiming refugee status in Canada. In March 2005 the Immigration and Refugee Board denied the claim.

20 For example, in 2005 Canada presented its country reports in relation to the *Convention against Torture* and the *Covenant on Civil and Political Rights* to the UN Committee against Torture and the UN Human Rights Committee, respectively.

21 For example, UN Human Rights Committee and *International Covenant on Civil and Political Rights*.

22 *Serbia and Montenegro v. Canada*, one of eight cases brought against NATO countries by Serbia and Montenegro on *the Legality of the Use of Force*. On 15 December 2004, the International Court of Justice dismissed the cases against Canada and other respondents for want of jurisdiction, having found that Serbia and Montenegro did not, at the

- presenting Canada's legal position on matters referred to the International Court of Justice for an advisory opinion;[23]
- presenting Canada's interpretation of its various international obligations when contested in domestic courts;[24]
- advising the federal government as to whether use of force by a state is or is not justified under international law in particular circumstances;
- providing the full range of legal advice relevant to armed conflict;
- advising on the legal dimensions of rules of engagement and on the application of international humanitarian law, other international laws, and domestic law in all Canadian Forces operations;
- advising on applicability of Canada's international humanitarian law, international human rights obligations, and domestic legal standards in particular circumstances where the Canadian Forces are deployed in international operations;
- advising on the legal dimensions of joint military operations or interoperability where partner states may have different international humanitarian law obligations and different interpretations of their international humanitarian law obligations;
- participating in international conferences on international humanitarian law and related subjects of international law;
- providing legal advice to the federal government on the development of principles of international humanitarian law and on positions to take on international humanitarian law-related matters before the UN Security Council or the UN General Assembly;[25]
- providing legal advice and assistance in the preparation to sign and ratify new international humanitarian law, human rights, or arms control instruments;[26]

---

time of the institution of the proceedings, have access to the court under either para. 1 or para. 2 of art. 35 of the ICJ statute.

23 A recent example being the UN General Assembly reference to the ICJ on the *Legal Consequences of the Construction of a Wall in the Occupied Palestinian Territory*, (ICJ Advisory Opinion of 9 July 2004).

24 For example, *Bouzari v. Iran*, above note 12.

25 For example, UN reform and the *Report of the Secretary General's High Level Panel on Threats, Challenges and Change*, the situation in Darfur, the initiative on *The Responsibility to Protect*, resolutions pertaining to various international and non-international armed conflict, etc.

26 For example, the *Protocol to the Conventional Weapons Convention on Explosive Remnants of War, Protocols to the Hague Convention on the Protection of Cultural Property in Times of Armed Conflict*.

- providing relevant Canadian expertise to support international tribunals; and
- developing international humanitarian law training for military personnel and other government officials to ensure they respect international humanitarian law when deployed on international operations; contributing Canadian expertise to international humanitarian law training programs around the world.[27]

G. THE CANADIAN NATIONAL COMMITTEE FOR HUMANITARIAN LAW

National implementation and compliance with international humanitarian law is a permanent process requiring the cooperation of different ministries and organizations. Establishment of national committees for the implementation of international humanitarian law is seen as an effective way to ensure that national implementation measures are undertaken by states. The Canadian National Committee for Humanitarian Law (CNCHL) was established in March 1998, with representation from the Departments of Foreign Affairs and Justice, the Canadian Forces, the Canadian International Development Agency, the Royal Canadian Mounted Police, and the Canadian Red Cross Society.

The mandate of the CNCHL is to facilitate the implementation of international humanitarian law in Canada, including the 1949 Geneva Conventions and the 1977 Additional Protocols. It serves as a forum for sharing information and discussing recent developments in international humanitarian law. The committee is still relatively new and its functions are evolving. The committee might play a useful role in encouraging the ratification of legal instruments pertaining to international humanitarian law, supporting the implementation of international humanitarian law obligations, and encouraging collaboration in dissemination and training in Canada. The committee might also stimulate the actions of governmental departments and other relevant organizations to strengthen compliance with and enhance the dissemination of international humanitarian law.

The committee might encourage study and development of recommendations on how best to promote national implementation of international humanitarian law into domestic law, in order to assist other countries by drawing on the resources and expertise available in Canada. It might also

---

27   For example, military personnel exchanges and partnerships with the International Institute of Humanitarian Law.

maintain an updated list of experts in international humanitarian law and share information on international humanitarian law with other national committees, as well as the International Committee of the Red Cross.

H. FUTURE CHALLENGES IN INTERNATIONAL HUMANITARIAN LAW

The nature of conflict has been changing in recent years, throwing up new challenges to international humanitarian law. While states continue to build national armies to protect territorial sovereignty, the nature of the "enemy" has shifted from identifiable state actors to non-state actors, making identification of the "enemy" more difficult. The new asymmetrical conflicts have given rise to heated political and legal debate challenging the notion that the Geneva Conventions are a universal code that all sides to a conflict must follow. The tactics of war have changed, with guerrilla groups using volunteer and coerced suicide bombers to target civilian populations. In response, national armies develop new weapons and methods of warfare that are better suited for armed conflicts with non-conventional enemies, but which may raise concerns about consistency with humanitarian law principles.

The use of child soldiers is a horrifying and persistent problem in some parts of the world. Militarized children present particular challenges in terms of educating them sufficiently to understand and obey the limits imposed by international humanitarian law and to understand there may be alternatives to war. The victimization of civilians in conflict, especially women and children, continues unabated, notwithstanding the established norms of international humanitarian law forbidding the targeting of civilian populations and the new articulation of offences against women in the Rome Statute.

There is increased use of civilian contract employees and private firms to perform functions that in the past would have been considered functions traditionally performed by regular armed forces. How international humanitarian law might apply to these contract workers, and whether they are properly trained to behave in accordance with its limits, is an open question. The drafting of defence procurement contracts involving such arrangements needs to consider any potential international humanitarian law dimensions. The issue of corporate social responsibility has particular resonance when private corporations are conducting business in war-torn or failing states.[28]

---

28 See, for example, *Embedding Human Rights in Business Practice*, a joint publication of the United Nations Global Compact and the Office of the United Nations High Commissioner for Human Rights, specifically, the discussion by Denise O'Brien & Melissa

Increasing awareness of the gulf in human rights and humanitarian standards recognized by different parties to a conflict raises many questions about how to ensure universal standards. Military coalitions may include nations with different commitments under international humanitarian law, international human rights, and other relevant international law and with widely varying capacity or willingness to meet their respective commitments. How does each coalition participant ensure that it meets its particular international law obligations and relevant domestic law standards, and still participate effectively in the coalition?

These are some of the difficult issues with which the International Committee of the Red Cross, national committees on international humanitarian law, and lawyers from national governments are currently grappling. While this chapter offers no solutions to these complex issues, it highlights how much more work needs to be done both to ensure humanitarian law is widely understood and applied, and to develop this field of law to meet the world's emerging needs.

I. CONCLUSION

These are significant issues that force us to rethink and reinterpret international humanitarian law, but history has always thrown up challenges to this body of law; yet, with international collaboration and leadership, international humanitarian law has persevered. The basic concerns addressed by it have been with us since ancient times, and admonitions to treat civilians and disarmed or wounded combatants humanely can be traced through the Hammourabi Code of Babylon four thousand years ago, the ancient Indian Mahâbhârata, and the law of Manu; the code of Japanese soldiers in feudal times; the Koran; Jean-Jacques Rousseau's *Social Contract* of 1762; the 1785 "Treaty of Friendship and Peace"; Henry Dunant's *A Memory of Solferino* of 1862; and the Lieber Code of the American Civil War.

In spite of the challenging issues we now face, international humanitarian law has never been stronger. Since its early modern beginnings in eighteenth-century Dutch diplomat Grotius's work *De Jure Belli ac Pacis*, international humanitarian law has developed into a vast infrastructure of law, including the recent enactment of the Rome Statute of 1998 and the creation of the International Criminal Court. It may be true that inter-

---

Powell on the Global Compact policy dialogue: "The Role of the Private Sector in Zones of Conflict" at 128.

national humanitarian law develops slowly, but progress is inexorable.[29] Government and military lawyers will continue to work in partnership to strengthen domestic understanding and implementation of humanitarian law concepts, and participate with the International Committee of the Red Cross and National Committees on International Humanitarian Law in the ongoing development of international humanitarian law.

---

29 When first engaged to examine the proposal for an ad hoc tribunal for war crimes in the former Yugoslavia, this author was surprised to discover departmental files on a proposed international criminal code and criminal court that dated back to the 1950s—what once may have seemed like a quixotic dream became reality as the twentieth century drew to a close.

Selected Bibliography

SECONDARY SOURCES: BOOKS

Alston, Philip & Madelaine Chiam, eds. *Treaty-Making and Australia: Globalisation versus Sovereignty?* (Sydney: Federation Press, 1995).

American Law Institute. *Restatement of the Law (Third): The Foreign Relations Law of the United States*, vol. 1 (St. Paul, MN: American Law Institute, 1987).

Aust, Anthony. *Modern Treaty Law and Practice* (Cambridge: Cambridge University Press, 2000).

Barker, J. Craig. *The Abuse of Diplomatic Privileges and Immunities: A Necessary Evil?* (Aldershot: Dartmouth, 1996).

Basson, Dion A. *South Africa's Interim Constitution: Text and Notes* (Kenwyn: Juta, 1994).

Bergsmo, Morten, ed. *Human Rights and Criminal Justice for the Downtrodden: Essays in Honour of Asbjorn Eide* (Leiden: Brill Academic Publishers 2003).

Bhagwati, Jagdish. *In Defense of Globalization* (London: Oxford University Press, 2004).

Blackshield, Tony & George Williams, *Australian Constitutional Law and Theory*, 3d ed. (Sydney: Federation Press, 2002).

Bradley, A.W. & K.D. Ewing *Constitutional and Administrative Law*, 12th ed. (London: Longman, 1997).

Broomhall, Bruce. *International Justice and the International Criminal Court: Between Sovereignty and the Rule of Law* (Oxford: Oxford University Press, 2003).

Brownlie, Ian. *Principles of International Law*, 6th ed. (Oxford: Oxford University Press 2003).

Burns, Peter. "The Convention against Torture and Diminishing Immunity." In *The Changing Face of International Criminal Law* (Vancouver: International Centre for Criminal Law Reform and Criminal Justice Policy, 2001).

———— & Sean McBurney. "Impunity and the UN Convention against Torture: A Shadow Play without Ending." In Craig Scott, ed. *Torture as Tort* (Portland: Hart Publishing, 2001).

Byrnes, Andrew, "Civil Remedies for Torture Committed Abroad: An Obligation under the Convention Against Torture?" In Craig Scott, ed. *Torture as Tort* (Portland: Hart Publishing 2001).

Cassese, Antonio. *International Law* (Oxford: Oxford University Press, 2001).

Charlesworth, Hilary *et al.*, eds. *The Fluid State: International Law and National Legal Systems* (Sydney: Federation Press, 2005).

Currie, John H. *Public International Law* (Toronto: Irwin Law, 2001).

Cygan, Adam J. *The United Kingdom Parliament and European Union Legislation* (The Hague: Kluwer Law International, 1998).

Devenish, G.E. *A Commentary on the South African Constitution* (Durban: Butterworths, 1998).

de Waal, Johan. "Constitutional Law." In C.G. van der Merwe *et al.*, eds. *Introduction to the Law of South Africa* (The Hague: Kluwer Law International, 2004).

Dicey, A.V. *Introduction to the Study of the Law of the Constitution*, 10th ed. (London: Macmillan, 1959).

Di Marzo, Luigi. *Component Units of Federal States and International Agreements* (Rockville, MD: Sijthoff & Noordhoff, 1980).

Dinwoodie, Graeme. "The International Property Law System: New Actors, New Institutions, New Sources." In *Proceedings of the 98th Annual Meeting of the American Society of International Law* (2004).

Dunsmuir, Mollie. *The Kyoto Protocol: Overview of Federal Legal Mechanisms for Implementation* (Ottawa: Library of Parliament, 2002).

Doeker, Günther. *The Treaty-Making Power in the Commonwealth of Australia* (The Hague: Martinus Nijhoff, 1966).

Driedger, E.A. *Construction of Statutes*, 2d ed. (Toronto: Butterworths, 1983).

Dugard, John. *International Law: A South African Perspective*, 1st ed. (Kenwyn: Juta, 1994).

————. *International Law: A South African Perspective*, 2d ed. (Kenwyn: Juta, 2000).

Dyzenhaus, David, ed. *The Unity of Public Law* (Oxford: Hart Publishing, 2004).

Evans, Malcolm D. & Rod Morgan. *Preventing Torture: A Study of the European Convention for the Prevention of Torture and Inhuman or Degrading Treatment or Punishment* (Oxford: Clarendon Press, 1998).

Fawcett, J.E.S. *The British Commonwealth in International Law* (London: Stevens & Son, 1963).

Fox, Hazel. *The Law of State Immunity* (Oxford: Oxford University Press, 2002).

Franck, Thomas M., ed. *Delegating State Powers: The Effect of Treaty Regimes on Democracy and Sovereignty* (Ardsley, NY: Transnational Publishers, 2000).

Gervais, Daniel. *The TRIPS Agreement: Drafting History and Analysis,* 2d ed. (London: Sweet & Maxwell, 2003).

———. *La notion d'œuvre dans la Convention de Berne et en droit compare* (Genève: Librairie Droz, 1998).

Giddings, Philip & Gavin Drewry, ed. *Britain in the European Union: Law, Policy and Parliament* (New York: Palgrave Macmillan, 2004).

Gotlieb, Allan E. *Canadian Treaty-Making* (Toronto: Butterworths, 1968).

Hall, Christopher K. "Contemporary Universal Jurisdiction." In Morten Bergsmo, ed., *Human Rights and Criminal Justice for the Downtrodden* (Leiden: Brill Academic Publishers, 2003).

Hannum, Hurst, ed. *Guide to International Human Rights Practice,* 4th ed. (Ardsley: Transnational, 2004).

Harris, Sally. *Out of Control: British Foreign Policy and the Union of Democratic Control, 1914–1918* (Hull, UK: University of Hull Press, 1996).

Hegel, Georg W.F. *Hegel's Philosophy of Right,* trans. by T.M. Knox (London: Oxford University Press, 1967).

Hogg, Peter W. *Constitutional Law of Canada,* 4th ed. (Scarborough: Carswell, 1997).

Jacomy-Millette, Anne Marie. *Canadian Provinces and Foreign Relations* (Ottawa: Library of Parliament, 1991).

———. *Treaty Law in Canada* (Ottawa: University of Ottawa Press, 1975).

Jacques, Geneviève. *Beyond Impunity: An Ecumenical Approach to Truth, Justice and Reconciliations* (Geneva: WCC Publications, 2000).

Janis, Mark. *An Introduction to International Law,* 4th ed. (New York: Aspen, 2003).

Jennings, Robert & Sir Arthur Watts, eds. *Oppenheim's International Law,* 9th ed. (New York: Longman, 1992).

Jones, Raymond A. *Arthur Ponsonby: The Politics of Life* (London: Christopher Helm, 1989).

Keyes, J.M. *Executive Legislation* (Toronto: Butterworths, 1992).

Kittichaisaree, Kriangsak. *International Criminal Law* (Oxford: Oxford University Press, 2001).

Koskenniemi, Martti. *The Gentle Civilizer of Nations: The Rise and Fall of International Law 1870–1960* (Cambridge: Cambridge University Press, 2001).

Leigh, Monroe *et al.*, eds. *National Treaty Law and Practice: Canada, Egypt, Israel, Mexico, Russia, South Africa* (Washington, DC: American Society of International Law, 2003).

Locke, John. *Second Treatise of Government*, ed. by C.B. Macpherson (Indianapolis, IN: Hackett, 1980).

Macedo, Stephen, ed. *The Princeton Principles on Universal Declaration* (Princeton, NJ: Princeton University, Program in Law and Public Affairs, 2001).

———. *Universal Jurisdiction: National Courts and the Prosecution of Serious Crimes under International Law* (Philadelphia: University of Pennsylvania Press, 2004).

Marquand, David. *Parliament for Europe* (London: Jonathan Cape, 1979).

———. *Ramsay MacDonald* (London: Jonathan Cape, 1977).

McKay, William, ed., *Erskine May's Treatise on the Law, Privileges, Proceedings and Usage of Parliament*, 23d ed. (London: LexisNexis U.K., 2004).

Munzer, Stephen R. *A Theory of Property* (New York: Cambridge University Press, 1990).

Ollivier, Maurice. *The Colonial and Imperial Conferences from 1887 to 1937* (Ottawa: Queen's Printer, 1954).

Oosterveld, Valerie & Alejanda C. Flah, "Holding Leaders Liable for Torture by Others: Command Responsibility and Respondeat Superior as Frameworks for Derivative Civil Liberties." In Craig Scott, ed. *Torture as Tort* (Portland, OR: Hart Publishing, 2001).

Opeskin, Brian R. & Donald R. Rothwell, eds. *International Law and Australian Federalism* (Melbourne: Melbourne University Press, 1977).

Ponsonby, Arthur. *Democracy and Diplomacy: A Plea for Popular Control of Foreign Policy* (London: Methuen and Co., 1915).

Ratner, Steven R. & Jason S. Abrams. *Accountability for Human Rights Atrocities in International Law: Beyond the Nuremberg Legacy* (Oxford: Oxford University Press, 2001).

Riesenfeld, Stefan A. & Frederick M. Abbott. *Parliamentary Participation in the Making and Operation of Treaties: A Comparative Study* (Boston: Martinus Nijhoff, 1994).

Roht-Arriaza, Naomi. *The Pinochet Effect: Transnational Justice in the Age of Human Rights* (Philadelphia: University of Pennsylvania Press, 2005).

Scherrer, S. "La Pratique québecoise en matière de traités, accords et autres instruments internationaux" (1992) *Actes de la XIe Conférence des juristes de l'État* (Cowansville, QC: Yvon Blais, 1992).

Scott, Craig, ed. *Torture as Tort* (Oxford: Hart Publishing, 2001).

Shaw, Malcolm N. *International Law*, 5th ed. (Cambridge: Cambridge University Press, 2003).

Stilborn, Jack. *The Kyoto Protocol: Intergovernmental Issues* (Ottawa: Library of Parliament, 2002).

Sullivan, Ruth. *Driedger on the Construction of Statutes*, 3d ed. (Toronto: Butterworths, 1994).

———. *Sullivan and Driedger on the Construction of Statutes*, 4th ed. (Toronto: Butterworths, 2002).

Swartz, Marvin. *The Union of Democratic Control in British Politics During the First World War* (Oxford: Clarendon Press, 1971).

Symonides, Janusz, ed. *Human Rights: International Protection, Monitoring, Enforcement* (Aldershot: Ashgate Publishing, 2003).

van Ert, Gibran. *Using International Law in Canadian Courts* (The Hague: Kluwer Law International, 2002).

van Wyk, Dawid *et al.*, eds. *Namibia: Constitutional and International Law Issues* (Pretoria: VerLoren van Themaat Centre, 1991).

Wildhaber, Luzius. *Treaty-Making Power and Constitution: An International and Comparative Study* (Basel: Basel, Stuttgart, Helbing & Lichtenhahn, 1971).

Zines, Leslie. *The High Court and the Constitution*, 4th ed. (Sydney: Butterworths, 1997).

SECONDARY SOURCES: JOURNAL ARTICLES

Akande, Dapo. "International Law Immunities and the International Criminal Court" (2004) 98 Am. J. Int'l L. 407.

Anderson, Winston. "Treaty-Making in Caribbean Law and Practice: The Question of Parliamentary Participation" (1998) 8 Caribbean Law Review 75.

Aucoin, P. & L. Turnbull. "The Democratic Deficit: Paul Martin and Parliamentary Reform" (2003) 46 Public Administration 427.

Bartsch, Kerstin & Bjorn Eberling. "*Jus Cogens v. State Immunity*, Round 2" (2005) 4 German Law Journal 5.

Bassiouni, M. Cherif. "World War I: The War to End All Wars and the Birth of a Handicapped International Justice System" 30 Denv. J. Int'l L.& Pol'y 244.

Beaulac, Stéphane. "National Application of International Law: The Statutory Interpretation Perspective" (2003) Can. Y.B. Int'l Law 225.

———. "On the Saying that 'International Law Binds Canadian Courts'" (2003) 29:3 Canadian Council on International Law Bulletin.

Bederman, David J. "Dead Man's Hand: Reshuffling Foreign Sovereign Immunities in U.S. Human Rights Litigation" (1995/96) 25 Ga. J. Int'l & Comp. L. 255.

Bianchi, Andrea. "Immunity Versus Human Rights: The Pinochet Case" (1999) 10:2 E.J.I.L. 327.

Bissonet, Michel. "The Participation of Parliamentarians in Trade Negotiations" (2004) 27 Canadian Parliamentary Review 10.

Botha, Neville. "The Coming of Age of Public International Law in South Africa" (1992/93) 18 S.A.Y.B. Int'l L. 36.

———. "Incorporation of Treaties under the Interim Constitution: A Pattern Emerges?" (1995) S.A.Y.B. Int'l L. 196.

———. "Interpreting a Treaty Endorsed Under the 1993 Constitution" (1993/1994) 19 S.A.Y.B. Int'l L. 148.

———. "Treaties after the 1996 Constitution: More Questions than Answers" (1997) 22 S.A.Y.B. Int'l L. 95.

———. "Treaty-Making in South Africa: A Reassessment" (2000) 25 S.A.Y.B. Int'l L. 69.

Bracegirdle, Allan. "Domestic Procedures for International Treaty Action: Description of New Zealand Procedures" (2003) 14 Public Law Review 28.

Burmester, Henry. "The Australian States and Participation in the Foreign Policy Process" (1978) 9 Federal Law Review 257.

Byrnes, Andrew. "The Implementation of Treaties in Australia after the Tasmanian Dams Case: The External Affairs Power and the Influence of Federalism" (1985) 8:2 B.C. Int'l & Comp. L. Rev. 275.

Calandrillo, Steve P. "An Economic Analysis of Intellectual Property Rights: Justifications and Problems of Exclusive Rights, Incentives to Generate Information, and the Alternative of a Government-Run Reward System" (1998) 9 Fordham I.P. Media & Ent. L.J. 301.

Caplan, Lee M. "State Immunity, Human Rights and *Jus Cogens*: A Critique of the Normative Hierarchy Theory" (2003) 97 Am. J. Int'l L. 741.

Capling, Ann & Kim Richard Nossal. "Parliament and the Democratization of Foreign Policy: The Case of Australia's Joint Standing Committee on Treaties" (2003) 36:4 Canadian Journal of Political Science 835.

Cassese, Antonio. "When May Senior State Officials Be Tried for International Crimes? Some Comments on the *Belgium v. Congo Case*" (2002) 13 E.J.I.L. 853.

Charlesworth, Hilary, *et al.* "Deep Anxieties: Australia and the International Legal Order" (2003) 25 Sydney L. Rev. 423.

Charnovitz, Steve. "Using Framework Statutes to Facilitate U.S. Treaty-Making" (2004) 98 Am. J. Int'l L. 696.

Chen, Mai. "A Constitutional Revolution? The Role of the New Zealand Parliament in Treaty-Making" (2001) 19 N.Z.U.L. Rev. 448.

Chiam, Madelaine. "Evaluating Australia's Treaty-Making Process" (2004) 15 Public Law Review 265.

Cranwell, Glen. "The Treaty-Making Process in Australia: A Report Card on Recent Reforms" (2001) Australian International Law Journal 177.

Crawford, J. "The International Law Standard in the Statutes of Australia and the United Kingdom" (1979) 73 Am. J. Int'l L. 628.

Devine, Dermott J. "The Relationship between International Law and Municipal Law in the Light of the Interim South African Constitution 1993" (1995) 44 I.C.L.Q. 1.

———. "Some Problems Relating to Treaties in the South African Constitution and Some Suggestions for the Definitive Constitution" (1995) 20 S.A.Y.B. Int'l L. 1.

Dinwoodie, Graeme & Rochelle Dreyfuss, "International Intellectual Property Law and the Public Domain of Science" (2004) 7 J. Int'l Econ. L. 431.

Dugard, John. "International Law and the 'Final' Constitution" (1995) 11 S.A.J.H.R. 241.

———. "International Law and the South African Constitution" (1997) 8 E.J.I.L. 77.

———. & Iain Currie, "Public International Law" (1995) Ann. Surv. S. Afr. L. 76.

———. "Public International Law" (1996) Ann. Surv. S. Afr. L. 145.

Duhl, Gregory M. "Old Lyrics, Knock-Off Videos, and Copycat Comic Books: The Fourth Fair Use Factor in U.S. Copyright Law" (2004) 54 Syracuse L. Rev. 665.

Dunworth, Treasa. "International Treaty Examination: The Saga Continues" (2002) N.Z.L. Rev. 255.

Geiringer, Claudia. "*Tavita* and All That: Confronting the Confusion Surrounding Unincorporated Treaties and Administrative Law" (2004) 21:1 N.Z.U.L. Rev. 66.

Gervais, Daniel. "Canadian Copyright Law after CCH" (2004) 18:2 I.P.J. 131–68.

———. "The Compatibility of 'Skill & Labour' with the Berne Convention and the TRIPS Agreement" (2004) 2 Eur. I.P. Rev. 75–80.

———. "Feist Goes Global: A Comparative Analysis of the Notion of Originality in Copyright Law" (2002–3) 49:4 Journal of the Copyright Society of the USA 949–81.

———. "The Internationalization of Intellectual Property: Challenges from the Very Old and the Very New" (2002) 12:4: Fordham I.P. Media & Ent. L.J. 929–90.

Goldklang, Jack M. "Current Developments: The Thirty-Fourth Session of the International Law Commission" (1983) 77 Am. J. Int'l. L. 323.

Harrington, Joanna. "Redressing the Democratic Deficit in Treaty Law Making: (Re-)Establishing a Role for Parliament" (2005) 50 McGill L.J. 465.
———. "Scrutiny and Approval: The Role for Westminster-Style Parliaments in Treaty-Making" (2006) 55 I.C.L.Q. 121.

Hustins, Nancy-Louise E. "British Court Grants Canadian William Sampson the Right to Sue Saudi Captors" 31:1 (2005) Canadian Council on International Law Bulletin.

Jones, Melinda. "Myths and Facts concerning the Convention on the Rights of the Child in Australia" (1999) 5:2 Australian Journal of Human Rights 126.

Keightley, Raylene. "Public International Law and the Final Constitution" (1996) 12 S.A.J.H.R. 405.

Keith, Kenneth. "New Zealand Treaty Practice: The Executive and the Legislature" (1964) 1 N.Z.U.L. Rev. 272.

Keyes, J.M. "Required Rule-Making: When Do You Have to Make Delegated Legislation" (2002) 15 Can. J. Admin. L. & Prac. 293.

Knop, Karen. "Here and There: International Law in Domestic Courts" (2000) 32 N.Y.U.J. Int'l L. & Pol. 501.

Koh, Harold. "Transnational Public Law Litigation" (1991) 100 Yale L.J. 2347.

Lacey, Wendy. "In the Wake of *Teoh*: Finding an Appropriate Government Response" (2001) 29:2 Federal Law Review 219.
———. "Prelude to the Demise of *Teoh*: The High Court Decision in *Re Minister for Immigration and Multicultural Affairs; Ex parte Lam*" (2004) 26 Sydney L. Rev. 131.

La Forest, Anne. "Domestic Application of International Law in Charter Cases: Are We There Yet?" (2004) 37 U.B.C. L. Rev. 157.

LeBel, Louis & Gloria Chao, "The Rise of International Law in Canadian Constitutional Litigation: Fugue or Fusion? Recent Developments and Challenges in Internalizing International Law" (2002) 16 Sup. Ct. L. Rev. (2d) 23.

Low, John C. "Finding the Right Tool for the Job: Adequate Protection for Research Tool Patents in a Global Market?" (2005) 27 Hous. J. Int'l L. 345.

Maskus, Keith E. & Jerome H. Reichman, "The Globalization of Private Knowledge Goods and the Privatization of Global Public Goods" (2004) 7 J. Int'l Econ. L. 279.

Molot, H.L. & M.L. Jewett. *The State Immunity Act of Canada* (1982) 20 Can. Y.B. Int'l Law 79.

Oddi, A. Samuel. "TRIPS—Natural Rights and a 'Polite Form of Economic Imperialism'" (1996) 29 Vand. J. Transnat'l L. 415.

Olivier, Michèle. "Exploring the Doctrine of Self-Execution as Enforcement Mechanism of International Oobligations" (2002) S.A.Y.B. Int'l L. 99.

———. "Informal International Agreements under the 1996 Constitution" (1997) 22 S.A.Y.B. Int'l L. 62.

———. "The Status of International Law in South African Municipal Law: Section 231 of the 1993 Constitution" (1993/94) 19 S.A.Y.B. Int'l L. 1.

Opeskin, Brian R. & Donald R. Rothwell. "The Impact of Treaties on Australian Federalism" (1995) 27 Case W. Res. J. Int'l L. 1.

Ostergard, Robert L., Jr. "Intellectual Property: A Universal Human Right?" (1999) 21:1 Hum. Rts. Q. 156.

Radin, Margaret Jane. "Property and Personhood" (1982) 34 Stan. L. Rev. 957.

Ratner, Steven R. "Belgium's War Crimes Statute: A Postmortem" (editorial comment) (2003) 97 Am. J. Int'l L. 888.

Ricketson, Sam. "The Boundaries of Copyright: Its Proper Limitations and Exceptions: International Conventions and Treaties" 1 (1999) Intellectual Property Quarterly 56–94.

Robinson, Darryl. "The Impact of the Human Rights Accountability Movement on the International Law of Immunities" (2002) Can. Y.B. Int'l Law.

Saunders, Cheryl. "Articles of Faith or Lucky Breaks? The Constitutional Law of International Agreements in Australia" (1995) 17 Sydney L. Rev. 150.

Schneeberger, JoAnn. "A Labyrinth of Tautology: The Meaning of the Term 'International Agreement' and its Significance for South African Law and Treaty-Making Practice" (2001) S.A.Y.B. Int'l L. 1.

Schoombee, J.T. "A Licence for Unlawful Arrests across the Border?" (1984) 101 South African Law Journal 713.

Setear, John K. "An Iterative Perspective on Treaties: A Synthesis of International Relations Theory and International Law" (1996) 37 Harvard Int'l L. J. 139.

Shearer, I.A. "International Legal Notes" (1995) 69 Australian Law Journal 404.

Stewart, David P. "The UN Convention on Jurisdictional Immunities of States and Their Properties" (2005) 99 Am. J. Int'l L. 194.

Strom, T. & P. Finkle. "Treaty Implementation: The Canadian Game Needs Australian Rules" (1993) 25 Ottawa L. Rev. 39.

"Symposium on Parliamentary Participation in the Making and Operation of Treaties" (1991) 67 Chicago-Kent L. Rev.

Lord Templeman, "Treaty-Making and the British Parliament" (1991) 67 Chicago-Kent L. Rev. 459.

Toope, Stephen J. "The Use of Metaphor: International Law and the Supreme Court" (2001) Can. Bar Rev. 534.

Turp, Daniel. "Un nouveau défi démocratique: l'accentuation du rôle du parlement dans la conclusion et la mise en oeuvre des traités internationaux" (1999) Canadian Council on Int'l L. Proc. 118.

van Ert, Gibran. "International Law Does Bind Canadian Courts: A Reply" (2004) 30:1 Canadian Council on International Law Bulletin.

———. "The Legal Character of Provincial Agreements with Foreign Governments" (2001) 42 C. de D. 1093.

Warbrick, Colin. "Current Developments: Treaties" (2000) 49 I.C.L.Q. 944.

Weiser, I. "Undressing the Window: Treating International Human Rights Law Meaningfully in the Canadian Commonwealth System" (2004) 37 U.B.C. L. Rev. 113.

Williams, Daryl. "Establishing an Australian Parliamentary Treaties Committee" (1995) *Public Law Review* 275.

———. "Treaties and the Parliamentary Process" (1996) 7 Public Law Review 199.

Wirth, Steffen. "Immunity for Core Crimes: The ICJ's Judgements in the *Congo v. Belgium* Case" (2002) 13 E.J.I.L. 877.

World Organization to Investigate the Persecution of the Falun Gong. "Searching for Justice: Counteracting Hate, Torture, and Crimes against Humanity" (conference document, 19 June 2004).

STATUTORY SOURCES: CANADA

Access to Information Act, R.S.C. 1985, c. A-1.

An Act to amend the Department of External Affairs Act and to make related amendments to other Acts, S.C. 1995, c. 5.

An Act to create a Department of External Affairs, 8-9 Edw. VII, c. 13.

An Act Respecting the Ministère des Relations Internationales, R.S.Q., c. M-25.1.1.

Export and Import Permits Act, R.S.C. 1985, c. E-19.

Extradition Act, R.S.C. 1985, c. E-23.

Extradition Act, S.C. 1999, c. 18.

STATUTORY SOURCES: OTHER JURISDICTIONS

Case-Zablocki Act, 1 U.S.C. § 112(b).

Commonwealth of Australia Constitution Act, 1900, 63 & 64 Vic., c. 12.

Constitution of Ireland, 1937.

Constitution of the Republic of Namibia, 1990.

Constitution of the Republic of South Africa, Act 32 of 1961.

Constitution of the Republic of South Africa, Act 110 of 1983.
Constitution of the Republic of South Africa, Act 200 of 1993.
Constitution of the Republic of South Africa, Act 108 of 1996.

Government of Wales Act 1998, c. 38 (United Kingdom).

Northern Ireland Act 1998, c. 47 (United Kingdom).

Ratification of Treaties Act 1987, No. 1 of 1987 (Antigua and Barbuda).

Scotland Act 1998, c. 46 (United Kingdom).
Statute Law (Miscellaneous Provisions) Act 1993 (Queensland).

Treaties Commission Act 1974 (Queensland).

JURISPRUDENCE

Azanian Peoples Organization v. President of the Republic of South Africa, 1996 (4) S.A. 671, 1996 (8) B.C.L.R. 1015 (Const. Ct.).

Baker v. Canada (Minister of Citizenship and Immigration), [1999] 2 S.C.R. 817.

Canada (A-G) v. Ontario (A-G), [1937] A.C. 326 (P.C.) [*Labour Conventions* case].
Commonwealth v. Tasmania (Franklin Dam Case) (1983), 158 C.L.R. 1 (Aust. H.C.).

European Roma Rights Centre v. Immigration Officer at Prague Airport, [2003] E.W.C.A. Civ. 666, [2004] 2 W.L.R. 147 (C.A.).

Harksen v. President of the Republic of South Africa, 2000 (2) S.A. 825, 2000 (5) B.C.L.R. 478 (Const. Ct.).
Hellenic Republic v. Tzatzimakis, [2002] F.C.A. 340 (Aust.).

Minister of State for Immigration and Ethnic Affairs v. Teoh (1995), 183 C.L.R. 273 (Aust. H.C.).

Pan American World Airways Inc. v. S.A. Fire and Accident Insurance Co. Ltd., 1965 (3) S.A. 150 (Appeal Division).
Pasini v. United Mexican States, [2002] H.C.A. 3 (Aust.).
Puli'uvea v. Removal Review Authority (1996), 2 H.R.N.Z. 510 (C.A.).
Tavita v. Minister of Immigration, [1994] 2 N.Z.L.R. 257 (C.A.).
Toonen v. Australia, Communication No. 488/1992, U.N. Doc. CCPR/C/50/D/488/1992 (1994).

GOVERNMENT DOCUMENTS: AUSTRALIA

Australia. Joint Standing Committee on Treaties, *Report 11* (1997).

650 THE GLOBALIZED RULE OF LAW

———. Joint Standing Committee on Treaties, *Report 14: Multilateral Agreement on Investment: Interim Report* (1998).

———. Joint Standing Committee on Treaties, *Report 16: OECD Convention on Combating Bribery and Draft Implementing Legislation* (1998).

———. Joint Standing Committee on Treaties, *Report 17: United Nations Convention on the Rights of the Child* (1998).

———. Joint Standing Committee on Treaties, *Report 18: Multilateral Agreement on Investment: Final Report* (1999).

———. Joint Standing Committee on Treaties, Parliament of Australia, *Report 24: A Seminar on the Role of Parliaments in Treaty-making* (1999).

———. Joint Standing Committee on Treaties, *Report 38: The Kyoto Protocol—Discussion Paper* (2001).

———. Joint Standing Committee on Treaties, *Report 40: Extradition—A Review of Australia's Law and Policy* (2001).

———. Joint Standing Committee On Treaties, *Report 45: The Statute of the International Criminal Court* (2002).

———. Joint Standing Committee on Treaties. *Report 61: Australia-United States Free Trade Agreement* (2004).

———. Senate Legal and Constitutional References Committee. *Trick or Treaty? Commonwealth Power to Make and Implement Treaties* (1995). Online: www.aph.gov.au/senate/committee/legcon_ctte/completed_inquiries/pre1996/treaty/report/index.htm.

Commonwealth of Australia. *Joint Statement by the Minister for Foreign Affairs, Senator Gareth Evans QC, and the Attorney-General Michael Lavarch MP: International Treaties and the High Court Decision in Teoh* (1995).

———. *Joint Statement by the Minister for Foreign Affairs, Alexander Downer MP, and the Attorney-General, Daryl Williams AM QC MP* (1996). Online: www.dfat.gov.au/media/releases/foreign/1996/fa29.html.

———. Attorney-General's Department. *Review of the Treaty-Making Process* (1999). Online: law.gov.au/agd/Attorney-General/Treaty-Making%20Process.htm.

———. Department of Foreign Affairs and Trade. *Signed, Sealed and Delivered: Treaties and Treaty-making: An Official's Handbook*, 3d ed. (2003).

Final Report of the Constitutional Commission. Canberra: Australian Government Publishing Service, 1988.

Parliament of Queensland. Legal, Constitutional and Administrative Review Committee. *Report 22: The Role of the Queensland Parliament in Treaty-making* (2000).

———. Legal, Constitutional and Administrative Review Committee. *Report 39: The Role of the Queensland Parliament in Treaty-making—Review of Tabling Procedure* (2003).

Parliament of Victoria. Federal-State Relations Committee. *International Treaty-making and the Role of the States* (1997). Online: www.parliament.vic.gov.au/fsrc/report1/contents.htm.

Parliament of Western Australia. Standing Committee on Constitutional Relations. *Report 38: Report in relation to a Seminar on the Role of Parliaments in Treaty-making* (1999).

GOVERNMENT DOCUMENTS: CANADA

Alberta. *Report of the MLA Committee on Strengthening Alberta's Role in Confederation.* Edmonton: Government of Alberta, 2004. Online: www.iir.gov.ab.ca/canadian_intergovernmental_relations/documents/mla_committee_report_003.pdf.

Government of Canada. "Government of Canada Releases International Policy Statement," news release no. 68 (19 April 2005). Online: webapps.dfait-maeci.gc.ca/MinPub/Publication.asp?Language=E&publication_id=382440.

———. "Government Statement on Proposals for Copyright Reform, March 2005." Online: www.pch.gc.ca/progs/ac-ca/progs/pda-cpb/reform/statement_e.cfm.

———. Privy Council Office, *Ethics, Responsibility, Accountability: An Action Plan for Democratic Reform* (Ottawa: Government of Canada, 2004).

———. Department of External Affairs. *Federalism and International Relations* (Ottawa: Queen's Printer, 1968).

Parliament of Canada. Special Joint Committee of the Senate and of the House of Commons on the Constitution of Canada. *Final Report* (Chairs: Molgat and MacGuigan) (Ottawa: Queen's Printer, 1972).

———. Standing Committee on Foreign Affairs and International Trade. *Bill S-22, An Act authorizing the United States to preclear travellers and goods in Canada for entry into the United States for the purposes of customs, immigration, public health, food inspection and plant and animal health: Eighth Report of the Standing Committee on Foreign Affairs and International Trade* (May 1999).

———. Standing Committee on Foreign Affairs and International Trade. *Canada and the Multilateral Agreement on Investment: Third Report of the Standing Committee on Foreign Affairs and International Trade: First Report of the Sub-Committee on International Trade, Trade Disputes and Investment* (December 1997).

————. Standing Committee on Foreign Affairs and International Trade. *The Free Trade Area of the Americas: Towards a Hemispheric Agreement in the Canadian Interest: First Report of the Standing Committee on Foreign Affairs and International Trade: First Report of the Sub-Committee on International Trade, Trade Disputes and Investment* (October 1999).

Report of the Royal Commission on Dominion-Provincial Relations (Rowell-Sirois Commission) (Ottawa: Queen's Printer, 1940).

Second Report of the [Ontario] Advisory Committee on Confederation: The Federal-Provincial Distribution of Powers (Toronto: Queen's Printer, 1979).

GOVERNMENT DOCUMENTS: SOUTH AFRICA

Republic of South Africa. Department of Foreign Affairs. Office of the Chief State Law Adviser (International Law). *Practical Guide and Procedures for the Conclusion of Agreements* (undated). Online: www.dfa.gov.za/department/law.doc.
————. Office of the President. *Manual on Executive Acts of the President of the Republic of South Africa* (May 1994).
————. Office of the President. *Manual on Executive Acts of the President of the Republic of South Africa* (1997).
————. Office of the President. *Manual on Executive Acts of the President of the Republic of South Africa* (March 1999).

GOVERNMENT DOCUMENTS: UNITED KINGDOM

United Kingdom. *Memorandum of Understanding and supplementary agreements between the United Kingdom Government, Scottish Ministers and the Cabinet of the National Assembly for Wales.* Cm 4444 (October 1999).
————. *Strengthening the Biological and Toxin Weapons Convention: Countering the Threat from Biological Weapons.* Cm 5484 (April 2002).
————. Foreign and Commonwealth Office. *The Ponsonby Rule.* London: Foreign and Commonwealth Office, 2001. Online: www.fco.gov.uk/Files/kfile/PonsonbyRule.pdf.
————. Foreign and Commonwealth Office. *Treaties and MOUs: Guidance on Practice and Procedure,* 2d ed. London: Foreign and Commonwealth Office, 2000. Revised May 2004. Online: www.fco.gov.uk/Files/KFile/TreatiesandMOUsFinal,0.pdf.
————. House of Commons Information Office, *Treaties* (House of Commons Factsheet No. 14, Procedure Series). Revised June 2003. Online: www.parliament.uk/documents/upload/p14.pdf

———. House of Commons. Select Committee on Procedure, *Second Report: Parliamentary Scrutiny of Treaties*, HC 210, Session 1999-2000 (26 July 2000).

———. House of Commons. Select Committee on Procedure, *Second Special Report: Government's Response to the Second Report of the Committee: Parliamentary Scrutiny of Treaties*, HC 990, Session 1999-2000 (22 November 2000).

———. House of Commons. Select Committee on Defence, *Third Report: NATO Enlargement*, HC 469, Session 1997-1998 (2 April 1998).

———. Joint Committee on Human Rights, *The Convention on the Elimination of Racial Discrimination*, HL Paper 88/HC 471, Session 2004-05 (16 March 2005).

———. Joint Committee on Human Rights, *The International Covenant on Social, Economic and Cultural Rights*, HL Paper 183/HC 1188, Session 2003-04 (20 October 2004).

———. Joint Committee on Human Rights, *Protocol No. 14 to the European Convention on Human Rights*, HL Paper 8/HC 106, Session 2004-05 (1 December 2004).

———. Joint Committee on Human Rights, *Review of International Human Rights Instruments*, HL Paper 99/HC 264, Session 2004-05 (23 March 2005).

———. Joint Committee on Human Rights, *The U.N. Convention on the Rights of the Child*, HL Paper 117/HC 81, Session 2002-03 (9 June 2003).

———. Royal Commission on the Reform of the House of Lords. *A House for the Future*. Cm. 4534 (January 2000).

GOVERNMENT DOCUMENTS: OTHER JURISDICTIONS

New Zealand. New Zealand Law Commission. *The Treaty-making Process: Reform and the Role of Parliament*. Wellington: The Commission, 1997.

United States. Library of Congress. Congressional Research Service. *Treaties and Other International Agreements: The Role of the United States: A Study Prepared for the Committee on Foreign Relations*, United States Senate, S. Prt. 106-71 (January 2001).

World Trade Organization. *Canada—Patent Protection of Pharmaceutical Products, Report of the Panel*, 17 March 2000. Document WT/DS114/R.

———. *Canada—Term of Patent Protection, Report of the Appellate Body*, 12 October 2000. Document WT/DS170/AB/R.

———. *United States—Section 110(5) of the US Copyright Act, Report of the Panel*, 15 June 2000. Document WT/DS160/R.

WEBSITES

Australia. Parliament. Joint Standing Committee on Treaties: www.aph.gov. au/house/committee/jsct/index.htm.

Canada. Treaty Information: www.treaty-accord.gc.ca.

United Kingdom. Foreign and Commonwealth Office. Treaties Information: www.fco.gov.uk/treaty.

Contributors

Dr. Natasha Affolder is assistant professor at the Faculty of Law, University of British Columbia. She completed her LL.B. at the University of Alberta, and a B.C.L. and Doctorate in Law (D.Phil.) at Oxford University, where she was a Rhodes Scholar. Before joining the University of British Columbia, Dr. Affolder held a research associate position at Harvard Business School, and practised law in private practice in Boston. She has worked in various capacities for international non-governmental and inter-governmental organizations including OXFAM and the United Nations Environment Programme (UNEP).

Dr. Stéphane Beaulac is an associate professor at the Faculty of Law, University of Montreal, where he teaches public international law and statutory interpretation. He started his career at Dalhousie Law School. He conducted his master's and doctoral research at the University of Cambridge and was a law clerk at the Supreme Court of Canada with Justice L'Heureux-Dubé.

Josée Boudreau holds a B.Sc.Soc. in political science and an LL.B. from the University of Ottawa. She is counsel with the Aboriginal Law and Strategic Policy section of the Department of Justice Canada. Josée Boudreau is co-author of the book *Standards of Review of Federal Administrative Tribunals* (2003).

Doug Breithaupt is senior counsel with the Criminal Law Policy section of the Department of Justice. During his career at Justice, he has worked on various criminal law-related legislative and policy initiatives, both national and international. More recently, he participated in the development of the *Corruption of Foreign Public Officials Act*, the *Crimes Against Humanity and War Crimes Act*, and the *Anti-Terrorism Act*. Internationally, he has represented Canada at the UN, the Organization of American States, the Organisation for Economic Co-operation and Development, and the Council of Europe, as well as at other international meetings.

Dr. Stephen Clarkson pursued graduate studies at Oxford as a Rhodes scholar and obtained his doctorate at the Sorbonne. Since that time, he has taught political economy at the University of Toronto, where he has devoted much of his time to Canada's position in the continent and the world. His principal publications in this regard are *An Independent Foreign Policy for Canada?* (1968); *Canada and the Reagan Challenge* (1982) [John Porter Prize]; *Trudeau and Our Times. Volume 1: The Magnificent Obsession* (1990) [Governor General's Award for non-fiction]; *Trudeau and Our Times. Volume 2: The Heroic Delusion* (1994) [John W. Dafoe Prize]; and *Uncle Sam and Us: Globalization, Neoconservatism, and the Canadian State* (2002). He is a Fellow of the Royal Society of Canada and is now writing a study of transborder governance in North America.

Maurice Copithorne is a professor of law at the University of British Columbia. Earlier in his career, he was a Foreign Service Officer in the Department of External Affairs, holding a variety of positions in Canada and abroad including that of Legal Advisor to the Department.

Armand de Mestral is Jean Monnet Professor of Law, McGill University; co-director Institute of European Studies of the Université de Montréal and McGill University; and former Acting Director of the Institute of Air and Space Law, McGill University. He is also the author, co-author, and co-editor of numerous publications, including *The Limitation of Human Rights in Comparative Constitutional Law* (1986); *An Introduction to International Law* (1987); *The Canadian Law and Practice of International Trade* (1991); and *The Canadian Yearbook of International Law/l'Annuaire canadien de droit international*.

Elisabeth Eid is Director and General Counsel, Human Rights Law Section, Department of Justice Canada. She received her B.A . from the University of Alberta), and her LL.B. and B.C.L. from McGill University (National Program). Her interests include international human rights law, equality rights, and human rights issues in the immigration context.

Dr. Oonagh Fitzgerald, B.F.A. (York University), LL.B. (Osgoode Hall Law School), LL.M. (Ottawa University), S.J.D. (University of Toronto), E.M.B.A Candidate (Queen's University), Senior General Counsel with the Department of Justice Canada. Dr. Fitzgerald served as Special Advisor International Law and Acting Chief Counsel Public Law while this project was developing. In these capacities, she represented the Department of Justice on the Canadian National Committee for Humanitarian Law and the Canadian Council of International Law. She organized regular discussions between Department of Justice international lawyers and Canadian international law professors, culminating in the production of this essay collection. Dr. Fitzgerald is currently studying the contribution of international business to the development of global standards of corporate social responsibility.

Donald J. Fleming, B.A. (Mount Allison), LL.B. (U.N.B.), LL.B. (International Law) (Cantab.), called to the bar of New Brunswick in 1975. He teaches at the Faculty of Law, University of New Brunswick, and his primary teaching interests are subjects in public international law, trade law, humanitarian law, and torts law. Professor Fleming has acted as counsel for government and aboriginal groups and has published primarily on international law and international human rights law. Professor Fleming is on the Roster for NAFTA Chapter 19 Binational Panels and is currently serving a two-year term (October 2004–October 2006) as president of the Canadian Council on International Law.

Dr. Evan Thane Fox-Decent, B.A. (Manitoba), M.A. (Manitoba), J.D. (Toronto), Ph.D. (Toronto). He is assistant professor, Faculty of Law, McGill University. Dr. Fox-Decent teaches and publishes in legal theory, administrative law, First Nations and the law, the law of fiduciaries, and human rights. He has worked on human rights and democratic governance reform in Latin America since 1987, beginning with advocacy and relief work in El Salvador under the auspices of Nobel Peace Prize Nominee Medardo Gomez.

Dr. Daniel Gervais is acting dean, vice-dean (Research), and Oslers Professor of Technology Law at the Faculty of Law (Common Law), University of Ottawa. Dr. Gervais holds a Doctor of Laws degree *magna cum laude* from Nantes University (France), a Diploma in International Copyright Law *magna cum laude* from the Graduate Institute of Advanced International Studies (Geneva), as well as an LL.M. and an LL.B. from McGill University and the University of Montreal. Prior to studying law, Dr. Gervais studied computer science in Montreal.

Hoori Hamboyan, B.A., B.S.W., M.S.W., LL.B., articled with the Human Rights Law Section, Department of Justice Canada, and now works as counsel with the Family, Children and Youth Section, Department of Justice Canada. Prior to attending law school, Ms. Hamboyan worked as a social worker in Montreal and Toronto, in the fields of youth protection, advocacy for refugees, and crisis counselling.

Joanna Harrington is an associate professor with the Faculty of Law at the University of Alberta. Her work on parliamentary scrutiny and approval of treaties is based, in part, on her experiences in Australia as a Visiting Fellow with the Gilbert & Tobin Centre of Public Law at the University of New South Wales, and in the United Kingdom as the parliamentary legal officer to Lord Lester of Herne Hill, QC, of the House of Lords. Her writings on treaty making have appeared in the *International and Comparative Law Quarterly*, the *McGill Law Journal*, and as a chapter in *Australia in the Fluid State: International Law and National Legal Systems* (2005).

John Mark Keyes is the Acting Chief Legislative Counsel in the Legislative Services Branch of the Department of Justice (Canada), having joined the Department in 1984. He is also an adjunct professor at the Faculty of Law, University of Ottawa, and has published a number of scholarly legal articles and casebooks, as well as a book entitled *Executive Legislation: Delegated Law-making by the Executive Branch* (1992).

Hugh M. Kindred, LL.B. (Bristol), LL.M. (London), LL.M. (Illinois), is professor of law at Dalhousie University, and a member of the bars of England and Nova Scotia. He is co-general editor (with Phillip Saunders) and a co-author of *International Law Chiefly as Interpreted and Applied in Canada* (2006), now in its 7th edition. In 2003, the Canadian Association of Law Teachers honoured Professor Kindred with its Award of Academic Excellence.

Anne Warner La Forest, LL.B. (U.N.B.) 1984, LL.M. (Cantab.) 1985, is professor of law and former dean of law, University of New Brunswick. A member of the bars of Ontario, Nova Scotia, and New Brunswick, she has been a Visiting Fellow in the Harvard Law School Human Rights Program and Visiting Scholar-in-Residence at the Department of Justice in Ottawa. She is a Fellow of the Cambridge Commonwealth Society and is currently a member of the Board of Governors of the National Judicial Institute.

Stefan Matiation is a lawyer with the Aboriginal Law and Strategic Policy group in the Department of Justice Canada. He has a J.D. from the University of Toronto (1995) and a Master of Laws degree in international law from Columbia Law School (2002), where he was a Human Rights Fellow.

John P. McEvoy, B.A. (S.T.U.) 1975, LL.B. (U.N.B.) 1978, LL.M. (Osgoode) 1982, LL.L. (Ottawa) 2004, was called to the bar of New Brunswick in

1978. He is a member of the Faculty of Law of the University of New Brunswick, where he teaches courses primarily in the areas of constitutional law, human rights law, Aboriginal Peoples, and private international law, and researches and writes on topics in these subject areas. Professor McEvoy has argued constitutional law issues before the courts of New Brunswick, the Court of Appeal of Prince Edward Island, and the Supreme Court of Canada. A former president of the Canadian Association of Law Teachers, he is also an active member of the legal community and has served as president of the Canadian Bar Association, New Brunswick branch, and as a member of the executive committee of CBA National. Professor McEvoy serves as a labour arbitrator and human rights mediator.

Lorraine Pelot, B. Comm., LL.B., is a Senior Research Officer at the Law Commission of Canada and is currently completing a Master's Degree in Public Administration (International Concentration) at l'École nationale d'administration publique. She has done extensive work in the areas of human rights and equality, health law, the health care system, and international law.

Linda C. Reif, LL.B. (Windsor), LL.M. (Cambridge), is a professor at the Faculty of Law, University of Alberta. She has written on national human rights institutions, international human rights law, and international business law in publications in Canada, the U.S., and Europe. Professor Reif is Editor of Publications of the International Ombudsman Institute.

Ruth Sullivan, B.A., M.A., B.C.L., LL.B., M.Leg., is a professor, Faculty of Law, University of Ottawa.

Gib van Ert is an associate with Hunter Voith Litigation Counsel in Vancouver. He has degrees from McGill, Cambridge, and the University of Toronto, and served as a law clerk at both the Supreme Court of Canada and the Court of Appeal for British Columbia. He is the author of *Using International Law in Canadian Courts* (2002) and the co-author of *International Human Rights Law* (2004).

Stepan Wood is an associate professor at Osgoode Hall Law School in Toronto, where he coordinates the joint Master in Environmental Studies/ LL.B. program. He was a Virtual Scholar in Residence with the Law Commission of Canada in 2004–5, helping with a project on Governing Beyond Borders. His current research interests revolve around environmental law, non-state transnational governance, and corporate social responsibility. His most recent publication, with Benjamin Richardson, is *Environmental Law for Sustainability* (2006).